THE 'GREGORIAN' *DIALOGUES* AND THE ORIGINS
OF BENEDICTINE MONASTICISM

STUDIES IN THE HISTORY
OF
CHRISTIAN THOUGHT

FOUNDED BY HEIKO A. OBERMAN †

EDITED BY

ROBERT J. BAST, Knoxville, Tennessee

IN COOPERATION WITH

HENRY CHADWICK, Cambridge
SCOTT H. HENDRIX, Princeton, New Jersey
BRIAN TIERNEY, Ithaca, New York
ARJO VANDERJAGT, Groningen
JOHN VAN ENGEN, Notre Dame, Indiana

VOLUME CVIII

FRANCIS CLARK

THE 'GREGORIAN' *DIALOGUES* AND THE ORIGINS OF BENEDICTINE MONASTICISM

THE 'GREGORIAN' *DIALOGUES* AND THE ORIGINS OF BENEDICTINE MONASTICISM

BY

FRANCIS CLARK

BRILL

LEIDEN · BOSTON

2003

This book is printed on acid-free paper.

BR
65
.G53
D532
2003

Library of Congress Cataloging-in-Publication Data

Clark, Francis, 1919-
 The 'Gregorian' *dialogues* and the origins of Benedictine monasticism / by
Francis Clark.
  p. cm. — (Studies in the history of Christian thought, v. 108)
 Includes bibliographical references and index.
 ISBN 9004128492
 1. Gregory I, Pope, ca. 540-604. Dialogi. 2. Benedict, Saint, Abbot of Monte
Cassino. 3. Miracles—History of doctrines—Middle Ages, 600-1500.
4. Immortality—History of doctrines—Middle Ages, 600-1500. I. Title.
II. Series.

BR65.G53 D532   2002
270.2—dc21   2002027833

Die Deutsche Bibliothek - CIP-Einheitsaufnahme

Clark, Francis:
The 'Gregorian' *dialogues* and the origins of Benedictine monasticism /
by Francis Clark – Leiden ; Boston : Brill, 2002
 (Studies in the history of Christian thought ; Vol. 108)
 ISBN 90–04–12849–2

ISSN   0081-8607
ISBN   90 04 12849 2

© *Copyright 2003 by Koninklijke Brill NV, Leiden, The Netherlands*

*All rights reserved. No part of this publication may be reproduced, translated, stored in
a retrieval system, or transmitted in any form or by any means, electronic,
mechanical, photocopying, recording or otherwise, without prior written
permission from the publisher.*

*Authorization to photocopy items for internal or personal
use is granted by Brill provided that
the appropriate fees are paid directly to The Copyright
Clearance Center, 222 Rosewood Drive, Suite 910
Danvers, MA 01923, USA.
Fees are subject to change.*

PRINTED IN THE NETHERLANDS

CONTENTS

PART IV
THE DIALOGIST AND HIS LEGACY: RETROSPECT AND FUTURE PROSPECT

ACKNOWLEDGEMENTS

I renew the grateful acknowledgements that I expressed in a foreword to my previous work, *The Pseudo-Gregorian Dialogues*, to the many scholars to whom I was indebted in the preparation and production of that work, major elements of which I retain and adapt in this volume. I express my appreciation also to those who have advanced the debate engendered by that book during the sixteen years that have elapsed since it was published. I pay tribute especially to the open-minded Benedictine commentators who have furthered the reception of its seemingly iconoclastic thesis, in particular the late Dom Robert Gillet, Dom Henry Wansbrough, Dom Benedict Guevin, Dom Claude Peifer, Dom Marc Doucet and the editors of *Revue Bénédictine* and *The American Benedictine Review*. I keep in specially grateful memory Fr Gillet, a master in the study of the spiritual legacy of St Gregory the Great. He was the first eminent scholar to recognize the cogency of the demonstration given in *PsGD* that the *Dialogues concerning the Miracles of the Fathers of Italy* were not written by that great Doctor of the Church, and over several years he gave me encouragement to persevere in correcting a thirteen-centuries-old error in Church history and tradition. I much appreciated his support, and the influence of his judgement, in the years when scholarly contention on the subject was often heated.

I must not fail to renew the respectful acknowledgement that I made in *The Pseudo-Gregorian Dialogues* to another renowned Benedictine scholar, Dom Adalbert de Vogüé, of the Abbey of La Pierre-qui-vire in Burgundy. In the study of the monastic history and texts of antiquity, and of the Gregorian *Dialogues* in particular, he has long been a distinguished master. From the time he first learned of my conclusions concerning the origin of that work, he has made clear his resolute disagreement with them, and has continued to oppose them with vigour. He has been the most prominent opponent of my thesis. Yet he was unsparing in giving me his time and advice in this field of such great interest to us both. I have profited much from his criticisms, and I thank him again warmly for his charity and for the many services he has rendered to me. My wider indebtedness to his writings, especially to his magisterial commentary in the

Sources Chrétiennes edition of the *Dialogues*, will be apparent throughout this book. I venture to suggest that some of my most telling
arguments are based on premises that have been established by his
own indefatigable researches.

This new volume, like its predecessor, *The Pseudo-Gregorian Dialogues*,
forms part of the series, *Studies in the History of Christian Thought*, published in 1987 by Brill of Leiden. I gratefully acknowledge my debt
to two distinguished Editors-in-Chief of that series. The first was the
late Professor Heiko A. Oberman of the University of Arizona, of
blessed memory, who welcomed *PsGD* for inclusion in the series (of
which he was the founder). He was the patron and staunch advocate of the work throughout the ensuing controversy, and was actively
promoting a republication and updating of it in the weeks immediately before his death in 2001. I likewise express my heartfelt gratitude to his successor as Editor-in-Chief of *SHCT*, Professor Robert
J. Bast of the University of Tennessee, who has warmly welcomed
this new volume for inclusion in the series and has effectively brought
it to publication. He it was who proposed its format, and he has
actively guided its preparation, giving valuable and much appreciated advice.

Lastly and most fervently, I express my gratitude to my long-
suffering wife Pauline, in whose life the "Gregorian" *Dialogues* have
loomed large, and who has made my writings on the subject possible, as well as contributing appreciably to their content and expression. The dedication of this new volume is therefore the same as in
previous works:

"DILECTISSIMAE SPONSAE PAULINAE"

ABBREVIATIONS

AA.SS	*Acta Sanctorum* (Brussels)
AB	*Analecta Bollandiana*
BAH	*Biblioteca de la [Real] Academia de Historia* (Madrid)
BHL	*Bibliotheca Hagiographica Latina*
BM	British Museum
BS	*Bibliotheca Sanctorum* (Rome)
CC	*Collectanea Cisterciensia*
CCG	*Corpus Christianorum, Series Graeca*
CCL	*Corpus Christianorum, Series Latina*
CETEDOC	*Centre de Traitement Électronique des Documents* (Louvain-la-Neuve)
CMH	Cambridge Modern History
CPL	*Clavis Patrum Latinorum*
CSEL	*Corpus Scriptorum Ecclesiasticorum Latinorum*
DACL	*Dictionnaire d'Archéologie Chrétienne et de Liturgie*
DCB	Dictionary of Christian Biography
DHGE	*Dictionnaire d'Histoire et de Géographie Ecclésiastique*
Dial.	*Dialogues* traditionally ascribed to St Gregory
DIP	*Dizionario degl'Istituti di Perfezione*
DS	*Dictionnaire de Spiritualité*
EH	Ewald-Hartmann edition of *Registrum Epistularum* of Gregory the Great
HJ	*The Heythrop Journal*
IGPs	The "Inserted Gregorian Passages" in the *Dialogues*
JEH	*Journal of Ecclesiastical History*
K	Cononian Abridgement of the *Liber Pontificalis*
LP	*Liber Pontificalis*
LT	*Liber Testimoniorum* of Paterius
MGH	*Monumenta Germaniae Historica*
PG	*Patrologia Graeca* (Migne)
PL	*Patrologia Latina* (Migne)
PsGD	*The Pseudo-Gregorian Dialogues* (Francis Clark, 1987)
RB	*Regula Benedicti*
RBS	*Regulae Benedicti Studia*
RGG	*Die Religion im Geschichte und Gegenwart*

Rev. Bén.	*Revue Bénédictine*
RHE	*Revue d'Histoire Ecclésiastique*
RM	*Regula Magistri*
RPTK	*Realencyklopädie für Protestantische Theologie und Kirche*
RSR	*Recherches de Science Religieuse*
SA	*Studia Anselmiana*
SC	*Sources Chrétiennes*
SM	*Studia Monastica*
SpM	*Spiritual Meadow* of John Moschus
SMGBO	*Studien und Mitteilungen zur Geschichte des Benediktiner-Ordens und seiner Zweige*
VB	*Vita Burgundofarae*
VF	*Vita Fructuosi*
VPE	*Vitas Patrum Emeretensium*
ZKT	*Zeitschrift für katholische Theologie*

INTRODUCTION

The authenticity of the famous book entitled *The Dialogues of Pope Gregory concerning the Miracles of the Fathers of Italy*, generally attributed to St Gregory the Great since the early Middle Ages, was first denied by some humanist and Protestant scholars in the sixteenth century. A heated inter-confessional dispute ensued during the following two centuries, which eventually petered out inconclusively. During recent years the origin of those *Dialogues* has again been the subject of lively controversy, following the publication in 1987 of my two-volume work, *The Pseudo-Gregorian Dialogues*,[1] the thesis of which is declared in its title. The renewed discussion has been conducted in new light, though still not without considerable heat. While some eminent critics have indignantly contradicted my findings, others have appraised them positively.

Recent developments (and a disconcerting discovery) in this sphere of historical and literary research have served to confirm that significant revision and correction of age-old assumptions is necessary. Indeed there is now discernible a turning of the tide in this long debate. A growing number of scholars are open-mindedly reassessing the historical and literary evidence relating to the origin and emergence of the *Dialogues*, and are coming to recognize the force of the revisionist case, despite the vehement protests of its critics. Traditional loyalties notwithstanding, monastic scholars are in the forefront of this movement of realistic reappraisal.

In *The Pseudo-Gregorian Dialogues* (to which I shall refer in these pages by the abbreviation *PsGD*) I put forward a converging series of arguments, based on both internal and external evidence, to show that the *Dialogues* for so long ascribed to St Gregory the Great were in fact not written by that pope in the year 593, as usually assumed, but by an unknown pseudepigrapher in an age considerably later than his. I showed reason for concluding that the real author (whom I call "The Dialogist")[2] was in all probability a scribe in the secretariate of the Roman see in the later seventh century, one of the

---

[1] E.J. Brill, Leiden 1987; Volumes 37 & 38 in *Studies in the History of Christian Thought*.
[2] I chose that title when first researching this field long ago; later I found that

most talented of the busy legend-spinners of that age. The 1987 edition of *PsGD* is now out of print. There is need both for an up-to-date account of the present state of the question and for a revised and more compact presentation of the massive case set out in those two volumes to be made available to the wider constituency of potentially interested readers in many lands, most of whom may as yet know of it only by hearsay. This new single volume is offered to meet that twofold need. In it the course of the present-day debate is surveyed and updated, and the essential substance of the case set out in *PsGD* is presented anew in reordered and condensed form.[3] A few needful *corrigenda* are noted, none of which affect the substance of the case.

Part I of this book presents a view of "The *Dialogues* in the tide of time". In the first chapter the long history and enduring influence of that enigmatic work is traced from the time at which it first emerged into the light, through the thirteen centuries of its chequered *Nachleben*, until the beginning of the renewed debate on the book's authenticity in the later twentieth century. I there discuss the relevance to the present debate of the earlier protracted controversy on the subject which began in the sixteenth century. My second chapter gives an overview of the recent developments in the controversy and of the present state of scholarly opinion on the issue. In the second and third parts of this book there follows detailed discussion of all the elements, singly and in their concordant unity. In *PsGD* the external historical evidence indicating the spuriousness of the allegedly Gregorian *Dialogues* was discussed first and the internal textual evidence second. In this new publication I reverse that order of treatment.

It is against the arguments based on external evidence that the group of determined critics of *PsGD* have concentrated their attack. Their objections are based on a few documents of debatable origin traditionally alleged to provide proof of knowledge in Gregory's own age of the existence of the *Dialogues* and of his authorship of them. I showed in *PsGD*, and now reinforce the demonstration in these pages, that the documents adduced do not provide the proof claimed

---

a seventeenth-century Anglican scholar, Robert Cooke, had chosen a similar title by which to refer to him—namely, "The Dialogian". I discuss Cooke's own researches in Chapter 2.

[3] For the purpose of cross-reference between chapters, I have divided each chapter into sections distinguished by letters prefixed to the subheads.

by the critics, and that the pleas which they base upon them are
flawed. In any case, those inconclusive pleas are positively discredited by the solid proof of the non-Gregorian origin of the *Dialogues*
jointly provided by the internal evidence of the text and by the external evidences relating to the first emergence of the *Dialogues* into historical record.

In the concluding fourth part of this volume I sketch a profile of
the author of the *Dialogues* as it can be traced from clues contained
in his text and in contemporary records which give indications of
the setting of his life and activity. Then I offer concluding reflections
on the turning of the tide in this debate, and on the history and
future of the legendary saga that has left an enduring imprint on
Christian history.

To achieve the required reduction of wordage required to make
this new publication more accessible I have been obliged to omit or
drastically abbreviate much of the collateral documentation by which
the principal arguments in *PsGD* were further supported. Those readers whose specialist research interests lead them to deeper study of
the relevant documentary data are recommended to seek out, in
libraries where *PsGD* can be found, the fuller discussion of those
data in that work. A major instance of such abbreviation is the omission in this new volume of the marked Latin text of the *Dialogues*
that was set out in the appendix to *PsGD*,[4] In those 114 pages I
identified and underlined what I call the fourscore "IGPs" ("Inserted
Gregorian Passages") which can be seen to be interpolated, often
incongruously, into the main narrative text of the *Dialogues*. Some of
those genuine passages were manifestly copied from Gregory's published works. The greater number of them, I conclude, were drawn
by the Dialogist from surviving unpublished *reportata* of Gregory's
scriptural commentaries which, we know, were long preserved in the
Roman *Scrinium*. In this new volume I do not reproduce the text of
the IGPs. In the appendix readers are given chapter and section references to enable them to pick them out in the Latin text of the
Sources Chrétiennes edition. I also briefly recall there some of the most
telling points in the detailed critique of the IGPs which filled 149
pages of *PsGD* (Chapters 13–17).

---

[4] Pp. 297–410. That text was reprinted from the edition in *Sources Chrétiennes*,
vols. 260 and 265.

PART I

THE *DIALOGUES* IN THE TIDE OF TIME

CHAPTER ONE

THE *DIALOGUES* IN HISTORY AND IN CONTROVERSY

a

The debate on the question of the authorship of the book of *Dialogues* traditionally ascribed to St Gregory the Great is no mere dry-as-dust discussion of recondite points of textual criticism, of interest only to those engaged in specialist study of ancient texts. Since its misty origins in the dark ages that book has had a major place in the living tradition of the Church. It is the sole source of all biographical data—with the exception of one vital fact—concerning the person of St Benedict, patriarch of Western monasticism and therefore honoured as patron of Europe. That vital fact, known independently of the *Dialogues*, is of course his authorship of the great monastic rule that bears his name. The *Regula Benedicti* has shaped the history and development of Christendom; in every age it continues to sanctify the lives of countless Christians.

Jean Leclercq declared the common verdict of historians of Christian culture: "The Western monastic tradition from the Middle Ages is, in its totality, founded principally on two texts constituting the Benedictine tradition: the Life of St Benedict in the book of *Dialogues* of St Gregory, and the rule for monks ascribed from time immemorial to St Benedict".[1] The emergence and widespread diffusion of the wondrous biography of St Benedict contained in the *Dialogues* bearing the name of the great Pope Gregory was a major factor in the spread and eventual pre-eminence of that monastic rule over all others. As P. Batiffol also observed, "There is no doubt that the second book of the *Dialogues* made St Benedict the patriarch of the monks of the West."[2] *When* and *how* it did so are significant questions

---

[1] *Cultura monastica e desiderio di Dio. Studio sulla letteratura monastica del Medio Evo*, Florence 1983, p. 11.
[2] *St Gregory the Great*, English translation, London 1929, p. 190.

to be discussed in these pages. Likewise, the colourful hagiographical narrative contained in the other three books of the *Dialogues*,
relating the lives and marvellous deeds of many other holy men completely unknown to historical record, also became etched into Christian
tradition in the course of centuries.

In many spheres that narrative made an enduring impress on the
religious culture of the Middle Ages. The stories of miracles, apparitions and other preternatural events that it contained were mirrored
in the religious folklore and pious practices of the following centuries. It provided many new names to be added (in much later
times) to the traditional calendars of saints.[3] Its influence is reflected
in mediaeval tales and artistic depictions of journeys to the other
world, and in concepts of the chastisement of departed souls expiating their unpurged sins. To it can be traced the origin of the pious
practice of the "Month's Mind", with special value for impetrating
the release of a suffering soul in purgatory. It provided patristic
precedent for the development of such numerical calculation of the
value of offerings made for the succour of departed souls.[4] Throughout
the Christian world the book was the mediaeval equivalent of a best-
seller. It had all the ingredients needed for success and acclaim: read-
ability, human interest, vivid tales of miraculous happenings and of
awesome doom, elevated theological passages, homely examples for
Christian living, spine-chilling stories of ghosts and devils, eye-wit-
ness accounts of what lay beyond the grave, colourful subject matter for sermons and for art. The veracity of all those tales was
vouched for by the authority of one who was a great pope, saint
and doctor of the Church.

No other work of any of the Fathers of the Church was more
eagerly transcribed and read. In the words of A. Ebert, historian of
the literature of those centuries, it "exercised the greatest influence
on the culture of the Middle Ages and on the literature of the
nations".[5] Copies of it were to be found on the shelves of libraries

---

[3] In Chapter 8.c below I cite the criticism of the Bollandist historian B. de Gaiffier
of the many unjustifiable additions to the calendars of names of saints taken from
the *Dialogues*.

[4] Cf. Chapter 4 of my book, *Eucharistic Sacrifice and the Reformation* (2nd edition,
Oxford 1967), entitled "Practical abuses and superstitious observances connected
with the altar in the pre-Reformation era", especially pp. 58–60.

[5] *Geschichte der christliche-lateinische Literatur*, vol. I, Leipzig 1874, p. 520.

throughout Christendom. In the Middle Ages it was translated from the Latin original into Greek, Anglo-Saxon, Old French, Castilian, Old Slavonic, Middle German and Dutch, Icelandic, Arabic, Anglo-Norman, early Italian, Czech, Bulgarian, Catalan, Sicilian, and later into all the modern languages of Europe.[6] The later Middle Ages saw the apogee of the *Dialogues'* fame and influence on popular religiosity. G. Dufner, who charted the fortunes of the book through the centuries, observed: "The great century for the *Dialogues* was the fourteenth. Virtually everywhere in Europe the work enjoyed a new surge, indeed an explosion, of popularity."[7] After the coming of printing in the fifteenth century it became still more widely accessible.

In the age of the New Learning, however, there came a change in religious culture. Reform-minded humanists drew critical attention to distortions and accretions that had appeared in mediaeval piety in the course of previous centuries. The criticism of the Protestant Reformers was still more radical. Their accusation against the mediaeval Church itself was that it "had fed popular religiosity on a diet of sensational miracle-tales, rather than on the pure bread of the Gospel".[8] They pointed to the *Dialogues* of Pope Gregory I as the main source of that radical debasement of belief and practice. Thus Philip Melanchthon, principal coadjutor of Martin Luther and humanist theologian, scornfully denounced the author of that book as "that Gregory whom they [the papists] call 'great', but whom I call the dance-leader and torch-bearer of a theology going down to ruin".[9]

However, there was soon to begin a further remarkable change of scholarly opinion on this matter. In the mid-sixteenth century another Protestant humanist, Huldreich Coccius (Koechlin) of Basel, published—on grounds of literary criticism—the first challenge to the age-old ascription of the *Dialogues* to Gregory. In so doing he implicitly distanced himself from the opprobrious judgement passed on that pontiff by Melanchthon and the other Protestant scholars who had assumed as certain his authorship of the work. In a preface to his

---

[6] Cf. G. Dufner, *Die Dialoge Gregors der Grosse im Wandel der Zeiten und Sprachen*, in *Miscellanea Erudita*, vol. XIX, Padua 1968, pp. 38–45.

[7] *Op. cit.* p. 32.

[8] I cite that phrase from my book, *Godfaring: on Reason, Faith and Sacred Being*, p.161.

[9] "... *Gregorius quem isti magnum ego praesultatorem* καὶ δᾳδοῦχον *theologiae pereuntis voco*" (*Corpus Reformatorum*, vol. 11, 1843) col. 16.

edition of Gregory's *Works*, published at Basel in 1564, Coccius
expressed his warm admiration of the writings and teachings of that
great pope and doctor, but significantly excepted the *Dialogues* from
that favourable judgement, voicing his strong suspicion that the work
was spurious: "As for the *Dialogues* in which he recounts the miracles of the Fathers of Italy, I hardly know what to assert, except
that I doubt whether they be written by Gregory—so much do they
differ from all his other works in character, form of expression, seriousness and purpose".[10]

b. *Heated counter-arguments*

Other Protestant scholars soon joined in challenging, with growing
emphasis, the authenticity of the *Dialogues*. The celebrated Lutheran
divine Martin Chemnitz, one of the Centuriators of Magdeburg,
pointed to the relevance of that challenge in the context of contemporary doctrinal controversy. Discussing the origins of the Catholic
teaching on purgatory, in his *Examen Decretorum Concilii Tridentini* published in the years 1565–1573, he commented as follows on the stories in the Gregorian *Dialogues* of spectres who declared that they
were suffering penal purgation for their sins in steamy ordeals in the
public baths of Italian towns:

> And yet Gregory himself did not see or hear those spectres, but he
> believed the tales that others told him. Then, with exceedingly rash
> credulity, he imposed them on the Church—if indeed those *Dialogues*,
> replete with prodigious happenings in Italy, were written by Gregory.
> Scholars not unjustifiably doubt this, since the work concords with
> Gregory's other writings neither in manner of expression nor in the
> nature of its contents.[11]

Protestant criticism of the *Dialogues* had parallels in that of some
Catholic scholars. The Dominican theologian Melchior Cano aroused
the indignation of his peers when he voiced daringly outspoken criticism of St Gregory for spreading such dubious tales as the book
contained. Baronius apostrophized him ironically: "How now, good

---

[10] *Opera D. Gregorii Papae huius nominis primi*, 2 vols. Basle 1564; prefatory letter to
W. Waidner (composed in 1551), vol. 1, fol. B2 verso.
[11] *Examen*, Frankfurt edition 1596, *pars tertia*, p. 100.

sir, are all others blind and you alone can see? Are all others asleep, and you alone are watchful?".[12]

The first challenge to the authenticity of the *Dialogues*, made by Coccius in the mid-sixteenth century, had been based strictly on grounds of literary criticism, without controversial motive. In the following decades a growing number of other Protestant and humanist scholars joined in recognition of the many indications of non-Gregorian origin in the text of the *Dialogues*, and came to conclude definitely that the work was spurious. Even though that conclusion gave the lie to Melanchthon's polemical argument, they realized that they could find in it a new argument for use in current controversy. They pointed to that literary forgery as one more instance of the mediaeval Roman Church falsifying the books, to rank with the forged Donation of Constantine, with the Pseudo-Isidorian Decretals, and with the mass of other apocryphal Acts, fictitious hagiographies and forged bulls that had been unmasked by Renaissance scholarship. The assumedly Gregorian *Dialogues* provided for polemicists one more instance of the Romanists' passing off spurious works as genuine patristic sources in order to justify innovations in Church doctrine and practice. Some tales in the *Dialogues* had evident relevance to matters of current inter-confessional dispute, especially Catholic teaching concerning purgatory and the power of the Mass-sacrifice. In reflex loyalty to their cause, Catholic apologists rallied strongly to defend the Gregorian authorship of the *Dialogues*. The dispute widened and intensified. It was conducted with special vigour during the seventeenth century. (Incidental confusion was introduced into the controversy by the discovery that some mediaeval Byzantines had given the title "Gregory the Dialogian" not to Gregory the Great but to Gregory II, who was pope from 715 to 731.)[13]

c. *Robert Cooke and his opponents*

Two of the ablest and most influential protagonists on the Protestant side, both of whom published works with the same general aim at

---

[12] Baronius, edition of the *Martyrologium Romanum*, Antwerp 1598, pp. 555–6.
[13] I discuss the effects of that discovery and the confused debate which followed in *PsGD*, pp. 33–4.

about the same time, were Robert Cooke in England and Robert
Rivet (Rivetus) in the Netherlands. That aim was to expose spurious Christian writings which (in the words of Rivetus) "either ignorance has attributed to, or deliberate fraud has fathered on, many
Fathers of earlier and purer centuries". Among such works they
included the *Dialogues* as a prime example. By the end of the first
quarter of the seventeenth century denial of the authenticity of the
work had become widespread, as William Forbes, who became the
first Protestant Bishop of Edinburgh during the reign of Charles II,
observed in an unusually urbane book about points of inter-religious
dispute. In that work he discussed, among other controversial issues,
that of the *Dialogues*:

> These dialogues are seen by many Protestants, and also by some other
> very learned men . . . to be supposititious and not the genuine work of
> Gregory I. To pass over in silence numberless other Protestants, there
> are the critics, Cocus, who maintains at much length that some other
> later author and not Gregory surnamed the Great was the author, and
> also Rivetus . . .[14]

The author Robert Cooke, there referred to by Forbes as "Cocus",
was a learned divine of the Church of England, sometime fellow of
Brasenose College, Oxford, and a canon of Durham. His detailed
argument for the spuriousness of the *Dialogues*, in a book published
in 1614,[15] was the most thorough of all those put forward in that
age. After quoting Melchior Cano's challenge to the credibility of
the stories it contained, Cooke declared his own more radical judgement: "But I call in question the very authorship of the work; for
it will be seen that I have many arguments—some concerning the
style of the book, some the matter it contains—which show that the
author of these *Dialogues* was a later writer, not Gregory surnamed
the Great." He introduced his discussion of those arguments with
this general comment:

> If in Gregory's writings there is always a balance of expression, always
> a great consistency in style and a harmoniously linked construction of

---

[14] *Considerationes modestae pacificae*, Oxford edition, 1856, pp. 69–70. The work was
written before 1634 but first published in 1658.
[15] *Considerationes quorundam scriptorum quae sub nominibus sanctorum et veterorum auctorum
Pontificii passim in eorum scriptis sed potissimum in quaestionibus hodie controversis, citari solent*
(London 1614).

clauses, as Sixtus of Siena attests, if Gregory surpassed Cyprian in eloquence, as Baronius (quoting St Ildefonsus) says, then we must dismiss these *Dialogues*. In no way can they have been written by Gregory the Great. In them the manner of expression is indeed very dissimilar to that used by Gregory in the writings which are acknowledged by all to be really his. In these *Dialogues* there is little of eloquence, but many barbarisms in language, phrasing and expression.

Whereas other critics were content to assert in general terms that the language and style of the *Dialogues* were uncouth and very different from Gregory's own, Cooke gave concrete instances. He proceeded to argue that the absurd and grotesque tales in the *Dialogues*, some of which he cites, could not have been written by Gregory the Great. "Who indeed could suspect, without injustice to Gregory, that he would himself accept such old wives' tales, or that he would wish others to believe them?" He further argued that there were doctrinal differences between the suppositions of the author of the *Dialogues* and the teaching of Gregory himself. The case set out by Cooke, based as it was on the convergent internal evidence of the language, syntax and style of the book, as well as on a critique of its contents, was frequently referred to in subsequent debate, both by friends and opponents. When examined, it can be seen to concord in essentials with the much fuller and more detailed case against the Gregorian authenticity of the *Dialogues* from the internal evidence of their language and contents that is now gaining increasing acceptance some four centuries later. However, we today have many cogent evidences that he lacked.

Catholic apologists reacted vehemently against the Protestants' challenge to the Gregorian authorship of the *Dialogues*. The major factor in their indignant defence of the authenticity of the work was loyalty to the age-old tradition of the Church concerning St Benedict, father of Western monasticism, whose life story was provided solely by the second book of the *Dialogues*. Among those who joined in the fray during the seventeenth century were John Picard, Possevinus, Benedict Van Haeften, Philip Labbé (Labbaeus), the English Jesuit James Mumford, Peter de Goussainville, the renowned Benedictine historian Jean Mabillon (who singled out Robert Cooke for particular obloquy for the "insolent audacity" of his denial of the Gregorian authorship), and the other Maurist scholars, especially Denys de Sainte Marthe, who worked on the great Paris edition of St Gregory's works published at the turn of the seventeenth century. Later in the eighteenth century another Benedictine historian, Remi Ceillier, repeated and amplified the arguments of his predecessors.[16]

d. *Later vicissitudes in the controversy*

Although Robert Cooke had effectively hit his target at essential points of internal criticism of the language and contents of the *Dialogues*, his treatment of the question of authenticity did not take account of the question of the emergence of the work into recorded history. He did not provide answers to counter-arguments based on other contemporary documents from Gregory's age which his Catholic opponents were soon to be urging with emphasis, and which they claimed were sufficient by themselves to discredit the evidence alleged by the Protestant critics from the internal evidence of the *Dialogues* text. Mabillon and his colleagues presented as their main counter-argument a letter from Gregory to Bishop Maximian of Sicily contained in the *Registrum Epistularum*, the curial record of the pope's letters, which patently referred to the *Dialogues*. They pointed to it (as many still do today) as decisive proof of Gregory's authorship of the *Dialogues* from his own words. No one in that age yet adverted to signs within the letter that it was counterfeit. Nor could those defenders of the Gregorian authorship imagine that several other contemporary testimonies which they adduced as attesting it would also be eventually discredited. A prime example is a spurious passage cited by Mabillon, supposedly written by St Isidore of Seville, stating that Gregory had written "four books in the form of a dialogue held with Peter concerning the virtues of the Fathers".[17] It is only in the present age, when one after another of those counter-arguments have collapsed, refuted by the exposure of interpolation and misdating of the alleged documentary testimonies, that the case disproving Gregory's authorship can be seen as a whole, in its cogent coherence.

The first author whom I find to have admitted that the available evidence was paradoxical, and that there seemed to be plausible

---

[16] I give references to the relevant writings of those authors in *PsGD*, p. 35.

[17] Mabillon's defence of the authenticity of the *Dialogues* is in the preface to *Acta Sanctorum Ordinis Benedicti*, Paris 1688; the words cited are on pp. xii–xiii.

arguments on both sides, was another Anglican scholar, Dr William Cave, a canon of Windsor, who in 1688 published a history of ecclesiastical writings.[18] He wrote:

> Not a few authors from the Reformed churches assail these dialogues, while writers of the Roman church strenuously defend them. For those who reject them, the first argument that makes for their case is the immense discrepancy in style . . .; and indeed it must be recognized that in these dialogues many expressions are used that are those of a man with only a mediocre competence in the Latin language, not to put it more harshly. Secondly, there are the silly and inept fables which occur throughout the work and which are wholly unworthy of Gregory the Great, and indeed of any prudent man . . . Thirdly, in these dialogues there are found things which are in contradiction with the doctrine that Gregory clearly teaches in his undoubted writings.[19]

On the other hand, Cave admitted, the defenders of the *Dialogues* had in their favour some impressive arguments based on early documents—especially the *Letter to Maximian*—which seemed to show that the work was known as Gregory's since his own age. Cave had studied the recent works of the Catholic apologists, and made specific reference to those of Labbaeus, Mabillon, Goussainville and, nearer home, of Mumford. He took note of the seeming conflict of evidence and offered a compromise judgement on the issue: "When, therefore, the arguments on both sides have been weighed, what emerges is that those dialogues are at least dubious—written, it would seem by Gregory the Great but amplified and interpolated by more recent hands." Cave's proposed solution, though inconsistent and inconclusive, had one feature of considerable interest. Out of all those who have written on the enigma of the *Dialogues* text, from his day until very recently, he alone observed that a key for unlocking that enigma lay in recognizing that there were disparate elements in the text, some of which were Gregorian and some were not. (My own use of that key, namely the identification of genuine Gregorian passages—the "IGPs"—inserted into his composition by the pseudepigraphical author, differs radically from Cave's, as will appear in the course of this book.)

---

[18] *Scriptorum ecclesiasticorum historia literaria*, London 1688. The work became well known; further editions were published at Geneva in 1693 and at Oxford in 1740.
[19] Oxford edition, 1740, vol. 1, p. 545.

Cave abandoned the second of Cooke's main arguments: namely, that the bizarre and superstitious tales in the *Dialogues*, being clearly alien to Gregory's own spiritual vision, proved that the work was not his. Instead, he was prepared to admit that many of the legendary tales were indeed narrated to and passed on by Gregory, and he accordingly found fault with the pope for excessive credulity. This was a significant modification of the position taken by the Protestant critics from the mid-sixteenth century onwards, who had denied Gregory's sponsorship of those tales. It was a step backwards towards the position of Melanchthon and the earlier Reformers, and marked a change of opinion among critics in the Reformed tradition that gained momentum during the age of the Enlightenment. At about the same time a growing number of Catholic scholars (notably L. Ellies du Pin and F. Bruys),[20] while assuming the Gregorian authorship of the *Dialogues*, expressed open agreement with the Protestant critics in recognizing the puerility of the stories in the book and the uncouthness of its language and style. More widely, in the secular and sceptical climate of that age, there was a withering away of interest in the old disputes between Protestants and Catholics on dogmatic and historical issues. The scholarly critics of the new age were concerned neither with the authenticity nor with the credibility of the *Dialogues*: they were generally agreed that its narrative was "entire nonsense", as Edmund Gibbon put it. With the fading of interest in the earlier inconclusive controversy about the book's origin, Protestant scholars saw little point in continuing their predecessors' challenge to Gregory's authorship. Indeed, they realized that it was polemically more effective to assume his authorship and accordingly to denounce him, one of the most famous and revered popes of Rome, for corrupting the mediaeval Church by that farrago of invented miracles and superstitious notions, thus promoting debased religious doctrines and practices in the following centuries.

In that vein Archibald Bower, in his *History of the Popes* published in 1750, deplored Gregory's culpable gullibility in repeating idle tales told him by worthless informants, thereby furthering unsound developments in belief, especially relating to purgatory. It could well be, he commented, that the Church of Rome is "indebted to some old

---

[20] E. du Pin, *Nouvelle bibliothéque des auteurs ecclésiastiques*, Paris 1691, vol. 5, p. 138; F. Bruys, *Histoire des Papes*, La Haye 1732, pp. 362–3.

man or woman for one of its most profitable articles".[21] That charge against Gregory was commonly pressed by later critics. The German historian Georg Lau, in his critical study of the life and teaching of Pope Gregory, unhesitatingly affirmed: "The Catholic Church is indebted to the *Dialogues* for its doctrine of purgatory".[22] When dealing with the question of the authenticity of that book, Lau, like his contemporaries, made no personal investigation of his own, but relied on the arguments from external evidence put forward by Mabillon and other Catholic apologists in the earlier controversy, which he reproduced with relish.

Likewise disowning the position taken by the post-Reformation Protestant protagonists, the Liberal Protestant scholars of the nineteenth century reverted wholeheartedly to Melanchthon's condemnation of Gregory for leaving the baneful legacy of his *Dialogues* to the mediaeval Church. For authoring that work Theodore Mommsen, eminent historian of the city of Rome, dubbed Gregory *"ein recht kleiner grosser Mann"*—"a truly little great man". The jibe was repeated by J. Haller in his history of the papacy[23] and by many others. It was Adolf Harnack, revisionist historian of Christian theology, who made the most forceful impact with his attack on Gregory as being, through his authorship of the *Dialogues*, the father of the *Vulgärkatholizismus*, or popular superstitious Catholicism, which he said had corrupted true Christian faith in the Middle Ages. That pope, he declared, thus "made miracle the distinguishing mark of the religious", and "fashioned the popular form of mediaeval Catholicism".[24] For begetting the *Dialogues*, Gregory was designated *"pater superstitionis"* by G. Wickert.[25] The same charge became standard in later German scholarship. Thus H. von Schubert roundly declared: "Through the 'Fourth Doctor of the Latin Church' *Vulgärkatholizismus* was permanently legalized and given official approval".[26] W. Walter admitted that the *Dialogues* showed some marked differences from Gregory's other works, but firmly excluded any attempt to exculpate Gregory

---

[21] *The History of the Popes*, London 1750, vol. V, p. 158.

[22] *Gregor der Grosse nach seinem Leben und seiner Lehre*, Leipzig 1845, p. 316.

[23] *Das Papstum*, Stuttgart edition, 1953, vol. I, p. 295.

[24] *Lehrbuch der Dogmengechichte*, vol. III, 3rd edition, Freiburg-im-Breisgau 1897, p. 241. In a footnote Harnack also acknowledged with respect the personal merits and sagacity of Gregory evidenced in his voluminous correspondence.

[25] In *RGG*, I, *s.v.* "Gregor I".

[26] *Geschichte der christliche Kirche im Frühmittelalter*, Tübingen 1917, p. 210.

by a return to the earlier denial of his authorship. "That the miracles that are recounted are frequently of a monstrous or ridiculous
kind", he insisted, "should not lead to any doubts about the genuineness of the book".[27]

A similar verdict was expressed more mildly by H.H. Milman,
Dean of St Paul's, London, in his *History of Latin Christianity*.[28] While
finding much to praise in Gregory's pontificate, he too deplored the
enduring endorsement given in his *Dialogues* to popular superstitious
religiosity. After recounting some of the strangest tales from that
book (in which he recognized not only superstition but also child-
like imagination and enduring social vitality), Milman reflected that
it was only after the later Schoolmen "began to aspire to higher
truths", and after the Protestant Reformers eventually set themselves
"to reform religion to its primal spiritual simplicity" that the influence
of the "prolific legendary Christianity" endorsed by Pope Gregory
in his *Dialogues* began to fade—although, Milman added, it was still
active and apparent in his own time. A Catholic author, P. de
Labriolle, has expressed a similar criticism more circumspectly: "One
must concede to Harnack, the great denouncer of *Vulgärkatholizismus*,
that popular Catholic imagination owes more to Gregory than to
any of the Fathers who preceded him."[29]

e. *Dudden's theory of a psychological dichotomy in Gregory*

A major study of Gregory's life and work, written from a standpoint
very similar to that of Milman but with new and distinctive insights,
was that of F. Holmes Dudden, *Gregory the Great: his Place in History
and Thought*, published in 1905. It was to become the standard biography of the pope in the English language, and it has had lasting
influence on later scholarly assessment of his character, teaching and
legacy to posterity. While tempering the contemptuous judgement
passed by the German Liberal Protestant historians on Gregory as
the "father of superstition", Dudden agreed with them that his authorship of the *Dialogues* was indeed of central importance for the under-

---

[27] *RPTK*, VII (1899), p. 87.
[28] 2nd edition, London 1857, vol. I, p. 443.
[29] *Histoire de la littérature latine chrétienne*, 2nd ed. Paris 1924, p. 685.

standing of his complex world-view. In his own judgement of Gregory he combined, on the one hand, admiration for his pastoral wisdom, and for his faithfulness to Scripture and tradition, with, on the other hand, pitying disapproval of the popular superstitious side of his character, revealed in the *Dialogues*. Gregory's theology, according to Dudden, had very different sources. As well as drawing from the well of traditional scriptural wisdom and patristic tradition (the writings of St Augustine in particular), he drew from another very different source, murky and potentially baneful. This, Dudden explained, like Milman before him, was "the body of common popular ideas, some of which were inherited from paganism, while others had sprung up in connection with the ritual and practice of the Church. These ideas were as yet undefined . . ." He summarized as follows Gregory's adoption and systematization of that body of popular ideas in his *Dialogues*:

> It was Gregory's work, however, to give shape to those vague conceptions, to define them with precision, and to restore them as doctrines to the consciousness of the Church. Thus we get the religious fancies of an ignorant clergy and laity expressed in dogmatic formulas; and the current conceptions of angels, saints, demons, miracles, penances, satisfactions, purgatory, heaven and hell are brought in to supplement the older theology. This is, perhaps, the most interesting part of Gregory's teaching, and also the part which at first sight appears the most original. It is clear, however, that Gregory was not initiating any new doctrine, but was merely treating systematically the vague notions of the people of his time.[30]

Dudden did not see the conjunction of those disparate elements in Gregory's thought as a coherent synthesis, but as a radical dichotomy, a psychological illogicality hardly open to rational explanation. His puzzled summing up of the paradox was as follows:

> Let me, in conclusion, once more call attention to the strange combination of shrewdness and superstition which characterized the mind of Gregory. It is certainly astonishing that the clear-headed man who managed the Papal estates and governed the Church with such admirable skill, should have contributed to the propagation of those wild tales of demons and wizards and haunted houses, of souls made visible, of rivers obedient to written orders, of corpses that scream and walk. And yet such is the fact. The landlord of the Papal Patrimonies and the author of the *Dialogues* are one and the same person.

---

[30] *Op. cit.* vol. II, pp. 294–5.

Dudden never thought of questioning the age-old assumption that he stated in the closing sentence of the passage cited above. That fundamentally false premise still strongly sways scholarly discussion of Gregory's thought and legacy. Commentators in recent times have generally accepted, to a greater or less degree, Dudden's regretful exposure of the contradictory strands and basic flaws in his psychology and religious vision. Not a few of them have accordingly come to agree that the greatness of Gregory the Great has been grossly overrated.

Discussion of the historical, literary, doctrinal and devotional questions arising from the *Dialogues* continues unabated today. In an attempt to resolve the paradox highlighted by Dudden, some authors attempt to vindicate Gregory by supposing that he did not relate his fanciful miracle-tales as being historically true, but as allegorical vehicles for conveying higher spiritual lessons. This is the position taken by Carole Straw, in her work *Gregory the Great: Perfection and Imperfection*. She sees the *Dialogues* as "reflecting a sacramental view of reality", and thus not detracting from the nobility of Gregory's overall vision.[31] An extension of such apologia, more rarefied and even less realistic, seeks a clue for interpreting such tales by situating the author in a thought-world that transcends factual veracity. Thus it is suggested that "if we can recover a state of mind in which all texts speak equally of an artistically shaped and fundamentally unreal, but true world, then the anomalies of miracle are far less troubling".[32] In his notable collection of studies on *Gregory the Great and his World*,[33] R.A. Markus gives only brief and passing attention to the *Dialogues*. He does not, as others do, see in that narrative a major source for the understanding of Gregory's world-view, but he interprets them benignly as "an expression of his pastoral concern", and even makes the unsubstantiated judgement that they are "as didactic in their aim as Gregory's preaching on the Scriptures".[34]

---

[31] University of California Press, 1988, Chapters 2 and 3.

[32] I cite these words from a footnote in an article by J.J. O'Donnell, "The Holiness of Gregory" in *Gregory the Great: a Symposium*, ed. J.C. Cavadini, Notre Dame 1995, p. 80.

[33] Cambridge 1997.

[34] *Ibid.*, p. 64. Apart from his summary comment on the *Dialogues* in pages 64–67 (in formulating which, he acknowledges, he was substantially indebted to the articles of S. Boesch Gajano) Markus makes virtually no other reference to that work in his valuable study of Gregory's life, work and thought.

In the common-sense judgment of many other critics, those attempts to rehabilitate the *Dialogues* and to exculpate their author by an enlightened higher criticism are unavailing; no interpretive alchemy can transmute the legendary dross of the *Dialogues* into the golden treasure of Gregorian wisdom. The puzzlement and disquiet that is commonly felt was eloquently expressed by Pierre Courcelle: "After having read the four books which constitute the *Dialogues* one feels oneself seized with nausea. How could Gregory, that great administrator revealed to us by his *Registrum Epistularum*, and that great contemplative revealed to us by his *Moralia on Job* and his *Homilies on Ezekiel*, have written such silly stuff? . . . And yet the authenticity of the *Dialogues* is not in doubt."[35] So too Owen Chadwick, eminent admirer of Gregory's greatness shown by his other works, qualified his admiration with the brusque rider: "But he also wrote a book, the *Dialogues*, full of strange miracles but not of good sense, and so unlike the rest of his works that some critics have tried to prove he did not write it".[36] In recent times many detailed studies of the *Dialogues* have been published, throwing light from various angles on the form and contents of that problematic book.[37] Especially noteworthy are the contributions to the debate made by A. de Vogüé.

f. *A tangled controversy and its renewal today*

That survey of criticism of the *Dialogues*, from the time of the Reformation until the twentieth century, is a necessary preliminary to our present investigation. The first challenge to the Gregorian authenticity of the work was in the arena of literary history and criticism. Coccius and those who followed him based their objections on the great difference in style and religious thought in that strange book, compared with Gregory's authentic works. That criticism was objectively based, and did not originate from anti-Roman bias. Soon, however, the question of the genuineness of the *Dialogues* became a bone of inter-confessional recrimination. In the face of the Protestants'

---

[35] "*Saint Benoît, le merle et le buisson d'épines*", in *Journal des Savants*, 1967, p. 154.
[36] *A History of Christianity*, Oxford 1995, p. 136.
[37] References in the Bibliography below, and more fully in *PsGD*, Chapter 18. See also references given by A. de Vogüé in *SC* 251, pp. 161–2, footnotes 73–8; and R. Godding, *Bibliographia di Gregorio Magno (1890–1989)*, Rome 1990, pp. 111–56.

critique, the Catholic scholars closed ranks and would not admit that there were any anomalies or faults in what they insisted was a Gregorian work. Earlier adverse criticisms even about its religious value, such as those of Melchior Cano, were suppressed.

Whereas sixteenth and seventeenth-century humanist and Protestant critics had impugned the *Dialogues* as a forgery, the argument faded from view after the eighteenth century. No doubt the critics from that time onward were impressed by the detailed defence that the Benedictine and other Catholic scholars had put forward. In any case, they were not inclined to continue the defence of St Gregory by probing the documentary record more closely, as is being done today. Taking a cue from William Cave, they realized that it was a much more effective criticism of the Roman Church to admit the authenticity of the *Dialogues* than to deny it, since thereby a radical deformation of Christian piety could be laid at the door of one of its most esteemed popes. The eventual withering and abandonment of the scholarly challenge to the authenticity of the *Dialogues* was not because Protestant and independent critics had found that the counter-arguments of the Catholic defenders were conclusive, but rather because they themselves had lost interest in that academic debate. By accepting the traditional ascription they could point to the papal *magisterium* itself as the origin and fount of a debased popular Catholicism. It is also instructive to follow the course of the Catholic reaction to criticism of the *Dialogues* from the sixteenth century to the present day. The argument of present-day defenders of the Gregorian authorship is basically the same as that of their predecessors in the seventeenth-century controversy, despite the serious cracks that have recently appeared in its structure.

My own investigation of the riddle of the *Dialogues* began more than fifty years ago, in my early research studies of Gregorian and other patristic texts. My suspicions were aroused when I turned from study of the treasure-chest of spiritual wisdom in Gregory's doctrinal and pastoral works, and in his enlightened letters guiding the life of the Church, to study of the text of *The Lives and Miracles of the Fathers of Italy*. Those suspicions were confirmed by discovery of many anomalies in that text, in language, style and contents, and by scrutiny of its historical origins. I studied with interest the course of the earlier and almost forgotten controversy, and the arguments then put forward on both sides. I wrote a research paper setting out the provisional results of my investigations at that time. Subsequently I set myself to a deeper and lifelong study of the question, moved by *pietas* towards St Gregory, the father of my nation's faith. My conviction that the work was a later forgery was confirmed as I found more and more evidence fitting into the overall pattern. Some time, I resolved, I must complete and publish that case, even *contra mundum*; but under the pressure of circumstances in a busy and not unchequered life that massive project was always supplanted by some other task with more immediate priority.

The spur that finally set me to work on the long-delayed project came in 1980. That year was celebrated as the fifteenth centenary of the birth of St Benedict of Nursia, which, from various historical references found in the *Dialogues*, was assumed to have occurred around the year 480. Accepting an invitation to participate in a scholarly colloquy held at Nursia as part of the year's celebrations, I there offered the first public statement of my reasons for concluding that Gregory was not the author of that book. As I expected, my thesis was received with astonishment and polite derision by most of the scholars present. However, in the following months some of them discussed it further with me in correspondence and by word of mouth. An invitation to read a paper at an international conference on Gregorian themes, held at Chantilly near Paris in 1982, gave me a wider opportunity to present my unorthodox thesis. That invitation was sent to me by one of the principal organizers of the conference, Dom Robert Gillet, a distinguished authority on the Gregorian writings, who was deeply interested in my findings and eventually became convinced by them. He wrote the first published report of them, a favourable summary included in his article on Gregory the Great in *DHGE*.[38]

The paper that I read at the Chantilly conference, entitled "The authenticity of the Gregorian *Dialogues*: a reopening of the question?" was heard with critical disapproval by many, but with an open-minded interest by some. Included in the *Acta* of the conference,[39] that summary led to further debate and comment in the following

---

[38] *Grégoire le Grand*, Paris 1986, pp. 429–44.
[39] "*Grégoire le Grand*" in *DHGE* vol. XXI, cols. 1387–1420.

months and years. Several correspondents wrote to me to discuss
the issue more fully, and a number of them expressed their substantial agreement with my conclusions. I continued preparation of
the full presentation of my complex case, which was eventually published in 1987 in the two volumes of *The Pseudo-Gregorian Dialogues*.

CHAPTER TWO

RECENT DEVELOPMENTS AND THE PRESENT STATE OF THE QUESTION

a

In the previous chapter I surveyed the *Nachleben* of the *Dialogues* through the ages from the time of its emergence into historical record in the early Middle Ages to the late twentieth century. In this chapter I survey the new developments in the story of that famous book since the long dormant debate on its authorship was recently reopened.[1] Soon after *The Pseudo-Gregorian Dialogues* was published in 1987, setting out in full the newly formulated case against the Gregorian authenticity of the *Dialogues*, it was vigorously assailed by three eminent critics. Dom Adalbert de Vogüé, renowned authority on the texts and history of early monasticism, and especially on the Gregorian *Dialogues*, wrote a spirited 58-page critique of the work in *Revue d'Histoire Ecclésiastique*[2] passing a comprehensively negative judgement on its arguments and conclusions. In several other writings since then he has maintained his inflexible opposition to the thesis of the book, dismissing it as "*brillante mais fausse*" and vigilantly countering favourable assessments of it as they appeared. Another renowned writer on the history and literature of late antiquity, Dr Paul Meyvaert, also wrote a scathing rejection of *PsGD* which filled 47 pages in *The Journal of Ecclesiastical History*.[3] He has been Vogüé's chief ally in opposing that book. A third influential critique was that of Fr Robert Godding SJ, published in *Analecta Bollandiana*.[4]

---

[1] In this chapter I recall and adapt passages from two more recent publications of mine: "Authorship of the Commentary *In 1 Regum*: implications of A. de Vogüé's discovery", in *Rev. Bén.* 108 (1998); and "Saint Benedict's biography and the turning tide of controversy", in *ABR* 53 (Sept. 2002).

[2] *RHE* 83 (1988), pp. 291–348.

[3] "The Enigma of Gregory the Great's *Dialogues*: a Response to Francis Clark", *JEH* 39 (1988), pp. 335–81.

[4] "*Les Dialogues de Grégoire le Grand. À propos d'un livre récent*", *AB* 106 (1988), pp. 201–29.

That trio of critics, to whose objections I made detailed reply in
a number of writings,[5] have been described by a commentator who
does not share their viewpoint as "the heavy artillery" of the initial
attack on *PsGD*.[6] Their adverse judgement was followed and echoed
by several writers of shorter dismissive reviews, who thought it unnecessary to spend time studying an unorthodox and dauntingly long
work that they assumed to have been effectively refuted by such
renowned authorities. However, it proved not so easy to suppress.
Notwithstanding the strongly negative verdict pronounced on it by
those three eminent critics, a number of other scholars no less eminent declared themselves convinced by the arguments and findings
of the book. Some of their testimonies are cited below. Although
the initial rejection of *PsGD* by those reputed critics did indeed inhibit
others from studying the case presented there, word of it continued
to spread in the succeeding years, and a growing number of scholars came to recognize the force of that case. A Church historian
who gave careful study, not only to the whole of the massive argument set out in those two volumes but also to the objections of its
principal opponents, was Professor C.F.A. Borchardt. In an article
published in 1990 he objectively assessed the arguments on either
side, and judged the case presented in *PsGD* to be "indeed very
strong". He summed up his verdict by citing a phrase written by
P. Meyvaert in a derisory sense and adapting it to express his own
positive endorsement of that case:

> This then is the thesis of Clark, in the words of Meyvaert, "a vast
> edifice where all the bricks have been tightly fitted together, each lend-
> ing support to the other, the whole forming an imposing structure that
> no onslaught can breach". With this last remark I fully agree.[7]

Similar recognition of the conclusive convergence of the arguments
presented in *PsGD* has been expressed by impartial observers from

---

[5] Most fully in: "The authorship of the Gregorian *Dialogues*: an old controversy
renewed", in *The Heythrop Journal* 30 (1989), pp. 257–72; and "St Gregory and the
Enigma of the *Dialogues*: a Response to Paul Meyvaert", in *JEH* 40 (1989), pp.
323–46. Other articles in which I defended the conclusions of *PsGD* and commented on the developments in the controversy are listed in the Bibliography below.

[6] Cf. Claude Peifer, "The origins of Benedictine monasticism: state of the question"; *ABR* 51 (2000), pp. 293–315.

[7] "The ongoing debate on the Gregorian *Dialogues*", in *Studia Historiae Ecclesiasticae*
18 (1992), pp. 96–107; the passage quoted is on p. 105. Cf. also Borchardt's review
in *Ned. Geref. Teologiese Tydskrif* 31 (1990), pp. 280–1.

different countries and traditions. Dom Henry Wansbrough commented: "Some are more probative than others, but the combined force is irresistible . . . It is a joy to follow an argument presented with such courteous cogency . . .[8] R.J.Z. Werblowsky reflected: "One wonders how, after this publication, it is still possible seriously to maintain the Gregorian authorship".[9] Several others have made similar judgements. Pre-eminent among all those who have closely studied and found convincing the case presented in *PsGD* was Dom Robert Gillet, master guide to the writings and spirituality of St Gregory, whose witness I have already mentioned. He found at last in that book the solution to the enigma posed by the stark contrast that he had long and uneasily discerned between the crude popular religiosity manifest in the *Dialogues* and the distinctive mind-set and sublime spiritual vision of the real Gregory. In a pregnant sentence at the end of his long and appreciative assessment of *PsGD*, he summed up that contrast, the explanation of which he had found in the demonstration given there of the spuriousness of the work:

> The *Dialogues* 'date', as much by their style as by the distance that separates them from our psychology and from our Christian devotion; whereas a doctor and a pastor of such exceptional depth of spirituality as St Gregory the Great spontaneously expresses himself, like a poet or a great artist, in a language that resists the passage of time and penetrates to what is most intimate and most profound in each of us.[10]

As well as those who have judged that the case argued in *PsGD* is conclusively proved, there are others who have conceded that the question has become at least an open one. Giuseppe Cremascoli, acknowledging the comprehensive strength of the case presented in *PsGD*, concluded that the authorship of the *Dialogues* was thereby shown to be open to doubt, and observed: "Indeed, if we accept as certain and unquestionable the Gregorian paternity of the *Dialogues*,

---

[8] *Heythrop Journal* 30 (1989), p. 366.
[9] *Numen* 39 (1992), p. 114. Similarly positive were the assessments made by Alf Härdelin in *Kyrkohistorisk Arsskrift* (1988), pp. 117–23), and (circumspectly) by H. Rosenberg in *Church History* 58 (1989), pp. 88–9.
[10] "*Les Dialogues sont-ils de Grégoire?*", in *Revue des Études Augustiniennes* 36 (1990), pp. 309–14. (His originally chosen title, as printed on the page proofs that he sent me before publication was, "*Les Dialogues du Pseudo Grégoire*". He changed it at the instance of the editors, who evidently thought it too provocative!)

too many things turn out to be incomprehensible and strange".[11]
Some other commentators, impressed by the non-Gregorian features
and striking anomalies that I had pointed out in the text of the
Dialogues, have proposed the compromise theory (similar to Cave's
long ago) that the text was reworked and interpolated by a later
hand than Gregory's. They included Stephan Kessler[12] and Giorgio
Cracco, both noted authorities on the history and literature of late
antiquity and the early Middle Ages. While unwilling to abandon
the traditional ascription of the *Dialogues* as a whole, Professor Cracco
made an assessment of the historical value of *PsGD* that contradicts
the opinion of its indignant critics: "Let it be made very clear: even
prescinding from its basic thesis, the book brings a fundamental and
decisive contribution to knowledge about Gregory the Great and
about the vicissitudes of his works in the seventh and eighth centuries... After it, the conventional landscape of Gregorian studies is
no longer the same".[13]

b. *Monastic historians and the question of the Dialogues*

The question of the authenticity of the *Dialogues* is naturally of special concern to monastic scholars. The colourful life of St Benedict
narrated there, and the account of his foundations, has been for
more than twelve centuries an integral part of the Benedictine heritage. I am well aware that the conclusions presented in *PsGD* have
seemed to many who have heard of them to present an affront to
traditional monastic loyalties. This factor has naturally coloured the
indignant opposition to that book. Yet even within that sensitive
sphere of study, in which monastic piety and regard for hallowed
traditions are a very pertinent factor, there is now critical reassessment of the religious value of the legendary tales told in the second
book of the *Dialogues*.

Dom Henry Wansbrough's comment on the apparently iconoclastic findings of *PsGD* was: "For this Benedictine at any rate, its

---

[11] "*Se i Dialogi siano opera de Gregorio Magno: due volumi per una vexata quaestio*", in
Benedictina 36 (1989), pp. 179–92; the comment quoted is on p. 189.

[12] "*Das Rätsel der Dialoge Gregors der Grossen: Fälschung oder Bearbeitung? Zur Discusion
um ein Buch von Francis Clark*", in *Theologie und Philosophie* 65 (1990), pp. 566–78.

[13] "*Francis Clark e la Storiographia sui Dialogi di Gregorio Magno*", in *Rivista di Storia e
Letteratura Religiosa* 27 (1991), pp. 115–24.

conclusions are liberating."[14] Another open-minded monastic reviewer, describing the book as "a magisterial study, disconcerting but also extremely enthralling", wrote: "We look forward with great confidence to the results of this renewed inquiry into the origin of the *Life* [of St Benedict]".[15] A strong statement of the irrelevance to Benedictine spiritual life of the life-story of St Benedict contained in the *Dialogues* was made in an article in *The American Benedictine Review* by J.B. More. Citing the verdict of *PsGD* on "the religious sensationalism, dubious theology and superstitious notions" to be found in the *Dialogues* narrative, he wrote: "My own conversations with a number of Benedictine monastics reveal that they regard *Dialogues II* as holding little relevance and no normative value in connection with their calling."[16]

The understandable disquiet arising from the implications of *PsGD* felt by many in the monastic tradition was voiced by another reviewer who, after giving a positive account of the close-knit case presented there, added: "There remains, nevertheless, a troubling fact: namely, the complete overthrow of what we thought we knew about the origins of Benedictine monasticism".[17] Other monastic reviewers made similar comments. "The point at which the argument from silence disquiets us most", wrote one, "is where it bears on the knowledge and cult of St Benedict, and on the first knowledge and spread of the Rule. There, indeed, Clark can find support from recent research . . .".[18] The recent research to which that writer referred was the process of significant revision and correction of the historiography of the origins of Benedictine monasticism that has gained growing momentum during the past half-century. A distinguished pioneer in that research was Dom Kassius Hallinger, who drew on, interpreted and added to a body of new evidence brought to light by other contemporary historians. He demonstrated the tardy and muted appearance of the *Regula Benedicti*, despite the praise accorded to it in the *Dialogues*, and also the absence of any observance of that monastic rule south of the Alps until the eighth century. In *PsGD*, while acknowledging my own debt to his ground-breaking study,[19] I

---

[14] *Art cit.*, p. 367.
[15] *Benediktyns Tijdschrift* 1987, p. 170.
[16] *ABR* 45 (1994), p. 142.
[17] Gueric Coilleau, in *Collectanea Cisterciensia* 50 (1988), p. 313.
[18] G. Mathon, *Bulletin de théologie ancienne et mediévale* 14 (1987), p. 458.
[19] "*Papst Gregor der Grosse und der heiliger Benedikt*", in *SA* 42, 1957, pp. 231–319.

amplified and further developed his findings, which have now to be modified on some secondary points. In this volume I summarize that body of evidence and the conclusions to be drawn from it. I also draw on the researches of the Benedictine scholars J. Deshusses and J. Hourlier, who documented the puzzling absence of any cult or liturgical honour of St Benedict during the seventh century.[20]

Hallinger himself did not explicitly challenge the traditional ascription of the *Dialogues* to Gregory the Great, but he did point out the singular isolation of the life-story of St Benedict, and of the reference to his monastic rule found in that book, when contrasted with the pontiff's total lack of knowledge either of the saint or of observance of his rule, as evidenced by his other writings. Indeed, he showed that in Pope Gregory's letters regulating monastic observance there was not only no mention of the rule that is given such superlative praise in the *Dialogues*, but he enjoined practice that was at variance with the provisions of the *RB*. He began by positing the following questions: "When and where did Benedict emerge into the light of history? When and where did he become the object of liturgical cult? By what course and in which century did that great servant of God attain his lasting fame?" Although Hallinger did not advert to the fact, those questions are essentially relevant to the question of the authenticity of the *Dialogues*. The substance of the answers that he gave to them, which provoked indignant reactions from critics, was adopted and developed in *PsGD* and is restated in this book. In a later article[21] Hallinger summarized the new radical clarification of early Benedictine history that was then in progress.

In later chapters I survey the significant implications of the pattern of events in the earliest records of Benedictine monasticism that has been brought into the light in recent times by the researches of Hallinger and other monastic historians. Such a survey provides a comprehensive historical argument showing the weakness of all attempts to claim that the *Dialogues* attributed to Gregory were known from his own lifetime onwards. I show that the first reliable evidence of the emergence into the light of the biography of St Benedict (and of the *Dialogues* as a whole) can be dated about the ninth decade of the seventh century. It was then that its existence was first attested

---

[20] Cf. Chapter 18.a below.
[21] *"Benedikt von Monte Cassino: sein Aufsteig zur Geschichte, zu Kult und Verehrung"*, in *Benedicti Studia*, 10/11 (1984) pp. 77–89.

by a group of half a dozen concordant testimonies, all occurring within the same period. I document the fact that it was not until the first quarter of the eighth century that the first mention of St Benedict appeared in any calendar of saints. From that time also dates the beginning of cult and liturgical commemoration of him.

If indeed in AD 593 the great Pope. Gregory had written in the *Dialogues* the wondrous life-story of St Benedict, how can it be explained that the first beginnings of cult and liturgical honour of the great monastic founder and thaumaturge so greatly lauded in that book did not occur until the first quarter of the eighth century? How was it, in that age of ardent devotion to the shrines and relics of saints, that pilgrimage to his burial place and relics (the location of which at Monte Cassino was expressly indicated in the *Dialogues*) did not begin until more than 120 years later? How explain that, while the first known records of the existence and introduction of the *RB* date from the mid-seventh century in Gaul, and esteem for that rule grew in the Frankish regions from then onwards, there is no evidence throughout the seventh century of its observance either in Rome, or elsewhere in Italy, despite the high commendation allegedly given to it by St Gregory in the *Dialogues*? And how was it that it was not until the middle of the eighth century that the great flowering and expansion of the Benedictine observance throughout the Frankish realms commenced? The answer to those puzzling questions, I submit, is to be found in realization that the marvel-filled biography of St Benedict, allegedly written by St Gregory in *Dialogues* II, did not become known until the closing decades of the seventh century; and that those remarkable developments during the pontificates of Gregory II, Gregory III and Zachary (AD 715–752) were the consequence of the tardy emergence and spread of the *Dialogues*, and of the subsequent *succès d'éstime* of that fascinating book. These developments are chronicled and discussed more fully below, in Chapter 18.

With the marked turning of the tide of debate in recent years, the reassessment of traditional assumptions has grown apace. Dom Benedict Guevin, observing that "Benedictine scholars have begun to adjust to the possibility that the *Dialogues* may not have been written by Pope St Gregory",[22] reassured his brethren regarding the consequences of such adjustment for monastic piety:

---

[22] "A new Gregorian controversy: the authorship of the Commentary on First *Kings* in doubt", *ABR* 50 (1999), pp. 437–43.

Whatever further scholarship on these questions uncovers, Benedictines need not, indeed should not, fear the truth of their origins or their place in history. As Clark himself writes, "although the facts of his life are hidden in the legendary mists of the *Dialogues*, Benedict's veritable and enduring monument stands like a beacon above the changing tides of time. It is the monastic rule that bears his name and that has shaped the lives of countless Christian men and women through more than a millennium".

In a valuable study entitled "The origins of Benedictine monasticism: state of the question",[23] Dom Claude Peifer situated the unfolding debate over the *Dialogues* within the wider context of the dramatic sea change in the historiography of early Benedictinism that has taken place during the past half century, which I have summarized above. While judiciously refraining from predicting an early resolution of the current debate, he concluded his study with a frank acceptance of the real possibility that the traditional assumption of the Gregorian authorship of the *Dialogues* will eventually be abandoned. His concluding reflections on the implications of such an outcome for Benedictine loyalties were as follows:

> If the *Dialogues* can no longer be considered a sixth-century witness to St Benedict and his Rule, then there will be no early sources left except the Rule itself and the piecemeal historical record of its gradual penetration. But would that necessarily be a loss? It is always a gain for us to discover the truth. In the entire process of revision that has taken place in the past half-century, it has not been a question of devout monks defending St Benedict from within against hordes of rationalists assaulting the ramparts. On the contrary, most of the protagonists in the controversies have themselves been monks who were trying to discover the truth about the origins of our way of life.

c. *A. de Vogüé's momentous discovery*

A significant new turn in the progress of this long-running controversy came in the year 1996, when the principal and most influential critic of *PsGD*, Dom Adalbert de Vogüé himself, announced a momentous documentary discovery which gave, *malgré lui*, weighty corroboration to the case presented in that book.[24] It related to the celebrated

---

[23] *ABR* 51 (2000), pp. 293–315.
[24] That discovery was announced by Vogüé in an article entitled, "*L'auteur du*

commentary on the first book of *Kings* (now *1 Samuel*) known generally as *In 1 Regum*. The question of the authorship of that truncated commentary is of immediate relevance to the *Dialogues* controversy, since the text contains verbatim citations from the rule of St Benedict and, like the *Dialogues*, high praise of its saintly author. Its Gregorian authorship, disputed in the past, had become widely accepted during the twentieth century, following the magisterial researches and edition of P.-P. Verbraken.[25] A. de Vogüé and P. Meyvaert had joined in pronouncing as certain Gregory's sole authorship of the whole text, and even affirmed (here disagreeing with Verbraken) that the great pope had personally approved the final recension and publication of the work. Accordingly both those authors, in their critique of *PsGD*, had pointed to the witness of *In 1 Regum* as decisively discrediting my demonstration that there is significant absence, in all the surviving historical and literary records, of any evidence to show that either St Gregory or any of his contemporaries had knowledge of St Benedict and his rule. Vogüé had derided as an absurd tissue of fantasy my conclusion, based on the internal evidence of the text, that the composer of *In 1 Regum*, and author of its Benedictine allusions was not St Gregory but a mediaeval Benedictine monk.[26] The disconcerting discovery that he has recently made is of cogent evidence in a twelfth-century chronicle showing that the real composer of *In 1 Regum* was in fact a mediaeval Benedictine monk, Peter of Cava, who became abbot of Venosa.

Constrained by that documentary evidence, which is reinforced by linguistic critique of the text, Vogüé abruptly abandoned his previous conviction that the commentary was entirely the work of St Gregory. Instead, swinging to the opposite extreme, he declared his judgement that it was entirely the work of the monk Peter of Cava. In concert with him, Meyvaert also changed his mind promptly and signified his agreement with that extraordinary reversal of judgement.[27] In an article commenting on his retraction,[28] I reiterated my

---

Commentaire des Rois attribué à saint Grégoire: un moine de Cava?", in *Rev. Bén.* 106 1996, pp. 319–31.

[25] Following his preliminary historical discussion in *Rev. Bén.* 66 (1956), pp. 39–62; Verbraken's annotated edition of the text of *In 1 Regum* was published in *CCL* 144 in 1963.

[26] *Art. cit. RHE* 83 (1988), pp. 318, 246 *et alibi*.

[27] As Vogüé records in *Rev. Bén.* 106 (1996), p. 323, note 25.

[28] Reference in footnote 1 above.

reasons for concluding that *In 1 Regum* does in fact contain a considerable quantity of genuine Gregorian commentary, abstracted by
the mediaeval author from a store of unpublished *reportata* of Gregory's
expository discourses, which—as I show in the following chapter—
was preserved for centuries after his lifetime. However, while retract-
ing his previous confident pronouncements on the Gregorian authorship
of that commentary on *Kings*, and having to admit accordingly that
one prominent bastion of his position on the question of the authenticity of the *Dialogues* had fallen, Vogüé did not withdraw or modify his resolute opposition to the main conclusions of the case presented
in *PsGD*.[29]

His embarrassing discovery has had a significant influence in the
ongoing change of opinion in the *Dialogues* debate. Although disproof
of Gregory's authorship of *In 1 Regum* does not by itself disprove his
authorship of the *Dialogues*, it has immediate relevance to the controversy over the latter question. It undermines the arguments (and
the credit) of those reputed critics who have appealed to the certain
authenticity of *In 1 Regum* as confirming the certain authenticity of
the *Dialogues*. It means, too, that others who have confidently relied
on their authority must now revise their own contentions—as is
already happening.[30] More widely, it serves to dispel an illusion that
for many minds has hitherto been a major obstacle to recognition
of the cogency of the multiple proofs that Gregory was not the author
of the *Dialogues*.

I have elsewhere[31] described the collapse of the argument that the
critics had based on Gregory's praise and citation of St Benedict's
rule, allegedly given by him in the commentary on *Kings*, as "the
fall of the penultimate domino in a row of false assumptions". The
assumptions referred to were a string of alleged testimonies from
authoritative seventh-century documents that had been traditionally
adduced as proofs that the *Dialogues* were known and attributed to
Gregory in his lifetime and in the following age. As I showed in

---

[29] He reaffirmed his opposition in an article, "*Du nouveau sur les Dialogues de saint
Grégoire?*" in *CC 62* (2000).
[30] For instance, Professor Robert Markus had cited what he thought was the
established fact of Gregory's authorship of *In 1 Regum* as "clinching" proof of the
pope's knowledge of St Benedict's rule. (*Gregory the Great and his World*, Cambridge
1997, p. 69.) I commented on his subsequent change of position in *HJ* 40 (1999)
pp. 207–9.
[31] In *ABR* 53.3 (2002).

PsGD and recall below in Chapter 12, those seemingly impressive pleas have been proved, one by one, to be unsound and to be based on later interpolations made in the MS tradition. In his article referred to above, "The origins of Benedictine monasticism: state of the question", Claude Peifer surveyed the continuing process of scholarly demolition of the vast structure of misconception, myth and literary forgery that has hitherto obscured the historiography of those origins a process that has recently culminated in the discrediting of the alleged testimony of *In 1 Regum*. He too marked the problematic isolation of the biography of St Benedict narrated in the putatively Gregorian *Dialogues*, doubtfully surviving, in his phrase, as "our only sixth-century source" for knowledge of early Benedictine history. The metaphor that Peifer himself used was not that of a solitary last domino beginning to fall but of a solitary foundation rock beginning to disintegrate. He wrote: "There is still the rock of the *Dialogues* to fall back upon. But this rock too is showing signs of threatening to break up, thanks to a massive attack launched upon it in the 1980s by Dr Francis Clark. This controversy ... has to be mentioned as being of crucial importance to the question of Benedictine origins."[32] He proceeded to give a clear and objective summary of the facts of that controversy.

Since Peifer wrote those words the unsubstantial rock has continued to crumble. He did not predict the time of its final disintegration, but at the end of his article he pointed, as other commentators have also done, to a parallel with another long-drawn-out controversy concerning the origins of the Benedictine tradition. That parallel had earlier been pointed out by an appreciative monastic reviewer of *PsGD*. Citing a comparison already made by Dom Robert Gillet in his article on St Gregory in *DHGE* in 1986, G. Mathon wrote: "It took 40 years and some 500 articles to bring into clear light the relationship between the *Regula Magistri* and the *Regula Benedicti*. In this debate we may expect something similar: a period of denial, maybe to absorb the shock, then a coming to terms with the facts."[33]

A notable contribution to the study of Benedictine origins is contained in the study of Marilyn Dunn, *The Emergence of Monasticism*,[34]

---

[32] *ABR* 51 (2000), p. 312.
[33] *BTAM* 14 [1988], p. 459.
[34] Oxford and Malden, 2000.

which has thrown much new light on early monastic history and has discredited some hoary misconceptions. Describing the authenticity of the *Dialogues* as now "highly controversial and problematic" in the light of *PsGD*, she brings further arguments from monastic history which indicate that the book was of post-Gregorian origin, to which I shall again refer in later pages. She concludes: "As for the disputed *Dialogues*, it appears increasingly likely that the first reliable witnesses to the existence of the text as a whole date from the later seventh century".[35] In ongoing work she offers further evidence for this conclusion.

---

[35] *Ibid.*, p. 131.

PART II

INTERNAL TEXTUAL EVIDENCE OF THE NON-GREGORIAN AUTHORSHIP OF THE *DIALOGUES*

CHAPTER THREE

AN ESSENTIAL KEY TO THE ENIGMA OF THE *DIALOGUES*: THE DETECTION OF GENUINELY GREGORIAN PASSAGES INSERTED INTO THE MAIN NARRATIVE TEXT

a

Undeniably, the *Dialogues* text presents a stylistic paradox. On the one hand there are cogent and convergent arguments, from both internal and external criticism, indicating that the author of that fanciful and home-spun narrative was not St Gregory the Great; on the other, there are recognizable within the text many discrete passages and fragmentary phrases that can be seen to bear the unmistakable stamp of his literary style and to reflect his doctrinal and pastoral wisdom. Defenders of the Gregorian authenticity of the work have singled out those passages to support their case. Some critics frankly admit, indeed, that they are in puzzling contrast with what Peter Goussainville recognized as the "barbarisms of phrase and style" in the main narrative. "Regarding the style", he wrote, "I acknowledge that there is some diversity, but it is not absolute. Who does not know that style varies according to the nature of the treatise and of the subject matter? . . . Nevertheless it is clear to the reader that in these *Dialogues* there are many things that do exhibit the style, power and elegance of Gregory's other works, indeed the loftiness of his wisdom as well".[1] The presence of many discrete pearls of Gregorian wisdom within the main narrative text of the *Dialogues* has undoubtedly been a powerful factor in persuading many scholars during the past four centuries to accept the work as authentically Gregorian, despite its other disconcerting features. The puzzling contrast between their elevated and euphonic style and the demotic and often inelegant style of the main narrative has been remarked by many scholars, and various strained theories have been advanced to explain them.

[1] *Vindiciae Dialogorum, PL* 77, col. 133–4; cf. *PsGD*, pp. 684–5.

The true resolution of that stylistic paradox, I argue, lies in realization that those unmistakably Gregorian passages, some eighty in
number and constituting nearly one quarter of the total wordage of
the *Dialogues*, were derived by the unknown author from a deposit
of genuinely Gregorian literary remains, most of which were never
edited or authorized by the pontiff for publication, but which were
preserved during his lifetime and for long afterwards in the Lateran
scrinium, the secretariate and archives of the Roman see. We have
clear proof of the existence of such a deposit, and much information about its contents.

In Chapters 12–17 of *PsGD* I set out at considerable length the
evidence relating to each of those authentic pericopes discernible in
the *Dialogues*, which I habitually refer to, both in that book and in
this, by the abbreviation "IGPs" = "Inserted Gregorian Passages".
I demonstrate their disparity from the main narrative text and their
often incongruous usage by the Dialogist. In this chapter I give an
abridged summary of that case. The sources available to the Dialogist
from which to draw such pericopes were threefold. The first was the
archive files of passages which Gregory had discarded from earlier
drafts of his expository and homiletic works, especially the *Moralia*.
There is documentary evidence of the survival of such excised passages, found in the anthology of Paterius[2] and elsewhere. The second and major source was the large collection of Gregorian *reportata*
and *inedita*: that is, the large archival reserve of transcripts of expository discourses that had been taken down by stenographers as
Gregory delivered them by word of mouth, but which he never had
opportunity to edit for public circulation. The third and most obviously recognizable source is the corpus of Gregory's published works,
chiefly his Gospel *Homilies*, from which the Dialogist transcribed a
number of passages verbatim. I discuss each of those three sources
in turn.

First, there are the reused passages from discarded drafts in the
archives. Gregory himself gave a description of his methods of composition, which shows how in the editing process discrete passages
from earlier drafts could be left aside. In a letter to Leander of
Seville, prefaced to his great commentary on *Job*, the *Moralia*, he
told incidentally of the work of the busy amanuenses who recorded

---

[2] To be discussed more fully in Chapter 21 below.

his words and of the processes by which his expository commentaries were amended and prepared for authorized publication:

> With the brethren assembled to hear me and with the book open before my eyes, I spoke my commentary on the earlier chapters straight out. For the later chapters, finding that I had more time at my disposal, I dictated the text reflectively. Finally ... I went through the whole text, which had been taken down as I uttered it, correcting and arranging it ... However, I have left the third section of the work as I uttered it by word of mouth, since the brethren, by drawing me away to other tasks, have not allowed me to amend it in more detail.[3]

How there came to be variant texts of Gregory's published homilies, reflecting different stages in their composition, is made clear in a letter he wrote towards the end of his life to Bishop Secundinus of Taormina, enclosing a copy of the finally authorized text of his *Homilies on the Gospels* and explaining how it had reached that form:

> During the sacred solemnities of Mass I expounded forty passages from the holy Gospel, which it is the traditional practice of this Church to read on fixed days. In some cases the exposition which I had dictated was read out by a notary; in others, I myself gave a spoken explanation while the people listened, and as my words were uttered so they were taken down in writing. But some of the brethren, fervent with zeal for the sacred word, reproduced what I had said before I could revise it by careful amendment ... Just as these homilies were delivered by me at different times of the year, so they were also transcribed by the note-takers into the codices at different times. If Your Fraternity should come across a transcript in which the text of the Gospel is expounded in an ambiguous manner you must realize that the transcripts in question have remained uncorrected ... The edited text is preserved here in the *scrinium* of our holy Church, so that [those in doubt] may find here, in our codices that have been duly amended, an exemplar from which they can resolve any uncertainties.[4]

Gregory's letter to Bishop Secundinus well illustrates the meticulousness—some might call it fussiness—with which he supervised the editing and inscribing of his works. He was closely concerned with the due functioning of the secretariate of the Roman see. There, as I shall recall many times in the following chapters, he had at his service a well-organized recording and filing system that enabled him

---

[3] Epist. V.53a; EH I.354–5; cf. *PsGD*, pp. 412–3.
[4] Epistola IV.17a; EH I.251–2.

to retrieve and adapt the text of his works for authorized publication. I describe more fully in Chapter 11 the circumstances in which
his *Homilies on Ezekiel* were originally preached: how, in the grim
winter of 593–594, with the army of the Lombard king Agilulf men-
acing Rome, Gregory could no longer prepare his sermons by careful forethought but spoke his commentary extempore from an anguished
heart while the notaries took down his words, until at length the
horrors of the siege of Rome made further preaching impossible.
The clerks' transcriptions of that series of homilies was left unrevised
for eight years, until Gregory was prevailed upon to edit them for
publication, as he related in a dedicatory letter to Bishop Marianus
of Ravenna, written in 601–2:

> Oppressed by a multitude of cares, I had left in oblivion the homilies
> on the prophet Ezekiel that had been taken down in writing just as I
> spoke them to the assembled people. But after eight years, at the urg-
> ing of the brethren, I took pains to send for the *schedae* of the notaries,
> and with the help of God I revised them. As far as the pressure of
> my afflictions permitted, I have corrected the text.[5]

The existence of several "lost" Gregorian passages from the *Homilies*
has long been recognized. The Maurists had already signalled the
existence of such passages in their edition of the seventh-century
anthology ascribed to Paterius. In 1769, in his collection of Gregory's
works,[6] J.B. Galliccioli printed an incomplete series of additional passages from those homilies which were not to be found in any existing MSS. In an article in 1958 R. Étaix supplemented the list of
fragments, and commented: "It may well appear astonishing that
authentic texts of St Gregory, published under his name in the Latin
Patrology, should never be utilized . . . From both external and internal criticism we are obliged to consider those pieces as being truly
Gregorian".[7] M. Adriaen reprinted a fuller collection of those items
in his critical edition of the *Homilies on Ezekiel*.[8] Asking where the
additional passages came from, Étaix inferred that they were drawn
from the notebooks of the notaries who took down Gregory's words
as he preached them in 593–4. Adriaen judged this "a shrewd hypoth-

---

[5] Epistola XII.16a; EH I.362–3.
[6] Venice 1769, VI, pp. 263–71.
[7] "*Le Liber Testimoniorum de Paterius*", in *RSR* 32 (1958) p. 76.
[8] *CCL* 142, 1971, introduction.

esis", and agreed "there can be no possible doubt about the Gregorian origin of these fragments".

Étaix also indicated, as a likely source from which some other unknown Gregorian fragments in the Paterian anthology were taken, "a first edition of the *Moralia*".[9] Some of the unknown Gregorian pericopes in the Paterian collection are in fact ascribed in early MSS to the *Moralia*, and others to the *Regula Pastoralis*. Gregory painstakingly amended successive drafts of that commentary on *Job*; the discarded pericopes would thus have been also available in the *scrinium*—to serve the Dialogist later as a source for some of his IGPs. Adriaen also alluded to the fact that several more of those "lost" Gregorian passages are also cited, usually in fragmentary or abbreviated form, by Tajo of Saragossa in his *Liber Sententiarum*. (I further discuss Tajo's use of those passages in Chapters 12.e and 21.b.) Étaix concluded his article on the "lost" Gregorian texts which survive in the Paterian anthology and elsewhere by raising the interesting question of possible reasons for their suppression in the editions authorized by St Gregory: "Was it in order to correct certain assertions that seemed inadequate or ambiguous, or simply to lighten the weight of its composition?"[10] This question may be relevantly adapted to a main concern in this book—that is, the provenance of the IGPs in the *Dialogues*. It would seem that in some cases the probable reason why certain IGPs had been excised from earlier drafts of Gregory's works was that they duplicated what he had said elsewhere—especially in the *Moralia*.

b. *The "Claudian Collection" of Gregorian* reportata

However, the codices of discarded drafts of Gregory's published writings constituted a relatively small part of the mass of Gregorian *schedae* filed in the Lateran archives.[11] A far larger potential source from which the Dialogist could draw his IGPs was the deposit of

---

[9] *Op. cit.*, p. 400.

[10] *Op. cit.*, p. 78.

[11] P. Meyvaert's derisory comments (in *JEH* 39, p. 360) about "accumulated fragments and snippets", in his critique of my treatment of the IGPs in *PsGD*, reflect only a cursory reading of what is actually said there.

unpublished *reportata* of expository discourses which had been delivered viva voce by the pontiff but which he never had time or energy
to edit and prepare for publication. Those discourses, too, had been
taken down by stenographers, either at dictation in his study or,
more usually, while he preached, as he put it, "with the Bible open
before my eyes". In one of his letters we find explicit reference to
a very considerable store of such unedited *reportata* of his spoken
scriptural commentaries. The letter was sent two years before his
death to his representative at Ravenna, John the Subdeacon, instruct-
ing him to recover from the monastery of Classis, and to send to
Rome for safe-keeping, a large collection of such texts which had
been ineptly recorded by a monastic amanuensis named Claudius,
lately deceased:

> My beloved son the late abbot Claudius was a hearer of discourses I
> delivered on *Psalms*, on the *Canticle of Canticles*, on the Prophets, on the
> *Books of Kings*, and on the Heptateuch. Because of my infirmity I could
> not put those discourses in written form; accordingly, lest they should
> perish in oblivion, he made transcripts of them according to his appre-
> hension. It was intended that when opportunity occurred he should
> bring his transcripts to me so that I might correct them for publica-
> tion. But when he read them to me I found the sense of my words
> altered in a very unsatisfactory manner. Wherefore you must without
> delay or excuse go at once to his monastery, call the brethren together
> and order them, under strictest precept, to bring out whatever manu-
> scripts on those various parts of Scripture that Claudius took there.
> Take possession of them and send them to me as speedily as possible.[12]

The surviving store of unpublished *reportata* of Gregory's commentaries on all the books of the Old Testament named in that letter
must have been extensive indeed. Transcripts of his expository discourses on *Proverbs*, on the *Canticle*, on the Prophets, on the books
of *Kings* and on the Heptateuch, the first seven books of the Old
Testament, would constitute a very large collection of *schedae*. That
store remained in the *Scrinium* after Gregory's death, and would have
been still available there to the composer of the *Dialogues* to use in
the later seventh century and thus give his narrative an appearance
of Gregorian authenticity.

Included among the transcripts specified in Gregory's letter, which
John the Subdeacon was ordered to retrieve from Classis, were his

---

[12] Epist. XII. 6; EH II.352.

unpublished commentaries on the books of *Kings* and on the *Canticle of Canticles*. Sections of clearly Gregorian commentary on both those scriptural texts, unpublished in his lifetime, have survived the centuries. I mentioned in Chapter 2 the survival of genuine sections of *In I Regum* that were recognizably incorporated by the mediaeval abbot Peter of Cava into a composition of his own. P.-P. Verbraken, who edited that truncated commentary in the *Corpus Christianorum* series, drew attention to a remarkable phrase in the *incipit* prefixed to the oldest extant MS, stating that the text had been taken "from the *exceda* of the Lord Gregory, pope of the Church of Rome". Verbraken noted that "*exceda*" was a variant form of "*scheda*", a term used to refer to booklets or loose folios. He commented: "This work, then, was drawn from the archives of the pope", and he concluded that the phrase in the ancient *incipit* "offers all the guarantees of an origin contemporary with Gregory".[13] In his criticism of *PsGD* R. Godding denied that the term "*schedae*" could have the meaning I attach to it in this context,[14] but his opinion is refuted by the findings of Verbraken and others. The author of the seventh-century Paterian anthology likewise states that some of his excerpts were drawn from Gregory's works contained "*in schedis suis*"—that is, in the draft transcripts in the papal archives. The meaning of these phrases is also illustrated by a remark of a Spanish writer in the mid-seventh-century, who (as related below in Chapter 21.b) referred to a search recently made for Gregorian writings "*in archivio Ecclesiae Romanae*" by Tajo of Saragossa.

It was to that same store of Gregorian literary remains that the ninth-century biographer of St Gregory, John the Deacon, referred when he attested that undivulged writings of the great pope were still strictly guarded in the Roman archives three centuries after his lifetime: "*reliqua ipsius opera nunc in sancta Romana Ecclesis retinentur adhuc sub custodia, ne penitus vulgarentur.*"[15] The concluding seven words may reflect a written injunction of Gregory himself repeating his stern prohibition of unauthorized publication of the *inedita* recalled by him to the curial *Scrinium*. John had access to some curial records that have since perished. One was Gregory's subsidy roll, which, he

---

[13] *CCL* 144, p. viii; cf. *PsGD*, p. 420.
[14] Cf. his article in *AB* 106 (1988), p. 206.
[15] *PL* 75, col. 223.

reported, was still in his day to be seen in the Roman *Scrinium*—"*in hoc sacratissimo Lateranensis palatii scrinio*".[16]

The large mass of unedited Gregorian *reportata* that was recalled to the Lateran archive by Gregory's orders will be seen to be essentially relevant in our examination of the constitutive elements of the *Dialogues*. In these pages I will call it "the Claudian Collection" of Gregorian literary remains. It was in all probability the source from which, in the seventh century, Paterius and Tajo drew excerpts of the otherwise "lost" Gregorian excerpts, which I will discuss more fully in Chapter 21. It was doubtless from that curial store of *reportata* texts that in later centuries the fragmentary text of the unpublished Gregorian commentaries on *1 Kings* and on the *Canticle* was retrieved. Likewise, I conclude that it was from the selfsame store in the Lateran secretariate that, in the last part of the seventh century, a *scriniarius* in the Roman secretariate was able to draw a considerable number of genuine Gregorian pericopes to insert in his fictional work put out under the great name of Pope Gregory I, thus giving it impressive verisimilitude.

c. *Identification and critique of the inserted passages*

In *PsGD* the inserted Gregorian passages discernible in the *Dialogues* are identified and delimited. To appreciate the dissonance between the IGPs and the main narrative text in which they are inserted, it is evidently requisite to have familiarity with Gregory's own vocabulary, intricate phrasing and elevated literary style. His Latin usage has a very distinctive character, as scholars down the centuries have remarked. Sixtus of Siena observed, in his work *De falsa librorum inscriptione* (written in 1566, when the new challenge to the authenticity of the *Dialogues* was a subject of current concern), "nothing is more difficult than to imitate the style of another". Of the writings of Gregory the Great, he declared: "In them there is such a consistency of diction, always such a similarity of style and such an aptly sustained order of expression, that it is impossible to discern in his writing anything which could seem to be imitated from elsewhere

---

[16] *Vita Gregorii*, II.11; *PL* 75.98. John also gives the information (probably from a MS annotation) that it was Aemilianus the notary who, with others, took down in writing Gregory's Gospel *Homilies* as he delivered them (*PL* 75.92).

or supplied by another author".[17] Gregory has been justly called "a lyrical poet in prose". As I show more fully in Chapters 5 and 6, his pastoral and expository writings have in common a distinctive character, in language and thought-content, that provides a sure recognition mark, or "literary signature", attesting his authorship. It is immediately recognizable in all his writings, including the more "popular" Gospel homilies. While that distinctive and harmonious pattern of Gregorian composition is significantly absent from the main narrative text of the *Dialogues*, it is recognizable throughout the eighty IGPs marked out in *PsGD*.[18]

While in *PsGD* the number of the IGPs is reckoned as eighty, (and in this book as eighty-one)[19] that number would vary if my subdivisions of individual IGPs were listed separately. Moreover, it could be somewhat increased if, as well as complete pericopes, we also counted the many discrete phrases studded by the Dialogist into his demotic narrative text to give it Gregorian verisimilitude, which likewise have the veritable ring of Gregory's style and choice of words. For instance, two such phrases, used in praise of St Benedict, occur in the first paragraph of the second book of the *Dialogues*. The first, "*soli Deo placere desiderans*", is found at least three times in Gregory's authentic works. The second, the pithy oxymoron "*scienter nescius et sapienter indoctus*", also has a truly Gregorian ring.[20] In several cases the source from which the Dialogist took his snippets of Gregorian phrasing can be recognized. Thus the phrase "*in quo mentis vertice stetit*" in *Dial.* III.16.4 is taken verbatim from the *Homilies on Ezekiel* II.6.9. Whereas in the *Homilies* Gregory uses it to refer to the exemplary humility of St Peter, the Dialogist applies it to a holy hermit Martin whose spiritual eminence is there demonstrated by the fact that he was able to live unharmed for three years with a sinister

---

[17] *Bibliotheca sancta ex praecipuis Catholicae Ecclesiae auctoribus collecta*, Venice 1566, IV, pp. 510, 374. There is a curious (perhaps prudent) ambiguity in Sixtus's own reference to the *Dialogues*. Did he privately share Coccius's opinion?

[18] A typical illustration of it, plucked at random, may be cited from IGP 3: "*Sed tamen sunt nonnumquam qui ita per magisterium Spiritus intrinsecus docentur, ut, etsi eis exterius humani magisterii disciplina desit, magisterii intimi censura non desit. Quorum tamen libertas vitae ab infirmis in exemplum non est trahenda, ne, dum se quisque similiter sancto Spiritu impletum praesumit, discipulus hominis esse despiciat et magister erroris fiat.*" (*Dialogues* I.1.6)

[19] See Appendix below, IGP 22.*bis*.

[20] Several others are indicated in *PsGD*, pp. 439–40. A. de Vogüé refers to many other instances of such Gregorian phrases within the narrative text. *RHE* 83 (1988) p. 330.

serpent in his cell. I discuss those discrete Gregorian phrases further
in Chapter 5.d, with further examples.

The main narrative text of the *Dialogues* constitutes just over three-
quarters (76%) of the total wordage. The IGPs which constitute the
remaining quarter (24%) are unevenly distributed. In the first three
books they occupy only 15% of the wordage, but in the fourth book,
which has a special character, they account for 40%. With the exception of a small group to be discussed below, the IGPs are all moral
and doctrinal passages of the same theological character and literary style that is found in the *Moralia* and Gregory's other scriptural
commentaries. Often it is possible to infer the context in which they
were originally written by Gregory. The insertion of those doctrinal
and expository passages into the narrative text is often abrupt and
artificial. A. de Vogüé calls them, appropriately, "*excursus*", and "pure
doctrine passages".[21] Tangential and digressive they are indeed, despite
the Dialogist's editorial attempts to make them seem relevant to his
narrative context. As more than one commentator has observed,
those elevated but digressive passages dislocate rather than integrate
the flow of the narrative.

Investigation of the context of the IGPs, and of the manner in
which the Dialogist made use of the pearls of Gregorian wisdom
which he had appropriated from the curial archives, leads to interesting discoveries. We find, time and time again, that after a picturesque tale or comments in his less than elegant Latin, there comes
a leading question from Peter the Deacon, Gregory's interlocutor in
the dialogue. Though often having only a strained connection with
what has just been related, the question proves to be a cue for bringing in a genuine Gregorian passage that the Dialogist has ready to
insert. In some cases Peter's question leads directly into the passage,
but in others the author puts into Gregory's mouth some sentences
or phrases of his own composition in order to link the question with
the authentic Gregorian passage which is to follow. After this pre-
amble, there follows an IGP in Gregory's distinctive language and
style, giving a moral or spiritual teaching based on scriptural teaching. The opening phrase of the pericope is sometimes adapted to
make it seem relevant to what has preceded. A frequent tell-tale
marker of the introduction of an IGP is the insertion of the voca-

---

[21] *SC* 251, p. 108.

tive *Petre*. (This feature is marked in the first three books of the *Dialogues*, but is almost completely lacking in the fourth, which contains the greatest number of IGPs. In later pages I discuss the special character of that fourth book, which has led several commentators to conclude that it was probably conceived and composed independently.) Very occasionally the Dialogist inserts extraneous words of his own into the text of a Gregorian excerpt, but as a rule he reproduces the pope's elevated wording verbatim. At the end of the borrowed pericopes there is often a remark by Peter the Deacon in praise of what has been said, followed by the return from elevated Gregorian doctrine to the Dialogist's fictional narrative and to his own lower level of language and thought. One tell-tale instance of such return, which he himself clearly signals, is in *Dial.* II.3.12. There, after interpolating a Gregorian reflection (IGP 18) on the fortitude and heavenly longings of St Paul, he marks the end of the borrowed pericope by making Peter the Deacon expressly ask his master to return to his narrative text: "*Sed quaeso ut de vita tanti patris ad narrationis ordinem redeas*".

In many cases the leading question put into the mouth of Peter is clearly forced and malapropos. I cite here two examples of such inconsequential cues. The first introduces IGP 38 (*Dial.* III.26.7–9 and 28.2–4). The Dialogist has just related a number of tall tales, concluding with a story about a holy hermit named Menas who demonstrated his supernatural insight by detecting and rejecting a concealed gift that had been sent to him by a wicked landowner. From his source of Gregorian *inedita* in the Lateran store the author has at hand a long and elevated passage on two kinds of martyrdom, actual and spiritual (which closely parallels, both in reasoning and in wording, a passage in Gregory's Gospel *Homilies*, 35.7). What cue can he give to Peter the Deacon in his dialogue to make that passage concerning spiritual martyrdom seem relevant to the stories he has just told, such as that of Menas's vatic perspicacity? The quite incongruous leading phrase that he chooses is: "Many of these men, I think, would have been able to undergo martyrdom if a time of persecution had come upon them". As a ploy to introduce the coming *excursus* of Gregorian wisdom concerning spiritual martyrdom, that remark is abrupt and inept. In his commentary on the text in his *Sources Chrétiennes* edition of the *Dialogues* A. de Vogüé remarks (with considerable understatement) that the connexion is "*un peu inattendue*".

My second example of a patently arbitrary cue used as a pretext to introduce a borrowed Gregorian pericope is in *Dial.* III.33.10. There the Dialogist has ready for use a long Gregorian passage (IGP 39, *Dial.* III.34.1–4),[22] in which the pontiff reflected on the virtue of compunction and holy tears, distinguishing two different kinds of compunction. To prepare for its use, the author introduces the preliminary remark that the holy abbot Eleutherius of Spoleto, whose deeds he is relating, was a man of great compunction and his tears were of much avail for obtaining miraculous favours. (*Soi-disant* Gregory testifies from personal experience to his thaumaturgic power; he relates that he himself had been cured by it when at the point of death from a syncope.) Then, at the end of the chapter, the Dialogist supplies the immediate cue by which Peter the Deacon solicits the recitation of the Gregorian pericope ready for use, on the virtue of compunction and its two main *genera*. That cue reads as follows: "Because you said that this man was of great compunction, I should like to learn more fully what is the power of tears. Wherefore tell me, please, how many kinds of compunction there are." The Gregorian theological pericope that follows, on the two *genera* of compunction, has no application to the narration that has preceded, and the cue that leads into it is patently inconsequential. Here again A. de Vogüé observantly remarks on the singular awkwardness of the author's device: "*Trop précise, la seconde demande de Pierre est bien gauche*".[23] In many other places in his commentary on the *Dialogues* Vogüé points out the logical disarray and inconsequence of the author's composition. He remarks that just as the chapters in Book IV on purgatorial sanctions are introduced abruptly by Peter the Deacon without apparent connexion with what had preceded, so "it is in a manner just as abrupt that he passes from purgatory to the questions concerning hell".[24]

I have already indicated probable sources in the files of the Roman *Scrinium* from which the IGPs were drawn: in particular, the successive drafts of the *Moralia* text and especially the large collection

---

[22] In Chapter 21.b below (and more fully in *PsGD* (pp. 512–7), I trace the close verbal connexion of IGP 39 with Gregory's letter to the princess Theoctista in 597, and compare it with the transcripts used by Paterius and Tajo, to which the Dialogist also had access.

[23] *SC* 260, p. 400.

[24] *SC* 251, p. 73.

of Claudius's unedited *reportata* of Gregory's commentaries on several books of the Old Testament. In some places the original source of the borrowed IGPs can be identified, but in most cases it can no longer be traced. We do not have access to the Claudian Collection or the other Gregorian remains which the Dialogist was able to exploit. Nevertheless, as well as being able to trace the source of some specific passages, we can make shrewd conjectures about the origin of many of his borrowings. We are also able to discern the start and finish of the Gregorian excerpts, to mark their linguistic difference from the text in which they are imbedded, and to recognize the awkwardness of their appropriation by the Dialogist. While the great majority of the IGPs are taken from unpublished Gregorian commentaries, not all of them are in that in the category. Nine of them are reproduced verbatim from Gregory's published writings. These are discussed below, in Section e. of this chapter.

In the Introduction I referred to the difference between my treatment of the IGPs in *PsGD* and in the present volume. In the 112-page appendix of Volume 1 of *PsGD* the whole Latin text of the *Dialogues* was printed, with the wording of all the IGPs marked out within the main narrative text by underscoring. In the 139 pages of Chapters 14–17 of that book I discussed in detail the content and context of each of the IGPs in turn, pointing out their incongruity with the main text in which they are embedded. That fuller documentation still remains needful for those who wish to pursue exhaustive research of all aspects of the question of the authorship of the *Dialogues*. In this volume, however, there is not space for the reproduction of that complete Latin text with the IGPs marked out in it, nor of the four chapters in *PsGD* in which they were exhaustively discussed. Many readers might naturally be daunted by the intricacy and length of the arguments in those chapters of *PsGD*, which demand close attention to the Latin phraseology and style of the inserted pericopes and to the manner of their insertion into the main narrative. As well as close scrutiny of the original text, there is required familiarity with Gregory's own sonorous style and vocabulary in order to recognize clearly the contrast between the borrowed passages and the Dialogist's distinctively different and less elegant Latin in the main body of his fanciful work. Here I wish to make my total argument accessible also to the general reader, and not to overlay it with technical minutiae. Accordingly I have listed all the IGPs in the Appendix to this volume, giving references to their place in the *Sources Chrétiennes* edition of the *Dialogues*, with brief comments on their incongruity in their context. My criteria for demarcation of those genuine Gregorian passages, and for distinguishing them from the alien narrative text into which they are inserted, are based on considerations of vocabulary, style, text-structure, linkages, thought-content and religious character. While the exact points of demarcation between the two disparate strata in the *Dialogues* are in places uncertain, I submit that the passages thus delimited are recognizably different in origin from the main narrative text, which has its own unmistakable characteristics. Here I select a single example out of the fourscore IGPs, in order to illustrate how the others demarcated in the Appendix may be fruitfully subjected to the same detailed criticism.

d. *Discerning the IGPs: one representative example*

The passage I propose to discuss as a typical example of the Dialogist's method is found at the conclusion of the biography of St Benedict (IGP 27, *Dial.* II.38.4). In that final chapter one may observe all the five elements habitually involved in the Dialogist's use of IGPs. First, there is the narration of supernatural events, which will be followed by the gem of Gregorian scriptural exposition that he has ready to introduce into his narrative; secondly, there is the leading question of Peter the Deacon, intended to provide the cue for its introduction; thirdly, there is a statement by *soi-disant* Gregory making the coming IGP seem relevant to the narrative context; fourthly, there comes the IGP itself; and finally there is an expression by Peter the Deacon of praise and admiration of his master's wise reflections. That concluding passage of Book II is the genuine Gregorian pericope that I list as IGP 27. It is inserted by the Dialogist as a doctrinal comment by Gregory following the relation of miracles at Subiaco connected with St Benedict. I reproduce here the three preceding paragraphs of the dialogue between the putative Gregory and the deacon Peter, leading up to the final pericope, IGP 27, which was written by the real Gregory and which I here put in italics. After describing the saint's death and glorious transit to heaven, and the burial of his body in the oratory of St John the Baptist at Montecassino, the dialogue in Book II continues with the final chapter, as follows:

(GREGORY) Yet in the cave at Subiaco in which he first dwelt, he still to this day shines forth with miracles, if besought by the faith of those who pray to him. I now relate an incident that happened there recently. A certain deranged woman, completely out of her senses, wandered day and night through mountains and valleys, woods and fields, only resting when weariness forced her to do so. One day, when she had strayed far afield, she arrived unknowingly at the cave of the blessed father Benedict, entered it and stayed there. When morning came she came out from it sound in mind, as if madness had never possessed her. She continued through all the rest of her life in the same state of sanity.

(PETER) How is it that we often find that it is like this, that heavenly patrons, the martyrs too, do not bestow such great favours through their bodies as they do through things that were associated with them, and that they perform greater wonders in places where they themselves do not lie buried?

(GREGORY) There is no doubt, Peter, that the holy martyrs can and do show many wonders in the places where they rest corporally, and that they vouchsafe countless miracles to those who ask with a pure mind. But since weak minds can doubt whether the saints are present to listen favourably to their prayers in places where they are certainly not bodily present, therefore it is necessary for them to show forth greater wonders in such places, where weak minds can doubt their presence. But the godly mind has so much the more merit of faith inasmuch as it realizes that while they do not lie there in body they are nevertheless at hand to listen favourably to prayers.

> *Wherefore Truth himself, in order to increase the faith of his disciples, said: "If I go not away, the Paraclete will not come to you". Now since it is certain that the Paraclete Spirit is eternally proceeding from the Father and the Son, why does the Son say that he is going away in order that the Spirit, who never leaves the Son, should come? It was because the disciples, beholding the Lord in the flesh, eagerly desired to see him always with their bodily eyes, that he indeed said to them. "Unless I go away, the Paraclete will not come". It is as if he clearly said, "If I do not withdraw my body, I cannot show forth the Spirit who is love, and unless you cease to behold me corporally, you will never learn to love me spiritually."*

(PETER) Well pleasing are your words.

The final italicized passage does indeed bear the hallmarks of Gregory's phraseology and expository teaching. His comment on the text from St John's Gospel (16.7) accords with his familiar heuristic manner of exegesis. He raises the question: how can those two scriptural truths be reconciled? He answers it by explaining that the Lord was drawing his disciples' understanding to a deeper spiritual level. The Dialogist had at hand this passage of typically Gregorian exegesis

and has cobbled it into his text as if it were an apt scriptural illustration of what he had just narrated, using it as a finale to his
biography of St Benedict. He has just related Benedict's burial at
Montecassino and the continuing miracles worked at his cave at
Subiaco. The cue that he puts into the mouth of Peter the Deacon
immediately follows his account of the cure of the demented woman
at Subiaco by Benedict's miraculous power. It is the question: Why
do the saints and martyrs work greater miracles in places where they
are not buried than at the places where their bodies rest? That question implies the sub-question: Why report miracles worked by Benedict
at Subiaco but not at Montecassino?

The answer to Peter's question which is put into Gregory's mouth
is indeed theologically odd. The martyrs and saints have to work
wonders in places other than where they are buried in order to reas-
sure those weak in faith of their miracle-working power, and also to
increase the merit of those of strong faith who do not doubt that
power. It is in corroboration of this quaint explanation that the
Dialogist introduces Gregory's elevated expository passage commenting
on *John* 16.7. His application of it to his own context is bathetic. In
its original context St Gregory reflected on the sublime meaning of
Christ's revelation to his Apostles of the coming of the divine Spirit
upon them that will follow the withdrawal of his own bodily presence.
The author of the *Dialogues*, assumedly Gregory, uses that exegesis
of the Gospel text as if it were apt comment on his musings about
the miracle-working powers of saints and martyrs even at a distance,
as instanced by his tale of the cure of the madwoman at the Subiaco
cave. The concluding comment that he puts into Peter's mouth parallels many similar self-satisfied comments elsewhere in his book.

IGP 27 has significant similarity to a shorter passage found in the
text of the *Moralia*; moreover, the lesson that the Dialogist seeks to
draw from it also has quaint and distorted echoes of a spiritual lesson taught by Gregory in one of his *Homilies on the Gospels* (II.32). I
will discuss each of those two parallels in turn. In the relevant *Moralia*
passage Gregory cites the same text from *John* 16.7 that is cited in
IGP 27, and gives a similar exegesis, but more briefly.[25] He uses it
as confirmation of his teaching that in order to attain higher divine
truth the soul must withdraw from all corporeal imagination. In

---

[25] *Moralia* 8.41. In this passage the emphasis is on attainment of divine truth; in
IGP 27 it is on attainment of divine love.

reproducing that passage from the *Moralia* I italicize words in the Latin text that appear in identical form in IGP 27:

Unde et eisdem suis dilectoribus *Veritas dicit*: "Regnum Dei intra vos est". Et rursum: *"Si ego non abiero, Paraclitus non veniet"*. Ac si aperte dice-ret: Si ab intentionis vestrae oculis *corpus non subtraho*, per consolatorem Spiritum ad intellectum vos invisibilem non perduco.	*Wherefore Truth himself says* to those who love him: "The Kingdom of God is within you". And again: *"If I go not away, the Paraclete will not come"*. *It is as if he clearly said: If I do not withdraw my body* from the sight of your eyes, I shall not bring you, through the strengthening Spirit, to understand what cannot be seen.

In the Dialogist's context, following on from his tale of the mad-woman in Benedict's cave, the gem of Gregorian exegetical wisdom is crassly misplaced. It is an evidently false note to make Gregory's reflection on *John* 16.7 seem to apply to the bizarre notion put forward in *Dialogues* II.38.3—namely, that the saints in heaven have to disregard the expected pattern and *locus* of their posthumous miracles by their clients in order to correct the misapprehensions of those of little faith about the range of their miraculous power. The Dialogist makes Gregory argue that Christ's words make it clear to clients of miracle-working saints that their patrons do not limit their favours to the places where their bodies are entombed. The real Gregory, so profoundly reverent to the words of Scripture and above all to those of Christ, *ipsa Veritas*, would not have made such a crude and distorted exposition of the words of the Gospel.

The original context of IGP 27 was doubtless the same as the elevated theological discussion in which the *Moralia* passage cited above was set. It seems quite likely that Gregory originally composed both those two similar passages in the course of his spoken commentaries on Scripture. It may well be that IGP 27 was originally a "doublet" of the passage cited above from the *Moralia*. In the successive stages of editing the *reportata* of his oral exposition (a process that Gregory described in his prefatory letter to Leander of Seville), he would naturally note that there were places in different parts of the script where he repeated himself in citing scriptural lessons, and would excise one of the duplicated passages. The excised passages would have been preserved with the other Gregorian remains in the archives of the Roman *Scrinium*, where they would still have been available for the Dialogist to find and reuse them in the following century.

As I have noted above, R. Étaix, when discussing the provenance of the otherwise unknown Gregorian passages preserved in the anthology ascribed to Paterius, suggested that some of them could have come from a first edition of the *Moralia*, and he cites a number of Paterian excerpts where this seems likely.[26]

The second parallel with IGP 27 in Gregory's genuine writings, which is found in his 32nd sermon in the second book of his Gospel *Homilies*,[27] is also revealing. That sermon, delivered to a Roman congregation at the shrine of the martyrs SS. Processus and Martianus, had as its text not *John* 16.7 but *Luke* 9.23–27, with its reference to those who lose their lives for Christ's sake and gain true life, a text evidently applicable to the martyrs whose feast-day was being celebrated. From it Gregory drew a pastoral lesson for his hearers, teaching them that it is necessary to raise the minds of simpler folk (*rudes*) above the quest for visible marvels and favours at the shrines of martyrs, to seek the eternal life of the spirit. If healing is provided for the living through the merits of the martyrs whose relics lie there, he reflects, how much greater is the heavenly life of those saints? If they gave their bodies to be put to death, is that not a proof of the supreme value of the eternal life for which they accepted bodily death? There are distorted echoes of that lesson in the Dialogist's usage of IGP 27. Applying it to his own agenda, he presents a different antithesis between the spiritually minded and the weaker brethren, and a different lesson for the latter to learn. For him, the former are enlightened not because they yearn for the divine gift of eternal life, but because they realize that the martyrs can hear prayers and work miracles even in places where their bodies are not buried. Very alien from the spiritual perspective of the real Gregory is the conclusion formulated by the author of the *Dialogues*:

> Since it can be doubted by weak minds whether the saints are present to grant answers to prayers even in places where their bodies do not rest, it is therefore necessary that they should show forth greater miraculous signs in those places where weak minds may doubt their presence.

I have chosen to discuss IGP 27 as a typical instance of the Dialogist's misappropriation of genuine Gregorian materials. It is only one out

---

[26] *RSR* 1958, p. 78; cf. further reference to Étaix's finding in Chapter 21.b below.
[27] *PL* 76, 1237–8.

of very many similarly revealing passages that are discussed at length in Chapters 14–17 of *PsGD*. Understandably, the daunting length and linguistic complexity of that massive dossier has deterred many from studying it in detail.[28] Dom Robert Gillet was one who did so, and found there not only the explanation of the clearly Gregorian character of some passages in the *Dialogues* but also a decisive confirmation of the spuriousness of the work as a whole.

e. *A special category of "IGPs"—reused Gregorian* exempla

Of the four books that make up the *Dialogues* the fourth is the longest of all, amounting to nearly a third of the whole work. In it I distinguish 37 IGPs, which thus make up a far larger proportion of the text than in the other three books. A. de Vogüé also points out that of the 62 chapters in Book IV no less than 25 are wholly composed of what he calls "pure doctrine passages", something that is found in only one chapter in the first three books. While the proportion of IGPs in the first three books of the *Dialogues* is approximately 15%, in the fourth book the proportion rises to approximately 40% of the whole text. Accordingly the IGPs in that book constitute just over 58% of the IGP wordage in the *Dialogues* as a whole.

A notable peculiarity of Book IV, and one very relevant to the present question, is the patent reuse therein of a group of seven truncated passages copied from Gregory's *Homilies on the Gospels*. In the first three books all but two of the 43 IGPs inserted there are not found elsewhere in any of the pope's known writings. (Those two exceptions are IGP 16, concerning fifty-year-old Levites, which is adapted from the *Moralia* 23.21, and IGP 39, a passage that is also found in the letter sent by Pope Gregory to Princess Theoctista, sister of the Emperor Maurice, in 597.) In Book IV we find seven more passages which are, beyond any possible dispute, "Inserted Gregorian Passages" since they are found verbatim in Gregory's authentic writings. I call these seven passages "the narrative IGPs" to distinguish them from all the rest, which are "doctrinal IGPs".

---

[28] A. de Vogüé, assuming *a priori* that the *IGPs* were a mare's nest, dismissed that dossier with the caustic comment: "*Je n'arrive même pas à m'y intéresser*" (*RHE* 83, 1998, p. 331).

They are taken from the text of Gregory's *Homilies on the Gospels*. (There is also an eighth passage which adapts wording from one of those homilies.) When retelling six of those narrative IGPs (nos. 52, 53, 54, 55, 59, 65) the *soi-disant* Gregory of the *Dialogues* acknowledges the source from which he has borrowed them, saying that he "remembers" that he has recounted them in his homilies, and reproducing them almost verbatim. That remark is another significant indication of the spurious character of the *Dialogues*, since the authorized edition of the *Homiliae in Evangelia*, the text of which the Dialogist faithfully reproduces, was not published until near the end of Gregory's pontificate, several years after the ostensible date of the composition of the *Dialogues* in 593.

While all the other IGPs are didactic passages containing exegetical, doctrinal or moral teaching, the inclusion of those seven "narrative IGPs" in Book IV is a novel element in the *Dialogues*. In preaching his sermons to the people of Rome, Gregory, like any good preacher, provided *exempla* to illustrate the pastoral moral that he was drawing for his flock from the Gospel reading of the day. In every case the moral teaching is paramount, and the vivid deathbed accounts of preternatural happenings, marking the merits of saintly persons and the demerits of the wicked, were added as *exempla* to illustrate that teaching. The Dialogist, in contrast, fastens solely on the preternatural details of those pious stories to add a truly Gregorian flavour to his own much more colourful tales of the existence and observance of the *RB* collection of prodigy-stories about departing souls, omitting the pastoral moral that was Gregory's chief intent and reason for telling them.

Out of all Gregory's genuine works, the fourteen pious anecdotes that he relates in his Gospel homilies provide almost the only "light relief" in the otherwise universal gravity of his writing and teaching. Although, as F.H. Dudden remarked, "it cannot be said that these anecdotes are particularly striking"[29] (and indeed as wonder-stories they are pale in comparison with the Dialogists' own bizarre tales), they were doubtless often retold by readers of Gregory's works. I suggest that it may well have been the presence of those few anecdotal exempla in his *Homilies on the Gospels* that later gave the Dialogist the idea of using them as a nucleus for composing a book of divert-

---

[29] *Op. cit.* I. p. 254.

ing stories with a Gregorian aura which would cater to the eager thirst for such literature. By interweaving them, together with numerous fragments of genuine Gregorian doctrinal teaching taken from the Roman archives, into his own concoction of much more sensational miracle-stories, he could plausibly present his book as the work of Gregory himself. I noted above that, in addition to the seven narrative IGPs borrowed from Gregory's Gospel homilies, we also find in Book IV two long doctrinal IGPs (IGP 71, on the Origenist objections to eternal punishment, and IGP 74, on the discernment of dreams), both of which are reproduced with identical wording from his *Moralia* (8.42–3) but without mention of the fact.

Many times in the course of these pages I shall have occasion to return to the essential need to distinguish the IGPs from the main narrative text in which they are embodied. They are a major element in the Dialogist's total pattern of literary invention and deception. I shall point out many other indications that he planned his work with much ingenuity in order to persuade his own generation (in particular his peers and superiors in the Roman curial secretariate in which he was employed) that this hitherto undiscovered work of hagiography had been written by Pope Gregory. The seventeenth-century scholars who detected the supposititious character of the *Dialogues* also realized that the author was a falsifier of great astuteness, who took extraordinary pains to give his falsehood impressive verisimilitude. They were ridiculed (as I have been in my turn) for concluding that he was *"tam peritus fallendi artifex"*—"such a skilled artificer of fraud";[30] but they are now being proved right.

---

[30] The phrase was used derisively by Peter de Goussainville; cf. Chapter 8.a below.

CHAPTER FOUR

EVIDENCE OF THE NON-GREGORIAN AUTHORSHIP OF THE *DIALOGUES* FROM VOCABULARY AND ORTHOGRAPHY

a

Of all the arguments against the Gregorian authorship of the *Dialogues* that which is based on the language and literary style of the book is the most obvious. It was on those grounds that in the sixteenth century the Swiss scholar Huldreich Coccius first raised the challenge to its authenticity. I quoted earlier Coccius's judgement that the *Dialogues* greatly differ from all Gregory's other works "in character, form of expression, seriousness and purpose". I also cited there similar judgements by other critics during the following two centuries, who on the same grounds concluded positively that the work was spurious. Robert Cooke, noting in the book "many barbarisms in language, phrasing and expression", found in them the paramount proof of its counterfeit character and concluded, "We must dismiss these dialogues; in no way can they be by Gregory the Great". Likewise William Cave, emphasizing "the immense discrepancy in style" of the book, observed that in it "many expressions are used which are those of a man with only a mediocre competence in the Latin tongue". Similar forthright judgement on the Latinity of the *Dialogues* has been passed by many scholars during the past four centuries. Even Peter de Goussainville, the seventeenth-century protagonist in the defence of the authenticity of the book, admitted the presence in it of "*phrases et dictiones barbarae*", but sought to excuse them. Present-day authors usually have no difficulty in recognizing what A. Haggerty-Krappe bluntly described as "the barbarous and annoying style" of the *Dialogues*.[1] The attempt of a few present-day apologists to dispute that judgement is generally recognized to be futile.[2] Others allow at least that Gregory often used popular and

---

[1] *Le Moyen Age*, 50 (1937), p. 272.
[2] Both Meyvaert and Vogüé, in their critiques of *PsGD*, attempt (in disagreement

inelegant language when writing that book, and they seek excuses for his doing so.

In this volume there is space only for an abridgement of the lengthier critique of the linguistic usages in the *Dialogues* narrative that was set out in *PsGD*. In this chapter I discuss the distinctive character of the vocabulary and phraseology of that narrative, and the original morphology of the text. The style and thought-content of the work will be discussed in the two following chapters. Several useful studies have been devoted to the language and style of the book,[3] but they are of course weakened by lack of discernment of the two contrasting elements in the text. Once the distinctively Gregorian IGPs have been separated from the main non-Gregorian narrative in which they are incongruously inserted, the debased character of the Latinity of the main narrative stands out unmistakably, and a surer perspective opens on the linguistic puzzle of the *Dialogues*. Even when the difference in genre between narrative and doctrinal works is duly taken into account, the author of the *Dialogues* can be seen to have a clearly diverse use of language than that of Pope Gregory himself in his undisputed writings. The arguments summarized in this chapter and the two following chapters, demonstrating the non-Gregorian character of the vocabulary, style and thought-content of the *Dialogues*, relate to the three quarters of the text that constitute the legendary narrative, but not to the IGPs that make up the other quarter of the text, which, although not placed there by Gregory, are authentically Gregorian.

When comparing the language and style of the *Dialogues* narrative with that of Gregory's undisputed works sound method also requires that such comparison be based mainly on the four principal works composed by him personally: namely the *Moralia in Job*, the *Regula Pastoralis*, the *Homiliae in Evangelia* and the *Homiliae in Ezechielem*. The exiguous commentary *In Cantica Canticorum*, never authorized by him for public circulation, is also relevant. The commentary *In 1 Regum*

---

with most other commentators) to deny the presence of linguistic barbarisms in the *Dialogues*, and also to argue that Gregory himself wrote in the same style elsewhere.

[3] They include: L. Wiese, *Die Sprache der Dialoge des Papstes Gregor*, Halle 1899; V. Stella, *I Dialoghi di s. Gregorio Magno nella storia del latino. Saggio filologico*, Cava dei Tirreni 1910; V. Diglio, *La bassa latinità e San Gregorio Magno*, Benevento 1912; A.J. Kinnerey, *The Late Latin Vocabulary of the Dialogues of St. Gregory the Great*, Washington 1935; A. Bruzzone, *Sulla lingua dei Dialoghi di Gregorio Magno* in *Studi Latini e Italiani* (1992), pp. 181–283.

is also germane to this discussion. Vogüé and Meyvaert now hold that none of that work was written by Gregory, while other authors agree with me that it includes a substantial element of genuine Gregorian exposition. The *Registrum Epistularum*, the large collection of Gregory's pontifical letters, is of limited relevance in our comparison, since, as D. Norberg has demonstrated,[4] the greater number of those letters were not composed by Gregory personally. He distinguishes three categories in the contents of the *Registrum*. In the first category are routine administrative letters which exhibit the stereotyped grammatical formularies of the papal chancery as used by Gregory's predecessors and successors, models of which can be found in *the Liber Diurnus*.[5] The second category is of letters written for special needs requiring the pontiff's authorization, yet which do not show the characteristic stamp of Gregory's own style. Thirdly, there is the relatively small group of letters that can be seen from internal evidence to have been written or dictated by him personally. Norberg shows that the letters in both of the first two categories exhibit a high percentage of the formalized accentual clausulae habitual in curial usage, whereas the group of letters in the "personal" category do not. Rather, the latter conform to the rhythmic and semi-poetic patterns of grammatical usage and style found in Gregory's pastoral and expository writings. (An attempt has in fact been made to base an argument in defence of the Gregorian authenticity of the *Dialogues* on the supposition that the pattern of final clausulae in sentence-endings in that work conform to a general pattern found throughout Gregory's works. I discuss this plea in *PsGD*[6] and show that it is based on fallacious suppositions, and is discountenanced by the findings of Norberg mentioned above.)

Study of the *Register* of Gregory's letters preserved in the papal secretariate is of major relevance to the subject of this book, as will

---

[4] *"Qui a composé les lettres de saint Grégoire?"*, in *Studi Mediaevali*, Series 3, 21 (1980), pp. 1–18. Cf. also Norberg's earlier work, *In Registrum Gregorii Magni studia critica*, Uppsala 1937, and the preface to his critical edition of the *Registrum* in *CCL* 140–140A, pp. 1–18.

[5] Cf. M.B. Dunn, *The Style of the Letters of St Gregory the Great*, Washington 1930.

[6] Pp. 688–701 ("The argument from formal clausulae"). The plea was based on the defective premises and findings of a dissertation by K. Brazzel, *The Clausulae in the Works of Saint Gregory the Great*, Washington 1939. A. de Vogüé makes appeal to her findings in *SC* 251, p. 34, to argue that the *Dialogues* text "in no way deviates in this respect from the Gregorian writings as a whole"; but her method and findings have been discredited by Norberg's critique.

appear from many arguments in the following chapters. Not only is there multiple evidence to show that the Dialogist had access to the file of those letters and borrowed names, phrases and themes from it, but, I shall argue in Chapter 10, he made a very significant inter-polation in it (Epistola III.50, the "*Letter to Maximian*"), and proba-bly, as I argue in Chapter 7, a lesser addition to an existing letter (Epistola XI.26).

In questions of disputed authorship, study of the "involuntary markers" discernible in an author's vocabulary may be just as significant, when tracing his literature signature, as study of his delib-erate choice of phrasing and habitual style. These markers may be provided by such textual features as frequency of individual words, recurring grammatical forms, word order and word clusters, prefer-ences in the usage of synonyms and alternative word-forms, inci-dental use of enclitics and adverbs, and other similarly unstudied usages. Examination of such features in the text of the *Dialogues* pro-vides a coherent argument which even by itself demonstrates that the book was not composed by Gregory the Great. In this field, evi-dently, the computer is now an indispensable tool. I used it as best I could when preparing my survey of the linguistic evidence for inclu-sion in *PsGD* more than twenty years ago. Today, after the great advances in cybernetic resources and techniques made since then, that demonstration can be considerably extended and strengthened. For my statistical survey I was indebted to the resources and tech-nical assistance of the staff of three institutions: the Open University Academic Computing Service, the Oxford University Computing Service, and especially to CETEDOC, the *Centre de Traitement Élec-tronique des Documents* of the University of Louvain-la-neuve.

CETEDOC's *Thesaurus Gregorii Magni* charts the frequency and dis-tribution in the individual writings of every one of the 1,172,830 words and 60,830 different verb-forms in the eight works that are commonly accepted as constituting the Gregorian corpus. Their wordage was counted as follows: *Moralia*, 483,569 words; *Regula Pastoralis*, 40,638; *Homilies on Ezekiel*, 112,035; the *Homilies on the Gospels*, 81,847; the fragmentary commentary *In Cantica Canticorum*, 7,483; the commentary *In 1 Regum* (180,165 words); the *Registrum Epistularum*, 211,341; and the *Dialogues*, 54,056. Thus our possession of a "con-trol text" of well over a million words in those seven works ascribed to Gregory provides a solid base for comparative investigation of the distinctive patterns of word usage and frequency in the *Dialogues*. For my pursuit of that comparison I necessarily separated the text of the eighty IGPs (inserted Gregorian passages) from the main narrative text of the *Dialogues*. I subjected each of those two elements in the book to a separate computer scrutiny, prior to comparing the linguistic patterns of each of them with those of the other works in the Gregorian corpus.

Two distorting factors in such comparative discussion of the Gregorian writings should be mentioned. The vocabulary of the register of the papal letters (which make up nearly a fifth of the total wordage of the Gregorian corpus, and are all included in the CETEDOC *Thesaurus Gregorii Magni*) does indeed have generic similarities to some usages in the *Dialogues* narrative. Nevertheless, as noted above, the greater number of the letters in that *Registrum* were not composed by Gregory personally but by secretaries, who would present their drafts for ratification by his authority. Thus the vocabulary of 211,341 words in the *Registrum* cannot simply be taken as Gregory's own, and its inclusion in our overall statistics necessarily introduces an irregular element into the resulting calculations. Indeed, we find many instances in which there is similarity of word-frequency between the *Registrum* and the *Dialogues* but not between those two works and the other writings in the corpus. That similarity is especially notable in the use of terms (to be discussed in the next chapter) that can be classified as "notarial" or clerkish. In Gregory's letters those terms are evidently to be attributed to the secretaries who composed his administrative letters and not to him; when found in the *Dialogues* they accord well with other evidence, to be considered later, that points to the conclusion that the author was himself a curial scribe.

A second distorting factor arises from the inclusion of the commentary in the CETEDOC survey of Gregorian word usages in the commentary *In 1 Regum*. As noted above in Chapter 2, A. de Vogüé and P. Meyvaert, constrained by a documentary discovery, have now acknowledged that fragmentary commentary to be non-Gregorian. In *PsGD* I showed that it was not composed by Gregory, but I still identified within it considerable elements of genuine Gregorian *reportata* tacitly included in the text by the mediaeval monastic author who fashioned the work.

Neither of those two distorting factors produce a bias in favour of the conclusions I am proposing. Rather, they produce some contrary statistical bias, since they both dilute the proportion of specifically Gregorian vocabulary contained in the control text used in the present comparison. Another very relevant consideration that must be given due weight is the narrative character of the *Dialogues* text, which naturally entails some diversity of vocabulary from that of Gregory's doctrinal writings because it requires the use of concrete rather than abstract terms. All three of the principal critics of *PsGD* stressed this point. However, when all due weight is given to that factor, the radical contrasts between the vocabulary of the Dialogist and that of the real Gregory are still too many and too stark to be explained away.

b. *Distinctively non-Gregorian vocabulary*

Before pursuing the statistical comparison of the vocabulary of the narrative text of the *Dialogues* with that of the main works in the Gregorian corpus, particular mention must first be made of the presence in the text of a relatively small but significant group of words which are not only absent from all Gregory's undisputed writings, but are not even found in any other known Latin texts before or during his age. A.J. Kinnerey pointed out the following words in the latter category: *praelatus* (used as a noun: *Dial.* I.1); *suppeditaneus* (used as an adjective: I.2) *tortitudo* (II.3); *falcastrum* (II.6); *posterga* (used as an adverb: II.7); *extremere* (II.7); *spatharius* (II.14); *refectorium* (II.22), *trepedica* (II.30); *primarius* (used as a noun: III.21); *exstringere* (IV.55). Kinnerey noted that *tortitudo, extremere* and *exstringere* are historical neologisms.[7] The word *mansionarius* (*Dial.* I.5) is found elsewhere only in one of the curial administrative letters in the *Registrum*. There are also the words *spatharius* and *bulgaricus*, which are found previously only on inscriptions. *Falcastrum* appears elsewhere only after Gregory's time, used by Isidore of Seville, who explains its origin. (I conclude, *pace* A. de Vogüé, that the Dialogist, who echoes that explanation, drew it from Isidore.) Can the defenders of the Gregorian authenticity of the *Dialogues* offer a plausible explanation of the presence in the book of that group of words which are not found anywhere in Gregory's own writings or in any other texts before and during his age?

Kinnerey also noted that the author of the *Dialogues* uses half a dozen medical terms, and 29 words derived from late Greek forms.

---

[7] *Op. cit.*, p. 121.

The latter can be seen to reflect the "hellenization" of Rome's culture in the course of the seventh century, described below in Chapter 23.c. A. Bruzzone augmented the trawl of rustic and other non-literary words found in the book by noting the following: *caballus, capisterium, coquina, doleus, ferrarius, ferula, fullo, mulomedicus, plantare, sagum* (of Gallic origin), *sudis*. Of special interest are three words of Germanic origin, *matta, vanga*[8] and *flasco*, doubtless imports to rural Italy resulting from the Gothic and Lombard conquests. The author of the *Dialogues* excuses himself for using such vulgar terms, and explains their meaning to his readers. Although the combined wordage of the seven works in the rest of the Gregorian corpus, as recorded in the CETEDOC *Thesaurus*, is twenty-two times greater than the total wordage of the *Dialogues* narrative, there are several words in the latter work that do not occur in any of the others. Fifteen examples of such distinctively non-Gregorian words, significantly pointing to other authorship, are: *aestuatio, albatus, accitus, armamenta, biduum, conlibertus, crepido, crepitus, crepusculum, crociare, devexus, dilaceratus, exfugare, maturescere, pons*. The adjective *"devexus"* merits particular remark. Although never used by Gregory in his undisputed works (nor even by the drafters of his letters) it is used by the Dialogist five times, always in a set phrase, which was evidently a favourite of his: *"devexum montis latus"*.

The presence in the *Dialogues* of those distinctive and non-Gregorian words, including neologisms and *hapax legomena*, provides a clear and major argument against the authenticity of the work. The comparative study of word frequencies in the *Dialogues* narrative and in the other works of the Gregorian corpus which now follows is presented as a further argument to the same effect. Although more complex and in places disputable,[9] it gives a general corroboration of the specific evidence provided by that first group of distinctively non-Gregorian words.

---

[8] *"ferramenta quae usitato nos nomine vangas vocamus"*; *Dial.* III.14.6. The Germanic word *vanga* entered late Latin in Italy as a substitute for the usual Latin word *bipalium*. Cf. *Dizionario Etymologico Italiano*, ed. C. Battisti & G. Alesso, vol. V, Florence 1957, p. 398.

[9] In their critiques of *PsGD* Vogüé and Meyvaert did indeed dispute several points in that case. I accept that some of their objections had force. Rather than quibble about individual words and inferences, I here point to the total import of the vocabulary of the *Dialogues* narrative.

Taking into account differences of genre, every author has a broad range of habitual word-usages which can be charted statistically. Duly noting the great difference in word-count between the two terms of the comparison, we can show for each word in the *Dialogues* narrative the statistical probability of the number of times it would occur in the other works if they were of common Gregorian authorship. (The word-forms listed in my survey include declined or conjugated forms of each word.) Conversely, we can select words found very frequently in the rest of the Gregorian corpus and calculate how often they would be expected *pro rata* to occur in the *Dialogues*, on the assumption of common authorship. Comparison of those projected frequencies with the actual textual frequencies shows in both cases a very wide discrepancy from the expected correlation, and thus provides further indication that the assumption of common authorship is erroneous.

Such comparative study reveals some significant contrasts. There are many word-forms found fairly often in the *Dialogues* narrative that occur far less frequently, *pro rata*, in the rest of the Gregorian corpus. In *PsGD* a table of about 40 such words is given,[10] showing first the number of times each word would be statistically expected to occur in those other works on the assumption of common authorship, and then the actual number of such occurrences. In every case the latter number is far less than the statistical expectation. For example, the word *alveus*, occurring 11 times in the *Dialogues* narrative would be statistically expected to occur 298 times in the other seven works; but in fact occurs in them only 8 times. Many other fairly ordinary words are likewise used by the Dialogist in striking disproportion to their much rarer occurrence in the other seven works in the Gregorian corpus. Examples are: *famulus*, of which the frequency in the seven works is, *pro rata*, 20 times less that in the *Dialogues* narrative; *defunctus* (14 times less frequent); *sepulchrum* and *sepelire* (14 times less); *quaeso* (26 times less); *familiariter* (10 times less); *urbs* (11 times less); *specus* (27 times less). *Specus* is the word that the Dialogist habitually uses to refer to caves. In his own writings Gregory uses it only in one sequence in the *Moralia* (30.26 seq.) where he expressly cites the word from the Latin text of *Job* 38.40 (". . . *et in specubus insidiantur*"). Apart from that scriptural citation, he never uses

---

[10] *PsGD*, pp. 701–2.

the word *specus* in all his writings, but instead uses the alternatives *spelunca, caverna* or *antrum.*

Conversely, I list in *PsGD* 54 words often found in the corpus of Gregory's writings that have a proportionate frequency in the *Dialogues* narrative that is very much less than the statistical norm.[11] Examples of words which are repeatedly used by Gregory himself in the other works, but which do not occur at all in the *Dialogues* narrative, are: *ambulare, annuntiare, apprehendere, conversio, delictum, dissipare, districtus, doctor, expressio, exprimere, interpretari, interpres, robor, roborare, sapientia, subditur, torpor, torpere, unctio, ungere, unitas.* The word *contemplatio* (*contemplare*), which occurs 971 times in Gregory's main works, and would be statistically expected to occur 36 times in the *Dialogues* narrative, occurs there only once. Other words which are especially prevalent in Gregory's usage are strangely sparse in the *Dialogues.* I cite here eight word-forms, as especially notable examples, most of which were connatural for Gregory to use:

- forms of *amare, amor*: occurring 1,165 times in the other writings, would be statistically expected to occur 43 times in the *Dialogues* narrative, but occur there only 11 times;
- forms of *desiderium*: occurring 1,056 times in the others, with statistical expectancy in *Dial.* of 39 appearances in that narrative, occur there only 9 times;
- forms of *cor*: occurring 2,210 times in the others, with statistical expectancy in *Dial.* of 81, occur there only 13 times;
- forms of *contemplare, contemplatio*: occurring 971 times in the others, with statistical expectancy in *Dial.* of 36, occur there only once;
- forms of *recte, rectus*: occurring 1,002 times in the others, with statistical expectancy in *Dial.* of 67, occur there only 3 times;
- forms of *robor, roborare*: occurring 358 time in the others, with statistical expectancy in *Dial.* of 13, do not occur there at all;
- forms of *sapientia*: occurring 654 times in the others, with statistical expectancy in *Dial.* of 24, do not occur there at all;
- *subditur*: occurring 690 times in the others, with statistical expectancy in *Dial.* of 25, does not occur there at all;
- instead of the Gregorian word *conversio* (referring especially to the embracing of the monastic life), which he does not use, the Dialogist uses as an equivalent *conversatio* 21 times.

---

[11] *Ibid.,* pp. 697–8.

For discernment of distinctive statistical patterns in an author's vocabulary, the evidence provided by study of his habitual usage of auxiliary parts of speech—conjunctions, prepositions and adverbs—are even more revealing than the evidence provided by study of his usage of nouns, verbs and adjectives. The overall pattern of those simple and ubiquitous words reflects an author's unstudied and ingrained linguistic habits, thus providing involuntary markers of his literary signature. His preferred usages of such minor parts of speech are largely independent of variations in literary genre, and when they occur very frequently they provide a significant volume of statistics for comparison. In *PsGD* (pp. 702–9) many examples are given of the very significant disparity between the text of the *Dialogues* narrative and all the other works in the Gregorian corpus in the choice and frequency of such everyday "marker" words. I cite a few examples. The adverb *aliter* occurs 519 times in those other works but only once in the *Dialogues* narrative—that is, 19 times less than the statistical frequency expected if the works had common authorship.[12] The adverb *hinc* occurs 1,408 times in the former but only 5 times in the latter—10 times less than the statistical norm. There are 699 genuine Gregorian uses of the word *profecto*, contrasted with 3 in the *Dialogues*—a variant factor of 9. The use of *tamquam* is variant by a factor of 6. On the other hand, the tables in *PsGD* show examples of disproportionate use by the Dialogist of the following everyday "marker words": *mox* (exceeding Gregory's usage by a factor of 5); *parum* and *repente* (both over-frequent by a factor of 5); *sese* (excess factor of 4); *statim* (excess factor of 6); *vehementer* (excess factor of 5); and *ulterius* (excess factor of 6). Some of these words would of course be expected to occur more frequently in narrative writing.

Even more telling is the relative usage of two conjunctions which are among the most ordinary and neutral words in the Latin language: *enim* and *ergo*. In *PsGD* I discuss those two test-cases in detail, comparing the usage of each of those words in the other works of the Gregorian corpus (here excluding the *Registrum*). The total wordage of those other works is 905,737. The word *enim* occurs in them 5,192 times; its mean frequency in them collectively is thus one occurrence per 174 words; the average variation from the mean in the six works

---

[12] In *RHE* 83 (1988), pp. 341–5 A. de Vogüé uses all his ingenuity to belittle these contrasts, but their overall force remains.

is 17%. In the *Dialogues* narrative *enim* occurs only 32 times, with frequency of one occurrence per 1,287 words, thus deviating from the mean by −740%. The relevant figures for *ergo* are: in the six works, the word occurs 4,699 times; the mean frequency of *ergo* in them is one occurrence per 193 words; the average variation in them from the mean frequency is 26%. In the *Dialogues* narrative the word *ergo* occurs only 14 times, with frequency of one occurrence per 2940 words, thus deviating from the mean by −1448%. In the short IGP texts there is a much higher relative frequency of both *enim* and *ergo* than in the narrative text, as is to be expected in texts of authentic Gregorian parentage. While taking due account of occasional anomalies in the data and of course the difference between narrative and teaching, the overall pattern is, despite the critics' insistence to the contrary, undeniably significant.

c. *Orthography and morphology*

The controverted question of the original spelling and word-formation of the *Dialogues* text is also very relevant to our discussion. In a study published in 1904–5, entitled *Le alterazione fonetiche e morfologiche nel latino di Gregorio Magno e del suo tempo*,[13] A. Sepulchri put forward weighty reasons for concluding that the original Latin word-forms in the Gregorian works, as written down in the papal secretariate and edited and authorized by Gregory himself, were surprisingly debased. He based his argument almost entirely on five early MSS of the *Dialogues*. Comparing the original orthography and morphology of the three principal writers in Latin in the second half of the sixth century, Gregory of Tours, Venantius Fortunatus and Pope Gregory I, Sepulchri acknowledged that in the writings of the first two of those authors "the echo of the classical tradition was not extinguished"; but he judged, from the evidence of the early manuscripts of the *Dialogues*, that in the writings of Gregory and his circle the standard was "*molto mediocre*". He showed that in those MSS there were phonetic and morphological characteristics, in spelling, word-formation, case-endings, etc., that were notably deviant from the more classical forms previously in use. He recognized that the

---

[13] In *Studi Medioevali* I (1904), pp. 171–235.

Dialogues were clearly a painstaking composition, and yet were first written in debased word-forms.

Because those linguistic barbarisms followed consistent patterns in the different MS families, Sepulchri concluded that they must be traced back to the original archetype of the work. His conclusions laid ultimate responsibility for the textual solecisms at the door of Pope Gregory himself. Even though the original archetype would not have been an autograph from the pope's own hands, since he habitually dictated his works to notaries, he would personally have edited it and authorized it for publication, according to his meticulous practice as attested in the preparation of his other writings. Before Sepulchri drew attention to them, the crude word-formations in the earliest *Dialogues* MSS had gone unremarked, since more literate scribes and editors in later centuries had corrected the spelling and morphology of the earliest manuscripts in order to make them conform more nearly to literary norms. In his edition of the *Dialogues*, published in Rome in 1924, U. Moricca embraced Sepulchri's findings and developed them further, paying particular attention to the two oldest (eighth-century) manuscripts, the Ambrosian and the Veronese. The latter was copied by an unlearned scribe who simply wrote out the vulgar forms in the exemplar before him. The scribe who penned the Ambrosian MS was more aware of due literary forms, and in several places corrected the barbarisms that he found in the text he was copying, while leaving others. Both Sepulchri and Moricca argued convincingly that the fact that those different copyists consistently reproduced the same misspellings and aberrant case formations in many places (even though varying in some others) indicates that those vulgar forms were not merely their own, but derived from a common original source. A recurrent instance of grammatical vulgarism in those early MSS of the *Dialogues* is the use of the accusative case instead of the nominative, both for nouns and adjectives (e.g. "*ad portam quae vocatur auream*", *Dial.* III.2.3.) That particular usage of accusative in place of nominative was endemic in popular parlance in late antiquity. It appears also in low Latin scripts of the Dark Ages, and it became institutionalized in the emerging Romance languages.[14]

---

[14] A notable instance of that incorrect use of the accusative case was in the title of a celebrated hagiographical work from Spain which will be discussed in Chapter 22 below, *The Lives of the Fathers of Merida*, which was originally entitled, and still is called to this day, *Vitas Patrum Emeretensium*.

Moricca was so impressed by the discovery of the debased word-forms of the original text of the *Dialogues* that in his edition of the work he sought to recover the primitive form of the text by printing the uncouth forms that the more literate mediaeval copyists had emended. This disconcerting feature of his edition was a main reason for its being set aside. Later critics indignantly rejected the conclusions of Sepulchri and Moricca—although D. Norberg was impressed by them. While Sepulchri was right about the original linguistic debasement of the *Dialogues'* narrative text, he was wrong in assuming that similar debasement could be found in the original texts of Gregory's undisputed writings. Proof to the contrary is found in contemporary documents.[15] One such proof is found in a manuscript of 150 folios of Gregory's *Regula Pastoralis* surviving from his own lifetime. That manuscript, now at Troyes, attests his practice of making successive revisions and redactions of his writings before he was sufficiently satisfied with the text to authorize its publication. Although the script was already a "fair copy", carefully inscribed in fine Roman majuscule, it was authoritatively amended, as E.A. Lowe observes: "There are numerous alterations, corrections over erasure and marginal insertions—all by a contemporary hand—which suggest that our manuscript presents the author's revision of a preliminary edition of his work; the corrected version is closer to the text as we have it today . . . Obviously it bears the marks of a book revised under the author's immediate supervision".[16] Significantly, the Troyes MS shows none of the verbal barbarisms found in the early MSS of the *Dialogues*, but conforms to classical standards of orthography and morphology.

---

[15] Cf. *PsGD*, pp. 713–4.
[16] *Codices latini antiquiores*, VI, p. 40.

CHAPTER FIVE

THE DISTINCTIVE LITERARY STYLE AND SYNTAX OF THE *DIALOGUES* NARRATIVE

a

Gregory's own distinctive style, permeating all his pastoral and expository works, has been analysed by many scholars. That style is signally absent from the *Dialogues* narrative. Again and again in his genuine writings we meet examples of the three "stylistic types" distinguished by P.-P. Verbraken in his acute study of Gregory's composition.[1] The first of them is the balanced juxtaposition of two adjacent syntactical elements which normally would be linked by co-ordinating conjunctions. Secondly, there is what Verbraken describes as the "cascade" type of sentence, in which supple developments of Gregory's thought, introduced by subordinating conjunctions or by relative pronouns, flow on one from another. Thirdly, there is another type of balance, or parallelism, between subordinate and principal propositions, often emphasized by the use of correlatives or alliterations. Recurring in the word patterns is the *cursus rhythmicus* that Verbraken points out as a hallmark of Gregory's style. He is a master of *homoteleuton*, of the rhyming clauses that so many later mediaeval writers were to seek in vain to imitate. Jacques Fontaine, who aptly called Gregory "a lyrical poet in prose", also highlighted the distinctive features of his writing: namely, the "psalmlike" enunciation of synonymous parallelisms; the density and intricacy of metaphors; the poetic rhythm of the stately periods and harmonized clauses; and the exceptional fidelity to the classical Latin order of words.[2]

A distinctive characteristic of Gregory's habitual style was described in a terse Latin phrase by the seventeenth-century Maurist scholar, Denys de Sainte Marthe: "*delectatur Gregorius quodam praepostero vocabulorum*

---

[1] *Art. cit. Rev. Bén.* 1956, pp. 179–81.
[2] In *Grégoire le Grand* (Acts of Chantilly conference of 1982), Paris 1986, pp. 499–509.

contextu, frequentibus transpositionibus ac veluti hyperbatis . . .".[3] That may
be paraphrased: "Gregory has a predilection for using a certain pattern of words whereby what would logically be put first is put last,
with frequent transposition of phrases and unexpected leaping ahead."
Countless examples of that literary mannerism can be cited from the
genuine works of Gregory, but it is singularly missing from the
Dialogues—except in the IGPs. Although there are some variations of
style within his vast master work, the *Moralia*, and in his Gospel
homilies, Gregory's underlying literary signature is everywhere recognizable. In the *Dialogues* it can be clearly recognized in the isolated IGPs; but it is significantly absent from the main narrative text
of that work.

b. "Un style de notaire"

In the introduction to his edition of the *Dialogues* A. de Vogüé draws
attention to the pervasive presence in the text of what he aptly calls
"un style de notaire", a repetitive and stilted style such as that used by
notaries in official documents. The phraseology is of the kind used
by clerks trained to write with legalistic and stilted precision in order
to make clear at every point who or what is being referred to. The
author of the *Dialogues* does so, as Vogüé observes, by "the use and
abuse of adjectives or *phrases de renvoi* (phrases of 'reference back')
every time that a person or thing previously mentioned reappears
in the text". Constantly we find such expressions: e.g. *praedictus* ("the
aforesaid"), *quem praedixi* ("whom I have named above"), *quem praefatus sum* ("whom I have referred to"), *cuius memoriam feci* ("of whom
I have made mention"), and the constant repetition of the word *idem*
("the same", "the selfsame") before the name of a person or place.
Sometimes we find a sentence so overloaded with repetition of such
reference terms that it reads like a clause of legal jargon. Here is
an example from the story of an advocate ("the aforesaid Valerian")
in whose house a prodigy occurred: *Cum vero eiusdem advocati domus
eadem clade vastaretur, isdem puer percussus est.* ("When the household of
the same advocate was afflicted by the same plague the same ser-

---

[3] *De commentario S. Gregorii Magni in librum primum Regum: Praefatio*, p. ii, in the
Maurist edition of Gregory's works, *PL* 79.11.

vant was stricken".) Again, the name of a venerable priest who is cited as a witness of a spectral apparition in the baths at Centumcellae is at once reidentified, and his location repeated, by the phrase *idem presbyter in eodem loco* ("the selfsame priest in the selfsame place").

Vogüé himself makes the following trenchant critique of the clerkly style so strangely manifest in the *Dialogues* narrative, a critique which should surely raise the question whether the author whose work betrays that peculiar trait can plausibly be assumed to be Gregory the Great:

> Even in a short narration, those phrases—such as "the same", "the aforesaid", "the abovementioned"—are multiplied with singular wearisomeness. There are instances in which three references of this kind are found in succession in the same phrase, or in which one such *idem* follows immediately after another. This literary *tic* springs from the legalistic style, in which it is important not to leave the slightest occasion for ambiguity. By linking every new mention of a person or thing back to antecedent mentions of it, the discourse is overburdened with interconnections. In this it relates to another characteristic of the style of the *Dialogues*: namely, the abundance of connecting relative pronouns, which are likewise multiplied, often in monotonous sequence. The same concern with precise reference and with verbal linkings shows itself in the frequent use of the adverbs *nimirum, scilicet, videlicet*, which generally have little or no real function there.[4]

That clerkish and legalistic style is distinctively present throughout the narrative text of the *Dialogues*. It is not similarly present in the IGPs, nor in the other works personally composed by Pope Gregory. Vogüé's exposure of the *style de notaire* of the author of the *Dialogues* is further confirmed by a cybernetic computation of the frequency of *phrases de renvoi* in that book compared with the works personally composed by Pope Gregory. For example, the referential adjective *praedictus*—"the aforesaid"—occurs in the main narrative text of the *Dialogues* with a frequency of once every 807 words; in those other works the frequency is once every 33,546 words; it is of course of much greater frequency in the administrative letters composed by the notaries. (Although the Dialogist and the curial secretaries have in common very frequent usage of the word *praedictus*, it is not so with the very similar alternative *antedictus*, which occurs 57 times in the *Registrum* but only once in the *Dialogues*—and not at all in the

---

[4] Vogüé, *SC* 251, pp. 81–2.

rest of the Gregorian corpus.) Reference back by forms of the word *idem*, "the same", in its different cases, is very common in the administrative letters—but not in those composed by Gregory personally—and likewise in the *Dialogues*. In the latter work one out of every 102 words is a form of *idem*; in Gregory's *Homilies on Ezekiel* the proportion is only once in every 460 words; and in his *Moralia* once in every 680 words. Similarly, the "abundance of connecting relative pronouns, often in monotonous sequence", which Vogüé points out as a prominent stylistic feature in the *Dialogues*, is not similarly obtrusive in Gregory's personal letters in the *Registrum*—nor are they in the main Gregorian works, nor in the IGPs.[5]

As well as bringing into relief those clerkish traits in the *Dialogues* narrative, Vogüé also draws attention to another obtrusive and unattractive aspect of the author's habitual phraseology. "We must note", he writes, "the heaviness and monotony of the titles accorded to sacred personages, even when they are simply introduced as informants. There are countless occurrences of phrases such as *"vir venerabilis, vir vitae venerabilis, vir venerandus."* By such usage, says Vogüé, the papal author pays "a heavy tribute to courtesy and convention", which he explains as follows: "The strictly hierarchized society of the late Empire is reflected in the Church, both triumphant and militant. Each personage has a right to his proper title, in which 'veneration' must be punctiliously observed".[6] It must be observed that proliferation of reverential expressions is not in fact found in Gregory's own literary usage, which reflected his love of simplicity and his distaste for clerical pomp and ostentation. His principle, *"me vana superfluitas non delectat"*, affirmed in one of his letters,[7] can be seen reflected not only in his pastoral writings and in the letters personally composed by him but even in the official letters drawn up for him by the curial *consiliarii*.[8] Doubtless they were duly mindful of their master's moderation in such matters. Although in the *Registrum Epistularum* there is careful observance of the customary titles of respect

---

[5] In *RHE* 83 (1988) Vogüé adduces, as an objection to my present argument, IGP 53 (*Dial.* IV.16.1–7), which is an anecdote extracted from Gregory's *Hom. Evan.* 34.18. In that passage there is indeed repetition of the word *"praefatus"* and of linking relative pronouns, but their use there is not comparable to the Dialogist's habitual and ungainly usage.

[6] *SC 251*, p. 82, note 165.

[7] Ep. I.39a; cf. Ep. VI.63: EH I.440.

[8] Cf. *PsGD*, pp. 429–30.

that protocol demanded, we do not find the "vain superfluity" of honorific epithets such as those applied in the *Dialogues* to any priest, monk or pious person, even if mentioned only in passing. Such fulsome language doubtless came to be freely used by others in the curial offices, including the scribes of the Lateran *Scrinium* in the later seventh century, among whom I locate the author of the *Dialogues*.

Still another distinctive feature of the *Dialogues*, also duly observed by A. de Vogüé,[9] is the contrast between the manner in which the various ranks of clergy are referred to in the *Dialogues* on the one hand and in Gregory's personal works on the other. In his scriptural commentaries and homilies, and in his *Regula Pastoralis*, Gregory habitually avoids the formal terms used to denominate the ranks of the clergy and used instead pastoral and "functional" descriptions when referring to those in holy orders. Throughout the *Dialogues*, however, the formal titles are used. While noting this remarkable fact, Vogüé comments that although such usage of direct nomenclature is not found in those other works of Gregory, it is found commonly in his letters. However, once again I have to recall that only a minority of the letters in the Gregorian *Registrum Epistularum* were composed by Gregory personally; most of them were composed by the curial notaries, and so reflect not his literary style but the formal conventions of the chancery. It is in those administrative letters that the ordinary direct and official descriptions of clergy are apparent. The fact that the author of the *Dialogues*, unlike Gregory, also habitually used such formal terminology accords with recognition of him as a curial scribe.

c. *Other distinctively non-Gregorian usages*

CETEDOC's *Thesaurus Gregorii Magni* provides, in addition to its main concordance, an alphabetical list arranged in reverse order of spelling of every word in the Gregorian corpus. This useful resource enables one to study the statistical patterns not only of suffixes but also the terminations of verb forms, and thus to make a comparative survey of the author's use of tenses and moods. Such comparison serves to confirm that the IGPs are of different authorship than the main

---

[9] *SC* 251, pp. 80–1.

narrative text of the *Dialogues*. In the latter text, compared with the rest of the Gregorian corpus, there is a markedly greater frequency of use of the imperfect and pluperfect subjunctive. In particular, the Dialogist uses with much greater frequency (but not with grammatical precision) the imperfect and pluperfect subjunctive forms, *haberet*, *esset, fuisset, potuisset* and *debuisset*. To take one instance, he uses *fuisset* some 50 times in his narrative. On the assumption of the same Gregorian authorship, that would give a *pro rata* statistical expectation in the other seven Gregorian works of about 1,350 occurrences of that verb form. In fact, it occurs in them only 130 times—that is, ten times less frequently that the projected probability. In the IGPs the word *fuisset* occurs only 3 times. Likewise *esset* occurs in the IGPs only 8 times, against 74 occurrences in the main text of the *Dialogues*. Comparative scrutiny of other verb forms also shows some distinctive patterns in the Dialogist's preferred usages, For example, his use of the present indicative passive is very much rarer, *pro rata*, than in the genuine Gregorian works.

One of the many valuable features of A. de Vogüé's commentary on the *Dialogues* is his grammatical index, in which he records some "phenomena" in the author's usage, with selected examples.[10] Almost all the forms and linguistic habits that he lists could profitably be made the basis for an extended study and comparison with usages in Gregory's undisputed works, from which they differ distinctively. For example, the luxuriant use of verbal periphrases was a common trait in late Latin, and can be found sometimes in Gregory's own writings; but the author of the *Dialogues* has a predilection for such usages that is obtrusive and disproportionate. He is especially fond of periphrases using the verbs *posse, valere, coepisse, consuevisse, debere* (the latter almost always in the subjunctive). To those must be added a further dozen favourite verbs which he uses to make similar periphrastic constructions.[11] Many other usages in the *Dialogues* also present a distinctive pattern. To take one out of many instances, Vogüé lists sixteen occurrences of the word *citius* in which this comparative form of the adverb is used instead of the positive *cito*, normal in literary Latin. *Citius* is indeed a favourite word of the Dialogist's. He uses it scores of time in his narrative, but it does not occur at all in the IGPs. In the rest of the Gregorian corpus it is found with

---

[10] *SC* 265, pp. 267–81.
[11] Cf. Vogüé, *ibid.*, p. 83, note 167 & pp. 275–6.

a frequency that is proportionately much less, and usually with its properly comparative meaning. The grammatical and stylistic peculiarities listed by A. de Vogüé, in his index of literary "phenomena" in the *Dialogues*, are found plentifully in the narrative text, but not in the genuinely Gregorian IGPs. While it is true that occasional instances can be found in Gregory's authentic works of late Latin usages that parallel some of those found in the *Dialogues* narrative, an overall comparison shows that the author of that book has a consistent pattern of usage of demotic grammar and syntax throughout his work that marks off his linguistic habits as habitually different from those of Gregory the Great.

Among other distinctive phenomena in the *Dialogues* noted by A. de Vogüé, special mention may be made of the following frequently occurring usages:

- use of the present tense instead of the future;
- use of the pluperfect subjunctive instead of the imperfect, especially in periphrastic constructions involving the verbs *debere* and *posse*;
- use of the indicative mood rather than the subjunctive in indirect questions;
- use of *valde* as an equivalent for a superlative;
- especially idiosyncratic use of "*cum*" as a linking relative word, to convey the meaning "and then . . .";
- consequential and pleonastic use of *quatenus* following *ut*;
- *sicut* used in an explanatory sense, with the meaning "seeing that . . .";
- use of the genitive case after an indefinite pronoun (e.g. "*aliquid caritatis*", in IV.57.14);
- replacing of the genitive by the preposition *de* (e.g. "*de domo utilitas*", in IV.4.4);
- clumsy interrogatives, e.g. "*quid est quod . . .?*", "*quid ergo quod . . .?*", "*quidnam hoc esset quod . . .?*";
- there are frequent pleonasms, much inelegant repetition of words and, not rarely, the grammatical sequence flounders in awkward anacoluthon.

d. *Gregorian eloquence evident in IGPs and in isolated phrases*

To counter my arguments showing the linguistic and stylistic disparity between the *Dialogues* and Gregory's acknowledged works,

defenders of his authorship of the book object that there are nevertheless not a few phrases, allusions and sentiments in the text that
closely parallel similar elements in the *Moralia* and other undisputed
writings of the great pope. Therefore, they argue, the evidence of
dissimilarity is contradicted by evidence of similarity. This objection
falls wide of the mark since it fails to distinguish between the two
essentially different strands in the *Dialogues* text—the main narrative
and the IGPs. By citing the latter, which collectively constitute less
than a quarter of the total text, it is easy to find a genuine Gregorian
flavour in the *Dialogues*, but that is just what is to be expected. As
remarked earlier in Chapter 3, one must also recognize the presence even within the main non-IGP narrative of not a few discrete
phrases that also have that flavour. The explanation of those isolated Gregorian snippets may again be found in the literary astuteness and duplicity of the Dialogist, of which I cite many instances.
He not only inserted into his own homespun tales sizeable pericopes
of Gregorian expository teaching drawn from the *schedae* in the Lateran
archives, but he also added to the Gregorian verisimilitude of his
counterfeit by interspersing in them expressions drawn either verbatim from Gregory's known writings or from the voluminous store
of Gregorian *inedita* in the Lateran *scrinium*. In Chapter 3.c I pin-
pointed some examples of such usage. I add some more here.

The stylistic balance and the sentiment of the clause in *Dial.* II.8.10
echoes words of Gregory in Epistola IX.147:[12] "*tanto ... graviora praelia
pertulit, quanto contra se aperte pugnantem ipsum magistrum malitiae invenit*".
The rebuke to the devil put into the mouth of Datius in *Dial.* III.4.2
seems to reflect a genuine Gregorian snippet. The quotation from
Isaiah cited there is abbreviated by Gregory in just the same way
elsewhere.[13] Likewise second-hand are the words put into the mouth
of Peter the Deacon in *Dial.* III.17.6; they are very similar to a
phrase used by the real Gregory in *Moralia* 27.77. Surely Gregorian
is the sonorous antithesis in *Dial.* III.15.5: "*quia antiquus hostis, unde
bonos cernit enitiscere ad gloriam, inde perversos per invidiam rapit ad poenam.*"
The reference in *Dial.* III.22.4 to the divine "*dulcedo*" towards men,
shown forth by works of miraculous power, echoes similar phrases
in the *Moralia* (16.33) and *Homilies on the Gospels* (2.66.3). Whereas in

---

[12] EH II.143, lines 16–7; cf. also Vogüé, *SC* 260, p. 440.
[13] Cf. Vogüé, *SC* 260, p. 272, footnote.

the two latter instances, however, the real Gregory referred to the kindly Gospel miracles of healing and succour worked by the Lord Jesus, the Dialogist sees "the divine sweetness apparent in joyful miracles" as exemplified in prodigious happenings such as the one he has just related, by which a thief who had stolen a sheep belonging to a church was struck with paralysis, still holding his booty, as he passed the grave in which a saintly priest had recently been buried.

Other examples of the numerous echoes of phrases from Gregory's genuine works in the narrative text of the *Dialogues* are the following: "*nosse velim*", "*pensandum ergo quantum . . .*", "*mira res valde*", "*in quanto culmine*", "*neque hoc silendum puto*", "*quo ordine*", "*manus locutionis*", "*aliis ad adiutorium, aliis vero ad testimonium*", "*innotescere*" (in the sense of, "to show forth". Dom Marc Doucet has made a trawl of a number of other instances in which there are verbal parallels between the *Dialogues* and the *Moralia*.[14] One direct and notably incongruous borrowing by the Dialogist is in *Dial.* III.1.9, where he puts into the mouth of Peter the Deacon a heartfelt and poignant phrase spoken by Gregory in one of his Gospel homilies (33.1): "*flere magis libet quam aliquid dicere*". The banal reason given there by Peter for his preference to weep rather than to comment on his master's narration of the wondrous deeds of saints is that he himself is unable to imitate them. R. Godding also compiles a relevant "*échatillon*" of typically Gregorian expressions embedded in the narrative text.[15]

e. *Literary level and intended readership of the* Dialogues

The apologists who vehemently defended the Gregorian authenticity of the *Dialogues* in the seventeenth-century controversy were constrained to admit the marked difference of the work from Gregory's other writings in language, syntax and literary style. They sought to explain that disparity by appealing to a difference of genre. Gregory deliberately chose to write in such demotic language, they asserted, in order to adapt the level of the book to that of the popular readership for whom it was intended. Such choice, wrote Peter Goussainville,

---

[14] In a study paper kindly communicated to me; he duly observes that "*enracinement n'est pas authenticité*".

[15] In *AB* 106 (1988), p. 228. He cited them as objections to my argument, but in fact they support it.

was not unusual among the Fathers, "who sought truth and simplicity rather than linguistic elegance". Did not Gregory himself, in
his letter to Leander, express his unconcern for literary elegance?[16]
Present-day authors commonly admit the lower standard of much
of the Latinity of the *Dialogues*, but excuse Gregory for writing in
such a style by putting forward pleas similar to those of Goussainville
and his fellow apologists in the seventeenth century. While supposing that Gregory adopted that style in order to cater to popular
taste, they observe that he nevertheless reverted in several places (i.e.
in the IGPs!) to his usual elevated style. Thus W. Ullmann, while
recognizing that Gregory's Latinity was normally of high quality,
judged, on the evidence of the *Dialogues*, that "he was nevertheless
capable of descending to an uncouth Latin when it was necessary
to reach the semi-literate lower clerical sections in distant regions".[17]
G. Pucci has a similarly strained explanation: "It was from direct
contact between the soul of the great pope and that of the people
that the very style and structure of the book, which reflect popular
influence much more than do Gregory's other writings, derive".[18]

One eminent commentator who distances himself from the general scholarly consensus on the frequently low level of the *Dialogues'*
Latinity is A. de Vogüé. In the introduction to his edition of the
work, he writes appreciatively of "the relationship which unites the
musicality of Gregory's style with his spirituality", and cites six "beau-
tiful passages" from the *Dialogues* as exemplifying that harmonious
style.[19] It is no surprise to find that all the six passages cited by him
are IGPs. He does indeed observe that to those "choice morsels" of
nobly expressed spiritual teaching there should be added similar
"examples of narrative passages" from the *Dialogues*—but he does not
adduce any such examples.

Vogüé likewise distances himself from the opinion of the commentators mentioned above who suggest that Gregory purposely
adopted an unwonted demotic style when writing the *Dialogues* in
order to direct his message to the common people, or at least to
"the semi-literate lower clerical sections in distant regions". He argues
on the contrary that "Gregory had principally in mind a religious

---

[16] *Vindiciae Dialogorum*, PL 77, col. 133–4.
[17] *A Short History of the Papacy in the Middle Ages*, London 1972, p. 51.
[18] *Novissima hominis nei Dialogi di Gregorio Magno*, Bologna 1979, p. 10.
[19] *SC* 251, pp. 83–4.

and social élite", and he notes passages which would have special interest for priests and clerics, for monks and even for prelates and nobles. He also highlights the author's disparaging attitude to rustics and indeed his pessimistic attitude to layfolk generally, a subject to which I will return in the next chapter. Such an attitude, Vogüé observes, would by no means commend the *Dialogues* to the common people or give them spiritual encouragement. Disagreeing with the general opinion of the other commentators, he writes:

> The popular character that is attributed to the *Dialogues* is, then, largely illusory. If by "the people" one understands the Christian layfolk, or the lower social classes, or persons without education, in each case one must necessarily recognize that the work is adapted just as well, if not better, to the opposite sector of society—that is to say, to the élite of consecrated persons, of notables and of educated minds.[20]

That perception of the intention of the author of the *Dialogues* is a pertinent corrective to current assumptions. Far from intending to sacrifice literary elegance for wider pastoral ends, he clearly had pretensions to it. He also took care to explain vulgar expressions for his prospective readers, and showed concern lest his reporting of the "*rusticanus usus*" of his lowly informants should appear unfitted to a proper "*stilus scribentis*".[21] However, Vogüé's corrective to those mistaken assumptions leaves another paradox to puzzle those who assume that the author of the *Dialogues* was St Gregory. If the book was not, after all, intended to be a "popular" work, why should Gregory have chosen when writing it to sacrifice his normal grace of style and subtlety of thought, and to adopt instead a low and often uncouth Latinity?

---

[20] *SC* 251, p. 42; cf. also pp. 37–40, 43, 83.
[21] *Dial.* I, Prologue, 10.

CHAPTER SIX

CONTRAST BETWEEN THE PERSONAL TRAITS AND ATTITUDES OF THE AUTHOR OF THE *DIALOGUES* AND THOSE OF ST GREGORY

> *God has no use for a lie, for Truth does not seek the aid of falsehood* (St Gregory, *Moralia* 12.37.)

a

In the preceding chapters I have already pointed to many distinctive differences between the character, pastoral attitudes and reasoning of the author of the *Dialogues* and those of the real Gregory, as known from his expository and pastoral writings. In this chapter I discuss more fully some of the most significant of those differences. Foremost among them is the contrast, remarked by many commentators through the centuries, between the mentality of the author of the *Dialogues* in relating his tales of fantastic marvels and that of Gregory in all his writings on Christian life. In the words of Robert Cooke cited earlier, "Who indeed could suspect, without injustice to Gregory, that he would himself accept such old wives' tales, or that he would wish others to believe them?" L. Ellies du Pin, *Professeur Royal* in the reign of Louis XIV, while admitting Gregory's authorship, still shared the criticism of him: "It seems nevertheless that this work is not worthy of the gravity and discernment of this great pope, so full is it of bizarre miracles and incredible stories. Admittedly, he relates them on the authority of others, but he ought not to have passed them on as veritable facts".[1] E. Auerbach expressed the general judgement of later commentators: "More astonishing, in a man such as Gregory, is the extent and nature of the credence given to prodigious happenings. The *Dialogues* show forth an almost childish fairy-

---

[1] *Nouvelle bibliothèque des auteurs ecclésiastiques*, V, Mons 1691, pp. 137–8.

tale world. Among the stories there are many of the utmost naïvety . . . Here the miraculous is frequently mixed with the grotesque".[2]

In Chapter 1 I cited the strictures of other critics, F.H. Dudden in particular, whose regretful belittlement of the greatness of St Gregory is shared widely today. Not only does the Gregory of the *Dialogues* tell tall tales in profusion, but he also goes to extraordinary lengths to provide spurious authentication for them. To appreciate what an extraordinary dossier of witnesses and informants is presented in the *Dialogues*, one must study it attentively. However remote in time or place, almost every one of his stories is vouched for by some informant with whom he claims to have had personal contact.[3] In some cases he directly vouches for a story from his own experience. He claims to have personally witnessed six of the miracles he relates. There is special insistence on recent testimonies, which are presented as most cogent. "These events are pleasing because they are marvellous, and especially because they are recent", comments Peter the Deacon in *Dial.* III.16.11. Vogüé notes that "the march towards the present moment and the immediate vicinity" in the presentation of the eyewitnesses' testimonies accelerates in Book IV.[4] In one case, related in *Dial.* IV.27.2, *soi-disant* Gregory repeats a dying prediction of a lawyer who had died only two days before he wrote it down, and he relates events at the funeral that could only have happened the day previously!

Dufourcq has shown that the "*souci d'authentifier*" is common to the authors of the fictitious *Gesta* which were rife in that age; the author of the *Dialogues* carries it to a ludicrous extreme. It is this consistent pattern of false authentication that invalidates the plea of modern commentators on the *Dialogues* who seek to justify its fictional narrative as a literary genre adopted by Gregory as a vehicle for an assumedly higher pedagogy. It is not only the fictitious nature of the stories told there that is the problem, but the author's mendacious insistence that their indubitable truth is guaranteed in every case by

---

[2] *Literatursprache und Publicum in der lateinischen Spätantike und im Mittelalter*, Bern 1958, pp. 73–4. He cites several of those stories, in which he recognizes "*eine richtige Heinzelmänchen Atmosphäre*".

[3] Lists of the informants are set out by Dufourcq, *op. cit.*, III, pp. 29–2; by Moricca, *op. cit.*, pp. xxiii–xxxii; and (better) by S. Boesch Gajano, *op. cit.*, pp. 642–3. J. Petersen's discussion of them is valuable (*op. cit.*, pp. 1–15).

[4] *SC* 251, pp. 46–7, 50, 63, 64.

the testimonies of witnesses known personally to himself—testimonies
that he has likewise invented.[5] No theory of literary genres can make
plausible the attribution of that pattern of falsification to St Gregory
the Great, the inflexible moralist who condemned any such deception with the trenchant phrase anglicized at the head of this chapter: "*Deus non eget mendacio, quia veritas fulciri non quaerit auxilio falsitatis*".
In the next chapter I discuss the theological aberrations contained
in the spurious narrative, and the impossibility of attributing them
to St Gregory.

An objection to what has just been said about the Dialogist's exaggerated *souci d'authentifier* may be put as follows. Is not that preoc-
cupation clearly attested in an undisputed work of St Gregory the
Great? In the small group of accounts in his Gospel homilies, relating edifying deathbed scenes accompanied by preternatural happenings, he takes pains to insist on the trustworthiness of the eyewitnesses
of those events from whom he had learned the details. When introducing one of those edifying anecdotes, in Homily 38.15, he stresses
the importance of such authentication:

> But because at times the example of faithful lives avail more than the
> words of teachers to convert the minds of hearers, I wish to relate to
> you something from near at hand. Since it comes from your own
> neighbourhood, your hearts will hear it with all the more concern. For
> the events we are speaking of did not happen long ago; we are recall-
> ing things for which there are living witnesses, who testify that they
> themselves were present.

So, it is objected, here we have Pope Gregory in an undeniably genuine work claiming the same sure authentication of his edifying stories by reliable witnesses that pervades the *Dialogues* narrative. Is this
not indication that he was the author of both works? No, that is a
non sequitur. Gregory did indeed consider, when putting before his
flock those unobjectionable examples of edifying deaths and divine
favours, that it was especially effective to cite instances that were
near to his hearers in time and place, and that were attested by

---

[5] An indignant protest against such attribution of falsehood to Gregory was made
by W.D. McCready in his study, *Signs of Sanctity: Miracles in the Thought of Gregory the
Great* (Toronto 1989), on which I have commented in *HJ* 33 (1992), pp. 339–40.
Such criticism, as found in McCready's work and in *PsGD*, is again dismissed by
Vogüé as ineptly "founded on a strict and anachronistic moralism" (*RHE* 83, 1988,
p. 334).

known and living witnesses. But from the fact that he took care to cite such testimony it by no means follows that his cited evidences are of the same spurious character as that of the vast muster of fictional witnesses who "authenticate" all the prodigious and bizarre happenings narrated in the *Dialogues*. Both the preacher of truth and the spinner of invented tales may cite their sources and authorities, but it does not follow that their procedures are the same. It may well be that St Gregory's care to cite recent and nearby witnesses for the few edifying episodes narrated in his Gospel homilies was a useful precedent for the Dialogist when he provided meticulous but spurious verification for all his own bizarre miracle-stories. His own constant and obtrusive insistence on authenticating his tales is carried to a ludicrous extreme. It is a caricature of Gregory's own careful attestation of those signs of divine favour that he related in those sermons.

b. *Banal reasoning and limping logic*

Among the obviously non-Gregorian features of the *Dialogues* a fundamental anomaly is the mediocre level of reasoning and argument in that book. Although in his writings the real Gregory can indeed be discursive and repetitive, his mental acuity and power of coherent argument is unwavering. By contrast, the level of thinking and reasoning of the author of the *Dialogues* is distinctively inferior. The rational links in his anecdotal narrative and commentary are laboured and weak, and his attempts to maintain a consequential argument often fail. In my detailed discussion in *PsGD*[6] of the manner in which the author comments on the IGPs that he has abruptly inserted into his narrative of miraculous events, I pointed out many instances of the inconsequentiality, naïvety and clumsiness of his discourse.

Although some commentators have tried to present the *Dialogues* as a skilful work of pastoral pedagogy, others have recognized more realistically that the logical sequence of the dialogic exchanges often limps painfully. As F. Bruys observed long ago, "The interventions of Peter are often irrelevant and always insipid".[7] A. Vitale Brovarone

---

[6] Chapters 14–17.
[7] *Histoire des Papes*, La Haye 1732, pp. 362–3.

describes the discussion between the two interlocutors as *"disarmonico"*, and judges it to be outside the main literary current of reasoned dialogue.[8] It is in the fourth book of the *Dialogues* that the author's banal reasonings and limping logic are most apparent, contrasting with the character of the genuinely Gregorian passages incorporated into the text. Can we assume that St Gregory the Great would have put forward the painfully thin, indeed puerile, "rational proofs" for the immortality of the soul offered in that fourth book? A. de Vogüé remarks on their lameness and inconsequence. He points out that merely to argue, as is done in *Dial.* IV.5, that bodily sight of visible things implies the existence of the invisible soul "proves nothing regarding the *future* life of the soul, which is the object of the debate".[9] In my detailed commentary on the context of the fourscore IGPs in the *Dialogues*, in Chapters 14–17 of *PsGD*, I have pointed out many other indications of the low level of the author's reasoning.

It is in Book IV of the *Dialogues*, where the author attempts to develop a structured treatment of chosen themes relating to other-worldly realities, that the weakness of his reasoning is most apparent. He there sets out, as he explains, to provide an apologetic demonstration of the immortality of the soul, using only *ratio* and *animarum exempla*—natural reason and reports of the vicissitudes of souls in or on their way to the afterlife. It would have been alien to the mentality and practice of the real Gregory to follow such a procedure. Divine revelation declared in Holy Scripture was determinative of all his thinking and writing. He would not have set out to prove eternal verities merely from human reasoning and reportage of preternatural apparitions, as though prescinding from the light of revelation in which he saw all reality. The theme of eternal life, of resurrection, of the future rewards and bliss that God bestows through the grace of the Saviour Jesus Christ on those he loves, is an ever resounding theme in his writings. It would have been strange indeed for him to speak of the world to come without placing in the forefront the New Testament teaching on which Christian faith is founded.

---

[8] *"La forma narrativa dei Dialoghi di Gregorio Magno: problemi storico-letterari"*, in *Atti della Academia delle Scienze di Torino*, 108 (1973–4), pp. 95–173.

[9] *SC* 265, p. 37; cf. *PsGD*, pp. 355–6. I analysed those feeble and inconsequential arguments in Chapter 17 of *PsGD*. A. de Vogüé, though sharply critical of them in his commentary on the text, when objecting to *PsGD* excused Gregory for using them with the remark: *"Ces gaucheries sont dans la nature des choses"* (*RHE* 83, 1988, p. 331).

In the following chapter I comment further on the manner in which the Dialogist, when reproducing verbatim in Book IV seven *exempla* that Gregory himself had related in his published Gospel homilies to the people of Rome, stripped those edifying accounts of the pastoral moral that was the pope's original intent in relating them. IGP 43, contained in that fourth book, contradicts the methodology chosen by the Dialogist there. In that genuine pericope Gregory reflects that the human mind is afflicted by spiritual blindness after the Fall. Among the *invisibilia* which the carnally minded doubt, he says, is the reality of the heavenly fatherland and of its citizens, the angels, with whom the souls of the just are companions. But Gregory does not there assume the premise attributed to him by the Dialogist when introducing Book IV: namely, that doubters are to be taught the truth of the soul's survival after death by rational argument or by ghost-stories. Rather, he expressly says that the reality of the *invisibilia* is now made known to our sense-bound race by the Incarnation of the Son of God, who has sent the Holy Spirit into our hearts "that we may believe what we can no longer know experientially". There are close parallels to IGP 43, with frequent verbal assonances, in Gregory's known works.[10] In them is presented a coherent teaching which illuminates the perspective of that pericope. It is a very different perspective from that of the Dialogist.

c. *Smug self-congratulation of the Gregory of the* Dialogues

Among the many distinctive contrasts between the *Dialogues* and all Gregory's undisputed works, in mentality and literary style, is a fundamental difference between the smug self-congratulation of the author of that book and the selfless objectivity of St Gregory. One cannot, of course, argue that he was a pseudepigrapher merely from the fact that he makes himself the protagonist in the dialogue. Earlier writers of repute had done the same. For instance, Sulpicius Severus (to whom the author of the *Dialogues* was considerably indebted for models for his own tales) made himself the principal speaker in his hagiographical dialogue about St Martin of Tours.[11] Gregory himself

---

[10] Cf. *PsGD*, pp. 528–30.
[11] Several examples of the genre of dialogue in patristic literature are given in the article, "*Dialogues spirituels*" in *DS* III.834–50.

adopted a dialogic form of exposition in a couple of passages of the *Moralia*.[12] What is anomalous in our *Dialogues*, and alien to Gregory's character, is the manner in which the author and chief speaker conducts the exchanges with his interlocutor Peter the Deacon, whom he portrays as naïve and uninformed. Particularly alien are the frequent eulogies of his own wisdom that he complacently puts into Peter's mouth. Again and again the latter is made to express his admiration of Gregory's magisterial answers to his questions, and of the profound explanations given in the IGPs, saying how clear they are and how completely he is convinced by them. The Gregory of the *Dialogues* is a papal Dr Johnson, so to speak, omniscient and oracular, who constantly enlightens his Boswell-like disciple Peter; but, unlike Johnson, he composes his own praises.

I give a few examples, out of very many, of that self-praise. These are some of the eulogies of his own sagacity that the Gregory of the *Dialogues* puts into the mouth of Peter: "Because your reasoning has laid bare the secret meaning, no trace of doubt remains in my mind" (*Dial.* I.8.7); "All that has been said is admirable; I had no inkling of it until now" (I.12.4); "I confess that what you say is altogether satisfying" (I.12.6); "You have unlocked the hidden sense of the text cited" (II.2.5); "You relate great things, which will profit for the edification of many" (II.7.4); "The posing of my little query gave occasion for your reasoning to make the matter plain" (II.16.9); "Cogent reasoning cries aloud that what you affirm is the case" (II.21.5); "Your words, I avow, are like a hand wiping away the doubts of my mind" (II.22.5); "That all is as you say is patently certain, because you prove your premises by facts" (II.32.4); "I rejoice that I was ignorant of what I inquired about, since through such subtle explanation I have been able to learn what I did not know" (IV.4.9); "What has been said is wholly right" (IV.5.5); "By your satisfying response to my question, reason has made the matter plain" (IV.37.1); "There is nothing that can be answered to such an evident argument" (IV.47.1). Shorter acclamations by Peter of his master's wisdom and acumen, such as "*placet quod dicis*", "*multum placet*", or "*valde placet*", occur very frequently in the dialogue.

Almost invariably those expressions of self-congratulation, ostensibly written by Pope Gregory himself, are found immediately following

---

[12] Cf. *PsGD*, pp. 628–9.

the insertion of genuine IGPs, and thus serve as external markers of such pericopes. They may be seen to reflect the Dialogist's satisfaction at being able to introduce so many gems of Gregory's spiritual wisdom into his own pseudo-Gregorian and fictional narrative.

d. *"Socio-religious snobbery"*

Another non-Gregorian trait of the author of the *Dialogues* is what may be described as his "socio-religious snobbery". He conveys a sense of the superiority of the clerical caste. He has no such esteem for the laity, even those of higher station, and he has a contempt for the peasantry. I have already mentioned that unpleasing trait in the previous chapter when discussing the intended readership of the *Dialogues*. Here I cite a further scathing criticism of that ecclesiastical élitism by A. de Vogüé (which sharply contrasts with what he writes elsewhere about Gregory's profoundly pastoral intent in writing his narrative!):

> Usually the *Dialogues* do not show much esteem for and interest in the *rustici*. When some of them appear, it is to bring out their lumpishness, their "stupidity", their incongruous judgements and attitudes towards the saintly and the sacred . . . As for the townsfolk, Gregory seems to be no more interested in them . . . In the main, the consecrated persons go to paradise and the layfolk to hell . . . Gregory seems to present monasticism and the ecclesiastical ministry as the normal paths to salvation . . . Indeed, the Christian people receive from the book only scanty encouragement to bring to fruition the spiritual values proper to their state and the riches of grace latent in everyday life.[13]

Vogüé makes a related comment on the social standing of Gregory's informants for his tales: "Most often they are persons of distinction: bishops and priests, abbots and priors, noblemen and high functionaries . . . If he happens to give the reports of inferior clerics or beggars he refrains from giving their names".[14] In a study of "Cultural class-distinctions and ecclesiastical power-broking in the *Dialogues*",[15] S. Boesch Gajano has also aptly described and documented the sacral élitism of the author whom she assumes to be St Gregory. She too

---

[13] *SC* 251, pp. 36–9.
[14] *SC* 251, p. 43.
[15] *"Dislivelli culturali e mediazione ecclesiastiche nei Dialoghi di Gregorio Magno"*, in *Quaderni Storici* 41 (1979), pp. 398–415.

points out that although the peasant world is the background to
many of the episodes, it is extraneous to the world of ecclesiastical
sacredness that the author takes as his norm. The lower orders are
just *there*, passive, subordinate, despised. The story of the strolling
minstrel who unwittingly offended Bishop Boniface of Ferentis, told
in *Dial.* I.9.8–9, typifies the socio-religious gulf between what she
describes as *"due mentalità, due monde contrapposti"*. In that story the
wretched fellow, seeking by his tricks and tunes to gain a bite to
eat, appears with his cymbals and his monkey at the door of the
hall in which the holy bishop is about to dine as guest of the charitable nobleman Fortunatus. His clanging disturbs the ritual prayer
and affronts the sacred dignity of the prelate, who, realizing that
because of that irreverent interruption the wretch is as good as dead,
exclaims: *"mortuus est miser iste"*. Nevertheless he bids them, "for charity", to give the doomed minstrel something to eat. The inevitable
sequel follows: as the man leaves the hall a block of masonry falls
on his head and kills him. A similar cautionary tale is told in *Dial.*
I.10.6–7. There a dweller in Todi is punished by the violent death
of his infant son for an apparently hospitable act, which is nevertheless implicit irreverence to a bishop.

Such stories tell us much about the mentality and clerical prejudices of the author of the *Dialogues*, but they do not square with
what we know of the pastoral attitudes of St Gregory himself. Although
in his homilies he does indeed speak severely of worldly vanities and
those who pursue them (as Vogüé points out),[16] he shows in his writings no class-distinction in his theology of salvation. In his letters he
shows himself intent on safeguarding and promoting the spiritual
welfare and human dignity of all classes and conditions of humankind—
layfolk as well as clerics and monks, poor as well as rich, *coniugati*
as well as *continentes* and *praedicatores*.

The "socio-religious snobbery" of the Dialogist is also manifest in
his wearisome profusion of unctuous terms of respect applied to any
clerical personage mentioned in his narrative, also described in my
previous chapter. Other major contrasts between the mentality of
the author of the *Dialogues* and that of St Gregory the Great are
pointed out in the following chapter, relating to the Dialogist's theological aberrations.

---

[16] *RHE* 83 (1988), p. 335.

CHAPTER SEVEN

DOCTRINAL ABERRATIONS AND ANOMALIES

a

There are many radical contrasts between the folkloric religious perspectives of the author of the *Dialogues* and the theological, spiritual and pastoral vision of St Gregory the Great. In this chapter I point out particular contrasts in the following spheres: in the use of Scripture; in eschatological doctrine—concerning final judgement, eternal life, heaven, hell and relief for souls suffering purgatorial chastisement; in attitudes to prophecy and miracles; in ecclesial and social perspectives; in beliefs about the intervention of the saints; in concepts of demonic activity.

A primary difference between the perspectives of the author of the *Dialogues* and those of Gregory the Great is in their use of Scripture. Gregory's thinking and writing is always Scripture-based; it is habitual to him to intersperse the words and lessons of Scripture within his discourses and theological explanations. In the main text of all four books of the *Dialogues*, however, the Scripture-based perspective of Gregory is lacking: it appears only in the IGPs. To explain that anomaly it is not enough to appeal to the narrative character of most of the work, which, it is argued, allowed little scope for mention of Scripture. Even in the narrative sections of Gregory's homilies to the people the habitually scriptural cast of his thought is apparent. The Dialogist's thought is not cast in the same mould.

In the previous chapter I pointed out the contradiction between, on the one hand, the Dialogist's attempts to prove the immortality of the soul by lame reasoning and by fictitious tales, and, on the other, the deeply theological meditations of Gregory on the way open to fallen mankind for salvific knowledge of God and of eternal life. The consistent teaching of Gregory, in his *Moralia* and *Homilies*, is that the human mind, darkened by the Fall and by sinfulness, is restored by the Redeemer's grace to know God by faith. It may transiently repress and transcend its bodily concerns and imaginings, and thus gain some measure of the lost contemplative awareness of divine reality. But only by grace and divine light can it penetrate through the obscuring veils and regain some knowledge of the *bona invisibilia*. In the fourth book of the *Dialogues*, contrariwise, *soi-disant* Gregory describes the world beyond the grave with a wealth of corporeal images, and finds a principal assurance of the existence of eternal world in his colourful ghost-stories and reports by revenants of their journeys to the Beyond. Here we are in a thought-world far from that of St Gregory.

Another distinctive characteristic of the *Dialogues* is the lack of the ecclesial and social perspective that is so prominent in Gregory's authentic writings. His homilies, commentaries and letters, and especially his *Regula Pastoralis*, testify to his constant awareness of the grave responsibility of bishops and shepherds of souls to lead and guard their flocks, using the means divinely provided in the Church's structures. The bishops and religious superiors must instruct, correct, guide, protect and assist all those committed to their care—priests and laity, monks and nuns, officials and servants of the ecclesiastical domains. They must build up, and where necessary reform the institutions of the Church—the diocesan administration, the organization of local churches and communities, the monasteries and nunneries—and must supervise the charitable provision for the relief of the poor and afflicted. Even though the recent Lombard invasions had wrought havoc in Church life in mainland Italy, Gregory still resolutely set himself to apply the Church's resources to alleviate the resulting disorder and distress in the everyday lives of the Christian people. That ecclesial and social perspective, so characteristic of Pope Gregory, is virtually missing in the *Dialogues* and from the author's portrayal of religious practice and piety in contemporary Italy. The Gregory who writes there shows no similar concern. Nor do the wonder-working bishops, monks and holy men who throng his pages show the same kind of pastoral care and institutional involvement that Gregory practised and held up as the norm for leaders of the Church's life.

S. Boesch Gajano has drawn attention to the strange "absence of any urban dimension" in almost all the stories of holy bishops told in the *Dialogues*. She observes that whereas in Gregory's normal perspective the bishop's office is intimately linked to the town that is his see and to its citizens, in the *Dialogues* "the holy bishops do not operate in a typically urban ambience . . . There is a kind of absorption of the city into the countryside, or rather a lessening of any precise delimitation between the two . . . The city is never presented as a spatial, social or institutional entity".[1] Indeed in that book the holy bishops usually have charismatic freedom from institutional constraints. Likewise, the abbots, monks and wonder-working saints who people those pages are remarkably free from the ecclesial structures and from episcopal oversight which Pope Gregory tried vigilantly to maintain. The Dialogist's viewpoint is individualistic, not social. When succour comes to the needy or afflicted it is not provided by the institutional Church, as in Gregory's Rome, but by the intervention of thaumaturges. For the consolation of those in affliction, he offers the reflection that those blessed men are channels for supernatural forces that can triumph over all the ills and adversities of life. As well as the absence of active ecclesial oversight in the religious world of the *Dialogues*, the secular structures of the late Roman empire, still surviving in Italian society in Gregory's day, are also missing. As R. Markus has remarked, "The *Dialogues* are set in a world in which the 'secular' is absent".[2]

So too the perspectives of the author of the *Dialogues* on monasticism differ notably from those of the real Gregory. The pontiff did indeed esteem the monastic life, and in his pastoral oversight of the Church did much to provide for its proper observance. He recalled with nostalgia the relatively brief period in which he himself had been "*in monasterio constitutus*", devoting himself to contemplative seclusion in the monastery of St Andrew that he had established in his ancestral home on the Coelian Hill. (Much has been unwarily assumed about that episode in his life. Outside the pages of the *Dialogues* there is no evidence either that he was himself abbot of that monastery, or that he was a professed monk of the community living there under monastic obedience.) When he was reluctantly raised to the episcopate and to the *culmen regiminis* he continued to hold the coenobitic life in high regard and took very seriously his responsibility as bishop and patriarch to provide for the due ordering of monastic observance. Nevertheless his understanding of that life and of the place of monks in the Church contrasts distinctively with that of the Dialogist.

---

[1] "*La proposta agiografica . . .*", pp. 632–3.

[2] In a paper read at the Ninth Oxford Patristic Conference in 1983 and included in its *Acta*. In *Dial.* III.10 there is a rare reference to one "*Johannes in hac modo Romana civitate locum praefectorum servans*". This reproduces a passage from one of Gregory's letters (*Epist.* X.8).

Although Gregory esteemed eremitical devotion, he saw the norm
of monastic observance as regular life in obedience to community
discipline. In the *Dialogues*, as Dom Robert Gillet pointed out,[3] we
find monks held up for admiration who lead an eremitical rather
than a coenobitical life. The individual abbots and monks whose
marvellous feats enliven those pages are put forward primarily as
objects of wonderment, not as teachers of godly living and models
of religious observance. In Gregory's own perspective of the life of
Christian perfection there is no such concern for miraculous powers
and clairvoyance, nor does he consider the life of holy hermits and
thaumaturges to be the summit of sanctity. Rather, as Gillet also
points out,[4] he holds up the mixed life of apostolic ministry and
humble devotion as the highest service of God. In his *Homilies on
Ezekiel* he describes the progress of contemplative souls who become
truly enlightened only when they "reluctantly accept the ministry of
souls". Both the spiritual humility and pastoral earnestness of St
Gregory are missing from the sensation-seeking narrative of the
Dialogues.

As well as holy hermits, there are indeed some coenobitical communities in the *Dialogues*. Features of their observance do not accord,
however, with Gregory's own strict standards. For instance, we find
the author of that book praising Galla, a nun of a convent in Rome,
and also Merulus, a monk of the community of St Andrew's, for
exercising the virtue of generous almsgiving. A. de Vogüé comments:
"It is surprising to find resources for almsgiving possessed by religious who have renounced proprietorship; it is still more surprising
to find such almsgiving praised as personal virtue by Pope Gregory,
who regarded any possession of money by monks as seriously wrong
and as a bane of peace and charity in a monastic community.[5]

b. *Theologically objectionable eschatology*

The eschatological beliefs presupposed in the stories told in Book IV
of the *Dialogues* are particularly bizarre and often theologically aber-

---

[3] "*Spiritualité et place du moine dans l'Eglise selon saint Grégoire le Grand*", in *Théologie
de la vie monastique*, Paris 1961, pp. 323–52.
[4] *Ibid.*, p. 350; cf. also his article in *DS* VI, pp. 886–7.
[5] *SC* 265, p. 170.

rant. Of those "visions of the life beyond the tomb, which are at times of extravagant realism", C. Dagens justly exclaims: "What a contrast there is between these representations of paradise and hell and the spiritual conception of the future life that we find in the *Moralia* . . .!"[6] Attempting to reconcile in Gregory's mentality "this diversity of literary genres that exists between the moralist who seeks to stimulate the desire for eternity and the popular story-teller who seems to give credence to naïve legends", he cites a text from the *Dialogues* that has "an almost total resemblance" to a text in the *Moralia*. We find (not unexpectedly) that the *Dialogues* text cited by Dagens, as reassuring evidence of Gregory's unitary vision in both works, is one of the genuine Gregorian passages incongruously interpolated into that text, discussed in *PsGD* and in the Appendix below as IGP 57b.

Although some apologists now seek to explain the fanciful tales which abound in the *Dialogues* as a pastor's allegorical pedagogy, skilfully adapted to the thought-world of the unlearned, the original character, meaning and literary genre of those yarns are too plain to be obscured by such pleas—as other commentators recognize. We read stories about souls who after departing from this world had strange adventures in the next, and returned to earthly life to report what they had seen. Similar fables can be found in the works of legendary hagiography from which the Dialogist borrowed. From Virgil, Cicero and other classical authors such imaginative myths were well known in the ancient world, and we find their influence in Christian apocryphal writings, such as the *Visio Pauli*, and even in some patristic writings. P. Riché also notes that "a great deal of Irish Christian literature is devoted to voyages to the other world and to supernatural visions. The Irish brought this literary genre to Gaul, as also to England."[7] It is an interesting possibility that the Dialogist knew such Irish writings, such as those of the seventh-century monk Lathcen. Although the authentic theology of St Gregory himself found no place for them, the fourth book of the *Dialogues* established their popularity in mediaeval Christendom. "In fact one may regard it as the chief Western source of those visions of heaven, hell and purgatory

---

[6] *Saint Grégoire le Grand: culture et expérience chrétiennes*, Paris 1977, pp. 401–2.
[7] In *Columbanus and Merovingian Monasticism*, ed. H.B. Clarke and M. Brennan, Oxford 1981, p. 70.

which formed an important genre in mediaeval literature and reached its highest point in Dante's *Divina Comedia*."[8]

In Chapters 37 and 38 of Book IV several bizarre stories are told of the uncertain predicament of souls trying to cross the gulf between perdition and paradise. Sometimes, it seems, souls are summoned to hell by error. In IV.37.1 Peter the Deacon asks: "But why is it that some persons are, as it were, called out of their bodies by mistake, and after returning from that exanimate state, each relates how he heard, down there, that he was not the one sent for?" *Soi-disant* Gregory replies: "When this happens, Peter, if you consider the matter well, it is not a mistake but a warning". Nevertheless in the remarkable case reported in that passage, the infernal judge himself declares that his minions have made a mistake in bringing before him Stephen the magnate instead of Stephen the blacksmith whom he had sent for.[9] There is more bizarre eschatology in the Dialogist's subsequent account, of an even direr predicament in which the same high-born Stephen found himself when he died for the second (and last) time. Because he had been partly good through generous alms-giving, and partly bad through unchastity, he was the object of a grim tug-of-war between devils and angels as he tried to cross the bridge over the waters of the infernal river, from which he eventually escaped. The real Gregory, in his *Moralia* 21.9, insists sternly that no good works can counterbalance grave sin in the final judgement.

Also in that chapter we read of the strange and equivocal sanction visited on those who have managed to cross the fateful bridge over the Stygian river to arrive on the heavenward side but were still sullied there by the delight they took in impure temptations while still on earth. Accordingly, while escaping damnation, they were subject to a lesser penalty: that is, their habitations were located near the infernal stream and they were affected by the *foetoris nebula*, a stinking vapour that arose from it. A similarly equivocal punishment was apparently meted out to the nun in the tale related in *Dial.* IV.53.1–3, referred to below, who was partly virtuous because of her continence and partly blameworthy because of her sins of the tongue. Her fate after death was to have one half of her person burned and the other half left immune. Such grotesque conceptions

---

[8] E. Colgrave and R. Mynors (editors), Bede's *Ecclesiastical History*, Oxford 1969, pp. 128–9, note 1.
[9] Cf. *PsGD*, pp. 594–5, where the antecedents of the tale are noted.

of other-worldly sanctions would have no place in Gregory's theological thinking. They do, however, reflect notions that were quite common in ancient mythology. The fateful bridge of souls in *Dial.* IV.37, which the saved manage to cross safely but from which the wicked fall into the nether abyss, was such a notion. (It would seem to derive ultimately from the Zoroastrian myth of the Bridge of Cinvat, "the Separator".)

There are many other eschatological oddities in the *Dialogues*. The author concretely locates hell in the volcanoes of Sicily and the Lipari islands. To those craters were ferried the doomed souls of the two young and dissolute laymen, Eumorphius and Stephen. Because the Arian king Theodoric the Ostrogoth had persecuted unto death Pope John I and the patrician Symmachus, he was justly condemned to torments there. In *Dial.* IV.31.2–4 we read how a hermit of great holiness saw the impious king being thrust down into hell in one of the craters of Lipari, watched by his two illustrious victims. K. Hallinger commented: "That Theodoric the Ostrogoth must repine in the volcano of Stromboli until Judgement Day is something that the theologically erudite Gregory would surely not have believed himself."[10]

c. *Strange accounts of release from purgatorial sufferings*

The ancient Christian belief in a purgatorial cleansing of departed souls not yet ready for heavenly glory and for the divine vision, which had already been made more explicit by St Augustine, underwent a new and crass development in the *Dialogues*. The conservative Augustinian teaching of the real Gregory (expressed in IGP 67) was distorted and eclipsed in the sensational accounts related in that book. Those accounts were to have great influence in shaping the popular mediaeval conception of purgatory, and also the practice of suffrages to succour those suffering there.

In two separate but remarkably similar anecdotes (in *Dial.* IV.42 and 57) *soi-disant* Gregory relates how two wretched spectres were found expiating their sins by performing menial labour in the steamy heat of the public baths in Italian towns. One of the sufferers was the deacon Paschasius, who was liberated from his torrid prison in

---

[10] *SA* 42, p. 243. This anecdote is discussed again in Chapter 22.b below.

the baths of Angulus by the prayers of Bishop Germanus of Capua. His sin had been obstinate schism against the legitimate pope Symmachus. (Vogüé justly queries whether that sin could be regarded as a pardonable matter, of the kind that Gregory considered could be purged after death.)[11] The other sufferer had in his lifetime been "lord of the baths" at Tauriana, and that same thermal establishment became the penitentiary to which he was consigned for the purgation of his faults. He was released from it when a sympathetic priest, meeting the sorry ghost there, offered a week of Masses for him. The notion of later mediaeval popular piety, that the suffering souls in purgatory were pleading piteously for succour from the living to procure their release from penal torments, drew strength from those fictitious tales.

The story of the nobly-born but bad-tempered nuns, in *Dial.* II.23.2–5, raises critical questions about its theological presuppositions. Those two nuns, failing to heed St Benedict's warning of impending excommunication, died under that ban. Thereafter, whenever the deacon pronounced the dismissal of non-communicants during the eucharistic liturgy, the spectral nuns were constrained to arise from their tombs in the church and to depart hurriedly. Eventually they were released from their predicament and posthumously restored to ecclesiastical communion by Benedict's intervention. When Peter the Deacon asks Gregory how the holy abbot while still in this life had such power "to absolve souls placed in the invisible judgement", the answer he receives is the citation of the genuine Gregorian exposition of Christ's words in *Matthew* 16.19, which I list as IGP 23.[12]

It was indeed a major theological anomaly to attribute to an unordained abbot the power of binding and loosing beyond the grave, and the answer given to Peter's question does not resolve it. A. de Vogüé calls the affair of the excommunicate nuns "one of the strangest in the life of Benedict", and remarks that the saintly abbot's act in lifting the ban of excommunication from departed souls is a great marvel, "even greater than one would realize".[13] By commending Benedict's act in the *Dialogues* account, he observes, Gregory departs from a principle firmly maintained by his predecessors Popes Gelasius

---

[11] *SC* 265, p. 153, note 4. Cf. *Moralia* 25.29 and IGP 67.
[12] Cf. *PsGD*, pp. 482–5, where the theological implications of the Dialogist's application of IGP 23 are examined in detail.
[13] *Vie de S. Benoît*, p. 146.

and Vigilius in the fifth century. Although pressed to do so, those pontiffs firmly refused to grant absolution from excommunication to the patriarch Acacius of Constantinople, who had died a century previously, for the reason that the power of binding and loosing given to his Apostles by Christ in the Gospel applied only to those who were still "on earth", as the Gospel passage made clear. Vogüé comments: "Gelasius denied that it was possible for him to absolve Acacius. Gregory affirms that Benedict did well and truly absolve those nuns", and he marks the puzzling contrast between the ruling of Gregory's papal predecessors when pronouncing on a principle concerning the whole church and his own complacent narration of the non-canonical act of an abbot who did what they declared could not be done. (Fr de Vogüé's puzzlement, here and in so many other anomalous features in the *Dialogues* that he so percipiently brings to light, would be resolved if only he could bring himself to recognize that their author was not Pope Gregory!)

It was not only the charismatic abbot Benedict who is related in the *Dialogues* to have procured the release of departed souls from other-worldly penalties. In *Dial.* IV.57.8–16, we read how Gregory himself was confidently able to obtain such posthumous release (even from perdition, it appears!) of a sinful monk Justus, who as he lay dying was found to have secreted some coins for his own possession. (In later pages I discuss the likely provenance of this story, from a work of the seventh-century Greek hagiographer John Moschus.) Thereupon Gregory decreed that the sinner be denied all consolation on his deathbed, and that his body be buried in a dunghill while his fellow-monks cast the coins on it crying, "Thy money be with thee unto perdition". Moved by compassion, the Gregory of the *Dialogues* later obtained his rescue from fiery torments by ordering a series of Masses to be offered for him for thirty days in succession, after which Justus appeared to his brother to announce his release. This anecdote provided precedent for the mediaeval observance of "the Gregorian trental" of Masses for departed souls.

It is mainly because of those tales in Book IV of the *Dialogues* that St Gregory has been called "the father of the doctrine of purgatory". In his controversial book, *La Naissance du Purgatoire*,[14] J. le Goff, while admitting that in the doctrinal passage in *Dial.* IV.41 (i.e. IGP

---

[14] Gallimard 1981, p. 125.

67) Gregory shows the same conservative restraint as Augustine before him when referring to purgatorial purification of souls after death, concludes that the *Dialogues* narrative introduced doctrinal innovation. Observing that "the novelty comes above all from illustration and anecdote", he adds: "Gregory's stories are all the more important because they became the model for the anecdotes by the aid of which the Church in the thirteenth century expanded the belief in purgatory". Le Goff realizes, however, that despite those novel anecdotes in the *Dialogues*, on the strength of which he calls Gregory "the final founder of purgatory", the pontiff was strangely silent in his doctrinal writings about the new understanding of purgatory that was to become so important in mediaeval Christendom: "For all that, Gregory accords to this belief only a very secondary interest. For him, the essential is still that at the Day of Judgement there will no longer be more than two categories—the elect and the reprobate".[15]

Several other critics agree that the Gregorian *Dialogues* marked a decisive departure from earlier Christian belief about the possibility of purification of souls beyond death. "With Gregory I there comes a complete change", commented C. Vogel: "That change in eschatology assumes a change in religious sensibility that is still insufficiently explained".[16] A sufficient explanation of the rise of what Vogel calls "*la nouvelle eschatologie*", is that the crasser sensibility manifest in the *Dialogues* was able to influence later mediaeval piety and practice because that book was universally, though erroneously, assumed to have the authority of Pope St Gregory the Great. In an article entitled "Pseudo-Gregory and the Doctrine of purgatory", Peter McEniery also wrote: "It is difficult to exaggerate the influence of Book IV of the *Dialogues* on the development of the doctrine of purgatory in the Western Church".[17] He welcomed the conclusions of *PsGD* as cogent, and saw the exposure of the spurious character of the *Dialogues* as opening the way to riddance from crude and often superstitious notions of the doctrine of purgatory common in the past.

Marilyn Dunn also finds in the suppositions about purgatory in the *Dialogues* a further indication of the book's origin in the later

---

[15] *Ibid.*, p. 129.

[16] In a paper for the Chantilly conference on Gregorian studies in 1982, published in the *Acta* of that conference: "*Deux consequences de l'eschatologie Grégorienne: la multiplication des messes privées et les moines-prêtres*". (*Gregoire le Grand*, Paris 1986, pp. 266–76.)

[17] *Pacifica* 1 (1988), pp. 328–34.

seventh century, pointing out that "its postulation in Book IV of a systematized process of intercesssion for the release of souls of the dead derives its basis from the evolution of a tariffed penitential system which had begun to develop in Britain and Ireland and was virtually unknown on most of the continent at this stage".[18]

d. *Aberrant attitude to the miraculous*

The Dialogist's attitude to the miraculous, and his purpose in telling miracle-stories, differed radically from that of the real Gregory. The latter's first concern in his writings was to teach the way of Christian living. He expressly taught that miraculous signs as such could not provide examples for the moral instruction and edification of the faithful. In a passage in his *Homilies on Ezekiel* (written at the very same time that he was allegedly writing the *Dialogues*) he insisted: "Miracles are not to be adduced as examples for living . . . What we learn as our rule of belief and conduct is one thing; what we know about miracles is another".[19] The same teaching about the *exempla sanctorum*, (also called *exempla patrum, exempla maiorum, exempla iustorum*) is found repeatedly in his writings. His sole concern when referring to works of spiritual power in the lives of the patriarchs, saints and servants of God is to stress their value as incentives to virtuous conduct: "The examples of the fathers of old strengthen us, and by applying them to ourselves we are emboldened to do what in our weakness we shrink from." (*Moralia* 27.17.) In Gregory's terminology those *exempla sanctorum*, so profitable to Christians as incentives to virtue, are never equated with *signa*. Although in later mediaeval usage the word *exemplum* came to mean any kind of anecdote, often a miraculous event, brought into a sermon by a preacher to hold the attention of his hearers, that was not Gregory's own usage. When he refers to the *signa, mira* or *miracula* wrought by the Apostles and others specially chosen by God he never calls them *exempla*.

Gregory would certainly not have made the assertion, ascribed to him in the prologue of the *Dialogues*, that a whole day would not be long enough for him to recite the wondrous signs and miracles of

---

[18] *The Emergence of Monasticism*, p. 137.
[19] ". . . *miracula in exemplum operationis non sunt trahenda . . . Sed aliud est quod nos de doctrinae usu atque disciplina discimus, aliud quod de miraculo scimus.*" (I.2.4.)

the countless thaumaurgic fathers of Italy known to him from recent
reliable reports. He himself held that after the establishment of the
Church miracles became no longer necessary and were of rare occurrence. Although in a few places in his letters (discussed below) there
is reference to the continued favours of miraculous healing and of
liberation from the powers of evil that were granted to the faithful
at the tombs and through the relics of the Apostles and martyrs,
and although he recognized that there was still need for miraculous
signs to corroborate the preaching of the faith to pagans placed "at
the ends of the earth" (as in newly evangelized England)[20] he plainly
supposed that the main incidence of miracles, and the need for them,
lay in the past, when they had served to authenticate the divine origin of the Church.[21] Then they were needed to overcome the
incredulity of unbelievers and the hostility of persecuting rulers.
Miraculous signs, he affirmed, quoting St Paul, are for unbelievers,
not for believers, and they should be viewed with reserve.[22] Although
the miracles of the saints can be seen as outward signs of God's
inward favour to them, miracles do not in themselves constitute victorious virtue, since, he pointed out, "sometimes they are given to
the reprobate too".[23] Whereas the Apostles performed outward miracles in order to plant the faith, the Church now daily performs
God's inward miracles by reforming hearts and instilling virtue. "Such
miracles are the greater, the more spiritual they are . . . For corporal miracles sometimes show forth sanctity, yet they cannot bring it
about; but these spiritual miracles, which are performed in the mind,
do not show forth virtuous living but bring it about".[24]

The Gregory of the *Dialogues*, on the other hand, claims that the
age in which he is writing is one of unprecedented disclosure of
supernatural "revelations and visions". (*Dial.* I, prologue, and IV.43.1.)
His principal aim in presenting his collection of sensational miracle-
stories is to excite in his readers a sense of excited marvel. The sentiment that he both arouses and feeds is expressed in the words that
he puts into the mouth of Peter the Deacon: "*Miracula quo plus bibo,
plus sitio*"—"The more I drink in miracles, the more I thirst for

---

[20] *Homilies on Ezekiel*, I.2.4.
[21] *Moralia* 27.21; Epist. XI.36 (EH II.395-6).
[22] *Homilies on the Gospels*, 4.3, 10.1 & 29.4; cf. also *Moralia* 27.36-7.
[23] *Homilies on Ezekiel*, II.5.2.
[24] *Homilies on the Gospels*, 29.4.

them". Rightly does A. Ebert comment: "Where the work has an effect, it is exercised on the imagination rather than on the spirit", and he criticizes the *Dialogues* for lack of moral purpose. In it, he observes, there is no sense of the spiritual value of asceticism, such as is conveyed by the hagiographical collection of Rufinus.[25] It was natural that Adolf Harnack, assuming without question the authenticity of the *Dialogues*, contemptuously concluded that for St Gregory the Great "miracle is the distinguishing mark of the religious".

The Dialogist may have known the teaching of St Gregory well enough to realize that a thirst for miracles for their own sake was incompatible with that teaching. Here and there he puts in a remark to admit that interior virtue is superior to external signs and wonders. Indeed that superiority is explicitly stated in genuine Gregorian passages that he incorporates in his text (e.g. IGPs 2, 14, 15, 17). Despite those occasional token admissions, he ignores them in practice. The whole thrust of his narrative is concentrated on the external marvels. As E. Auerbach observes,[26] even when Peter the Deacon acknowledges (after IGP 15) that "*vita et non signa quaerenda sunt*" he goes straight on to clamour for more miracle-stories. S. Boesch Gajano has compiled a weighty dossier of instances in the *Dialogues* in which the author concentrates solely on the wonder-working of his holy men, saying nothing about their inward virtue, and simply presents those miracles as proof of sanctity and spiritual power without using them as pedagogical incentives to virtuous living.[27] She also recalls the few contrasting passages in which the author acknowledges the superiority of interior virtue, but (not doubting that Gregory was the author of the *Dialogues*) she concludes that the book leaves an unresolved inconsistency on the relative value of inward sanctity and outward wonders. In a four-page commentary on IGP 2 in *PsGD*,[28] I discuss at greater length the Dialogist's attempt to gloss over the contradiction, and to make Gregory equate *miracula* and *signa* with *exempla patrum*.

---

[25] *Op. cit.*, I, p. 523.

[26] *Op. cit.*, p. 73.

[27] "*La proposta agiografica*", pp. 637–8 & footnote 98.

[28] Pp. 443–7. I point in one place to an evident substitution by the Dialogist of the word "*signorum*" in place of "*exemplorum*"; that the latter word was used in the original is indicated by the two-fold repetition of *exempla* in the sentence immediately following.

It is then commonly agreed that Gregory's purpose, when in his sermons he occasionally narrates episodes in which preternatural events occur, is always to draw a pastoral moral from the narration that all Christians can apply to themselves for their own conduct. The Dialogist, contrariwise, relates the outward marvels but omits any pastoral moral—even when he reproduces Gregory's own *exempla* from his Gospel homilies. A. de Vogüé observantly marks this change from "the original tenor" of those borrowed narratives: "In the *Homilies* those deaths accompanied by supernatural phenomena serve only to confirm a moral lesson, which is the principal purpose of the recital . . . In the *Dialogues*, on the contrary, those moral elements are not made the object of any comment . . . Now it is the supernatural phenomena surrounding the death that become the direct object of the narration".[29] Vogüé doubtless realized that this admission did not tally with pleas he advanced elsewhere; he added a footnote reassuring his readers that this concentration on the extraordinary phenomena was not "a play on the imagination and catering for curiosity", but had an underlying purpose of edification.[30] *Mais comment?*

e. *Grotesque and sub-Christian miracle-stories*

Can the prodigious and often superstitious tales that make up the bulk of the *Dialogues* be ascribed with any reasonable probability to the great pastor and master of the spiritual life who was Pope St Gregory? For centuries those tales have been seen to present a major contradiction to his reputation for spiritual greatness and wisdom. They were a principal reason why the sixteenth and seventeenth-century Christian humanists denied his authorship of the book, and also why the later Liberal Protestant scholars condemned him as *"pater superstitionis"*. It must be recognized that ascription of those pseudo-miraculous tales to Gregory is not only to represent him as credulous and gullible, (and indeed as culpably deceitful in relating and authenticating them while knowing them to be false, fabricated

---

[29] *SC* 251, p. 93. Vogüé cites several passages in Gregory's works in which the true Gregorian meaning of *exempla patrum* as models of godly living is apparent; I add more in *PsGD*, p. 443.

[30] *SC* 251, p. 93 and footnote 49; cf. also p. 76.

by himself), but also as a pope responsible for spreading superstitious and theologically objectionable notions, not only to his own flock but to the Church of posterity. I cite here a dozen representative examples of such doctrinally aberrant tales in the *Dialogues*. It is not from a Gregorian or an orthodox Christian thought-world that such stories as the following emerged:

- The tale of the half-saved and half-damned nun of Sabina, who preserved her chastity but gave rein to her vicious tongue. After her burial in church, a sacristan saw in a vision her body cut in two, one half being burnt and the other remaining intact. On the morrow the vision was confirmed when the marks of burning were found on the marble flagstones before the altar. (*Dial.* IV.53.1–3.)
- The tale of the horde of caterpillars in a vegetable garden, which were adjured by Bishop Boniface in the name of Jesus Christ to desist from eating the vegetables and to depart. The creatures obeyed the sacred injunction and departed. (1.9.15.)
- The tale of the five-year-old boy whose father did not correct his habit of repeating blasphemous words that he had overheard. Because he could speak, the child was liable to damnation; dying from the plague, he was borne away to hell by demon blackamoors. (IV.19.1–4.)
- The tale of Bishop Sabinus of Piacenza, who, when the rising Po flooded his church's domains and a disobedient deacon would not bear a message to the invading river, summoned a notary and dictated a written injunction to bid it retreat. As soon as the document was thrown into its waters the Po obediently retired to its bed, "and did not presume thenceforth to rise up into those domains". (III.10.2–3.)
- The tale of the grim and unmerited fate of a bishop of Brescia. A sacristan was charged by St Faustinus to warn the bishop that unless he ejected the corpse of an aged rake from his tomb in the city's church he would die after 30 days. Frightened by the vision, the man failed to deliver the message. Despite his inculpable ignorance of the saint's warning, the bishop was duly struck down by sudden death on the thirtieth day. (IV.54.1–2.)
- The tales of the prodigious fauna in the life of the holy hermit Florentius. His tame bear tended his sheep for him, strictly observing the due hours for its return home, according to the dictates of the monastic *horarium*. When four envious monks trapped and

slew his pet bear, Florentius cursed them, so that they were all immediately struck down with leprosy. Their members putrified and they died—to the remorse of the holy hermit. When innumerable snakes infested his cell, his prayer immediately called down a thunderbolt that killed them all. The sanitary problem of disposing of the multitude of dead reptiles was solved by another prayer and heavenly intervention. At once there swooped down from the sky exactly as many birds as there were carcasses to remove, and the area was cleared. (III.15.2–12.)

- The tale of a young novice monk who left the abbey to visit his parents' house without the permission of St Benedict, and who accordingly fell dead on the same day that he arrived home. His body, when buried, was found repeatedly cast out of its grave, until Benedict gave it rest by having the Eucharist placed upon it. The purpose of the prodigy was to show that "the earth itself would cast out the body of one who had departed this world out of Benedict's favour". (II.24.1–3.)

- The tale of the unintentional but fatal irreverence shown to Bishop Boniface of Ferentis by the mendicant minstrel, related above in Chapter 6.d. (I.9.8–9.)

- The tale of a nun who, fancying a lettuce she had seen in the convent garden, ate it without first blessing it with the sign of the cross, and was thereupon possessed and tormented by a devil. When the holy abbot Equitius came to exorcize the indigestible imp, it cried out to him from the nun's mouth, in self-excuse: "What have I done? I was sitting there on the lettuce and she came and bit me." (I.4.7.)

- The futile tale of what befell Theodore, a sacristan of Palestrina. Having risen before dawn one morning to tend the lights in the church of that town, he was standing on a step-ladder carrying out his task when St Peter suddenly appeared on the pavement below him and called out: "Comrade, why have you risen so early?". The Apostle vanished immediately, but the shock of the apparition prostrated the poor sacristan for several days. (III.24.1.)

- The tale of the venerable Valerian priest Stephen, who, returning home from a journey, spoke with unguarded ribaldry to his servant, "Come, devil, take off my boots!" Thereupon the fastenings of the priest's boots began to loosen very quickly, "so that it should clearly appear that he who had been called on, the devil, obeyed the order to pull off the boots". The priest hastily explained that

he had intended to address his servant, not the demon, who therefore desisted. (II.23.2–5.)
• The tale of the acid-tongued nuns who, despite being warned by St Benedict that he would excommunicate them if they did not check their abusive speech, died unreformed. When during the liturgy the deacon dismissed all who were non-communicants, the spectres of the bad-tempered nuns were seen to rise from their tombs and to depart hurriedly. The saint eventually lifted their other-worldly excommunication by having a Mass-oblation made for their repose. (II.23.2–5.)

Those dozen tales may be taken as typical of the kind of anecdote that the author of the *Dialogues*, supposedly St Gregory, delights to tell. I have discussed in *PsGD* several other theologically objectionable fantasies found in his work.[31] It is understandable that many commentators have judged such tales, which abound in those pages, to be evidence of a primitive and theologically debased mentality. With astonishment and regret, H.H. Howarth expressed that common criticism of the book:

> It is full of naïve and childish tales, many of them grotesque and some of them touching and beautiful, but they hardly reconcile the reader to the thought that their author was a Doctor of the Church and an infallible pope; yet he published these fairy tales (which were believed by himself and taught to others) as if they were true, and thus steeped the theology of the succeeding centuries with a great mass of crude materialism and paganism.[32]

f. *Objection: did not the real Gregory relate strange tales?*

It is objected, however, that to show that the stories in the *Dialogues* are legendary and often bizarre is not a cogent reason for concluding that they were not written by St Gregory. It is alleged that there is other evidence that he was, like most of his contemporaries, naïvely (even superstitiously) credulous in his acceptance and narration of miraculous events. Appeal is made to the seven *exempla* in his *Homilies*

---

[31] *PsGD*, pp. 636–8, and *passim* in my examination of the context of the 80 IGPs in Chapters 14–17 of that book.
[32] *Gregory the Great*, London 1912, pp. xxxvi–vii.

on the Gospels, already referred to above (in Chapter 3.e), which have echoes in the *Dialogues* and which show his belief in contemporary visions and supernatural boons, which he described to his flock. Other similar evidence is adduced. There are three Gregorian letters sent to ladies of high rank at the imperial court at Constantinople which include reports of preternatural happenings and sanctions. A letter of his to the empress Constantina tells her how some who had temerariously handled the relics of martyrs came to an untimely end. In a letter he sent to Rusticiana, who was a benefactress of St Andrew's monastery in Rome, four stories (*"pauca de multis"*) are related. Vouched for by the abbot and prior of that monastery, they describe how erring monks were recalled to rectitude by preternatural signs.[33] Moreover, continuing the custom of previous popes, Gregory sent to persons whom he wished especially to honour keepsakes from the shrine of St Peter fashioned in the form of gold-filled keys, and also filings from the Apostle's chains. Such hallowed objects, it was said in the letter, when "placed on the sick are wont to show forth many miracles".[34] In another letter of Gregory's to the emperor's sister Theoctista there is narrated a dire punishment for irreverence that had happened in a previous pontificate. An impious Lombard, trying to extract the gold from one of those keys with a blade, transfixed his own throat and expired.[35] If therefore Pope Gregory could believe and narrate such things, it is objected,[36] why could he not have similarly believed and narrated the miracle-stories of the *Dialogues*?

A first reply to that objection is that there are substantial differences between the stories in the *Dialogues* and the references to preternatural *exempla* both in Gregory's Gospel homilies and in the letters sent to the pious ladies in Constantinople. The real Gregory accepted, of course, that the accounts of miracles in the Scripture were divinely revealed truth. He also accepted as a fact that miracles still occasionally occurred in the Christian age, although he expressly stated that they were no longer necessary for confirming the faith as they had been at the time of the Church's origins. When we examine the accounts of supernatural happenings that Gregory himself credited, in the writings referred to above, we find that they differ

---

[33] Epist. IV.30 & XI.26; EH I.263–6; II.288–9.
[34] Epist. 1.25; EH I.39.
[35] Epist. VII.23; EH I.468.
[36] Especially and strenuously by A. de Vogüé, *RHE* 83 (1988), pp. 332–3.

significantly in kind from the tales in the *Dialogues* that have provoked so much astonishment and derision. The few edifying *exempla*
narrated by Gregory in his homilies on the Gospels to the people
of Rome are, in comparison with the Dialogist's stories, religiously
sensitive and sober in content and style. We recall that F.H. Dudden
found them "not particularly striking" and "uninteresting".[37] They
tell especially of deathbed consolations bestowed upon saintly persons, of visions welcoming them to their eternal reward, of heavenly
psalmody heard at their passing, of sweet fragrance lingering about
their bodies, of divinely granted healing both spiritual and corporal,
of cases of preternatural knowledge and foresight. Such supernatural phenomena have been seriously recorded in the Church down
through the centuries in the biographies of saints (for instance, in
recent times, St John Vianney, St Gemma Galgani, St John Bosco.)
Christian belief finds nothing objectionable in accounts of providential divine intervention to protect the just, to recall erring sinners and to punish the ungodly. Indeed, it finds a providential
meaning in everyday events.

In recognizing the possibility of supernatural favours divinely granted
to the faithful through the offering of Mass, and through devotion
to the saints and their relics and shrines, Gregory was at one with
the tradition of the Church in all ages, in both West and East. It
is not the acceptance of the miraculous as such that distinguishes
the mentality of the author of the *Dialogues* from that of the real
Gregory, but a basic difference of genre in his miracle-stories and
of purpose in the telling of them. As many sensitive Christians have
objected, the miracle-stories of the *Dialogues* are often sub-Christian,
as well as being grotesque and absurd. We are not here comparing
the book with other ancient or mediaeval works of legendary hagiography: in such a comparison the *Dialogues* would not stand out as
different in character from many others, though it would rank among
the most sensational of them all. What we are comparing is the religious character, theological presuppositions and mentality of the tales
in that book with what St Gregory writes in his undisputed works.
It is in such a comparison that the *Dialogues* stands out clearly as
non-Gregorian.

---

[37] *Op. cit.*, p. 254. They are less sensational than the series of some two dozen
miracles appended to St Augustine's *City of God* (22.8).

The four stories of preternatural events retailed in the letter (Epistola XI.26) sent by Gregory to Rusticiana in Constantinople have been singled out by the critics as more closely approaching the mental climate of the *Dialogues*, and therefore as confirming his penchant for fantastic tales. Those stories do not, in any case, have the bizarre and theologically objectionable features apparent in so many of the miracle-tales in the *Dialogues*. However, there are good reasons for supposing that the last section of the letter, which contains the four anecdotes in question, was not personally composed by Gregory. The first and main section of the letter is obviously his own composition. It a personal message to an old friend, whom he had known when he was at the imperial court in Constantinople, and it bears the stamp of his own phrasing and flowing style. He first expresses his warm solicitude for Rusticiana's well being, and then goes on to thank her for her generous alms sent to the monastery of St Andrews that he had founded on the Coelian Hill. The appended second section of the letter, relating the four stories of preternatural events, is in a different style, and displays the clerkish traits that have been described above in Chapter 5 as belonging to the formal and stilted style of the curial secretaries (which A. de Vogüé calls the "*style de notaire*"). For instance, in that brief appendix there are a number of uses of phrases of "reference back", which A. de Vogüé points out as a peculiarity of the notarial style: e.g. "*de eodem pretio*", "*in eisdem tenebrosis latibulis*", "*ex eodem miraculo*". All four stories concern the monastery of St Andrews, and they are introduced by the explanatory remark of the author of the letter that he has "learnt them from the narration of the abbot and prior of that monastery". One may well ask how that appendix in clerkish style came to be added to the letter. One possible answer but less likely answer is that Gregory, wishing to associate the abbot and prior of St Andrews with his letter of appreciation to their benefactress, asked them to provide the secretary who had taken down his personal message to Rusticiana with some edifying stories connected with the monastery to add to his own personal message of thanks and friendship. Byzantine piety took special delight in such colourful *exempla*. On this explanation, the recording and editing of their narrations by the papal secretary, for addition to the first section of the letter composed and dictated to them by Gregory, would account for the clerkish traits in that concluding section of the letter. There is nothing in them that Gregory would have to exclude on theological grounds.

Another possible answer to the question, to my mind more probable, is that the clerkish appendix was written by a later curial scribe—the *Dialogist* himself. In later chapters I will show plentiful evidence that he was very familiar with the file copies of Gregory's letters preserved in the Lateran archives, and made repeated use of them for names and details to add verisimilitude to his fictional narrative. In particular, I give in Chapter 10 multiple and weighty reasons for concluding that he interpolated into that file a spurious "*Letter to Maximian*" (a former abbot of St Andrews) as a "supporting forgery" to allay possible suspicions that the newly produced *Dialogues* bearing Gregory's name were not authentic. Very frequently the Gregory of the *Dialogues* asserts that the miraculous happenings which he narrates were reported to him personally by the abbots and monks of his monastery of St Andrews. In the suspect appendix to Gregory's letter to Rusticiana we find a phrase very similar to that with which his many other tall tales are attributed in the *Dialogues* to the same informants—"*quod abbate ac praeposito monasterii narrantibus agnovi*". The Dialogist may well have added that appendix to the file copy of the letter to Rusticiana as an astute device, aptly confirming the forged testimony of the *Letter to Maximian*, in order to allay the suspicions of his peers and superiors in the papal *Scrinium* and of others. Such addition would also provide for suspicious peers in the *Scrinium* and others a further illustration, otherwise lacking outside the *Dialogues*, of Gregory's predilection for such colourful hagiography. Critics will doubtless object that such an explanation is too far-fetched to be plausible, just as they also make the same objection to the arguments that expose the *Letter to Maximian* as counterfeit. However, it is not at all implausible to attribute such deceptive astuteness to the author who is caught in the act of counterfeiting in so many other instances. In this case truth may well seem stranger that fiction; the Dialogist's fictions are strange indeed.

g. *The folkloric demonology of the* Dialogues

It is instructive to compare the fantastical stories about demons told by the Dialogist and the teaching of St Gregory about the hidden powers of darkness, which recurs as a sombre strand in his scriptural commentaries. When in his genuine works he speaks of the menace of demonic powers he does so in words of grave warning, never with derision and trivializing imagery.[38] Satan, the apostate archangel and prince of darkness, is the *antiquus hostis* and universal agent of evil, who with his host ever campaigns to bring humankind to spiritual ruin. He assures the Christian people that, humbly relying on God's grace and almighty power, they need fear no lasting harm from the ancient enemy. But when we turn from Gregory's sombre reflections on the menace of the powers of evil to the pages of the *Dialogues* we find a very different picture of diabolical activity in the world of human experience. That picture was well described by F.H. Dudden:

> Gregory's *Dialogues* have a peculiar interest in this connection, because in them we meet, for the first time, with the fully developed conception of the mediaeval devil. Here Satan is represented, no longer as the portentous power of darkness, but as a spirit of petty malice, more irritating than awful, playing all manner of mischievous pranks and doing at times serious damage, but easily routed by a sprinkling of holy water or the sign of the cross . . . He is represented at one time as making his appearance all on fire, yet condescending to make a pun on the name of a saint; at another time, disguised as a physician, riding on a mule; again, under the form of a little black boy, or a bird with flapping wings. He haunts a house in Corinth, rendering it uninhabitable by his imitation of "the roaring of lions, the bleating of sheep, the braying of asses, the hissing of serpents, the grunting of hogs, and the squeaking of rats". (III.4) . . . He lives for three years, under the form of a serpent, in the cave of a holy hermit of Campania. In such representations as these the devil has lost much of his terror and has become comparatively innocuous. He is already the cunning impostor, full of tricks and devices, with whom the Middle Ages were familiar. And his attendant demons have undergone a similar transformation.[39]

The malicious imps of the *Dialogues* are akin to the crafty hobgoblins of pagan folklore. Aptly does Auerbach describe the air we breathe in those pages as "*eine richtige Heinzelmännchen Atmosphäere*". The notions there expressed were doubtless common in the superstitious world of the countryfolk which that book reflects. They can also be found reflected in the hagiographical *Gesta*-tales of late antiquity; but that was not the thought-world of St Gregory. In his dis-

---

[38] E.g. *Moralia*, 2.4, 2.38, 14.46, 16.47, 32.27 & 51, 33.37.
[39] *Op. cit.*, II, pp. 367–8.

cussion of Gregory's teaching on "Demons and the Devil", Dudden documents the paradoxical contrast between the sobriety of his teaching in the *Moralia* and the fantastical tales about devils in the *Dialogues*, and concludes: "Gregory's most important contribution to the science of demonology is the collection of stories in the *Dialogues*".[40] Since Dudden assumes without question the Gregorian authorship of the latter work, he has to dismiss the peculiar demonology that it contains as one more instance of the inexplicable paradox in Gregory's character as presented by that book. Rather, the paradox that he points out can be seen as further evidence of the non-Gregorian authorship of the *Dialogues*.

h. *Some other doctrinal contrasts and anomalies*

In my detailed discussion in *The Pseudo-Gregorian Dialogues* of the 80 genuine Gregorian passages incongruously inserted by the Dialogist into his narrative, I noted a large number of other doctrinal anomalies in his text. That discussion is recalled in abridged form in the Appendix to this volume. I conclude this chapter by citing four such instances of the disparity between the notions of the Gregory of the *Dialogues* and the theological premises of the real Gregory. Summarizing them here, I give in each case the number of the IGP in question and must refer researchers to the fuller discussion of them in *PsGD* and in the Appendix below, where similar disparities in many of the other IGPs are also pointed out.

• In *Dial.* II the phrase *"prophetiae spiritus"* is repeatedly applied by soi-disant Gregory to Benedict's capacity for clairvoyant predictions, a usage that contrasts with that of the real Gregory, who uses it only to refer to the Holy Spirit's inspiration of the prophets of Scripture.[41] The Gregory of the *Dialogues* also attributes the prophetic spirit to other holy men in his narrative: Cerbonius, Sabinus and Isaac. Apart from those problematic uses in the *Dialogues*, the word *prophetia* is used exactly 200 times in the corpus

---

[40] Cf. also D.L. Walzel, *The Sources of Mediaeval Demonology*, chap. 5, "Gregory the Great: *imprimatur* on popular beliefs"; *Medioevo Latino*, Spoleto 1980.

[41] Cf. Appendix below, in the discussion of IGPs 21 and 22; also *PsGD*, pp. 481–2 & 477–9.

of Gregory's writings, always with reference to biblical prophecy. Often it occurs in the phrase *"prophetiae spiritus"*, the spirit possessed by the prophets of Scripture. In his *Homilies on Ezekiel* he says "we cannot see through the spirit of prophecy", and in *Moralia* 34.7, when recalling the divine signs no longer given in the Church, he writes *"prophetia absconditur"*. Yet the Gregory of the *Dialogues* attributed "the spirit of prophecy" to Benedict and other contemporary wonder-workers on several occasions.

- In *Dial.* III.24.2–3 there is the tale, already referred to above, of the sudden apparition of St Peter to a sacristan in Palestrina to ask him, "Friend, why did you get up so early?". This so frightened the man that he lost all bodily strength and was confined to bed for many days. The *soi-disant* Gregory explains as follows St Peter's reason for giving him that disagreeable surprise: "What else did the blessed Apostle wish to show thereby but his constant vigilance of those who serve him, since whatever they do to venerate him he would count towards their eternal reward?" Once again the Dialogist strikes a patently false note. It would be far from the spiritual vision of the real Gregory to suppose that the Apostles and the other saints are unceasingly concerned for their own honour on earth. The Dialogist's report of the unpleasant consequences for the poor sacristan of St Peter's early-morning vigilance is introduced, it becomes clear, in order to provide a niche for the insertion into his narrative of IGP 37, which is evidently a pericope of Gregorian commentary on *Daniel* 8.27. The same exegesis is found in *Moralia* 4.67; also relevant is Gregory's comment *Homilies on Ezekiel* I.8.19.[42]

- In *Dial.* I.8.5–6 a genuine Gregorian passage (IGP 9), giving a theological reflection on the place of men's prayers on God's predestinatory plan, is introduced by the quaint story which purportedly gives an example of predestination "helped" by prayer. (The Dialogist expressly uses the word *iuvari* in I.8.6). It tells how the holy abbot Anastasius of Suppentonia—an ex-notary of the Roman Church—and eight of his monks were one night given notice of their impending summons to their heavenly reward by a voice calling their names in succession from a nearby cliff-top.

---

[42] Cf. my further discussion of IGP 37 in the Appendix below and in *PsGD*, pp. 507–9.

They died during the following days, in the order in which their names had been called. There was one monk, however, whose name had not been called, who begged the dying Anastasius to obtain for him too assured passage to eternal life. He duly died the following week. *Soi-disant* Gregory comments as follows on the special dispensation granted to the supernumerary monk: "This was to make it clear that he was able to obtain his passage only through the intercession of the venerable Anastasius." In other words, the monk, although not previously predestined, became predestined through the holy abbot's intervention! The Dialogist doubtless considered this tale to be an apt introduction for his borrowed pericope of Gregorian teaching on predestination; it provides one more tell-tale instance of the gulf between his own mentality and theological understanding and the spiritual insight of Gregory himself.[43]

- A further instance in which the Gregory of the *Dialogues* sanctions conduct contrary to traditional Church teaching and discipline is found in III.37.19–20. There he highly praises the wonder-working but illiterate priest Sanctulus with whom, he says, he has for many years been on intimate terms. He states, without any hint of regret but rather with complaisance, that this priest may never have read in the New Testament St John's words about Christ's sacrifice, that he did not know the Commandments, indeed that he was unfamiliar with the very rudiments of letters and learning. For the real Gregory such a state of affairs would have been scandalous, and he would have given it no countenance. He held that ability to read the sacred books was essential to priestly life, and that it was a grave abuse for priests to be illiterate. In his letters reinforcing the Church's discipline he sternly opposed the ordination or promotion of such men.[44] A. de Vogüé understandably commented on Gregory's apparent tolerance of such abuse in this case: "*Prêtre connaissant mal l'alphabet et la Bible: l'aveu est remarquable*".[45]

---

[43] Cf. Appendix, on IGP 9 and *PsGD*, pp. 450–1.
[44] Cf. *Epist.* II.37, IV.26, V.51, X.15; EH I.133, 261, 351; II, p. 247.
[45] *SC* 260, p. 425.

i. *The anomaly of Book IV of the* Dialogues

The fourth book of the *Dialogues* is the longest and most elaborately structured of all the four parts of the work. Patently its scope and theme do not correspond to the overall intent announced in the prologue of the *Dialogues*, which was to show that saintly thaumaturges had been numerous and active in Italy. Instead, the theme of the fourth book (announced at the end of the third) is to show "that the soul does not end with the flesh". In Book IV we meet a motley host of departing and departed souls: among them some saints, some imperfect folk and—in increasing numbers—sinners, the reprobate and the damned. We have seen also that the fourth book contains a disproportionately large number of IGPs, in comparison with the other three. A. de Vogüé also points out that of the 62 chapters of that book, no less than 27 are what he calls "pure doctrine" without narrative episodes—something that is found in only one chapter in all the other three books. Those "pure doctrine" elements are the 39 passages which I identify in the appendix as IGPs 43–80.[46] Constituting just over 58% of the total IGP wordage of the *Dialogues*, the IGPs of Book IV give impressive verisimilitude to the ascription of the whole work to Gregory. As well as containing a greater proportion of borrowed doctrinal material, Book IV is unique in being systematically arranged. In the first three books the wonder-stories are narrated in no particular order. In the fourth book they are arranged in three different groups, corresponding to three groups of IGPs which are inserted successively into the narrative. The IGPs in the first group (IGPs 43, 44, 45, 47, 48, 49) concern the reality of the spiritual world of *invisibilia*. Those in the second group (IGPs 57, 60, 61, 63, 69, 70, 71, 72) relate to eschatological doctrine—in particular, to speculative questions concerning hell, which can hardly be considered relevant to the hagiographical theme of the *Dialogues* as declared in the prologue. The third related group of pericopes (IGPs 76, 77, 78, 80) concern the eucharistic oblation and its salvific effects for the dead.

There are other distinctive features in the fourth book of the *Dialogues*. Indeed, some commentators have conjectured that it was conceived and commenced independently. "It has a kind of priority

---

[46] They are analysed in Chapter 17 of *PsGD*.

over the three preceding books", observes A. de Vogüé, "and it may be that Gregory wrote it, at least in part, before them".[47] One may speculate that in planning it the Dialogist had in mind the literary dialogue of Gregory of Tours with one of his priests (in his *Historia Francorum*)[48] concerning the Last Things, and in particular "the life of the soul after its departure from the body". The Gallic Gregory's discussion of the Beyond would be matched and surpassed by one bearing the august name of the Roman Gregory. Patently the main content of the fourth book of the *Dialogues* does not correspond to the intent announced in the prologue to the whole work, which was to show that saintly thaumaturges had been active and numerous in Italy. The intent of Book IV (announced in the closing paragraph of Book III), is to show "that the soul does not end with the flesh". Some manuscripts of the *Dialogues*, in fact, give it a composite title, "*De miraculis patrum italicorum et de aeternitate animarum*". While at the beginning of the work it is announced that its subject will be the life and deeds of the Fathers of Italy, in the last book those Fathers are largely lost from sight. Instead, we meet a motley host of departing and departed souls, among them some saints, some imperfect folk, and also—in increasing numbers—sinners, the reprobate and the damned.

---

[47] *SC* 251, p. 65. P. Boglioni advanced a similar view, in a communication to the international conference held at Norcia in September 1980 to commemorate the putative 15th centenary of St Benedict's birth.

[48] 10.13; cf. Vogüé, *SC* 251, p. 42, note 65.

CHAPTER EIGHT

HISTORICAL DISCREPANCIES AND ANACHRONISMS

a

The book of the *Dialogues* is presented by the author as a recital of historical facts, supported by circumstantial references to people and places known from historical record. The events reported are linked with Gregory's own acts and experiences and with those of other persons associated with him. There are chronological indications of when and where those events occurred. Commentators have taken these features as proof of the book's authenticity and of its value as a historical source. When, however, one attempts to test the historical setting of the *Dialogues* against an objective framework of fact known from the records of Gregory's age, one encounters a tangle of inconsistencies and contradictions. In this chapter I indicate some of the main historical discrepancies that tell against Gregorian authorship of the book. Others will be discussed in Part II, especially in Chapters 13–16, where it is shown that the early history of Benedictine monasticism, as now critically revised, provides a major argument against the supposition that Book II of the *Dialogues* originated in the age of St Gregory and was known throughout the seventh century.

The astuteness of the Dialogist in contriving to situate his pseudepigraphical work in the age and ambience of Pope Gregory was recognized by the humanist and Protestant scholars who denied the Gregorian authenticity of the book three centuries ago. Goussainville took account of their arguments but derided them: "But, you will say, the author of the *Dialogues*, who chose to disguise himself as if in the person of Gregory, had steeped himself in the history of the holy Father by assiduous reading of his writings, and so took pains to depict and adorn himself in those colours."[1] Such a degree of skilful guile, he retorted, was beyond reasonable possibility. "*Quasi*

---

[1] *Op. cit.*, *PL* 77, col. 139.

vero tam peritus fallendi artifex esse potuisset!", he scoffed. However, as we shall see, scholars now admit—A. de Vogüé in particular—that the author (assumedly Gregory) was adroit in disguising his borrowing and in adaptation of motifs from earlier sources. Several times in these pages I have occasion to refer to him by that apt description, "a skilled artificer of fraud". There is much evidence to show that he sought to set his fabricated narrative in the historical setting of Gregory's pontificate. He did indeed strive, with considerable ingenuity, to maintain an overall historical consistency in his narrative. While he succeeded in giving it verisimilitude at some points, he failed at others.

We have seen that many clues in his work indicate that he had access to the records preserved in the papal library, including the archive copies of Gregory's letters, which he sometimes uses as a source for names of characters mentioned in his tales. Usually he avoids possible inconsistencies by peopling his pages with characters completely unknown to historical record and situating their deeds in vague locations. From time to time, however, he does make references to persons and events in Gregory's lifetime and circle that can be tested against historical records of that age. It is then that his narrative includes some significant historical errors. I do not argue that the real Pope Gregory would have been incapable of making mistakes in historical record (in fact he did so on one or two occasions). My argument is that there are historical discrepancies in the *Dialogues* that cannot plausibly be attributed to the real Gregory, in the light of what we know from other sources of his experience and attitudes. In particular, he had special knowledge of the recent history of the Roman imperial dominions from his six years of residence in Constantinople as *apocrisiarius* of Pope Pelagius II at the Emperor's court.

I cite three examples of such historical blunders in the book, which may be taken as test cases. The first is found in the repetition, in *Dialogues* III.32.1, of a well-known story concerning some bishops whose tongues were cut out by order of the persecuting Arian king of the Vandals in North Africa. Wondrously, though thus mutilated, the heroic confessors were still able to speak. They took refuge in Constantinople, where their prodigious speech was witnessed by many. The episode had been narrated by no less than six earlier authors who wrote before the time of Gregory's pontificate: namely, Victor

Vitensis, Marcellinus, Procopius of Caesarea, Victor Tunnensis, Justinian and Aeneas of Gaza.[2] It must have been well-known in Constantinople. The Gregory of the *Dialogues* affirms that, while living in that city as papal representative at the imperial court, he himself had spoken with an old prelate who had personally known those bishops and heard them speaking. Yet, in spite of his special familiarity with the facts, he makes what F. Dudden rightly calls the "extraordinary mistake" of affirming that the episode occurred during the reign of the Emperor Justinian—that is, only about fifty years before the date at which he was ostensibly writing. In fact, as the contemporary historians all make clear, it occurred during the Arian persecution in North Africa under the Vandal king Huneric—a century before the time of Justinian.[3] This glaring historical blunder cannot with any plausibility be attributed to Gregory, who was in a position to know the true historical framework.

A second test case of historical error that cannot reasonably be laid at the door of Gregory the Great is in *Dial.* III.1. There a long and edifying story is told about an act of heroic charity by St Paulinus of Nola, which parallels similar themes in other hagiographical collections.[4] When the Vandals were ravaging Campania they carried off the son of a poor woman to be the slave of the son-in-law of the Vandal king. Hearing of this, Paulinus chose to take the captive's place in Africa. When his identity was preternaturally revealed, he was honourably sent back to Italy with all his fellow-captives from Nola. The author of the *Dialogues* knows and refers to the account of St Paulinus's death by Uranius—a rare instance in which he explicitly makes mention of a written source for his narrative. However, he is strangely ignorant of the century in which the renowned Paulinus lived. The Vandal invasions did not begin until well after the saint's death at an advanced age in AD 431. The real St Gregory would surely have known that the active life of St Paulinus, friend and correspondent of St Ambrose, St Augustine, Pope Anastasius and other famous contemporaries, antedated by many decades the Vandal onslaughts on Italy, which culminated in their capture of Rome in 455. Ellies du Pin pointed out this strange chronological error long

---

[2] Cf. Dudden, *op. cit.*, I, p. 341, note 2; also Vogüé, *SC*, pp. 390–1.
[3] Dudden, *op. cit.*, I, p. 342.
[4] Cf. Vogüé, *SC* 260, p. 259.

ago. Dudden commented on it: "It is certain that Gregory made a serious mistake". A. de Vogüé sees that anachronism as indication of the legendary character of the narrative. J. Petersen makes similar excuse, explaining that "Gregory was not writing history but following the conventions of hagiographical writing in his own day".[5]

b. *Role attributed to Hermenigild in the conversion of Spain*

A third test-case and most significant test-case in which the Gregory of the *Dialogues* gives a version of historical events that the real Gregory would not have given is the graphic account, narrated in *Dial.* III.31, of the circumstances of the death of the Visigothic prince Hermenigild, and the consequent conversion of the Spanish kingdom to the Catholic faith. It merits a lengthier examination, since it concerns contemporary events of which Gregory himself was sensitively aware and can be seen to be incompatible with his own understanding of those events, as revealed in his personal letters. The account in the *Dialogues* describes how the wicked king Leovidgild attempted to force his Catholic son Hermenigild to apostatize by accepting the Arian heresy to which he himself adhered. The heroic prince, who had been converted to the true faith by his relative Bishop Leander of Seville ("with whom", *soi-disant* Gregory remarks, "I have long been joined in familiar friendship"), was cast into a dungeon bound in chains. There, by constant prayer and asceticism, he attained deep spiritual insight and saintliness. Resolutely rejecting his father's attempt to make him receive Easter communion from an Arian bishop, he was consequently put to death at the king's order. Miraculous phenomena around the martyr's body attested his heavenly glory, and he was venerated by the faithful in Spain. Leovidgild, vainly remorseful on his deathbed, commended his other son and successor Reccared to Leander, begging the bishop to lead him too, like Hermenigild, to conversion. After ascending the throne Reccared duly embraced the Catholic faith, through the merits and noble example of his martyred brother, and thereby the whole Visigothic kingdom was converted. The Gregory of the *Dialogues*

---

[5] Dudden, *op. cit.*, I, p. 341; Vogüé, *SC* 260, p. 257; Petersen, *The Dialogues of Gregory the Great in their late antique cultural Background*, Toronto 1984, p. 20.

stresses that the principal credit for this glorious triumph of the faith
was due to Hermenigild, whom he calls "God's confessor" and "the
man dedicated to God". He insists repeatedly on the decisive role
of the saintly prince in the conversion of Visigothic Spain. It was,
he declares, "through the merits of his martyred brother" that
Reccared "obtained help from above to lead many souls back to
God's fatherly embrace. We must realize that all this would never
have come to pass had not royal Hermenigild died for the truth.
For as the Scriptures tells us, 'A grain of wheat must fall into the
ground and die, to yield rich fruit' . . . In the Visigothic nation one
died that many might have life. One grain was sown in faith that
an abundant harvest of faithful souls might spring up therefrom".

That insistence of the Gregory of the *Dialogues* on Hermenigild's
essential role in the conversion of Spain contrasts strangely with the
viewpoint of the real Gregory, expressed in his personal letters commenting on those events shortly after they occurred. It also contradicts the account of them given by contemporary chroniclers. St
Isidore of Seville, brother of Gregory's friend Leander and chief
luminary of Visigothic Catholicism, sees Hermenigild not as a martyr but as a usurping leader of a faction in a civil war. He does not
mention his death or the manner of it, but tersely reports that
Leovidild "besieged Hermenigild his son, who was tyrannizing over
his realm, and vanquished him".[6] Another contemporary Spanish
writer, John of Biclaro, who had himself endured the Arian persecution of Leovidgild, likewise describes Hermenigild simply as a rebel
who was eventually captured by his father and sent to Tarragona,
where he was put to death, not by Leovidgild but by his father-in-
law Sigbert.[7] Gregory of Tours, though not as near to those events
as the Spaniards Isidore and John, adds some further details. Like
them, he does not regard Hermenigild as a martyr, but describes
him as a rebel against the king, as a fomenter of domestic strife and
as a wretch who was "unmindful of divine justice". He does, however, mention his acceptance of Catholicism (made at an earlier time,
through the influence maybe of his Frankish wife) and his confirmation
at his viceregal residence in Seville by Bishop Leander.

---

[6] "*Hermenigildum deinde filium imperiis suis tyrannizantem obsessum [Leovidgildus] superavit*"
(*Historia Gothorum* 49 & likewise *Historia Suevorum* 91; *MGH Auct. Antiqu.* XI, 1893,
pp. 287, 303).
[7] *Chronicle*, anno 585; *MGH Auct. Antiqu.* XI, 1983, p. 217.

From the writings of those three contemporary chroniclers and other sources we can establish the dates and sequence of those stirring events in Spain. Hermenigild's insurrection against his father began about AD 579; he was exiled in 584 and put to death in 585; Leovidgild died in 586. In those very years Gregory and Leander were living at the imperial court in Constantinople, bonded in friendship. Gregory later referred to their years there together in the dedicatory letter to Leander that he prefaced to his *magnum opus*, the *Moralia*. All three contemporary chroniclers record Reccared's adherence to the Catholic faith, and the convening of the Third Council of Toledo in the spring of 589, establishing Catholic orthodoxy as the national religion. Early in his pontificate, in April 591, Gregory wrote to Leander in Spain, replying to a letter in which his friend had informed him of Reccared's conversion and merits and expressing his great joy at the news. In his reply Gregory made no mention of the dramatic events which, according to the account in the *Dialogues* that (supposedly) he was to write only two years later, had led to that conversion. In it there is no word of Leander's own central role in the events reported in the *Dialogues*, first by converting Hermenigild, then by carrying out Leovidgild's dying commission to him to convert his brother Reccared. Nor does Gregory make any mention in his letter of 591 of the crucial part played in those events by the royal martyr Hermenigild, to whom (allegedly) he soon afterwards gave superlative praise in his *Dialogues* as the Christ-like martyr who by his piacular death brought the whole Visigothic nation to the way of eternal life. In the *Registrum* there is also a later letter from Gregory to Reccared himself, dated August 591, warmly praising the king's great achievement, "by which the whole nation of the Goths has been brought from the error of the Arian heresy into the firmness of right faith".[8] There is again no mention in that letter of the part of Hermenigild in bringing about that national conversion, which Gregory is assumed to have declared publicly in the *Dialogues* to have been of decisive importance.

Another odd feature of the account in the *Dialogues* is that, while attributing Hermenigild's conversion to the spiritual counsel of "the most reverend bishop of Seville, Leander, to whom I have long been joined in familiar friendship", the Gregory of the *Dialogues* nevertheless

---

[8] Epist. IX.228 (EH II.221–5).

gives, as his source for knowledge of the facts, not Leander but reports he has heard from "many people who have come hither from Spanish parts". Despite his assertion that the martyred Hermenigild's "true glory was quickly made known to all by signs from heaven", and that "as a result the faithful began to show his body due veneration", there is in fact no trace of any such cult either in the records of the Visigothic period or in the Mozarabic liturgy, which testifies to the ardent devotion of the Spanish Christians under alien rule to their earlier saints and martyrs. Even the author of the *Vitas Patrum Emeretensium*, who copied passages from the *Dialogues* when writing his legendary tales of saints in the Visigothic period, refused to reproduce the phrases that represented the rebel Hermenigild as a martyr for the Catholic faith, and substituted a corrective phrase of his own.[9] It was not until the later Middle Ages, through the influence of the *Dialogues* in resurgent Spanish Catholicism, that Hermenigild's reputation was rehabilitated in his own homeland, a process that led eventually to the approval of cult of St Hermenigild by Pope Sixtus V in 1586—a millennium after his death.

F.H. Dudden severely criticized Gregory for error and invention in the telling of his story about Hermenigild and the conversion of the Visigoths. He commented: "The account which Gregory gives of the 'martyrdom' of Hermenigild cannot be credited for a moment in view of the silence of the Spanish historians and the glaring inaccuracies of the narrative itself. It is pure fiction."[10] B. Saitta likewise concluded that Hermenigild "certainly did not favour or hasten the passage of the Visigothic world to Catholicism".[11] Some authors have attempted to mitigate the problem by various strained conjectures—perhaps to take account of the Church's official approval of his cult a millennium after his putative martyrdom.[12]

I cite a further instance in which the Dialogist's usage is significantly at variance with that followed in Gregory's letters. In *Dial.* IV.37.3, the country named as Iberia (or Hiberia), is evidently Spain—a usage that became usual in the early Middle Ages as an alternative for Hispania. That was not the usage of the real Gregory: when he sent

---

[9] Cf. *PsGD*, pp. 665 and 131–56.
[10] *Op. cit.*, I, p. 342; cf. pp. 403–11. So also R. Altamira, *CMH* XI, 1913, p. 170.
[11] "*La rivolta di Ermenigildo*", in *Quaderni catanesi di studi classici e medioevali*, I (1979), pp. 81–134.
[12] Cf. *PsGD*, pp. 664–5.

a letter (XI.52) to the Catholic bishops of Iberia (Hiberia) he meant the Caucasian country of Georgia, to which that name was still commonly applied in his time.

c. *Discordances with sixth-century Italian history*

The social and economic background of contemporary Italy reflected in the *Dialogues* does not correspond to the more organized social and political system which still survived in the age of Gregory's pontificate, and which is well documented in his letters. In the everyday world depicted in that book there is virtually no evidence of administrative control either by the imperial exarch of Ravenna or by his subordinates. Imperial control, taxes and soldiery, which were still in Gregory's age (as his letters show) grievous burdens for the countryfolk in those regions of central Italy, do not feature in the *Dialogues*. In so far as there is authority in those regions it is exercised not by civil officials but by miracle-working bishops, abbots and other holy men.

In Gregory's day the Byzantine emperor's overlordship over the city of Rome was still acknowledged, both in theory and in practice. F. Gregorovius assesses its exercise at that time as follows: "Besides the City Prefect and the *Magister militum* or *Dux*, there were in Rome other imperial officials . . . Occasionally an imperial messenger appeared, whose despotism occasioned no slight dismay . . . Although the records of the government of the city at this time are very scanty, so much at least is certain, that the military, civil and political power in the city was in the hands of the Emperor's officials, while a certain supervision belonged to the Pope, to whom recourse was made in case of appeal."[13] However, in the Rome reflected in the pages of the *Dialogues*, that imperial presence has faded; a later stage has been reached in the evolution of the ecclesiastical city-state towards independent authority. C. Diehl has well documented that evolution, and the age in which it happened. He shows both the reality and officiousness of imperial control in the exarchate and in Rome during Gregory's pontificate and its erosion and disintegration

---

[13] *Op. cit.*, II, p. 51; cf. also P. Llewellyn, *op. cit.*, pp. 93–4, and J. Richards, *op. cit.*, Chapters 6 & 7.

during the turbulent seventh century.[14] By the end of that period
(the time, that is, when the *Dialogues* first emerged into the light), he
wrote, "for those Byzantines of the seventh century the influence of
the Roman Church on the civil administration had become an evident and undeniable fact."

When we turn from the wider sphere of contemporary history to
the regions of central Italy in which most of the *Dialogues* narrations
are set, we find there too that several of the assertions attributed to
St Gregory in that book are incompatible with what we know from
other sources, and that most of the events and situations he supposedly recounts are in a realm of fantasy beyond historical verifia-
bility. U. Moricca tried to draw up some chronological framework
into which those events would fit coherently, but found it impossible. He remarked, in the preface to his edition of the *Dialogues*, that
while the narrative abounds in "indications of a historical character", it is so lacking in precision that one finds oneself "sailing in
the midst of dense darkness" and unable to give any firm dating or
verification of the events related.[15] V. Recchia set out to write a
study of what can be learned about the rural society of Gregory's
age, using the data provided both in the *Registrum* of his letters and
from the *Dialogues*, but found himself confronted with a puzzling
incompatibility between those two sources. Concluding that "the picture of agricultural society that is drawn from the *Dialogues* is very
different from that presented in Gregory's administrative letters", he
decided to leave out of account the data of the *Dialogues* and to base
his research only on the evidence of the *Registrum*.[16]

In the past, not a few commentators on the *Dialogues* have drawn
reassurance from the author's careful attestation of his sources, naming informants, often eyewitnesses, who vouched for the truth of
what he reports. This they saw as an index of his concern for accuracy, even though they conceded that he might have been misled
by some of those informants. The assurance of those commentators
is now shown to be unfounded. The constant appeal of the author
to the witness of named informants provides, on the contrary, a
telling counter-argument against both the historicity and the Gregorian

---

[14] *Etudes sur l'administration byzantine dans l'Exarchat de Ravenne (568–751)*, Paris 1888,
pp. 133–90.
[15] *Op. cit.*, p. XLV.
[16] *Gregorio Magno e la Società Agricola*, Rome 1978, p. 6.

authorship of the book. It is now commonly admitted—notably by
A. de Vogüé—that it is no longer possible to exculpate the author
of the *Dialogues* by supposing that he passed on, in good faith, the
untrustworthy reports of others. It is recognized that in many cases
he himself was the inventor both of the idle tales and of their spurious authentication. Hence the piling up of those first-hand testimonies to the truth of his narrative, far from enhancing his credit,
decisively undermines it.

Despite his clear-sighted recognition of the author's inventiveness,
and of his wiliness in concealing it, A. de Vogüé still judges the
Dialogues valuable as a historical source. "It is above all in the area
of regional and local history that the *Dialogues* are precious", he
writes. Not only does the work provide "a very lively picture of
Italian society in the sixth century", but, he affirms, "there is also
in it an abundant documentation of prosopography and topography.
Moreover many persons, monuments and sites of Italy in that epoch
are known to us solely, or for the first time, in the *Dialogues*".[17] It
cannot be said, however, that the historical credit of the book is
restored by those circumstantial details which Vogüé finds so precious. The author of the *Dialogues* does indeed give a picturesque
and lively picture of Italian society, and sets his miracles in a homely
setting which he evidently knows well from personal experience. Yet
that does not authenticate his fictions about people and events within
that setting.

Vogüé considers that the information furnished by the *Dialogues* is
particularly important for the history of the monasteries of Italy in
the dark age in which Gregory lived. "Without those indications",
he argued, "we should know nothing of Honorius and of Fondi, of
Equitius and his Valerian foundations, of Anastasius and of Suppen-
toma, nor of so many other coenobitical foundations . . ." One may
comment, on the contrary, that it is surprising that such notable
saints and such important foundations should be otherwise so completely unknown, unmentioned in any authentic documentary record.
In Chapter 18 I point out the singular lack of any trace, in any
record before the close of the seventh century, of biographical knowledge of St Benedict, who should surely have been the most remarkable Italian saint of that age—if St Gregory had written the *Dialogues*

---

[17] *SC* 251, p. 155.

at the close of the sixth century. Similar critical doubts arise about most of regional "history" in that book, and about the lives and deeds of the other miracle-working saints related there, whose very existence was for long unrecognized in the localities in which they are alleged to have been active. The artificial renown they acquired in later centuries, when the *Dialogues* had made them famous, could not supply for the lack of any cult or knowledge of them in their presumed homelands. B. de Gaiffier justly described the tardy introduction of such "new saints" into the Roman sanctoral calendar as unjustified, "since there is not the least trace of any cult rendered to them".[18]

A particularly striking example of that strange historical *incognito* of the saints of the *Dialogues* can be shown from critical consideration of the narration in *Dial.* III.27–28.1. There we read how in or about the year 578 (the date is given by indications in the text) 440 Italian countryfolk died as steadfast and glorious martyrs at the hands of the Lombards. First 40 captive peasants were slain because they refused to eat food immolated to idols; then no less than 400 others were martyred for refusing to adore a goat's head which the impious Lombards had sacrificed to the devil. (The Dialogist may have drawn this detail of his story from a letter of Gregory to the Frankish queen Brunhild, dated 597, in which he urged her to restrain her subjects from "sacrilegious sacrifices with the heads of animals", and from "the cult of devils".)[19] Now if such an extraordinary demonstration of the highest Christian virtue and valour by so many hundred Italian countryfolk who chose martyrdom rather than deny their faith had really occurred at that time, only a dozen years before Gregory became pope, how is it that—outside the pages of the *Dialogues*—there is no trace of remembrance of it either in his lifetime or throughout the following century? No place can be identified as the site of the martyrdom or of the martyrs' tombs, no local church claimed them, no pilgrimage or cult arose to venerate them and to enlist their heavenly power. Surely Pope Gregory himself, if he knew and had lauded so highly the glorious constancy of those 440 martyrs, would have ensured that the place of their martyrdom and of their tombs should be made known and honoured by the

---

[18] "*Les héros des Dialogues de Grégoire inscrits au nombre des saints*", in *AB* 83 (1965), pp. 53–74; the words cited are on pp. 72–3.
[19] Epist. VIII.4; EH II.7.

Christian world? Commentators today are prepared to recognize that the story must be classified in the genre of fictitious hagiography; but how can we assume that St Gregory would impose on the faith and piety of his flock by putting out such a false report of that allegedly recent martyrdom? At all events, if in AD 593–4 he had announced that event in the *Dialogues*, surely his report of that mass martyrdom in his book, which allegedly rose to rapid fame, would have made some discernible impression in the century following, an age when the cult of martyrs was at its height?

There are many other instances in which we are able to compare the assertions of the Dialogist with those of Gregory himself in his authentic writings and to observe that they do not tally. In the previous chapter I have already referred to one in particular which is fairly representative of many. In *Dialogues* III.7 Gregory tells of prodigious happenings relating to Bishop Andrew of Fondi, which he there authenticates with the assurance that "there are as many witnesses to them as there are inhabitants existing in that place". The real Gregory, however, writing to the exiled bishop Agnellus of Fondi the year before he allegedly wrote that story, lamented that "because of the destruction of war it is impossible for anyone to dwell either in that city or in your church".[20]

It is remarkable how many of the episodes in the *Dialogues*, especially in Books I and III, are connected with the region of central Italy embracing the provinces of Valeria, Sabina, Tuscia and Umbria. In Book II, the biography of St Benedict, the setting is first in the Sabine hill country east of Rome and later in the region traversed by the Via Latina towards Campania. In Chapter 23, where I discuss the biographical background of the Dialogist himself, I will say more about the significance of his topographical references. It appears that he (unlike Pope Gregory) had personal familiarity with those particular regions. I will argue later that he may well have had a function in the administration of the Roman church that gave him occasion to become familiar with the papal patrimonies, estates that still survived during the seventh century in central Italy and Campania, despite the earlier Lombard conquests which had led to the establishment of the Lombard dukedoms of Spoleto and Benevento. He shows no similar familiarity with the important papal patrimonies in

---

[20] Cf. *PsGD*, p. 669.

Sicily. Although many of Pope Gregory's letters were concerned with
Sicily, where there were estates of his own family and where he himself founded six monasteries,[21] we find in the *Dialogues* only very occasional mention of that island, and no stories about particular towns,
local churches, monasteries and ecclesiastical functionaries, such as
are abundantly related about the regions of central Italy.

Another historical incongruity in the *Dialogues*, relating to the role
of abbots and monks in rural society and giving further evidence of
the post-Gregorian origin of that book, is pointed out by Marilyn
Dunn:

> The *Dialogues'* picture of monks as evangelists and of monasteries which
> served as pastoral centres appear out of place in sixth-century Italy,
> but it is much more appropriate to another area and a slightly later
> stage of monastic history.[22]

d. *Historical incongruities relating to the city of Rome*

When we turn to the later pages of the *Dialogues* in which the city
of Rome is the setting for a number of miracles and visions, we
again find some strange features of the narrative. First, it is extraordinary that so many of the community of the monastery of St
Andrew that Gregory had founded in his family home on the Caelian
Hill were witnesses to or even participants in such prodigious happenings. K. Hallinger lists no fewer than 27 such instances.[23] We
note too that a curiously high proportion of those informants in the
Roman monastery were knowledgeable about events in the remoter
regions of central Italy, especially Valeria and the country in the
neighbourhood of Spoleto and Nursia, spanning southern Umbria
and the old Sabine region.

The references made by the Gregory of the *Dialogues* to the abbots
of "my monastery", when taken in conjunction with firm facts known
from the Gregorian letters, present an incongruous pattern of names
and dates. The first abbot of the monastery that we hear of in the
Dialogues (IV.22) is Valentius, from Valeria, who is said to have ruled

---

[21] Cf. F. Gregorovius, *History of the City of Rome in the Middle Ages*, English trans.
vol. II, London 1894, p. 31.
[22] *The Emergence of Monasticism*, p. 137.
[23] "*Papst Gregor der Grosse und der heiliger Benedikt*", SA 42 (1957) pp. 252–4.

the community while Gregory was a monk there. (John the Deacon, the ninth-century biographer of St Gregory, says however that he wore the monastic habit under two abbots, Hilarion and Maximian.)[24] In *Dial.* IV.22 it is stated that Maximian was abbot of St Andrew's when Gregory was papal representative in Constantinople—that is, from about 579 to 586. A letter sent by Pope Pelagius II to Gregory in the imperial capital,[25] which seems to refer to Maximian (described there as "*presbyter*") demands that the latter should return to Rome because he is needed "in our monastery" and also by Pelagius himself for some specific task. However, in *Dial.* IV.57 the author presents Gregory himself as exercising abbatial authority at St Andrew's after his return from Constantinople. Some commentators suggest that Gregory was not then acting as abbot but as patron of the monastery. On that hypothesis, the office of abbot was presumably vacant, since in the fanciful tale of the fate of the sinful monk Justus Gregory issued his instructions through the prior, named there as Pretiosus. In the *Registrum* there is a letter of Gregory's dated from the end of the year 590, mentioning that Maximian was abbot of St Andrew's at that time.[26] By October 591 Maximian had left Rome to become bishop of Syracuse and papal vicar in Sicily. In *Dial.* III.49.5 *soi-disant* Gregory states that a monk called Peter was head of the monastery of St Andrew's at the time of writing (i.e. ostensibly 593); this Peter had been abbot long enough to have prepared a tomb for himself some time previously. There is also a letter of Gregory to a priest named Marianus who was made bishop of Ravenna in July 595 and who had previously exercised the *regimen monasterii* at St Andrews.[27] Finally we know from a genuine record in the *Registrum* (*Epist.* VIII.12) that in the year 598 the abbot was Candidus. That confusing tangle of data and dates is indeed difficult to make sense of. If all those depositions were true, one would have to conclude that eight different superiors governed the monastery of St Andrew's in uncertain succession during the fourteen years from 584 to 598 (including in that number Pretiosus and Gregory himself), and that Maximian had two spells of abbotship separated by an intermission. If, however, we discount the historical credit of the

---

[24] *Vita Gregorii* I.6.
[25] EH II.440–1.
[26] *Ibid.*, I.14.
[27] I owe this additional reference to A. de Vogüé, *RHE* 83 (1988), p. 338.

Dialogues we have sure knowledge of only two abbots or perhaps three in that period—Maximian, Candidus and Marianus.

Another curious feature to note in the *Dialogues* narrative is the pattern of localization and sequence of the events narrated. Rome appears late in that sequence. In the first three books of the *Dialogues* the persons and events mentioned are almost all located in provincial and rural areas. In Book II Rome is mentioned as the place from which the youthful Benedict fled, but the theatre of his activities is elsewhere. Only in the second part of Book III does Rome begin to be a place of supernatural occurrences. Then in Book IV the Roman episodes multiply. A score of stories tell of marvellous events there, six of them in the monastery of St Andrew. There is, however, a dearth of thaumaturges in the city, compared to the country regions. Although prodigies occur in Rome, they are visions of the Beyond rather than miraculous deeds. The healing of a paralytic girl by Acontius, a sacristan of St Peters (*Dial.* III.35), is a rare exception. If, as several scholars think likely, Book IV was originally planned as a free-standing opuscule, the non-Roman perspective of the first three books stands out even more clearly. The centre of gravity of the miraculous narrative is not in Rome but in its hinterland. That would be a surprising bias if the author of the book were Gregory the Great, Roman of the Romans. It seems to point rather to an author who, though familiar with Rome and the administration of the papal Curia, was more familiar (and perhaps connected by origin) with the countryside, towns and monasteries of provincial Italy.

More than one author (Moricca in particular) has commented on the extraordinary longevity of Gregory's informants. In his desire to authenticate his tales of long ago by the evidence of informants known to Gregory personally, the author of the *Dialogues* cites several witnesses who lived for improbably long periods. I cite two instances. The first is provided by the testimonies authenticating the miracles of the holy abbot Equitius, as related in the fourth chapter of the first book. U. Moricca, after wrestling with the difficulties encountered in attempting to date the life and activity of Equitius, concluded: "Concerning the time in which Equitius lived, and in which the miracles narrated by Gregory can be located, there exists discord and confusion in the sources".[28] Confusion there is indeed

---

[28] *Op. cit.*, p. 27, note 2. Vogüé, although ready to admit that Gregory invented

in the *Dialogues*, the sole source for any information about Equitius. It arises mainly from the extraordinary length of the abbot's active life as described there, and also of the life span of those who attested his miraculous deeds. The Dialogist presents him as already a renowned abbot when he unmasks the magician Basilius. The existence of the latter is attested in historical record. The legal process against him and his accomplice Praetextus, who were arraigned for practising magic arts, is recorded by Cassiodorus, and can be dated accurately to the year 510 or 511. According to the *Dialogues* (I.4), the wonder-working ministry of abbot Equitius continued for many years. We read there of his being summoned to Rome by a pope, whom Dufourcq thought was John III (pope from 561 to 574), but who Vogüé suggests was Agapitus, who was pope for a year, 535–6.[29] (Despite his scepticism elsewhere about the historicity of the tales in the *Dialogues*, Vogüé assumes without question that Equitius really existed.) The Gregory of the *Dialogues* asserts that at the putative time of writing (the year 593, as indicated by the *Letter to Maximian*), "many are still alive" who had witnessed the marvellous life and deeds of Equitius. The longevity of those many witnesses, who could all recall in 593 events that occurred before 510, is surely another marvel! Even more extraordinary was the longevity and memory of an aged cleric who was still alive and able to inform Gregory about deeds worked by Bishop Boniface of Ferentis while still a child in his mother's care—at a date which, from the indications given in the text, must have been nearly a century earlier.

In Chapter 23 I signal yet another significant historical discrepancy in the *Dialogues* narrative relating to local Italian history, which even by itself is cogent evidence that the *Dialogues* were written many years after Gregory's death. In *Dial.* III.29.1–4 the author retells a story about a miracle which foiled an attempt by an Arian bishop in Spoleto to take possession of a Catholic church. Ecclesiastical rivalry between Arians and Catholics in the churches of Spoleto arose in the mid-seventh century because of Arianizing measures introduced in the reign of the Lombard king Rothari 636–652).[30] As originally told that story was relevant in that specific historical context;

---

both tales and informants, finds nothing surprising in the extraordinary longevity of the informants cited in the *Dialogues*: cf. *RHE* 83 (1988), p. 338.

[29] Dufourcq, *op. cit.*, III, p. 73; Vogüé, *SC* 260, p. 436, *and "Le pape qui persécuta S. Equitius"*, in *AB*, 100 (1982), pp. 319–25.

[30] Cf. Chapter 9.d below.

to present it as told by Pope Gregory at the end of the sixth century, and as referring to the first period of the Lombard conquest, is another tell-tale anachronism.

e. *Reuse of names and a pattern of literary impersonation*

Despite the rich profusion in the *Dialogues* of personal names and topographical references, it proves impossible to obtain from them any historical confirmation of the book's Gregorian authenticity or early date of origin. Many names of individuals who are mentioned in the *Registrum* of Pope Gregory's letters are also found in the *Dialogues*, either as witnesses to miracles, or as relatives or associates of other characters, or sometimes as participants in the episodes narrated. Yet although the author of the book supplies further particulars about those individuals which give his narrative some verisimilitude, nothing in his book adds convincingly to the knowledge we have from Gregory's official letters and other contemporary sources. The Dialogist evidently had first-hand access to those letters in the papal archives, and made skilful use of them. Although in the later seventh century (the period indicated as the probable time of the *Dialogues'* origin) copies of Gregory's letters were not publicly circulated, and were accessible only to the clerkly *coterie* of notaries and scribes who staffed the papal secretariate in Rome, it may well have appealed to his inventive mind to introduce into his narrative historical characters mentioned by Gregory himself. That ploy could be a persuasive factor in convincing his peers and colleagues in the *Scrinium* of the Gregorian authorship of his pseudography.

Studying those personal names, two categories may be distinguished. First, there are several instances in which it is clear that the author of the *Dialogues* intended to identify a character in his narrative with a person named in the papal letters. In some of these cases the same names appear in both sources and seem evidently to refer to the same persons, but there are historical circumstances that make such identification incongruous. Secondly, there are numerous other instances in which there is identity of names in both, yet it is quite clear that the characters mentioned in the *Dialogues* could not be the same as their namesakes in the *Registrum*. In such cases it appears that the Dialogist plucked names from the *Registrum* to give to the fictitious characters of his tales, without any attempt to identify those characters with the individuals whose names he was borrowing.

A notable example in the first of those two categories is the story about Exhilaratus narrated in *Dial.* II.18. This individual, mentioned a number of times in Gregory's letters, was an important notary in the papal secretariate—indeed, his name may well have been still familiar to the clerks and other officials in the papal Curia a century later. According to the tale in the *Dialogues*, Exhilaratus had in his youth been a servant, and was sent by his master to take a gift of two wine kegs to St Benedict at Cassino. Dishonestly, he delivered only one, having hidden the other by the wayside for his own use. The prescient abbot warned the servant not to drink from the keg he had hidden, but to tilt it cautiously to see what was inside. When Exhilaratus, covered with confusion, did as he was bid, a serpent emerged from the keg. In telling this tale (which has several parallels in antiquity)[31] *soi-disant* Gregory identifies the one-time dishonest servant (who, he says, later became a monk) as "*Exhilaratus noster*", and he reminds his interlocutor Peter the Deacon, "You yourself knew him after his conversion". The possessive pronoun "*noster*" is habitually applied by Pope Gregory in his writings to one who was a member of the papal household. The Dialogist is plainly introducing as a character in his own fictional narrative the well known official Exhilaratus who was the *secundicerius*, or second-in-rank of the guild of notaries of the Roman church, and who is historically known from references to him in the *Registrum*. In *Epist.* V.6, written in the autumn of 594, in which Gregory recalls his earlier intention of sending Exhilaratus on a mission to Constantinople, he refers to him by the same familiar phrase, "*Exhilaratus noster*" that the Dialogist uses in *Dial.* II.18 to identify the reformed rogue of his wine-keg story. It is not unlikely that this high-ranking curial official was afterwards raised to the episcopate and that he was the "*coepiscopus noster Exhilaratus*" whose unjust conduct in Sicily Gregory reprehends in a letter of September 603.[32] (Did that malfeasance of Exhilaratus in later years suggest to the Dialogist the idea of attributing to him dishonesty in his youth?)

---

[31] Cf. *PsGD*, p. 671, note 34.
[32] *Epist.* XIV.4; EH I.477.

The story of Exhilaratus and St Benedict is in itself very suspect.
It is a "doublet" of a tale told of Isaac of Spoleto and a deceitful
servant in *Dial.* III.14.9, where all the circumstances are practically
identical. A. de Vogüé points out that duplication, which, he agrees,
indicates legendary creation. He argues, however, that it is the event
at Spoleto rather than the one at Cassino that should be judged
fictitious—his reason being that "Exhilaratus plays there a role that
is little to his credit, which Gregory could hardly have attributed
gratuitously to a person of his court".[33] (With this remark concerning Gregory himself, I fully agree!) It appears that Vogüé, though
critically sceptical of tall tales elsewhere in the *Dialogues*, here accepts
the veracity of the tale about Exhilaratus and the serpent in the
stolen wine keg because he assumes, on the evidence of that book,
that it was public knowledge.

Another Roman ecclesiastic known from the records of Gregory's
pontificate is mentioned in the *Dialogues* in connection with another
story of St Benedict's prescience. He is the subdeacon Florentius,
referred to in a letter of Gregory's (*Epist.* III.15) whose grandfather,
a priest also named Florentius, was the villain of a story told in *Dial.*
II.8. There it is narrated how the latter first attempted to poison
Benedict, but was frustrated by the saint's clairvoyance. He then
tried to seduce the minds of Benedict's disciples by sending seven
naked maidens to dance in the monastery garden, and he rejoiced
when Benedict left the monastery in disgust. Divine justice punished
him as he stood gloating at Benedict's departure: he was crushed to
death by a prodigious fall of masonry. In the *Dialogues* Gregory
identifies the wicked priest as "*huius nostri subdiaconi Florentii avus*".
Commentators agree that this is meant to be a reference to the same
Florentius, likewise described as "*subdiaconus noster*", whose pusilla-
nimity the pope deplores in a letter of December 592, relating how
the man had fled in order to avoid being consecrated as bishop of
Naples. He was probably the same as "our beloved son the deacon
Florentius" mentioned six years later in a letter of Gregory dated
September 598.[34] Here once again, as in the case of Exhilaratus, we
find a Roman official who is referred to (unfavourably) in one of
Gregory's letters and who is also mentioned in the *Dialogues* in con-

---

[33] *SC* 251, p. 159, note 68; cf. *SC* 260, p. 310, note 9.
[34] *Epist.* III.15 and IX.8 (EH I.174 & II.46). Cf. also Vogüé, *SC* 251, p. 159,
note 68.

nection with a story of wickedness detected by St Benedict's preter-natural insight. Here likewise A. de Vogüé considers that the attri-bution of a discreditable grandfather to the Roman subdeacon Florentius provides confirmation of the historical existence and mis-deeds of the wicked priest Florentius of Spoleto. He comments: "Even if the pope had reason to be indignant with this faint-hearted sub-deacon, can one imagine that he would have calumniously attrib-uted to him so dishonourable a grandfather?"[35] Again, as in the case of Exhilaratus, I concur with Vogüé: such calumnious invention can-not indeed be laid at the door of the real Gregory! Fiction there was in those circumstantial tales of Exhilerataus and Florentius, but it must be attributed to someone else at a later date. Vogüé him-self points out that the story of the wicked priest Florentius of Spoleto contains parallels to a passage in the *Life of St Martin* (27.3) by Sulpicius Severus, and even echoes its phraseology.[36]

Several other Roman ecclesiastics and members of the papal Curia who are named in Gregory's letters appear in the *Dialogues*, either as informants about miraculous happenings or even as involved in them. Those cross-references give the narrative an impression of his-torical verisimilitude. They show the author's ingenuity and his famil-iarity with the Lateran archives. I cite here three representative instances out of many. The first is the mention in *Dial.* III.20.1 of "our deacon and paymaster (*dispensator*) of the church, Boniface", who is introduced as a near relative of Stephen, the priest of Valeria who made an unguarded imprecation which led to his bootlaces being immediately untied by an invisible devil. The intended refer-ence is evidently to the Roman deacon Boniface who is repeatedly mentioned in Gregory's letters. His function as an official treasurer is referred to in a letter of 598.[37] It is probable that he was the future pope Boniface IV (AD 608–615). The Dialogist may even have known that (as recorded in the *Liber Pontificalis*) Boniface IV was a native of Valeria, which would make appropriate the location of his loose-tongued relative Stephen in that province.

My second instance of the Dialogist's adoption of characters and formulae from the curial file of Gregorian letters shows direct ver-bal borrowing from that source. In *Dial.* II.35.1 there is mention of

---

[35] *SC* 251, p. 159, note 68.
[36] *SC* 260, p. 161.
[37] Cf. *PsGD*, p. 673.

Servandus, who was Benedict's companion in the tower from which the saint had his great vision, and who is described there as *"abbas monasterii quod a Liberio quondam patricio in Campaniae partibus fuerat constructum"*.[38] The identical Latin words used in that description are found twice in the *Registrum Epistularum*, in two separate letters of Gregory dating from the year 599. There, however, they were applied not to an abbot Servandus but to an abbot Theodosius, who was in each letter is described by the selfsame formula, "abbot of a monastery which had been built in the region of Campania some time before by a certain patrician Liberius".

My third instance of borrowing of titles from the *Registrum* relates to the story in *Dial.* I.8.1, telling of supernatural portents that preceded the death of one Anastasius, who had once been a curial notary. The Dialogist, in mentioning the man's office, makes Gregory pompously refer to his own sacred dignity as Roman pontiff by using a stereotyped official formula. Anastasius, he pronounced, "was a notary of the holy Roman Church to which, by God's authority, I minister"—*"sanctae Romanae ecclesiae, cui Deo auctore deservio, notarius fuit"*. The phrase used there was a standard formula of the papal secretariate before, during and long after the time of Gregory I. As Dobschütz notes, it is found in stylized form (*"sanctae Romanae cui Deo auctore deservimus ecclesiae"*) in the oldest part of the *Liber Diurnus*, and also in letters dating from the pontificates of Gregory II and Gregory III in the eighth century.[39] In making Gregory use that formula when referring to Anastasius's previous employment the Dialogist gave one more indication of his familiarity with secretarial usage and with the file copies of Gregory's letters.

I pass now to consider the second category of personal names in the *Dialogues* which duplicate names taken from Gregory's letters and other contemporary sources, but which clearly cannot refer to the same persons. Mere coincidence of names, of course, is not a proof of counterfeiting; many personal names were of general currency in late antiquity and in the early Middle Ages. However, in the *Dialogues* there are several instances which indicate that the author casually

---

[38] *Epist.* IX. 162 and 164 (EH II.162–3).

[39] *Op. cit.*, p. 234. He cites six instances from Sickel's edition of the *Liber diurnus*. M.B. Dunn finds that in the *Registrum* of Gregory's letters the phrase *"Deo auctore"* occurs 64 times. (*The Style of the Letters of St Gregory the Great*, Washington 1931, pp. 63–4.)

borrowed names for some of his characters from Gregory's letters without troubling to avoid incongruity. I cite one remarkable example which, for those who suppose that Gregory wrote the *Dialogues*, is indeed difficult to explain. In the account of Benedict's earlier monastic life at Subiaco, in *Dial.* II.1.5, we read how he was befriended by a person named Romanus who dwelt in a nearby monastery ruled of an abbot named Adeodatus. Now in the *Registrum* we find a letter written by Gregory in the year 600 to an abbot named Adeodatus, whose monastery near Naples was established in a house belonging to a person named Romanus. A. de Vogüé himself remarks that the same two names that are linked in the *Dialogues* story are also linked together, "*curieusement*", in the Gregorian letter. Yes, it is indeed curious to find in those two texts mention of an abbot named Adeodatus who was dwelling in the same place as an associate named Romanus, yet the pairs in question are clearly separated by about a century. It becomes "curiouser and curiouser" (to use Alice's phrase) when we see it as one item in a wide pattern of strange coincidence of names.

As well as noting the occurrence in the *Dialogues* of names that seem to be plucked from the Gregorian letters, we find in that book an even larger number of names that replicate names found in the corpus of hagiographical writings of late antiquity, and especially in the legendary *Passiones* and *Gesta* of the fifth, sixth and seventh centuries which the Dialogist knew so well. Some of those names, of course, were common throughout the Latinate world; but since the Dialogist's borrowing of plots and situations from those legendary writings is proved, his frequent use of names that occur in them is evidently more than mere coincidence. We find in the *Dialogues* narrative the following personal names which are also borne by heroes of the *Gesta*: Anastasius, Euticius (and Euthicius), Proculus, Juvenal, Sabinus, Faustinus, Maximus, Donatus, Frigidianus, Gaudentius, Boniface, Spes, Eleutherius, Herculanus, Isaac and Severus. Although those names are given to different fictional characters in the legendary texts, there is in several cases a recognizable connection between the situations in which those names occur in both *Gesta* and *Dialogues*. Dufourcq's pages contain many suggestive indications of such correlation. In his own speculation about the dating and literary interdependence of the texts, however, his judgement is necessarily coloured by his assumption that St Gregory wrote the *Dialogues* in the last decade of the sixth century, which leads him to conclude that the seventh-century *Gesta*-writers were copying names and themes from that work. In the next chapter I examine the links between the *Gesta* and the *Dialogues* more in detail.

f. *The incongruity of Peter the interlocutor*

The persona of Peter the Deacon, Gregory's companion in the dialogue, and his contributions to the discussion, presents many puzzles and incongruities. *Soi-disant* Gregory begins by introducing his interlocutor as *"dilectissimus filius meus Petrus diaconus"*—the same phrase that is used by the real Gregory in his letters to describe one of the prominent officials of his court. Was this individual identifiable with the Peter the Deacon who was repeatedly mentioned in Gregory's letters as rector of two papal patrimonies, first in Sicily and then in Campania? Although K. Hallinger considered that to be "a mere opinion", most other commentators, following the Maurists, accept it as sure. A. de Vogüé marshals the arguments in favour of that identification and finds it to be "altogether probable".[40] I too agree that it was what the author clearly meant to convey. However, like Hallinger, I recognize puzzling uncertainties in the historical evidence relating to deacons named Peter in Gregory's pontificate, and I link them with incongruities in the portrayal of the interlocutor in the *Dialogues*. It does indeed appear that the Dialogist (*"tam peritus fallendi artifex"*) chose the persona of Gregory's interlocutor with shrewd attention to particulars and dates in the curial file of the papal correspondence. It also appears that, despite his astuteness in doing so, he overlooked other evidence in Gregory's correspondence pointing to the existence of at least two diaconal Peters in the papal service (whom I will call here Peter the rector and Peter the *defensor*) and that his oversight unwittingly betrayed the incongruity of his artifice.

What is clear is that he supposed that there was only one deacon Peter who was at that time a prominent official of the Roman Church, whom he assumed to have been elevated to that rank before Gregory began to write the *Dialogues*—that is, in the summer of 593. As a trusted and familiar member of the Gregory's immediate circle, this Peter would be a suitable character to portray as the pope's

---

[40] *SC* 251, pp. 44–5; cf. *SC*. 260, pp. 11 & 435.

partner in the dialogue. The Peter of the *Dialogues* recalls (in *Dial.* IV.59.6) the time when he was "*in Sicilia positus*", thus identifying himself with the Peter who, while still a subdeacon, was appointed rector of the papal patrimonies in Sicily in AD 590. The real Peter was transferred to the rectorship of the Campanian patrimony at some time before June 593, as we know from a letter (Epist. III.39) which Gregory addressed to him there in June of that year. In that letter (written a month before the date of Gregory's alleged *Letter to Maximian* announcing his current project of writing a book on the lives of the Fathers of Italy) Peter the rector was still addressed by the pope as a subdeacon; yet in the *Dialogues* he is given the title of deacon. We know that he was subsequently elevated to the diaconate, some time before March 595, from a letter (V.28) sent to him by Gregory in that month addressing him as deacon.[41]

However, only a month after Gregory had sent the letter to the subdeacon Peter in Campania in July 593, he made mention in another letter (III.54), written to the bishop of Ravenna, of a deacon Peter, sometime *defensor* of the Roman Church, who had been entrusted by the pope with an important mission to the court of the imperial exarch in that city. His mission is repeatedly mentioned in Gregory's correspondence. Most of those who assume the Gregorian authorship of the *Dialogues* conclude from its text that the deacon and *defensor* Peter who was Gregory's emissary to Ravenna was one and the same as the subdeacon Peter who was rector of the papal patrimony in Sicily from 590 and of the patrimony in Campania in 593 and ordained deacon thereafter. A. de Vogüé had no doubt of this identification.[42] More cautiously, L. Hartmann described that it was "a conjecture", albeit one that was "not inept".[43] The complexity of the question becomes apparent when one follows up the many references, in the index of the Ewald-Hartmann edition of Gregory's *Registrum*, to "Peter" as subdeacon, deacon and *defensor*. From close scrutiny of the Gregorian letters it becomes evident that there was indeed more than one deacon named Peter prominent in the papal service at that time. Those who conclude that there was only one are basing their conclusion on the evidence of the *Dialogues*, which

---

[41] Epist. V.28; EH I.308.
[42] *SC* 251, p. 44 & notes 79 & 81.
[43] EH I.308, note 2.

is assumed to clarify the puzzling uncertainties of the *Registrum* which Hallinger and others have highlighted.

In any case, there is a clear contrast between the experienced and shrewd deacons named Peter who are known to us from Gregory's letters, and from whom the pope expected a high level of intelligent judgement, and on the other hand the obtuse interlocutor depicted by the author of the *Dialogues*, who is deficient both in understanding and in general knowledge of the Italian scene, and whose contributions to the debate are often naïve, banal and inconsequential. There is also a great difference between the courteously dignified tone of the pope in his letters to the curial deacons named Peter and the attitude of the *soi-disant* Gregory of the *Dialogues* to the simpleton Peter whom he there enlightens—and into whose mouth he puts constant praise of his own masterly wisdom and lucidity. If the plea is made that in portraying Peter's character Gregory is merely using literary licence, one must comment that it would be very unlike the real Gregory to publish such a travesty, exposing a loyal and able assistant to misjudgement and ridicule. The ignorance attributed to Peter the Deacon is remarkable. Although he is supposedly identified with the deacon Peter who had been rector of the papal patrimonies both in Sicily and in Campania, he has never heard of the great saint and thaumaturge of Campania, Benedict of Cassino. K. Hallinger notes the strangeness of that admission.[44] Nor indeed has Peter heard of any of the multitude of other holy Fathers who worked stupendous miracles in the regions of central Italy in very recent times. The Dialogist's tissue of historical anomalies cannot be disentangled.

---

[44] *Op. cit.* (*Papst Gregor*), p. 258.

CHAPTER NINE

OLD TALES IN NEW GUISE: ANTECEDENTS AND
SOURCES OF THE DIALOGIST'S LEGENDARY *GESTA*:
BORROWINGS FROM POST-GREGORIAN SOURCES

a

Although the author of the *Dialogues*, speaking in the persona of
Gregory, claims to have heard his accounts of sensational miracles
at first hand from numerous named informants, many of them said
to have been eyewitnesses of the events described, it is now established that a large number of them are old tales in new guise. In
this chapter I summarize major instances of such borrowings taken
from the fuller dossier that I set out in *PsGD*. Of particular significance
is the evidence, resumed in the final section of this chapter, indicating
that the author not only took many of his plots from pre-Gregorian
sources but also took some of them from fictitious hagiographical
narratives dating from the period *after* Gregory's lifetime.

The discoveries made in modern times of the author's literary
artifices and dissimulation in composing his book provide further
cogent disproof of the theory of Gregorian authorship. With change
of names, places and circumstances, he appropriates and adapts stories from earlier sources to use in his own fictional tales, while insisting that the events related have been recently reported to him
personally by reliable eyewitnesses. Those earlier sources include both
the Bible and the legendary literature of late antiquity. In a number
of cases he himself alludes to those resemblances. He acknowledges
in passing that the marvellous works of Benedict, Libertinus, Equitius,
Nonnosus and other holy men in his narrative recall both the deeds
of great scriptural figures and those of saintly thaumaturges narrated
in earlier hagiographical legends. In a moment of truth, when narrating miracles worked by Nonnosus, he makes both the interlocutors in the dialogue comment expressly on his use of such models.[1]

---

[1] *Dial.* I.7.3–5.

The reuse of biblical models by the author of the *Dialogues* has long been recognized, from the seventeenth century onwards. F.H. Dudden summed up the suspicions of many: "It is suspicious that many of the recorded wonders exhibit striking analogies with the Bible miracles. Gregory himself noticed this (*Dial.* II.8). The miracles of Elijah and Elisha in particular seem to have furnished suggestions to the reporters of Benedict's acts."[2] The dossier of evidence of the reuse of biblical models in the book has been considerably augmented by many detailed studies of the *Dialogues* published since Dudden wrote those words.

Gradually defenders of the *Dialogues* ceased to defend Gregory from the suspicion of copying the plots of his stories from biblical models. Admitting that he did so, however, they sought to excuse him. A monastic commentator, M. Mähler, pointed out many biblical *évocations* (especially relating to *Kings*) in the stories of St Benedict's wondrous works told in the second book of the *Dialogues*,[3] as well as many echoes of tales told in hagiographical legends, and was ready to allow that those stories were not only fictitious but in many cases were borrowed from elsewhere. Whereas other commentators had been reluctant to admit any covert plagiarism on Gregory's part, preferring to lay the blame for misinformation solely on the pontiff's deceitful informants, Mähler concluded that Gregory himself had deliberately reused earlier models, not merely communicated to him by unreliable informants but even drawn by himself directly from older sources, biblical and hagiographical. He did so "without much concerning himself of the historical value" of the tales newly reported. Mähler explained that Gregory "recognized" the similarity between Benedict's reported deeds and those told of the prophets and saints, and that, "going further, by a subtle transposition", he gave to his narration of those deeds a "*Sitz in Leben*" copied from those sources. Even though that borrowed aureole "obscures from our eyes the historical implications", Mähler saw it as a gain that "we possess a recital that, rather than keeping to the constraints of the original facts, has the aim of disclosing their meaning". Similar uneasy pleas are now commonly put forward by other commentators.

---

[2] *Op. cit.*, vol. II, pp. 167–8, footnote 2.
[3] *Évocations bibliques et hagiographiques dans la vie de saint Benoît par saint Grégoire* in *Rev. Bén.* 83 (1973), pp. 398–429.

More forthright was the judgement on the second-hand character of the *Dialogues* narratives expressed by A. de Vogüé, in the invaluable commentary prefaced to his edition of the text. His study brought a new dimension to the scholarly discussion on the antecedents, both biblical and hagiographical, of the stories in the *Dialogues*. As he rightly observed at the outset, "Here we enter on a new domain, that of the unavowed antecedents of the *Dialogues*".[4] A major concern in his exploratory study, he explained, was "to recognize the literary *arrière-plan* of the book, and to seek out the models that Gregory deliberately chose, or followed in a more or less conscious fashion, showing their diverse elements and entering into the details of their narrations". That literary search led Vogüé to recognize what he called "a disturbing fact" about Gregory's choice of models: namely, that "the similarities are not limited to formal resemblances but often involve the very substance of the events narrated . . . This disconcerting observation calls in question the historical character of the work . . ." Even less circumspectly, Vogüé later affirmed that in several instances "there is little doubt that the author himself consciously arranged or even fabricated the tale altogether by copying what he had read in previous literature".[5]

Commenting in particular on the resemblance of the tales in the *Dialogues* to scriptural antecedents, Vogüé remarked: "If some of them—not all—probably bear the stamp of pure literary imitation of biblical models, their openly avowed character is less disquieting than other parallels which remain unexpressed".[6] He went on to identify instances in the latter category, "not rare and more disturbing", in which "a story in the *Dialogues* strangely resembles an event from the Bible without any mention of it". As a primary example of such dissembling he cites the story (in *Dial.* I.10.17–18) of the raising to life of Marcellus of Todi by Bishop Fortunatus, alleged to have been reported to Gregory by an unnamed old man, the circumstances of which are very similar to the Johannine account of the raising of Lazarus from the dead by Jesus. "Everything suggests an imitation of the Gospel", Vogüé observes, "one that is all the more suspect because it remains unavowed. If Gregory does not

---

[4] *SC* 251, p. 112.
[5] *Hallel* 11 (1983), p. 66.
[6] *SC* 251, p. 137.

breathe a word here about the Gospel model, is it not because he means to hide it?"

Thus Vogüé was one of those who came to terms with the new realism concerning what he recognized as "the unavowed antecedents of the *Dialogues*", and candidly criticized the author's surreptitious borrowings from earlier sources. Commenting on the reuse of a *"récit fictif"* based clearly on a tale told earlier by Lucian of Samosata and adapted by Augustine, he wrote rather caustically: "This time Gregory has not gone to much trouble to disguise his borrowing."[7] In *PsGD*, making frequent use of the findings of Vogüé himself, I discussed in detail several of those unavowed antecedents of the tales told in the *Dialogues*. Here there is not space to rehearse that lengthy dossier, which amply repays close study. I mention a single striking example, from *Dialogues* III.7.1–9.[8] The tale in question is the racy adaptation of a story about the thwarting of diabolic plans to bring a soul to ruin, which had been previously told by Cassian and more briefly in the Latin translation of the Greek *Apophthegmata*. The Dialogist's revised version of it, making it relate to Bishop Andrew of Fondi, is indeed artistically told. He makes Gregory assure his readers that the facts narrated are indubitably true because "there are as many witnesses to them as there are inhabitants in that place". (I noted earlier[9] that owing to the Lombards' depredations, as we know from Gregory's letters, Fondi was completely deserted during Gregory's pontificate.) A. de Vogüé finds "particularly disturbing" this earnest attestation of a story which is recognizably another form of one narrated by previous hagiographers. His detection of disguised plagiarism throughout the text of the *Dialogues*, though now widely accepted, brought dismayed reaction from some of his monastic brethren, who thought that it impugned the hallowed traditions deriving from the biography of St Benedict contained in that book.[10] He himself addressed their concern:

> Here we touch a delicate point, at which my edition of the *Dialogues* has provoked mixed reactions among monks. Some have thought that the door has been opened to a radical demythologizing of the whole

---

[7] *SC* 251, pp. 134–5; cf. *PsGD*, p. 595 and note.

[8] It is discussed at length in *PsGD*, pp. 591–4; see also p. 497.

[9] In Chapter 8.c.

[10] E.g. P. Murray, "The miracles of St Benedict: may we doubt them?", in *Hallel*, 9 (1981), pp. 46–52.

work, and especially of the life of St Benedict. With the unmasking of so many antecedent models lurking in the mind of St Gregory, which he consciously used, is one not led to see the *Dialogues* as a work of pure fiction? Others have expressed their anxiety—and even their indignation—at seeing this venerable Life of the saint and of other similar figures made to appear "a school of error, a workshop of fraud and imposture".[11]

Vogüé attempted to provide his disconcerted brethren with a solution to the problem that he had brought so clearly into the open. He assured them that to conclude that Gregory himself fabricated those stories, using earlier models, "is not to do an injustice to the great pope". The disquiet felt at the revelation of such apparently disingenuous dealing, he explained, is due to a legacy of a "naïvely strict concept of veracity", which leads to a misplaced search for historicity in ancient texts which have a different genre of religious purpose. He reassured his brethren:

> Instead of crying fraud and imposture, it is fitting, it seems to me, to appreciate the literary creativity and pedagogical talent of this pastor who is so concerned to edify his people. The suspicion that Gregory may have embellished or even completely invented some episodes in no way diminishes the esteem and confidence he inspires . . . When we seemingly catch him in the act [i.e. of falsification] we will respectfully consider his narration as a language which demands to be understood. Happy are those who are capable of imagining such fine and striking stories in order to communicate a spiritual message![12]

This apologia sits uneasily with Vogüé's frank avowal, cited earlier, that in relating preternatural events the author of the *Dialogues* was concerned not with pointing a moral but with providing sensational pabulum for his readers. When he reuses the few edifying stories of deathbed visions related by the real Gregory in his sermons to the people, he omits in every case the moral of the original *exemplum*. Nevertheless, despite his frank criticism elsewhere of the author's duplicity, Vogüé seeks to defend him here with the plea that his motive in counterfeiting was pastoral and edifying! Similar pleas are now put forward by a number of other writers, but ridiculed by others, who have no difficulty in recognizing in the *Dialogues* the same genre of sensational miracle-fiction that was the stock-in-trade of the

---

[11] *Vie de S. Benoît*, Bellefontaine 1982, pp. 11–12.
[12] *Vie de S. Benoît*, p. 13.

many legend-spinners of that age. Patently, the author of the *Dialogues*
is intent on catering to that taste; far from seeking to edify, he
attaches no spiritual message to his sensational yarns. I cited earlier
the words that he puts into the mouth of Peter the Deacon words
that express the popular craving to which he caters: "the more I
drink in miracles, the more I thirst for them".

b. *Borrowings from the later* Gesta *literature*

While there are indeed several instances of the Dialogist's use of biblical models when telling his tales, it is the evidence of his borrowings from the hagiographical literature of late antiquity that has the
greatest significance in our present inquiry. In that literature we may
make a distinction—which is not hard and fast—between two categories. In the first category are the works of authors of renown, such
as Rufinus, Evagrius, Jerome, Sulpicius Severus, Paulinus, Augustine,
Cassian and Gregory of Tours; also the collection of *Vitae Patrum*
translated into Latin by the deacon Pelagius. In the second category
are the less reputable writings of the numerous and usually nameless
legend-spinners who fed the popular taste for sensational miracle-
stories, and whose fictions were expressly disapproved by the so-
called *Gelasian Decree* sanctioned by the Roman church in the sixth
century.[13] In his narrative the author of the *Dialogues* included motifs
borrowed freely from both those categories of writings. It is the evidence of his familiarity with and use of fantastic *Gesta*-writings in the
second of those two categories that has special importance for our
present inquiry. It provides many indications, not only of models
used by the author for his own legend-spinning, but also of the historical situation, circle and period in which he lived. Most significant
of all is the evidence showing that some of the legendary *Gesta* that
he reused (and improved upon) originated in the seventh century,
after Gregory's lifetime. That evidence will be discussed below, in
Section d.

The author's plagiarizing from those sources became progressively
clearer to historians of ancient literature in the course of the twen-

---

[13] Cf. F.E. von Dobschütz, *Das Decretum Gelasianum*, Leipzig 1912, pp. 271, 345,
351.

tieth century. In his pioneer study, *Étude sur les Gesta Martyrum romains*,[14] written in the early years of the twentieth century and still invaluable despite its much-criticized shortcomings, Albert Dufourcq was the first to recognize the Gregorian *Dialogues* as an integral part of what he called "the legendary movement" of the sixth and seventh centuries. He referred by that term to the proliferation of fictional hagiography relating both to the city of Rome and what he called "the duchy of Rome", the central region of Italy. Much of what he brought to the attention of the learned world had never been observed before. He distinguished two historical phases in that movement: the earlier phase spanning the period from the Ostrogothic dominance in Italy to the pontificate of Gregory the Great, the later phase spanning the seventh century. He pointed out specific resemblances and links between the Gregorian *Dialogues* and those fictional *Gesta*, which he saw as providing the historical and literary context for that work. "St Gregory is only the illustrious emulator of a hundred obscure writers", he concluded. "By seeing him in the same literary setting as his contemporaries one can readily explain the origin, and more precisely appreciate the character, of his hagiographical work."

Dufourcq called the earlier phase of the fictional *Gesta* literature (up to the end of the sixth century) "the Ostrogothic legendary movement". Assuming unquestioningly that the *Dialogues* were written prior to the seventh-century *Gesta*, Dufourcq inappropriately gave the general title of "the Gregorian legendary movement" to that second phase in the current of fanciful hagiographical writings that welled up after Gregory's lifetime.[15] I say more below about Dufourcq's dating of those developments. He made the following criticism of the author of the *Dialogues*, whom he unquestioningly assumed to be Gregory the Great: "The writer who takes pleasure in writing so many trivial or futile stories, who records them without making any comment—but rather, who presents them as worthy of faith and praise—that man is on the same level as the compilers of the Roman *Gesta*. What wonder that he underwent their influence?"[16]

In order to appreciate what Dufourcq rightly called "the strict solidarity" between those legendary *Gesta* and the *Dialogues*, and moreover to recognize the dependence of the latter on the former, it is

---

[14] 4 vols. Paris 1900–1910.
[15] *Op. cit.*, vol. III, "*Le mouvement légendaire grégorien*" (1907), preface.
[16] *Op. cit.*, I (1900), p. 379.

necessary to make critical comparison of the texts themselves, with the aid of the contextual and topographical commentary that Dufourcq and other literary historians have provided. Between the two terms of comparison there are, of course, not only close resemblances but also differences.[17] Among these is a difference of literary convention. The authors of the *Gesta* usually (but not always) situate their tales in a distant age of persecution and fantasy, while the author of the *Dialogues* situates his in a more recent past, from the time of Ostrogothic rule onwards. For all that, both they and he live in the same mental climate. Both imagine the same kind of conceits and envisage the same kind of readers. They share the same religious sensibilities, the same hagiographical motifs and the same geographical knowledge of the towns and territories of central Italy reached by the Roman roads radiating from the City.

In his edition of the *Dialogues*, published in 1924, U. Moricca further developed that critique of the book in its historical setting and continued the detection of its hagiographical antecedents. He recognized that there are not merely generic analogies between the *Dialogues* and the contemporary Roman *Gesta* but close affinities between them, of which the explanation must be either dependence of one on the other or their common dependence on earlier sources. Like Dufourcq, he saw those resemblances with the *Gesta* as essentially significant for understanding the origins and nature of the Gregorian *Dialogues*. He commented:

> We find parallels between them indicating that both reflect the same political, ecclesiastical and religious situations. The same preoccupations occur in both, the same anti-Arian motives, the same legendary themes, the same incidents in the struggle between Christianity and the still surviving rural paganism. In a word, the two groups of testimonies fit into one framework, and each illuminates the other. By bringing them together we can reconstruct the totality of the process of legend-formation, of which each is one part. The *Gesta* sing the praises of the martyrs, the *Dialogues* those of the confessors.[18]

Although the findings of Dufourcq, complemented by those of Moricca, were for long unduly neglected, twentieth-century scholars, Bollandists among them, came progressively to recognize their importance, and proceeded to explore that new field of research more thoroughly.

---

[17] J. Petersen points out such differences; *op. cit.*, pp. 88–9.
[18] *Op. cit.*, p. xxi.

They came to recognize more clearly the correspondence between the motifs in the miracle-stories of the *Dialogues* and similar themes found in the wide range of earlier sources which Dufourcq had first explored.

c. *St Gregory's awareness of and attitude to legendary tales*

It is, then, commonly recognized that the author of the *Dialogues* was very familiar with the legendary hagiographies of late antiquity, that he borrowed many tales from them to use anew in changed guise and that he dissembled those borrowings, claiming to have heard the facts related directly from the mouths of eyewitnesses. Is it plausible to assume that Pope Gregory himself had familiarity with and predilection for that literature, and engaged in such borrowing and dissembling? What light do other sources throw on his knowledge of and attitude to the legendary sub-culture of that age?

Leaving aside the *Dialogues*, there are two explicit references in Gregory's letters, and a single reference in his other pastoral and expository works, to the popular hagiographical writings narrating the lives and deeds of the saints.[19] The sole instance in those other writings is contained in a homily preached in the basilica of St Felicity on that martyr's feast day. He refers there to an episode in her passion which, he said, could be read "in the more reliable Acts relating to her life" ("*in gestis eius emendatioribus legitur*"). Here he is clearly alluding to the *Passio SS Perpetuae et Felicitatis*, a third-century writing that is a classical example of the sober martyrology of earlier times. The implied comparison is with the fictional composition *Passio S. Felicitatis cum vii filiis*, which was a product of "the legendary movement" of later centuries that Dufourcq and others have chronicled. Gregory's qualifying phrase implies his critical awareness of *gesta* that were not *emendatiora* but rather suspect. Elsewhere in his Gospel homilies he makes occasional references to the constancy and virtues of the Roman martyrs, but in doing so makes no use of the legendary *passiones martyrum* that had gained wide popularity during the fifth and sixth centuries.

---

[19] References in *PsGD*, pp. 597–600.

The two references to hagiographical collections in Gregory's personal letters indicate that he had little personal knowledge of or any interest in such writings. One is an incidental remark in a letter of June 601 to Aetherius, bishop of Lyons, who had asked him for a transcription of the *gesta vel scripta* of St Irenaeus. Gregory replied that the writings requested could not be found in the Roman Curia. The other reference, in a letter from the pope to Eulogius of Alexandria, is noteworthy. The latter had asked him for a copy of the book of the *gesta* of all the martyrs said to have been compiled by Eusebius. Gregory replied that an exhaustive search in the Roman archives had revealed nothing answering that description, apart from a file which contained a few items ("*quaedam pauca*"), of which he evidently had been previously unaware. He continued:

> We do however have here the names of almost all the martyrs collected in a single codex, with their different passions assigned each to its proper day, and on the respective dates we celebrate the solemnities of the Mass in their honour. However, in this volume the manner in which each suffered is not indicated, but all that is recorded is his name, the place and the day of his passion . . . But Your Beatitude has these particulars, I think. We have then searched for, but not found, what you requested. Nevertheless, although we have not found it we will go on searching, and if it can be found we will send it.[20]

The single codex Gregory referred to was evidently the sanctoral calendar dating back to the time of Pope Damasus I in the fourth century, later to be called the *Martyrologium Hieronymianum*, which, apart from listing the particulars of names, places and dates as specified in Gregory's letter, gave no biographical information about the saints named. Some commentators, Dufourcq in particular, have found the disclaimer in that letter perplexing, since it accords ill with the evidence of the *Dialogues* that apparently attests Gregory's access to and familiarity with a very wide range of hagiographical *Gesta*—and indeed with his own composition of such fables. Dufourcq's quaint solution to this puzzle was to surmise that when writing that letter Gregory was not revealing the "pious interests of his soul", but "restrained himself by a measure of prudence when an inquiry was put to him as Pope, the successor of Peter".[21] In other words, in

---

[20] *Epist.* VIII; EH II.28–9.
[21] Dufourcq, *op. cit.*, I, 1900, p. 383, footnote.

order not to disedify the bishop of Alexandria, Gregory dissembled his own familiarity with and addiction to such fanciful literature, and pretended that there was none to be found in his possession or in the libraries of his see!

Gregory's complete disregard of the popular hagiographical *Gesta* already proliferating in his age, none of which was to be found in his curial archives, reflects the strict attitude to such effusions that still prevailed in the sixth-century church of Rome. The pontiffs remained faithful to the sober tradition witnessed to by Pope Damasus, which honoured the memory of the martyrs but did not permit imaginative fiction to supply for the lack of historical facts about their lives. That faithful vigilance is expressed in the fifth and last part of so-called Gelasian Decree, *De libris recipiendis et non recipiendis*—"On the writings that are to be approved and those that are not". That admonitory text did not originate in the pontificate of Pope Gelasius I (492–496) but later. It is known to have been current during the pontificate of Hormisdas (514–523) and seems to have been augmented after that time. It was enforced by the Roman see during the sixth and seventh centuries and undoubtedly expressed its orthodox reaction against the wave of spurious hagiography that continued to well up in that age. The *Gelasianum* proscribed the public reading of those "*novellae relationes*" and upheld the "*antiqua consuetudo*" and "*singularis cautela*" of the Roman church. It affirmed that although no Catholic could doubt the power of God manifested through the passions of the martyrs, the unauthorized *Gesta Martyrum* were not to be approved: "In accordance with ancient custom, and observing strict caution, they are not to be read in the holy Roman church; not only because the names of their authors are completely unknown, but also because misbelieving and simple folk apprize in them things that are preposterous and unreal."[22] The document went on to express the same cautious reserve to the wave of fanciful *vitae patrum*.

The stern reaction of the Roman Church, expressed in the decree "*De libris non recipiendis*", attests the extent and contemporary impact of the fictitious hagiographical works which, as P. Llewellyn observes, "were beginning to gain currency as the staple Christian literature for the masses, filling out the bare list of names in the martyrologies

---

[22] E. Von Dobschütz, *Das Decretum Gelasianum*, Leipzig 1912, pp. 271, 345, 351.

with all the wonders of the novelette, which the great families and political factions were to find a convenient genre for propaganda in internal disputes."[23] The chief practical effect of the official disapproval was the prohibition of reading the discredited *Gesta* in church. (Since the church in a town or village was usually the only building in which the whole community could gather, its availability for the reading aloud of the *novellae relationes* to an illiterate populace could be of considerable concern both to would-be hearers and to the purveyors of such legendary entertainment.)[24]

The reaction of the new and ever more enterprising school of inventive hagiographers against the conservatism of the Church authorities is reflected in a curious preface, headed "*Omnia quae a sanctis gesta sunt*", which is found prefixed to a number of those fabulous narratives.[25] It was evidently a sequel and a direct retort to the *Decretum Gelasianum*. It defends "the *gesta* of the saints which we studiously record", and challenges the attitude, as lacking in pious sensibility, of "those of you who judge that they should be dismissed among the apocryphal writings". (The word *apocryphus* occurs 61 times in the *Gelasianum*.) "The censorious may issue prohibitions, the timid may bid us to be silent, the despisers may attack us and may rebuke those who read these works aloud and those who eagerly listen to them"; but, the authors of the defensive preface retort defiantly, "We will continue to speak of, write and preach those deeds of divine power". It appears that the anti-Gelasian preface reflects a situation in the latter part of the sixth century. It expresses the resentment of the *Gesta* writers and pedlars at the continuing force of the official disapproval of their popular products, a ban which must have had considerable effect. Copied and prefixed to diverse *Gesta* texts, their protest indicates that the controversy remained topical in later decades of the sixth century and afterwards.

Gregory would certainly have been fully aware of the discipline enforced by his predecessors. Faithful as he was to the sacred responsibility laid upon him as Roman pontiff and as guardian of right belief and of the Church's tradition, he would have continued that

---

[23] *Op. cit.*, p. 39.

[24] Cf. Chapter 16.c below, where I cite a reference by St Aldhelm to the reading of such *Gesta* in England "*in pulpitu ecclesiae*" at the end of the seventh century.

[25] Cf. B. de Gaiffier, "*Un prologue hagiograpique hostile au Décret de Gelase?*", in *AB* 82 (1964), pp. 341–53; the text of the hostile prologue is given on pp. 343–4.

discipline vigilantly. His expressed concern for *gesta emendatiora*, his assurance to Bishop Eulogius that rumoured *gesta martyrum* were not to be found on the shelves of his libraries, and his complete disregard for the fabulous *Gesta*-literature in his genuine writings are indications of his attitude. The prudent policy of the Roman see, prohibiting the reading of such literature in church, endured long after his age, as I note below. It is only because of his assumed authorship of the *Dialogues* that Gregory is judged to have abandoned that vigilance and to have opened the door to official tolerance of superstitious fables. P. Llewellyn, for instance, expressed this judgement:

> The *Dialogues* and the histories they present point to the changes in Roman thinking . . . Gregory's encouragement and adoption of those spontaneous, uncritical, unintellectual literary forms, which were to remain the staple of religious reading for centuries, is marked . . . His work was to be the most perfect of the genre.[26]

Llewellyn is doubtless right in concluding that the *Dialogues*, bearing the great name of Pope Gregory, were historically a potent factor in eventually bringing about the change of official attitude. His critique of Gregory himself is nullified, however, once it is realized that the *Dialogues* did not originate at the end of the sixth century but in the late seventh century, and that it was their rise to fame and influence in the eighth century that led on to the subsequent change of official attitude later in that century. It is indeed a fact, as B. de Gaiffier has shown, that the prudent policy of the Roman see, prohibiting the reading of such literature during the liturgy or in church, remained in force long after the age of Gregory the Great. It was not until the pontificate of Hadrian I (772–795) that it was relaxed. "It was only from the end of the eighth century", Gaiffier concluded, "that the Roman Church abandoned its attitude of disapproval".[27] This fact, together with the earlier evidence outlined above concerning the official Roman policy in Gregory's age, shows the ineptitude of supposing that he had written the *Dialogues* near the close of the sixth century. Defenders of his authorship of that book have to suppose that the great pope abruptly abandoned that traditional doctrinal vigilance of his Church, and that in defiance of it he himself wrote, published and sowed abroad throughout Christendom the

---

[26] *Rome in the Dark Ages*, London 1970, pp. 98–9.
[27] B. de Gaiffier, "*La lecture des Actes des Martyrs dans la prière liturgique en Occident*", in *AB* 72 (1954), pp. 141–2.

most luxuriant and influential of all those *novellae relationes* which his predecessors had condemned "because misbelieving and simple folk apprize in them things that are preposterous and unreal".

d. *The Dialogist's borrowings from post-Gregorian* Gesta

The corpus of legendary *Gesta* so far discussed in this chapter, and shown to have provided models for the second-hand tales told in the *Dialogues*, can be pieced together from a wide range of documentary sources that originated during the fifth, sixth and seventh centuries.[28] Now I go on to point to evidence that is even more directly relevant—indeed decisive even in itself—in the present inquiry: namely, indications that some of the legendary narrations borrowed and adapted by the author of the *Dialogues* were taken from *Gesta* that originated in the seventh century, *after* the lifetime of St Gregory the Great, and therefore that he could not have been the author of that book.

The researches of Dufourcq and others so far discussed relate mainly to the earlier phase of the development of that fictitious martyrology: that is, to the period spanning the fifth and sixth centuries, during which the first great wave of apocryphal *Gesta* relating to martyrs of the city of Rome were composed. It was the period of the Ostrogoths' domination of Italy, for which reason Dufourcq named that earlier phase of *Gesta*-spinning "the Ostrogothic legendary movement". It was the proliferation of the counterfeit *Acts* during that period that provoked the Roman Church's reaction against such literature, expressed in the *Gelasian Decree*. Still more directly relevant to our present inquiry is the later phase in the proliferation of the *Gesta* literature, which Dufourcq, because of his unquestioning assumption of St Gregory's authorship of the *Dialogues*, misnamed "the Gregorian legendary movement". He inferred that the current of apocryphal hagiography, after continuing "feebly" during the last part of the sixth century, was "reanimated" during the subsequent period, especially during and after the pontificate of Boniface V, who

---

[28] Dufourcq prints a considerable quantity of that material in his valuable (but little used) volumes. Many other such texts are to be found in the Bollandists' *Acta Sanctorum* and in later editions of individual *Gesta*.

died in 625, and was still vigorous in the second half of the seventh
century.

In that later phase, Dufourq pointed out, the authors of the fabulous *Gesta* embraced a wider range of characters and themes than
that of their fifth and sixth-century predecessors. Whereas the latter
had provided life-stories for martyrs whose names at least were known
from historical record, the authors of the seventh-century wave of
mainly provincial hagiography invented not only life-stories of saints
but the saints themselves—not only martyrs but also non-martyr
thaumaturgic saints. Whereas those earlier *Gesta* had related mainly
to the city of Rome and its environs, the later ones related mainly
to the rural hinterland of Rome and to the provinces of central Italy
in the corridor of imperial territory running between Rome and
Ravenna. The saints who are the heroes of the saga of the "Twelve
Syrian Brothers" (which is set in Tuscia and Umbria,[29] and to which
the *Dialogues* have close affinities) are patently invented. While Dufourcq
traces the origin of many of the *Gesta* relating to Rome and its hinterland back to the earlier phase of legend-spinning, he concludes
that some of them reflect later situations and particular concerns
that only became topical in the course of the seventh century. For
instance, he dates the fictitious passion of the martyr St Boniface to
the first quarter of that century. Its purpose, it would seem, was
to provide a life-story of the titular patron of a church dedicated to
that saint which was built on the Aventine hill about that time.[30] It
is those spurious *Gesta* of the later period, traceable from the beginning of the seventh century and continuing with important developments around the middle of that century, that provide the closest
links with the *Dialogues*.

Dufourcq misnamed that later current of legendary hagiography
"the Gregorian movement", because he supposed it to be subsequent
to the *Dialogues* attributed to St Gregory, but in reality it is the
Dialogues that reflect those seventh-century *Gesta* and not *vice versa*.
Dufourcq pointed out certain distinctive tendencies in that seventh-
century current of hagiographical literature. After Gregory's time, he
wrote: "The two traits that are properly *Gregorian* become accentu-
ated: that is, the Gothic type of legend wanes, and the miracles and

---

[29] The *Gesta* of Abundius, Carpophorus, Anastasius and their Brethren: in *BHL*,
1620–6.
[30] Dufourcq, *op. cit.*, I, pp. 166–8.

bizarre elements multiply. The later texts are indirectly influenced
by the work of Rothari and the restoration of the bishoprics".[31] (The
reference is to the work of consolidation of the Lombard kingdom
under Rothari, AD 636–652.) He also showed that the seventh-century *Gesta* were much influenced by the ecclesiastical hellenization of
Italy during that period, which is well documented. In contrast, the
greatest of the *Gesta*-writers, namely the Dialogist, was to react against
the prevailing hagiographical fashions by patriotically asserting the
existence of a multitude of Italian thaumaturges to outshine those of
eastern Mediterranean (and Gallic) origin. (I return to this theme in
Chapter 23.) He also made the saintly heroes of his narrative confessors from the recent past instead of martyrs from antiquity, as in
most of the prevalent *Gesta* literature.

Of special relevance is the saga of *The Twelve Syrians*. The reasons
given by Dufourcq for dating that work to the second half of the
seventh century are cogent. He also shows that there are clear literary interrelationships between that text and several other seventh-
century *Passiones* relating to the same regions.[32] Throughout the
abundant legendary literature of that period we find many names
and situations that have intriguing echoes in the *Dialogues*. Although
the Dialogist has his own creative talent, and has fashioned anew
his stories of those mythical worthies of the duchy of Rome, it is
surely more than a coincidence that his pages repeatedly evoke names
and legends that we find scattered through those seventh-century
Gesta. (The names of many such names reused in the *Dialogues* have
been cited above in Chapter 8.e.)

In this volume there is not space to study all the remarkable parallels, both in themes and in wording, between the *Dialogues* and the
fabulous *Gesta* literature of the seventh century. Here I reproduce
five test-cases in which the textual inter-relationship is clear, and
point out evidence showing that it is the text of the *Dialogues* that is
dependent on the corresponding *Gesta* text, and not vice versa.

First test-case: My first instance is the story of the martyrdom
of Bishop Herculanus of Perugia at the hands of the Gothic king
Totila. In the *Dialogues* the story is told in III.13. We find another
version of the same story in the *Acts of Abundius and the Twelve Syrians*.

---

[31] *Ibid.*, III, pp. 283–5.
[32] *Op. cit.*, III, Chapters 2–7.

The latter is described by Dufourcq as a "cyclical text", that is, one in which diverse traditions are combined. Although he thinks it includes sixth-century material, he dates its composition to after the middle of the seventh century, and infers from internal evidence that is was the work of a writer who was "in the papal administration". He sets out the two texts recounting the martyrdom of Herculanus in parallel columns, where their remarkable correspondence can be studied. There can be no doubt that the two forms of the story are closely related. The essential elements are the same. In both accounts it is related that Totila besieged Perugia for seven years (both thus stating an historical error); in both, famine is indicated as a main cause of the eventual capture of the city; both describe in gory detail the manner in which the perfidious king dealt with Herculanus, the bishop of Perugia—namely, his decree that a long thong of skin should be stripped from the bishop's body, "from head to heel", and that he should then be beheaded on the city wall; both relate that his body was later found to be intact and incorrupt in its grave, without any trace of lesion; both also relate that a child's body was placed in the same tomb.

Yet for all the striking resemblances between the two accounts, there are also intriguing differences (—which, later in the Middle Ages, gave rise to the cult of *two* saints Herculanus at Perugia; they were elided into one in 1940.)[33] In particular, they give quite different accounts of what befell the child's body in the tomb. In the *Gesta Abundii* there is a further miraculous sequel, missing in the *Dialogues*. Because of those differences Dufourcq judges that "the two texts are independent of one another", and that "both derive from an oral tradition".[34] I would dissent from that view, for a number of reasons, of which I give two here. First, there are several verbal assonances that argue connection between them.[35] I put a further objection to Dufourcq's supposition that the *Gesta* text originated later than and independent of the *Dialogues* account. If, as he shows, the text of the story of *The Twelve Syrians* was composed after the middle of the seventh century, and if, as he and others assume, the *Dialogues* of St Gregory had been published over sixty years before that time and were everywhere famous, how can one explain that the author

---

[33] Cf. A. Brunacci, "*Ercolano*", in *BS*, Rome 1964, cols. 1302–8.
[34] *Op. cit.*, III, p. 71.
[35] I set them out in parallel columns in *PsGD*, p. 613.

of those *Gesta* gave a version of the events that differs on substantial points from that given by the great pope? Why should he rely on "independent oral tradition" when he had available so authoritative and renowned a source from which to draw the facts?

Throughout the legendary *Gesta* Dufourcq marks a consistent pattern of apocryphal martyrdom-stories. He shows that the events described, and often the persons mentioned, are fictitious. The *Acts of Abundius and the Twelve Syrians*, in which the story of Herculanus is contained, are patently a tissue of bizarre romancing. (He also shows that in still later Umbrian *Gesta* there is more about Herculanus, and that in them "he tends to move out of his secondary role and to become the principal hero".)[36] Why then suppose that in the particular instance of Herculanus's martyrdom the seventh-century author of the *Gesta Abundii* had inherited a genuine "oral tradition" from more than a century earlier to incorporate into his fanciful narrative? Dufourcq's reason for that supposition is that he assumes without question that the Gregorian *Dialogues* had been written at the end of the sixth century and that the story of the martyrdom of Herculanus given there, on the authority of a bishop named Floridus, was a proof of its earlier origin. But since the author of the later *Gesta* gives the story in a strangely variant form, Dufourcq concludes that he must have had it from another tradition. If we prescind from his initial assumption, there is no reason to regard the story of Herculanus as any less fictional than the rest of the *Gesta* of which it is a part. Dufourcq thinks that the *Dialogues* account appears "simpler and truer than that in the *Gesta*". On the contrary, it appears that the shorter form in the *Gesta*, while no truer, is the prior and original form of the story, and that it has been picturesquely embroidered and expanded by the Dialogist in accordance with his usual practice when reusing and adapting earlier hagiographical models.

Second test-case: My second instance is a tale found both in the *Dialogues* (I.12.1–3) and in the *Gesta* of Severus of Valeria, which F. Lanzoni dates "after the sixth century" and Dufourcq "about the middle of the seventh century".[37] The central character in that narrative is a high-born and learned priest who was martyred in the

---

[36] *Op. cit.*, III, pp. 71–2 & note 2.
[37] Text in *BHL* 7685; cf. Lanzoni, *Le Origine delle Diocesi antichi d'Italia*, Rome 1923, p. 231; Dufourcq, *op. cit.*, III, p. 268.

time of the persecuting emperor Maximian. There are a number of tell-tale signs in the wording which indicate the independence and priority of the *Gesta* text. The first is a reference to a local place-name. Introducing Severus, both texts record in identical wording that he lived "in a valley named Interorina, which is called by many folk, using a rustic form of the word, Interocrina" (*"in eo etiam loco Interorina vallis dicitur quae a multis verbo rustico Interocrina nominatur"*). The place (now called Antrodoco) is in Valeria, north of Rieti. It is understandable that the seventh-century *Gesta* author, whose legendary account is located in that region, should mention the slightly variant form of the name in local rustic usage. The Dialogist simply repeated his explanatory gloss when reproducing the story. But it is surely implausible to suppose that Pope Gregory would have known the way that the local countryfolk pronounced the name of their village, or that he would have given such information in his narrative.

Another pointer to the priority of the *Gesta Severii* to the *Dialogues* is found in the story there about a *paterfamilias* who, at the point of death and wishing to put his soul to rights, sent for Severus. However, the priest delayed in order to finish tending his vines, and the man died before his arrival. Severus prayed for him with bitter tears, and the dead man returned to life to relate what had happened to him in the Beyond. Fire-breathing captors had been leading him away when a young man of resplendent appearance, with supporting companions, stood in their path and commanded them: "Send him back, since Severus the priest is lamenting him bitterly!" Hearing of Severus's prodigious power, the Emperor Maximian had him beheaded in the same valley. (A. de Vogüé has pointed out that there is an earlier literary antecedent for the story in a narrative in the *Life of St Martin* by Sulpicius Severus.)[38] Most of this legend is also contained in the *Dialogues*, where it is linked with other prodigious events related to Gregory by a venerable abbot Fortunatus. In this instance there can be no doubt that the account in the *Gesta Severii* and the *Dialogues* present the selfsame text, since there is substantial verbal identity in the account of the experiences of the *paterfamilias* in the other-world. However, in two sentences comprising 29 words,[39] citing the words

---

[38] *SC* 260, pp. 114–5.
[39] *Dialogues* I.12.2, lines 27–33; the corresponding passage in the *Gesta Severii* is in Dufourcq's third volume, p. 266.

in which the *paterfamilias* described his rescue from his demonic captors, there is a seemingly minor verbal discordance which provides
another indication that the story as told in the *Dialogues* is secondary
to that in the *Gesta Severii*. Though otherwise reproducing verbatim
the wording of those *Gesta*, the Dialogist omitted three words which
were evidently original, and in so doing showed that he was the
later writer. I cite that passage here, underlining the three omitted
words:

> *Cumque per obscura loca diutius ducerent, subito pulchrae visionis iuvenis cum
> aliis <u>sodalibus suis iuvenibus</u> nobis euntibus obviavit qui me trahentibus dixit:
> "Reducite illum, quia Severus presbyter amarissime eum plangit".*

The *Gesta Severii* have what is evidently the fuller original text.
According to the full sentence given in the *Gesta*, the *paterfamilias* said
that as his demonic captors led him away through dark places "suddenly a young man of gracious appearance, with his young companions, barred our way as we went along". According to the shorter
reading given in the *Dialogues*, what the *paterfamilias* said was that the
angel barred the way "to us, as we were going along, with others".
The casual omission of the three words "*sodalibus suis iuvenibus*" after
the word "*aliis*" somewhat obscures the sense. There is another indication from a verbal variation in the text that the form of the story
in the *Dialogues* is secondary. It is an apparent correction by the
Dialogist of a grammatical form in the original. In the *Gesta* text,
the angelic rescuer, referring to Severus's tears and prayers for the
deceased *paterfamilias*, says "*Suis enim lacrymis et intercessionibus Dominus
ei vitam reddidit*". In reproducing the text the Dialogist changed the
possessive pronoun "*suis*" to the more correct form "*eius*", which is
required because the subject of the sentence is "*Dominus*". Would a
plagiarist writing in the mid-seventh century, reproducing a narrative
written by Pope Gregory in a book known far and wide, change the
grammatically correct "*eius*" to the demotic "*suis*"? More significantly,
one may ask also: would he adapt and augment the story related
by Fortunatus, speaking from his knowledge of the local worthies of
Valeria, and give the lie to the great pope by making Severus a
martyr of the early centuries who suffered under the emperor
Maximian? While it must appear improbable that a seventh-century
plagiarizer should make such bold changes and additions to a well-
known history narrated by St Gregory, it is not at all improbable
that another *Gesta*-spinner writing at a later date, namely the Dialogist,

should borrow and adapt the provincial yarn from the *Gesta Severii* for use in his own rich collection of such tales, as he did in several other cases.

Third test-case: My third instance of interdependence is the strange duplication, in the *Gesta Felicis* and in the *Dialogues*, of a story about vegetable thieves and tools called *vangae*. Dufourcq judges that this text, in which the chief character is Felix, a priest from Nola, originated during the first quarter of the seventh century.[40] His reasons for that dating are fair but not apodictic; a still later date is quite probable. The same story that is told in the *Gesta* about Felix of Nola is told in the *Dialogues* about a prescient abbot Isaac of Spoleto. In both texts, apart from the saints' names, all the essential elements are identical. The thieves enter the saint's garden to steal vegetables. There they find *vangae*, or rustic spades. The would-be thieves feel themselves constrained to till the ground all night. In the morning, still labouring, they are kindly addressed by the holy man, and they confess how the Lord had turned them away from their dishonest intent. The author of the *Gesta Felicis* uses the word *vangae* without explanation—he assumes it is known to his readers; but the author of the *Dialogues* adds one, specifying that they are "iron tools which we call by the colloquial name of *vangae*"—"*ferramenta quae usitato nos nomine vangas vocamus*". (Who, one may well ask again, are "*we*"? Is it supposed that Pope Gregory the Great belonged to a circle in which that demotic name for the rustic tool was current?)

Because of his unquestioned assumption of the Gregorian authorship of the *Dialogues*, Dufourcq assumed that the Spoletan setting of the tale was the original, since there *soi-disant* Gregory, when relating it about Isaac of Spoleto, testifies that he has learnt much about the deeds of that holy man from "monks of our monastery", as well as from a holy virgin Gregoria and from a venerable abbot Eleutherius. (The latter is an enigmatic figure. There are *Gesta* of a martyr named Eleutherius, composed, as Dufourcq argues, in the first quarter of the seventh century, after which he is frequently referred to.)[41] Nevertheless Dufourcq sees no need to conclude that the story of Isaac of Spoleto in *Dial.* III.14 influenced the author of the *Gesta* of Felix of Nola. Both he and J. Petersen[42] surmise that the two stories

---

[40] *Op. cit.*, III, pp. 236–7.
[41] Dufourcq, *op. cit.*, I, pp. 319–20.
[42] *Op. cit.*, pp. 80–2.

borrowed independently from an earlier model. He suggests that the model may have originated in Umbria. *Contra*, I submit that an objective comparison between the two known versions of the story points to the conclusion that the short and unadorned episode related in the *Gesta Felicis* presents the original form, and that the longer and more circumstantial narrative in the *Dialogues*, where the plot and the denouement are developed with dramatic irony, is a later elaboration of that original short form. Such a pattern can be traced in the tradition of many a mediaeval legend.

Fourth test-case: Other tell-tale indications that the author of the *Dialogues* copied from seventh-century *Gesta*-writers and not vice versa can be seen in the grouping of stories in his work, especially in the third book. In its topography and hagiography, Book III has numerous links with the legendary *Gesta* of central Italy, relating to Tuscia, Umbria, Valeria and Sabina. In its middle chapters we find brought together a succession of anecdotes that are strikingly paralleled by similar anecdotes and allusions that are to be found in several different *Gesta* texts. From a critical standpoint one may ask, which is the more probable: that the several authors of those diverse legends, which we find dispersed in many different texts, separately drew their legendary models from that one group of narratives in a single section of the *Dialogues*; or that the single author of the *Dialogues* (who, it is now generally admitted, was an assiduous borrower of themes from a wide range of hagiographical literature) brought together in that one section of his work scattered stories based on models and motifs which he had garnered from several diverse *Gesta*-tales of central Italy?

An instance of those literary interconnections can be found in Chapter 14 of *Dialogues* III, which tells another tale about the holy abbot Isaac of Spoleto. Immediately before the anecdote about Isaac and the vegetable thieves, which as we have seen was a doublet of a story in the *Gesta Felicis*, there is an account of Isaac's arrival at Spoleto from Syria which, as Dufourcq demonstrates, is a doublet of a story in the *Gesta* of John Penariensis.[43] Both John of the *Gesta* and Isaac of the *Dialogues* were holy strangers who arrived in Umbria from Syria. Each made his way to Spoleto, each conversed there with God, and each resolved to make his abode here. The sanctity

---

[43] Dufourcq, III, pp. 61–2; the text is also reproduced in *BHL* 4420.

of each was revealed to the inhabitants of Spoleto by a miracle (different in either case); each exorcized demoniacs; each founded a monastery at Spoleto, and each attracted there a multitude of disciples. Thus we find that in adjacent paragraphs of the *Dialogues* Isaac of Spoleto has two doubles who are found separated in different *Gesta*—Felix the priest of Nola and John Penariensis from Syria. This is surely a clear sign of the Dialogist's borrowing from those earlier separate texts.

Isaac is the only one of the holy "Fathers of Italy" in the *Dialogues* who is not of Italian but of Eastern origin. In the *Gesta*, however, John of Penariensis is just one of many saints who have come from the East to central Italy. In particular there is "the great legend" of the Twelve Syrians who came to Rome in the time of Julian the Apostate, and who dispersed to Sabina, Valeria and Umbria—regions that are also the setting for many episodes in the *Dialogues*. The interconnections appear still further tangled when we find that one of those Twelve Syrians who is connected with Spoleto is in fact named Isaac. Dufourcq observes that he is evidently identifiable with his namesake in the *Dialogues*.[44] So we find that the Dialogist's Isaac not only impersonates two other characters from the *Gesta*, Felix of Nola and John Penariensis, but is also given the name and the persona of a third such character—the Isaac who is one of the Twelve Syrian Brethren. Among those Twelve Syrians was bishop Herculanus of Perugia, whose presence in the *Dialogues* has been discussed above. The more we explore, the more we find evidence of the Dialogist's knowledge of and special interest in the characters and themes of those seventh-century *Gesta*, which he mingles with his own fictions.

Fifth test-case: The last instance that I cite is one of unique interest, in which the author of the *Dialogues* explicitly refers to models of his miracle-tales in previous hagiographical writings, one of which proves to be post-Gregorian.[45] It is found in *Dial.* I.7.3. Recounting two miracles of Nonnosus, prior of a monastery on Monte Soracte, the author remarks that in performing them Nonnosus "imitated" two miracles from earlier times.[46] The first of those two models

---

[44] *Op. cit.*, III, p. 72.

[45] Relevant references to the original and secondary sources mentioned here are given in *PsGD*, pp. 620–2.

[46] "*Sicque in duobus miraculis duorum patrum est virtutes imitatus: in mole scilicet saxi factum Gregorii, qui montem movit, in reparatione vero lampadis virtutem Donati, qui fractum calicem pristinae incolumitati restituit.*"

was the prodigious moving of a gigantic rock by Gregory the Wonder-worker, a story found in the fourth-century *Historia Ecclesiastica* of Rufinus. It is the second model that is of decisive relevance to our present inquiry. It is the miraculous restoration to wholeness of a glass vessel that had been shattered into pieces, a tale that is told in the *Passio Donati*, one of the legendary *Gesta* dating from the seventh century. The evidence pointing to the post-Gregorian dating of the *Passio Donati* is very strong. Its author emphasizes that Donatus went to Rome to be consecrated as bishop of Arezzo by the Roman pontiff, a feature of the narrative that significantly reflects a dispute concerning the metropolitan rights of the Roman pontiffs in the province of Tuscia-Umbria. As Dufourcq and other scholars have recognized, that dispute did not arise in the sixth century but only in the course of the seventh, when the newly restored Catholic bishops of Spoleto, capital of the powerful Lombard duchy in central Italy, began to vindicate for themselves metropolitan rights over that Apennine region. Moreover, there is scholarly agreement[47] that another contemporary text, the *Gesta* of Juvenal of Narnia, originated likewise in the seventh century and came in all probability from the same workshop as the *Passio Donati*. The author of those *Gesta Iuvenalis* likewise insists on the ecclesiastical subordination of Tuscia to the Roman church. Jesus Christ himself, he claims, confided the evangelization of that province to Saints Peter and Paul; accordingly he relates that it was to Rome that Juvenal went to be consecrated there by the pope as bishop of Narnia. There are also reflections of the same controversy over jurisdiction in the *Gesta* of Felicianus of Foligno, which as Dufourcq points out were evidently closely related in origin with the *Gesta Iuvenalis*.

Dufourcq and the later commentators were all faced with what seemed to them to be a puzzling contradiction to the evidence clearly showing that the *Passio Donati* and the related *Gesta* were of seventh-century date: namely, the paradoxical fact that a miracle from that *Passio* was explicitly referred to in the *Dialogues*, which they assumed to have been written by Gregory the Great in AD 593. How could he have had knowledge of a seventh-century hagiographical work? Dufourcq met this serious difficulty by postulating that there was an earlier, pre-Gregorian, form of the text of the Donatus legend, which

---

[47] Notably by F. Caraffa and G. Luchesi: references in *PsGD*, p. 622.

Gregory must have known and referred to in the *Dialogues*, and that it was "reworked" after his time to reflect the ecclesiastical preoccupations of the seventh century. (Dufourcq also recognized that certain features of the *Passio Donati* reflected those of the *Gesta* of Victorianus-Severinus and of Agapitus, which were evidently written—or, he suggested, "reworked"—in the earlier part of the seventh century.) G. Luchesi proposed an alternative solution to the puzzle, which he saw as simpler and more plausible than Dufourcq's theory of textual reworkings: namely, that Gregory had the anecdote of Donatus's miraculous repair of the shattered vessel not from an earlier and more jejune text of the *Passio* but from an independent "oral tradition" which was later incorporated into the seventh-century text.[48] Such a conjecture, Luchesi claimed unconvincingly, "removes any solid basis for dating the *Passio* to an epoch earlier than that of St Gregory the Great"—a dating, he realized, that was contradicted by the multiple evidences of the seventh-century origin of that text.

Instead of those contorted attempts to resolve the paradox of the reference to the *Passio Donati* in the *Dialogues*, the simple solution is surely to recognize that the legendary document did indeed originate in the course of the seventh century, but that it antedated the *Dialogues*. The Dialogist, writing later in the seventh century, may not have adverted to the fact that the *Passio Donati* was too recent in date to have been known to Gregory; but by expressly citing an anecdote from it, and by assuming that it was well known, he unwittingly betrayed the non-Gregorian origin of his own pseudepigraphical *Gesta*.

The relevance of the legendary *Gesta* to the question of the authorship of the *Dialogues* has hitherto been widely ignored in the controversy over the authenticity of the *Dialogues*. Those texts survived only in scattered manuscripts and remained virtually unexamined until Dufourcq rescued them from oblivion. During the half century following the publication of his four-volume work, only Moricca and a few other scholars gave appreciative attention to his findings. A. de Vogüé, when writing the commentary on his edition of the *Dialogues*, firmly refrained from taking any account of Dufourcq's researches,

---

[48] *BS* IV, Rome 1964, *s.v.* "*Donato*", cols. 778–9.

as being "too uncertain".[49] The Bollandist H. Deleheye, who was at first the most severe critic of the faults of Dufourcq's work, later came to admit its essential value. The store of little known manuscript texts that Dufourcq brought to light and published has been supplemented and surpassed by the scholarly editions in the *Bibliotheca Hagiographica Latina*.

In his critique of the arguments of *PsGD*, R. Godding passed over the evidence there brought to the fore to show that the author of the *Dialogues* drew on seventh-century *Gesta*. Vogüé judged it enough to dismiss that evidence by a simple appeal to the generic assertion the Bollandists: "*Finalement, c'est au jugement des Bollandistes qu'il faut revenir: les gesta copient Grégoire*". As proof that their assumption was correct Vogüé referred to the account of the death of a bishop Brice written by the anonymous author of the *Gesta Abundii*. That account, he asserts, is "a veritable cento" of snippets from the *Dialogues*, which he identifies in a footnote reference.[50] When we examine the seven snippets alleged to have been dredged together by the author of those *Gesta* from different places in the *Dialogues*, we find that they do not provide the proof that Vogüé claims. Of the seven supposed borrowings that he adduces, all but one of the alleged citations from the *Dialogues* are found to be assonances of commonplace themes and expressions, some of which are also found in the Gregorian *inedita* preserved in the Roman archives. (It is in any case a strange supposition that Vogüé makes: that the author dredged through the *Dialogues* picking out those six everyday phrases to stud into one of his stories!) The one exception, a longer passage, is at first sight impressive. Vogüé points triumphantly to a passage in the *Gesta* text which he claims is copied almost verbatim from *Dial.* IV.15.4, in the story of the holy death of a poor woman named Romula. The passage is in fact genuinely Gregorian. But what Vogüé does not advert to is that it is one of the seven edifying *exempla* from Gregory's *Homilies on the Gospels* that are reproduced verbatim in the *Dialogues*. (I discuss it in *PsGD*, pp. 542–3 as "IGP 52".) The author of the *Gesta Abundii* copied it not from the *Dialogues*, which did not yet exist,

---

[49] "*En préparant l'édition des Dialogues, nous avions évité de confronter ceux-ci avec les gesta, comme le faisait souvent Moricca. La raison en est que les travaux bien connus d'A. Dufourcq nous avaient paru trop peu sûrs pour qu'on en pût exploiter cette mine*": RHE 83 (1988), p. 339.

[50] *Ibid.*, p. 340, note 2.

but from a celebrated work of Gregory himself. His reuse of it is indeed noteworthy, since it provides a precedent for the Dialogist's own similar borrowing, and an insight into the practices of the *Gesta*-spinners of that age.

One of the few who have given serious study to Dufourcq's findings is Joan Petersen; in her book, *The Dialogues of Gregory the Great in their late antique cultural Background*, she acknowledges their value. One of her references in that book to post-Gregorian *Gesta* is observantly noted by Marilyn Dunn as relevant to the *Dialogues* controversy: "J.M. Petersen maintains the authenticity of the attribution of the *Dialogues* to Gregory, but her discussion of the Equitius-narrative [*Dial.* I.4] reveals its resemblance to one of the Italian *Gesta Martyrum*".[51]

e. *Borrowings from Gregory of Tours, Moschus and Jonas of Bobbio*

There are a number of other hagiographical texts of later date, of better literary repute than those sheaves of legendary *Gesta* composed by nameless scribes, to which the *Dialogues* show significant similarities and which may likewise be counted among the sources that provided motifs for the tales in that work. Out of those discussed more fully in *PsGD*, I make special mention here of works written by Gregory of Tours, John Moschus and Jonas of Bobbio. The possible relatedness of the *Dialogues* to the writings of the Gallic Gregory, especially to his works *In Gloriam Martyrum* and *In Gloriam Confessorum*, has been much discussed, notably by J. Petersen, who points out the manifest resemblances between miracle-stories told by the two authors. In his commentary on the *Dialogues* A. de Vogüé also signals the striking and frequent parallels. "In points of detail", he writes, "the narrations in those works, like others in the *Historia Francorum*, are often so similar to those in our *Dialogues* that one cannot help asking whether Pope Gregory did not read and draw upon the writings of his namesake."[52] He calls this "a delicate question", since the relative dating of the writings of the two Gregories presents a disconcerting problem. It is indeed difficult to maintain that Pope Gregory could have known those contemporary and still unedited

---

[51] *The Emergence of Monasticism*, p. 236.
[52] *SC* 260, p. 120; cf. *SC* 265, pp. 300–1.

writings of his Gallic namesake at the time at which he was allegedly composing the *Dialogues*. Vogüé wrote a further article on the subject[53] in which he recognized "the almost insoluble problems presented by this embroiled chronology", and passed on leaving those problems unresolved. While it is indeed implausible, in view of those problems, to assume that the legendary compositions of Gregory of Tours could have been available in Rome in AD 593 to stimulate Pope Gregory "to achieve for Italy what had just been done for Gaul",[54] it is altogether probable that the later seventh-century author of the *Dialogues*, while borrowing from the narrations of Gregory of Tours, had such a motive.

While the *Dialogues* clearly have close affinity with, indeed dependence on, the narrations of Gregory of Tours there is one notable difference between the two collections of wonder-stories that has understandably puzzled the commentators. Vogüé pointed it out: "It is a curious fact that our author has almost nothing to say on a subject in which his contemporaries were passionately interested, namely, the miraculous cures and wonders of all sorts that happened at the tombs of saints. Whereas the work of Gregory of Tours abounds in stories of this kind, in the *Dialogues*, by contrast, there is a dearth of them". Such stories, Vogüé commented, "make the writings of the bishop of Tours a veritable guide to the miraculous shrines of Christendom".[55] I see a clear reason for that apparently puzzling contrast. Although the stories of Gregory of Tours were, like those of all the hagiographers of that age, replete with legendary miracles, he was at least writing about real places of pilgrimage, where there was historical record and present cult of the holy persons whose tombs and relics were venerated there. A practical function of his writings was indeed to serve as a guide and incentive for pious pilgrims journeying to those shrines. The *Dialogues*, on the other hand, had no such function. The author, like other seventh-century writers of legendary *Gesta*, invented not only his miracle stories but also the characters who feature in them. Although he presented the lives of his holy thaumaturges in the setting of central Italy, most of them belonged to a never-never-land of fantasy, without anchorage in existing centres of devotion and pilgrimage. They had no home, cult or

---

[53] A. de Vogüé, "*Grégoire le Grand, lecteur de Grégoire de Tours?*", in *AB* 94 (1976).
[54] Vogüé, *SC* 226, p. 120.
[55] *SC* 251, p. 94 and footnote 52.

tomb-shrines to which his wonder-stories could guide his readers. Cultic devotion to them came only in later centuries, as a consequence of the spurious fame given to them by the *Dialogues*.

There lies the explanation of the "curious" contrast noted by Vogüé between Gregory of Tours and the author of the *Dialogues*, whose works are otherwise so alike. The stories of the Gallic Gregory related stories of saints whose shrines were actual centres of pilgrimage and cult; those of the Dialogist lacked any such historical or geographical base. A similar contrast is recognizable between the fifth and sixth-century authors of the *gesta martyrum* of the city of Rome, who provided legendary lives for historically commemorated saints and for existing shrines, and, on the other hand, the later authors of the seventh-century *Gesta* relating to the wider region of central Italy, whose bizarre stories featured previously unknown provincial saints for whom there were no existing shrines or cult.

The close parallelism between a tale narrated by the Greek hagiographer John Moschus concerning Gregory himself and one narrated in the *Dialogues* is also relevant to this discussion. Moschus, it has now been established,[56] sojourned in Rome from about AD 614 until his death in 628 or 629, and during that time wrote out his Λειμών, or *Spiritual Meadow* (here abbreviated as *SpM*). There is no trace of a Latin translation of the work until much later. A. de Vogüé asserted that *SpM* "certainly depends" on the *Dialogues*, and that it reveals "the first literary trace" of the rapid diffusion of that Gregorian work. In support of that assertion he cited Moschus's story of an excommunicate monk which, he said, "reproduces in a moderately altered form" the story, told in *Dialogues* IV.57.8–16 (and recalled in Chapter 7 above), of the monk Justus who sinned against the law of monastic poverty by secretly retaining three gold pieces. Vogüé surmised that Moschus took the story "from an oral tradition derived from the *Dialogues*". I have argued,[57] on the contrary, that textual comparison shows that the story in the *Dialogues* is later in date and is dependent on that in *SpM*, at least indirectly. It is unlikely that the Dialogist knew Greek, but he could have heard the substance of Moschus's tale in later seventh-century Rome, by which time Greek-speaking monks had become numerous in the city. (One should also

---

[56] Cf. *PsGD*, p. 104.
[57] *Ibid.*, pp. 104–6.

take account of the fact that the text of *SpM* was added to and
revised in the course of its manuscript transmission.)

The tale of the sinful monk as told in *SpM* is simpler and less
dramatic than its longer counterpart in the *Dialogues*—which is a
pointer to its priority in date. The author of the *Dialogues* introduces
into the plot Gregory's behest that the culprit should die a lonely
death deprived of all consolation, that he should be buried in a
dunghill, and that his brethren should throw the three gold pieces
after him, exclaiming, "May your money go with you unto perdition". The Dialogist then adds the sequel, likewise missing in Moschus's
account, in which Gregory orders that a trental of Masses be offered
posthumously for the sinful soul, who at the end of the month appears
to his brother to announce his release from fiery torments. In the
widespread hagiographical borrowing in that age it was common
practice for the later writers to refashion, augment and embroider
the materials they were reusing, and this was evidently what the
Dialogist did. Another obvious objection to Vogüé's assertion may
be stated as follows: Would Moschus, writing in Rome some 25 years
after Pope Gregory had published a report of supernatural happenings in which he himself was the chief protagonist, have omitted
substantial elements in the story and changed others, thus directly
contradicting the testimony of the great pope concerning himself?
Would not Moschus realize that such omissions and changes would
be recognizable and objectionable to the many who knew that papal
work which, according to Vogüé, had gained rapid fame and was
well known at the time the *Spiritual Meadow* was written?

There are also significant similarities between the miracle-tales in
the *Dialogues* and those told by another seventh-century hagiographer, Jonas of Bobbio. Vogüé judges that Jonas "seems to have in
mind Book IV of the *Dialogues* in his narration of holy deaths in his
Vita Burgundofarae", and cites a dozen accounts in the *VB* of such
pious deaths, together with two of a contrary character.[58] He marks
out six passages in particular as indications of Jonas's knowledge and
reuse of the *Dialogues* narrative. I agree that the remarkable similarities in the plots and details of the prodigious stories related in both
works strongly argue dependence of one on the other. I even find
some assonances of phrasing that can hardly be mere coincidences.

---

[58] *SC* 260, p. 141.

For example, in the *VB* the dying nun Willesuinda greets her heavenly sisters with the words, "*Benedicite dominae meae, benedicite dominae meae*". This recalls the greeting of the dying priest of Nursia, in *Dialogues* IV.12.4, when he sees the Apostles Peter and Paul coming to summon him: "*Bene veniunt domini mei, bene veniunt domini mei*". However, I again see the literary dependence of one text on the other to be the reverse of that assumed by Vogüé. As in the case of the interconnection between the *Dialogues* and Moschus's *Spiritual Meadow*, the evidence of Jonas's *Vita Burgundofarae* points to its prior origin. His homogeneous collection of edifying deathbed stories is triter and less colourful than the Dialogist's tales with similar themes, which greatly excel Jonas's in their dramatic presentation, in their wealth of picturesque details and in the variety of persons, places and circumstances described.

It has been claimed that echoes of the *Dialogues* can be found in some other seventh-century texts, but on close examination all those claims are found to be likewise unsubstantial. Later, in Chapters 21–22, I discuss them more fully.

PART III

EXTERNAL EVIDENCE OF THE NON-GREGORIAN
AUTHORSHIP OF THE *DIALOGUES* FROM OTHER
DOCUMENTS AND FROM THE HISTORY OF
BENEDICTINE ORIGINS

CHAPTER TEN

THE "BEDROCK PROOF" ON WHICH DEFENDERS OF THE *DIALOGUES*' AUTHENTICITY NOW BASE THEIR CASE: THE COUNTERFEIT *"LETTER TO MAXIMIAN"*

a

The defenders of the Gregorian authorship of the *Dialogues* now base their case on the evidence of some problematic documents which, they claim, attest the ascription of the work to St Gregory in his own age or soon afterwards. All but one of the documents now alleged by them date from the seventh century, after Gregory's death. One alone is claimed to date from his own lifetime, and to be no less than a letter written by the great pope personally, testifying that he was setting about the writing of the *Dialogues*. That is, they appeal first and foremost to a brief *Letter to Maximian* which is found in the curial collection of Gregory's letters (Epistola III.50). As their chief secondary arguments they appeal to passages in the seventh-century anthology of Gregorian scriptural commentary compiled by Paterius, which allegedly contain quotations from or references to the *Dialogues*. Brushing aside my protest against his failure to take into account the multiple convergent proofs of non-Gregorian authorship based on the internal evidence of the text, P. Meyvaert insisted that he rested his case squarely on two documentary sources: "I refuse to be distracted", he wrote; "It is the witness of the letter to Maximian of Syracuse, together with that of Gregory's secretary Paterius that remain the bedrock historical evidence for asserting that Gregory the Great is indeed the author of the *Dialogues* that bear his name".[1] A. de Vogüé has likewise reiterated the palmary importance of the *Letter to Maximian* for vindicating Gregory's authorship.[2] He too included the Paterian anthology among a number of other problematic texts in which he, like R. Godding, thought that echoes of the *Dialogues* could be detected. I examine the critics' first "bedrock"

---

[1] *JEH* 40 (1989), p. 346.
[2] *CC* 62 (2000), p. 186.

argument in this chapter, and their other secondary arguments later, in Chapters 21–22.

They insist that in the problematic *Letter to Maximian* lies conclusive documentary proof from Gregory's own hand, dated in July 593, that he was then engaged in writing a book on the miracles of the Fathers of Italy—the very title of the *Dialogues* as given at the beginning of that work. In the letter he asks his correspondent for details of the deeds of a holy abbot named Nonnosus, who duly appears in the pages of the *Dialogues*. The letter was recorded and filed in the curial collection of Gregory's correspondence, which in a later century was transcribed under the title of *Registrum Epistularum*. It has been flourished as a trump card by defenders of the authenticity of the *Dialogues* from the seventeenth century to the present. With the collapse of so many traditional arguments for authenticity that are now shown to be fallacious, this plea is urged as the uniquely decisive issue in today's debate.

Before discussing the origin and import of that celebrated letter, I must observe that no argument based on it, however seemingly impressive, can avail to overthrow the force of the massively convergent case set out elsewhere in this volume which independently demonstrates, both from the internal evidence of the text of the *Dialogues* and from the external evidence of contemporary documents, that Gregory the Great was not the author of that work. Thus any *prima facie* assumption in favour of the genuineness of the *Letter to Maximian* must necessarily yield to truth in the light of that contrary evidence. Confirming that prior and conclusive argument, I now proceed to show that there are several features of that letter, both in its wording and in its putative setting, that give strongly positive indications that it was supposititious, a counterfeit inserted at a later date into the collection of copies of Gregory's letters in the Roman archives. I will show, from the history of the manuscript transmission of the copies of Gregory's letters, that there is no guarantee of the original authenticity of that item in the *Registrum*. Rather, there are strong reasons to make the further inference that the author of the letter was the pseudonymous Dialogist himself, who placed it in those files as a supporting forgery to authenticate his fabricated narrative. As I show more fully in later pages, there are several probable indications from the *Dialogues* text that he was himself a curial *scriniarius*, and that he had access to the register of Gregory's letters, the wording of which he echoes in places. Furthermore, examination of the historical records of Gregory's situation and occupations in the second half of the year 593 shows the extreme implausibility of the supposition that he was composing the *Dialogues* in that period, as the dating of the *Letter to Maximian* would require.

The argument based on that letter is *prima facie* impressive. Before commenting on it I give its text here, in the Latin original and in translation:

EPISTOLA III.50, dated July 593

Gregorius Maximiano
Episcopo Syracusis

Gregory to Maximian
Bishop of Syracuse

Fratres mei qui mecum familiariter vivunt omni modo me compellunt, aliqua de miraculis patrum quae in Italia facta audivimus, sub brevitate scribere. Ad quam rem solatio vestrae caritatis vehementer indigeo, ut quaeque vobis in memoriam redeunt, quaeque cognovisse vos contigit, mihi breviter indicetis. De domno enim Nonnoso abbate, qui iuxta domnum Anastasium de Pentumis fuit, aliqua retulisse te memini, quae oblivioni mandavi. Et hoc ergo et si qua sunt alia tuis peto epistolis inprimi, et mihi sub celeritate transmitti, si tamen ad me ipsum non proferas.

My brethren who live with me in my household are by every means urging me to write a brief account of miracles worked by Fathers in Italy, of which we have heard. For which purpose we urgently need the help of Your Charity, that you would briefly indicate to me whatever may recur to your memory, whatever you may happen to know. For I recall that you related something about the lord abbot Nonnosus, who was in the company of the lord Anastasius of Pentoma, which I have quite forgotten. In a letter, therefore, pray write that down, and anything else there may be, and send it to me quickly—that is, if you do not bring it to me in person.

Maximian, the addressee of that letter, is a historical figure known to us from several of Gregory's letters and from a reference in his *Homilies of the Gospels*.[3] He had earlier been abbot of the monastery that Gregory had established about the year 574 in his family home on the Coelian Hill in Rome. In October 591, the second year of his pontificate, we find Maximian already in post as bishop of Syracuse. In a letter of that date the pope appointed him vicar of the Apostolic see with delegated authority "over all the churches of Sicily".[4] During

---

[3] 38.18; *PL* 76, col. 1257–8.
[4] *Epist.* II.8; EH I.106–7.

the three succeeding years Gregory addressed a dozen official letters
to him, all phrased in the usual dignified and authoritative style. We
know that Maximian died before November 594.[5] Gregory's reference to him in his Gospel homily is of particular interest in the present context, since there he cited Maximian by name as his source
of information for an edifying episode concerning a monk who, while
praying in secret, heard a voice declaring that his sin was forgiven,
whereupon his abbot perceived a heavenly light falling upon him.
One may well surmise that it was that *exemplum*, related by Gregory
on the authority of Maximian, that gave the Dialogist the idea of
using the latter's well-known name to vouch for several of the tales
told in his *Dialogues*. In one of these tales, describing a miraculous
escape from shipwreck, Maximian himself is given a central role in
the drama. Significantly, when introducing him there (*Dial.* II.36),
the *soi-disant* Gregory of the *Dialogues* reproduces the very same descrip-
tive phrases that the real Gregory had applied to him in his Gospel
homily. The name of so celebrated an associate of Pope Gregory,
who was a former abbot of the monastery established by him and
later a bishop and Apostolic Vicar in Sicily to whom Gregory
addressed several letters, would be a suitable choice as the addressee
of a fictitious papal letter designed to provide external authentication for the *Dialogues* when they were published in the later seventh
century. To that persuasive evidence the Dialogist's clerical colleagues
in the Roman curia could be referred if they were tempted to suspect that the previously unknown Gregorian work was merely one
more of the legendary *Gesta* familiar in that age.

b. *Suspect features in the* Letter to Maximian

There are several indications from the contents, wording and style
of the *Letter to Maximian*, and from the historical circumstances in
which it is assumed to have been written, that tell against the traditional assumption that it was written by Pope Gregory. First, there
are anomalies in language and phrasing. In the letter there are indeed
a couple of phrases that have a formal turn, echoing similar phrases
found in the *Registrum* of Gregory's letters: "*quaeque vobis in memoriam*

---

[5] From *Epist.* V.20; EH I.302–3.

redeunt, quaeque cognovisse vos contigit . . ." There are also two occur-rences in that short message of the modal or adverbial use of the preposition *sub* with the ablative, which could have been modelled on the same usage often found in the papal administrative letters and other documents. "*Sub brevitate*", which occurs at the end of the first sentence in the letter, is paralleled elsewhere, e.g. in *Epist.* III.63: ". . . *epistolis tuis sub brevitate respondeo*". But whereas in the latter exam-ple the expression does really mean that the papal reply is succinctly brief, one suspects that in the *Letter to Maximian* it was brought in merely because it was a standard expression in the papal corre-spondence with which the scribes were familiar, for in this instance it is not apposite. According to the assertion in that sentence, Gregory reports that the monastic brethren were using every means to induce him to write a book on the miracles of the Fathers of Italy; it is not likely that they were also insisting that he should do so only briefly, "*sub brevitate*", as is stated there. Here can be detected one more instance of the Dialogist's "*style de notaire*" discussed in Chapter 5 above, which points to his being a *scriniarius* in the seventh-century papal secretariate.

Another such tell-tale pointer can be recognized in the wording of the final sentence of the *Letter to Maximian*, which likewise has the ring of a stereotyped chancery formula: "*Et hoc ergo et si qua alia sunt tuis peto epistolis inprimi at mihi sub celeritate transmitti*". The requirement, "*sub celeritate*", chimes with the similarly official "*sub brevitate*" just mentioned. The phrase "*et si qua alia sunt*"—"if there be any other such items"—reflects a common notarial usage that is also found in the administrative correspondence of the pontiffs, including that of Gregory I. In the Gregorian *Registrum* the phrase "*si qua sunt alia*" occurs five times.[6] In the *Dialogues*, while that usage does not occur in the 80 IGPs, it occurs five times in the narrative text, put into the mouth of the curial official Peter the Deacon in order to voice a request very similar to that expressed in the *Letter to Maximian*. While the occurrence in that letter of the clerkly phrase, "*si qua sunt alia*", is not in itself proof of the non-Gregorian origin of that let-ter, it may be seen, taken in conjunction with other clues, as one more probable sign of the hand of a pseudepigrapher. I also note a curious change within that short letter in Gregory's manner of

---

[6] There are a further 50 occurrences of stilted "*si qua . . .*" phrases in the *Registrum*.

addressing Maximian. In the first part he thrice addresses him formally in the second person plural; in the second part he thrice addresses him familiarly in the second person singular.

Among other suspect features in that short letter is the reason given there by *soi-disant* Gregory for writing to Maximian. He explains that he greatly needs the former abbot's help to recall details of the miracles of Italian holy men, in particular of an abbot named Nonnosus. He remembers only that Maximian formerly retailed some facts about that worthy, but what they were has completely passed out of his mind. It is surely strange that he should have to write to Maximian in far off Syracuse to obtain a reminder of those facts when there were so many articulate monks in the monastery of St Andrew in Gregory's ancestral mansion who would have heard the same stories related by Maximian when he was abbot there. Again and again in the *Dialogues* we are told of the miracle-stories vouched for by those monks. Surely from their rich store of such knowledge they would have been able to recall for Gregory's use those narrations of Maximian about the wondrous deeds of the abbot Nonnosus?

Moreover, when we look at the *Dialogues* to see what particulars are related there about Nonnosus, we find (in *Dial.* I.7) that not only Maximian but also another monk named Laurio is cited as Gregory's authority for those stories. Laurio is said to be not only still living and well known in Rome but to have been educated by the abbot Anastasius, who was a close associate of the holy man Nonnosus. Why then were the first-hand recollections of such a privileged witness not adequate by themselves for Gregory's purposes? Why did he have to send a request all the way to Sicily to obtain Maximian's reminiscences about Nonnosus when there was so authoritative a witness to the details available on the spot? We are also told that the abbot Anastasius, companion of Nonnosus and master of Laurio, had been *praepositus* of a monastery on Monte Soracte, nor far from Rome. Again, one would assume that the general fame of the stupendous miracles of Nonnosus and Anastasius would not have passed into oblivion in the city, and that Gregory would not have to send afar for news of them.

It is also relevant to recall that Maximian is cited as Gregory's authority for other stories in the *Dialogues* as well as that concerning Nonnosus in *Dial.* I.7. In *Dial.* IV.32, for instance, we find the story of a dreadful judgement upon a wicked courtier, a story which, Gregory says, "Maximian, bishop of Syracuse and a man of holy life who was a long time abbot of my monastery in this city often related (*narrare consuevit*)". For a story that Maximian recounted repeatedly, there would presumably be no such "oblivion" on Gregory's part as confessed to in the problematic letter III.50, and he would be able to rely on his own memory instead of having to wait for information to be sent to him in reply to his letter of July 593. The wording of that letter does not square with the supposition that he already had available for his projected hagiographical work a miracle-story that Maximian had often recounted in previous years.

Another point in the short letter that gives rise to suspicion is the opening phrase, "*Fratres mei qui mecum familiariter vivunt omni modo me compellunt . . . scribere*", which matches expressions used by the real Gregory when introducing two of his main works, the *Moralia* and the *Homilies on Ezekiel*. The similarity is particularly notable when that phrase is compared with words found in the dedicatory letter to Leander of Seville prefaced to the text of the *Moralia*, Gregory's most famous work. In that preface Gregory recalled his fellowship with Leander in Constantinople in earlier years, and how his friend had joined his voice to those of the monks from Gregory's own monastic foundation who were with him in the imperial city when they pleaded with him to expound the meaning of the book of *Job*. There is close similarity between the opening phrase of the *Letter to Maximian* quoted above and the following words from Gregory's preface to the *Moralia* recalling the earnest request of those monks: "*eisdem fratribus . . . placuit ut importuna me petitione compellerent . . .*" (One may note that, whereas according to the *Letter to Maximian* it was the monastic brethren who importuned Gregory to write a book about the miracles of the Fathers of Italy, in the prologue to the *Dialogues* Gregory relates that he did so at the urging of Peter the Deacon, a curial official.) However, the circumstances in which the monastic brethren pressed Gregory, then papal envoy in Constantinople, to comment on the book of *Job* were very different from those in which the pontiff found himself in the troubled summer of 593. The picture painted in the *Dialogues* of those monks living in an atmosphere of peaceful prayer and study with Gregory in the papal palace, urgently pleading with him to write a book of miracle stories, accords ill with what we know of his situation at that time, as I shall show more fully in the following chapter.

Also suspect is the concluding phrase of the letter. There we read Gregory's injunction to the bishop of Syracuse to send the information

he requires as quickly as possible, to which he adds the qualifying
clause: ". . . that is, if you do not bring it to me in person". It is
highly questionable whether the pope would have written that. From
his authentic letters to Maximian and others, written within a few
weeks of the date of the suspect letter, and from what we know of
the ecclesiastical discipline of his time, it is clear that he took it for
granted that the bishop of Syracuse, his vicar in Sicily, was reliably
stable in the position of sacred responsibility in which he had been
placed, devoting himself to the service of his flock with the same
dependable dedication that Gregory himself had firmly enjoined upon
all bishops in his *Regula Pastoralis*. From the concluding words of that
letter it is made to appear that the pontiff contemplated with equa-
nimity the possibility that the bishop of Syracuse might decide to
make the journey to recount to him those fanciful tales, despite the
pressing responsibilities that he had to carry out in his diocese and
vicariate. It can be seen as a blunder on the part of the fabricator
of Epistola III.50 to make Gregory thus imply that Maximian was
at liberty to leave his post and to decide to go off to Rome as he
chose to tell his tales to the pope.

c. *Gregory's relations with Maximian at the material time*

It is instructive also to examine the genuine letters that Gregory sent
to Maximian during the period in which the suspect letter was ostensibly written. Those letters, together with others sent earlier, throw
much light on the relationship between the pope and his vicar in
the island of Sicily. They express Gregory's earnest concern with the
manner in which Maximian was carrying out his responsibilities. The
content and tone of those admonitory letters of Gregory accord ill
with the familiar and permissive message that he had assumedly sent
to Maximian shortly before, requesting his help in compiling a collection of miracle stories. In them Gregory wrote with the courteous dignity of a superior giving firm instructions to his vicar. In a
letter filed in the *Registrum* almost immediately after Epistola III.50,
and also dated in July 593, he gave instructions to Maximian to
make provision for the support of a deposed bishop.[7] (In the letter

---

[7] Epist. III. 53; EH I.210.

in the *Registrum* immediately preceding III.50, likewise dated July 593, there is instruction to another Sicilian bishop, Theodorus, bidding him to refer some matters of clerical discipline to Bishop Maximian as higher authority.)[8] From two further letters of Gregory to Maximian, written within the three months following the alleged date of Epistola III.50, we gain revealing indications of the nature of the pope's relations with his vicar in Sicily and the manner in which he dealt with him, which also show the lack of verisimilitude of that suspect letter. The first of the two letters is dated in September 593. It contains a dignified rebuke to Maximian for failing to observe the pontiff's earlier instructions to correct ecclesiastical abuses in Sicily, and a renewed exhortation to him to exercise greater vigilance:

> By our authority the duty has been laid on Your Fraternity to correct on our behalf any abuses that might be committed in the churches and other venerable places in Sicily, or any things that may be done amiss. However, since despite those injunctions complaints have reached us of neglected discipline in some matters, we perceive that it is especially necessary to arouse Your Fraternity again to correct those matters.[9]

Gregory then proceeded in the same letter to detail the abuses and the required remedies. A month later he wrote to Maximian again, lamenting the tidings of evil deeds that had continued to reach him from Sicily, which, he said, led him to fear that the whole province would perish for its sins. He ordered Maximian to rectify a scandalous injustice committed by agents of the bishop of Messina, namely, the forcible separation of a bondswoman from her husband and her resale to another. Gregory further ordered Maximian to warn the bishop that if the Pope learned of any such evil in the future, canonical punishment would be visited not merely on the bishop's men but on the bishop himself.[10] These contemporary letters, vibrant with zeal and personal solicitude for the flock of Christ in the churches of Sicily and written by Gregory in the later summer and autumn of the year 593 (the period in which he was supposedly writing the *Dialogues*), stress Maximian's pressing responsibilities at that time and the Pope's insistence on his unremitting devotion to the duties he had deputed to him. In comparison, Epistola III.50, supposedly

---

[8] Epist. III.49; EH I.205–6.
[9] Epist. IV.11; EH I.243–4.
[10] Epist. IV.12; EH I.245–6.

written by Gregory to his vicar in July about a comparatively trivial matter, with its lame concluding clause which seems to ignore
the grave responsibilities on which Gregory insisted so strongly in
his other letters to Maximian, is shown up as incongruous and
implausible.

To those who assume that message to be genuine, one might put
a further objection, already alluded to above. What if Maximian,
justifiably taking the concluding words of Gregory's letter in July 593
as implicit encouragement to go off to Rome bearing the desired
sheaf of miracle tales, had acted on it? Would it not occur to the
pope, writing to his vicar in Sicily in September and October of
that year with instructions to carry out serious disciplinary measures,
that the bishop might well not be there to execute his stern injunc-
tions, since his own letter of July had equivalently allowed him freedom to leave his post and to journey to Rome to recount the
requested stories if he was so minded? It will not do, as an answer
to that objection, to suggest that perhaps Gregory was expecting
Maximian to travel to Rome for one of the *ad limina* visits that the
Sicilian bishops were obliged to make in order to consult and pay
homage to the successor of St Peter. In *PsGD* I recalled, with documentary confirmation, that Gregory had decreed that such visits
should take place only once every five years, to coincide with the
feast day of the Apostle, June 29th, and that the previous quin-
quennial visit of the Sicilian bishops had taken place the year previously, in 592.[11] It is quite clear that they were not free to leave
their sees when they felt inclined, either collectively or singly.

Gregory's ostensible timetable in composing the *Dialogues* is also
relevant to this discussion. It is commonly assumed that Maximian,
responding to his master's urgent request for the swift despatch of
hagiographical material, wrote back promptly as bidden, and that
Gregory received that material in time to use it when writing his
tale about Nonnosus. Although he wrote letters to Maximian in September and October that year, in neither of them does he make any
acknowledgement or mention of any such materials sent to him by
his vicar in Sicily. Nor, anywhere in his letters of that time or later,
does he refer to the literary project that was then assumedly engross-
ing him, in which Maximian is mentioned several times as an author-

---

[11] *PsGD*, pp. 70–71.

itative informant. That bishop was in the pope's disfavour at that time, and died some time before the end of the summer of 594.

There is another cogent reason against supposing that Gregory would have felt any need to appeal to Maximian to send him the details of miracle-stories that had "passed into oblivion" in his memory, for inclusion in a book of dialogues that he was preparing to write. It is the fact—already discussed at length in Chapter 9 above and now reluctantly admitted by defenders of the authenticity of the *Dialogues*, with confirmation from the researches of A. de Vogüé— that the author of that book was not reliant on the information of others for his tall tales but freely plagiarized and adapted his themes from other hagiographical sources and legends, and in many cases invented them himself! Why should he have to send to Sicily for details of such fantasies, and even prompt his Apostolic Vicar in that island to come to Rome to give him such details, when he could simply have invented them, as he did freely throughout his fictional narrative?

In Chapter 24 I answer the objection to my conclusion that the *Letter to Maximian* was a later "supporting forgery" is too far-fetched to be true. I show, on the contrary, that there is much historical evidence relating to the activities of the notaries and clerks in the Roman *Scrinium* in the later seventh century (among whom the Dialogist can be numbered) that makes such a conclusion not only possible but very probable. In the following chapter a further argument against the genuineness of the *Letter to Maximian* will appear: namely, that Gregory's situation and current preoccupations would have precluded his composition of the *Dialogues* at the time implied by the dating of that letter.

CHAPTER ELEVEN

INCONGRUITY OF THE ALLEGED DATE OF THE *DIALOGUES*' COMPOSITION, JUDGED IN THE CONTEXT OF CONTEMPORARY HISTORY

a

Clearly, the question of the putative date of the composition of the *Dialogues* is closely connected with the question of the dating of the *Letter to Maximian*. The ostensible *terminus ante quem non* for the composition of the book is provided by that letter, dated in July 593, announcing Gregory's intention of writing a book on the miracles of the Fathers of Italy and asking for details to include in it. The *terminus post quem non* is a letter in the register of Gregory's correspondence sent to his vicar in Sicily, Cyprian the Deacon, in which he recalled that the news of Maximian's death had reached him in November 594.[1] In the *Dialogues* Maximian is referred to three times as still living at the time of writing (*Dial.* I.7, II.36. IV, 33). On the supposition that Gregory was the author of that book, its final redaction and publication must therefore have been completed some time before that date—otherwise the author would surely have amended the textual references to Maximian to take account of his death. That time-span, from the summer of 593 to the autumn of 594, during which the *Dialogues* were ostensibly composed, can be narrowed down still further. The date 593 accords neatly with the threefold mention in the *Dialogues* of the plague that had ravaged Rome "*ante triennium*". That plague, mentioned in Gregory's *Homilies on the Gospels* and by Gregory of Tours, broke out in January 590 (and carried off Pope Pelagius II in February). It seems to have been over by January 591.[2] Another clue comes from *Dial.* IV.49, where the *soi-disant* Gregory refers to the burial of a monk John that had occurred "*ante hoc triennium*" when he himself was still living in the

---

[1] Epist. V.20; EH I.302.
[2] Cf. Vogüé, *SC* 265, p. 73, footnote.

monastic community of St Andrew and was thus not yet pope—presumably shortly before September 590 when he was elected. It is remarkable how the author of the *Dialogues* inserts these and other chronological references, as if to give historical consistency to his composition.

There are, however, some disagreements about the data. In *Dial.* III.19 there is mention of the great flood of the Tiber that inundated Rome "*ante hoc fere quinquennium*". This flood is usually dated by reference to a passage in the *Historia Francorum* of Gregory of Tours (10.1), which indicates its occurrence in November 589. Five years after that date would take us to November 594. Accordingly A. de Vogüé surmises that the flood reference in Book III of the *Dialogues* may have been written in the autumn of 594, even though the three plague references in Book IV date those chapters to the autumn of 593. He also tentatively suggests that two references to Bishop Venantius of Luna (in *Dial.* III.9.1 and IV.55.1) may be indications that those sections were being written shortly before May 594.[3] O. Chadwick (pointing out the relevance of his findings to the dating of the *Dialogues*) has argued that the passage referring to the flood in the *Historia Francorum* may be an interpolation made in the eighth century. In any case, the adverb "*fere*" in *Dial.* III.19 indicates only an approximate dating.

Apart from Vogüé, the historians who have discussed the issue agree that the *Dialogues* must have been completed around the end of the year 593. Why do they find it necessary to squeeze the time of its composition into the later months of that year? As well as the date of the *Letter to Maximian* and the thrice repeated "*ante triennium*" in the *Dialogues* references to the plague, which imply that the author was writing the book at that time, there are seen to be extraneous constraints that make it necessary to constrict still further the time-span of its composition. (It appears that the Dialogist himself was not sufficiently aware of those constraints when he devised a chronological pattern into which to fit the origin of his pseudo-Gregorian work.) We find that the putative starting date of the work, indicated by the *Letter to Maximian* dated in July 593, would have to be set still later to allow time for the final redaction and publication of Gregory's *Homilies on the Gospels* in that year. Moreover it appears

---

[3] Cf. *SC* 251, pp. 25, 26 (note 8) and *SC* 260, p. 287, note 1.

that the putative finishing date of the work must be set, not merely before news of Maximian's death reached Gregory in November 594, but no later than the autumn of 593, in order to take account of the date both of Gregory's preaching of his *Homilies on Ezekiel* and of the campaign of the Lombard king Agilulf culminating in the siege of Rome. When we examine these factors more closely we find that the ostensible date of the composition of the *Dialogues* can be seen to be clearly unrealistic.

The dating of the final redaction and publication of the authorized text of Gregory's *Homilies on the Gospels*, which, it is universally assumed, he preached to the people of Rome during the first three years of his pontificate, is found to be very relevant to the question of the dating of the *Dialogues*. Those homilies contain fourteen edifying stories of supernatural happenings, mainly at the deathbeds of saintly persons. Of those fourteen *exempla* no less that seven are retold in the *Dialogues*, with exact verbatim quotation in many places,[4] but in every case minus the moral that was the purpose of their telling in the original sermons. (They are the "narrative IGPs" discussed in Chapter 3.e above.) *Soi-disant* Gregory expressly says that he is repeating the narratives that he has earlier related to the people of Rome in his sermons on the Gospels. In a dedicatory letter (of uncertain date)[5] to Bishop Secundinus of Taormina prefixed to the *Homiliae in Evangelia*, Gregory recalled that at an earlier stage an unauthorized text of them, based on *reportata* taken down by "the brethren", had been in circulation; and that later he himself had corrected that defective text and had sanctioned an authorized edition. He further stated that any unamended codices could be corrected by reference to a master copy kept in the Roman *Scrinium*. Since the *Homilies on the Gospels*, in the authorized text as it has come down to us, were cited at length in the *Dialogues*, and since time must be allowed for the earlier issue and widespread circulation of the unauthorized version, the dating of the production of the *Homilies* sets some seemingly insoluble problems.

---

[4] G. Pfeilschifter gives a useful table of those duplications, showing the correlations between them, in his study, *Die authentische Ausgabe des 40 Evangelienhomilien Gregors der Grosse*, Munich 1900 (reprinted 1970).

[5] Ewald-Hartmann assumed, because they accepted unquestioningly the authenticity and dating of the *Dialogues*, that this dedicatory letter was written in the middle of 593. (Cf. EH I.251 & note.)

Ewald and Hartmann indeed deduced that the last homily, preached on a second Sunday after Pentecost, must be dated as late as May 1st 593, which implies an impossibly short time between the delivery of that sermon and the composition of the *Dialogues* in the late summer or autumn of 593. On their hypothesis, it would be necessary to fit into those four or five months the following sequence of events: the transcription and widespread circulation to distant places of the first and unauthorized edition of the Gospel homilies; the subsequent recall of those *reportata*; and the redaction of an emended and authorized edition by Gregory, to be available for verbatim citation in the *Dialogues*. Understandably Pfeilschifter found that hypothesis too difficult to accept. His alternative solution—which nevertheless has its own serious difficulties—is to compress the preaching of Gregory's Gospel homilies into a short cycle at the beginning of his pontificate, and to date the issue of "the authentic edition of the *Homilies* in the first half of the year 593, if not already in the second half of the year 592".[6] This theory is contradicted by the documentary evidence.

I would argue, therefore, that the common assumption referred to above, namely that the authorized edition of Gregory's *Homiliae in Evangelia* must have been completed before the autumn of 593 (i.e. in order to be available for them to be quoted verbatim in the *Dialogues* at that time), needs critical reconsideration and correction. If one prescinds from the supposition that the *Dialogues* were written by Gregory in that year, it will be seen to be much more reasonable to assign the date for the finally authorized redaction of those Gospel homilies to a later period, nearer the end of his life. It will also be reasonable to doubt the assumption that all those sermons were preached in the earliest period of his pontificate.

Another consideration which naturally weighs heavily with Pfeilschifter and other authors is the need to allow time for Gregory to write the *Dialogues* before he became taken up with the preparation and delivery of his *Homilies on Ezekiel* in the late autumn. Thereafter followed the desperate winter of the Lombard onslaught and siege of Rome, during which, as Pfeilschifter repeatedly observes, further literary composition on Gregory's part was out of the question. Although the exact dating of those events is not without obscurities,

---

[6] *Op. cit.*, p. 95.

there is sufficient historical evidence to demonstrate the dire threat that the Lombard army presented to Rome and its bishop in the closing months of the year 593.[7] It is instructive to examine the dating of events in that period more closely, since it is very relevant to the supposed dating of the composition of the *Dialogues.*

b. *The Lombard onslaught and the dating of the* Dialogues

Ever since the Lombard duke Ariulf had come to power in the duchy of Spoleto in 591 he had menaced the Roman territory. In the summer of 592 he invaded it, while the other Lombard duke, Arichis of Benevento, ravaged Campania to the south and threatened Naples. When Ariulf advanced on Rome, Gregory succeeded in buying him off with tribute from the papal treasury.[8] A counter-attack against the Lombards in central Italy by the imperial exarch provoked the Lombard king himself to intervene. In 593 Agilulf set out with a formidable army from his capital at Pavia, which crossed the Po and marched south, conquering, slaughtering and pillaging as it went. After capturing Perugia, Agilulf's host continued Romewards and arrived before the walls to lay siege to the city. At the same time Arichis moved up from the south with a force to support his overlord. That Agilulf's descent upon Rome took place in the second half of the year 593 is clear, but it is disputed whether it happened earlier or later in that period. Weise and Dudden argued that the later summer was a more probable time, on the grounds that a winter campaign would have been unfeasible in that age. However, an autumn march southwards to Rome and a winter siege of the city would have been quite possible in the Italian climate. There are many other examples of winter campaigning in the peninsula. During the Gothic wars the army of Belisarius was active in central Italy during the winter of 536–7, when the Ostrogothic king Vitigis marched against him near Ravenna. The fighting of those winter months led up to a great siege of Rome early in March 537. Again, if it is objected that Agilulf could not have made a winter march from Pavia to Rome, it may be replied that one of his successors, the

---

[7] Cf. J. Richards, *Consul of God*, pp. 181–7.
[8] Epist. II.45; EH I.144.

Lombard king Aistulf, did just that in the winter of 754–5, arriving before the walls of Rome in January.[9]

Against the theory of a date in late summer for the invasion is the fact that we possess several routine letters of Gregory from those months in 593 which give no hint of a crisis or any special danger at that time. A positive proof that Agilulf had not yet marched on Rome before the autumn can be seen from two letters written by Gregory in September of that year.[10] One was to Constantius, archbishop of Milan, in which he asked that prelate to send him a discreet report on what Agilulf was doing, and authorized him to intimate to the latter that the pope himself would be willing to act as a mediator between the king and the imperial exarch. Such instructions are not reconcilable with the hypothesis that Agilulf's southward march to besiege Rome was already in progress at that time. The other letter was to Queen Theodelinda, Agilulf's wife. It concerned the schism and theological controversy over the "Three Chapters" dispute and the dogmatic definition of Chalcedon—which would hardly have been an apposite subject for discussion if at that very time the queen's fierce husband was threatening slaughter and ruin to Gregory's city and people.

The opinion of Weise and Dudden, dating Agilulf's descent upon Rome in the late summer of 593 is a minority one. From all the available indications, Ewald-Hartmann and other authors judge that the Lombard siege of Rome lasted from about December 593 to March 594. (It ended, apparently, when Agilulf agreed to accept payment by Gregory of a ransom of 500 pounds of gold.)[11] A significant pointer to those dates is provided by the complete cessation during those four months of all recorded pontifical correspondence.[12] If the siege itself began in or shortly before December the beginning of Agilulf's preliminary campaign must be set considerably earlier. Even with forced marches and swiftly successful fighting it would have taken his army at least two months to make its way from northern Italy across the Po valley, then southwards through the Apennines, defeating the hostile forces in its path, besieging and

---

[9] P. Llewellyn, *Rome in the Dark Ages*, London 1970, pp. 213–4.
[10] Epist. IV.2 & IV.4 (EH I.233–5, 236).
[11] Cf. *Continuation of the Chronicle of Prosper of Havnium*, in *MGH, Auctores antiquissimi*, IX, 339.
[12] Cf. EH I.319, note 2.

capturing Perugia before marching down the Tiber valley to the
walls of Rome.

The most informative source we have concerning Agilulf's siege
of Rome is the text of Gregory's *Homilies on Ezekiel*, which, according to M. Adriaen, the editor of the *CCL* edition, were delivered in
the closing months of the year 593.[13] In this he follows the sequence
of events established by Pfeilschifter. Those homilies bear the marks
of intense meditation and laborious preparation—for example, in the
carefully worked out explanation, given in the first homily, of the
various kinds of prophecy. Although, as Gregory afterwards recalled
when editing them, they were preached *coram populo*, it would seem
that he had chiefly in mind the clerics and monks who would hear
and read his words. The ordinary populace of Rome would not have
found it easy to follow the mystical profundity of his exposition. It
is relevant to cite his references in those sermons to contemporary
events, since they throw a vivid light on his preoccupations at the
very time in which he is supposed by some authors to have been
also composing the *Dialogues*. He had begun the series of sermons
before the threat to Rome by Agilulf had arisen. In the first eight
of them there is no hint of anything untoward. In the ninth homily
there is what seems to be a reference to the hostile incursions of the
Lombard dukes, when he speaks of his people as being "*afflicti, obsessi,
conclusi*". Then, in the thirteenth homily, there is news of a dramatic
development: news has come of impending attack from the north
by the army of the Lombard king. Gregory announces that he is
now so oppressed by anxieties that he cannot proceed with an orderly
commentary on the scriptural text; omitting some 36 chapters of the
sacred book, he will go straight on to expound the meaning of
Ezekiel's culminating vision in Chapter 40:

> Under the pressure of many cares, I cannot expound before you the
> book of the prophet Ezekiel in due order. Nevertheless, your good
> desires have led you to ask that at least I should expound the prophet's
> final vision . . . And indeed I feel bound to comply with your wish, but
> there are two things that here dismay my spirit. The first is that the
> vision is shrouded by such dark mists that whatever it contains can
> hardly be perceived by our mind's light. The other is that we have
> learned that Agilulf the king of the Lombards has already crossed the
> Po and is hastening with all speed to besiege us.

---

[13] "*anno 593 exeunte*"; *op. cit.*, p. V.

Gregory's ever increasing distress and his pressing responsibilities in the defence of the city were reflected in subsequent homilies. He spoke of his duties both in providing for those in need and in "keeping watchful guard over the defences of the city against the swords of enemies, lest the citizens should perish from a sudden assault". When he came to preach his eighteenth homily the Lombard army was closely investing Rome and bringing terror and death to its citizens. He recorded: "We see men led away into slavery, others have their limbs cut off, others are slain . . . Swords and tribulations now oppress us daily . . ." At the end of his twenty-second homily he announced with anguish that he could not go further:

> Let no one blame me if after this address I preach no more, since, as you all see, our tribulations have increased beyond measure. On all sides we are surrounded by swords and face fearfully the imminent peril of death . . . For how can one to whom life itself is denied find pleasure in declaring the hidden meaning of sacred Scripture? And how can I, who am forced to drink daily from a bitter cup, offer sweet draughts to others?

Defenders of the authenticity of the *Dialogues* would have us believe that in those same months of the Lombard offensive Gregory had the time and inclination to devote himself to the exacting literary task of composing that complex narrative of miracles and apparitions. Try as they may, they find it virtually impossible to disengage the period in which the *Dialogues* were ostensibly being composed from the period of Gregory's greatest distress and his daily involvement in urgent pastoral and civic duties. We have seen, from the *Letter to Maximian* and from the chronological clues that the author of the *Dialogues* gives in his text, that the substantial work of composing that book was supposedly being carried out in the last four or five months of the year 593. Yet firmer chronological evidence indicates that in those very same months Pope Gregory was first engaged upon the preparation and delivery of his earlier expository homilies on *Ezekiel* and then plunged into the prolonged crisis and terror of the Lombard siege.

Pfeilschifter tries to reconcile the conflicting data by postulating an implausibly short time for Gregory's composition of the *Dialogues*, thus supposing that it was squeezed in before the commencement of the delivery of the *Homilies on Ezekiel* in the late autumn, and the subsequent onset of the Lombard campaign. On close consideration of the period in which that series of homilies were preached it appears that to assign such a late date to their commencement is unrealistic. According to the commonly agreed chronology, the siege of Rome began in or shortly before December 593. As we have seen, the first reference in the *Homilies* to the siege of Rome was in the eighteenth sermon; the thirteenth sermon announcing Agilulf's crossing of the Po must be dated many weeks before that. Thus, even though the earlier homilies were preached at much shorter intervals, the start of the series cannot reasonably be dated any later than about the beginning of October 593.

It is clear, then, that there are serious difficulties in the traditional view, based on indications in the text of the *Dialogues*, that Gregory was engaged in writing that book in the autumn of 593, and that it was substantially completed by the close of that year, apart from some final touches in 594. We know that those autumn months were a time of emergency, of anguish and of unremitting responsibilities for the pope and his staff. His pastoral zeal motivated him to continue the preparation and delivery of his sermons on *Ezekiel*, but as time went on he was worn down by the Lombard menace and atrocities, and by his own daily duties in maintaining the defence of his flock and city. Eventually he no longer had the time, energy or heart even to continue the sacred task of expounding the word of God for his trembling flock. It is implausible indeed to suppose that in that autumn fraught with dangers, distress and unremitting duty, Gregory chose to compose the fanciful book of *Dialogues*.

The *soi-disant* Gregory of the *Dialogues* does indeed remark that at the time of writing he has many cares and distractions, and expresses nostalgic longing for his lost peace.[14] Some commentators have expressed the view that Gregory wrote the *Dialogues* as a pleasant *jeu d'esprit* and a relief from official preoccupations. So E.R. Hardy writes: "One cannot help feeling that the *Dialogues* have rather the character of a recreation among his more serious works and business activities".[15] However, those who suggest that Gregory turned to writing the *Dialogues* as a diversion can hardly have considered the time and circumstances in which he is supposed to have done so. Even if he had been able to find the time, energy and opportunity to write such a work in those months of constant duties and dangers, is it

---

[14] *Dial.* Prologue, 1–4; & III.38.5.
[15] "Servant of the servants of God", in *Church History*, XII (1943), p. 22.

plausible to suppose that the real Gregory, whose character and spirit we know so well from the works in which he pours out his pastoral zeal and his spiritual ideals, would have considered it a worthy use of his time and talents in that time of crisis to devote himself to writing a book of fictional folk-tales as an escape from the stern demands of his apostolic duty? Composition of the *Dialogues* would have been no brief task. It is a complex and carefully crafted work which (even in the pontiff's normal situation, with its manifold and inescapable demands on his time) would have required several months to compose. The author clearly went to considerable pains to collect and arrange his material, and to weave his narrative with an undeniable artistry.

So we see that, despite the many attempts that have been made to reconcile the conflicting data, there remain insurmountable difficulties which show that the *Dialogues* could not have been composed by St Gregory at the date ostensibly indicated by the *Letter to Maximian* and by references in the text of the book. After tracing the intricacies of this tangled skein, perhaps some puzzled readers may put forward the following objection to the case I have presented here: "According to your analysis, the Dialogist deliberately chose a clearly delimited span of time, the fourth year of Gregory's pontificate, in which to situate the alleged composition of the *Dialogues* by the pope. In the *Letter to Maximian* which he interpolated into the files of Gregory's letters, and also in the text of the *Dialogues* itself, he provided chronological indications that restrict the period of the book's composition to a period of a few months in the second half of the year 593. Now if, as you argue, the Dialogist was sufficiently well-informed and astute to achieve chronological consistency in thus setting the stage for the book's origin, why did he fall into what can be seen to be an obvious blunder by making Gregory compose the *Dialogues* in that most traumatic period of his pontificate, during the same months that he was first engaged in the preparation and preaching of his *Homilies on Ezekiel* and then overwhelmed by the cares and tribulations of the Lombard onslaught and siege of Rome? His incessant responsibilities and afflictions during that period of crisis are well documented. Surely the Dialogist, if he was as astute as you claim, would have chosen a more peaceful year of Gregory's reign as the setting for his pseudepigraphical work?"

I reply that I do find the Dialogist to be astutely alert to observe chronological consistency, doubtless mindful of possible suspicions of colleagues and rivals in the papal *Scrinium* in his own day who, like himself, had access to the archive record of Gregory's letters and other relevant sources. In that very archive he had at hand an accurate framework of historical time-reference, namely the dating given there of all Gregory's letters by the year and month of the relative Indiction. That framework would normally have enabled him to choose an appropriate point in Gregory's pontificate at which to situate the composition of the *Dialogues*. He also had the aid of some datings given by Gregory of Tours, and there were some other chronological indications to be gleaned from the *Homilies on the Gospels* and the *Moralia*. However, although we now have fuller documentary information, the Dialogist would not have available any clear indication of the *year* in which the *Homilies on Ezekiel* were delivered and Agilulf's siege of Rome occurred. The register of Gregory's letters has a significant gap in the very period during which the Lombard offensive against Rome was taking place. It appears that none were sent or written during those months of crisis and siege. Moreover, nowhere in Gregory's surviving correspondence is there any indication of the date either of the Lombard offensive against Rome or of the delivery of the *Homilies on Ezekiel* within that period. The only letter in the register in which Gregory refers to the siege (written to the Emperor to justify his conduct and that of the Roman officials in that hour of crisis) was dated in June 595, and it makes no mention of the date at which the crisis occurred. The Dialogist might reasonably have supposed from the date of the letter that the Lombard offensive, and Gregory's delivery of the *Homilies on Ezekiel* which refer to it, had occurred in the period immediately preceding the letter to the Emperor (that is, 594–5) and not in the previous year. He would therefore have mistakenly assumed that the autumn of 593 was a plausible time in which to set the composition of his pseudepigraphical fiction.

c. *Other constraints precluding such composition by Gregory*

I draw attention to another alien feature of the *Dialogues*. It has already been referred to above. Leaving aside the *Dialogues*, it can be seen that after the completion of his magisterial *Regula Pastoralis* in the first year of his pontificate, he never again had time for laborious literary composition. The sequential structure of the works that

he produced after that was determined by their character as homilies and expositions of Scripture. They followed the order of the
sacred text or the homiletic task before him. The *Dialogues* on the
other hand, although inferior to all Gregory's works in expression,
content and spiritual perspective, have a carefully designed character, and are the product of literary striving and wide use of previous hagiographical sources. They "smell of the lamp". The fourth
book in particular, despite its limping logic and inconsequentiality,
has pretensions to be a laboured mini-treatise demonstrating the
immortality of the soul.

All the works that Gregory produced after AD 591 were originated by the spoken word. To meet the administrative and pastoral
needs of his office he dictated his letters to secretaries, or approved
drafts that they had prepared. His scriptural commentaries or homilies were likewise taken down in the first place by stenographers
from his spoken word. Sometimes he would prepare the text by med-
itative reflection and then deliberately dictate it to secretaries for
later use and publication. More often his method was simply to
expound the word of God by commenting viva voce on the book
of Scripture open before him (*"ante oculos"*), while scribes took down
his extempore reflections as he uttered them. Later, he edited and
amended their transcripts when that proved possible. Thus originated the large body of Gregorian *reportata* referred to in a letter
written by Gregory near the end of his life (the "Claudian Collection"
referred to in Chapter 3.b above). He expressly stated the reason
why literary composition, even editing, had been impossible for him
in the preceding years: "Because of my infirmity I could not put
those discourses in written form". Habitually weighed down by the
pressing cares of his office and his chronic maladies,[16] Gregory had
less and less time to devote to laborious literary work. Although his
Homilies on Ezekiel were prepared and delivered around the time of
Agilulf's offensive against Rome in 593, they were not edited by him
and authorized for publication until eight years later, shortly before
the end of his life.

The story of the revision and publication of Gregory's main work,
the *Moralia*, is also relevant to the present question. In a letter of

---

[16] J. Richards well documents Gregory's "crippling burden of illness"; *op. cit.*, pp.
45–7.

April 591 Gregory told his well beloved friend and former associate at the imperial court in Constantinople, Bishop Leander of Seville, at whose urging that great commentary on *Job* had first been undertaken and to whom it was dedicated, that he had been labouring to put into book form the shorthand notes of that dictated commentary taken down by the monks who had heard it uttered, and now hoped to send it to him very soon. The scribes, he said, were already busy on the codices. However, so busy and harassed by tribulations was he during the four years from 591 to 595 that it was not until the end of that period that he could complete the editing of the main section of the *Moralia*, which one would suppose would have been a first priority in his literary activity. It was not until July 595 that another letter to Leander announced the sending off of the long-delayed codices, which even then lacked two out of the six parts which made up the whole. At the same time Gregory apologized for writing such a short note, explaining that he was overwhelmed by the pressure of his official duties: "The brevity of my letter shows Your Charity how much I am weighed down by the massive force of the affairs of this Church, seeing that I say so little in it to the one whom I love above all others".[17] Yet although he never found time or opportunity during those four years to see to the completion and despatch of the missing parts of his major doctrinal work, which he had promised as a debt of friendship to his dearest friend, it is supposed that he chose to devote considerable time and effort during the busiest and darkest months during those four years to the writing of a substantial and detailed legendary work, the *Dialogues*, which he was under no similar obligation to produce and which could not have been seen to be a necessary and urgently pressing task.

---

[17] Epist. V.53; EH I.58.

CHAPTER TWELVE

THE *DIALOGUES* UNKNOWN IN GREGORY'S AGE AND FOR LONG AFTERWARDS: TELL-TALE INTERPOLATIONS IN MANUSCRIPT RECORDS IN LATER TIMES

a

A principal reason that has persuaded many scholars to accept the *Dialogues* as a genuine work of Gregory the Great is the assumption that a continuous chain of documentary evidence, reaching back to the end of the sixth century, attests his authorship. They take it as proved that the book was known in his own lifetime; that it enjoyed fame among his contemporaries; and that during the first half of the seventh century and later it became ever more widely read and quoted. When the early records are critically scrutinized, however, those confident claims collapse. There proves to be no reliable contemporary evidence that anyone knew of the existence of the *Dialogues* either in Gregory's own lifetime or for some eighty years after his death. Rather, we find that sources that would surely be expected to attest the existence of the work are significantly silent about it.

It is of course no sufficient proof of Gregory's authorship to show that it has been traditionally assumed for some thirteen centuries. There are many once traditional attributions of ancient works that have been disproved by the advance of literary criticism. Nor is it a sufficient proof of authenticity to argue that the *Life* of St Benedict narrated in the Gregorian *Dialogues* has been a foundation document in the development of Western monasticism. There are not a few legendary works that have influenced the expression of Christian piety in the history of the Church. However, defenders of the Gregorian authorship of the *Dialogues* have not relied only on such general suasions, but have put forward explicit arguments which, they claim, show that the work was known as authentically Gregory's in his own age and in the period immediately following. The chief of those arguments, based on the putative *Letter to Maximian* and claimed by the modern-day defenders of the authenticity of the

Dialogues to be the principal "bedrock proof" of their case, has already been discussed in the Chapters 10 and 11 and shown to be non-probative. In this chapter I discuss some supposedly authoritative testimonies dating from the seventh century that have been widely influential in building up the general conviction that the *Dialogues* were known and accepted as Gregorian in that period. In the light of the documentary evidence now available, not one of them survives critical scrutiny. Instead, that evidence indicates positively that there was a long-continuing silence about the very existence of the *Dialogues* in Gregory's age and for long afterwards, which is all the more remarkable in view of the great renown of his writings. His published works were known, referred to and quoted as his in contemporary writings during that period—but the *Dialogues* were not. It was not until the close of the seventh century that the work emerged into the light of history, and not until the first quarter of the eighth century that it began to provide inspiration for the great new expansion of Benedictine monasticism in that century.

From his letters we see that Gregory was much concerned with the editing and transmission of his writings. In them is found repeated mention of all the authentic writings that he authorized for publication. We have seen that he took particular care with the revision of the text of his works before he would authorize them for circulation. Yet, although the *Dialogues* ostensibly date from the earlier part of his pontificate and show evidence of careful planning and contrivance, we search in vain for any mention of them in the hundreds of letters that he wrote after that date. We find there record of his sending presentation copies of his works to bishops and priests in different regions. There are explicit references to his *Moralia*, or *Commentary on Job*, which is prefaced with a letter dedicating it to his friend Leander of Seville. There are several references to his *Regula Pastoralis*, of which he sent copies to Bishop Leander, to a priest Columba and to Bishop Venantius of Luna.[1] From a letter of 603 we learn that the Emperor himself had requested a copy of that work, which was also in the possession of a deacon Anatolius, and that Bishop Anastasius of Antioch had it translated into Greek.[2] He sent an authentic copy of the two codices of his *Homilies on the Gospels*

---

[1] Epist. V.53,17; EH I.352, 299.
[2] Epist. XII.6; EH II.352–3.

to Bishop Secundinus of Taormina, with a letter carefully explaining how those homilies had been composed, and urging the bishop to see that any incorrect copies were duly emended according to the authorized text.[3] With a letter of 599 he sent another presentation copy of those *Homilies* to a hermit, likewise named Secundinus.[4] There is also a letter sent by Gregory in AD 601 to Marinianus, bishop of Ravenna, together with an edited copy of his *Homilies on Ezekiel*, which he had authored in the dark days of 593 and which he had never in the intervening eight years had time to revise for publication.[5] The commentary was nevertheless in unauthorized circulation, since in his letter to Gregory the Irish monastic founder Columban requested a copy of the work, the fame of which had reached him.[6]

However, despite the fame of those writings, and Gregory's constant concern for their editing and transmission, there is nowhere in the *Registrum* of his letters (leaving out of account the discredited *Letter to Maximian*) any mention of the *Dialogues*, which one would surely expect to be known and eagerly sought after if they then existed. According to a statement attributed in the book to Gregory himself, that account of so many miraculous events was compiled at the request of the brethren in the papal household, and would thus surely have become widely known after publication. The inclusion of Peter the Deacon, a prominent Roman cleric, as the pope's interlocutor in the book would naturally add to its interest in curial circles. Well-known contemporary personalities, including correspondents of the pope, are referred to in the text, all of whom would have been keenly interested in what was said there. I comment below on the special significance of the lack of all mention of the *Dialogues* in contemporary Spain, where Gregory's writings were avidly sought.

Before turning to the evidence from the seventh century, showing the continuing *incognito* of the *Dialogues*, I recall a remarkable speculation of P. Meyvaert, one of the three chief critics of *PsGD*. He was sufficiently impressed by the case made there to be ready to concede that Gregory purposely withheld publication of that book during his lifetime. He commented:

---

[3] Epist. IV.17a; EH I.251–2.
[4] Epist. IX.147; EH II.148.
[5] Epist XII.16a; EH II.363.
[6] "*mihi idcirco tua sitienti largire precor, quae in Ezechielem miro modo ut audivi elaborasti ingenio*" (*PL* 80.263).

Each of Gregory's other works has a dedicatory letter to a particular
person . . . These dedicatory letters are integral parts of the works they
introduce; they get transmitted with these works and not through Gregory's correspondence in the *Registrum*. It seems to have been Gregory's
practice to attach such a letter as an indication that he was publishing the work. No such letter is attached to the *Dialogues*. We are therefore entitled to ask whether the *Dialogues* were ever published, that is,
released by the author to be copied and read outside his own immediate circle.

Pondering on those facts, Meyvaert concluded: "It is the absence of
any evidence regarding the circulation of the *Dialogues* that presents
us with an enigma that is still unresolved". He proceeded to speculate subtly on the reasons that may have led Gregory not to publish the work.[7] He even remarked in conclusion: "We can be grateful
to Francis Clark for calling attention to an anomaly in the early history of the work". A. de Vogüé objected to the concession of his
confrère on this issue, and wrote a rebuttal of his speculations.[8]

b. *Alleged testimonies*: In 1 Regum *and a letter to a queen*

The *Letter to Maximian* is not the only document supposedly written
by Gregory himself that has been traditionally alleged to confirm
the authenticity of the *Dialogues*. The scriptural commentary on the
first book of *Kings*, likewise commonly ascribed to him, was presented
as corroboration of his authorship of the *Dialogues*. In that work the
text of the *Regula Benedicti* is cited, and its author is lauded in a
phrase that evokes the parallel praise of St Benedict and his rule
found in the *Dialogues*. When I, with K. Hallinger and others, pointed
out the strange absence of any proof of observance of the Benedictine
rule in Gregory's lifetime—and, indeed, the positive indications to
the contrary—the defenders of the traditional assumptions, A. de
Vogüé and P. Meyvaert in particular, ridiculed my arguments and
insisted on the certainty of Gregory's authorship of *In 1 Regum* as
confirming beyond doubt that the *RB* was already famous and that
Gregory must have been the author of the biography of St Benedict

---

[7] *JEH* 39 (1988), pp. 372–81.
[8] In his article, "*Les Dialogues, oeuvre authenique et publiées pas Grégoire lui-même*", in
the symposium, *Gregorio Magno e il suo tempo*, Rome 1991, vol. II, pp. 27–40.

in the *Dialogues*. Others, including a distinguished historian of late antiquity, R.A. Markus, have relied on their authoritative assurance. I recalled above, in Chapter 2.c, how those two distinguished critics, constrained by a disconcerting discovery made in a mediaeval chronicle by Vogüé himself, have abruptly changed their minds and now jointly affirm that the composer of the commentary *In 1 Regum*, with its eulogy of Benedict and his rule, was a twelfth-century Benedictine abbot—as indeed I had argued in *PsGD* from the many discrepancies and anachronisms discernible in the text. Since they have now disowned their previous certainty that the commentary was wholly and solely the work of Gregory, and now ascribe it to Peter of Cava, it seems unnecessary to rehearse here the multiple arguments presented in *PsGD* to demonstrate that the work was not fashioned by Gregory and that the references in it to the *RB* and its author were of twelfth-century date.[9]

Apart from the supposititious *Letter to Maximian* and the commentary *In 1 Regum*, there is another documentary reference which has been traditionally adduced as proof that the *Dialogues* were extant in Gregory's lifetime. It is claimed that he himself sent a presentation copy of the book to the Lombard Queen Theodelinda, who was a Catholic (though inclined to favour schismatic clerics).[10] The claim, based solely on an unsubstantiated assertion by Paul Warnefrid in his *History of the Lombards*, written about AD 787, has been given wide credence. It was even conjectured by the Maurist editors of Gregory's works that the eventual conversion of the Lombards to the Catholic faith was largely promoted through that putative gift to their queen, who, they supposed, used the book to convert her husband, King Agilulf, and the whole Lombard nation. From that supposition they derived a quaint argument for the credibility of the stupendous miracles related in the book: "Therein many miracles are narrated which were performed before the very eyes of the army of the Lombards. Now unless those miracles were certainly evident, and confirmed by the testimony of them all, the Lombards—whom, because of their ferocity, Gregory describes as more like bears than

---

[9] The arguments are set out in Chapter 11(E) of *PsGD*. They are summarized in my article in *Rev. Bén.* 108 (1988), pp. 67–70. Against Vogüé and Meyvaert, I argue nevertheless that *In 1 Regum* contains many insertions of genuine Gregorian material.

[10] For fuller discussion of these issues, cf. *PsGD*, pp. 59–64.

men—would have voiced their derision, and would have burned with greater hatred than before against the Catholic faith and the Roman Church".[11]

There is a strong antecedent improbability that Pope Gregory would have sent any such work as a gift to the Lombard queen. The villains of the *Dialogues* are unmistakably the Lombards. The book resounds with bitter denunciations of their cruelty and perfidy and with descriptions of their sacrilegious atrocities. It can be seen to reflect the horrified folk-memories of the monks and countryfolk of seventh-century Italy, still under threat from marauding Lombards. We have letters from Gregory to Theodelinda, dating from the very months in which Gregory is assumed to have been writing the *Dialogues*, in which he shows himself earnestly concerned to influence her, and through her, her fierce husband Agilulf, towards a policy that would bring some measure of peace to the troubled Italian peninsula and of reassurance for the Church and city of Rome. In his letters and in his *Homilies on Ezekiel* Gregory does indeed lament the miseries inflicted on the people of Italy by the *"nefandissima Langobardorum gens"*; but in his letters to Queen Theodelinda and the Lombard court he is intent on winning their goodwill. In the period in which he allegedly sent to the queen a gift of the *Dialogues* his relations with the Lombard rulers were particularly difficult and delicate. Only a short time previously Agilulf's army had ravaged central Italy and besieged Rome, committing atrocities before Gregory's own eyes, withdrawing only after exacting a heavy tribute. In that time of constant danger and political uncertainty, would the prudent Pope have sent to the Lombard court a book, written by himself, that depicted the Lombards in the worst possible light, as sadistic murderers, as enemies of God, as seemingly fiends incarnate?

There are phrases in Paul Warnefrid's eighth-century report of Gregory's gift to the queen that have assonances with phrases from the pope's letters to her preserved in the *Registrum* of his correspondence. Paul was given to romancing, as editors of his work have noticed. (Waitz describes his history as *"narratio vivacior quam verior"*.) References in Gregory's letters to the queen's admirable faith and good works, and to some gifts that he was sending her, seem to be echoed by the phrases used by Paul in the passage in question. Why,

---

[11] In the preface to their edition of the *Dialogues, PL* 77, col. 139.

one may ask, would Paul link the *Dialogues* and the Lombards in an invented episode? He knew well and treasured that book, which in his day had emerged into the light of fame. He was himself a leading figure in the rise of Benedictine monasticism which had been spurred by the biography of St Benedict assumedly written by St Gregory in his *Dialogues*. In his *History of the Lombards* (his *magnum opus*), how could he relevantly bring in a reference to that Gregorian work? An answer to the difficulty would be to make Gregory send a copy of it to the most famous of Lombard queens, Theodolinda.

c. *The alleged witness of the* Liber Pontificalis

I now take account of the traditional claims that explicit mention of Gregory's authorship of the *Dialogues* can be found in documents which date from the period following his pontificate and which refer to and list his writings. The most impressive and influential of those claims was the appeal to the allegedly certain attestation of Gregory's authorship of the work contained in the *Liber Pontificalis* (*LP*), the official chronicle of the Roman see. It has been edited both by L. Duchesne and by T. Mommsen, with detailed documentation of the manuscript tradition and variant MS readings.[12] The brief biographical record of the pontificate of Pope Gregory I given there can safely be dated to the early years of the seventh century. Duchesne gives good reason for concluding that it was written very soon after his death. The *LP* record, preserved in the curial archives, seems to provide decisive proof that the *Dialogues* were the work of Pope Gregory and were known as such by his contemporaries. It provides a list of his writings, as follows: "*Hic exposuit omelias evangeliorum numero XL, Job, Ezechielum, Pastoralem et Dialogorum et multa alia quae enumerare non possumus*".[13] Here it appears that the *LP* chronicler expressly included the *Dialogues* (albeit in an oddly inapposite genitive case) in the list of Gregory's extant works, together with the names of all his main expository and pastoral writings.

---

[12] Duchesne, *Le Liber Pontificalis: texte, introduction et commentaire*: original edition, Paris 1886–92; reprinted, with additions and corrections by C. Vogel in the supplementary vol. III, 1955–1957. I refer also to Mommsen's edition, *MGH*, Berlin 1898.

[13] Duchesne, *op. cit.*, I, p. 312.

Until very recently the testimony of the *LP* has been generally accepted by scholars as conclusive contemporary proof of Gregory's authorship of the *Dialogues*. Understandably, appeal to it was the first objection brought to refute my challenge to the authenticity of the work when I presented it at the Chantilly conference in 1981.[14] Nevertheless, that consensus has now been effectively confounded. In *PsGD* I showed, from investigation of the manuscript history of the text, that, far from attesting Gregory's authorship of the work, the *LP* provides a striking argument against that attribution. My detailed proof that the words "*et Dialogorum*" were not in the original seventh-century text of the *LP* but were interpolated into the MS transcription of that text in a later century, fills nearly five pages in *PsGD*.[15] Crucial is the fact that those two words are found to be lacking in four different manuscript families in the earliest tradition. I do not reproduce that lengthy demonstration here, since it is now generally admitted to be conclusive, even by the chief defenders of the authenticity of the *Dialogues*. R. Godding conceded that the absence of the *Dialogues* from the original text of the *LP* list has been shown to be *réel*.[16] A. de Vogüé eventually recognized the fact, though at first reluctant to do so.[17]

At what probable date was the interpolation in the MS tradition of the *LP* made? The scribe who first made it evidently lived at a period when the *Dialogues* had become the most famous of St Gregory's writings, and it would have appeared strange to him when transcribing the official record not to include that work in the list of those writings. The oldest surviving MSS in which the words "*et Dialogorum*" are found point to their interpolation in the eighth century, even as early as the pontificate of Gregory II (715–731).[18] It was during his reign that the fame and influence of the *Dialogues* began to spread widely, leading to "the new Benedictine movement" and the building up of the monastery of Montecassino—a development that I trace in Chapter 19.

[14] The objection was raised there by Professor G. Cracco, who later gracefully acknowledged that my detection of the spuriousness of that mention of the *Dialogues* in the *LP* record was conclusive.
[15] *PsGD*, pp. 54–58.
[16] *AB* 106 (1988), p. 203.
[17] Cf. *RHE* 83 (1988), p. 296, note 1.
[18] Cf. *PsGD*, p. 58.

I add a concluding comment on a tenuous plea that has been put forward as an explanation of the omission of the *Dialogues* from the list of Gregory's writings in the *LP*. It had been inferred (by P. Llewellyn)[19] that after Gregory's death there was reaction against his memory on the part of the Roman clergy, who resented his employment of monks in the papal Curia and the diminution of their own privileges. A. de Vogüé argued accordingly that it is not surprising if a Gregorian writing favouring monks remained in eclipse at that time, and that omission of its title in the *LP* entry may reflect such feeling.[20] I answer that even though such a factor may have been operative in Rome (and in any case whatever anti-Gregorian feeling there may have been among the Roman clerics was limited and short-lived) it is a far-fetched conjecture to suppose that the *notarius* in the Roman Curia who wrote the notice on Gregory in the *LP* would have been constrained by it to omit mention of a principal work of the pope when listing his writings. Moreover such a postulated inhibition would not apply to the rest of Christendom. Vogüé's strained plea could not explain why other seventh-century authorities also omitted mention of the *Dialogues* when listing and lauding Gregory's works. Later in this chapter I recall how avidly the works of St Gregory were copied and sought in his own lifetime and throughout the seventh century, especially in Spain and England. "We are yours, and it is in your writings that we take delight", wrote Bishop Licinianus of Cartagena in a letter to the pope lauding his *Regula Pastoralis* and begging for a copy of the *Moralia*.[21] As R. Wasselynck put it, in an expressive phrase, "Spain was during the first half of the seventh century a solid Gregorian fief".[22] The English were no less devoted to the memory of good Pope Gregory, to whom they owed their conversion to the Christian faith. There is a letter of Pope Honorius I, written about 630 to King Edwin of Northumbria, exhorting him "to be frequently occupied in the reading of your teacher and my master, Gregory of apostolic memory".[23]

---

[19] "The Roman Church in the 7th Century: the legacy of Gregory I", in *JEH* 25 (1974).

[20] This plea is put forward by Vogüé in his critique of *PsGD*, in *RHE* 83 (1988) p. 296.

[21] "*Tui enim sumus, tua legere delectamur*"; cf. EH I.58–61.

[22] "*Les Compilations des 'Moralia in Job' du VIIe au XIIe siècle*", in *Recherches de théologie ancienne et médiévale* 30 (1982), p. 11.

[23] Epistola VI, *PL* 80.476.

d. *The interpolated witness of St Isidore of Seville*

A second significant instance of interpolation of the missing title of
the *Dialogues* is found in the list of Gregory's writings given by St
Isidore of Seville, a younger contemporary of the pope who outlived
him by thirty years. He was a brother of Leander, Gregory's close
friend at Constantinople and correspondent in later years. When
Leander died in AD 600 Isidore succeeded him as bishop of Seville.
Until his own death in 636 his contacts and scholarly interests spanned
the Roman world. Like other churchmen and scholars in seventh-
century Spain, he had special admiration for the great Pope Gregory.
In compiling his *Sententiae*, a manual of Christian doctrine and practice, he drew both on the works of Augustine and on the *Regula
Pastoralis* and *Moralia* of Gregory. We have a positive indication that
he was unaware of the existence of the *Dialogues*. When he listed the
chief writings of Pope Gregory as known to him, that allegedly
famous work was not included in his list.[24] The passage attesting that
significant omission is in his work *De viris illustribus*, written between
616 and 618.[25]

Isidore's failure to include the *Dialogues* in his list of Gregory's
known writings was doubtless puzzling to mediaeval readers to whom
the book was the most familiar of all his works. The missing title
was eventually supplied (with others) by a thirteenth-century interpolation in the MS tradition of *De viris illustribus*, which was to provide
Mabillon[26] and other seventeenth-century defenders of the Gregorian authenticity of the *Dialogues* with a prime but fallacious argument
to use against their opponents. In the following century P. Arevalo,
editor of Isidore's writings, recognized from the manuscript evidence
that the mention of the *Dialogues* in that work was *"intrusa"*; today
the spuriousness of Isidore's alleged testimony is universally admitted.
It is not usually acknowledged, however, that the common assumption of the Gregorian authorship of the *Dialogues* has been bolstered

---

[24] *PL* 83.1102. Although Isidore's *De viris illustribus* was amplified by Braulio of
Saragossa, it is established that Chapter 40, containing the particulars about Pope
Gregory, belongs to the main body of the work composed by Isidore himself.

[25] The dating is well established in a monograph by Franz Schütte, *Studien über
den Schriftstellerkatalog des hl. Isidor von Sevilla*, in Band I of *Kirchengeschichtliche Abhandlungen*,
Breslau 1902, pp. 220–1.

[26] Preface to *Acta sanctorum ordinis S. Benedicti*, Paris 1668, p. xiii. Peter Goussainville,
however, was silent about Isidore's alleged testimony in his *Vindiciae Dialogorum*.

in the past by that false evidence, as also by several other similarly spurious testimonies.

Vogüé and Godding concede that Isidore did not know the *Dialogues* at the time he was writing his *De viris ilustribus*, but seek to minimize the significance of his silence.[27] If he had only hazy knowledge of Gregory's other writings, why should he be expected to mention the *Dialogues*? There are very good reasons for such expectation. One of them has already been alluded to in my previous chapter. It is the fact that the *Dialogues* (III.31) present Pope Gregory's revisionist account of the dramatic circumstances surrounding the conversion of Visigothic Spain to the Catholic faith, which would have been of concern to all contemporary Spaniards and of especially close interest to Isidore personally. Bishop Leander of Seville, who was Isidore's brother and predecessor in that see and a dear friend of Gregory's, features as a main actor in that drama. The other principal actors named there, Hermenigild and Kings Leovidgild and Reccared, were personally known and indeed related to Isidore.

Out of all Isidore's voluminous writings there are two passages that defenders of the authenticity of the *Dialogues* allege as implicit evidence that Isidore knew the work. One is a short doctrinal passage on the two kinds of martyrdom, which does indeed contain some expressions that are also found almost verbatim, in a section of *Dialogues III*. I discuss that passage in the Appendix below, as IGP 38. I show there that it was taken by the Dialogist from the archival store of genuine Gregorian expository *reportata*, and inappropriately applied by him to his own chosen context. But how, it may be asked, could Isidore have known of that text in the Roman archive? It is established that the *Etymologiae* was a later and unfinished work of Isidore's, and was edited and completed by his disciple Braulio of Saragossa. The indications are that it was the latter who added to the work the passage in question. As will be shown in the next section, Braulio sought from his friend Tajo copies of the rich collection of transcripts of Gregorian writings, published and unpublished, that he had brought back from a journey to Rome before the middle of the seventh century. There he could have transcribed from the *schedae* in the curial archives the same text that the Dialogist was later to use and embellish as an inserted doctrinal *excursus* in his own fanciful narrative.

---

[27] Vogüé, *RHE* 83, p. 297; Godding, *AB* 106, p. 211.

The other passage which, according to Vogüé and Godding, was taken by Isidore from the *Dialogues*, is a snippet of half a dozen words, found both in a story told in *Dialogues* II.6, and also in Isidore's *Etymologies*. The phrase is: *"ferramentum . . . quod a falcis similitudine falcastrum vocatur"*. (Both authors stress that it occurs in the main narrative of the *Dialogues*, and that therefore I cannot explain it as taken from an IGP!) Vogüé attaches particular significance to the identical explanation in both works of that etymological derivation of the word *falcastrum*, seeing there proof that Isidore, though ignorant of the *Dialogues* when writing his biographical notice of Gregory, went to that book for his explanation of the origin of the word *falcastrum*.[28] It is indeed a quaint argument. Is it supposed that Isidore, with his wide knowledge of Latin literature and mastery of language, should have to rely on the text of the *Dialogues* to find that derivation? The word *falx*, meaning a scythe or sickle, was in universal use in Latin both in classical times and later. The linguistic connection between *falx* and *falcastrum* is straightforward, and Isidore would not need to bring in a verbatim quotation from another author to explain it. The cognate words, *falcarium, falcatus, falcifer*, also in common use, were similarly linked with *falx*. The proof that Vogüé and Godding adduce from that item in Isidore's *Etymologies*, to demonstrate his knowledge of the *Dialogues* and so to refute my whole case, is tenuous indeed. They can find no explicit reference to the *Dialogues* or attribution of them to Gregory in any of Isidore's works. Out of the vast corpus of his writings the only indication that they can produce to show his knowledge of the supposedly famous Gregorian narrative is an implicit allusion to an etymological aside contained in that text. In any case, their alleged disproof of my conclusion is a *petitio principii*. The simple explanation of the duplication of that phrase in the two texts, I answer, is that the Dialogist, writing half a century later, copied it from Isidore's work.

e. *The silence of Braulio and Tajo*

The writings of Isidore's disciple Braulio of Saragossa provide further evidence of the continuing *incognito* of the *Dialogues*. He edited

---

[28] *RHE* 83 (1988), pp. 297–8.

and supplemented his master's *De viris illustribus*. If he knew of the existence of the Gregorian *Dialogues* one would assume that he would surely have noted and rectified the surprising omission of that title from Isidore's list. Yet he reproduced that list without any such addition.[29]

Also very significant is the silence of Braulio's friend, correspondent and successor as bishop of Saragossa, the abbot Tajo, already introduced above. One of the most renowned of the Spanish Church leaders and scholars of that age, he not only knew Gregory's writings thoroughly but showed deep devotion to the saintly pope, which he expressed in a letter to Bishop Eugenius of Toledo which has been preserved. It is from that letter that we know details of Tajo's visit to Rome, at a date before 649, to seek out and transcribe writings of St Gregory that the Spaniards lacked.[30] During that visit he gained access to the unpublished remains of the pope's expository commentaries preserved in the archival *schedae* of the Roman secretariate, several passages from which he transcribed for use in an anthology of Gregorian teachings that he was planning. (He even mentions contact there with still surviving *notarii* and *familiares* of the great pope.) Defenders of the authenticity of the *Dialogues*, R. Godding in particular, have argued that he tacitly copied some of his excerpts from the latter work. I show in Chapter 22.b, where I discuss Tajo's anthologizing of Gregorian expository passages more fully, that their arguments are flawed. Here I stress the fact that in spite of his fervent admiration for Gregory and his works, Tajo makes no mention of Gregory's authorship of the *Dialogues*, nor even of the title of that book, supposedly already famous and so relevant to the recent history of Visigothic Spain. If it had then been extant and known Tajo would surely have had tidings of it, at least after his journey to Rome in search of Gregorian writings. Through him and his correspondents it would have become widely known throughout the Visigothic kingdom. We have record that on his return to Spain from that stay in Rome he received an earnest entreaty from his friend Braulio, asking for copies of the Gregorian texts that he had brought back with him. Braulio added that his brother John (to whom he was to succeed as bishop of Saragossa) was likewise eager

---

[29] Cf. *PsGD*, pp. 116–7, and p. 53, note 16.
[30] *PL* 80.723–8. There is also a legendary account from another source of marvellous happenings that befell him on that visit (*PL* 80.989–92: cf. *PsGD*, p. 101).

to obtain copies of those newly acquired codices. His letter is worth quoting, for it well illustrates the intense interest of seventh-century Spanish churchmen and scholars in the writings of St Gregory:

> And there is one thing, so far unobtained, which is above all others needful for me. That is, I pray Christ himself should so crown your good intent that you would send me, as quickly as possible, the undivulged codices of the holy pope Gregory, which were lacking in Spain and which by your diligence and labour were brought hither from Rome, in order that I may have them transcribed. Not I alone petition you for this boon, but also my lord and brother-german, who loves you. Wherefore if you grant this favour to one of us, you will satisfy both of us, but if you fail one you will spurn both. Your Charity can certainly trust me to send those codices back to you within whatever time you may stipulate.[31]

Tajo's journey to Rome and diligent search for Gregorian writings in the papal *Scrinium* and library will be factors to bear in mind when we come to discuss the date at which the *Dialogues* became known. All the indications are that the work was not yet known in Spain in the middle years of the seventh century. Tajo's account of his researches in the Lateran archives are also relevant confirmation of the existence of the store of unpublished Gregorian literary remains in those archives—the source from which the Dialogist was later to draw the IGPs for insertion in his fictional narrative.

f. *The interpolated witness of St Ildefonsus of Toledo*

Likewise significantly unaware of the existence of the *Dialogues* was another celebrated disciple of St Isidore, namely St Ildefonsus of Toledo. Born about 607, he became bishop of Toledo in 657 and died in 667. During his ten-years episcopate he wrote a work which was transcribed as a continuation of Isidore's *De viris illustribus*, with a linking phrase ascribing it to Ildefonsus. In later MSS it was to be entitled *De virorum illustrium scriptis*. J. Madoz showed cogent reasons for concluding that the work did indeed originate in the episcopal office of Ildefonsus himself. He placed it as part of a "family patrimony" of such writings in the Visigothic Church, begun with

---

[31] Braulio, Epist. XLII, to the abbot Tajo: *PL* 80, col. 690.

the *De viris illustribus* of Isidore and continued, with successive augmentations, by Braulio, Ildefonsus, and later by Julian and Felix.[32]

Defenders of the Gregorian ascription of the *Dialogues* have traditionally claimed Ildefonsus as a prime witness for their cause, pointing to an explicit affirmation of that ascription in one particularly informative chapter of his work. There indeed is found a passage in which Ildefonsus recalls that Isidore had already written about Gregory's writings, but declares that he, with fuller knowledge of the blessed pope's writings, would give further information about them. He duly lists them, and there follows the explicit statement that Gregory "also wrote four books on the lives of Fathers who had dwelt in Italy, and brought them together in one volume, which he chose to call the codex of dialogues".[33] Since other early testimonies alleged to prove Gregory's authorship of that work had been proved to be spurious, that of Ildefonsus assumed particular importance for modern historians concerned with the subject. G. von Dzialowski commented: "Because he is the first to give information about the *Dialogues*, his witness is very valuable, especially for establishing Gregory's authorship, which has been doubted".[34]

Some fifty years ago I reached the conclusion that the supposedly pioneer testimony to the existence of the *Dialogues* attributed to Ildefonsus was, like the testimonies attributed to Isidore and to the author of the *LP*, a later interpolation in the manuscript transmission. My findings were based especially on discernment and analysis of the stylistic differences and anachronisms in the contents of that chapter in the work of Ildefonsus. Those arguments were set out at considerable length in *PsGD* (pp. 121–30), but I do not repeat them here since they are no longer necessary to prove the points at issue. Until 1970 I was alone in my conviction that the alleged witness of Ildefonsus was unauthentic. In that year Professor Codoñer Merino, who had hitherto shared the universal assumption that the relevant chapter of his work was genuine, published a study in which she highlighted the striking fact that the chapter was missing from

---

[32] "*San Ildefonso de Toledo*", in *Estudios Eclesiasticos*, 26 (1952), pp. 468, 476.

[33] "*De vitis patrum per Italiam commorantium edidit etiam libros quattuor, quos volumine uno compegit, quem quidem codicem dialogorum maluit appellari*" (*PL* 96.199).

[34] "*Isidor und Ildefons als Litterarhistoriker: eine quellenkritische Untersuchung der Schriften 'De viris illustribus' des Isidor von Sevilla und Ildefons de Toledo*", published in *Kirchengeschichtliche Studien*, Münster 1898, IV.2, p. 133.

all the earlier mediaeval manuscripts of the Ildefonsian opusculum, and first appeared in a fifteenth-century MS.[35] She did not immediately reject it as an interpolation, but suggested a strained hypothesis to explain its survival despite its absence from the manuscripts. However, by 1972, when she published her critical edition of the text, she had come to recognize the untenability of the traditional opinion and firmly rejected the problematic chapter as spurious.[36] Her magisterial study of the external evidence showing the late origin of that supposedly Ildefonsian testimony concerning the *Dialogues*, together with my detailed demonstration of its fraudulence from the internal evidence of the text, have combined to discredit that interpolated passage decisively. Disconcerted, the defenders of Gregory's authorship of the *Dialogues* no longer include it in their armoury.

We have seen that sources in Western Christendom that would surely have mentioned the *Dialogues* during the course of the seventh century if they existed are silent about them. Nor is there any trace of them in any of the Eastern Mediterranean lands. Yet when in the course of the eighth century that book of wonders eventually became known in the Greek-speaking world, it was very soon translated and rapidly gained great fame and popularity. Indeed because of the renown of that book in the East Pope Gregory I was thereafter known to the Greeks by the title of "The Dialogian".

---

[35] "*El libro De Viris Illustribus de Ildefonso de Toledo*", in the volume *La Patrologia Toledano-Visigoda*, Madrid 1970, pp. 337–48.
[36] El "*De Viris Illustribus*" *de Ildefonso de Toledo: estudio y edición crítica*, Salamanca 1972, pp. 29–30, 71–3.

CHAPTER THIRTEEN

POST-GREGORIAN ORIGIN OF THE *DIALOGUES*
CONFIRMED BY THE HISTORY OF BENEDICTINE
ORIGINS: OBSCURE FIRST APPEARANCE OF
THE *REGULA BENEDICTI*

a

In our discussion of the external evidence relating to the authenticity of the *Dialogues* one most important field remains to be further explored. It is the question of the origins and first diffusion of Benedictine monasticism, developments which are clearly related to the *Life* of St Benedict supposedly narrated by St Gregory in that book. The newly clarified historiography of those developments provides further conclusive confirmation of the post-Gregorian origin of the *Dialogues*. In this chapter I give first a summary overview of that field, and in following chapters will discuss the individual issues in detail.

Until recently there was general agreement among monastic historians on the following points: that St Benedict of Nursia was born about AD 480 and died *circa* 550; that during the first half of the sixth century he composed the rule for monks that has come down to us under his name, and made the first foundations of Benedictine monasteries at Subiaco and later; that the observance of his rule, later established at his abbey of Montecassino, thenceforward spread widely throughout Western Europe; and that, through the authoritative approbation given to it by Pope St Gregory in his *Dialogues* and through its own intrinsic excellence, the *Regula Benedicti* proceeded during the seventh century to supplant all rivals, to become the norm for monastic life in the western Church. In this process, those historians have stressed, a decisive influence was St Gregory's glowing biography of the saintly founder in the *Dialogues* and his eloquent encomium of the *RB* in that work. In the words of P. Batiffol quoted at the beginning of Chapter 1, "There is no doubt that the second book of the *Dialogues* made of St Benedict the patriarch of the monks of the West." However, in the second half of the twentieth

century monastic historians began to ask the question, with increasing disquiet, "*When* did that happen?" Previously, the answer generally given to that question had been: "At once: that is, spreading
widely from Montecassino in the sixth century and powerfully promoted by the authoritative approval given to it by Pope St Gregory,
the *RB* soon reached pre-eminence to eclipse all other monastic rules
in the West." Yet the advance of historical scholarship in recent
years has shown that this answer is wrong. One by one, those centuries-old assumptions about the early flourishing and triumph of
Benedictinism have been exposed as unfounded.[1] In the light of
searching studies devoted to the history of monasticism in that dark
age a puzzling new picture has appeared.

From Book II of the *Dialogues* one would naturally conclude that
the great wonder-working abbot St Benedict of Nursia and Montecassino was already famous in the pontificate of Gregory I and that
his rule was widely observed and honoured at that time. Yet it proves
to be strangely impossible to establish from any other contemporary
source that there was any such fame of St Benedict or of his rule
in that age; rather, the indications are to the contrary. There is no
sign that anyone, either in Gregory's lifetime or for long years afterwards, took any notice or had any awareness of the approbation
putatively given by that pontiff to the monastic rule of the great
saint and thaumaturge of Cassino. Although the *RB* eventually
emerged, obscurely, into recorded history in Gaul during the seventh century, we find that in Italy and in Rome itself, despite that
papal commendation supposedly given to it in the *Dialogues* in AD
593, it was nowhere observed during the century following that date.
Pope Gregory himself, in his pastoral vigilance to promote and reg-
ulate monastic life, never once proposed adoption of the Benedictine
rule. Nor did he make any mention of it in any of his letters or
other authorized writings, as L. Salvatorelli pointed out as long ago
as 1929.[2] He did not introduce that rule in the monastery that he
himself founded in his home *ad clivum Scauri*, nor anywhere else.

---

[1] It would of course be an anachronism to speak of a recognizable "Benedictine
order" at that time. I use the term "Benedictinism" not supposing that there was
an institutional entity corresponding to it, but to refer generally to monastic activity associated with the *Regula Benedicti* and with the name of St Benedict.

[2] *San Benedetto e l'Italia del suo tempo*, Bari 1929, p. 196: "... *in tutto suo epistolario
non v'è un solo caso in cui s'imponga o si raccomandi di un monasterio l'adozione della Regola.*"

Some 200 out of his more than 850 letters contain reference to monastic observance. (In the index to Ewald-Hartmann's edition of them the entries under *monasteria, monachus,* and kindred words fill nearly five columns of print.) Yet, as Baronius observed and K. Hallinger demonstrated in detail, the monasticism there reflected in those letters is not that of the Benedictine code, of which there is not the slightest mention. Commentators ask with puzzlement: If the great pope had acclaimed the *RB* as of outstanding worth, why is there no trace of its observance in his age, from which we have record of the existence of more than two dozen Latin rules?

Moreover, we read in the prologue to the second book of the *Dialogues* that Gregory learned his facts about Benedict's life and teaching from four of the saint's close disciples and successors as abbots: first, Constantinus, his immediate successor at Montecassino; then Simplicius, his second successor; also Valentinian "who was for many years abbot of the Lateran monastery"; and Honoratus, who at the time of writing was abbot at Subiaco. Surely, with such first-hand testimonies to rely on, Gregory would have made some mention, either in his letters of monastic concern or in his homilies addressed to monks, to the great miracle-working saint who (if the *Dialogues* are to be believed) must have been the most illustrious abbot and monastic founder of that time, nor to the monastic tradition derived from him?

Of primary importance, therefore, is a document from south-west Gaul, dating from the second quarter of the seventh century, in which we find what is apparently the first historically verifiable mention of the existence and observance of the rule for monks that bears St Benedict's name. It is discussed more fully below, in Section c. From the middle of the seventh century onwards the *RB* gradually emerged as one of several monastic codes in partial use in seventh-century Francia, while still not recorded in any other land save England. In Frankish usage in that period it is mentioned only as one element of a mixed rule, usually in composition with the rule of the Irish missionary saint Columban. Not until the eighth century did the Benedictine observance begin—suddenly and rapidly—to rise to pre-eminence in monasteries in Francia and beyond the Rhine. That development, evidently spurred by the recent diffusion of the *Dialogues,* began during the pontificate of Pope Gregory II (715–731), after that pope had introduced the *RB* in the newly built abbey of Montecassino. While the hitherto prevalent "mixed-rule monasticism" was slow to disappear, the sole observance of the *RB* was thereafter found in an increasing number of monasteries in those northern lands (though not likewise in Italy or Spain), through the influence of the new "mystique of Montecassino" and the zeal of St Boniface and others. From the middle years of the eighth century it was used by the Anglo-Saxon missionaries and Frankish rulers as a potent instrument for the Christianization of still largely pagan regions of Germany.

In the light of the facts summarized above, which will be more fully documented in the following pages, the historical paradox is apparent. On the traditional supposition that in his famous *Dialogues* written in the year 593 Pope St Gregory narrated the life and miracles of St Benedict, and singled out his monastic rule as "*discretione praecipua, sermone luculenta*", there is no satisfactory explanation of that very tardy and geographically incongruous flowering of Benedictine monasticism. On the traditional assumptions, it cannot be explained why the first emergence into history of the Benedictine observance occurred not in the land of its origin nor in the age of St Gregory, but many decades in remote parts of Gaul, in which land it was used later in the second half of the seventh century as an occasional and non-dominant element of mixed rules. It cannot be explained why the wide diffusion and pre-eminence of that rule did not begin until that late date. Even more difficult to explain is the fact that for nigh on a hundred years after the date at which Pope Gregory supposedly wrote St Benedict's biography there was no indication of knowledge of the life of that great saint himself—as distinct from his rule—nor any cult or liturgical honour of him, until the eighth century. That extraordinary silence will be the subject of Chapters 16 and 18 below.

All those puzzles are resolved, however, once it is recognized that the *Dialogues*, the book that eventually "made St Benedict patriarch of the monks of the West", to repeat Batiffol's phrase, was not written by St Gregory in the last decade of the sixth century but by a later pseudepigrapher, and that it did not emerge into the light until the close of the seventh century. Thus an essential aid to unravelling the tangled skein of evidence relating to the origins of Benedictine monasticism is to realize that the *Regula Benedicti* was publicly known well before the *Life* of St Benedict; and that the *RB*, after its first obscure appearance in recorded history in Gaul, had been unobtrusively progressing towards wider observance and esteem for many years in Francia before it received its decisive endorsement in the pseudo-Gregorian *Dialogues*.

b. *Modern critical reappraisal of early Benedictine history*

That outline statement of the historiographical problems and their solution must now be justified by reference to the details of the very intricate pattern of those events. A first step is to review the remarkable reappraisal of early Benedictine history that took place during the second half of the twentieth century. That work of critical reappraisal has to a large extent been led by Benedictine scholars. It had previously been assumed by monastic historians that the *RB* must have been widely observed and celebrated during the sixth century. Thus A. Zimmermann confidently affirmed that "at the close of the sixth century the rule was diffused in the whole of Italy; Gregory the Great marks only the conclusion of this development"; he further claimed that Pope Gregory himself was a Benedictine monk and abbot, hailing him as "the greatest son of our Father Benedict".[3] The same claim was made by O.M. Porcel: "In truth, St Gregory is the noblest example of monastic life that the Rule of St Benedict has ever produced".[4] The first assertion that Gregory was himself a Benedictine monk can be traced back to the ninth century, when it was made by Amalarius of Metz and by John the Deacon in his *Life of St Gregory*. When Baronius and some of his disciples challenged the view that Gregory gave Benedict's rule to his monastery of St Andrew and was himself a Benedictine, he was caustically refuted by Mabillon and the other Maurist scholars.[5]

Monastic historians generally have until recently accepted the Maurists' assumptions. They have agreed that, following St Gregory's authoritative approval of the *RB* as the highest model of monastic observance, it rapidly outstripped all other rules and became everywhere predominant during the seventh century. That impressive

---

[3] *Kalendarium Benedictinum*, Metten 1933, vol. I, p. xl.

[4] *La Doctrina Monastica de San Gregorio Magno y la "Regula Monachorum"*, Madrid 1950, p. 214.

[5] J. Mabillon, *Dissertatio de monastica vita Gregorii papae primi*, in *Vetera Analecta*, Paris 1676, II, pp. 145–212. Cf. the Maurist editors' *Life of St Gregory*, *PL* 75.252–62. References to other works mentioned in this section may be found in *PsGD*, pp. 189–92, and footnotes.

fabric of assumptions about the rise of the Benedictine observance
had since the seventeenth century been buttressed by the erudite
arguments of Mabillon and his associates. Yet today hardly a stone
of it remains erect. The process of demolishing it began in the earlier part of the twentieth century. Scholars began to advert to strange
facts, such as the lack of evidence of any Benedictine observance in
the island of Britain for a large part of the seventh century.[6] What
then of the common supposition that St Augustine of Canterbury
and his companions who came to convert the English in AD 597
were Benedictine monks? Finally there came scholarly recognition
that the claim that Gregory's missionaries to Kent were Benedictines
was unfounded, as also was the claim that there were monasteries
solely observing the *RB* in seventh-century England.[7]

Further problems about the earliest sightings of the *RB* began to
be raised insistently. The challenge, first raised by Baronius, to the
assumption of St Gregory's Benedictine affiliation and of his cham-
pionship of the *RB* was renewed and presented more cogently. In
Italy the work of Dom G. Penco (especially his monograph, *La prima
diffusione della Regula di S. Benedetto*)[8] showed how unsubstantial were
the common assumptions about the early renown and prevalence of
the *RB*. Other studies revealed the ubiquity and continuing vigour
of non-Benedictine forms of monastic observance throughout the seventh century and for much of the eighth.[9] Deeper study of the early
history of Christianity in the eastern Frankish territories,[10] and of the
monastic background and activity of the missionaries who worked
to Christianize the German tribes, also showed how tardy was the
intervention of Benedictine monks. The work of H. Tausch was a
notable contribution to that new critical historiography of Benedictine
origins in the German-speaking lands.[11]

---

[6] E.g. R. Ewald, in his edition of *Aldhelmi Opera*, 1919, p. xv.

[7] Cf. J. Winandy OSB, *Mélanges Bénédictins*, St Wandrille 1947, pp. 244 seq.; N.
Mayr-Harting, *The Coming of Christianity to Anglo-Saxon England*, London 1977.

[8] *SA* 42, 1957, pp. 321–45; also his book, *Storia della monachesimo in Italia*, Rome
1960.

[9] Cf. *Mélanges Columbaniens: Actes du Congrès Internationale de Luxeuil*, Paris 1950; and
Columbanus and Merovingian Monasticism, ed. H.B. Clarke and M. Brennan, Oxford
1981 (especially the essays of P. Riché and F. Prinz).

[10] There is a good summary by T. Schieffer, *Wilfrid-Bonifatius und die christliche
Grundlegung Europas*, Freiburg 1954.

[11] *Benediktinisches Mönchtum in Oesterreich*, Vienna 1949.

At almost the same time that Penco's monograph appeared, G. Ferrari published a study of the archaeological and historical evidence concerning the monasteries of Rome in the early Middle Ages.[12] The author began his work without particular awareness of the problems of early Benedictine history, but found himself constrained by his findings to add his voice to that of the historians who were challenging long-cherished illusions in this field. He recorded his surprise at finding that the traditional view about the prevalence of Benedictine observance in the Roman monasteries from the time of Gregory I onwards was mistaken. His statement of his discovery is worth citing, since it marks a watershed between the old historical illusions and the new realism that was dawning.)[13] He wrote:

> Originally I undertook this work with the hope of tracing the introduction and adoption of the rule of St Benedict as the sole norm of monastic life in these monasteries. I somewhat unconsciously presumed that this could be reliably documented as early as the period beginning shortly after Gregory the Great. I soon became aware, however, that such was not the case . . . Ever since the time of Mabillon there has been an unquestioned assumption on the part of most scholars and monastic historians that the monasteries of Rome (and elsewhere for that matter) founded during and after the time of Gregory the Great were automatically Benedictine. This supposition was so widespread and is today so well known that it needs no documentation. Even a cursory inspection of the sources collected for this history of Roman monasteries, however, will show that there is no evidence to support this conclusion.[14]

Among other writers who have contributed to the recent critical revision of the history of Benedictine monasticism special mention must be made of the works of S. Brechter OSB,[15] J. Winandy OSB,[16]

---

[12] *Early Roman Monasteries. Notes for the History of the Monasteries and Convents at Rome from the V through X Century*, Rome 1957.

[13] I mark one obvious slip in his summary. He says that he could find no evidence for esteem of the *RB* in Rome "and elsewhere" before the tenth century; I show below, in Chapter 15.a, that such evidence exists from the eighth century onwards—above all, in the policy of Pope Gregory II. In *RHE* 83 (1988), pp. 322–3, A. de Vogüé rightly criticizes Ferrari's tenth-century dating, but mistakenly suggests that my argument in *PsGD*, pp. 191–2, is somehow dependent on that dating.

[14] *Op. cit.*, pp. xvii, 379–80.

[15] In several articles, some of them cited below, from the 1930s and 1940s.

[16] "*L'œuvre de S. Benoît d'Aniane*", in *Mélanges bénédictins* 1947.

T. Leccisotti,[17] F. Prinz,[18] and above all Kassius Hallinger OSB. The latter had already exposed as fallacious the accepted opinion that the Benedictine rule was prevalent among the Anglo-Saxons in the century following the sending of St Augustine to Canterbury by Pope Gregory. In 1957, in his ground-breaking monograph, *Papst Gregor der Grosse und der heiliger Benedikt*,[19] he traced the steady erosion of the traditional assumptions about the first appearance and spread of Benedictine monasticism. Piece by piece, he showed how the hoary tradition attesting the fame and prevalence of that observance in the sixth and seventh centuries had been built up in large measure on legendary, falsified or misinterpreted evidence. Monastic loyalties and ambitions over more than a millennium had woven a vast tissue of unhistorical assertions, and its unravelling and dissolution by critical scholarship was often painful to traditional sensibilities. Hallinger himself became a target of indignant protests. In his exposure of that wide canvas of pseudo-history, he listed and critically refuted many circumstantial claims about early observance of the *RB*. Some of them were also pointed out by other scholars, whose further findings corroborated his own.

Exposed as spurious are the *Acta* of two Roman synods, in AD 601 and 610, the first allegedly presided over by Pope Gregory himself and the second by Pope Boniface IV, which were alleged to have given the formal stamp of papal approval to the Benedictine rule.[20] Then there was the letter of an abbot of Fondi to Simplicius, assumed to have been the third abbot of Montecassino, which was taken as proof that the *RB* was established throughout Italy in the second half of the sixth century, to the exclusion of all other observances. That letter too was an invention, forged centuries later. Spurious too were the verses attributed to Abbot Simplicius himself, which have often been adduced as evidence of the sixth-century propagation of that rule, but are now known to have been composed at Reichenau between AD 790 and 806.[21] Other age-old frauds,

---

[17] *"Le Consequenze dell' invasione longobarda per l'antico monachesimo Italico"* in *Atti del Congresso di Studi Longobardi*, Spoleto 1951; and *"Aspetti e problemi del Monachesimo in Italia"*, in *Il Monachesimo nell' alto Medioevo*, Spoleto 1956.

[18] *Frühes Mönchtum im Frankenreich*, Munich 1965.

[19] Published in the volume, *Commentationes in Regulam Sancti Benedicti*, ed. B. Steidle, *SA* 42 (1957), pp. 231–319.

[20] *Papst Gregor*, p. 235 & note 16.

[21] S. Brechter, *"Versus Simplicii"*, in *Rev. Bén.* 54 (1935), pp. 98–135; cf. also

on which much local piety was later grafted, were the fictitious *Lives* of St Benedict's chief disciples Maurus and Placidus, who are known otherwise only from their legendary appearance in the pages of the *Dialogues*. The *Life* of Maurus was fabricated in the ninth century by Abbot Odo of Glanfeuil, or "St Maur-sur-Loire"—for it was claimed that St Maurus's body, like that of his master,[22] was transferred from Italy to the Loire valley, to become a focus of pilgrimage there. A similarly fictitious "Passion of St Placidus" was written by one "Gordian", a twelfth-century romancer.[23]

My own critical reappraisal of the traditional historiography of the origins of Benedictine monasticism, set out more fully in *PsGD* and summarized in the following chapters, can be seen to owe much to the pioneer work of Kassius Hallinger. I treasure a letter from him, urging me to pursue further the path that he himself had pioneered, undaunted by the indignant opposition that I should meet.

c. *The first appearance of the* RB *in historical record*

Leaving aside the suspect testimony of the *Dialogues*, we ask: When and where did the monastic rule that bears the name of St Benedict first emerge into the light of recorded history? The answer given by Ludwig Traube, in his classic study *Textgeschichte der Regula S. Benedicti*,[24] an answer that has been generally accepted by scholars, is that the earliest known reference to the *RB* is found in a letter sent to a prelate named Constantius, who was bishop of Albi in the province of Narbonensis in south-western Gaul from about AD 620 to 630. The sender of the letter in which the reference occurs was a certain magnate named Venerandus, who was founder and patron of a monastery at Altaripa in the bishop's diocese. The purpose of his letter was to give instructions for the introduction at Altaripa of a new monastic rule in substitution for the one hitherto observed there. He enjoined upon the abbot and monks, under severe sanctions, the

---

N. Huyghebaert, "*Simplicius, 'propagateur' de la Règle bénédictine: legende ou tradition?*", in *RHE* 73 (1978), pp. 45–54.

[22] See Chapter 20 below.

[23] *Acta Sanctorum*, October III, pp. 114–38; cf. *PsGD*, p. 248, note 210.

[24] Munich 1898; in *Abhandlungen der königliche Bayerischen Akademie der Wissenschaften*, XXXV, no. 2, Munich 1911.

obedient acceptance and exact observance of the new rule. With his
letter to Constantinus he sent a copy of the text of that substitute
rule, which he described as "*Regula sancti Benedicti abbatis Romensis*",
and enjoined that it be kept in the cathedral archives at Albi as an
authentic text for permanent record. As Traube observes, the *RB*
must have been previously unknown in those parts. Nor is there any
previous or contemporary record showing knowledge of it anywhere else.

Venerandus's designation of St Benedict as "a Roman abbot" has
been understandably described (by G. Penco) as "enigmatic". According
to the *Dialogues*, Benedict of Nursia studied in Rome in his youth,
but then permanently turned his back on that city to lead the monastic life. We read that he was abbot first at Subiaco, and finally at
Montecassino, but never in Rome. Surely anyone who knew Pope
Gregory's life of St Benedict would refer to him, not as a Roman
abbot, but as the abbot of the monastery of Montecassino, made
famous in that book as the place where he lived longest, taught,
worked great miracles and died. Why then did Venerandus call him
"a Roman abbot"? A. Mundó commented: "Perhaps Venerandus
and his circle did not know the second book of the *Dialogues* of St
Gregory, or they would have found a fitter patronymic to ascribe
to Abbot St Benedict".[25] Traube tried to meet the difficulty by making the forlorn surmise that the puzzling description of Benedict as
a Roman abbot could have been in use during the seventh century
because, following the putative destruction of Montecassino by the
Lombards in 581, the "home town of the Benedictines" ("*die Heimstätte
der Benediktiner*") was "the monastery of St John in the Lateran".[26] As
J. Chapman and S. Brechter[27] and others have shown, the theory
of a surviving Benedictine monastery in the Lateran between 581
and 717 is another later figment without any historical foundation.

There is more to be said about that problematic phrase, "a Roman
abbot". It cannot be explained away as just a misconception on the
part of Venerandus, or (as one commentator proposed, as merely
the way a magnate in Gaul would vaguely refer to "an abbot from
the Roman region"). The phrase in Venerandus's letter has parallels in two other early documents. One is a manuscript of the *RB*

---

[25] *SA* 42, p. 149.
[26] *Op. cit.*, p. 79.
[27] *SMGBO* 56, 1938, pp. 109–50.

which bears the title, "*Regula a sancto Benedicto Romense edita*". It is found in a codex that was probably transcribed at Verona around the year 800, but the archaic character of the phrasing indicates that it may have been copied from an original going back to an even earlier time.[28] The other document is particularly interesting, since in it the same phrase is used with an addition that clarifies the meaning of the term "Roman abbot" as applied to Benedict. The phrase occurs in a reference to a mixed monastic observance consisting of elements of three rules, namely those "of Anthony, of Pachomius, and, not far from our own times, of Benedict, that abbot of this city of Rome" ("... *haud procul a nostris temporibus Benedicti abbatis istius Romae huius urbis*"). Although this formula is found embedded in a falsified papal privilege, composed in a Frankish monastery around the end of the eighth century, the text "certainly follows an older Merovingian document", as Traube recognizes.[29] Hallinger likewise thinks that it points to a text originating before the eighth century.[30] Those three documents, all seeming to err by locating Benedict's abbacy in Rome, and especially the letter of Venerandus, which can be dated fairly accurately, raise a further problem for those who hold the traditional view that the *Dialogues* had been written by Gregory at the end of the sixth century. Surely the fame of those *Dialogues*, with their detailed account of the life and deeds of the great abbot Benedict, should have prevented Venerandus and those other Frankish scribes from attaching to the Cassinese patriarch a description that was patently incorrect? Traube showed himself aware of the problem raised by those three testimonies. Acknowledging that they were "not yet explained", he wrote: "To be sure, ever since 593, through Gregory's *Dialogues*, it would have been possible for more accurate knowledge about the Father of the Order to become well known in the circles to whom those copies of the Rule were directed. Yet the letter of Venerandus shows that the error was still flourishing in southern France half a century later".[31]

Traube added an interesting comment: "On the other hand, one must indeed take it as certain that those manuscripts [of the *RB*],

---

[28] MS Verona LII; cf. Traube, *op. cit.*, pp. 58–9. Others, including E.A. Lowe (*Cod. Lat. Antiqu.* IV, Oxford 1947, no. 505) judged that the MS originated in a Burgundian monastery.

[29] *Op. cit.*, pp. 78–9.

[30] *SA* 42, p. 264, note 100.

[31] *Op. cit.*, pp. 78, 79.

which were apparently labelled with that false title by the recipients themselves, did in truth come from Rome." It is indeed not unreasonable to infer that the MSS of the *RB* that reached France in the first half of the seventh century originated in Rome. But instead of assuming without question, as Traube did, that Venerandus's description of the author of the rule as a "saintly abbot of Rome" was an "error" and a "false title", it may be that it was a correct one. His phrase provides us with the only three firm biographical facts that we have about the author of the *RB*, the great saint and founder who was to became the patriarch of religious life in the West and sanctifier of Europe. Those three facts can be stated as follows: (1) that Benedict was an abbot of Rome; (2) that he was reputed for sanctity; and (3) that he wrote an admirable rule for monks. From the date of that first historical reference to the existence of the *RB*, in the second quarter of the seventh century, one may infer with probability that it had originated several years earlier. One may conjecture that the author was a younger contemporary of Gregory the Great; as an abbot of one of the numerous monasteries in Rome, he may have been known to the pontiff. However, as we have seen, the prescriptions for monastic observance that Pope Gregory enjoined in his letters differed in several respects from those of the *RB*, as Hallinger and others later have pointed out in detail.

A further notable indication that the *RB* may reflect original usage in the city of Rome has been recently highlighted by Marilyn Dunn. She points out that the liturgical instructions contained in Chapter 8–18 of that rule appear to be based on the liturgy of the major public churches of Rome.[32] Thus the *RB* may well have originated for use in one of the sixth-century basilical monasteries, the monks of which served public churches in the city. This is further support for the conclusion that Venerandus's adjective describing the author of the *RB* was not an error. However, as Marilyn Dunn herself observes, "Many unresolved questions still surround the Benedictine *Rule*". The nature of its relationship with the *Regula Magistri* is still unclear. She has pointed to "the very different geographical backgrounds of the two rules", and that the *RM* "contains a liturgy where the content of the night office is modulated to take account of a very noticeable variation between the length of winter and summer

---

[32] *The Emergence of Monasticism*, pp. 129–30.

nights".[33] It remains possible that both rules originated around the end of the sixth century or in the first part of the seventh.

Since I discussed Traube's findings in *PsGD* doubt has been cast on the authenticity of Venerandus's letter because its oldest surviving MS is of very late date. The considerations indicated above, about the corroboratory references to "the city of Rome" found in early MSS of the *RB*, tell in favour of the letter's authenticity. However, it is singular because it is the only evidence purporting to date from the seventh century to refer to the *sole* observance of the *RB* in any monastery, and because it relates to south-west Gaul and not to the main Frankish regions where all the subsequent appearances of elements of the *RB* are located. In the light of the total evidence, the issue is still *sub iudice*. Whatever may emerge from this debate, it remains true that, since no earlier record of the existence and observance of the *RB* is known, the letter of Venerandus at least provides a *terminus ante quem non* of c. AD 625, before which we have no such record. Those who do not accept the authenticity of the letter now identify, as the earliest known evidence of the presence of the *RB*, its use as an element in the mixed rule for nuns, the *Regula Donati* introduced at Jussa-Moutier in Burgundy not long before 660. The case for this conclusion is argued by Michaela Zelzer in her study "*Die Regula Donati, der alteste Textzeuge der Regula Benedicti*".[34] If it prevails, still further adjustment may have to be made to traditional theories about the date of origin of the *RB* and of the lifetime of its author. Such later dating of the first appearance of the *RB* would support the possibility that it was composed even after the lifetime of Gregory the Great, during the first part of the seventh century. I prescind here from the further debate, now ongoing, on the question of "Irish monastic influences" in the *RB* and of possible "interpolations" in the surviving MS text.[35]

In the history of the Church there have been many great movements of new religious vitality stemming from the initiative of charismatic founders and leaders. The initial impetus and influence given

---

[33] *Ibid.*, p. 128.

[34] In *RBS* 16 (1989), pp. 23–6; also her later paper, "*Die Regula Donati als frühestes Zeugnis des 'monastischen Gebrauchstextes' der Regula Benedicti*", at the 50th Anniversary Symposium of the Monastic Institute of S. Anselmo, Rome, in May–June 2002.

[35] Cf. the study of Klaus Zelzer, "*Zu Geschichte und Überlieferung des Textes der RBen: Der status quaestionis*", in the *Acts* of the Symposium referred to in the preceding footnote.

to religious orders by the master founders—St Columban, St Odo, St Bernard, St Francis, St Dominic, St Ignatius, St Teresa of Avila and others—can be seen reflected in the early history of the institutions that developed from their charismatic initiatives. So too the influence of their first companions and successors is seen to have been of major importance in that development. However, in the greatest monastic movement of all—the Benedictine—it is otherwise. There we find no record of a historically rooted tradition, spreading the new monastic pattern by organic development from its charismatic source. When the *Regula Benedicti* does eventually emerge for the first time into historical record, in seventh-century Gaul, there is no sign of historical continuity with a living tradition of Benedictine observance elsewhere, no mention of an existing "mother house", nor of other monasteries following that rule, nor of successors of the charismatic founder. Benedictine monasticism appears hazily in recorded history, not as an already active religious movement transmitted from a famous founder through his devoted disciples, but as a previously unknown text introduced into observance at some date between 625 and 659.

CHAPTER FOURTEEN

GROWING REPUTE OF THE BENEDICTINE RULE IN SEVENTH-CENTURY FRANCIA, AS AN ADJUNCT TO THE PREVAILING COLUMBANIAN OBSERVANCE

a

After the first record of the existence and observance of the *RB* in the middle decades of the seventh century all the evidence concerning it during the subsequent years of that century relates to its use in the Frankish realms as one element of mixed monastic observance in which provisions from different rules were combined.[1] (There is no record of the use and knowledge of it in any other country during that period, save in England in the latter part of the century.) The extent of its spread and influence in the Frankish realms during that century has been much exaggerated in the past by a "pan-Benedictine apologetic". It is now well established that the predominant influence in Frankish monasticism throughout the seventh century was that of the rule of the Irish founder St Columban. The *RB*, though eventually growing in esteem and influence through its own intrinsic merit, was in that period still a relatively minor element.

The circle of rulers, bishops and nobles of the Merovingian kingdom are known to have been enthusiastic patrons of the Irish-Frankish monastic movement stemming from St Columban and his disciples. How did some of them come to favour the introduction of elements from the *RB* in the observance of monasteries under their patronage? F. Prinz conjectured that it was Bishop Constantius of Albi, to whom Venerandus sent the first known text of the rule, who planted the seed in that wider circle.[2] If it was from the Albi copy that they knew the text of the *RB* they would also have known the description

---

[1] What is summarized in this chapter is set out lengthily in *PsGD*, Chapter 11, with detailed references.

[2] *Op. cit.*, p. 288. A. de Vogüé criticized Prinz's theory, proposing instead the arbitrary conjecture that Columban himself knew the *RB* and may have commended it to his sons. Cf. *SC* 181, pp. 163–9 and *RHE* 77 (1982), pp. 109–13.

of the author given there, as "an abbot of Rome", which would thus be the single salient fact known about the saintly Benedict in seventh-century Francia.

There has been much dispute between historians about the interconnection of the rule of St Benedict with that of St Columban, and the relative importance of those two rules during that century. Comparison of what historical records can tell us about St Benedict and his disciples with what they tell us about St Columban and his disciples is revealing and instructive. The Irish abbot migrated with a group of his followers from the fringe of the Christian world shortly before the end of the sixth century to pursue a wide-ranging monastic mission on the Continent, first in Merovingian Gaul and then in northern Italy. His introduction of Celtic practices aroused hostility in many quarters. Although he wrote a letter to St Gregory, his monastic rule obtained no such magnificent approbation as that given by the great pope, according to the *Dialogues*, to St Benedict's rule. Yet in a comparatively short span of time Columban's influence revitalized monasticism and Christian life in large areas of Europe. The impact of the monastic movement that he initiated, the activities of his disciples, and the pattern of monasteries founded by him and them, are well documented during the century following his death in AD 615. Far from declining because of the assumed breakthrough of the *RB*, Columbanian monasticism continued its upward progress throughout that period, as the main force revitalizing religious life in Western Europe.

We have a biography of Columban, written by his disciple Jonas of Bobbio, which we may compare with the biography of Benedict given in the *Dialogues*. Both works contain legendary hagiography, but Jonas's narrative differs markedly from Book II of the *Dialogues* in being firmly anchored in verifiable contemporary history. When the legendary genre is allowed for in the *Vita Columbani*, a solid and extensive substrate of historical fact can be discerned, which is not only corroborated by other sources but adds substantially and verifiably to our knowledge of the history of the time. That Jonas's account of St Columban's life draws on genuine personal reminiscences is apparent. Not only do we learn from it the names of many of the saint's chief companions and disciples, but we have independent proof from plentiful cross-references in other authentic documents that they really existed, and made their mark on their time and place.

Thus we possess solid factual information about the persons, travels and foundations of more than a score of disciples and successors of St Columban—abbots and bishops who played a formative part in the development of seventh-century Christendom. I give here a list of that important group, both original companions and second-generation followers, including persons who are known from independent references in many historical sources and place names, as well as from mention in Jonas's *Life of Columban*. They were, namely: Acharius, Athala, Audomar, Autbert, Bertulf, Chagnaold, Cumanus, Dicuil, Donatus, Eligius, Eustacius, Gall, Jonas, Potentinus, Ragnachar, Romaric, Sigbert, Ursicinus, Walaric, Waldebert, Wandrille, Winnochus. To those names must be added that of the abbess Fara and those of several other early alumni of the monastic school at Luxeuil, whose existence and activity is likewise historically attested.[3]

The firm anchorage in history of St Columban and his disciples, and of their acts and foundations, is therefore a very different case to that of St Benedict and his disciples, about whom no biographical facts are known from any independent source apart from the wonderland of the *Dialogues*. Whereas the first expansion of Columbanian monasticism is richly documented in the records and on the historical map of seventh-century Europe, there is no genuine historical evidence of the multiplication of Benedictine foundations that is alleged to have been proceeding apace since the sixth century. While there is abundant and historically verifiable evidence of the activities of Columban's disciples and successors, nothing provides similar verification of the legend of Benedict and his disciples, of which the sole source is the Dialogist's uncorroborated and unhistorical narrative.

Of special significance is the evidence of the two seventh-century prototypes of the so-called Hieronymian Martyrology, the calendar of saints accorded cult and liturgical honour in the Church, which I will discuss at greater length in Chapter 18. They show clearly that St Benedict was not included in the calendars throughout that century. On the other hand St Columban was included in them, although he had died as recently as the second decade of that century, over sixty years after the putative death of St Benedict, and although he had been accorded no such praise and esteem as the

---

[3] For relevant references and sources, cf. *Mélanges Columbaniens* (1950) and Prinz, *op. cit.*, Chapters IV, V & VI.

Dialogues give for the latter. Rather, Columban had been a controversial figure in his lifetime because of his non-Roman monastic provisions. Yet not only was he included in the ecclesiastical list of saints
but even two of his disciples, St Athala and St Eustasius, were
accorded the same honour. Their life story, like that of their master, had been recorded by Jonas of Bobbio in his *Vita Columbani*.
There is no hint of any similar honour paid to St Benedict's putative disciples named in the *Dialogues* attributed to St Gregory.

b. *Prescriptions of the* RB *and the* Regula Columbani *combined*

The history of Columbanian monasticism in Francia does indeed
provide the context in which the first recorded spread of the Benedictine observance occurred. It was through conjunction with Columban's rule that the *Regula Benedicti* made progress and gained growing
esteem. The introduction of the *RB* at Altaripa (assuming that it
occurred) was a unique instance in the seventh century of the adoption of that rule for use by a community of monks as their sole
observance. In all the other historically documented instances of its
use it appears to have been only a part of a mixed rule in which,
according to the normal eclecticism of that age, prescriptions from
different rules were combined. Deeper and more sympathetic study
has now confirmed that in that *Mischregelzeitalter* the monastic code
that had major prestige and spiritual power in Merovingian Christendom was that of St Columban. In his study of *The Frankish Church*,[4]
J.M. Wallace-Hadrill concluded that the *Regula Benedicti* was "certainly not widely known" in that period, though later partially inserted
in several monasteries and contributing a growing influence. In the
northerly Frankish region the Columbanian tradition retained its primacy. In southern Gaul the monastic traditions of Lérins and Arles
remained the most influential.

Despite many later references to the combination of monastic practices from both the Columban and Benedictine rules, there is no
documentary record of an established rule for monks composed of
specific sections of those different rules. We do, however, have the

---

[4] Oxford 1983, pp. 59, 63–74.

text of such a composite rule for two convents of nuns in which the *RB* figures prominently. The first of those two notable instances, already mentioned above, was the *Regula Donati*, compiled not long before AD 660 for the convent at Jussa-Moutier by Bishop Donatus of Besançon, which was made up of excerpts from the three rules of Caesarius of Arles, of Benedict and of Columban. In the other, called the *Regula cuiusdam patris ad virgines*, composed about the same time for the nuns of Faremoutier, probably by Abbot Waldebert of Luxeuil, the two components are from the rules of Columban and Benedict alone. In the *Regula Donati* 43 out of 77 chapters were taken from the *RB*; in the *Regula cuiusdam patris* no less than 70% was taken from the *RB*. Those two rules for nuns are the principal evidence for use and esteem of major elements of the *RB* in seventh-century monasticism.

Rival claims for the rules of St Benedict and St Columban were made in a seventeenth-century controversy between the Maurist historians on one side and the Bollandists and the Oratorian Le Cointe on the other. While the latter emphasized the continuing predominance of non-Benedictine forms of monasticism in France throughout the seventh century and beyond, Mabillon and his brethren piled up all the argument they could find to support their theory of pan-Benedictine observance. They and their later successors made much appeal to surviving monastery charters assumedly dating to that age in which they found several instances of prescription of observance of the *Regula Benedicti*. True, almost all those phrases in the charters enjoined observance of the *RB* not as the sole form of monastic life, but as one element combined with the rule of St Columban, and occasionally with other monastic codes. Nevertheless, the apologists made the most of the inclusive wording of those charters, which usually named the *RB* in first place: i.e. "*secundum regulam sancti Benedicti et sancti Columbani*". On the strength of such phrases in those charters an impressive structure of inference was built up by the Maurists and others later, arguing for a flourishing Benedictinism in Francia even in the middle of the seventh century. It came to be commonly assumed that there were very numerous monasteries in which a compound Benedictine-Columbanian rule was observed, and that, with the growing success of the *RB*, the Columbanian component of the mixed rule rapidly waned, to be displaced completely by its erstwhile partner.

According to the thesis of A. Malnory,[5] as updated by A. Zimmermann, P. Schmitz[6] and especially F. Prinz,[7] that development took its rise in the abbey of Luxeuil in the Vosges, which had been founded by St Columban as the mother-house of his movement about AD 590. From the evidence of later monastic charters and other mediaeval documents, those authors argued as follows: that about the year 630 (that is, just after Venerandus's introduction of the *RB* at Altaripa) the monks of Luxeuil mitigated the over-harsh rule of their Irish founder by blending it in a composite rule with the gentler code of St Benedict; that this composite rule (which those authors called the *Regula ad modum Luxoviensis*) was soon afterwards attested by the foundation charter of the abbey of Solignac and also by that of Rebais; and that thereafter, through the paramount influence of Luxeuil (and in particular of its third abbot Waldebert, who ruled there from 629 to 670) it spread rapidly and widely, being adopted for the foundation of new monasteries or for the reform of older ones.

Those authors made the further inference that because of the known interrelations between Frankish monasteries, and between leading churchmen, it can be assumed that the hypothetical "*Institutum Luxoviense*" was introduced into many other foundations, even though evidence to that effect is missing in the individual cases. Thus they reached the following conclusion; that the two-fold observance of Luxeuil was adopted by some hundred religious houses in Neustria in the course of the seventh century; that the pious queen Baldhild must have been the principal patron of these developments; that, thanks to her, the Benedictine-Columbanian mixed rule was established at Corbie, Luxeuil's most famous daughter monastery (founded about 660) as well as in dozens of other royally sponsored foundations and in the major basilicas in the towns of the kingdom; and that, through its association with that network of Columbanian foundations in the great movement of monastic vitality in that age, the *Regula Benedicti* spread ever more widely until it eventually overshadowed and supplanted the Irish-Frankish rule with which it had been temporarily blended. Impressive lists of the very numerous monasteries

[5] *Quid Luxovienses monachi discipuli Sancti Columbani ad regulam monasteriorum atque ad communem ecclesiae profectum contulerint*, Paris 1894.

[6] *Histoire de l'ordre de saint Benoît*, Maredsous 1948.

[7] *Frühes Mönchtum in Frankenreich*, Munich 1965.

that are alleged to have adopted the Benedictine-Columbanian rule are given by Zimmermann[8] and Schmitz.[9] From reading the arguments of those apologists one would assume that a large number of monastic charters dating from that age contained the key mention of the rule of Benedict in conjunction with that of Columban. C.R. Montalembert roundly asserted that almost all of them did so. I discuss the falsity of that assertion below, in Section d. of this chapter.

The bold claims of those apologists have been progressively discredited. Before describing that process I make one preliminary and obvious objection to them: if an assumedly famous *"Institutum Luxoviense"*, a composite monastic rule combining the rules of St Benedict and St Columban, was indeed so prevalent and successful that it was eagerly embraced by more than a hundred different monasteries throughout the Frankish realm, how is it that no manuscript or even MS fragment of the text of that assumedly triumphant and ubiquitous rule has survived? We do have complete texts of the mixed rules introduced into the two convents of nuns mentioned above, one at Jussa-Moutier, the other at Faremoutier; but we find not one trace of the putative rule of Luxeuil supposedly observed by more than a hundred communities of Frankish monks in that age. I return to this point below, when I discuss the comprehensive collection of monastic rules compiled by Benedict of Aniane in the early ninth century. I remark here that whether the impact of the *RB* on Columbanian monasticism was greater or smaller, it still remains disconcerting and inexplicable, for those who hold that the rule and its author had been made famous by the *Dialogues* of St Gregory the Great so many years previously, that it remained for so long merely a relatively minor component of a hybrid rule, without any reference to its origin or to its exceptional papal authority.

c. *The exclusivist decree of "the Council of Autun"*

Another very impressive but now discredited apologia for the theory of early predominance of the *RB* in Francia must be mentioned here. It has been commonly assumed that there is clear proof, from the

---

[8] *Kalendarium Benediktinum* I, p. xlvi.
[9] *Op. cit.*, I, Chapter 3.

Acts of a Council of the Frankish Church convened at Autun soon after the middle of the seventh century, that the *Regula Benedicti* was not simply a partner of the rule of Columban but was prescribed by that council as the sole monastic rule to be observed by all monks thenceforward. Once again it was Mabillon who first formulated this argument[10] which has been accepted by many scholars until recently as probative. He adduced two separate documents. One of them related that a synod of 54 bishops, convoked by the Frankish king Thierry III at a place called *Christiacus locus* (Cressy-sur-Somme?), solemnly approved a disposition of land known as the *Testament of St Leodegar*.[11] The other was a collection of prescriptions of uncertain origin and date attributed to a "Council of Autun". It contained the following impressive decree: "As for abbots and monks, they must fulfil and safeguard in all particulars whatever is taught by canonical order or by the Rule of St Benedict."[12] Mabillon brought those two apparently unconnected documents together to formulate his argument. He suggested that the putative synod of the 54 bishops under King Thierry which ratified the *Testament of Leodegar* was the same body as the "Council of Autun" which decreed those canons. "Perhaps in the same place and at the same time", he wrote, "there was held the synod known as that of Autun, in which canons were decreed to approve and enjoin upon monasteries the discipline of the Benedictine rule". Why, it might be asked, should that assembly of bishops held at *Christiacus locus* be called the Council of Autun? "Perhaps", replied Mabillon, "for no other reason than that it was principally through the influence of Leodegar, the bishop of Autun, that its canons were enacted".[13]

Following Mabillon's lead, later authors have until recently attached great importance to "the Council of Autun" which, they assumed, by ratifying "the canons of St Leodegar" promulgated the exclusivist decree that all monasteries should follow the rule of St Benedict to the exclusion of all others. They have seen that event as marking the moment of victorious breakthrough of the Benedictine observance and the achievement of its hegemony. Even Abbot Fernand Cabrol allowed himself to be led into unsubstantiated rhetoric about

---

[10] *Annales Ordinis S. Benedicti*, I. pp. 518–9, Paris 1723.
[11] The text is given in *CCL* 117, pp. 513–6.
[12] Text in *Concilia Gallica 511–695*, ed. C. de Clercq; *CCL* 148A, p. 318.
[13] *Annales*, p. 519.

that assumed triumph of the *RB*: "A council of Autun prescribes the observance of the Rule for all monks. From that moment onwards councils in uninterrupted succession apply themselves to establishing uniformity in monastic life by means of the adoption of this Rule, considered henceforward as the sole rule for monks."[14] Although it proved to be strangely difficult to assign an exact date to that momentous "Council of Autun" (suggested dates ranged between 662 and 679), or even to prove that it ever took place, those authors assumed its reality and visualized it as a not merely local synod. Its linking with the assembly of 54 bishops convened by royal command argued that it was a council of the whole Merovingian empire, or at least all Neustria and Austrasia. On the strength of his assumed insistence on general observance of the *RB*, it is also argued that St Leodegar (St Ledger) must also have established that rule earlier in his native province of Aquitaine, where he had been abbot of a monastery at Poitiers.

It must be said bluntly that this impressive structure of assertions, often repeated since it was first constructed by Mabillon, is simply illusory. It was by a series of unsound conjectures that he reached his conclusions. *The Testament of St Leodegar*, assumedly approved by an assembly of 54 bishops at *Christiacus locus*, is a highly suspect document. The earliest mention of it is found in a document dating from the late Middle Ages, when it was adduced by a monastery at Autun in a dispute about land ownership. Modern scholars (notably J. Pardessus, C. de Bye, B. Krusch and A. Hauck) have, like the seventeenth-century Bollandists, exposed it as a forgery—one of many such mediaeval stratagems to establish land rights by fictitious authorization. (Mabillon himself had at first judged it to be spurious, recognizing in it some patently false chronological references, but later changed his mind.) As for the "Council of Autun", assumed to be the same assembly as the meeting of 54 bishops at *Christiacus locus*, there is no reliable evidence for the convening of such a council in the seventh century. Nor can any firm facts be established about the date, origin or authority of the brief collection of "canons" attributed to St Leodegar. That collection, which was kept in the library of the cathedral at Angers (known therefore as the *Collectio Andegavensis*), is a disjointed group of prescriptions of general monastic interest and

---

[14] *DACL* II, p. 670.

evidently of different provenance.[15] The earliest record we have of it is in two MSS dating from the ninth century, a time when the Benedictine observance was spreading widely. The item relating to the *RB*, evidently originating at that later time, is numbered 15 in an abbreviated series in which several of the earlier numbered items are missing.

The implausibility of the appeal to an exclusivist decree supposedly passed by "the Council of Autun" or by St Leodegar is further apparent from the fact that the Columbanian and other forms of non-Benedictine monasteries remained prevalent for long after the seventh century, both in Burgundy and in Merovingian Gaul as a whole—including Aquitaine, where Leodegar is alleged to have previously introduced the *RB*. In Tours itself the Benedictine observance had still not been introduced by the time of Charlemagne at the end of the eighth century. Even Alcuin failed in his attempt to impose it there. G. Penco observes that "more than two centuries after the death of St Benedict a monastery in Aquitaine, that of Ligugé, had not yet undergone Benedictine influence; there are other historical testimonies to the same effect."[16]

Other cogent reasons also exclude the possibility that Leodegar, or a Frankish council of his time, would have decreed the sole observance of the Benedictine rule to the exclusion of the Columban. F. Prinz pointed out (following similar observations by G. le Bras) that Leodegar was made bishop as the protégé of Queen Baldhild, who greatly favoured the Irish monastic movement; that he collaborated with her in her programme of Church reorganization; that both Autun and Poitiers (where Leodegar had previously been abbot) were meeting points of earlier and still vigorous monastic traditions from both the north and south of France; and that Leodegar had lived for a long time at Luxeuil, the mother-house of the Columban tradition.

---

[15] Mansi traced them there: cf. *PL* 96, col. 377.
[16] "*La prima diffusione . . .*", pp. 334–5; Penco refers also to the evidence presented by H.M. Rochais in *Rev. Bén*, 63 (1953), p. 287.

d. "Saint Benoît s'est couché dans le lit de Saint Columban"

Although there was no surviving order of Columbanian monks to make a contrary case against the theories of the Maurists, Malnory and others, scholarly criticism has since shown the arbitrariness and weakness of those theories. Le Cointe and the seventeenth-century Bollandists have their later successors, who rebut the pleas outlined above. That the alleged textual testimonies to early observance of the *RB* were unauthentic was already shown by J.M. Pardessus in his edition of the Merovingian charters published in the mid-nineteenth century.[17] Later critical studies have further highlighted the fact. Particularly significant are the instances in which it can be recognized that in the key phrase found in some later mediaeval charters, namely, "*regula sancti Benedicti et sancti Columbani*", the reference to the *RB* was an addition made to texts that had originally named the Columbanian rule only. In several cases it can be clearly demonstrated that such interpolation was made in the manuscripts in later centuries, after the monasteries concerned had gone over to the Benedictine observance. The same can be reasonably inferred in the other cases. That discovery also discredits the arguments, referred to above (in Section b.) of apologists who have sought to multiply the number of monasteries claimed to have observed at an early date a rule which combined the monastic codes of Benedict and Columban. That is, because the key phrase is assumedly found in the early charter of one monastery, they inferred that the combined rule must have been observed in a string of other monasteries, either because they were affiliated to that one monastery or because they had a common patron. Many instances of such extrapolation are documented in F. Prinz's study of this field.[18]

Modern critical study of Irish-Frankish monasticism has confirmed its preponderance and enduring strength in the Merovingian realms.[19] The monastic movement introduced by St Columban and continued by his successors and disciples was by far the most active and

---

[17] *Diplomata, chartae et instrumenta aetatis Merovingicae*, 2 vols. Paris 1843–9.

[18] *Op. cit.*, especially in pp. 270–84.

[19] Cf. H. Clarke & M. Brennan (editors), M. *Columbanus and Merovingian Monasticism*, Oxford 1981. The spread and influence of Columbanian monachism in the seventh-century Frankish realms is presented in new light by Marilyn Dunn in Chapter 8 of The *Emergence of Monasticism*, entitled "Irish *peregrini* and European monasticism".

widely diffused in that age. It was by no means exclusivist. It reformed and built on the older monastic forms observed in Gaul and flexibly adopted elements from several non-Columbanian rules—including the *RB*. Malnory's postulate of an *"Institutum Luxoviense"*, a supposedly dominant hybrid rule promoted widely by Abbot Waldebert in which the *RB* was pre-eminent, has been challenged and discredited by several scholars, in particular by A. Hauck, J.M. Wallace-Hadrill, I. Zibermayr and J. O'Carroll. Hauck showed that it was the predominant Columbanian rule that motivated the great movement of monastic vitality radiating from Luxeuil in the seventh century; and that the phrases alleged from the later charters, linking the *Regula Benedicti* as partner with the *Regula Columbani* in that age, could be proved in almost every case to be later pro-Benedictine interpolations. In particular, it is proved that the mention of St Benedict's rule was later interpolated into the documents relating to the original statutes of both Solignac and Rebais, the two main Irish-Frankish monasteries in which, according to Malnory and others, the hybrid *"regula Luxoviensis"* was established in the earlier part of the seventh century. It was also proved that the few authentic texts containing a dual reference to the Columban and Benedictine rules reflected a situation after that century; that in any case they were of minor significance.[20] Similarly I. Zibermayr[21] showed that the undiluted Columbanian rule remained in full vigour right up to the time of the Bonifatian mission to Germany in the eighth century, and that it provided the monastic ethos of so notable a figure as Pirmin from Aquitaine, founder of Reichenau in 724, which the Maurists and their successors had claimed to be the mother-house of the Benedictine observance in Germany.[22]

The *Acts* of the international congress on the life and achievement of St Columban held at Luxeuil in 1950, and of the 1981 symposium on *Columbanus and Merovingian Monasticism*, served to bring into juster perspective the work and legacy of the great Irish monastic founder, and further illustrated the primacy of his new form of monastic observance, still in its first vigour, in seventh-century France.

---

[20] Cf. F. Prinz, *Kirchengeschichte Deutschlands*, 8th edition, Leipzig-Berlin 1954, I, pp. 272, 288–9. Prinz identified many instances of such interpolation, especially in pp. 270–84.

[21] *Noricum, Bayern und Österreich*, Munich-Berlin 1944, pp. 192–213.

[22] Cf. also H. Traube, *op. cit.*, pp. 16–19.

Another significant but insufficiently known contribution to this debate was that of James O'Carroll. In a study entitled "Monastic Rules in Merovingian Gaul"[23] he set out to answer the question: "At what period did the Rule of St Benedict begin to make its way into the Columbanian monasteries in Gaul?" He based his answer on a painstaking re-examination of the MS copies of individual monastic charters which had for so long been claimed to support the traditional theory of the prevalence in the seventh century of the *Regula Benedicti* in conjunction with the *Regula Columbani*. He reported his findings as follows:

> Of those documents, we have for the 7th century about 95 which may be accepted as probably more or less accurate copies of the original grants. In them, however, not "nearly always" [as Montalembert claimed] but only in 12 is there mention of the two rules, and it is not certain that even the evidence of these is to be taken at its face value.[24]

O'Carroll found that out of those 95 monastic charters of seventh-century origin no less than 79 described the rules observed within the individual monasteries in generic terms, such as *"iuxta regulam coenobiorum"*, *"iuxta traditionem patrum"*, *"iuxta religionis normam"*, *"sub sancta regula"*, *"regulariter viventes"*, *"secundum ordinem et monita antiquorum patrum"*. Like Hallinger, O'Carroll showed that a conservative eclecticism in monastic usage prevailed. Columban himself did not stress observance of a textual rule, but rather faithfulness to "the customs of the ancient Fathers". When drawing up a statute for the government of a monastery, a good abbot or patron would select elements from a number of rules, "making store for the future like a provident bee", as was said of St Filibert.[25] The very few authentic instances in which the charters record that the monks observed a combination of the rules of Columban and Benedict must therefore be seen in that setting. It would be anachronistic to see them as evidence of a "pro-Benedictine movement". O'Carroll, like Hauck and the earlier Bollandists, exposed as a later interpolation the reference to the *RB* in the Solignac charter, from which so much has been inferred. As for the few instances (found in 8 out of nearly 100 charters) in which there is mention of the sole observance of the *RB*, he

---

[23] In *Studies* (Dublin) 42 (1953), pp. 407–19.
[24] *Ibid.*, p. 408.
[25] *Ibid.*, pp. 411–2.

observed, "Hardly one of these can stand examination", and he saw strong reasons for rejecting them all as later forgeries.[26]

O'Carroll duly took account of the evidence that in the two mixed rules for nuns, introduced in the convents of Jussa-Moutier and Faremoutier, extensive extracts from the *RB* were combined with passages from the rule of Columban (and, in one of them, from the rule of Caesarius of Arles). It is indeed noteworthy that those two rules for nuns, composed by abbots who came from the Columbanian tradition, should contain a large proportion of borrowings from the *RB*. It is a sign that the spiritual and practical merits of the latter were beginning to be recognized and prized in some circles. O'Carroll also stressed the point that there is no evidence that any similar composite code for monks, drawing elements from the twin rules of Columban and Benedict, ever existed as a formal text. Rather, he argued, there is indication to the contrary in the collection of monastic rules brought together by Benedict of Aniane in the time of Charlemagne. In his *Codex regularum monasticarum et canonicarum*, giving the text of rules formerly observed, the Benedictine reformer and systematizer of the *RB* duly reproduced the text of the two composite rules for nuns, the *Regula Donati* and the *Regula cuiusdam patris*, but did not reproduce any composite text of a similar rule for monks, bringing together the rules of Columban and Benedict. According to the traditional apologetic, a hybrid rule of this nature had been used in scores of monasteries in seventh-century Gaul. As I remarked earlier, if any such standardized formulary had existed, one would expect it to have been a major item in the collection of rules painstakingly assembled by Benedict of Aniane. O'Carroll reasonably suggests that, since there was evidently no such standardized text, the use of the phrase *"secundum regulam sancti Columbani et sancti Benedicti"* in the few cases in which it is genuinely found, may refer to adoption by some Columbanian foundations of useful juridical provisions from the *RB*—in particular, the wise procedure for the election of an abbot.[27] A case in point may be the Columbanian foundation of St Wandrille about AD 690, for which Bishop Ansbert decreed *"ut per succedentia tempora secundum sancti patris Benedicti regulam abbatem eligerent"*. F. Prinz too facilely concluded that this text attests the com-

---

[26] *Ibid.*, p. 413.
[27] *RB*, Chapter 64.

plete supplanting of the Columbanian by the Benedictine rule, which is manifestly not the case. Later I refer to two similar instances from Northumbria in which it was stipulated that the procedure of the *RB* for election of abbot be followed. O'Carroll's answer to the question that he set out to answer is worth citing here, for it serves as a prelude to my fuller discussion (in Chapters 18 and 19) of the later developments to which he refers:

> We may say that this search for a notable Benedictine influence on the Columbanian abbeys before well on in the 8th century has met with little success. Its first real appearance is to be found in what may be called the "Austrasian movement". This was mainly the work of Carloman, Duke of Austrasia . . . By the middle of the 8th century we discern therefore the first dawning in Gaul of the "Benedictine Centuries", when abbeys already famous attained a new splendour: Luxeuil and St Gall, St Wandrille, Jumièges, Corbie, St Valéry, Faremoutier and Jouarre, and so many others which owed their existence to an Irish monk and to the Gallo-Romans and Franks who received his teaching. It was then that Benedict's sons began to erect the shining edifice of which it has been said, "*Saint Benoît s'est couché dans le lit de Saint Columban*".[28]

O'Carroll's findings were corroborated by G. Penco's study, published not long afterwards, in which he too pointed to the factors that had promoted false claims to antiquity and priority by Benedictine monasteries in the Middle Ages:

> As a parallel to the well-known tendency of parishes and dioceses to boast for themselves an Apostle or a direct disciple of an Apostle as their founder, so a large number of monasteries, especially in Gaul, attributed to themselves a very early adoption of the Benedictine rule, which, so it was claimed, had been delivered directly to them by one of St Benedict's own monks. In the Carolingian epoch there occurred an inevitable levelling out when the monasteries were submitted to a uniform legislation and brought into a firm monastic *Ordo*. Then the more powerful and long-established among them sought to equip themselves with a noble pedigree by demonstrating—using any means—their pristine adoption of the Benedictine rule . . . We know, moreover, that many documentary reports of the foundation of monasteries in the sixth and seventh centuries reflect a state of affairs existing about the tenth century. In order to make the later situation seem to accord with that of the period of the foundation, there was inserted into the original document, or more often into a copy of it, mention of the

---

[28] *Op. cit.*, p. 418.

Benedictine rule also, which had by then reached a general diffusion
unknown two or three centuries previously.[29]

In Chapter 19 I shall say more about the significance for our present question of what O'Carroll calls "the Austrasian movement" of
monastic refoundation in the eighth century. Here I offer some general comments on the long controversy about the date and extent
of the penetration of Benedictine observance into Columbanian-
Frankish monasticism. There is as yet no scholarly consensus on this
subject, and opinions are still swayed by traditional misconceptions.
Although the original thesis of the Maurists has been effectively
refuted, it is still widely influential. Governing much of the speculation on these issues is the traditional assumption that the *Dialogues*
had been written by Gregory the Great at the close of the sixth century, and therefore that the great rise to fame and pre-eminence of
the Benedictine monastic movement must have begun in Gregory's
age and must have been in full vigour and success during the seventh century. Authors who accept those assumptions without question
naturally tend to have a preconceived picture of the seventh-century
developments in monastic history.

The pro-Columbanian school of thought, on the other hand, also
over-emphasizes some of the data. The paucity and obscurity of the
seventh-century sources leaves wide scope for conjecture and differing
interpretations of some disputed points. In his major study of the
history of early Frankish monasticism, F. Prinz dissented on some
key points from the position of Hauck and even favoured the thesis of Malnory, but some of his own interpretations of the relevant
documents are open to serious question. In his densely informative
chapters he acknowledges again and again the uncertainty that surrounds so many of the relevant documents by reason of later falsifications and interpolations of the records. While his postulate of
"the predominant Benedictine-Columbanian rule" is a misnomer,
there is also exaggeration by some in the pro-Columbanian camp
who would have it that a unitary Columbanian observance prevailed
until the middle of the eighth century. As we have seen, it is unrealistic to attribute the ideal of a standardized monastic code, or
loyalty to a rule-book, to seventh-century founders and monks. Irish-
Frankish monastic observance in that age was not exclusivist. While

---

[29] *Op. cit.*, ("*La prima diffusione . . .*"), pp. 322–3.

specially treasuring the heritage of its patriarch St Columban, it also laid under contribution the legacy of St Martin of Tours and the other Gallo-Roman rules; it drew on the traditions of Lérins, of Arles and of Agaunum, of Italy and the East—and it also increasingly drew elements from the newly emerged and admirable rule attributed to an otherwise unknown Roman abbot named Benedict.

One must allow for some unconscious bias in the writing of some of the protagonists on both sides in this celebrated controversy. The Lutheran historian A. Hauck made very notable contributions to understanding of the pattern of events, and succeeded in discrediting the "pan-Benedictine" theories of the Maurists and their successors. But even he seems to have been swayed at times by antecedent favour for Celtic monasticism, which he saw as non-Roman and dissident, and by a corresponding disfavour for the *RB* as "the Roman rule". However, such tendency does not invalidate his substantial contribution to clarification of the main historical pattern. A balanced view must allow that a mixed observance of some provisions of the *Regula Benedicti* along with those of the *Regula Columbani* (and other rules) was used in several Frankish monasteries in the later seventh and early eighth centuries, and that such usages grew more frequent as the great virtues of the *RB* became more widely appreciated. On the other hand, it must be recognized that there was as yet no sign of general and exclusive favour for that rule; it had not yet been singled out from all other forms of monastic observance as of superior authority. The campaign to make it preponderant and to supplant all rivals was a later phenomenon which arose and met with rapid success in the first half of the eighth century. The reason for that phenomenal development was, I will argue in subsequent chapters, the emergence around the turn of the seventh century of the *Dialogues* attributed to Gregory the Great, which extolled the sovereign merit of that rule, and which ushered in a new era of cult of its miracle-working author and of pilgrimage to his shrine in the newly built monastery of Montecassino. The mission of St Boniface and of his collaborators to the territory of Austrasia brought that new Benedictine movement to the notice of the Frankish rulers and nobles, and enlisted their support for its victorious breakthrough.

CHAPTER FIFTEEN

STATUS OF THE *REGULA BENEDICTI* BY THE CLOSE OF THE SEVENTH CENTURY: ITS ARRIVAL IN ENGLAND, AND ITS CONTINUING NEGLECT IN ITALY

a

In this chapter I resume what is firmly known about the standing of the *Regula Benedicti* at the close of the seventh century, not only in Francia but in the rest of Europe. In subsequent chapters its relative obscurity at that time will be compared with its meteoric rise to fame and privileged observance in the following century—as a result, I shall argue, of the recent emergence of the assumedly Gregorian *Dialogues*.

After the first mention of the *RB* in historical record (either at Altaripa or later in the introduction of the *Regula Donati* at Jussa-Moutier) its merit gradually become more widely known during the second half of the seventh century. There was as yet no trace of Benedictine observance in southern Gaul, which remained attached to the older monastic traditions of Lérins and Arles. The potent new Irish-Frankish monastic movement initiated at the beginning of the century by St Columban and his disciples remained a paramount influence in the rest of Gaul and in the Germanic borderlands of Christendom. Among the Belgians, Frisians, Rhinelanders and "Bavarians" there was as yet no sign of predilection for the *RB*. The earlier missionaries in those lands, whether Irish-Frankish or Anglo-Saxon, used and transmitted the mixed monastic rules, in which the Columbanian rule was prominent, but in which the *RB* featured as an occasional component. Hallinger has shown how untenable was the older theory that the first monasteries founded in those regions were Benedictine.[1]

Monastic developments in the Anglo-Saxon kingdoms differed in some respects from those that had earlier occurred in Gaul. In

---

[1] "*Römische Voraussetzungen der bonifatianischen Wirksamkeit im Frankenreich*", in the symposium, *Bonifatius: Gedenkgabe zum zwölfhundertsen Todestag*, Fulda 1954.

England there was only distant influence from the movement of Columbanian monasticism radiating from Luxeuil. On their frequent journeys to and from Rome Anglo-Saxon churchmen and other pilgrims came into contact with the older Roman traditions (especially with Rhone Valley monachism inspired from Arles and Lérins), as well as with the newer Irish-Frankish foundations further north. A nearer and at first stronger influence, especially in Northumbria, was that of the Celtic monks coming directly from Ireland and western Scotland. After the Council of Whitby in 664, and still more after the coming of Archbishop Theodore and Abbot Hadrian from Rome to Canterbury in 669–70, Roman usages were reverently adopted throughout the Anglo-Saxon Church. There was as yet no existing Roman usage of that time encouraging them to observe the Benedictine rule or to honour its miracle-working author. In the following chapter I will show positive reason to conclude that neither Theodore or Hadrian (who came from a region of Italy not far from Montecassino) had knowledge of the *Life* of St Benedict contained in the *Dialogues*. As in contemporary continental monasticism, it was also in England still the age of the mixed rule. In the new monasteries arising there several different codes were blended. A revealing instance is in the foundations of St Benedict Biscop, who studied no less than seventeen monastic rules when composing his own.[2] One of them was the *RB*.

The earliest evidence of English appreciation of the Benedictine rule comes from the later *Life* of St Wilfrid by Eddius, who relates that at a synod of Edwinspath in AD 702 Wilfrid claimed the merit of having been the first to introduce use of that rule into the northern realms.[3] From Eddius's pages it would seem possible that he did so when abbot of Ripon, about AD 665–8. His own three years of monastic formation had been in the Rhone Valley tradition. At some time in his frequent continental travels he must have obtained the text of the *RB*. Like the Frankish archetype assumed to have been possessed by Venerandus, and also the two other early MS referred to earlier, it would probably have borne the ascription "*Regula sancti Benedicti abbatis Romensis*". That would have commended it to Wilfrid, so devoted to Roman ways. His dislike for the customs and even

---

[2] Bede, *Historia abbatum*, cap. 11: *Opera*, ed. C. Plummer, Oxford 1896, pp. 374–5.
[3] *Vita Wilfridi*, 14 & 47; *MGH, Scriptores Rerum Merovingicarum* 6, 1913, pp. 168, 209, & 242.

the persons of the Celtic monks is well documented; it would be natural for him to prefer what he thought was a Roman observance to the prevailing Columbanian rule of Irish origin that he encountered in Francia. However, some of Wilfrid's provisions for monasteries under his jurisdiction seem to be at variance with Benedictine conceptions. As E. John pointed out,[4] he built up a "monastic empire" of his own, in which he induced abbots and prioresses to make over the ownership of their properties to him, in the interests of continuity.

Although Wilfrid may have introduced the Benedictine rule in his homeland, it appears that it was not widely used there. According to a theory in vogue until quite recently, it has indeed been assumed that England was a stronghold of "pure" Benedictine observance at the time when continental monasteries were using the *RB* only as one component of a mixed rule. That theory, as we have seen, was a corollary of the now disproved assumption that Pope Gregory himself was a Benedictine monk and abbot, who sent Benedictine monks to convert England to the Christian faith, and that therefore the integral Benedictine rule must have been observed in the English monastic foundations throughout the seventh century. The evidence to the contrary is now too plain to be denied.[5] We seek in vain for any sign of the sole observance of the *RB* in any Anglo-Saxon monastery in the seventh century. The norm there, as in Francia, was the mixed rule. Nevertheless, there are indications that the merit of one particular element of the *RB* was recognized in England. Benedict Biscop stipulated before his death in AD 689 or 690 that the provisions of that rule for the election of an abbot should be followed; the same provisions were referred to in AD 716 by Abbot Ceolfrid as applicable to the monasteries of Jarrow and Wearmouth. This development parallels the indications from continental Europe that it was especially for the resolution of the vexed problem of appointment of abbots that the precept of the *RB* was used in mixed rules. It is of interest that the oldest surviving MS of the *RB* was transcribed in England in the eighth century (Oxford Hatton 38).

The pattern traced in the two previous chapters of the gradual and partial usage of the *RB* north of the Alps during the last sixty

---

[4] *Rev. Bén.* 75 (1965), pp. 219–21.
[5] The evidence is further detailed in *PsGD*, pp. 242–4.

years of the seventh century showed it puzzlingly as "the foreign flowering of an Italian plant", to borrow L. Salvatorelli's phrase.[6] When and where do we find the first authentic record of its presence and observance in the land in which all agree it originated? Not until the early eighth century is there evidence of its use in Italy as part of a mixed rule. (Although not currently observed there, the *text* of the *RB* was of course not unknown in seventh-century Rome. Venerandus's copy of it came from Rome, and the Dialogist, writing towards the end of that century, would have known it at least by repute—no doubt from pilgrims travelling to Rome from Francia and England—and probably had access to its text.)[7]

Columbanian monasticism had entered Italy early in the century. When Columban was expelled from Luxeuil in AD 610 by the rulers of the Burgundian sub-kingdom he and his companions made their way, after a stay at Lake Constance, into northern Italy. There he founded the monastery of Bobbio near Piacenza in 614, and died there three years later. Older writers used to claim that the Benedictine observance was introduced at Bobbio itself in the first half of the seventh century, but this claim was based on a spurious bull of Pope Theodore I, fabricated centuries later, long after the Bobbio monastery had gone over to the Benedictine observance.[8] The seventh century was for the most part a dark age for monasticism in Italy. While a vigorous monastic renaissance was gathering momentum in Merovingian Gaul, long years of war and Lombard pillage had broken down much of the old fabric of Italian society and had brought religious life to a parlous state in many parts of the peninsula. In so far as there was a significant monastic development in Rome and southern Italy it came from the Greek-speaking East, which increasingly influenced Roman life in that period. Certainly, there is no trace of Benedictine foundations in Italy during that century.

It was not until the reign of the Catholic Lombard king Perctarit (AD 671–88) that a more peaceful age and a monastic revival could come to the Church in Italy. As the seventh century drew to its close the new wave of vitality from the monasteries beyond the Alps

---

[6] *Op. cit.*, p. 196: "...*fioritura prevalentamente straniera dell'istituto benedettino, pianta italiana*".

[7] As I argue below, in Chapter 24.b.

[8] Cf. G. Penco, *Storia del Monachesimo*, Rome 1960, p. 103, and *La prima diffusione*, p. 336; also K. Hallinger, *SA* 42, p. 264, note 101.

was transmitted to the Lombard dominions in northern Italy. Like
the Frankish kings and nobles earlier, the Lombard kings and dukes
became zealous patrons of new monastic foundations. The most
famous of those foundations was the abbey of Farfa, founded in AD
705. It is there that we find the first probable sign of use of the *RB*
in Italy. The observance introduced there, following the familiar pattern of the age, was a *regula mixta*. We have a later Carolingian document, expressed in fairly standardized terms, that seems to reflect
the founding statute of Farfa, and thus to provide us with the earliest glimpse of partial use of the *RB* in Italy. It was stipulated that
the new abbey was to be "like the other monasteries following the
ways of Lérins, Agaunum and Luxeuil, where the pristine rule of
Basil, of Benedict, of Columban and of other Fathers, is seen to be
observed".[9] (It is of course possible that the words "of Benedict"
were added later, as in so many other cases.) The same mixed rule
was subsequently observed at Farfa's daughter house, St Vincent on
the Volturno. Some twenty years after the founding of Farfa we have
the first record of the introduction of the *RB* as the sole observance
of an Italian monastery. That came about with the foundation of
the new abbey of Montecassino under Pope Gregory II.

b. *The "yawning gulf" in the history of the* RB

So we find that study of the *Mischregelzeitalter*, the age of the mixed
monastic rule, provides significant pointers for our inquiry into the
emergence of the *Dialogues* and their relevance to early Benedictine
history. The Maurist historians and their successors, taking for granted
the widespread knowledge of St Benedict's life and rule in the age
of St Gregory, were likewise convinced of the prevalence of the *RB*
in the subsequent age and of its rise to supremacy in the seventh
century. They and their successors assumed that the rule written by
the famous thaumaturge and monastic founder whose *Life* St Gregory
had written, a rule that the great pope had singled out for the highest approbation, must have been, as P. Schmitz put it,[10] "the monas-

---

[9] *MGH, Diplomata Karolinorum* I, 1956 edition, p. 141; cf. Hallinger, *SA* 42, p. 264,
note 103.
[10] *Histoire de l'ordre de saint Benoît*, Maredsous 1948, I. p. 64.

tic rule *par excellence*" from that time onwards. But, as is now more and more recognized, it was not so. After reviewing the evidence to the contrary, K. Hallinger summed up:

> Since therefore—as we must firmly conclude—the system of the mixed rule was everywhere predominant at the *end* of the century, it is simply untenable to postulate for the *beginning* of the seventh century the very reverse of that situation, namely, a uniformity that everywhere in the West belongs to a much later phase of development. So, try as one may, one cannot take what is the end-result of the historical development—that is, the sole hegemony of *one* rule—and make it into the starting-point of the historical process.[11]

In that historical setting the *RB*, while having as yet only a subordinate place as one of the many rules in use, at the same time stands out in its own right as a major synthesis of monastic wisdom. In accordance with contemporary custom, the author borrowed from pre-existing formularies—particularly, it seems, from the *Regula Magistri*. Thus the *RB* was itself a "mixed rule". Nevertheless it had an original power and attractiveness that ensured its survival and increasing use among the many rival forms of coenobitical observance. It had special qualities of moderation, flexibility and enlightened common sense, not indeed previously unknown in monastic codes, but not elsewhere blended in such masterly fashion. In particular, there is the author's insistence on what is of lasting importance, in contrast to ritual minutiae and secondary details; his concern to adapt his prescriptions to the diverse requirements of persons, conditions and circumstances; his readiness to leave flexible disposition of everyday matters to the judgement of the abbot; his realistic understanding of human nature as it is, and his avoidance of excessive rigorism; his far-ranging perspectives, which make his rule suitable not merely for one community, or for one region or climate, but universally; and especially his serene balance of judgement and his ruling aim to link the abbot with his sons, through charity and obedience, into one stable family united in devotion to the will of God.[12] With those intrinsic merits it is not surprising that the *RB*, after its first obscure emergence into history at Altaripa in the second quarter of the seventh century, gained an ever wider (albeit still modest) diffusion. The

---

[11] *SA* 42, pp. 265–6.
[12] Cf. A. Lentini OSB, *San Benedetto: la Regola*, Montecassino 1980, pp. xxviii–xxix.

decisive extrinsic reason for its eventual prevalence, namely, the
renown that would accrue to it and its author from the pseudo-
Gregorian *Dialogues*, still lay in the future. K. Hallinger's objective
survey of the monastic pattern in western Christendom at the beginning of the eighth century shows that there was still no sign of the
breakthrough to unitary observance of the *RB* that was to begin in
the middle years of that century. He sums up as follows:

> It is now plain to see, in the documentary records of western Europe,
> how tardily Benedict began to move into the foreground. We know
> that the pattern of his rule, hitherto submerged, began to rise in the
> eighth to ninth centuries, on the wings of the *Romidee*,[13] until it attained,
> over a span of no more than 250 years, to sole dominance in the
> sphere of monastic and religious life. Between that high period in which
> it rose to dominance and the period of the late sixth century there
> lies a yawning gulf, which one must not unwarily attempt to bridge
> with modern modes of thought . . . The second book of the *Dialogues*
> counts for nothing in this connection. That book stands out in isola-
> tion from all the other Gregorian works—a fact that has not been
> observed. In his *Homilies*, and moreover throughout the wide range of
> commentaries on Scripture that Gregory delivered to his monks, Benedict
> plays no part. Still more unbelievable for the present-day mentality is
> the fact that nowhere in his official letters does he make any mention
> of the great abbot. In them, he does indeed constantly deal with monas-
> tic affairs; surely, therefore, there would have been plentiful occasion
> to mention, at least once, the name of the venerable lawgiver?[14]

The older historiography of Benedictine origins looked for and claimed
to find abundant proof of the observance of the *Regula Benedicti* in
St Gregory's lifetime and throughout the following age. The new
historiography, correcting those hoary illusions, has set the record
straight and established the complete dearth of reliable evidence of
Benedictine observance in that early period. In this new situation,
the witness of *Dialogues* II.36 stands out, as Hallinger shrewdly observed,
as a strangely isolated and anachronistic phenomenon. Hallinger pon-
dered uneasily over that paradox, but since he did not then openly
question the traditional ascription of the *Dialogues* to Gregory he
could not offer a satisfactory explanation of it. At that time he con-
tented himself with a brusque judgement on the irrelevance of the

---

[13] I.e. the Romeward-looking ideas and polity of the Frankish renaissance, based
on special reverence for the see and successor of St Peter.
[14] *SA* 42, pp. 270–1.

isolated passage in Book II when compared with all the contrary evidence: "*zählt hier nicht*". The eighth-century upsurge in observance of the *RB* to which he referred will be traced more fully below, in Chapter 19. Here I would draw attention once more to a very significant problem closely linked with the puzzle of the belated ascendancy of the *RB*, which defenders of the Gregorian authorship of the *Dialogues* cannot satisfactorily solve: namely, the absence in all the seventh-century records of any indication of cult, or even of biographical knowledge, of the miracle-working author of the *RB*, St Benedict.

c. *Why was knowledge and cult of St Benedict so long delayed?*

Although there are many references to the *RB* in the records of the seventh century, there was before the closing decades of that century nothing to link the author of that rule with the great thaumaturge of Cassino whose *Life* had been assumedly written by Pope Gregory I in his *Dialogues*. St Benedict is thought to have died about AD 552, and the *Dialogues* telling the story of his life are thought to have been written in 593. Yet for nearly a century after the putative origin of that book there is no trace of knowledge anywhere of the details of St Benedict's life described there in such graphic detail. He appears only as a name in the title of a monastic rule written by a holy abbot of Rome. Like many another he is called *sanctus*, but that adjective was commonly applied to venerable persons and did not imply that the person so described was an object of cult and one of the intercessory saints honoured in the Church's liturgical worship and in popular piety. In fact there is no evidence throughout the whole of the seventh century of any cult or liturgical honour of Benedict, or pilgrimage to his shrine, despite the extraordinary holiness and thaumaturgic power attributed to him in the *Dialogues*. Not until the first quarter of the eighth century do we find any devotional veneration or liturgical commemoration of him—as a consequence, I shall argue, of the publication of his *Life* in the *Dialogues* not long before.

Those significant facts cannot simply be brushed aside, as "a mere argument from silence" of no consequence. If, as has been commonly assumed, Pope Gregory's celebrated biography of the great miracle-working abbot-founder was known and widely diffused throughout the seventh century, it is indeed an extraordinary silence. We have seen that, according to the Maurists and many other scholars in later times, the influence and diffusion of the Benedictine monastic rule is assumed to have been very considerable, indeed paramount, in that century. Yet the greater that influence is assumed to be, the more difficult it becomes to answer the present objection. If there was a widespread pro-Benedictine movement which superimposed the *Regula Benedicti* on the *Regula Columbani* in numerous Frankish monasteries in that age, all the more should we expect to find, somewhere, some authentic mention of personal details about the life, miracles and cult of the great saint who was the author of the *RB* and whose wondrous power had been assumedly made famous by Pope Gregory. Yet no such authentic mention can be found in that long period. I shall return to the question of the long and strange *incognito* of St Benedict in Chapter 18, when tracing the beginning of cult of the saint in the eighth century.

Here I again draw attention to the similarly strange lack, not only in the seventh century but for long afterwards, of any genuine historical record concerning the reputed disciples and successors of St Benedict. In the *Dialogues* we read of noble and pious families honouring him at Subiaco and committing their sons to be his disciples. Among the latter Maurus and Placidus have special mention. Benedict, we read, constituted twelve abbots for twelve monasteries that he founded in the neighbourhood of Subiaco. Later there were his very numerous disciples in his main foundation at Montecassino, with its daughter house at Terracina to which the noble brothers Speciosus and Gregorius belonged. The author of the *Dialogues* claims to have received first-hand information about the saintly abbot from four of his chief disciples, Constantinus, Valentinian, Simplicius and Honoratus, three of whom succeeded to his abbatial authority. Yet outside the pages of the *Dialogues* there is not the slightest historical indication that any of those disciples and successors of St Benedict ever existed. Unlike the disciples of St Columban, and of other great founders before and since, they left no mark on the religious traditions of their own or the following age. This evidence should surely raise sceptical questions. Did none of them go further afield, handing on the torch they had received from their illustrious master? Did none of them follow his example and make further monastic foundations of their own? How is it that, apart from the *Dialogues*, the hagiography and sanctoral calendars of the sixth, seventh and eighth centuries have no mention of them, that there is no echo of their lives, deeds and words, and that cultic devotion to them was likewise lacking? As noted earlier, in Chapter 13.c, attempts to fill that gap began only in the ninth century, with the appearance of the forged *Life* of St Maurus. The fictitious *Life* of St Placidus came much later.

CHAPTER SIXTEEN

THE FIRST EMERGENCE OF THE *DIALOGUES* INTO HISTORICAL RECORD IN THE LATE SEVENTH CENTURY

a

I return now from discussion of the origins and first appearance of the *Regula Benedicti* to discussion of the origins and first appearance of the *Dialogues*. Despite many strenuous attempts to prove the contrary, not only can no contemporary witness to the existence of the *Dialogues* in the age of Gregory the Great be found, but the same eloquent silence persisted throughout the greater part of the seventh century. When was that silence at last broken? The answer is: not until the closing decades of that century. From that time we have a remarkable group of documentary evidences, from England, France and Spain, all showing knowledge of the existence and contents of the *Dialogues* and all appearing within the same short span of years. In *PsGD* I discussed the testimonies of four contemporary authors clearly demonstrating such knowledge: Aldhelm of Malmesbury, Adamnan of Iona, Julian of Toledo and Defensor of Ligugé. Thanks to additional and corrective information given by R. Godding in his critique of *PsGD* (for which I express my appreciation) I can now add to that list two more contemporary witnesses, namely the authors of the *Visio Baronti* and of the *Passio Proiecti*, hagiographical works that can be dated to the same period in which the four witnesses named above were writing their concordant testimonies.

Marilyn Dunn also signals the pioneer witness of the *Visio Baronti* to the existence of the *Dialogues*. She sees in it a significant reaction against the still novel system of "tariffed penance" imported from Ireland and reflected in the tales in the *Dialogues*. She argues that its reflection there provides further evidence of the recent origin of that book (and thus implicitly discredits the many earlier sightings alleged by the critics of *PsGD*):

> The *Vision of Barontus* is one of the earliest authentic witnesses to the existence of the *Dialogues* as a whole and clearly takes issue with the

idea that a sin such as that of Justus [in *Dial.* IV.57] may be purged in the afterlife through the offering of the eucharist for a set period of time.[1]

Coupled with the evidence of those six contemporary writers, there is tangible proof of the existence of the *Dialogues* at the end of the seventh century in the shape of four surviving MS fragments of the text, all of which can be dated around the turn of that century or in the first quarter of the eighth. Those MSS will be discussed in the following chapter.

Here I will first discuss the early evidence of knowledge of the *Dialogues* in the writings of St Aldhelm of Malmesbury, a key witness. Three of his works are relevant here: (1) his prose work, *De laudibus virginitatis*; (2) his later verse paraphrase of that work, entitled *Carmen de virginitate*; and (3) his *Epistola ad Acircium*. Their date of origin can be determined with fair accuracy to the ninth and tenth decades of the seventh century. For this dating I use the findings of R. Ewald, G. Browne, W. Wildman and M. Manitius.[2] Aldhelm's three works attest his progressive awareness and acceptance of the legends told in the *Dialogues*. The origin of the prose work, *De laudibus virginitatis*, can be dated as certainly not prior to AD 686 but not after 690. The reasons for that dating are as follows. In his prefatory dedication of the work to the abbess Hildilid and the nuns of Barking, Aldhelm named as a member of that community his kinswoman Cuthburga. That princess, a sister of King Ine of Wessex, had been married in the year 685 to Aelfrid (or Aldfrith), king of Northumbria, but their union had been of very short duration. Cuthburga separated from Aelfrid and took the veil in the nunnery of Barking, moving not long afterwards to Wimborne as abbess. Aldhelm's prose work *De laudibus virginitatis* must therefore have been composed during the relatively short period in which she was still at Barking. The indications in the text point to its date of origin between 686 and 690.[3]

---

[1] *The Emergence of Monasticism*, p. 189. She notes on p. 246, nn. 124 & 126, that J. Hillgarth also indicates some direct quotations from the *Dialogues* in the *Visio Baronti*.

[2] Ewald, *Aldhelmi Opera, MGH*, Berlin 1919 & "*De aenigmatibus Aldhelmi et acrosticis*", in *Festschrift Albert von Bamberg*, Gotha 1905; Browne, *St Aldhelm: his Life and Times*, London 1903; Wildman, *Life of St Ealdhelm*, London 1903; Manitius, *Geschichte des lateinischen Literatur des Mittelalters*, Munich 1911, vol. I, pp. 134–41; also his *Zu Aldhelm und Baeda*, Vienna 1886.

[3] Cf. Wildman, *op. cit.*, pp. 127–8.

In the thirtieth chapter of that prose work of Aldhelm we find biographical and devotional references to St Benedict (as distinct from mention of his name as author of the *RB*). In it Aldhelm as yet made no mention of Pope Gregory as the author of Benedict's life-story, as he was to do later with enthusiasm. What he said there about St Benedict was strangely vague and inaccurate. He made no specific reference to Benedict's miracles, as he was to do in his later poetic work *Carmen de virginitate*. His concern in that earlier prose work was to cite Fathers and monastic founders who were models of consecrated chastity, of whom he mentions Benedict as an eminent Western example. He remarked on the meaning of the name *Benedictus*, with its scriptural and liturgical allusions. He went on to say in general terms that because "Christ's recruit" preserved spotless chastity he enjoyed divine protection, attested by heavenly signs and miracles. A large section of the passage devoted to Benedict was taken up by a long and complicated metaphor, devoid of any biographical illustration, in which he presented the saint as an evangelical harvester in the Lord's vineyard, whose husbandry brought good grapes to be pressed in the mystic winepress, there to be made into spiritual wine to be stored by the angelic taverners for the celestial banquet. The contrast between this vague verbiage and the explicit biographical knowledge about St Benedict shown in Aldhelm's later verse work is evident, and has been remarked by commentators. Rudolf Ewald, editor of his works, commented as follows on the oddity of what he says about the saint in that earlier text: "What he there brings forward in praise of Benedict he seems to have composed out of his own head (*de suo*)".[4] There are indeed in that prose work *De laudibus virginitatis* several indications that Aldhelm already had some general knowledge of the stories contained in the *Dialogues*, but it was unspecific and garbled. Chief among those indications is the chapter referring to an episode concerning St Scholastica, which clearly relates to the same event recounted in *Dial.* II.33, but in a manner strangely discordant from Aldhelm's understanding of the episode in his subsequent poetic work.[5]

In that poem, the *Carmen de virginitate*, written during the last decade of the seventh century, Aldhelm paraphrased and greatly extended the themes of his earlier prose work. In it the short and unspecific

---

[4] *Op. cit.*, p. 268, footnote.
[5] Cf. *PsGD*, pp. 164–70.

references to Benedict were replaced by 39 lines of verse, explicitly recalling the saint's miracles and evidently based directly on the text of Book II of the *Dialogues*. Aldhelm concluded his eulogy with the express statement in metrical Latin that Pope Gregory, to whom the English people owed their faith, had written the *Life* of the holy abbot Benedict:

> His matchless life, from its first beginning
> Until he ascended in bliss to the heavenly citadel
> Was once described by illustrious Gregory in writing.
> We, the citizens whom fecund Britain carries in her bosom
> Are joyfully gathered into the number of his disciples;
> From him the grace of baptism first flowed to us,
> From him the venerated band of teachers hastened hither.[6]

In his *Carmen de virginitate* Aldhelm amplified, in a form more fully in accord with the text of the *Dialogues*, the story he had earlier told about Scholastica. He still did not enhance the credit of that story by making reference to the authority of St Gregory, as he did in his references to Benedict. Instead he said, rather oddly, that the tale about Scholastica was very widely told by *rumusculus*, that is, by popular gossip.[7] Whatever successive stages there may have been in Aldhelm's coming to knowledge and acceptance of the *Dialogues*, there is very clear evidence that, by the time he wrote his *Epistola ad Acircium*, around the turn of the century, he had studied the text carefully. He there cited verbatim two phrases from it, expressly referring to a grammatical usage by Pope Gregory "in the third volume of the dialogue".[8] That allusion by Aldhelm is the first known reference to the short title by which the supposedly Gregorian work became universally famous, and to its division into four books. I say more about the significance of his testimony and of his association with other Anglo-Saxon scholars in Section c. below.

One of the nine Barking nuns to whom Aldhelm dedicated his earlier prose work was in fact named Scholastica. Although there is no trace of devotion to the sister of Benedict who features in the *Dialogues* anywhere else before the middle of the eighth century,

---

[6] *Opera* (ed. Ewald), pp. 389–90; lines 844–80.
[7] *Ibid.*, lines 2082–9.
[8] "*Et notandum quod Focas grammaticus praeteritum tempus frico fricui exposuit, Gregorius vero in tertio dialogi volumine non fricuit retulit, dicens: faciem defuncti fricavit, et infra, cumque diutius fricaretur et cetera*" (*Opera*, p. 191; the citation is from a passage in *Dial*. III.17.4.)

A. de Vogüé assumes that the Barking nun had been named after
her, and concluded from that reference that she must therefore have
been venerated in England previous to that time.[9] It would be strange
indeed (but not impossible) for a recently professed nun to have
taken the name of a saintly virgin known from current *rumusculus*;
more probably, Aldhelm's reference shows that the name was not
unique but was already in use in late antiquity.

b. *Other earliest witnesses to the emergence of the* Dialogues

The other five pioneer testimonies to the emergence of the *Dialogues*
into public awareness are all contemporary with that of Aldhelm.
Although less explicitly, they likewise give satisfactory evidence, from
Scotland, Spain and France, of the rise and spread of knowledge of
the book in the last decades of the seventh century. In his *Life of St
Columba* Adamnan of Iona, though making no explicit mention of it,
in at least three places clearly borrowed phrases from its narrative
to weave into his own.[10] As in the case of Aldhelm's relevant writings, the dating of Adamnan's work can be determined fairly precisely. He was born in Ireland about 628 and died in 704. After
early training in his homeland he entered the monastery on the
island of Iona off the north-west coast of Scotland, and in the year
679, on the death of Failbe, became abbot there. In 686 he went
on a mission to the court of King Aelfrid of Northumbria. Two
years later, in 688, he returned to Northumbria, where he studied
(and adopted) the Roman customs of the Anglian monks. On his
second visit he spent some time at Ceolfrid's monasteries of Wearmouth
and Jarrow, in the libraries of which was the rich store of books
brought back to Northumbria from Rome and Gaul by Benedict
Biscop and by Ceolfrid himself. The editors of Adamnan's work have
shown from several indications in the text that he composed his *Life
of Columba* in Iona while he was abbot there, at a date subsequent
to his second visit to Northumbria in 688.[11] The work must therefore have been written during the sixteen years between that date

---

[9] *RHE* 83 (1988), p. 314.
[10] A. and M. Anderson, *Adomnan's Life of Columba*, edited with translation and
notes, London 1961, pp. 20, 23, 204n, 302n.
[11] *Ibid.*, p. 94.

and his death in 704; probably it was completed during the reign of King Domnall Dond of Dall-Réti (688–696). Finally, after considering all the evidence, those editors conclude: "Adomnan must have written the Life of Columba between 688 and 704, and almost certainly between 688 and 692".[12] Since it is sure that Adamnan's *Life of Columba* contains, in A. de Vogüé's words, some "*réminiscences indubitables des Dialogues*",[13] it follows that a text of the latter work had reached the abbot of Iona at almost the same time from which we have evidence that it had come to the knowledge of Aldhelm in Wessex. Adamnan's contacts with the Northumbrian court and scholars, in particular with Benedict Biscop and Ceolfrid (whose monasteries at Wearmouth and Jarrow he visited in 688), suggest the probable source from which he himself gained knowledge of the *Dialogues*.

A third early sighting of the *Dialogues*, from Spain, can be dated with precision to the very same period in which those two other primary testimonies from the island of Britain originated. It is found in the last work of St Julian of Toledo, entitled *Prognosticon futuri saeculi*, which, it is generally agreed, can be dated with exactitude to the years 688–689. A modern critical edition of the work by J.N. Hillgarth has been published in the *Corpus Christianorum* series.[14] Born about 642, Julian became a disciple of Eugenius of Toledo, was consecrated as archbishop of Toledo in 680, and died in 690. As well as writing historical, grammatical and theological works of his own he was, like many in that age, a zealous anthologizer. His *Prognosticon futuri saeculi* was a collection of opinions of the Fathers on the afterlife, particularly on the state of souls before the final resurrection. He quoted such opinions verbatim, mainly from the works of Saints Augustine, Gregory and Isidore. That the work dated exactly from the year 688 appears from the author's prefatory letter to Idalius, Bishop of Barcelona, and from the latter's reply also given in the text. That exchange of letters was the fruit of a colloquy between the two bishops at Toledo just before Easter in 688. Idalius's presence at Toledo at that time is explained by his attendance at the fifteenth Council of Toledo. The *Prognosticon* must therefore have been finished

---

[12] *Ibid.*, pp. 55–96.
[13] Cf. *SC* 251, p. 142, note 6. For the relevant *loci* in Adamnan's work, cf. A. and M. Anderson, *op. cit.*, pp. 20, 23, 204n, 302n.
[14] *S. Juliani Opera*, I, *CCL* 115.

by the end of that year, or at least by 689, the year before Julian's death.[15]

In that work Julian quoted a large number of passages, sometimes in abbreviated form, from the works of St Gregory the Great. Among them are some ten excerpts which, in the Gregorian corpus, appear only in the *Dialogues*.[16] Those citations, which are introduced by phrases expressly naming Gregory as their author, are all found among the borrowed doctrinal passages that I have marked out as the "IGPs". That Julian is quoting them directly from the text of the *Dialogues* (and not from the surviving store of unpublished Gregorian *reportata* brought to Spain by Tajo of Saragossa) appears from a single phrase introducing one of them.[17] There he does not merely use the expression "as blessed Gregory says", as in all the other instances, but writes: "We read that when Peter asked about this matter Gregory replied as follows . . ." This explicit phrase indicates that Julian was quoting directly from the *Dialogues* narrative. We know of channels by which that work could have reached him in the years immediately preceding. From the time that he became archbishop of Toledo in 680, he was in frequent communication with the Roman Curia, especially because of the theological controversies in which he was involved.[18]

One may remark a strange feature of Julian's choice of Gregorian passages to include in his anthology of teaching on the life of departed souls. It is his omission of any quotation from or reference in his work to the abundant descriptions of life in the Beyond contained in the main narrative text of the *Dialogues*. The graphic accounts of events in the other-world contained in that text, especially in Book IV, would have provided him with many very relevant "prognostications of the world to come" for inclusion in his collection of Gregorian passages specifically relating to the afterlife. One could speculate whether Julian's omission of any mention of those accounts,

---

[15] Cf. C. Pozo, "*La doctrina escatologica del 'Prognosticon futuri saeculi' de S. Julian de Toledo*", in *Estudios Eclesiasticos*, 45 (1970), pp. 175–201.

[16] I list them in *PsGD*, p. 174, note 32.

[17] It is the passage in *Prognosticon* II.8, where Julian cites a passage from *Dial.* IV.26.1–4 (IGP 57). Cf. my discussion of this passage, and of Peter's inept cue-question, in the Appendix below, IGP 57, and more fully in *PsGD*, pp. 547–8.

[18] Cf. J.N. Hillgarth, "*El Prognosticon futuri saeculi de san Julian de Toledo*", in *Analecta Sacra Tarraconensia*, 30 (1957), pp. 5–61; see also his edition of Julian's *Opera*, p. x, note 2.

which were vouched for in that newly appeared and assumedly Gregorian master-work, may not indicate that he had scholarly reserve about the authenticity of that newly emerged *Gesta*-text, and that he prudently confined his quotations to passages in that book that clearly had the stamp of the great pope's own doctrinal teaching.

I acknowledge that the two further early sightings of the *Dialogues* signalled by R. Godding, in the *Visio Baronti* and the *Passio Praeiecti*, are sure. Marilyn Dunn also recognizes those two texts as among "the first secure evidence" of the beginning of circulation of the *Dialogues*.[19] Godding concludes that the *Visio Baronti* dates from "a short time after the event to which it relates, which is given as March 25th 678–679." We do not know how many years after 679 the work was written, but it is reasonable to suppose that it was about the same time that the testimonies of Aldhelm, Adamnan and Julian were written and circulated: that is, during the 'eighties or early 'nineties of the seventh century.

The same can reasonably be inferred of the *Passio Praeiecti*, which refers at least twice to the *Dialogues* written by St Gregory, and which Godding, following Krusch, dates as "written not long after 676".[20] From it he cites the words: "The most blessed Gregory, pontiff of the Roman Church, to whom the secrets of heaven lay open, recorded in the book bearing the title of *Dialogues* the ordeals of the saints, recounting there their manifold and beatific deeds". Godding also confidently adduced another and allegedly much earlier seventh-century testimony to knowledge of the Gregorian *Dialogues* in the seventh century, a sentence in the "*Chronicle of Fredegar*", for which he makes the bold claim that it is "the most ancient explicit attestation of the existence of the *Dialogues*".[21] I remit until Chapter 22 my discussion and refutation of that unsustainable claim, as also of other claims similarly based on texts of dubious origin and date.

A few years after the publication of the group of the earliest five testimonies to the emergence of the *Dialogues*, all dating from about the same time, a sixth is found in a work by Defensor of Ligugé

---

[19] *The Emergence of Monasticism*, p. 192.

[20] Cf. Godding, *op. cit.*, p. 218. He refers to the texts of the two works in *MGH, Scriptores rerum Merovingicarum*, V, Leipzig 1910. He also refers, somewhat diffidently, to another work that refers to the *Dialogues* as Gregory's, the *Vita Adelphi Habendensis* (*BHL* 73), which Levison dates to the end of the seventh century but which other scholars date much later, to the Carolingian age.

[21] *AB* 106 (1988), p. 220.

(near Tours), entitled *Liber Scintillarum*. It is an anthology of some 1,800 excerpts culled from writings of the Fathers. In his critical modern edition of the work H.-M. Rochais gives the results of his researches on Defensor's citation of the individual Church Fathers.[22] After Isidore, Gregory is the author whom he quotes most frequently. From the *Homilies on the Gospels* he cites about 110 excerpts; from the *Homilies on Ezekiel*, about 40; from the *Regula Pastoralis*, about 40; from the *Moralia*, about 30. In addition he cites nine passages that appear in the text of the *Dialogues*.[23] All but one of the latter belong to the category of IGPs. The one exception is a single sentence that is found in *Dial.* III.14.5, spoken by the wonder-working abbot Isaac: "*Monachus qui in terra possessionem quaerit monachus non est.*" That citation can be taken as probable confirmation that Defensor drew those nine Gregorian excerpts directly from the *Dialogues*. Thanks to Rochais's researches, we can fix fairly accurately the date of that anthology. From several indications, he concludes ("*avec une quasi-certitude*") that "the *Liber Scintillarum* was the work of the monk Defensor, writing in the monastery of St Martin of Ligugé under the rule of his abbot Ursinus, about the year 700.[24]

c. *Anglo-Saxon churchmen and books from Rome*

I return now to the discussion of Aldhelm's pioneer testimony and his relevant links with other Anglo-Saxon churchmen and scholars. We have seen that he came to awareness of the existence of the biography of St Benedict as related in the *Dialogues* in the ninth decade of the seventh century. Someone may object, to counter the evidence presented above, that it need be no matter for surprise that the work arrived so late in England, a remote and semi-barbarian land on the fringe of the Christian world to which travel was difficult and communications were uncertain. A first answer to this objection is to reiterate that there is no genuine reference to the *Dialogues* (or to the life-story or cult of St Benedict) in any of the historical and literary sources from *anywhere* in Europe throughout the preceding

---

[22] *Defensoris Locogiacensis monachi Liber Scintillarum*. CCL 117, Turnhout 1957; also his *Defensor de Ligugé: Livre d'Étincelles, SC* 77 & 86; and his article, "*Defensoriana*. Archéologie du *Liber Scintillarum*", in *Sacris Eruditi*, 9 (1957), pp. 199–264.

[23] I list them in *PsGD*, p. 176, note 38.

[24] *SC* 77, p. 21.

fourscore years since the time of their alleged origin, and in any case the primary testimonies from Francia and Spain are no earlier than those of Aldhelm and Adamnan.

Moreover Aldhelm and his fellow-scholars in Britain were by no means ecclesiastical backwoodsmen. The objection outlined above does not square with what we know of cultural communications between Rome and England at that time, and of Aldhelm's own scholarly contacts in particular. Between 688 and 693 he visited Rome, acquiring more codices for the English libraries. (There he may well have met the future Pope Gregory II, then a senior official in the papal *Scrinium* from which the northern book-seekers obtained their transcripts.) In the last forty years of the seventh century no part of Christendom was more fervently attached to the Holy Roman see and to Roman ways than England. With the Christian faith now generally established in the Anglo-Saxon kingdoms, there were frequent communications with Rome. The number of travellers from England—royalty, nobles and merchants, as well as numerous bishops, monks and other ecclesiastics—who made the long and often difficult journey to and from Rome during that period is truly remarkable. Bede's *Historia Ecclesiastica* and other early records testify to the zeal and enthusiasm of those Englishmen who journeyed Romewards, as pilgrims to the tombs of the Apostles Peter and Paul, as collectors of books and relics, as students of Roman learning and customs, or as seekers of papal favour and privileges.

Those Anglo-Saxon churchmen and scholars who travelled to Rome and other places on the Continent were especially concerned to seek out and bring back to England books for the new centres of Christian learning that were beginning to flourish in Kent, Northumbria, Wessex and elsewhere. The English venerated with special piety the memory and writings of good Pope Gregory. Had there been in existence, for nearly a century, a book by St Gregory so fascinating as the *Dialogues*, one would evidently expect it to have been known to Aldhelm at least during his studies at the school of Canterbury from the year 670, several years before he composed his *De laudibus virginitatis*. So too, Aldhelm's two famous masters at Canterbury, Archbishop St Theodore of Tarsus and the abbot Hadrian (St Hadrian of Africa), both of whom could attest at first hand Roman traditions and learning, would surely not have been ignorant of the Gregorian *Dialogues* if the work had been known in Italy at that time.

It was about the year 666 that the kings of Kent and Northumbria had sent to Rome a priest called Uighard with a request to Pope Vitalian to consecrate him as the new Archbishop of Canterbury. Shortly after arriving there Uighard fell ill and died—a fate that befell not a few other Anglo-Saxon pilgrims to Rome, including King Caedwalla just after his baptism by Pope Sergius in 688.[25] Pope Vitalian, anxious to provide a worthy primate for the English Church who would be staunchly attached to Rome and Roman ways, chose Hadrian, a monk held in high repute for learning and piety, who had been abbot of an abbey near Naples. Hadrian humbly begged to be excused from the honour, and recommended instead his friend the learned Theodore of Tarsus, offering to accompany the new Archbishop of Canterbury to assist him in his high responsibilities. Accordingly Theodore was consecrated in Rome in 668 and made his way to Kent, where Hadrian joined him in 670. Together they founded the school of Canterbury, where Aldhelm was one of their first pupils. Hadrian's work in educating and organizing the Anglo-Saxon Church in the latter part of the seventh century was very influential.[26] In our search for contemporary signs of the existence of the *Dialogues* he is an especially significant witness. Coming from the neighbourhood of Campania, he would surely have known of a *Life* of the great miracle-working abbot of Montecassino written by Pope Gregory if such a book had existed at that time. Yet not only is there a lack of evidence that he had knowledge of it, but there is a positive indication (discussed below in Chapter 18.c) that he did not know it.

When discussing the awareness of the existence of the *Dialogues* shown by Aldhelm and his contemporaries it is relevant to take account of the evidence of the traffic of copies of hagiographical writings from Rome to England. We know that the legendary *Gesta* from Italy were eagerly sought and read in England as elsewhere. A. Dufurcq pointed out that Aldhelm in particular "made numerous borrowings from all that literature".[27] He listed, among the hagiographical *exempla* that Aldhelm drew from those apocryphal *Acts*, the stories of saints named Christina, Eugenia, Cecilia, Agnes, Agatha,

---

[25] CF. W.J. Moore, *The Saxon Pilgrims to Rome*, Freiburg 1937.
[26] Cf. G. Mazzuolo Porru, "*I rapporti fra Italia e Inghilterra nei secoli VII e VIII*", in *Romano-Barbarico*, 5 (1980), pp. 117–69; esp. pp. 126–7.
[27] *Op. cit.*, (*Études sur les gesta*), I (1900), p. 395.

Lucia, Justina, Constantina, Chionia, Irene and Agape, Rufina and Secunda, Chrysanthus and Darius, Anatolia and Victoria. Aldhelm's use of the contemporary legends of the two last-named saints is of special interest. He quoted the actual text of their *Gesta*, which he said were being read in his day "*in pulpito ecclesiae*". Interestingly, we note a development in his references to Anatolia and Victoria, occurring between his prose work and his poem. In the former they are not related; in the latter they become sisters. Dufourcq suggested, as an explanation of that evolution, that two different texts of the legend had come successively to Aldhelm's hands, the second of which was fuller and more fanciful. The origin of both forms of the story can be dated with probability to the later part of the seventh century.[28]

Another celebrated monk-scholar who did much to further the foundation of the school at Canterbury, and who must therefore have been one of Aldhelm's masters there, was St Benedict Biscop, a scholar and bibliophile of Northumbrian origin. He it was who guided the newly consecrated Archbishop Theodore from Rome to Canterbury, becoming abbot (for two years) at the monastery of SS. Peter and Paul there. He had considerable familiarity with Rome and with the wider world of continental scholarship. Before 674 he made three separate journeys to the Eternal City and other places in Italy (the first in 653, in company with St Wilfrid of York, another indefatigable traveller and pilgrim to Rome), and he lived for some years as a monk in the famous abbey of Lérins off the southern shore of Gaul. On a later visit to Rome Benedict Biscop was accompanied by Ceolfrid, future abbot both at Wearmouth and at Jarrow, who went there "seeking to learn the duties of his station more fully than he could in Britain".[29] An enthusiast for Roman culture and practices, Ceolfrid was very diligent in collecting codices abroad for the libraries of monasteries in England. For instance, he bought a large collection of books at Vienne and took them back to his homeland, where they became the nucleus of the library at Wearmouth. He obtained another notable collection of books at Naples. His fourth journey to Rome in 679 and his fifth in 684 were also undertaken to procure books and relics for the English monasteries of Wearmouth and Jarrow. During the fourth he persuaded Pope Agatho to send

---

[28] *Op. cit.*, III (1907), pp. 259–65.
[29] Ewald, *op. cit.*, p. 512, note 1.

back with him to England the celebrated John, abbot of the monastery of St Martin and archcantor of St Peter's, to instruct the English in Roman liturgical and monastic practices. Those two visits, in 679 and 684 have interest for our present investigation. Among the codices he brought back from Rome on one or other of those two journeys may have been the pristine copy of the *Dialogues* that was the source from which, directly or indirectly, Aldhelm first gained his knowledge of the work.

The newly appeared *Dialogues* would naturally be attractive to the eager book-buyers from north of the Alps. There are other possible avenues by which Aldhelm could have gained knowledge of the *Dialogues* recently divulged in Rome, or at least of the stories from it that were bruited abroad by *rumusculus*. Whether or not he first gained access to the text of the work through the book-seeking expeditions of Benedict Biscop, or from the reports of visitors such as Abbot John, he would eventually have been able to obtain his own copy of it when he paid a visit to Rome in person. We know of at least one visit that he made to Rome, during the pontificate of Pope Sergius I (687–701), from which he brought back to England texts and canonical documents. His mediaeval biographers coloured the story of that visit with legendary accretions, but the fact of it is now accepted as sure. A letter survives in which an unnamed Irishman petitioned Aldhelm to accept him as a pupil, saying "You understand the minds of those who journey afar to learn wisdom, since you yourself were a sojourner in Rome". Ewald concludes that Aldhelm, as abbot of Malmesbury, visited Rome after 688 to seek papal protection and privileges for his monasteries.[30] As we have seen, by the time he wrote his later *Epistola ad Acircium* he certainly had exact knowledge of the text of the *Dialogues*.

Another early English witness to the currency of the *Dialogues*, dating from the beginning of the eighth century, is the anonymous monk of Whitby who wrote the first *Life* of St Gregory shortly before the year 714. The early date of that work has been satisfactorily confirmed by Bertram Colgrave.[31] As argued above, it is probable that knowledge of the existence of the *Dialogues* had been transmitted to the Northumbrian monasteries through the travels of St Benedict

---

[30] *Op. cit.*, (1919), pp. 494 & xiv.
[31] Cf. *PsGD*, p. 177, note 30.

Biscop and his associates about the same time that it reached St Aldhelm in Wessex. To find that the nameless monk of Whitby was familiar with the work in 714 is, therefore, according to expectation. He makes several allusions to its contents, and expressly says that Gregory, "in his historical writings narrated many miracles relating to the passage of souls to the world beyond". He repeated the story from *Dial.* IV.55 of the monk whom Gregory ordered to be buried excommunicate and whom he later freed from other-worldly torment by the offering of a trental of Masses. During the subsequent decades of the eighth century recorded references to the *Dialogues* multiply. A notable literary testimony is that of Bede in his *Historia Ecclesiastica Gentis Anglorum*, finished by the year 731. He quotes the prologue to the *Dialogues* verbatim (in II.1), stating expressly that the great pope Gregory "wrote four books of dialogues on the miracles of the Fathers of Italy".[32]

The keen interest of Anglo-Saxon scholars in *Gregoriana*, and the relevance of some aspects of the *Dialogues* to contemporary developments in England, has led Marilyn Dunn to speculate that the book may have been composed in Northumbria, and that "the 'unpublished' Gregorian material in the *Dialogues*" (i.e. the IGPs) could have been acquired by Benedict Biscop and Wilfrid during their several journeys to Rome.[33] From what I say below, in Chapters 23 and 24, about the Dialogist's familiarity with the rural provinces of central Italy and his connection with the Roman *Scrinium*, it will be seen that I do not regard it as likely that he was an Englishman.

d. *Some indications of the date of composition of the* Dialogues

We have seen, from the converging indications given by the documentary testimonies listed above, that the *Dialogues* became known in England, Francia and northern Spain in the 'eighties of the seventh century and in the following decades. What approximate date for the original composition and first publication of the *Dialogues* can be inferred from that evidence of its first circulation and fame? The possibility cannot be excluded, of course, that the author composed

---

[32] Edition of C. Plummer, Oxford 1896, reprinted 1946, pp. 74 & 76.
[33] *Op. cit.*, pp. 199–200.

the work some considerable time before he made it public. One can, however, make a reasonable estimate of the time it would take, after its first appearance in Rome, for a previously unknown work of that nature to become known and accepted by readers in those distant regions. In doing so one must allow for the time it would take for the work to emerge from its initial obscurity, for it then to gain acceptability as a genuine work of Gregory's, and for its fame to spread across Europe,

By extrapolation backwards from the years in which the *Dialogues* first became publicly known, one may reasonably estimate that the work originated in the eighth (or possibly even the seventh) decade of the seventh century. However, the rapid and widespread *succès d'estime* which it attained very soon after those first testimonies to its existence, and the extraordinarily rapid expansion of the Benedictine monastic observance in the eighth century as a consequence of its publication, suggest that the initial acceptance of that previously unknown and ostensibly Gregorian work may have been speedier than one would normally expect. In Chapters 23 and 24 I will return to the question of the time and circumstances in which the Dialogist composed his work, considered in the light of all the evidence that we have concerning the historical setting in which he did so.

CHAPTER SEVENTEEN

APPROXIMATE DATING OF THE ORIGIN OF THE
DIALOGUES IN THE LIGHT OF THE EARLIEST
MANUSCRIPT EVIDENCE

The dating of the earliest surviving manuscripts of the *Dialogues* is clearly relevant to discussion of the period in which the work first emerged into the light. In this summary of available evidence on this question I refer especially to the work of E.A. Lowe, who, in a monumental survey[1] encompassed the task of locating, listing, describing and approximately dating all the surviving Latin manuscripts that originated before the ninth century. I also take account of the work of other authors who have devoted particular study to individual MSS that he catalogued. From the findings of Lowe and others, four manuscripts containing sections of the *Dialogues* text in fragmentary form can be identified as the earliest in date. I detail those four MSS below, giving in each case the location and shelfmark of the MS as given by Lowe, the volume and number of its listing in his survey, the approximate date of origin assigned to it there, and some comments on its provenance made by him and others.[2]

(1) *Trier Stadtbibliothek Fragment s.n.* (Lowe, *Supplement*, no. 1808.) Closing years of the seventh century (*"saeculo VII exeunte"*). One mutilated leaf survives, bearing the first lines of Book III of the *Dialogues*. "Inscribed in the style named Luxeuil miniscule, it originated in the monastery of Luxeuil itself or in an associated monastery."

(2) *Stuttgart Landesbibliothek Theologische und Philosophische Quellen 628.* (Lowe, vol. IX, no. 1356.) Seventh to eighth century. Four mutilated folios in uncial, containing passages from Book III of the *Dialogues*. "Origin uncertain, probably from a centre with Insular

---

[1] *Codices latini antiquiores: a Palaeographical Guide to Latin Manuscripts prior to the Ninth Century*, 7 vols. & supplement, Oxford 1934–71.

[2] I must signal here a relevant article by M. Iadanza, *Il Tema della paternità Gregoriana dei Dialoghi e la Tradizione Manoscritta nei Secoli VII e VIII*, in *Benedictina* 42 (1995), pp. 315–34. I acknowledge the validity of the author's criticism of some minor points in Chapter 10 of *PsGD*, none of which affects the substance of my argument.

connexions on the Continent, to judge from the abbreviations, spelling and the use of parchment as against vellum" (Lowe, IX, p. 54). Those two bifolia were found in 1938 in the binding of an *incunabulum* in the Stuttgart library. Correcting erroneous views on the date and origin of those fragments advanced by A. Dodd, who first discovered and edited them,[3] Lowe judged them to be part of a manuscript originating around the turn of the seventh century, and recognized indications that it came from "an Anglo-Saxon milieu".

(3) *Barcelona Bibliotheca Capitular, s.n.* (Lowe, vol. XI, no. 1626.) Seventh to eighth century. This one folio in uncial characters, in poor condition, is a page from Book IV of the *Dialogues*. Lowe noted that it was manifestly written at the same centre as the following item in his survey (XI, no. 1627), which is a codex comprising 337 folios of Gregory's Gospel *Homilies*. Of the latter MS, Lowe wrote: "Origin uncertain; other possibilities apart, South France seems most probable since it explains the known influences better than any other region; the representation of what may be a flamingo . . . would favour a Mediterranean centre. Corrected by an Anglo-Saxon reader in the eighth century".[4] Lowe also observed a feature of the prickings of this MS which is "usually found only in Insular MSS or under Insular influence".

(4) *Wroclaw, University Library, Akc.* 1955/2 + 1969/430. (Lowe vol. XI, no. 1595 and *Supplement*, p. 31.) Five mutilated bifolia, containing passages from Book III of the *Dialogues*; plus a further two bifolia containing passages from Book II which were found a few years later. "Written presumably by a Northumbrian scribe, to judge by the general resemblance to English uncial and specifically to certain features of the Northumbrian capitulary type. It is significant that two other items, in the same type of English uncial, also relate to works of England's favourite Church Father."[5] D. Yerkes has devoted special scrutiny to those seven bifolia in the Wroclaw library.[6] Whereas Lowe dated the MS fragment to around the turn of the seventh century, Yerkes assigned a later date to it, contemporary with Bede's

---

[3] Cf. *PsGD*, p. 180.
[4] *Ibid.*, p. 14; I confess that in Lowe's facsimile the bird does not look to me like a flamingo, but rather like a duck!
[5] *Op. cit.*, IX, p. 34; see also A. de Vogüé, *SC* 251, p. 171, footnote.
[6] "Two early manuscripts of Gregory's *Dialogues*", in *Manuscripta* 19 (1975), pp. 171–3.

works. He showed that it was used as the exemplar for another copy of the *Dialogues*, which Lowe had judged to have been made "in a West German scriptorium with Anglo-Saxon connections, possibly at Lorsch or its vicinity".

Thus, of the four earliest surviving manuscripts of the *Dialogues*, three are found to date from the period of a few years before or a few years after the end of the seventh century, and the fourth from about two or three decades later.[7] The lettering of three of them shows Anglo-Saxon influence. From this survey of the earliest MS evidence it appears that there is an interesting chronological correlation between the period in which the first literary allusions to the *Dialogues* appeared and the period in which the earliest known batch of MSS were inscribed. While the relevant texts of Aldhelm, Adamnan and Julian can all be dated with quite remarkable precision to about the last dozen years of that century, the dating of the three earliest surviving MSS is inevitably less precise, but can be dated soon afterwards.

One must, of course, observe the limitations of any argument drawn from manuscript survival, which was always haphazard. Of many ancient works we have only relatively late copies. While one may infer from historical evidence that the *Dialogues* were unknown for the greater part of the seventh century (i.e. because of the omission of their title from authoritative lists of Gregory's writings, and because of lack of any cult or biographical knowledge of St Benedict throughout that time), such inference cannot be drawn from the fact that no manuscript fragments survive from before the close of that century. The work could have originated earlier and become known later. However, the correlation between the dating of the earliest group of MSS and that of the first group of literary testimonies to the book's existence does provide some suasive indication that it originated in the later seventh century. The witness of those four earliest MSS (three of them showing Anglo-Saxon or Insular influence), all appearing within the same period, concords with that of the first literary testimonies to the book's existence which had appeared not long previously.

We may compare the complete absence of *MSS* of the *Dialogues* before that time with the surviving MS evidence relating to other

---

[7] To them may be added another almost contemporary fragment, now at Halle; cf. *Erbe und Auftrag*, 1988, p. 261.

works of the Gregorian corpus. From Gregory's own lifetime we have a surviving manuscript of a large part of his *Regula Pastoralis*, an edited text which was evidently amended under his personal direction. From the early seventh century there survive two MS folios from his *Moralia* and four fragments from his *Homilies on Ezekiel*. Two of the latter, Lowe judges, may well have been inscribed during his lifetime, or very shortly afterwards.[8] Once the *Dialogues* rose to fame, from the eighth century onwards, they outstripped in popularity all the other Gregorian writings. From then onwards through the centuries the transcriptions of the *Dialogues* far exceeded those other works in number. If the work had been known in the 85 years following its supposed publication by Gregory in 593–4 one would naturally suppose that there would already have been in that period similarly avid interest in that spell-binding work; that accordingly many copies of it would have been transcribed. Thus it would have been likely that some fragments of them would have survived, as did fragments of those other less popular Gregorian writings.

---

[8] Lowe, *op. cit.*, IX, no. 1348 & 1597.

CHAPTER EIGHTEEN

FIRST BEGINNINGS, IN THE EARLY EIGHTH CENTURY, OF CULT AND LITURGICAL MENTION OF ST BENEDICT

a

The question, already raised at the end of Chapter 15, recurs: why, outside the pages of the *Dialogues*, is there no discernible sign of cult and liturgical devotion to St Benedict, or of pilgrimage to his tomb and relics for over 100 years after the putative date of publication of that work? The seventh century was an age of ardent veneration and supplication of the saints, including now confessors as well as martyrs. It was an age of eager pilgrimage to their tombs, of translation of their relics, of erection of shrines in their honour, of constant recourse to those sources of miraculous healing. According to the supposedly already famous *Dialogues* of St Gregory, the body of St Benedict, who in his lifetime had performed stupendous miracles and who continued after his death to do so for pious clients, was still lying—in company with the body of his saintly sister St Scholastica—in a tomb on the mountain top at Montecassino, the precise location of which was given (*Dial.* II.37.4). The author recorded that Benedict had founded a monastery at Montecassino on the site of a former temple of Apollo, and it was there that he died and was buried, together with his saintly sister. He also recorded that at the time of writing (putatively about half a century after Benedict's death) that monastery lay in ruins after destruction by the Lombards, and that the monks had escaped from that disaster without harm—as Benedict had prayed and predicted that they would. Surely one would assume that those monks would have kept in devout memory the place where their saintly founder's body lay, and would return there to pay it due honour when peace returned to that region? Would not the *Dialogues* of the great pope Gregory have been an enduring signpost to that hallowed place throughout the seventh century, to lead pilgrim throngs thither? Surely during all that time there would have been many people with the necessary authority and means—popes, bishops, abbots, rulers or devout layfolk—who, reading in Gregory's famous book of the dereliction of St Benedict's tomb, would have taken steps to rescue it from neglect and to ensure that the sacred relics of the great thaumaturgic saint and his holy sister were enshrined there with due reverence and honour? There were many years of peaceful and settled conditions in the region when that would have been perfectly feasible. Yet there is no record of any such initiative being taken during the century following the date of the supposed publication of the Gregorian *Dialogues*. Paul Warnefrid, in his *Historia Langobardorum*, recalled that the saint's tomb was left in a state of abandonment in that *"vasta solitudo"*.[1] Such apparent neglect, H. Leclercq remarked with puzzlement, "is all the more extraordinary because devotion to relics held a preponderant place in the piety of the faithful in the seventh century".[2] According to D. Galli, it "proves that the patriarch had been forgotten by his sons".[3] The Montecassino site did not begin to be built up as a centre of pilgrimage and of Benedictine monasticism until more than a century and a half after the traditional date of the saintly founder's death, in the pontificate of Gregory II (715–731). Nor is there any traceable link between the monastic activity of the saintly author of the *Regula Benedicti* which first appeared in historical record at Altaripa about 625 and the new foundation that was made at Montecassino in the eighth century.

We have seen that it was not until near the close of the seventh century that the first reports of biographical knowledge about St Benedict emerged, all within the same short span of time. However, even then there was as yet no historical trace of cultic devotion to him or of pilgrimage to his shrine. Clearly it is relevant to ask: from what time do we find the earliest mention of the saint and of his anniversary in the Church's calendar of saints and in liturgical commemoration? The answers to that question provide a significantly corroborative sequel to our previous conclusions about the date at which the *Dialogues* first emerged into public knowledge. The early

---

[1] IV.17, VI.2 & VI 40. I do not ignore the picturesque but spurious legend of the theft by Franks in the latter part of the seventh century of the bodies of St Benedict and his sister from Montecassino and their transferral to Fleury and Le Mans. See Chapter 20 below.

[2] *DACL* XI.2459.

[3] Galli, *St Benoît en France*, Fleury 1940, p. 23.

historical and liturgical material relating to cult of St Benedict is sifted, described and clarified in a magisterial study by Dom J. Deshusses and Dom J. Hourlier, *Saint Benoît dans les livres liturgiques*,[4] to which I make frequent reference in the following pages. Briefly, the facts they bring into the light are as follows. Before the eighth century there is no documentary testimony of any liturgical recognition of an anniversary of St Benedict, but rather positive indication that there was none; his name is missing from the calendar of saints in which one would naturally expect to find it; he is mentioned in none of the saints' calendars, sacramentaries or lectionaries before the eighth century.

The so-called Hieronymian Martyrology is our principal source of information about the names and feast-days of saints—not only martyrs, but confessors as well—whose cult or at least commemoration was observed in the sixth, seventh and eighth centuries. Updated during each of those centuries, it gave lists of saints' names, grouped under the days of the year, thus indicating the anniversaries of their passage to eternal life, on which they were especially venerated. Often, too, it named the localities in which the passions of the martyrs occurred and those in which the saintly confessors died or were buried with honour. Study of the successive texts of the sanctoral calendars throws remarkable light on our present question, confirming the conclusions reached on other grounds that show the late date at which knowledge of St Benedict's life-story first appeared.

There are many ramifications of the Hieronymian calendar, reflecting the differing devotional concerns of different regions and communities. Thus successive additions and modifications were made to it during those three centuries. Although the oldest surviving manuscripts of those variant recensions date from the eighth century, from those and from later MS families it is possible to discern with considerable accuracy the earlier stages and strata of the compilation. The principal texts and their derivatives were edited, compared and annotated by J.B. De Rossi and L. Duchesne in the *Acta Sanctorum*.[5] In their preface those editors argued cogently that the prototype of

---

[4] In *SM* 21 (1979), pp. 143–204.
[5] *Martyrologium Hieronymianum ad fidem codicum*, AA.SS, *Novembris* II/I, Brussels 1894, pp. iv–lxxxi, 1–195. The further derivatives and amplifications of the Hieronymian calendar in the Middle Ages were studied by H. Quentin, *Les Martyrologies historiques du moyen age*, Paris 1908.

the Hieronymian calendar as we know it, incorporating earlier Eastern, Roman and African materials, took its shape in sixth-century Italy. Names of confessors begin to appear there as well as those of the martyrs. The compilers' own main sources were collections of saints' names and anniversaries from numerous locations in the peninsula. (From a recognizable description in the papal correspondence it seems likely, as Duchesne observed, that the Hieronymian Martyrology in its primitive form was known to Pope St Gregory.)[6] While the greater number of Italian entries in that sixth-century form of the sanctoral calendar relate to the northern part of the peninsula and to Rome, there is also an interesting group of notices about saints venerated in the region of Campania. The places mentioned in those notices are: Capua, Naples, Nuceria, Puteoli, Terracina, Baiae, Benevento and Formia. I call this "the first Campanian list" to distinguish it from a fuller list found in the seventh-century recensions of the calendar. Cassino is not far from several of those places. There are also entries relating to the saints of Sabina, which spans the country from Nursia to Subiaco. Although it is traditionally assumed that St Benedict died in the mid-sixth century, no clear significance can be attached to the fact that his name is missing from that list, which could have been based on a record dating from his lifetime or not long afterwards. In different case, however, is the continuing omission of his name from "the second Campanian list" found in the seventh-century recensions of the calendar, which are of central importance for our inquiry and which now demand scrutiny.

b. *Continuing absence of St Benedict's name from the calendars*

By the end of the sixth century the Hieronymian calendar had been amplified by the addition of names of numerous saints of Gaul, mainly those honoured at Lyons, Autun and Auxerre. From the number and character of the Auxerre entries, Rossi-Duchesne inferred that the recension that combined those Gallic commemorations with the earlier strands was made in that town before the death of Bishop Aunacharius, which occurred in 605. In it there is still no mention of St Benedict. From that Auxerre text, which they call "X", Rossi-

---

[6] Namely, his letter to Eulogius of Alexandria; cf. reference in Chapter 9.c above.

Duchesne judged all known codices of the Hieronymian calendar to be descended.[7] A different view was taken by B. Krusch, who argued that "X" was compiled not at Auxerre before 605 but at Luxeuil about 626–7, but his view has not gained general support. This difference of opinion is not of consequence for our present inquiry. If Krusch's later dating of "X" were proved to be correct, it would make the omission of St Benedict's name from it all the more surprising, coming nearly 30 years after the putative publication of the Gregorian *Dialogues*.

During the seventh century the sanctoral calendar continued to grow and to ramify. Its transmission during that century was canalized through two distinct branches of the manuscript tradition— neither of which commemorated the supposedly famous name of St Benedict of Montecassino. One MS branch is that later represented by the Echternach Codex, known to have been inscribed in Anglo-Saxon circles in the early years of the eighth century. (That codex is of special interest in the present context, because a subsequent interpolated addition to its text provides the first documentary evidence of devotional commemoration of St Benedict.) A firm *terminus post quem* for its origin is set by mention in it of Pope Sergius I, who died in AD 701.[8] The second and main branch of the MS tradition reflects Gallic usages—especially of Poitiers—which are absent from the branch represented by the Echternach Codex. It has been established by Rossi-Duchesne that all the derivative MSS in the family of the second branch must ultimately go back to a common parent, called "Y", which was inscribed in Francia not later than AD 647. The contents and special properties of "Y" can be reliably deduced from study of the common phrasing and position of entries in the later variant MS texts which are its mediaeval progeny.

Now while St Benedict may well have been unknown when the commemorations of Italian saints were recorded in the primitive sixth-century prototype of the *Hieronymianum*, the situation should surely have been different when the seventh-century recensions of the sanctoral calendar were made. As time went on, its contents were updated and many new names were added of saints who had come to be venerated in the previous century and a half. By this

---

[7] *Op. cit.*, pp. xl–xliii.
[8] Cf. R. Aigrain, *L'Hagiographie*, Paris 1953, p. 40.

time the so-called *martyrologium* now contained, as well as commemorations of additional martyrs from the age of persecution, also
anniversaries of numerous non-martyr confessors from more recent
times. As already noted, a very significant feature of the seventh-
century calendars—both in the tradition of "Y" and in that to which
the Echternach Codex belonged—was that both now gave an anniversary feast-day of St Columban, the Irish monastic founder who had
died in AD 615, while remaining completely silent about St Benedict.
It was in vain that Dom John Chapman, in an article written in
1903, argued from the evidence of entries in post-eighth-century families of MSS that the prototypal "Y" must have included a commemoration both of the burial day of St Benedict and of its octave.[9]
That plea was soon disproved by H. Quentin, who showed convincingly that the commemorations of St Benedict and of his feast-
days in those later MSS were so disparate in character as to preclude
a common origin for them in "Y" itself. Today scholars in this field
are agreed that there is no known liturgical reference to St Benedict
that can be dated before the first quarter of the eighth century.[10]
Although Chapman himself did not recognize the full significance of
the documentary evidence he had brought into the light, I cite his
comment on the evidence of the Echternach Codex as corroboration of the arguments that I put forward here:

> It is nevertheless curious that this venerated name was not inserted
> in England . . . Some saints were interpolated into this martyrology.
> That was evidently done in Northumbria, for the majority of them
> are from the north. St Augustine of Canterbury, naturally, is not forgot-
> ten, and the pope of the English, Pope St Gregory, figures there also . . .
> The addition was also made of the feasts of Campania introduced at
> Canterbury by the abbot St Hadrian in 669. Yet among the feasts
> which feature in the liturgical annotations which (as Dom G. Morin
> has proved) have preserved for us the calendar of Canterbury at the
> end of the seventh century, one does not find the name of St Benedict.
> It is also absent from the fragmentary marginal notes in another man-
> uscript of the same date, now at Oxford . . . It is a clear conclusion
> that the interpolator who added, in the archetype of E [the Echternach
> Codex], the Campanian names found in his lectionary and yet lack-

---

[9] "*À propos des martyrologes*", in *Rev. Bén.* 20 (1903), pp. 285–313; from p. 295 he
directly addressed the subject of "*Les fêtes de S. Benoît aux VIIe–IXe siècles*".

[10] E.g. Deshusses-Hourlier, *loc. cit.* Cf. A. Lentini, in *BS* II, s.v. "*S. Benedetto*", col.
115.

ing in the martyrologies, did not encounter a feast of St Benedict to insert there.[11]

The Echternach sanctoral calendar is recognized to be of Anglo-Saxon origin. Written in an Insular hand, its contents reveal the special devotional concerns of late seventh-century England; its use on the Continent was within the circle of the English missionary saint Willibrord, the founder of the Echternach monastery. It testified to the special concerns of contemporary Anglo-Saxon piety, which had added to the calendar the commemorations of saints especially honoured by the English: St Augustine of Canterbury, St Paulinus of York, St Oswald, St Cuthbert, St Ethelwald. Mention of those five saints is proper to the Echternach Codex.[12] Whether the manuscript was inscribed in Northumbria, as Chapman supposed, or at Echternach itself, as Deshusses-Hourlier judge more probable, it was clearly copied from a Northumbrian model. Inclusion of commemorative anniversaries of St Cuthbert (who died in 687) and of St Ethelwald of Farne (whose death was later still, between 699 and 705) provides a *terminus ante quem non* for the completion of the MS. Since this formulary of saints' anniversaries reflects the usages of England, the absence from it of the name of St Benedict is all the more significant. In that land Pope St Gregory—whose own feast-day appeared, of course, both in the Echternach calendar and in "Y"— was universally revered as the Father-in-faith of the nation. If in a famous book he had singled out St Benedict for the highest praise and honour, if the English had long known Gregory's *Life* of the author of the *RB* (a rule which is supposed by many to have been the norm of Anglo-Saxon monastic observance!), then surely we should expect to find St Benedict's name among the saints honoured by St Gregory's spiritual children in England? And yet at the close of the seventh century the name of St Benedict was still not included in their calendar of venerated saints, nor was there any liturgical devotion to him.

---

[11] *Rev. Bén.* 20 (1903), p. 300.
[12] Cf. Rossi-Duchesne, *op. cit.*, p. viii.

c. *Other significant features of the calendars and sacramentaries*

Although the original manuscript of the Echternach Codex still contained no mention of St Benedict, his name was in fact inserted into it by a later hand. Since that interpolated entry is the earliest mention in any known documentary record of an anniversary of the saint in the sanctoral calendars and sacramentaries, it calls for special attention. The scribe who penned the original text of the Echternach Codex in the early years of the eighth century was named Laurentius. In all probability he is to be identified with the monk of that name, a companion of St Willibrord, who wrote letters to the latter during the years 704 to 711. At some time after he had copied the text of the calendar in the Echternach MS, a different but contemporary hand made the momentous insertion into it, adding at the end of the list of saints commemorated on March 21st the abbreviated phrase: "*et sci Benedicti abb*".[13] Deshusses-Hourlier judge that the interpolation was made not long after the manuscript was inscribed, and in any case no later that the first quarter of the eighth century. Soon after that first recorded liturgical mention of St Benedict's name, made by the interpolator of the Echternach calendar, we find two further indications of the newly kindled cult of the saint. The first is an explicit commemoration of his name under March 21st in the text of the so-called Calendar of St Willibrord, which can be dated not later than 728,[14] and which originated in the same milieu as the Echternach Codex. A curious error in the Calendar of St Willibrord is the designation of St Benedict as "*martyr*". This may be seen as one more indication of the newness and unfamiliarity of his cult. The second early reference to him in a sanctoral calendar is in that of St Bede, written between the years 725 and 731, which includes a simple mention of St Benedict's name under the date March 21st.

Two further features of the Echternach manuscript are very pertinent to our present question, First, I draw attention again to the fact that not only did it contain an anniversary of St Columban (as did "Y" too), but it also contained (proper to itself) anniversary notices of St Columban's two chief disciples, St Athala and Eustacius.[15]

---

[13] *Ibid.*, p. 35.
[14] Deshusses-Hourlier establish that dating, *op. cit.*, pp. 156–7, thus correcting a slightly earlier dating by Rossi-Duchesne.
[15] *Ibid.*, p. xliv.

We do not know whether the addition of those two seventh-century abbots to the roll of saints was first made in England or whether (as seems more likely) it was introduced into a continental recension of the calendar which was already distinct from "Y", and which was a progenitor of the Northumbrian-Echternach tradition. Why, one may ask, were the names of Athala and Eustacius added? The answer is to be found in the *Vita Columbani* written by Jonas of Bobbio[16] (referred to above in Chapter 9.e). That work was divided into two *libri*. The first and longest recounts the *Life* of St Columban himself; then, in the shorter section, Jonas goes straight on to relate the *Lives* of those two chief disciples and successors of St Columban. It is a reasonable inference that whoever added the names of those two saintly disciples to the prototype from which the Echternach Codex was derived did so because of the influence of Jonas's biographical work.[17] By contrast, the absence of St Benedict's name from the *Hieronymianum* before the eighth century appears even stranger. If the influence of Jonas's *Lives* of those two disciples of St Columban, who were in comparison lesser figures in the hagiography and monastic loyalties of that age, could prompt the inclusion of their names in the list of venerated saints, how much more should we expect the influence of the *Life* of St Benedict in the supposedly famous *Dialogues* of Pope St Gregory to ensure the inclusion there of the name of the glorious monastic patriarch and thaumaturge whose sanctity and miraculous power the great pope had extolled above all others.

The other feature of the Echternach Codex has already been referred to in the previous section, in the citation from an article by J. Chapman. It is the presence there of several names of saints of Campania and adjoining regions, additional to those already given in what I called above "the first Campanian list", contained in the earlier strata of the *Hieronymianum*. Those additional names are twelve in number.[18] Of special interest to us here is the fact that they include the anniversaries of two saints of Cassino—St Severus and St Constantius.[19] How did that further group of saints from the region of

---

[16] *Vitae Columbani abbatis discipulorumque eius libri II*; edition of B. Krusch, Hanover and Leipzig 1905, pp. 1–257.

[17] A. de Vogüé cavils with this conclusion, on the grounds that Jonas does not give the day of Athala's decease! (*RHE* 83, 1988, p. 326.)

[18] They are picked out by Rossi-Duchesne, *op. cit.*, p. ix.

[19] For July 19th, "*In Casino Severi*"; for Sept. 1st, "*In Casino Constanti*"; *ibid.*, p. ix.

Campania and Naples come to be included among those venerated
in distant Northumbria? The explanation, already referred to in previous chapters, is to be found in a study by Dom G. Morin of two
very early MSS in the British Museum, which show the Gospel readings used in the church of Canterbury towards the end of the seventh century.[20] Morin established the surprising fact that the liturgical
calendar then used in England was modelled on that of Naples, and
he was able to reconstruct the latter from the evidence of the English
MSS. He also pointed to the explanation of the remarkable fact that
he had discovered: it was to be found in the influence of the abbot
Hadrian, who in the year 669 set out from Rome for Canterbury
as companion and helper of Archbishop Theodore, and who was
for the following forty years a principal agent in the revitalizing of
ecclesiastical life and learning in England. Before leaving Italy, Hadrian
had been abbot of the island monastery of Nisita, near Naples, and
his presence and activity in England are the explanation of the apparently puzzling introduction of the Neapolitan church calendar among
the Anglo-Saxons, not only in Kent and the south but also in
Northumbria. Theodore and Hadrian, bearing gifts of codices, made
a visitation of Northumbria, even reaching Lindisfarne. Using Morin's
findings, Duchesne was able to identify the means by which the additional commemoration of Campanian saints' names was brought into
the Northumbrian recension of the sanctoral calendar—namely,
through the person and influence of Hadrian.

If Pope Gregory's *Life* of St Benedict had been known in the mid-
seventh century when Hadrian was an abbot of a Neapolitan monastery, the learned reformer could not have been ignorant of the fame
and heavenly power of the great saint who had been founder and
abbot of the neighbouring monastery of Montecassino, situated on
the Via Latina where Campania merged with Latium Adiectum.[21]
Hadrian, at least, could have alerted the English to their singular
neglect of the cult of so great a saint. Yet despite his close familiarity with the devotional usages of that region of Italy south of

---

[20] "*La Liturgie de Naples au temps de saint Grégoire, d'après deux évangeliaires du septième
siècle*", in *Rev. Bén.* 8 (1891), pp. 481–93 & 529–37. Cf. also *Analecta Maredsolana*, I,
p. 436.
[21] Cf. F. Lanzoni, *Le Origini delle Diocesi antiche d'Italia*, Rome 1923, p. 102. He
notes that in late antiquity towns in the southern parts of Latium Adiectum, such
as Cassino and Terracina, were reckoned as belonging to Campania.

Rome, when Hadrian introduced into England the cult of the twelve additional Campanian saints—including two from Cassino itself—he did not introduce the cult or the name of the saint who should have been the most famous of all the spiritual heroes of that region, St Benedict of Montecassino, supposedly so highly lauded by St Gregory in his *Dialogues*.

d. *Eighth-century beginning of liturgical honour of St Benedict*

The same silence about St Benedict that we find in the seventh and early eighth century recensions of the Hieronymian calendar is found in other liturgical documents reflecting devotion to the saints in that age. The ancient sacramentaries set out the order of the Mass liturgy for the use of the officiating clergy. They gave formularies for Masses in honour of particular saints, and the lectionaries provided the readings for their feasts. We possess the text of three sacramentaries which give precise information about usages in the city of Rome during the seventh century. They are: the Gregorian Sacramentary (type I), used doubtless for the papal liturgy; the Gelasian Sacramentary, of which the essential part is a book used in a titular church in Rome (probably St Peter ad Vincula) about the middle of that century, but which reflects adaptation for use in another church about the year 670; and the Gregorian Sacramentary (type II), which was probably compiled for use in St Peter's basilica about 680. "Not one of those books makes the slightest mention of St Benedict", Deshusses-Hourlier observe, "which leads us to think it probable that his feast was not celebrated in Rome in the seventh century".[22] If there had been any such liturgical honour of him, one would surely expect to find it in those Frankish monasteries in which elements of the *Regula Benedicti* came to be used in conjunction with the *Regula Columbani* during the course of the seventh century. But there is no trace of mention of the saint in the Frankish liturgies (not even at Luxeuil, where, Vogüé asserts, the *Dialogues* were "certainly" known),[23] or in any other place in the Christian world in that age. Deshusses-Hourlier observe: "the books of readings completely ignore St Benedict,

---

[22] *SM* 21, p. 160.
[23] *RHE* 83 (1988), p. 321.

no matter what the type or family to which they belong".[24] That surprising silence of the Frankish documents had also been pointed out long before by the bewildered Dom Chapman:

> In the course of the seventh century Benedictine and Columbanian-Benedictine foundations multiplied in France, but in the lectionary of Luxeuil Benedict has no place. Nor does he appear in an ancient calendar of Luxeuil dating from the end of the seventh century. The Martyrologium Gallicanum copied by Martene . . . contains no mention of St Benedict. Nor is there any in the ninth-century MS which came from St Martial of Limoges, the original of which was probably composed for the abbey of Marmoutier.[25]

Unlike Chapman, Deshusses-Hourlier and other Benedictine historians, A. de Vogüé finds nothing strange in that long omission of St Benedict from cult and liturgical honour. After all, he argues, the names of several saints of earlier centuries whose lives were famous, including Ambrose, Augustine and Caesarius, are not to be found in the sanctoral lists, either in the most ancient sacramentaries or in the martyrologies.[26] To this one must reply that the introduction of the names of saintly confessors as well as of martyrs into the texts of the *Martyrologium* was a later development. By the mid-seventh century it had become common. Despite Vogüé's complex pleas, which are not shared by other commentators, it remains astonishing that St Benedict was not included in the sanctoral calendar of that age, while other Campanian confessors, and also St Columban and his two disciples, were commemorated there.

From the second quarter of the eighth century onwards the references to St Benedict in the liturgical documents begin to multiply.[27] We find him commemorated in the Wissembourg codex of the *Hieronymianum*, which reflects a MS model that left the abbey of Fontenelle between 734 and 772. Some *abrégés* of the sanctoral calendar dating from not later than about 740 contain commemora-

---

[24] *Ibid.*, pp. 167–8.
[25] *Rev. Bén.* 20 (1903) p. 299.
[26] Cf. *RHE* 83 (1988), pp. 324–8. Vogüé also objects that motivation to include saints' names such as those of Athala and Eustacius in the sanctoral calendars could not be "*d'origine livresque*". Indeed their cult was not originated by their written *Lives*, but it was furthered by them. The saints whose cult was truly and solely originated by a book were the belatedly honoured heroes of the *Dialogues*!
[27] The MS tradition of these texts was set out and commented on by R. Grégoire in *SA* 54 (1965), pp. 1–85.

tions of the saint.[28] The day allotted to his anniversary, originally March 21st, underwent a somewhat puzzling variation. Even before the middle of the eighth century a commemoration on July 11th is found, as well as on March 21st. From about the middle of that century, too, special devotion to St Benedict is attested by commemoration of his name in the canon of the Mass. This is found in a copy of the Gelasian Sacramentary made in north-eastern France (probably at Chelles) and in the Bobbio Missal. In both those liturgical documents St Benedict's name is added to those of a group of confessor saints named in the *Communicantes* prayer in the canon of the Mass—"Hilary, Martin, Ambrose, Augustine, Gregory, Jerome, Benedict". Not long afterwards appears the earliest known formulary for a feast-day Mass of the saint, found in the Frankish-Gelasian Sacramentary compiled at Flavigny about AD 760–770, in which his feast is added to the feasts received from Rome in the older Gelasian and Gregorian Sacramentaries.[29]

Deshusses-Hourlier place the most important period for the development of liturgical devotion to St Benedict in the third quarter of the eighth century, while noting that the way had been prepared for those developments during the preceding quarter. They also note that this process was associated particularly with the court circle of the Frankish kingdom, and that "one can also, in many cases, discern an influence of St Boniface, above all after his intervention in the disciplinary reform of the Frankish church".[30] In the next chapter I shall discuss the momentous breakthrough of the Benedictine observance to special favour in the mid-eighth century, and eventually to pre-eminence, a movement in which St Boniface of Crediton was a principal protagonist.

---

[28] Cf. Deshusses-Hourlier, *SM* 21, pp. 170–2.
[29] For fuller references to the documents mentioned in this paragraph, cf. Deshusses-Hourlier, *SM* 21, pp. 153, 160–1, 166, 184–5, 200, 203.
[30] *Ibid.*, p. 184.

CHAPTER NINETEEN

THE "MYSTIQUE OF MONTECASSINO": EIGHTH-CENTURY UPSURGE OF BENEDICTINE MONASTICISM PROMOTED BY THREE POPES, BY ST BONIFACE AND BY THE FRANKISH RULERS

a

We have seen that before the eighth century the *Regula Benedicti* had a secondary but increasingly respected place as one of several elements in the pattern of Western monasticism. In the age of the mixed rule there was no single written code that stood out as superior to all others. In Rome and in Italy generally, in Spain and in southern Gaul, the older elements of monastic life, from East and West, remained in honour, adapted to the episcopal organization and urban civilization of the Mediterranean world. Among the Christianized Franks, Goths, Lombards and Anglo-Saxons, the newer pattern of large land-owning abbeys, influenced by the missionary and pastoral ideals of the Irish monks and by royal favour, marked a new flourishing development of monastic life. Even among the Gallo-Franks in the seventh century, while Columbanian monasticism was undoubtedly the most vigorous and favoured influence, there was no concerted trend towards a unitary code of observance. There was still a wide choice of existing statutes that a founder or abbot could use in the governance of his community. I cited earlier the eclecticism of the English founder-abbot St Benedict Biscop, who consulted no less than seventeen monastic rules, including the *RB*, when composing his own. When we look ahead to the late eighth century we find that a remarkable change from that eclectic pattern of monastic observance had by then taken place. In the Carolingian age the *Regula Benedicti*, from being as formerly one of many rules, relatively minor and mentioned mostly as one component of a mixed rule, became predominant north of the Alps and was systematically imposed by Frankish rulers and reformers. The decisive measures of Carloman and Pepin in the eighth century and by Charlemagne and his son

Louis in the ninth, implementing the reforms of St Benedict of Aniane, set the seal on that process. From then onwards came the great flowering of monastic life and influence in mediaeval Christendom during what are aptly called "The Benedictine Centuries". In this chapter I address the question: when and how did that breakthrough of the Benedictine observance come about?

When considering that question the significant period to be studied is not that of the general triumph of the *RB* from the later eighth century onwards, but the earlier and middle periods of that century, when its rise towards eventual pre-eminence began. The period of that development can be marked out as that covered by the pontificates of three popes: Gregory II (715–731); Gregory III (731–741) and Zachary (741–752). It is from those years that we first find record of the kindling of cult and devotion to St Benedict in his own homeland. In that period rose lively interest in the site of Montecassino and pilgrimage to St Benedict's tomb-shrine there. Then over ruins on the Cassinese mountain top was built a new Benedictine abbey which soon became a centre of monastic revival and mission. The monasticism based on the *RB* and on devotion to its illustrious author, radiating from Montecassino with papal encouragement and with the active support of the secular rulers, was a principal organ for the Christianization of the German territories evangelized by St Boniface and his fellow-missionaries, and it also became widely established as the norm for observance throughout the Frankish realms. The *RB* itself, from being only one among many rules, rapidly began to emerge in its own right, as a code of superior prestige and authority.

Several factors conspired to bring about that remarkable upsurge in the Benedictine observance in the short span of some four decades. As the essential determinant among those factors, I point to the emergence and diffusion, from the end of the seventh century onwards, of the *Dialogues* attributed to St Gregory the Great, with their *Life* of St Benedict which provided the golden legend and the title deeds of the new Benedictine movement. We can thus mark a clear chronological correlation between the first appearance and spread of knowledge of the *Dialogues*, in the closing decades of the seventh century, and the first beginnings of cult of St Benedict in the first quarter of the eighth century, followed soon afterwards by the new and triumphant rise of Benedictine monasticism. All the other developments that I am now going to summarize can be recognized as consequent

upon that first determinant factor. Although I shall discuss them separately, they combine to make up a unitary historical pattern, in the
study of which each serves to throw light on the others.

Those new developments began quite suddenly in the second
decade of the eighth century, when the initial stimulus was given by
Pope Gregory II. Shortly after his election in AD 715 he demonstrated devotion to St Benedict by deciding to restore honour to the
saint's neglected grave at Montecassino, which he had evidently found
described in the pages of the *Dialogues* bearing the name of his great
predecessor and namesake, Pope Gregory I. To that end he directed
Petronax of Brescia to go to Montecassino to initiate a revival of
coenobitical life in that long-neglected site, known to have been
ruined by Lombard marauders some 140 years previously.

The *Dialogues* contain plentiful references to a monastery founded
by St Benedict at Montecassino in the first half of the sixth century.
Apart from the *Dialogues*, what firm historical evidence is there of
the existence of a monastery there previously? There is Paul Warnefrid's
mention of its destruction by the Lombards around the end of the
sixth century, but his account, written in the late eighth century, is
reliant on the *Dialogues*. We do know that on the mountain top of
Montecassino there was in late antiquity a fortress built for the
defence and control of the town of Cassino below and the surrounding district, which was renowned as "The Citadel of Campania".[1]
Would there have been a monastery on the same mountain-summit
site? There is no archaeological proof of it.[2] What would have been
visible in the Dialogist's day were the ruins of the large fortress complex that had been destroyed by the Lombards a century earlier.
There were also on the mountain crest the ruins of pagan shrines
(also referred to in the *Dialogues*), perhaps replaced by a Christian
place or places of devotion. Excavation has also revealed the presence there of a cemetery in ancient times. Paul Warnefrid cites a
record that when Petronax went there at the bidding of Pope Gregory
II there were living on the summit a group of *simplices*, probably
devout men living an eremitical life.[3]

---

[1] Cf. L. Tosti, *St Benedict, an Historical Discourse on his Life*, trans. W. Woods,
London 1896, pp. 83–6.
[2] It is assumed, but not proved, in the book of S.A. Pantoni, *L'Acropoli di Montecassino
e il primitivo Monasterio di San Benedetto* (Montecassino 1980). The author's assumption is based on the *Dialogues*, but not demonstrated by the archaeological evidence.
[3] *Historia Langobardorum* VI,40; *MGH* edit. p. 178.

According to Paul Warnefrid, Petronax made his way, as instructed, "*ad sacrum corpus beati Benedicti patris*", and he and his successors proceeded to foster a monastic community there. During the following decades the new abbey and shrine of Montecassino grew to become a major centre of devotion and religious revival. Eager new recruits, including the sons of noblemen, pressed for admission to the community there. We read of a priest from Spain who went there as a pilgrim and remained as a cloistered monk. Writing some 50 years after the foundation, Paul Warnefrid related of Petronax: "He became the father of many monks, both nobles and commoners. Setting out to live under the yoke of the holy rule and institution of the blessed Benedict, and restoring the dwellings, he built up this holy monastery into the state in which we now behold it".[4] The principal factor in the spread throughout Europe of "the mystique of Montecassino" was its fame as a pilgrimage centre, and as the shrine of the great wonder-working saint who thus became the heavenly lord and protector of a territorial domain. It was not primarily esteem for the devout monks or for their holy rule that drew men's hearts and feet to Montecassino. They went "*ad sanctum Benedictum*". The cult and fealty paid to a saint was above all relative to his miraculous power and his fame as a healer and helper. St Benedict's power, proclaimed in the *Dialogues* of St Gregory, was known to be present in the new shrine where his relics, rescued from oblivion, were now venerated, and his pious clients went there to seek and gratefully experience it.

b. *The monastic mission of Boniface and Willibald*

Although Gregory II wished to promote veneration of the memory, tomb and monastery of St Benedict at Montecassino, it appears that he did not promote the observance of the *RB* as a general norm for monastic life elsewhere. When in 716 he sent three legates on a reforming mission to the Bavarians, bringing them directly under Roman religious governance, the introduction of the *RB* did not feature among the reforms his legates were instructed to make. It was Columbanian monastic observance that continued to hold sway among the Bavarians until late in the eighth century.[5] Neither did monasteries

---

[4] *Op. cit.*, pp. 178–9.
[5] Cf. B. Krusch, *MGH, Script. Rer. Merov.* 6, Hanover 1913, p. 498; K. Hallinger, *Römischen Voraussetzungen*, pp. 340–7; Tausch, *op. cit.*, p. 17.

existing in central and southern Italy during Gregory II's pontificate—
even the important abbey founded at St Vincent on the Volturno,
in the vicinity of Montecassino itself—adopt the Benedictine rule in
that age. I noted earlier that, despite conjectures to the contrary by
some writers, there was no survival of Benedictine observance in a
putative "Lateran monastery" during the previous 140 years. Such
a notion was a later myth originating from a cue in the *Dialogues*
and from the fancies of Leo Marsicanus in the eleventh century.[6]
Gregory II's initiative in sending Petronax to establish monastic life
at St Benedict's tomb was a new beginning; there was no existing
Benedictine observance there to revitalize. Nor did that pontiff introduce the *RB* in the city of Rome—either in his monastic reorganization of the basilica of St Paul's, or in the monastery that he
(following the example of Gregory I) founded in his family home.

There are no indications that when Wynfrith of Crediton, alias
the great St Boniface, went to Rome about 718 to secure the blessing of Gregory II for his missionary work, he was sent to Germany
with a mandate to promote observance of the *RB*. His apostolate in
those earlier years among the Frisians, Bavarians, Thuringians and
Hessians did not change the pattern of mixed-rule monasticism that
he found already established in those Christian borderlands. News
of his missionary success prompted Gregory II to call him to Rome
again in 722 in order to consecrate him bishop and to make him
the legate of the Apostolic see in that missionary region. In 732 he
was invested with the pallium by the new pope Gregory III. However,
that phase of his activity in north-central Germany, up to the year
735, was still not pro-Benedictine in its monastic policy.[7] The older
theory that single-rule Benedictine monasteries were founded east of
the Rhine in those earlier years of Boniface's mission lacks reliable
basis. Pirmin from Aquitaine, apostle of the Alemans and founder
of Reichenau, is often claimed as a leading promoter of the *RB*, but
the evidence is otherwise. While he knew the *RB*, he still stood in
the traditions both of the Irish-Frankish monks and of the older
Gallo-Roman observances. His foundations followed the pattern of
mixed-rule monachism.[8]

---

[6] Cf. P. Meyvaert, *Rev. Bén.* 65 (1955), pp. 63–7; H.S. Brechter, *SMGBO* 56
(1938), pp. 118–26; J. Chapman, *St Benedict and the Sixth Century*, pp. 130–4.
[7] Cf. C. Holdsworth, "St Boniface the Monk", in *The Greatest Englishman: Essays
on St Boniface*, Exeter 1980, p. 59.
[8] Cf. A.E. Angenendt, *Monachi peregrini. Studien zu Pirmin und den monastischen
Vorstellungen des frühen Mittelalters*, Munich 1972. Cf. also Chapter 14 above, note 21.

A vital role in the wider promotion of the Benedictine observance was played by Boniface's cousin Willibald, from Waltham in Wessex (not to be confused with a namesake who later wrote the Life of St Boniface). After first visiting Rome in 722–4, he spent six years as a pilgrim to the Holy Land and other eastern shrines. Returning in 730 with his Frankish companion Tidbercht and others, he was directed by the bishop of Teano to St Benedict's shrine at Monte-cassino, and there entered Petronax's community as a monk, per-suading his companions to do the same. His ten years' sojourn there was an important factor in the wider establishment of Benedictine monasticism.[9] His biographer and cousin, the nun Huneberc of Hei-denheim, later recorded: "For ten years he sought to observe, as far as possible, every detail of the monastic observance as laid down by the rule of St Benedict . . . He learned much from the brethren, but he in turn taught them more by his conduct; he showed them what was the real spirit of their institute, not so much by words as by the beauty of his character".[10] It is not unlikely that Willibald may have heard of the *RB* during his youth in Wessex, but his biogra-pher never mentions that rule in her account of his early monastic experience in England. She mentions St Benedict's name and rule for the first time—and then repeatedly—only when she records Willibald's arrival at Montecassino in 730.

During the subsequent ten years Willibald was closely associated with the Benedictine renaissance at Montecassino initiated by Pope Gregory II and Petronax. In his biography we find one of the earliest evidences of the newly established pilgrimage "*ad sanctum Benedictum*". In the year after Willibald entered the abbey Pope Gregory II, author and protector of the new foundation, died, to be succeeded by another pro-Benedictine pope, Gregory III (731–41). During the latter's pontificate the seed sown by his predecessor continued to grow towards maturity. In 739 Petronax sent Willibald from Montecassino on an errand to Rome. There he was summoned by Gregory III and told that his kinsman Bishop Boniface had asked for him to be sent from Montecassino to join him as a fellow-worker in the Lord's vineyard in the still semi-pagan Frankish lands east of the Rhine. Accordingly the pope instructed Willibald to leave the abbey-shrine

---

[9] Cf. S. Brechter, "*Die Frügeschichte von Montecassino*", in *Liber Floridus*, ed. Bischoff & Brechter, St Ottilien 1950, pp. 271–86.

[10] *Hodoeporicon Willibaldi*; text in C. Talbot's *The Anglo-Saxon Missionaries to Germany*, London 1954, pp. 172–3.

of Montecassino and to go to Boniface in Germany, which he did
in 740. After his ten years in the Cassinese monastery, playing a
prominent part in its establishment as the beacon of the new Benedictine movement, the English monk and future apostle of Franconia
was well placed to become a propagator of the *Regula Benedicti* in
the German frontier-lands. He was ordained priest by Boniface in
741, at 41 years of age. His biographer relates that he set to work
installing the pattern of Cassinese observance in his new mission
field: "He began to build a monastery in a place called Eichstatt.
There he put into force the sacred discipline of monastic life that
he had practised in the preceding years, which he had seen at St
Benedict's shrine (*ad sanctum Benedictum*); and not only there but also
in other monastic houses that he had examined with his experienced
eye as he travelled through various lands."[11] F. Prinz points to the
probability that it was Willibald who, after arriving in Bavaria in
741, was influential in promoting veneration of St Benedict at Freising,
where the dedication of the monastic cathedral was changed at that
very time from the patronage of St Martin to that of St Benedict.[12]

The first certain evidence of predilection for the Benedictine observance east of the Rhine appears soon after Willibald had joined his
cousin in Germany. Then the missionary strategy of Boniface, in
concert with that of the Frankish rulers, entered on a new phase. It
is only after that time that we find mention of St Benedict and his
rule, in the correspondence of Boniface and in other records relating
to him. It was then that the movement for monastic conformity
based on the *RB* took its rise. In these developments, and in the
wider spread of the Benedictine observance outwards from Montecassino, a central place must be attributed to the newly arrived
Willibald.

c. *The* Concilium Germanicum *and the exaltation of the* RB

The fifth decade of the eighth century was decisive for the new
Benedictine movement. It was during those years that the *Romidee*
and the spreading fame of Montecassino began to exercise widespread influence in the Frankish realms, where a Church revival was

---

[11] *Vita Willibaldi*, cap. 6.
[12] Prinz, *Frühes Mönchtum*, p. 391.

already in progress.[13] In those developments a decisive part was played by the two sons of Charles Martel, Pepin and Carloman. Charles Martel, overlord of much of Europe (and frequent misappropriator of Church property) had to some extent favoured the reforming elements in the Frankish Church. He issued a document of protection to Boniface in 723, and established courteous relations with Popes Gregory II and III. His two sons, between whom his dominions were divided on his death, both vigorously supported the long overdue reform of the Frankish Church and the new missions in Austrasia, the borderlands to the East. Both continued, like their father, to support Boniface and to honour the see and successor of St Peter. Both proved to be active patrons of the new Benedictine monasticism. Innovation was more immediately feasible in Austrasia where Carloman ruled, which was Boniface's main mission-field and in which ecclesiastical and monastic organization was still in a formative stage. Neustria and Burgundy, ruled by Pepin the Short, had long-established monastic traditions that were more resistent to change. The regions further south and west were still more conservative, retaining the ancient ecclesiastical loyalties of the land that had been the principal province of Roman Gaul.

On the accession to power of the two vice-regal brothers, Boniface was given authority to carry out a reform of the whole Frankish Church. From that time we find evidence of a definite policy on the part of Boniface and his associates, Willibald in particular, to promote the *RB* to a position of pre-eminence, at the expense of the many other rules or mixed rules, especially the hitherto prevalent Irish-Frankish forms of Columbanian monasticism. The collaboration of Boniface and Carloman in what J. O'Carroll calls "the Austrasian monastic movement" culminated in 743 (or 742) in a decree of the *Concilium Germanicum* that was the first great landmark of the triumphant rise of the new Benedictine movement. That council of the eastern Frankish Church, convened by Carloman and presided over by Boniface, ordained that thenceforward the rule of St Benedict should be the norm of observance for monks and nuns: "*Decrevimus . . . ut monachi et ancillae Dei monasteriales iuxta regulam sancti Benedicti vivere et vitam propriam gubernare studeant*".[14] What had not happened at the

---

[13] Cf. Hallinger, *Römischen Voraussetzungen*, pp. 320–7.
[14] *Ibid.*, p. 341.

imaginary "Council of Autun" in Burgundy in the previous century did happen at that German Council. A few months later its decree was reaffirmed by another Austrasian council held at Leptines in Belgium. Soon afterwards the pan-Benedictine policy was extended to the western part of the Frankish realm when it was approved by a synod held at Poitiers in 744, presided over by Pepin.

Also in 744 came another landmark, the founding of the abbey of Fulda, which became the centre of Benedictine observance across the Rhine.[15] The excitement of that period is reflected in the accounts which tell of the eagerness of the monks of Fulda to learn their new code of life. "For this purpose", it was related, "Boniface sent his disciple Sturm, a man of noble family and excellent character, to Montecassino so that he could study the regular discipline and the monastic customs that had been established there by St Benedict".[16] Sturm, the first abbot of Fulda, was accompanied on his journey by two companions. The spirit of their Benedictine quest is recaptured as follows by his biographer and third successor, Eigil:

> When the brethren had conceived a burning desire to follow the rule of the holy father St Benedict, and had striven to conform their ideas and actions to the discipline of the monastic life, they formed a plan of sending some of their members to well-established monasteries in other places, so that they might become perfectly acquainted with the customs and observances of the brethren. When this prudent plan was submitted to the bishop he heartily approved of it and commanded Sturm to undertake the expedition himself... [On the latter's return] there was great desire in the community to adapt their way of life to the observances either described or shown to them, or exemplified in the lives of the saints, and they carried out in every detail the rule of St Benedict which they had vowed to follow.[17]

In AD 751 the link between Fulda and Montecassino was further strengthened when Boniface petitioned the Cassinese abbot and community for the two abbeys to be joined in a special bond of spiritual friendship.[18] In his correspondence with Rome at the same time he sought and obtained papal privileges for the forest monastery of

---

[15] C. Holdsworth points out that even at Fulda the observance was not strictly based on the *RB*.

[16] *Vita Leobae*, cap. 10; translation of text is in C. Talbot, *op. cit.*, pp. 213–4.

[17] *Vita Sturmi*, cap. 14; text in *MGH, Scriptores* II, pp. 371–2; this translation by C. Talbot, *op. cit.*, pp. 191–2.

[18] Prinz, *op. cit.*, p. 249, note 394.

Fulda, in which he had placed "*monachos sub regula sancti patris Benedicti viventes*".[19]

d. *The age of the triumphant breakthrough of the* RB

K. Hallinger has emphasized the suddenness of Boniface's adoption of a uniformly pro-Benedictine policy from 740 onwards (calling it "*ungewohnt neu*"), and the consequent change in the pattern of continental monachism that came about as a sequel to the Frankish legislation of 743–4. He wrote: "Instead of the merely concomitant role it had played up to that point, the Rule of St Benedict would thenceforward be abruptly elevated to the leading place. It was thus that the *RB* ascended above its hitherto secondary position".[20] After the German Council of 743 the *RB* was set firmly on what W. Levison termed "its victorious career".[21] There are indications that about 759 (and certainly before 770) even the famous Columbanian foundation of St Gallen, south of the lake of Constance, went over to the *RB*. However, the Columbanian rule, mixed with others, still continued in vigour in some other regions, Bavaria in particular, until late in the eighth century. H. Tausch likewise marked that as the point after which the Irish-Frankish Columbanian observance, "which until then had prevailed almost everywhere in the realm of the Franks", began to decline.

Pope Gregory III had died in 741, to be succeeded by another enthusiastic patron of Montecassino, Pope Zachary (741–752.) Paul Warnefrid's account makes it clear that some considerable time had elapsed between the first arrival of Petronax among the group of *simplices* who were dwelling on the summit of Montecassino and the firm establishment of Benedictine observance in the reconstructed abbey. Other sources indicate that the material rebuilding of the edifice was not substantially achieved until the pontificate of Zachary. There is an entry in the *Cassinese Chronicle* that tells how Gisulf II, the Lombard duke of Benevento, bountifully endowed the hill-top

---

[19] *Bonifatii Epistolae*, nn. 86 & 87.
[20] *Römischen Voraussetzungen*, p. 343.
[21] *England and the Continent in the Eighth Century*, Oxford 1946, p. 104. It was then, he remarked, that "we hear of monasteries that abandoned another rule for that of St Benedict".

shrine, while his wife Scauniperga provided for the construction of holy places in the town below.[22] The rule of Gisulf began only after the year 742. H. Brechter distinguished two stages in the restoration of Montecassino, which spanned 40 years. The first was the initial building and recruitment programme, commencing about 717; the second was the full establishment of Benedictine life in the rebuilt abbey, completed in the pontificate of St Zachary. That pope is reported to have sent there a codex of the *RB* claimed to have been transcribed by St Benedict with his own hands.[23] His greatest contribution to the spread of the cult of St Benedict was the Greek translation of the *Dialogues* that he commissioned. Thenceforward the fame of St Gregory the Great as a hagiographer and the golden legend of St Benedict were diffused together, not only in Latin Christianity but also in the Byzantine world, including the Greek-speaking southern region of the Italian peninsula (of which Pope Zachary himself was a native). Perhaps the readers immediately envisaged were the numerous monks of the Greek-speaking monasteries in the city of Rome itself.

Among the indications of the now flourishing "mystique of Montecassino" may be included the apocryphal documents relating to its earlier history: namely, the poem of Mark of Montecassino, and the verses attributed to Simplicius, Benedict's supposed second successor as abbot there, which have been mentioned in Chapter 13.c above. Those were imaginative attempts to bridge the wide gap that separated the new Benedictine movement from the distant age of Benedict himself. Mark's poem is ostensibly set in that age; modern scholarship assigns it to the eighth century. His obscure references to improvements carried out in the area of the monastery may well refer to the new works carried out on the mountain site under abbot Petronax. The verses attributed to Simplicius, who is known only from the pages of the *Dialogues*, may be placed earlier in the eighth century. Those and other similar writings were signs and expressions of the new Benedictine myth which, deriving from the spread of the *Dialogues*, was seizing the imagination of many during the course of that century. G. Penco observes: "While diverse in nature, such apocryphal documents clearly indicate that both in Italy and in Germany at

---

[22] *MGH, Script. Rer. Lang.* Hanover 1878, pp. 279–80.
[23] *SMGBO* 56 (1938), p. 121.

that time the rule of St Benedict was becoming the norm for the monastic life—hence the desire to fill the gaps left by the lack of earlier documents".[24]

The rise of the new monastery of Montecassino to international renown was hastened when members both of the Frankish and the Lombard ruling houses took the monastic habit there. In 748, the eighth year of the pontificate of St Zachary, Carloman himself, ruler of the Austrasian Franks and ally of Boniface in his campaign to establish the Benedictine rule everywhere, renounced his worldly power and went to Italy to become a monk, first at Monte Soracte and finally under the Benedictine statute at Montecassino itself. In the years that followed the presence of Carloman in that abbey still further enhanced its prestige throughout Europe. In 755, during the abbacy of Optatus, a group of fellow-monks from "the venerable monastery of St Benedict" accompanied Carloman on a mission to the court of his brother Pepin.[25] Rachis, the pious king of the Lombards, also became a monk at Montecassino. Other illustrious scions of the once barbarian peoples swelled the number of St Benedict's new disciples in the community at his shrine. Among them, after the Lombard kingdom had been suppressed by Frankish conquest, was the historian and poet Paul Warnefrid. He composed a heroic poem about the life and miracles of St Benedict as told in the *Dialogues*, and also wrote a *Life* of St Gregory and made a selection of his letters.

After Carloman's retirement to the cloister his brother Pepin assumed supreme rule over all the Frankish territories. He was already showing himself a staunch patron of the Benedictine movement and he too gave Boniface energetic support. In 751 came the momentous take-over by Pepin of the royal dignity from the *fainéant* Merovingian dynasty, for which he sought and obtained the spiritual sanction of Pope Zachary. He was anointed as the new king of all Francia by Boniface in the following year. The sequel was the forging of a still stronger bond between the Frankish monarchy and the papacy. I. Zibermayr saw that bond as a chief factor in bringing about the eventual triumph of the Benedictine rule over all others.[26]

---

[24] "*Là prima diffusione . . .*", p. 337.
[25] Letter of Pope Stephen II, *MGH, Epistolarum Tomus III*, Berlin 1892, p. 507.
[26] *Op. cit.*, p. 210 *seq.*

At all events it served to accelerate the process already begun in the preceding decades. After the overthrow of the Lombard kingdom in Italy and the establishment of an independent papal state with the aid of Frankish power, the *Regula Benedicti* became a chief instrument of the Carolingian religious renaissance. Pepin's son Charlemagne, the great patron of Benedictine monasticism, himself visited Montecassino in 787 to pay his homage to St Benedict. After his death his son Louis the Pious continued his father's patronage. Thanks to the reforming zeal of St Benedict of Aniane, observance of the *RB* was made universal in the whole Frankish empire by the *Capitulare Monasticum* of the Council of Aachen in AD 817. Although the hegemony of Benedictine monasticism was at that time still limited to the Frankish empire, it was progressively extended to the rest of Europe in the following centuries.

The mediaeval chronicle listing the abbots of Montecassino gives the length of Petronax's tenure of office there as 32 years. Assuming that the period was dated from the time he was first sent there by the pope, it would mean that he was abbot at St Benedict's shrine until about the year 750, not long before the death of Pope Zachary. At the close of his life Abbot Petronax must have looked back with wonder at all that had come to pass since the time that he had first arrived on the mountain top at Cassino, charged by Gregory II to rescue from oblivion the memory, cult and monastic observance of St Benedict. A combination of factors had, in a comparatively brief span of years, laid down a pattern of monastic life that would have decisive influence on the future history of Europe and of worldwide Christendom. Those factors were: first, the powerful impact of the newly disseminated legend of Book II of the *Dialogues*; then the initiative and support of three popes, the successful establishment of the new abbey as a centre for pilgrimage and monastic expansion, the mission of Boniface and Willibald inspiring the Austrasian movement, the ever widening recognition of the unique merit of the *RB*, and especially the effective favour of the Frankish rulers. It was then, in the middle years of the eighth century that the strangely delayed flowering of Benedictine monasticism occurred. It was from that time forward that, as Batiffol put it, "Book II of the *Dialogues* made St Benedict patriarch of the monks of the West".

CHAPTER TWENTY

FLEURY'S CLAIM TO POSSESS ST BENEDICT'S BODY AND ITS IMPLICATIONS FOR STUDY OF THE HISTORY OF THE *DIALOGUES* AND OF THE NEW BENEDICTINE MOVEMENT

a

There are other documentary traditions that are also relevant to study of the remarkable upsurge of Benedictine monasticism in the eighth century as a result of the spreading fame of St Benedict's life-story newly revealed in the *Dialogues*. Among them a special place must be given to a celebrated legend that provided the title deeds of the monastery of St Fleurie-sur-Loire near Orleans. I refer to the narrative of a pious theft of the bones of St Benedict and St Scholas-tica from their tomb at Montecassino and their translation to that Frankish abbey. The rival claims of the abbeys of Montecassino and of St Benoït-sur-Loire to possess the bodily relics of St Benedict pose a historical and devotional problem. Controversy on the subject has continued since the Middle Ages. Four centuries ago Baronius described this question as a thicket of thorns ("*densum spinetum*"), and since his time that tangled controversy has been made denser and thornier by a mass of further writings on the subject. Here we cannot enter into all the intricacies of this hoary dispute, which have been dis-cussed at great length by monastic historians, but we must at least consider its bearing on our investigation of the dating and influence of the *Dialogues*. The study of the Fleury tradition was considerably advanced by the publication of a volume of *Studia Monastica*[1] devoted expressly to the issue. Entitled *Le culte et les réliques de saint Benoît et de sainte Scholastica*", it included studies of the many different aspects of the question—the historical, literary, archaeological and liturgical data, as well as the anatomical evidence of the surviving relics. The Montecassino tradition was re-examined and restated in two volumes,

---

[1] Vol. 21 (1979), fasc. 1–2.

Il Sepolcro di S. Benedetto.[2] The second of those two volumes contains studies directly relevant to the Fleury claims.

The abbey of Fleury, founded anew in AD 651, was in the succeeding years a main centre of the expanding Irish-Frankish monastic reform. Its founders and patrons were promoters of the new dynamic movement stemming from St Columban and his disciples. It is a fond anachronism to see it as already a centre of Benedictine observance in the mid-seventh century. In the days of "pan-Benedictine" apologetic history, it used to be claimed that the *Testament* of Leodobulus, the founding abbot, attested Fleury's contemporary observance of a joint rule of St Benedict and of St Columban, the text of which was adduced in proof of the assertion. However, that text has been shown to be unauthentic, having been reworked in the eleventh century. As Dom J. Hourlier has shown,[3] it cannot be cited as proof that the rule of St Benedict was partially used in the regimen of the abbey of Fleury in its early period. As in so many other instances (referred to above in Chapter 14), the mention of the *RB* in that document must be recognized as an interpolation added in the Carolingian age, when Fleury had become the most famous Benedictine abbey in France. We do not know when Fleury adopted the Benedictine observance exclusively; most probably it was about the middle of the eighth century, when, following the divulgation of the *Dialogues*, the new Benedictine movement, promoted by three popes, by St Boniface and his associates and by the Frankish rulers, had brought about a dramatic extension of St Benedict's fame and cult, and the *RB* was being singled out as the norm for Frankish monastic observance.

The fully developed form of the Fleury claim to possess the relics of St Benedict, as presented in a narrative written in the ninth century by a monk of that abbey named Adrevald, can be summarized as follows.[4] He relates that at some time after the original foundation of the monastery dedicated to St Peter and St Mary at Fleury, but seemingly in the latter part of the seventh century, an abbot of that monastery named Mummolus decided, after reading the *Life* of

---

[2] Vols. 27 and 45 of *Miscellanea Cassinese*. The first volume was published in 1951, the second 31 years later, in 1982.

[3] *SM* 21, pp. 112 & 132. F. Prinz also recognizes the anomalies and uncertainties of the relevant documents.

[4] I make abbreviated use here of the summary of A. Davril in *SM* 21, pp. 423–4.

St Benedict written by St Gregory, to send an expedition led by a monk called Aigulf to seek and rescue the relics of that saint which (as indicated in the *Dialogues*) were lying abandoned and unhonoured in the ruins of Montecassino after the Lombards' ravages. At the moment when the caravan was about to depart for Italy there arrived at Fleury a group of clerics and monks sent by the bishop of Le Mans, Berarius, who were setting out on a like mission. The two groups then joined together for their journey. Arrived eventually at Montecassino, they discovered the tomb of Benedict and Scholastica. Pretending a desire to keep prayerful vigil by it, they persuaded the custodians of the place to allow them to remain there overnight, and then surreptitiously smuggled out the bones of the saintly brother and sister under cover of darkness. Outwitting their pursuers, they bore away the precious relics and conveyed them safely to Francia. Arrived at Fleury, they separated the relics and sorted them according to size. The relics of St Benedict were then enshrined in the Loire abbey with great honour, while those of St Scholastica were carried onward to Maine by the party from Le Mans for due enshrinement there. Adrevald's narrative of the relic-stealing expedition is rich with circumstantial details of miraculous events and of the actors involved, who are duly named. Ascribed to him, too, is a compilation of *Miracula* associated with the Fleury shrine.

Coupled with Adrevald's narrative, which relates especially to the transfer of the relics of St Benedict, there are contemporary documents relating to the supposed transfer of St Scholastica's relics to Le Mans: namely, the *Relatio* and certain episcopal *Acts* of that diocese.[5] The inter-relationship between the Fleury and Le Mans accounts is still unclear. They differ considerably from one another in their details, but agree on the substance of the story. Adrevald's *Historia Translationis* exalts the place of the monks of Fleury in the achievement of the pious theft of the relics. The Le Mans accounts relate some additional miracles, and give prominence to the part played in the episode by Bishop Berarius.

---

[5] These and other relevant documents are described and discussed by J. Hourlier in "*La translation d'après les sources narratives*", in *SM* 21 (1979), pp. 213–39.

b. *Historical incongruities and a context of "sacred thefts"*

In this chapter I recall the cogent reasons for concluding that the colourful Fleury story of the relic-stealing expedition cannot be accepted as veridical history, but was a later fiction. Before tracing the rise and growth of that legend and its relevance to the question of the *Dialogues'* date of origin, I situate it in the wider contemporary context of pious counterfeits, in which it appears as one out of very many instances of that genre. Underlying all historical assessment of the documents relating to the Fleury claim to possess the body of St Benedict must be awareness of the prevailing culture of devotion to the miracle-working remains of the saints and of pilgrimage to their shrines, from which emerged many fabulous accounts of finding and transfer of their relics. The fortunes of a town or monastery could depend on the fame of the relics reputed to be enshrined in it, repute that brought to it throngs of pilgrims from afar and endowments from devout patrons. As a consequence there was a thriving *"commerce de reliques"* (to borrow the phrase of J. Guiraud).[6] There are many accounts of "pious thefts" of saints' relics carried out to provide such centres of pilgrim devotion and quest for heavenly favours. In his book, *Furta Sacra: Theft of Relics in the Central Middle Ages*,[7] Patrick Geary further described many of those accounts and critically examined their credentials. Not surprisingly, that prevailing devotional culture brought forth a crop of fictitious legends to supply for the lack of historical authentication of many of the relics and of their provenance. An earlier instance of procurement of spurious relics in the Roman cemeteries is found in a letter written by Pope St Gregory himself, who related one such fraud as follows:

> Certain Greek monks who came here more than two years ago dug up, in the silence of the night, near the church of St Paul, the bodies of dead men buried there in the common ground. Concealing those bones, they kept them until they were ready to depart. They were arrested and closely questioned about their reasons for doing what they had done. They confessed they were going to transport those bones to Greece, to pass them off as relics of the saints.[8]

---

[6] His work, *"Le commerce de reliques"*, in *Mélanges G.B. Rossi*, École Française de Rome 1892, was a pioneer study in this field.

[7] Princeton 1978.

[8] *Registrum Epistularum*, IV.30.

Gathering strength in the seventh century, the quest for and traffic in the relics of the saints rose to new heights in the West from the eighth century onwards. In that age of ripening renaissance in the Frankish Church, monasteries, cathedrals and churches were avid to obtain relics that would bring them the patronage and miraculous power of a renowned saint, and which would consequently draw to them a constant influx of pilgrims. Saints' relics, too easily assumed to be genuine, were eagerly brought from Rome and other parts of Italy to be enshrined in new pilgrimage centres north of the Alps. There are many known instances of impostures and unscrupulous means used to pass off dubious relics. We even find the bold claim, made by the church of St Médard at Soissons, to have obtained the body of Pope St Gregory himself. It precisely dates the alleged removal of the saintly pope's body from Rome in AD 826. That story of the pious theft of St Gregory's relics is remarkably similar to the Fleury story of the theft of St Benedict's relics related by Adrevald. Four other towns have claimed to possess the skull of St Gregory.[9]

Geary marks out the first half of the ninth century as the time of most intense activity by the purveyors of relics from Rome and Italy to the churches and monasteries north of the Alps.[10] The best known of the dealers in what he calls "the Italian trade" was a Roman deacon named Deusdona, whom Geary describes as "the head of a large and highly organized group of relic merchants". He shows evidence that Adrevald, who wrote the circumstantial history of the "sacred theft" of the bones of Benedict and Scholastica from which Fleury benefited, was well acquainted with the literature relating to the quest for relics. Adrevald's *Historia Translationis* describing the procurement of St Benedict's relics was, Geary observes, "directly modelled in style and material" on an earlier account by an earlier writer named Einhard, entitled *Translatio SS. Marcellini et Petri*, in which Deusdona himself features.[11] "The similarities of [Adrevald's] account to Einhard's are evident: the two expeditions, the dalliance in Rome, the dreams revealing the location of the tomb, the assistance, the deception on the part of the groups, the pursuit of the pope, the

---

[9] Cf. Dudden, *op. cit.*, II. pp. 273–5.
[10] *Op. cit.*, pp. 52–9.
[11] *Ibid.*, pp. 145–8.

final revelation of the deceit, and the settlement of all claims to
the relics."[12] A Dominican scholar, M. Laurent, commented: "It is
sufficient to compare this Fleury story with similar narrations—and
they are legion—to realize that here one is in the presence not of
history but of a legend (I use the word in a hagiographical sense)
relating to a transfer of relics. It presents all the characteristics of
that type".[13] W. Goffart has pointed to Le Mans also as the place
of origin of a number of literary falsifications in the ninth century.[14]

c. The growth of the Fleury legend

The antecedents of Adrevald's legendary story and the other ninth-
century narratives go back to the previous century. The very first
references to veneration of St Benedict's relics at Fleury can be dated
to the 'thirties or 'forties of the eighth century. They are entries in
sanctoral calendars commemorating an anniversary (on July 11th but
in some MSS on December 4th) of an "*adventus*" or "*adventio*" of the
saint. In most of those calendars there is nothing in the MSS to
explain what that vague term refers to, but in one homogeneous
group of *abrégés* of the *Hieronymianum* the reference is made explicit:
"In the monastery of Fleury, the arrival of the body of St Benedict
from the parts of Rome" ("*in monasterio floriaco a partibus Romae adventus corporis sancti Benedicti*"). Although the text of those *abrégés* of the
Hieronymianum is known to us only from documents dating from the
end of the eighth century and later, Deshusses-Hourlier show that
their common source can be dated back to the second quarter of
the eighth century—not later, they judge, than about the year 740.[15]
In those earliest known (albeit cryptic) references to an "arrival" of
relics of Benedict's at Fleury, there is as yet no mention of a pious
theft of them from Montecassino. In Chapter 18 I documented the
tardy development of liturgical commemoration of St Benedict. No
commemoration of the *adventus* of St Benedict in Francia is found
either in the Echternach Martyrology, or in the Calendar of St

---

[12] *Ibid.*, p. 148.
[13] *RHE* 47 (1952), p. 659.
[14] *The Le Mans Forgeries: a Chapter from the History of Church Property in the Ninth
Century*, Cambridge, Mass. 1966.
[15] *SM* 21, pp. 171–4; cf. p. 214.

Willibrord, or in the Martyrology of St Bede, all of which mention
only the saint's anniversary on March 21st. P. Visentin drew attention to that significant silence.[16] Deshusses-Hourlier have shown that
it was not until the middle of the eighth century that liturgical cult
and commemoration of the saint began to spread generally, and they
indicate the third quarter of that century as the decisive stage of
that development.

When Book II of the *Dialogues* first became famous in the early
eighth century it provided a clear pointer in its text to the neglected
tomb of St Benedict on the mountain top at Cassino, which inspired
Gregory II to restore the ruins as his shrine. That life-story of the
great saint also motivated Petronax, Willibald, Boniface and many
others to spread anew the Benedictine observance. It would be no
wonder if relic-mongers were ready to provide for pious Franks bones
of the saintly abbot and author of the *Regula Benedicti* which was
already esteemed in Francia. It is indeed quite likely that the text
of the *Dialogues* would have reached Fleury not long after its first
appearance, as it reached English monasteries at that time. (From
the Italian provenance of the earliest group of codices in the mediaeval library of Fleury it can be inferred that the abbey was acquiring codices from Italy from the latter part of the seventh century.)[17]

The fame of St Benedict was spreading rapidly in the second quarter of the eighth century—the period from which dates the earliest
mention in a sanctoral calendar of an *adventus* of St Benedict at
Fleury. At that time of *commerce de réliques* no extraordinary means
would have to be taken for Fleury to obtain relics of the saint "from
the parts of Rome". Dom A. Mundó suggests, in a provocative aside,
that the phrase in the sanctoral calendars "*a partibus Romae*" may
truly have been meant to refer to Rome, not Cassino, and that the
bones obtained may have been taken from the Roman cemeteries.[18]
Even if they were only fragmentary, the Fleury abbey could still
claim to possess the body of St Benedict, since the presence of even
a minor part of a saint's remains was considered to bring access to

---

[16] In his article, *"La posizione di S. Beda e del suo ambiente riguardi alla traslazione del
corpo di S. Benedetto in Francia"*, in *Rev. Bén.* 67 (1957), p. 34 *seq*. See also Deshusses-
Hourlier, *op. cit.*, pp. 157–8 & note 15.
[17] Cf. D.B. Grémont and J. Hourlier, *"La plus ancienne bibliothèque de Fleury"*, in
SM 21, pp. 253–64; also p. 426.
[18] "... *à moins que les ossements ne fussent vraiment des cimetières romains*"; cited from
his article, *SA* 42, p. 149, note 136.

the total presence and power of the sacred *corpus*. One may conjecture that it was during that second quarter of the eighth century
that the abbey of Fleury acquired bones "from the parts of Rome"
that were thenceforward revered as those of St Benedict. The new
fame of the relics doubtless spread during the middle years of that
century, when Frankish dominion was being consolidated in the territory between the Loire and the Garonne. It was the period when
Médon was abbot of Fleury, in which the abbey rose to importance
and influence, as documentary records show. There is record of "a
surge of donations" to the abbey, which J. Laporte[19] dates as probably occurring at that time.

It is too easily assumed that the story of the transfer of the relics
of St Benedict was already known in its fully developed form in the
middle of the eighth century. J. Hourlier observed: "The Fleury
sources leave a gap of about a century in the history of the relics,
and the tradition seems to have been interrupted for a period, until,
in the ninth century, it was decided to modify the initial data".[20]
During the hundred years following the first mention of an *adventus*
of St Benedict's relics in Francia, there was indeed a progressive
addition of circumstantial details, culminating in Adrevald's colourful story in the ninth century. In *PsGD* I discussed at some length
three documents marking stages in that process;[21] I summarize below
their bearing on the present issue. Those documents were:

> (i) a suspect letter attributed to Pope Zachary, appealing generally to
> the Franks for the return of St Benedict's body, which, it said, had
> been "furtively removed from his tomb";
> (ii) a reference by Paul Warnefrid (c. 780–790) to a theft of the relics
> by men from Le Mans and Orleans, ostensibly about the year 700;
> he makes no mention of the many marvellous happenings and other
> circumstantial details that were to be so vividly related in the ninth-
> century accounts;
> (iii) a vague narration by an anonymous Bavarian monk around the
> end of the eighth century. (As J. Hourlier points out, he provides no
> chronological clues as to when the transfer of relics supposedly occurred,
> and he is ill informed about Fleury and its situation.)[22]

---

[19] *SM* 21, p. 214.
[20] *SM* 21, p. 236.
[21] *PsGD*, pp. 261–71.
[22] *Ibid.*, p. 222. I do not discuss this nugatory testimony here, but simply refer
to my treatment of it in *PsGD*, pp. 264 & 278.

In addition to Adrevald's *Historia Translationis*, which was mainly influential in giving substance and wide currency to the story, there were references to it in mediaeval charters and annals. Of the latter, most significant are certain MSS of the Fleury *Annals* which, although inscribed in a later century, reflect the earlier text of the abbey's chronicle. From them it can be inferred that the earliest text of those annals, while commemorating the anniversary of the death of St Benedict (and also that of St Leodobulus, the abbey's founder), made no mention of the transfer of St Benedict's body to Fleury— which, one would suppose, would have been regarded as a principal event in the history of the abbey.

d. *The putative date of the transfer of the relics*

What indications do the documents in question give of the putative date and manner of the transfer of St Benedict's relics to France? Only the fictional ninth-century accounts give historical allusions that can be connected with known dates in the mid-seventh century or soon afterwards. In particular, Adrevald's references to Abbot Mummolus and Bishop Berarius have been claimed to offer such an "anchor in history". From those clues, first detected by Mabillon and since his time accepted as probative by many, it is conjectured by some that the pious theft of St Benedict's relics occurred as early as the year 653. Marilyn Dunn comments on this: "it seems likely that if the expedition ever took place it was not at that early date, but only after the *Dialogues*, with their second book devoted to Benedict's life and miracles, had begun to circulate in Francia".[23] Indeed those fanciful ninth-century accounts are spurious. They contain patent chronological and historical errors, as well as being self-contradictory. Leaving them aside, the two documents that seem most relevant in our search for the historical origins of the story, and for the supposed date of the relic-stealing episode, are the problematic letter of Pope Zachary and the passage in Paul Warnefrid's *Historia Langobardorum*, dating from around 779.

The letter of Pope Zachary, supposedly antedating Paul Warnefrid's account by about 30 years, has been much discussed. Its provenance

---

[23] *The Emergence of Monasticism*, p. 192.

is dubious: ostensibly it dates from about 750 but it cannot be traced to any Roman source, being first found in a collection of letters in a French monastery dating from the end of the eighth century. The letter is strangely vague. It would appear from it that the pope had no information as to when, how or by whom the saint's body had been taken to France, or where it was to be found there. Moreover, his initiative in sending such a generic appeal to the bishops and priests of the Frankish church is puzzling. Is it supposed that the pious theft had occurred only recently? Or if it was supposed to have happened in the previous century, why had it become a pressing and seemingly novel concern at that point in the middle of the eighth century? Why had not Zachary's predecessors, Gregory II and III, who like him were ardent patrons of the Montecassino shrine, made such an appeal for restitution of St Benedict's relics during the previous thirty years? Why, in making his appeal, did Pope Zachary address it so randomly? If it was common knowledge that the monastery of Fleury had organized and benefited from the theft of the saint's body from his tomb at Montecassino, why did Zachary not direct his appeal to the bishop of that diocese and to the abbot of that monastery and to the Frankish rulers, instead of merely generally to all and sundry? Why indeed did he not direct his appeal to the one person who more than any other could have effectively secured what he desired: namely, Pepin the Short, who, since his brother Carloman had retired to monastic life in Italy in AD 747, had been supreme ruler of the Frankish realms, including Orléannais in which Fleury was located?

This leads to what would seem to be the most puzzling and obvious question of all: if Pope Zachary and his contemporaries were convinced that the body of St Benedict had been furtively removed to Francia, why did St Benedict's shrine at Montecassino remain a principal centre of pilgrimage? From the time that Gregory II first initiated the building up of the new Cassinese monastery, it was above all the pilgrimage *ad sanctum Benedictum* that made that monastery the focal point of the new monastic movement that was to secure the triumphant diffusion of the *Regula Benedicti* in that age. If St Benedict's body was known to be no longer at Cassino but at Fleury, why did the eager throng of pilgrims *ad sanctum Benedictum* continue to travel to Montecassino in quest of the blessings and boons to be granted through his favour and power? Why did Pope Zachary himself continue to be the chief patron of devotion to St Benedict at the Cassinese shrine and to foster support for it throughout Christendom? The many anomalous features of Zachary's letter give grounds for concluding that it was one more example of the genre of "supporting forgery".[24]

Paul Warnefrid's story is the first to mention the removal of the relics of St Scholastica. Up to that time, in the second half of the eighth century, there is as yet no mention of the relics of St Benedict's sister, nor had she yet entered the sanctoral calendars. However, a question would naturally arise for readers of the *Dialogues*, where it is made clear that the body of St Scholastica had been laid to rest in the same tomb as that of her saintly brother. They would ask: If the tomb had been rifled to remove the body of St Benedict, what had happened to that of St Scholastica? The passage in Paul's *History of the Lombards*, written in the later part of the century, shows that by then account had been taken of that difficulty. It was now explained that St Scholastica's relics too had been removed to Francia by the predatory party. Indeed, Paul's report that the Frankish relic-raiders had come "*de celmanicorum vel aurelianensium regione*", from Orléannais or Maine, may well imply that the story as he knew it already included the claim of Le Mans to have acquired the bones of St Scholastica. Or perhaps, as W. Goffart proposes,[25] was Paul's loose topographical reference later taken as a cue for the invention of that claim? He points out that there is no trustworthy evidence for the existence of a monastery at Le Mans supposed to have contained the relics of St Scholastica.

Since the story of the pious theft of the saints' relics is patently fictional it is of little relevance to discuss the various dates assigned by commentators to the relic-stealing episode. The date that is implied by the chronological references in Warnefrid's account is later than that implied by Adrevald's. Paul implicitly places the occurrence of the pious theft within the period of rule of the Lombard duke Gisulf I of Benevento, which was from 690 to 707. Some authors see confirmation of Paul's implied chronology in a late entry in the mediaeval annals of the German abbey of Lorsch, which chronicles "the translation of the body of St Benedict from Montecassino" and assigns

---

[24] My conclusions here about the putative letter of Zachary are an advance on what I wrote on the question in *PsGD*.

[25] *Op. cit.*, pp. 118–9.

it to the year 703. Among those who have declared in favour of that putative dating of the episode are F. Chamard, L. Duchesne and H. Leclercq.[26] Theoretically, such a dating could be reconciled with the dating of the early diffusion of the *Dialogues* at the close of the seventh century, as shown above in Chapter 16. However, Paul Warnefrid is notoriously unreliable as a historian, and there is nothing to substantiate his version of the legend, or to show that the supposed sacred theft ever occurred. On the historical value of his testimony Dom J. Hourlier commented:

> Everyone will easily recognize that it provides a very firm proof of the belief that was widespread in the second half of the eighth century, in the regions of Gaul that he has visited and in some others, especially Austrasia ... He does not settle the question whether the relics that were transferred were authentic, but he regards them as being so ... He says, but he does not demonstrate, that the bones came from Montecassino; he says, but he does not prove, that they were those of St Benedict and St Scholastica ... The question remains whether the opinion of Paul Warnefrid corresponded to reality.[27]

While the Fleury legend is not history but fiction it serves as a pointer in our inquiry. The fact that its first beginnings can be dated in the second quarter of the eighth century serves to confirm the emergence of the *Dialogues* at the end of the seventh and their subsequent diffusion in Francia.

e. *Montecassino's counter-claim: overview of the controversy*

So far I have concentrated on the Fleury claim and the testimonies relating to it. Also to be critically considered is the counter-claim made by the defenders of the Montecassino tradition, which asserts that the bodies of St Benedict and St Scholastica never left Cassino and that their sacred relics are still preserved in that shrine today. The aerial bombardment of the historic abbey of Montecassino during the Second World War destroyed virtually all the buildings, but the shrine-tomb itself escaped destruction although buried under tons of rubble. The reconstruction of the abbey and the restoration of

---

[26] Chamard, *Les réliques de saint Benoît*, Paris 1882; Duchesne, *Fastes épiscopaux* II, Paris 1989; Leclercq, *DACL* XI, 2461. Cf. J. Hourlier, *SM* 21, p. 217, note 15.
[27] *SM* 21, pp. 209–11.

the shrine provided opportunity for a new scientific investigation of the whole site, of the tomb, of the relics, and of their history. The results were published in the first of the two volumes mentioned above, *Il Sepolcro di S. Benedetto*, published in 1951. The case vindicating Montecassino's claim to possess the veritable relics of St Benedict and St Scholastica is most fully set out in the second volume, published 31 years later.[28] The defenders of the Montecassino tradition press the same critical objections about the Fleury claims that have been outlined above, and indeed add others.[29]

In the Cassinese shrine there are bones dating from the early Middle Ages of an elderly man and of an elderly woman; in the shrines of Fleury and Juvigny there are likewise bones dating from the same period of an elderly man and an elderly woman. Although in both cases the remaining bones are very incomplete, there are enough of them to show that there is duplication of distinctive bones. Thus it is now established that the male bones in Italy are from a different individual than those in France; and that the same dichotomy exists between the two sets of female bones. It had been previously suggested, as a conciliatory theory, that there had been a partial transfer or donation of the saints' bones from Cassino to the northern abbeys, so that the Italian and French shrines genuinely shared possession of the relics of St Benedict and his saintly sister; thus the claims on both sides could be justified and reconciled. In the light of the anatomical investigations, however, it is now clear that this solution is not possible and that the rival claims cannot both be valid. The conclusion emerges inescapably that at some time in the early Middle Ages, in at least one of the two localities—either at Cassino or in western France—individual remains of an elderly man and an elderly woman were enshrined as being those of St Benedict and St Scholastica but were not such. In the light of the evidence showing that the *Dialogues* are not history but fable, both claims must be equally suspect. M. Laurent was one of those who have declared themselves convinced neither by the claim of Fleury nor by that of Montecassino to possess the genuine relics of St Benedict. After reviewing the arguments of the apologists for Montecassino, he concluded that "neither medicine, nor archaeology, nor history authorize

---

[28] Vol. 45 of *Miscellanea Cassinese*, 1982. There was a critical appraisal of the case by A. Davril of Fleury in *SM* 21, pp. 377–408.
[29] Cf. *PsGD*, pp. 272–3.

us now to consider as authentic the bones exhumed at Cassino in 1950".[30]

We are left with the agnostic reflection that the truth about the grave and remains of St Benedict, author of the great rule that has inspired Western monasticism and patron of Europe, lies beyond our reach. It has been obscured by age-old literary falsifications and pious frauds, leading to age-long historical misapprehensions. The only source of knowledge about his life, death and original burial place, the pseudo-Gregorian *Dialogues*, is now exposed as fictional and untrustworthy. Examination of the credentials of the Fleury legend has served to provide further pointers to the spuriousness of that book.

---

[30] *RHE* 47 (1952), p. 659.

CHAPTER TWENTY ONE

THE PATERIAN ANTHOLOGY, CLAIMED TO BE THE SECOND "BEDROCK PROOF" OF THE AUTHENTICITY OF THE *DIALOGUES*, AND THE TESTIMONY OF TAJO

a

Ever since the earlier controversies about the Gregorian authorship of the *Dialogues*, in the sixteenth and seventeenth centuries, the principal argument advanced by the defenders of their authenticity has been appeal to the *Letter to Maximian*, which has already been discussed in Chapter 10, where cogent reasons were given for concluding that it was a later counterfeit. As well as basing their case primarily on that letter, the three principal critics of *The Pseudo-Gregorian Dialogues*, Vogüé, Meyvaert and Godding, adduced a number of post-Gregorian texts, dating from the first half of the seventh century or not long afterwards, which they claimed also showed knowledge of the *Dialogues* and thus contradicted my thesis. In this chapter and the following I survey this remaining dossier of objections and address them in detail. Before doing so I begin by offering three general comments.

I observe in the first place that those critics, while now basing their case on passages found in a number of obscure texts of seventh-century date which supposedly include citations from the *Dialogues*, gloss over, as of no consequence, the body of evidence set out in *PsGD* demonstrating that contemporary authors and sources of established fame and authority significantly failed to make any mention of the book when expressly listing and discussing Gregory's works. (That evidence is summarized anew in Chapter 12 above.) They cannot explain away the contrary witness of the *Liber Pontificalis*, of Isidore of Seville, of Braulio of Saragossa, and of Ildefonsus of Toledo. Mention of the title of the *Dialogues* was interpolated into the MS tradition of those early lists of Gregory's writings in later centuries. The critics ignore the fact that the traditional apologetic for the book's authenticity, from the time of the Maurists onwards, has been bolstered largely by those false testimonies.

Secondly, I observe that the arguments they adduce are based on inference from passages found in seventh-century documents which, they claim, are implicit citations from the *Dialogues*; they cannot produce a single text genuinely dating from the seventy years after Gregory's death which explicitly names the book and mentions Gregory's authorship of it. Is it not strange that during all that time no author or source makes any express mention of it and its author? Nor indeed can any of the passages they claim to be tacit citations from the book be proved to be such, as I show in the following pages.

A third general comment of their apologia is to point out once more that even if (*dato non concesso*) the testimonies they allege could be truly shown to reflect knowledge of the *Dialogues* in the earlier seventh century, that would not prove that Gregory was the author of the work. The overwhelming proof from internal and other external evidence, set out in this volume, proves that he was not. If a genuine testimony dating from the 65 years following Gregory's death could be found that attests knowledge of the existence of the book and of its ascription to him, that would mean that the date of the composition of the pseudepigraphical *Dialogues* and of their first emergence into the light would have to be set earlier than that argued in this volume. It would not prove that they were of genuinely Gregorian origin.

b. *The three parallels to IGPs found in the Paterian anthology*

After the *Letter to Maximian* all three of those critics adduce, as a major documentary testimony contradicting the conclusions of *PsGD*, the citation of passages from the *Dialogues* in the Paterian anthology of Gregorian expository passages. I recall P. Meyvaert's emphatic affirmation, quoted earlier, that those two testimonies together constitute the foundation upon which the argument refuting my case is essentially based: "It is the witness of the letter to Maximian of Syracuse, together with that of Gregory's secretary Paterius that remain the bedrock historical evidence for asserting that Gregory the Great is indeed the author of the *Dialogues* that bear his name". The first of those "bedrock proofs" has been shown in Chapter 10 to be unavailing. The same must be said of the second, traditional though it is. Already in the seventeenth-century controversy Peter Goussainville had singled out Paterius as a prime witness to the authenticity of the *Dialogues*:

> Of the authors who lived after Gregory, I cite in the first place Paterius, his familiar companion and disciple, a notary and *secundicerius* of the holy Roman Church, of whom there is mention in the *Register* [of Gregory's letters]. He wrote the *Liber Testimoniorum*, drawn from all Gregory's works—indeed, as he states in his preface, he did so with the encouragement of the holy Father himself. In this work he adduces, in exactly the same words, more than twenty passages from the *Dialogues*.[1]

The anthology in question, usually entitled *Liber Testimoniorum*, but also (inaccurately) *Liber de expositione veteris ac novae testamenti*, is traditionally ascribed to the notary Paterius who is mentioned repeatedly in Gregory's letters.[2] The prologue of the work does not identify the author as Paterius, but it does attest that it was written by one of Gregory's household who had received fatherly encouragement from the pope himself to persevere in his proposal to construct an orderly scriptural commentary out of extracts from his master's works. The author describes how he scrutinized for this purpose not only Gregory's exposition of *Job* in the *Moralia*, but also other dispersed writings which he said the pope had preserved "*in schedis suis*"—this is, in the archive of Gregorian texts preserved in the papal Curia. The *Liber Testimoniorum* comprises excerpts of Gregorian commentary arranged according to their order in the Old Testament books. Some other compilations and commentaries were also attributed to Paterius in former times, but these have been shown to be spurious. Scholars are now also agreed that much of the text of the *LT* formerly ascribed to him originated in a later age, and that the excerpts relating to the later books of the Old Testament, at least from *Isaiah* to *Malachi*, did not belong to the original text of the anthology but were added by a later continuator of the work. R. Étaix considers it probable that also those passages relating to *Proverbs* and the *Canticle* were not in the original text.[3]

No documentary mention of the *LT* can be found throughout the seventh century. The first known mention of it is a reference by

---

[1] *Vindiciae Dialogorum*, *PL* 77.129.
[2] Epist. V.26; VI.12; IX.15.
[3] *Op. cit.*, pp. 68–9, 72.

Bede, dating from shortly before AD 731. The earliest surviving manuscripts of the text, one at Amiens (derived from Corbie) and the other at Fleury, are dated by A. Wilmart[4] as from the years 772–780. There are fragments which seem to date from earlier in that century. The eighth and ninth-century MSS belong to two different families. The earliest manuscripts of the *LT* do not give the name of the author; the name of Paterius was added in the ninth-century MSS. In view of the obscurity surrounding the first emergence of that anthology into historical record, and the evidence of multiple alterations and accretions in the text, I raised questions in *PsGD* about the origins and original form of the text, and suggested that the prologue, with its personal reminiscences, may have been added by a later hand. I there concluded that it could be reasonably assumed that the original core of the work was written not long after Gregory's death by one of his assistants, who had access not only to his published works but also to the file transcripts of earlier drafts of them and to the unedited *reportata* of his spoken commentaries on Scripture. I now recognize that some of the reservations I made in *PsGD* about the origins the *Liber Testimoniorum* were unduly cautious. I duly acknowledge the force of the joint critique of Vogüé, Meyvaert[5] and Godding on some points, and also of their comments about the author's stated methodology. I agree that, although the ascription was not made in the earlier MSS, it is quite probable that the original core of the anthology was indeed composed by Paterius the *secundicerius*. (For convenience, I adopt that ascription when referring to the author in the following pages.) However, my necessary admissions on those secondary points leave the main issues unchanged.

The impressive claim of Peter Goussainville that more than twenty passages from the *Dialogues* are cited in the original text of the Paterian *LT* has been drastically discredited by more recent scholarship. Correcting his inflated estimate, U. Moricca reduced to six the number of genuinely original passages thought to have been excerpted by Paterius directly from the *Dialogues*.[6] In the course of the twentieth

---

[4] "*Le Recueil Grégorien de Paterius*", in *Rev. Bén.* 1927, pp. 81–104.

[5] I acknowledge in particular Meyvaert's long discussion of the Gregorian anthology of Paterius (and that of Tajo) in *JEH* 39 (1988) pp. 351–66, which contains some useful observations and correctives.

[6] *Gregorii Magni Dialoghi*, Rome 1924, p. xii.

century that figure has been further corrected. Now the number of excerpts common to his work and the *Dialogues* is recognized to be no more than three. They are as follows: (1) Paterius, *In Genesim* LI (cap. 54) ≠ *Dial.* I.8.5–6; (2) Paterius, *In Numeros* IV ≠ *Dial.* II.2.4; (3) Paterius, *In Librum Josue* I ≠ *Dial.* III.34.1–5. Those three passages are identified in *PsGD* and in this volume as IGPs 9, 16 and 39. From those three passages the present-day defenders of the Gregorian authorship of that work draw a twofold argument. They claim, first, that identity of wording proves the dependence of Paterius on the *Dialogues*; and secondly that in two of the three items such dependence is conclusively confirmed by introductory headings which expressly name the *Dialogues* as the source from which they are quoted.

In *PsGD* I discussed each of those three passages in detail, and pointed out features in them which indicate that in reproducing them Paterius was independent of the *Dialogues*, but was citing them from the codices of Gregorian exposition available to him in the papal *Scrinium*[7]—the same source from which, I argue, the Dialogist later drew his IGPs. That evidence remains firm. That Paterius had access to an archival store of original Gregorian texts that have not come down to us in any of Gregory's published works is not mere conjecture: we have proof of it from the fact that in the *LT* he includes a number of other evidently Gregorian passages that have survived only through his transcription of them. In Chapter 3 I commented on the significance of 28 otherwise unknown Gregorian passages, for the transmission of which we are indebted to Paterius. From their style and teaching, as R. Étaix remarked, "it is impossible to doubt the Gregorian origin of those fragments". The fact that Paterius had access to those otherwise unknown Gregorian pericopes undermines the assumption that he must have been dependent on the *Dialogues* for the reproduction of the three Gregorian excerpts that are our present concern. If, as Étaix and others show to be the case, he was able to reproduce such unknown IGP gems from the *schedae* of reportata in the Lateran archives, so also could the Dialogist do so at a later date, by recourse to the same curial archive of Gregorian *inedita*.

The presence of otherwise unknown Gregorian passages in the text of the *LT* had already been recognized by the Maurist editors.

---

[7] *PsGD*, pp. 453–6, 466–9, 512–7.

As far as they could, they identified the source in Gregory's known works of most of Paterius's excerpts, but they admitted they had been unable to trace the origin of some. An interesting example, and very pertinent to the present question, is a passage (no. 54) in Paterius's compilation, which reproduces a lengthy section of Gregorian commentary on *Genesis* 24 concerning the divine promises to Abraham fulfilled through Isaac and his seed. The Maurist editors observed that the passage cannot be found anywhere in Gregory's works, but that nevertheless the style is indubitably Gregory's.[8] Now the very next excerpt in Paterius's compilation (no. 55) relates to the same theme, and expounds texts from the following section in *Genesis*. Whereas the Maurist editors had declared the preceding excerpt, no. 54, was derived from an unknown Gregorian source, when they came to its sequel, no. 55, they identified its source as *Dialogues* I.8.5–6 (i.e. IGP 9). Given the context, that conclusion is evidently questionable. If Paterius was able to extract the long preceding passage 54 from a source other than the *Dialogues*, why infer that he must have taken the succeeding passage 55, which is closely associated with that passage in its subject matter, from the *Dialogues*? Rather the obvious inference is that he took both those linked passages from another source—namely, from what he himself referred to as the "*schedae*" of Gregory's expository teaching, the archive in which were preserved both his published writings and the *inedita*. It was doubtless from that reserve in the Lateran archives of unpublished commentaries that Paterius also copied all the other 27 quotations of otherwise unknown Gregorian passages.

That same source would still have been available to the Dialogist in the later seventh century from which to draw the three pericopes (IGPs 9, 16 and 13) in his book that have parallels in the *LT*. It is probable that the Paterian anthology was also available to him there, and that he may have referred to it. However, there are several features in Paterius's citation of those Gregorian texts that differ from their wording in the *Dialogues*. I have pointed out those differences in *PsGD* when discussing in detail the three relevant IGPs.[9] Together they provide a cogent argument showing that Paterius was not copy-

---

[8] "*Quae sequuntur nullibi reperiuntur apud Gregorium . . . Gregorianum tamen stylum sapiunt*"; *PL* 79, col. 704.

[9] *PsGD*, pp. 454–6, 466–9, 512–6.

ing from the *Dialogues* but from another source. I also set out there several other indications, textual and historical, confirming that in reusing those three excerpts he did so without dependence on the *Dialogues*. In the next section I discuss the witness of Tajo of Saragossa, who knew and consulted the Paterian anthology when seeking Gregorian writings in the Roman archives in the mid-seventh century. He too composed an anthology of Gregorian passages, and included in it some of Paterius's excerpts, as well as some Gregorian passages that Paterius did not cite. Significantly, Tajo and Paterius agree in their reproduction of the wording of a Gregorian pericope commenting on a text from *Joshua*, concerning two kinds of compunction, but the presentation of the passage in the *Dialogues* (IGP 39) discords in points of wording and grammatical usage from the text as cited by both those two authors. If they were copying from the *Dialogues*, would they both have departed from the text at those points? The confusion becomes worse confounded when we find that the substance of the same expository passage, supposedly composed by Gregory in 593, was included in a letter he sent to the imperial court at Constantinople in 597 for the edification of the Empress Constantina, but is there found in a quite different order, with different wording in places.[10]

The critics' second and allegedly conclusive argument relates to the introductory headings in the *LT*, also called *lemmata* or *praefatiuncula*. As A. Wilmart observes, those preliminary headings in the anthology, which the author promises in his prologue to supply, are set out "like a kind of title or rubric", meant to indicate the scriptural *locus* of each item, its place in the Gregorian writings, and its theme. Of the three passages that have doublets in the *Dialogues* (though with several variations in wording) two are prefaced in the surviving Paterian MSS with reference *lemmata* stating their source as "*in codice Dialogorum*". The third contains some wording found in the *Dialogues* but consists mainly of a citation from the *Moralia*; it is prefaced by a *lemma* indicating the *Moralia* as its source. (I leave aside A. de Vogüé's intricate but inconclusive theory about the genesis of this third passage.[11] A simple and satisfactory explanation of the textual puzzle is that the text as found both in the Paterian anthology

---

[10] *Ibid.*, pp. 515–6.
[11] *RHE* 83 (1988), pp. 303–5.

and in the *Dialogues* derived from an original variant text of Gregory's exposition of *Numbers* 8.24–6 surviving among the papal *schedae*.)[12]

The dispute about the testimony of the Paterian anthology, which is alleged to attest knowledge of the *Dialogues* in Gregory's own age, now centres on those two *lemmata* in the *LT*, expressly naming the "*codex Dialogorum*" as the source of the two passages cited. Understandably, the trio of critics all seek to refute my demonstration that the *LT* is prior to the *Dialogues* by pointing insistently to those two subheadings. In brief, my answer to their argument is that it cannot be proved that the two *lemmata* in question were present in the seventh-century text of the *LT*; rather, there are sure indications in the MS tradition that some of the introductory *lemmata* in the *LT* were inserted by later hands—doubtless in an attempt to fill the gaps where the author of the original MS had failed to give the source of some items (as is the case with the 28 "unknown" Gregorian pericopes pointed out by Étaix).[13] Indeed, one must observe that the *lemmata* assigned to the individual extracts in the anthology are not consistent, but vary in the different families of the early MSS, as Étaix and others have noted. That is a tell-tale sign that, despite the author's stated intention to specify the sources of his excerpts, in several cases he could not do so—doubtless because he had copied them from unpublished folios of Gregorian literary remains filed in the *Scrinium*. That would explain why some of the introductory subheadings were not present in the original prototype but were added later. Moreover, in the earliest surviving MSS several of the references to the sources of the excerpts are erroneous. It cannot therefore be assumed that the two *lemmata* naming the "*codex Dialogorum*" were present in the original Paterian compilation in the seventh century. That the variant source-reference headings in the MSS tradition of the *Liber testimoniorum* are dubious and of later origin is confirmed by the judgement of the editor of the new critical edition of the work in the *CCL* series, R. Vander Plaetse.[14] Marilyn Dunn also observes the weakness of the appeal of Godding and others to the *lemmata* as allegedly dating from the earlier seventh century:

---

[12] Cf. *PsGD*, pp. 467 ff.

[13] Cf. Chapter 3.a above.

[14] He expressed that judgement in discussions at the Oxford Patristic Conferences of 1991 and 1995. I repeat my grateful acknowledgement to Mr Vander Plaetse for his kindness in providing me with the text of his new edition in advance of its publication.

Godding . . . shows that the earliest MSS of the *Liber testimoniorum*, an anthology of Gregorian material composed by the notary Paterius, date from the eighth century, so that the *lemmata* identifying excerpts as coming from the *Dialogues* could have been added long after the compilation was made and once the *Dialogues* as we know them came into circulation.[15]

The intention of Paterius, as announced in the prologue of the work, was to compile a collection of Gregorian comments on texts from all the books of the Bible, in three volumes. Whether or not he actually did so, the fact is that only a truncated text survived in the eighth century, contained in one codex. It is possible that the original text was left unpublished for many years before someone decided to copy it in an incomplete state, after which substantial additions were progressively made. That later hands edited the subheadings in the text is shown by the fact that a number of those *lemmata* are given differently in different MSS. That the two explicit references to the "*codex Dialogorum*" were not in that original text is in any case proved by the overriding demonstration that the *Dialogues* were not written by St Gregory, and so could not have been known to Paterius. The further inference can be made that those two *lemmata* on which the critics of *PsGD* base such impressive conclusions, were inserted after the seventh century, when the *Dialogues* had emerged to public knowledge and fame.

c. *The citation of Gregorian excerpts by Tajo of Saragossa*

I return to the question, broached in Chapters 3.a and 12.f, of the citation by Tajo of Saragossa of Gregorian passages closely akin to IGPs found in the *Dialogues*. As in the case of Paterius, so here the apologists for the authenticity of the *Dialogues* in the seventeenth century and today have taken Tajo's supposed citation of passages from the *Dialogues* as evidence that the latter work was known at an early date. Their plea does not have serious weight, but it must have some discussion here. Tajo first appears as a bishop in the Acts of the eighth Council of Toledo, held in the year 653. In a prefatory letter to Bishop Eugenius of Toledo he describes his earlier research

---

[15] *The Emergence of Monasticism*, p. 237, note 116.

visit to Rome to seek, study and transcribe Gregorian writings in
the papal library: "I went through all the documentary records (*moni-
menta*) of his writings, and the testimonies concerning almost the
whole of sacred Scripture that are contained in the different parts
of his works, which serve for proving or expounding each subject in
turn."[16] A contemporary account of his visit to Rome, which is
embellished with legendary details, relates that while he was searching "*in archivio Romanae Ecclesiae*" for certain Gregorian texts that were
missing in Spain, he was aided by an angelic vision to locate them.[17]

On his return from Rome bearing his hoard of Gregorian texts
Tajo set about composing his own anthologies of the great pope's
expository and theological wisdom, evidently making direct (and unac-
knowledged) use of Paterius's *LT*.[18] In the first of two distinct collections, which was also entitled "*Liber testimoniorum*", he arranged the
Gregorian excerpts according to the order of the books of the Bible.
In his second anthology (entitled *Libri quinque Sententiarum*) he subsequently arranged them according to an order of theological themes.[19]
Most of the text of his first anthology has been lost, but it can be
inferred that the excerpts it contained were later substantially reproduced in the *Libri Sententiarum*, in rearranged order. (The latter work
includes some excerpts from writings of St Augustine and St Isidore
as well.) In the earliest MSS of the *LS* no indications were given of
the sources Tajo used for his compilation, but they were supplied
later by the Maurist editors. Almost all the very numerous excerpts
are taken from the four Gregorian works, the *Moralia*, the *Homiliae
in Evangelia*, the *Homiliae in Ezechielem* and the *Regula Pastoralis*.

In *PsGD* I expressed doubt whether Tajo had drawn on the Gregorian anthology of Paterius, but in the light of the facts and arguments adduced by Vega, and also by Meyvaert and Godding, I now
recognize that he did indeed know and make use of that anthology,

[16] *Ibid.*, col. 726.

[17] *PL* 80, col. 989.

[18] I here draw on useful clarifications made by P. Meyvaert in *JEH* 30 (1988),
pp. 361–6, which supplement and in some respects correct my treatment of Tajo's
activities in *PsGD*, pp. 100–4, 117–9. Of particular interest are his observations
about Tajo's tacit plagiarism from Paterius.

[19] The text of the surviving sections of the first anthology, identified by R. Vega,
is given by him in *España Sacrada*, 56 (1957), pp. 225–399; it is also in *PL*, Supplement
IV, 263–419. Both Meyvaert and Godding duly take me to task for failing in *PsGD*
to mention Vega's findings.

sometimes reproducing Paterius's editorial retouchings and rearrange-
ments of Gregory's wording. However, it is certainly not the case
that he was wholly dependent on Paterius for his recording of unpublished Gregorian passages. Proof to the contrary lies in the fact that
he himself cites six other passages that are not found in the Paterian
anthology—but which do reappear in the *Dialogues*! Moreover there
is one instance in which Tajo supplies six lines obviously belonging
to the preface of Gregory's *Regula Pastoralis* (doubtless drawn from a
fuller text in the *scrinial* archives) yet which are found neither in the
text of that work as it has come down to us in the MS tradition,
nor in the anthology of Paterius, nor in any other surviving document. In several other places he gives a slightly fuller text than that
reproduced by Paterius. Most significant of all is the fact that, whereas
Paterius cites only three texts that are also found in the *Dialogues*,
Tajo cites no less than eight.[20] It is then clear that Tajo, as well as
reusing the anthology of Paterius and freely intermingling its text
with other elements, also had direct and independent access to the
same sources that Paterius used—namely, the Gregorian texts, published and *inedita*, that survived "*in archivio Romanae Ecclesiae*", which
he had studied and copied during his research visit to Rome. Thus
his compilation gives further pointers to the survival of that curial
store of unedited *reportata* of Gregorian commentaries—the same
source from which the *Dialogist* was later to take his IGPs.

Unlike Paterius, Tajo gives no references to the Gregorian sources
from which his excerpts are drawn, so the question of introductory
lemmata does not arise in his case. The critics infer that he copied
from the *Dialogues* the eight passages that are common to that work
and to his *Sententiarum libri*. I must point out that this is *petitio principii*: the fact that there is verbatim correspondence between Tajo's
anthology and the *Dialogues* does not prove that the former depends
on the latter. In the light of the total evidence, the conclusion must
be that Tajo, like Paterius, copied from the Gregorian codices, including unpublished texts, that were available to both of them at different
times in the Lateran library. In some cases Tajo cited passages directly
from those MSS (as in the case of the excerpts that are not in
Paterius); in others he copied them from the collection of Paterius,

---

[20] They are listed by Meyvaert, *op. cit.*, pp. 364–5; six are listed by Vogüé, *op. cit.*,
p. 306.

reproducing the latter's modifications of the text. When discussing IGP 74 in the Appendix (and much more fully in *PsGD*, pp. 566–72), I point to a signal instance in which Tajo and the *Dialogues* cite verbatim a Gregorian passage which Paterius does not, and in which Tajo's citation clearly demonstrates that his presentation of the total pericope is fuller and more faithful to the original source than the Dialogist's shorter text.

I sum up the evidence about the works of those two anthologizers. Leaving aside the inflated estimates made by the Maurists and others, scholars now agree that there are only three passages of Gregorian exposition in Paterius's anthology and eight in Tajo's which are found in substantially the same form in the *Dialogues*. The assumption that their citations were derived from the *Dialogues* can be seen to be unproved and vitiated by incongruities. One further incongruity may be noted here. In the *Dialogues* those eleven excerpts (all of them IGPs) are embedded in a context in which not only Peter the Deacon but also *soi-disant* Gregory himself makes further comments on and applications of the themes of those passages of scriptural exposition. Nowhere in the eleven parallel passages in the collections of Paterius and Tajo is there to be found any phrase or echo of that further commentary on the same themes supposedly given by Gregory in the *Dialogues*.

CHAPTER TWENTY TWO

OTHER ALLEGED INDICATIONS OF EARLY
KNOWLEDGE OF THE *DIALOGUES*: THE *CHRONICLE*
OF FREDEGAR, THE *VITAS PATRUM EMERETENSIUM*
AND THE *VITA FRUCTUOSI*

a

There remains a motley collection of other documentary items, of debatable date and provenance, which the defenders of the authenticity of the *Dialogues*, R. Godding and A. de Vogüé in particular, now adduce as evidence of knowledge of the *Dialogues* during the half century following Gregory's death in 604. Before considering those pleas individually, I must again point out how tenuous and incongruous they appear when contrasted with the totality of converging proofs, set out in the previous chapters, firmly validating the conclusion that the *Dialogues* were not written by St Gregory or known in his age. Against the critics' objections, based on assonances and allusions to the work supposedly found in that dossier of obscure minor texts, there stands the solid mass of evidence demonstrating that in its vocabulary, style and thought-content the book differs distinctively from Gregory's own writings; that it contains many theological and historical anomalies that cannot be attributed to him; that its title was absent from the seventh-century lists of Gregory's writings, an absence significantly marked out by later attempts to remedy it by manuscript interpolations; that it did not emerge to fame until nearly a century after the date of its supposed origin, and then with relative suddenness; and that biographical knowledge, cult and liturgical honour of the great saint and monastic founder lauded in it, St Benedict, did not commence until after that time. Against the background of that evidence, the critics' objections based on words and phrases in those few and problematic seventh-century texts can be assessed in due perspective. Before commenting on the specific texts which they allege as evidence that the *Dialogues* were known in the first half of the seventh century, I remark once again that even if solid proof of such knowledge could be found, it would

not prove that the work was written by Gregory. The conclusion
following from such a discovery would not be that the work was
authentically Gregorian, but that its pseudepigraphical author composed it at a somewhat earlier date than that estimated in these pages.

With the exception of three or four documents of dubious date,
to which I give fuller consideration below, none of the texts adduced
by those critics contain any explicit statement referring to the *Dialogues*,
nor any mention of Gregory as the author of those texts. They are
alleged to depend on the *Dialogues* solely because of parallelism of
wording and theme. In their most simplistic form, the arguments of
those apologists belong to the category aptly classified by the term
"*Gleichklangargument*", used by K. Hallinger when refuting claims that
the *RB* was cited in Gregory's lifetime. That is, because words or
phrases found in a seventh-century texts have assonance with expressions found in the *Dialogues*, the apologists assume that it is an implicit
quotation from the latter work. However, as well as such over-sim-
plistic arguments, the critics also bring some others based on passages and themes in seventh-century texts which show more substantial
affinity with counterparts in the text of the *Dialogues*. These call for
more serious attention. Several of their arguments again suffer from
the defect of *petitio principii*. That is, when pointing to evidence of
verbal correspondence between passages in certain seventh century
texts and passages in the *Dialogues*, they assume the temporal priority of the latter. In the instances alleged the evidence may equally
well—indeed better—be interpreted in the inverse sense, as showing
the dependence of the *Dialogues* on those earlier seventh-century texts
and not *vice versa*. Such is the case, I argue,[1] with the parallel passages recognizable in the *Vita sancti Columbani discipulorumque eius* of
Jonas of Bobbio and in the *Pratum Spirituale* of John Moschus.

In the category of *Gleichklangargument* may be placed the appeal of
those critics to a single phrase found in the *Vita Fursei*. St Fursey of
Lagny, an Irish missionary monk, died in Peronne before AD 652,
probably in 649. Krusch's arguments showing that his first biographer wrote during the seventh century, not long after Fursey's death,
are persuasive.[2] That biographer introduced his subject with the

---

[1] Cf. *PsGD*, pp. 104–10, and Chapter 9 above.
[2] In his edition of the work, in *MGH, Scriptores Rerum Merovingicarum*, IV, Hanover
1892.

phrase, "*Fuit vir vitae venerabilis Furseus nomine . . .*" Godding, with others, supposes that Fursey borrowed his introductory phrase from the exordium of Book II of the *Dialogues*, in which the first four words are the same: "*Fuit vir vitae venerabilis, gratia Benedictus et nomine . . .*" Here, he pronounces, "we have another indication of the existence of the *Dialogues*, this time from Irish *milieux* in the north of France".[3] I remark, first, that this conclusion too begs the question: it may just as well be that verbal dependence, if such there be, is the reverse of what he supposes, and it is the *Dialogues* text that is dependent on the *Vita Fursei*. The same must be said about the presence in both texts of themes relating to visions of the other-world, to which Godding also makes appeal. Moreover, Godding pays no heed to the pertinent data, recalled in *PsGD*, showing that there were pre-seventh-century models for the introductory phrase in the *Vita Fursei*.[4] After observing that part of the phrase was a not uncommon usage of earlier hagiographers, echoing the opening words of the *Book of Job* in the Latin Bible: "*Fuit vir . . . Job nomine*", I went on to point out a sixth-century prototype which the exordium of *Dialogues II* closely resembles in wording and grammatical construction. It is at the beginning of Cassiodorus's *Life* of St Augustine, where we find the phrase: "*Vir venerabilis Augustinus vita clarus et nomine*". I consider that while it is possible that the Dialogist knew and echoed a phrase from the *Vita Fursei*, it is alternatively quite possible that he drew his exordial phrase from Cassiodorus.

I also noted in *PsGD* the conclusion of recent scholarship that the *Vita Fursei*, as we have it, is not the original text of the seventh-century biographer, but a later composition reproducing the main features of that earlier text but with much interpolation. Thus we cannot even be sure that the exordium to the *Vita Fursei* about which so much has been written was actually there in the seventh-century original. The phrase, "*Fuit vir vitae venerabilis*", was indeed echoed in at least three biographies of saints in the eighth and ninth centuries. There it may well directly reflect the phrase in the *Dialogues*.[5]

---

[3] *AB* 106 (1988), p. 217.
[4] *PsGD*, p. 111.
[5] Cf. *PsGD*, pp. 110–11.

b. *Alleged reference to the* Dialogues *in the* Chronicle of Fredegar

The principal argument of R. Godding is based on a single sentence in the *Chronicle of Fredegar*, which he produces as a trump card with which to discredit the conclusions of *PsGD* and to prove the authenticity of the *Dialogues*. That problematic text, which, as he remarks, "has not ceased to intrigue scholars",[6] contains diverse elements evidently of different provenance. Scholars have indeed differed about its dating and about the number of authors who contributed to the text as we have it. Some of them favoured the theory of a plurality of authors who produced different parts of the work at different dates, ranging between AD 613/4 and 660; others, more recently, have concluded that there was a single author who composed the work in 659/60. Godding prefers to follow the opinion of the former group of authors, and to assign the origin of the key sentence that is our present concern to the earliest suggested date, namely 613/4. However, he has to admit that the opinion of the later authors who date the origin of the whole work some forty years later is tenable. He sums up his conviction of the decisive importance of the passage to which he appeals as follows:

> We may have, then, dating from the years 613/4, an explicit mention of the *Dialogues* and of their diffusion in Burgundy, the probable cradle of the *Chronicle of Fredegar* . . . However, even if it proved necessary to accept the thesis of a single author of that work, it would be difficult to admit for it a date of origin later that 642 (the date at which the chronicle is cut short). Thus the *Chronicle of Fredegar* constitutes the most ancient explicit testimony of the existence of the *Dialogues*.[7]

I observe once more that whether the chronicle originated at the earlier or the later of the two dates allowed by Godding, it still would not provide proof that the *Dialogues* were authentic. However, I present a more direct and decisive rebuttal of the argument that Godding bases on that sentence in the *Chronicle of Fredegar* as proof that the Gregorian *Dialogues* were known in the earlier seventh century. It is drawn from closer examination of the wording of the sentence itself. That sentence refers to the story "in the dialogues of

---

[6] *AB* 106 (1988), p. 218; B. Krusch's critical edition of the work was in *MGH, Scriptores rerum Merovingicarum* II (Hanover 1888), pp. 1–193.
[7] *Ibid.*, p. 220.

Saint Gregory" which relates how a certain priest saw the king
Theodoric, who had put to death the pope John and the patrician
Symmachus, being thrown by his victims into a fiery crater in Sicily.
This sentence (which expressly refers to the account of the event
given by Gregory in *Dial.* IV.31) connects with the immediately preceding sentence, which records the slaying of Theodoric by his
brother, whereby divine wrath punished him for his unjust execu-
tion of those two illustrious victims. In that preceding sentence it is
through the slaying of Theodoric by his brother that divine wrath
strikes the wicked king. In the succeeding sentence he is further punished by being hurled by his victims into the infernal fire of a Sicilian
volcano. I see cogent reasons for judging that the latter sentence,
referring to Gregory and the *Dialogues*, was a MS interpolation added
to the text at a later time by a less literate scribe when copying the
text. I cite here the two sentences, underlining in the second sentence the word-forms, usages and spellings in it which depart from
the level of Latinity in the rest of the document:

> *Theudericus cum papa Romensis apostolicum virum Iohannem sine culpa damnas-
> set et Symmachum patricium nullis causis extantibus itemque trucitare fecisset, ira
> percussus divina, a germano suo Gaisirico interficetur.*

> *Fertur in dialiquos sancti Gregorii a quaedam sacerdoti visibiliter ab ipso pontefici
> et patricio Theudericus vinctus tragetur Sicilia in olloam ignis.*

The Latinity of the first of those two sentences (and indeed of the
chronicle generally) conforms reasonably well to the ordinary standards of grammar and morphology observed by literate writers in that
age. Its overall structure is coherent and correct, even by classical
standards—apart from an inappropriate sequence of tense in the last
verb. The Latinity of the succeeding sentence, on the other hand,
is crude, ungrammatical and disjointed. It has errors in grammar
and orthography, and does not have a coherent structure. The adverb
visibiliter incongruously serves instead of a main verb in the sentence.
Cases of nouns and participle are incorrect. Even the key word
dialiquos is in incorrect case and oddly spelt. It is not difficult to recognize that the second sentence, containing the sole mention of the
Dialogues in the work, was interpolated into the manuscript tradition
of the *Chronicle of Fredegar* by a later scribe considerably less literate
that Fredegar himself, who felt that the latter's relation of the manner
of Theodoric's death should be supplemented by a reference to the
sensational sequel related in the Gregorian *Dialogues*, which had by

his time come to light and to fame. The immediately following word, *Explicit*, marked the end of the transcription of one section of the original text. Before inserting it, it seems, the scribe decided to insert a knowledgeable comment of his own on the concluding passage.

c. *The tangled tale of the* Lives of the Fathers of Merida

We have seen that in the surviving documentary sources from Spain, as elsewhere, there is found no mention during the first three quarters of the seventh century of the existence of the *Dialogues* or of Gregory's supposed authorship of that book.[8] Rather, sources that would surely have referred to it, if it had then been known, fail to do so. Spanish churchmen and scholars who were most devoted to the memory and writings of St Gregory, namely Isidore, Braulio, Tajo, and Ildephonsus, even when they explicitly praised and named his writings, did not include the title of the *Dialogues* among them. The later interpolation of that title into their lists of his works only accentuates its original absence there. The attempt to infer that Tajo, who sought out Gregorian writings in Rome, referred to the *Dialogues* implicitly, because some passages are found in his anthology that are paralleled by passages (IGPs) found in that work, has been shown in the previous chapter to be unsound.

However, the claim is made by the defenders of the authenticity of the *Dialogues* that there is after all a document dating from the first half of the seventh century in which the author explicitly and emphatically declared that Gregory wrote a book of dialogues relating miracles of saints, which had already become famous by the time he was writing. I refer to a text known as *Vitas Patrum Emeretensium* (hereafter abbreviated as *VPE*), ascribed to a deacon of Merida named Paul.[9] This too has been traditionally appealed to by defenders of the authenticity of the Dialogues—though some of them significantly refrained from doing so. A. de Vogüé continues to insist that it is of primary importance, as does Godding less emphatically.[10]

---

[8] M.C. Diaz y Diaz listed some 380 surviving works or fragments from the seventh century in his *Index scriptorum latinorum medii aevi Hispanorum*, 2nd edition, Madrid 1959.

[9] *PL* 80; editions by C. De Smedt in *AA.SS* 63, November 1st, Paris 1897, and by J.Garvin, Washington 1946.

[10] Cf. Vogüé, *RHE* 83 (1988), pp. 300–1, and in *CC* 62 (2000), p. 196, note 14; Godding, *AB* 106 (1988), pp. 214–5.

The *VPE* is a composite work, comprising two main elements. Recognition of the distinction and disparity between them is necessary for due assessment of the dating of the references found there to the Gregorian *Dialogues*. The second and longer section is a narrative of the miraculous *gesta* of five bishops of Merida (Paul, Fidelis, Masona, Innocentius and Renovatus) who lived in the period spanning the second half of the sixth century and the first half of the seventh. The first section, which I shall refer to here as "the prefix", consists of a preface and three chapters of miraculous *gesta* relating to individuals who were not bishops of Merida. In that preface is found the affirmation of Gregory's authorship of the *Dialogues* to which present-day apologists make appeal. As well as explicitly affirming in his preface that Gregory wrote the *Dialogues*, the author of the prefixed section of the book uses verbatim, in his three following chapters, five phrases evidently borrowed from passages in the *Dialogues*.[11] Each of those two disparate elements has its own preface. In "the preface to the prefix" the author states the motive, truly extraordinary in the time and context supposed, that induced him to write it: namely, to defend Pope Gregory against the calumnious suspicion that in writing the *Dialogues* he was spinning idle and spurious tales. By telling his own tales of the miracles worked by those Fathers of Merida in more recent times, he would dispel such doubts and strengthen the faith of readers to accept as true Gregory's narrative of miracles long ago. He explains that motive as follows:

> No one among us of right belief, and especially Catholics, should doubt that those miracles are utterly true which the most holy and excellent sage Gregory, pontiff of the city of Rome, inflamed by the truth-declaring inspiration of the Holy Spirit, described in his books of dialogues . . . Lest anyone be troubled in heart with doubts about any of those miracles, on the grounds that they are put forward as having been worked in former times, and thus might not give them full credence, and lest anyone should imagine that the aforementioned most holy man, that vessel of election and shrine of the Holy Spirit, obscured those matters with idle and nebulous words, we narrate events that have taken place in modern times in the city of Merida.[12]

In view of the importance that some (but by no means all) commentators attach to the *VPE*, as supposedly attesting knowledge of the *Dialogues* at an early date, I must discuss that alleged testimony

---

[11] Garvin lists them on p. 553 of his edition of the *VPE*.
[12] Garvin's edition, p. 136.

at some length. Before doing so, I emphasize how singular and anachronistic are the sentiments expressed in it. The period in which the *VPE* was supposedly written was an age in which the fabulous *Gesta* literature proliferated, and was eagerly sought and read. The kind of sceptical criticism of such tales that is referred to in the preface of the *VPE* would have been strange indeed in that age. The only criticism of those hagiographical fables of which we have record from those centuries came from papal authority, as reflected in the *Gelasian Decree*, which forbade reading of such suspect texts in church. Can it be plausibly suggested that in rural Spain in the middle of the seventh century critical doubts were being raised about the credibility of similar tales told by the great Pope Gregory, so widespread that the author of the *VPE* preface found it necessary to counter them? Bizarre, too, is the notion that the author of the *VPE* would vindicate the veracity of Gregory's tales of Italian miracles by telling similar tales of his own about miracles in Merida. I will indicate below a later period and setting in the history of mediaeval Spain when such sceptical doubts about the credibility of the *Dialogues* narrative would not have been so unlikely.

It was a seventeenth-century Spanish editor, Thomas Tamayo de Vargas (himself one of the notorious "False Chroniclers")[13] who first introduced the *VPE*, which had been brought to light only shortly before, into the controversy concerning the *Dialogues*. Apostrophizing the Protestant scholars, especially Martin Chemnitz, one of the Centuriators of Magdeburg, who challenged both the credibility and the Gregorian authorship of that work, he exclaimed: "Hear, O innovator, the judgement of this ancient writer on the *Dialogues* of Gregory. Give precedence to antiquity over novelty and, whether you be a Centuriator or anyone else, be silent!"[14] In the introduction to his *SC* edition of the *Dialogues* A. de Vogüé cited the *VPE* as being the first explicit testimony to the influence of that work in the seventh century. In his critique of *PsGD* he repeated his conviction on that point, but abstained from entering into the complex question of the dating of the *Vitas*. R. Godding gave more attention to the latter question, seeking to contradict the arguments in *PsGD* that point to a considerably later date of origin. Both authors resolutely reaffirmed

---

[13] Cf. *PsGD*, p. 135.
[14] *PL* 80.117.

their conviction that the *VPE* dates from well before the end of the seventh century, so differing from many other scholars who date it either from the last part of that century or later still, and who are readier than they are to recognize the many strange and suspect features of that problematic compilation. In his edition of the *Vitas*, J. Garvin reviewed the opinions of scholars during the past three centuries on the date of origin of that work. While he himself inclined to the opinion that it originated before the Moorish invasion of Spain in 711, he recognized that such dating was uncertain: "To attribute any dates for the composition of the *Vitas* is to rely upon hypothesis".[15]

It was Tamayo de Vargas who surmised that the *VPE* originated around the middle years of the seventh century. He based his argument on the premise that the last of the five bishops whose lives Paul the Deacon related was Renovatus, who "ruled that church in blameless fashion for many years". The successor to Renovatus, according to the annalist Franciscus Padilla, was a Bishop Stephen who subscribed to the Fourth Council of Toledo, held in 633 during the reign of King Sisenand, and died in 638. Tamayo argued that Paul the Deacon must have written his work during the episcopate of Stephen, since he did not record that bishop's life and deeds. "It is obvious". He asserted, "that Stephen lived on to a later date than Paul, since Paul concluded his work with the death of Renovatus." Strangely, most of the later writers who followed Tamayo in thus ascribing a mid-seventh century date of origin to the *VPE*— they included Mabillon, Flores, Görres and not a few commentators in recent times, including Vogüé—did not advert to the *non sequitur* and the singular weakness of his argument. As Paul the Deacon himself says, he was not reporting recent events but those of a distant past. The point was noted by Nicolas Antonio, a diligent bibliographer of the literature of Spain, who in 1672 published a polite critique which still effactually punctures the hypothesis of Tamayo and of the many others who have relied on it until the present day. He wrote:

> I do not see, however, why we should necessarily admit that Paul lived and died under this bishop Stephen rather than under another bishop. He was not intending to write a history of the bishops of the city of Merida that must include them all . . . And it would seem that the

---

[15] *The Vitas Sanctorum Patrum Emeretensium*, Washington 1946, p. 3.

author himself signifies that his was a later age when he says, speaking of events in the time of Leovidgild, that they occurred "many cycles of years ago".[16]

Authors who defend Tamayo's early dating also cite the assurance of Paul of Merida that the events he was relating had come to him by firsthand report from persons involved in them—who therefore must have lived no later than the episcopate of Renovatus, whose episcopate was in the first quarter of the seventh century. Against that argument is the fact that it was a commonplace in the fictitious hagiography of late antiquity and the early Middle Ages to present the tales told as nearly contemporary records of the events related, vouched for by recent eyewitness accounts from reliable informants. (The *Dialogues* provide a prime example of that genre!) It should also be noted that the chronological references in the *VPE* differ according to the different elements of the work. The setting of the main element, the *Lives of the Five Bishops*, is clearly intended to be in fairly recent times. However, in the "pro-Gregorian preface" and in the following three chapters the chronological references refer vaguely to a distant past. In the third chapter some stories are related of an abbot Nanctus who lived "many cycles of years ago (*ante multa iam curricula annorum*) in the time of Leovidgild, king of the Visigoths". The author contrasts the "*prisca maiorum gesta*" of that time with the recent events ("*novella*") that he narrates concerning a boy named Augustus and a monk of Cauliana.

Even though there are in the *Lives of the Five Bishops* many references to names and events of Visigothic history, there are no reliable indications that the narrative originated in that age. None of these references give us any independent and trustworthy historical knowledge of the period. They can be seen to be simply legendary embroidering of particulars given by earlier writers on Spanish affairs, principally Gregory of Tours, John of Biclaro and Isidore of Seville. Long ago, in 1742, the Spanish historian Gregorio Mayáns (Maiansis) wrote: "For many years now I have realized that the *Vitas Patrum Emeretensium*, published under the name of Paul the Deacon, are apocryphal. I will demonstrate this in due time, adducing many arguments to prove it." [17] The whole climate of the work is indeed that

---

[16] *PL* 80, cols. 162–4, footnote a.
[17] G. Mayáns y Siscar, in the preface to the posthumous work of N. Antonio,

of fanciful fable, not of contemporary history. There are numerous false notes in the narrative, and points at which it does not square with what is known from the sources of genuinely early date. Several such points are indicated by J. Garvin in his commentary on the text. A notable example is the account given in the *Vitas* of the rebellion led by the Arian bishop Athalocus of Narbonne.[18] C. De Smedt concluded that the author had used no independent sources for his narrative.

It is now generally agreed that the two main component parts of the *VPE* (one being the *Lives* of the five bishops, the other the prefixed section comprising the "pro-Gregorian" preface and the three following chapters) are of different authorship and date. The manuscript tradition indicates that the collection of bishops' biographies was of independent and earlier origin, and that the disparate prefix was added at a later date, composed by another writer and editor who gave final form to the *VPE*. The chronological allusions to which the defenders of the authenticity of the *Dialogues* appeal, as supposedly indicating a mid-seventh-century origin of the *VPE*, are contained in the second section, which narrates the lives of the five bishops; but the preface referring to the book of Gregory's *Dialogues* is contained in the prefixed section, which is of different and even later origin.

The strange duplication of prefaces in the *VPE* has been remarked on by several authors, especially by P.B. Gams.[19] While the prefixed section of the work begins with the problematic pro-Gregorian preface, the later group of chapters narrating the lives of the five bishops have their own independent preface, which is misplaced in the text. That second preface begins with an introductory promise by the author to write his narrative truthfully and simply, putting aside pompous and pretentious rhetoric (a promise that he expresses in a phrase of orotund pomposity!).[20] As it stands in the earliest MSS (which lack the prefixed section and give only the five episcopal biographies),[21] that grandiloquent preface is in its natural place at

---

Censura de Historias Fabulosas, Valencia 1742, p. XXXIV. It does not appear that his demonstration was ever published.

[18] Garvin, pp. 511–2.

[19] *Kirchengeschichte von Spanien*, II.2, Regensburg 1874, pp. 114–8.

[20] *"Omittentes phaleratas pompas, et praetermittentes garrulas facundiae spumas . . ."*: Garvin's edition, p. 160.

[21] BM, Add. 17357 and *BAH*, *Aemilianensis* 10.

the head of a book entitled *Lives of the Fathers of Merida*. In the longer form of the *VPE*, which eventually prevailed in the MS tradition, it is incongruously placed. It there purports to be an introduction to a narrative of miraculous events yet to be related; but it has already been preceded by an earlier introductory preface followed by three chapters recounting miraculous events.

Another incongruity in the placing of the pro-Gregorian preface was pointed out by P.B. Gams. In all the surviving MSS the work is entitled *Vitas Patrum Emeretensium*. Would a book about the lives of the episcopal Fathers of Merida have as its first chapter the story of an unknown peasant boy, Augustus, who died in childhood? How could that boy be included among "the Fathers of Merida"? One may add that it is equally inappropriate to include in a book about the lives of the episcopal Fathers of Merida the gluttonous monk of Cauliana to whom the second chapter of the suspect prefix is devoted. In fact the title of *VPE* applies only to the second and larger of the two main elements of the book as we have it, not to the prefix containing the pro-Gregorian preface. I point out several other incongruities in *PsGD* (Chapter 8).

Some historians of renown have concluded that the *VPE* originated after the conquest of Spain by the Moors in 711. Menendez Pelayo remarked that no credence need be given to stories in that legendary work, proceeding, he said, "from the head of an eighth-century writer". F.L. Lembke (who referred to the author as "*dieser Legendschreiber*") also judged that the *VPE* originated later than the seventh century, pointing out that the language of the text belonged to a much later period.[22] An even more radical judgement was that of the celebrated historian of Spanish culture J.F. de Masdeu. He began by expressing his agreement with Nicolas Antonio that the usual argument for an early seventh-century date for the *VPE*, based on the mere fact that Renovatus was the last bishop of Merida mentioned in the text, was unsubstantial. He went on to conclude that Paul the Deacon of Merida showed, "from his very manner of expression", that he was a writer of the ninth century—indeed he judged that Paul was among the most notable writers of that age.[23] I say more about those views later.

---

[22] *Geschichte von Spanien*, Hamburg 1831, p. 69, note 4.
[23] *Historia Critica de España y de la Cultura Española*, vol. XIII, 1794, p. 183.

In spite of those forceful counter-indications, many authors have continued to hold (for reasons indicated more fully below) that the *Vitas* must have originated before the conquest of Spain by the Moors in AD 711. Some, following the unsubstantial argument of Tamayo (based on the lack of mention of Bishop Stephen in that narrative) still uncritically accept his dating of the *VPE*'s origin in the middle of the seventh century. Several others judge that it dated from later in the seventh century. They indicate as a probable period of its origin that covered by the reigns of the Visigothic kings Recesvinth (653–672) and Wamba (672–688). M.C. Díaz y Diaz at first estimated the date of the *VPE*'s origin as "about 650", but later says more generally that the work was "composed in the second half of the seventh century".[24]

The conclusion of the scholars who have corrected Tamayo's dating of the origin of the *VPE* before the middle of the seventh century and who now place it later, has evident relevance to the question of the dating of the emergence of the *Dialogues*. Since it is now increasingly recognized that there is no cogent reason for concluding that the *VPE* originated at a date before the last part of the seventh century, Godding, Vogüé and other apologists cannot convincingly claim that it demonstrates earlier knowledge of the *Dialogues*. An index of the frailty of the argument based on the supposed witness of the *VPE* to early knowledge of the *Dialogues* is the fact that some authors of repute who seek for signs of such knowledge omit any appeal to the evidence of that text.

In favour of the amended theory which dates the origin of the *VPE* in the later part of the seventh century, it is argued that such a dating accords with recent advances in the historiography of Visigothic literary activity in that period. Then commenced what M.C. Díaz y Diaz has called "an extraordinary flowering of the hagiographic genre" in Spain, and "a cultural unfolding" through the influence of St Isidore's writings.[25] Under the stimulus of liturgical needs, a number of martyrs' *passiones* were composed at that time. These and other legendary narratives were brought together

---

[24] *Passionaires, légendiers et compilations hagiographiques dans le haut Moyen Age espagnol*, in *Hagiographie, cultures et sociétés, IVe–XIIe siècles*, Paris 1981, pp. 54 & 60. The similar opinions of other authors are outlined in *PsGD*, p. 144.

[25] *De Isidoro al siglo XI: ocho estudios sobre la vida literaria peninsular*, Barcelona 1976, pp. 51, 54.

in a hagiographical collection of texts known as the *Compilación Valeriana*, the original core of which is traced back to the last quarter of the seventh century, and which was transmitted as a recognizable group in the mediaeval manuscript tradition, progressively augmented by some later additions. The adjective "Valeriana" was adopted because it was formerly thought that all the texts in that collection had been written by Valerius of Bierzo, who was active in the later Visigothic period. There will be more to say later about that "shadowy" figure. Here it is enough to note that it is now generally recognized that only a small number of the opuscula in the original core of the *Compilación Valeriana* can be ascribed to Valerius. That group of texts are grouped together in the MS tradition until the thirteenth century.[26] It is claimed by some that the *VPE* is one of the texts found included within it. It is evidently very pertinent to the question of the date of origin of the *VPE* to ascertain when it was added to that fairly coherent group of texts in the MS tradition. The answer, confirmed by recent scholarship, is that it did not do so until the ninth century.[27] The significance of that fact will be discussed in the following section.

Here I observe that if, as J. Rodriguez de Castro and many other authors estimate, the *VPE* originated in the 'seventies or 'eighties of the seventh century, that estimate would not contradict the conclusions I have presented above, namely, that the *Dialogues* first became known in England, France and Spain during the last quarter of that century. If the *VPE* testified to such knowledge at the same time, that would be no argument for the *Dialogues*' authenticity. Thus the question whether the *VPE* originated at a still later date is an issue of secondary interest in the present inquiry. However, since A. de Vogüé and others continue to attribute importance to that work as witness to the early date of the *Dialogues*, I summarize in the following section the cogent case for concluding that the *VPE* originated long after that pseudo-Gregorian work appeared in the later seventh century.

---

[26] Diaz y Diaz, "*La Compilación hagiografica de Valerio del Bierzo*", in *Hispania Sacra* 4 (1951) pp. 3–25.
[27] Cf. *PsGD*, p. 148.

d. *The case for dating the* VPE *after the seventh century*

A very significant chronological pointer to the dating of the *VPE* comes from the strangely late, and faint, emergence of cult of St Masona in Spain. The author of the *Lives* of the five bishops of Merida attributes special eminence to that saintly prelate, and gives a glowing and graphic account of his heroic life and labours for the Catholic faith against the tyrant Leovidgild at the end of the sixth century. According to his account, it was Bishop Masona who thwarted the machinations of that wicked king and his agents, and who with the aid of miraculous power emerged as victorious champion of the Catholic cause which eventually triumphed under Reccared. However, leaving aside the witness of the *VPE*, we have only scanty historical references to the activity of the real Masona. In his *Chronicle* for the year 573, John of Biclaro records that "Masona, bishop of the church of Merida was a clear exponent of our dogma". Masona is also listed as a principal signatory at the Council of Toledo in 589, when Catholicism was established as the religion of the Visigothic kingdom, and again at another synod in 606. Isidore wrote a letter to him in 605 or 606. Those are the only details about Masona and his life given in surviving contemporary records. The Catholic historians in the Visigothic age who relate the events of Leovidgild's reign and its aftermath show no awareness of the extraordinary role in the resistance to the royal tyrant that is attributed to that bishop of Merida in the *VPE*.

If the account given in the *Vitas* of the heroic sanctity and miracles of Masona had been known and published in Spain in the mid-seventh century, as the authors named above so confidently maintain, and if, as is further affirmed in the *VPE*, there were innumerable miraculous cures at Masona's tomb at that time, we should surely expect to find signs of devotion and cult to so great a saint, thaumaturge and champion of Catholic Spain during the following centuries. Yet, disconcerting though it may be to those authors, there are none. It is indeed a singular fact that, until four hundred years after the seventh-century date at which the *VPE* is supposed to have been composed, there is no trace, in any liturgical calendar or other document of the period, of any such cult, nor any mention of details from the life either of Masona or of any of the other four episcopal saints eulogized in the *Vitas*. Although the Mozarab Christians zealously honoured the memory of their earlier saints, the names of the five wonder-working bishops of Merida are all missing from the Mozarabic calendars published by Ferotin.[28]

When eventually, in the eleventh century, a liturgical mention of St Masona and St Innocentius of Merida does appear, together with evidence of cult of their relics, those developments are significantly limited to two neighbouring monasteries in the Rioja region of Castille, the abbeys of San Millán de la Cogolla and of San Domingo de Silos. It was at San Millán that the earliest known manuscript of the *VPE* was transcribed, and the parentage of all but one of the other surviving mediaeval MSS can be traced to the same regions. It seems evident that it was the emergence of the Merida *Vitas* that aroused tardy devotion to the principal character and hero of that work, Masona, and that subsequently led the monks of that abbey to seek relics of the holy bishop, with which were also honoured the relics of his successor, St Innocentius. The author of the *VPE* had reported that their tombs were still to be seen in the basilica of St Eulalia at Merida. That may well have prompted the monks of San Millán to seek relics of them for a shrine in their own abbey to provide a centre of cult. At all events, relics of St Masona and St Innocentius are listed in a thirteenth-century inventory of the treasures of the Cogolla monastery.[29] The earliest reference to liturgical honour paid to St Masona is likewise found in an eleventh-century missal at San Millán. Similar commemorations are found in missals and breviaries of San Millán and San Domingo dating from the following three centuries. H. Delehaye appropriately calls this "an artificial cult". J.N. Garvin frankly avows: "The indications of a cult of Masona and probably of Innocent at San Millán de la Cogolla and San Domingo de Silos from the eleventh to the fourteenth century are undoubtedly due to the presence of the manuscripts of the *Vitas Patrum Emeretensium*".[30] J.F. Alonso expresses the same judgement.[31] This tardy and restricted commencement of liturgical recognition of SS. Masona and Innocentius, arising from possession of MSS of the *VPE* by the Rioja monks, is another significant pointer

---

[28] *Liber Ordinum en usage dans l'Eglise wisigothique et mozarabe d'Espagne du cinquième au onzième siècle*, Paris 1904; cf. also, edited by the same author, *Le Liber mozarabicus sacramentorum*, Paris 1912.

[29] Cf. B. de Gaiffier, *AB* 53 (1935), pp. 90–100.

[30] *Op. cit.*, p. 540.

[31] *BS* IV, p. 1172.

to the late date at which the work emerged into public knowledge.

I return to the question of the relation of the *VPE* to the *Compilación Valeriana*, which is thought to have been first assembled by Valerius of Bierzo. Since in the mediaeval codices the *VPE* is included in that standardized collection of hagiographical narratives, it seemed a plausible conclusion to ascribe its origin to the same period in which the original nucleus of that group of texts originated—which, as we have seen, is dated by scholars of repute to about the last quarter of the seventh century. Against that conclusion, however, stands the awkward fact, now firmly established, that the *VPE* does *not* belong to that original nucleus of the *Compilación Valeriana*. It entered that group of MSS only in a later century, and then appears only in the slender Rioja branch of that manuscript tradition. M. C. Díaz y Diaz, admitting that it originated "later than Valerius", surmises that it was added to the so-called Valerian Collection before the time of Alcuin, in the ninth century.[32] No existing MS of the *VPE* antedates the tenth century, and the record of its early textual formulation is confused. The fact that it did not belong to the original core of the *Compilación Valeriana*, but appears much later and then in one locality only, is a significant contradiction to the assumption that it was part of the Visigothic literary movement of the seventh century. Arguments from its language and style also tell against that assumption, as Lembke and Masdeu pointed out long ago.

A reason that has persuaded many authors that the *VPE* must date from the period of the Visigothic monarchy is their assumption that such a work of Christian hagiography could not have been written after the traumatic date in Spanish history, AD 711. In that year the Moorish invaders swept into Spain, extinguishing the Visigothic kingdom and its institutions and subjecting Merida and most of the Iberian peninsula to alien rule and Islamic culture. Thus, commenting on Masdeu's judgement that the *VPE* was written long after that date, J. Amador de los Rios scornfully retorted: "Why, if Paul the Deacon wrote under the Saracen yoke, is there not to be found in his whole work even the remotest allusion to indicate that it was so? How is it that, when devoting himself to extolling the celebrated men who flourished in the basilica of St Leocadia [Eulalia] during the period of the Visigoths, he did not shed a single tear to deplore

---

[32] *Passionnaires*, pp. 55–6.

the captivity in which that shrine was then lying?"[33] Even J.N. Garvin echoed the same reasoning: "It cannot be that our author would have passed over the Mussulman conquest of Spain in 711."[34]

At first sight, that argument may impress. Yet the origin of the *VPE* in that later age is fully consonant with what has emerged from modern studies of the situation and cultural concerns of the Christians under Moorish rule, both of the majority who preserved the old faith under that rule and of the minority who maintained an embattled independence in the mountains of the north. They looked back to an idealized golden age in which the Spanish nation and Church had flourished in a brilliant Christian civilization in the century following the conversion of the Visigothic kingdom from Arianism to Catholicism under Reccared. They treasured and educated themselves from the vast literary legacy of St Isidore of Seville, the great luminary of that age. Their nostalgic devotion concentrated on the shrines, saints and legends of that vanished age before the Crescent had supplanted the Cross. One can understand how, to meet the pious demand, legendary hagiographical writings such as the Merida *Lives* were composed.

That religious patriotism was fanned into flame especially in the Christian principality of the Asturias. There the seed of the *Riconquista* was already sown in the eighth century, to become a sturdy sapling in the ninth. It was especially during the reign of Alfonso II, king of the Asturias (789–842), that the Visigothic myth took its distinctive form in Spanish consciousness. It provided the Christian realm with a principle of unity in an age of warfare and confusion. Alfonso II explicitly claimed to be the successor of the Visigothic kings and continuator of their rule. In his court at Oviedo and in the other institutions of his government he imitated with deliberate archaism the organization of the Visigothic court at Toledo long before. Elsewhere too there was a reintroduction of old customs of the Church in the Visigothic age. There was ever-growing devotion to saints of pre-conquest Spain and enshrinement of their miracle-working relics, which were eagerly sought out in the towns and monasteries of central and southern Spain that had been the heartland of Visigothic Catholicism. There was eager demand, too, for codices relating the

---

[33] *Historia Crítica de la Literatura Española*, I, Madrid 1861, p. 409, note 1.
[34] *Op. cit.*, p. 6.

lives and wondrous deeds of those saints. Set in the idealized golden age of the Visigothic kingdom and church, those hagiographical legends and fictitious histories grew in volume as the *Riconquista* proceeded. One can well understand how, to meet that pious demand, writings such as the *VPE* were composed.

We know that in the eighth, ninth and tenth centuries many relics of saints were transferred from their resting places in the conquered south to churches and monasteries in the Christian north.[35] Financial inducements for such transfers were provided, to the benefit either of the Mozarab custodians of the relics or even of the local Muslim rulers. It is relevant to our present inquiry to observe signs of special interest on the part of northern Christians to the patron saint of Merida, St Eulalia, in whose honour Paul the Deacon of Merida declared that he had written his history of the Fathers of that city. There are mediaeval accounts, seemingly garbled, of a transfer of the body of St Eulalia from Merida to the Asturias at the end of the eighth century. The saint's relics were said to have been brought first to a new church at Pravia, then installed by Alfonso II in a shrine at Oviedo.[36] (Much later, in the eleventh century, relics of St Eulalia were obtained from Merida for a new cathedral in Narbonne.) There were close cultural links between the Christians of northern Spain and their Frankish coreligionists. The new interest in the history and historiography of Christian Spain was quickened by the influence of the Carolingian renaissance from beyond the Pyrennees. It was in the reign of Alfonso II that the momentous discovery of the tomb of the Apostle St James was made at Compostela. Then began the great pilgrimage to his shrine which served to bring the Christian kingdom of northern Spain into the mainstream of European culture. While a firmly independent base of Christian power was being consolidated in the Asturias, Cantabria and Galicia, most Spanish Christians still lived under Muslim rule. In the main, it was not the policy of the emirs of Cordoba and of the rulers subordinate to them to persecute their Christian subjects or to suppress their religion. The subjugated Christians, the Mozarabs, continued to constitute by far the greater part of the population of the peninsula. Although their civil status was inferior, they were allowed their own

---

[35] Masdeu, *op. cit.*, XIII, pp. 372–83.
[36] *Ibid.*, p. 374.

ecclesiastical organization and communal life. We know that in Merida
in particular they had guaranteed rights after the Arab conquest and
continued to worship in their churches and shrines. Situated as they
were, one would not expect the Mozarab authors of pious legends
of the vanished Visogothic past to include in them protests or laments
about the Muslim domination of their country.

The origin of the *VPE* was placed by Menendez Pelayo in the
eighth century, and by Masdeu and Lembke later still. While a dating of the work in the reign of Alfonso II is a reasonable conjecture, there are even better reasons for assigning its origin to the
second half of the ninth century, the age of Alfonso III, called "the
Great", who ruled the kingdom of Asturias-León from 866 to 911.
We have an intriguing reference to the *VPE*, attributed to Alfonso
III himself, which may be the first historical evidence of the existence of that problematic work. In a letter to the clergy and people
of Tours in western France, dated to the year 906, the king informed
them of the existence of a work which the Frankish scholars did not
possess but which he was willing to send to them from León—namely
the *VPE*. He wrote: "Moreover we have, clearly and learnedly written, the lives, virtues, and miracles of many illustrious men, namely
of Merida. As I recall, the text is not in your archives. If it would
be of use to you, we will arrange to have it sent to you".[37] The
king's words seem to suggest that the Merida *Lives* were of fairly
recent origin. There is, however, dispute about the genuineness of
that letter. A.C. Floriano, who summarizes the arguments on both
sides,[38] judges that "the question is almost insoluble", but thinks it
more probable that the last section of it, which contains the sentence quoted above, was added in the twelfth century. If so, one
may speculate on reasons why a twelfth-century interpolator should
show this special interest in enhancing the reputation of the *VPE*,
and why he should suggest that it was not widely known even then.
If on the other hand the letter was genuine, it provides a *terminus
post quem non* for the composition of that text.

There are other indications pointing to the middle years or second half of the ninth century as a likely date for the emergence of
the *VPE* in its final composite form. That was a time not only of

---

[37] Text in *Diplomatica Española del Periodo Astur (718–910)*, ed. A.C. Floriano, II,
Oviedo 1951, p. 341.
[38] *Ibid.*, pp. 343–5.

much literary activity among the resurgent Christians of the peninsular, but also of increased cultural and political contacts between
the Christian territories of the north and the Mozarab communities
in the centre and southern regions under Moorish rule. Politically,
the ninth century was a time in which the Muslim power in Spain
was fragmented into numerous small principates, which took the
overlordship of Cordoba lightly. At one time in that century Muslim
Toledo accepted client status to the Christian kingdom of León. The
cora or province of Merida (Badajoz) was for periods in that century
virtually independent of Cordoba. We possess a letter of Charlemagne,
written to the people of Merida in 830, urging them to throw off
the yoke of Cordoba.[39] It was not until the tenth century that central authority in *Al Andalus* was eventually restored, during the Caliphate
of Abd-ar-Rahman III (912–961).

R. Altamira observes that St Eulogius of Cordoba (martyred in
859) and others sought "to foster a renaissance among the Mozarabs
of Latin studies in the Visigothic tradition", and there were "several
notable Mozarabic writers in Latin, especially on religious themes",
who were influenced by the Carolingian and Ottonian renaissance
in Francia.[40] It was among those ninth-century writers that Masdeu
placed "Paul the Deacon of Merida", "*por su mismo modo de hablar*".
In this period there was a notable quickening in the process of relic
transference from the old Christian centres to the churches and
monasteries which were being built or enlarged in the north of Spain
and beyond the Pyrenees. Emigration of Mozarabs northwards,
observes S.G. Payne, "helped to make known and to reinvigorate
the Visigothic tradition".[41] In such a cultural setting the composition
and peculiarities of the *VPE* are readily explicable.

Among those peculiarities was the concern of the author to counter
current suspicions that in writing the *Dialogues* St Gregory was telling
"idle and nebulous tales". Since early mediaeval Christians were
extremely docile, indeed gullible, in their acceptance of pious fictions
and marvellous hagiographical tales, commentators have naturally
found it astonishing that the supposedly seventh-century author of
the preface to the *VPE* should have found it necessary to defend the

---

[39] Florez, *De la Lusitania antiqua*, pp. 416–7; Garvin, *op. cit.*, p. 271.
[40] *A History of Spain*, English trans., Toronto & London 1949, p. 10.
[41] *A History of Spain and Portugal*, University of Wisconsin 1973, vol. I, p. 133.

credibility of the colourful tales told by Gregory in the *Dialogues* against doubters. While such irreverent sceptics are hardly imaginable anywhere in newly Catholicized Visigothic Spain, or elsewhere in seventh-century Europe, there was one region in which they might well have been present in a later age—namely, in the sophisticated literary culture of the caliphate of *Al Andalus*, where the legacy of classical Greek philosophy was being rediscovered. In that intellectually liberal epoch the *muwalladun*, the numerous class of Spanish neo-converts to Islam, may well have scoffed at the fanciful beliefs and naïvety of their erstwhile coreligionists. Even the Christian Mozarabs were influenced by the pressures of that culture.[42] The pro-Gregorian preface to the *VPE* prefix could well have been topical in that brilliant and sophisticated epoch in the history of Muslim Spain that culminated in the reign of Abd-ar-Rahman III.

To sum up, then, the *VPE* is a work of inventive hagiography of a type commonly found in mediaeval ecclesiastical literature. It contains explicit evidence of the existence of the *Dialogues* and its Gregorian ascription. The assumption given currency by Tamayo de Vargas in 1638 and uncritically repeated by so many commentators from that day to this, namely that the work originated in the first half or middle of the seventh century, must be discarded as unfounded and as refuted by contrary evidence. Relinquishing that theory, many modern commentators hold that the *VPE* should be dated to the later part of that century. Their view does not conflict with my conclusions in this book that the emergence of the *Dialogues* in that same period predates the first appearance of the *VPE*. However, I have shown solid grounds for ascribing the work to a much later age, and to agree with those historians of Spain who judge that it originated after the Visigothic era. There are indications (more fully discussed in Chapter 8 of *PsGD*) that the origin of the main section of the work, the episcopal *Lives*, was probably in the ninth century; and that the disparate prefix, with its pro-Gregorian preface, was added to it (after some textual permutations) some time before the middle of the tenth century. After that the tenuous manuscript tradition attests the continuation of two forms of the work: one, consisting of the original text of the *Lives* only, the other augmented by the prefix.

---

[42] Cf. R. Hitchcock, "Muslim Spain", in *Spain: a Companion to Spanish Studies*, ed. T.E. Russell, London 1973, p. 47.

While obscurities remain in the history of this celebrated text, it is at least clear that the *Vitas Patrum Emeretensium* can no longer be adduced as evidence of knowledge of the Gregorian *Dialogues* before the closing decades of the seventh century.

e. *The problematic witness of the* Vita Fructuosi

Also to be considered is the short hagiographical work known as the *Vita Fructuosi* (*VF*),[43] which from the sixteenth century until recently was generally attributed to Valerius of Bierzo, whose literary output is usually dated in the last decades of the seventh century. Defenders of the authenticity and early fame of the *Dialogues* have traditionally cited the testimony of the *VF*. A. de Vogüé likewise asserts: "Shortly after the *Lives of the Fathers of Merida*, the *Vita Fructuosi* in its turn attests the influence of the *Dialogues*".[44] The *VF* is indeed found to have close links with the *VPE*. The two works not only have evident textual parallelisms but are also closely linked in the manuscript tradition. Although no explicit mention of the *Dialogues* is found in the *VF* there are clear parallels, including a passage of 17 words in the tenth chapter which is verbally identical with a passage in a tale told in *Dial*. III 15.5 about Florentius and his pet bear.

It is now generally agreed, as J.A. Alonso records, that the *VF* was "*falsamente attribuito a s. Valerio*".[45] Its provenance has been significantly reassessed since 1946, the date of a ground-breaking study by F.C. Nock.[46] It was she who first brought convincing arguments to show that the ascription of the work to Valerius of Bierzo, originally made by Ambrose de Morales in the sixteenth century, was an unfounded conjecture. Criticizing what she called the traditionally "superficial treatment of the authorship of the *Vita*",[47] she demonstrated that the work is distinctively different from the genuine opuscula of Valerius, in content, in mental attitudes, in use of biblical

---

[43] Edition and commentary by M.C. Diaz y Diaz, *La Vida de San Frutuoso de Braga*, Braga 1974.

[44] *SC* 260, p. 451. In his critique of *PsGD* (in *RHE* 83 (1988), p. 315) Vogüé insistently repeats his contention that Valerius is a witness to the fame of the *Dialogues* in the latter part of the seventh century.

[45] *BS* V, p. 1295.

[46] *The Vita Sancti Fructuosi*, Washington 1946.

[47] *Ibid.*, p. 17.

quotations and above all in vocabulary. Her refutation of the traditional assumptions was disconcerting but eventually commanded
assent.

In his edition of the *VF* the renowned authority on Spanish writings of that period, M.C. Diaz y Diaz, estimated the probable date
for the origin of the work as not earlier than about 670–680. I point
out, as I did when discussing the date of origin of the *VPE*, that
such an estimated dating for the origin of the *VF* is reconcilable with
my conclusion, argued in Chapter 16 above, that the *Dialogues* first
emerged into the light of history about that very time. If the *VF* did
date from that period it would have been possible for its author (and
indeed for Valerius of Bierzo himself) to acquire knowledge of the
Dialogues about the same time that a Spanish contemporary, Julian
of Toledo did so. Such tardy testimony would be of no avail to
prove that St Gregory had written the hitherto unknown *Dialogues*
nearly a century earlier. My arguments challenging some common
assumptions by setting the probable date of the origin of the *VF*
considerably later than the seventh century, are here recalled in summary form because of the further light they throw on a field of legendary literature that has been obscured by mediaeval inventions
and traditional misconceptions.

F.C. Nock made a painstaking analysis of the text of the *VF*, and
gave solid reasons for concluding that it was composed by more than
one author. Diaz y Diaz, though somewhat reserved in his agreement with Nock's findings, also recognized in the *VF* elements from
very different sources, including one especially connected with Merida.[48]
In Chapters 3–7 the text repeatedly betrays a grammatical peculiarity in the use of present participles in place of finite verbs. After
Chapter 7 this peculiarity ceases abruptly, and in the remaining thirteen chapters it is not found at all. Arguing from the verbal assonances between the *VF* and the *VPE*, and also from the anomalies
in the MS record, Nock persuasively suggested that the second and
larger part of the *VF*, relating to the miracles of the saint, were composed by the same author who wrote the *VPE*:

> Though "Paul of Merida" is a fictitious person to whom the *Vitae et
> miracula patrum Emeretensium* was attributed, the author in the present
> case may have been the one who composed this account of the church

---

[48] "*Notas para una cronología de Frutuoso de Braga*", in *Bracara Augusta*, 21 (1967),
p. 215. For his reservations, cf. his *Vida de S. Frutuoso*, p. 17, note 27.

at Merida. The number of expressions in the latter part of the *Vita sancti Fructuosi* which are similar to those found in the *Vitas sanctorum patrum Emeretensium* seems to support this conjecture.[49]

Nock was content to accept the current assumption that the *VPE* dated from the later period of the Visigothic kingdom. Accordingly, although she refuted the theory that Valerius of Bierzo had written the *VF* in the last quarter of the seventh century, she did not seriously question the common assumption that the *VF* itself dated from about that time. The unknown author makes several references which seem to imply that he was writing not long after the lifetime of his subject, St Fructuosus of Braga. Nock surmised that the *VF* was the work of "some writer of the seventh or early eighth century", but she did not take account of the possibility that he wrote after the fall of the Visigothic regime and during the succeeding age of Moorish rule in Spain, when so many similarly fanciful and nostalgic hagiographies were composed. A main reason why the *VF* has until fairly recently been assigned to the late seventh century was the unquestioned assumption that its author was Valerius of Bierzo who was active at that time. Since the ascription of the *VF* to Valerius has now been overthrown (by the painstaking work of Nock herself), a mainstay of the traditional dating has been removed. The *VF* is a typical work of mediaeval legend-mongering, replete with picturesque anecdotes and pious superlatives, but with no reliable anchorage in verifiable history. As Nock herself points out, "There is no date in the whole work. Even indirect means of dating are almost completely lacking".[50] Diaz y Diaz admits that his own estimate of the *VF*'s date of origin is conjectural, and that in discussing the problem of its dating "we have to move on uncertain ground, which offers us only very tenuous footholds". He points out that the author had a tendentious aim, which was to exalt the monastic life as the fundamental form of religion. "Rather than an historical source", he writes, "the *VF* presents us with a handbook of lofty imagination and devotion". Moreover, he recognizes within the *VF* "the presence of previous materials which the author, whoever he may have been and wherever he was active, sewed together and reconstituted for his own purpose".[51]

---

[49] *Op. cit.*, p. 38.
[50] *Op. cit.*, p. 99.
[51] *Op. cit.*, (*Vida*), pp. 15, 20, 23.

Diaz y Diaz and those who follow him base their approximate estimate of the *VF*'s date of origin (as c. AD 670–680) on two main assumptions: first, that Valerius of Bierzo, who is thought to have written his opuscula between c. 680–690, refers to it; and secondly, that the *VF* formed part of the earliest core of the *Compilación Valeriana*, thought to date from the late seventh century. To take the latter assumption first, it can be seen to be no sounder that the similar assumption (now generally discredited) of the presence of the *VPE* in the original core of that *Compilación*. I gave summary indications to that effect in *PsGD*.[52] The first assumption merits more attention. What can be said with certainty about the writings of Valerius of Bierzo? He is indeed a shadowy figure, who may reasonably be supposed to have lived in the latter part of the seventh century. It used to be assumed that he was abbot of the celebrated Asturian monastery of San Pedro ad Montes, but it now appears that he was not an abbot but a lay recluse of limited learning.[53] It is now generally recognized that he was the author of only a small part of the corpus of writings formerly attributed to him. Little is known of his life. A rare biographical clue is found in an opusculum bearing his name that seems to be authentic. In it he refers to the consecration of a chapel, and to the ordination of a priest at the same time, carried out by the Asturian bishop Aurelius, whose episcopate can be reliably dated from the year 681 onwards. Relating it, Valerius speaks of the event as coming "at the extreme end of his life". From this and other indications Aherne concludes that he died about 695, an approximate date now commonly accepted. However, that isolated clue cannot be taken as certain proof of the age in which Valerius lived. B. Gaiffier remarks on the continuing obscurity that surrounds Valerius, whom he describes as "this mysterious personality", and the writings attributed to him.[54] A number of allusions and assonances found in his writings have been adduced as evidence that he

---

[52] P. 160, note 103. R. Godding criticizes the "*style télégraphique*" of those indications, but did not attempt to bring contrary proof to demonstrate the presence of the *VF* in the primitive stratum of the *Compilación Valeriana*. He appeals instead to the opinion of Diaz y Diaz, expressed in a work dated 1951, before that author had renounced his earlier view that the *VPE* was included in the primitive *Compilación*.

[53] Some hoary misconceptions were exposed in the study of C.M Aherne, *Valerius of Bierzo*, Washington 1949; cf. also her article on Valerius in *BS* XII, cols. 917–9, Rome 1969.

[54] *AB* 77 (1959), pp. 192, 194.

knew the *VF*.[55] Although none of these references are free from uncertainty, it is a reasonable hypothesis that he did have knowledge of some constitutive sections of the *VF*. Did he also have knowledge of the *Dialogues*? Godding urges two passages as evidence that he did.[56] One of them parallels *IGP* 38 in the *Dialogues*; the other is debatable. I remark again that even if it were established that Valerius knew the *Dialogues*, that would be of no avail to prove that Gregory wrote the work, or that it was known earlier in the seventh century. However, there are several indications that Valerius lived and wrote at a date considerably later than traditionally supposed.

In view of the obscurities and misconceptions about the genesis and history of the *Vitas Patrum Emeretensium*, the close links between the *VPE* and the *VF* in the manuscript tradition are very relevant in this discussion. As I have noted above, they are found together, as parts of a sequence of connected opuscula in a small group of MSS dating from the tenth century onwards. Their provenance is linked to the Riojan monastery of San Millán de la Cogolla. Secondly and still more significantly, there is a close textual concordance between the *VF* and the *VPE*. The same phraseology, including rare and unusual expressions, is found in both works. J.N. Garvin has listed 19 such duplications.[57] A single telling example is a phrase that is found verbatim in both works (though in quite different contexts): "*divina percussus ultione crudeli exitu vitam finivit*". R. Godding, who adopts the estimated datings of Diaz y Diaz, also recognizes the evident linkage between the *VF* and the *VPE* (especially regarding the "central core" of the *VF*, chapters 8b–15), and is prepared to admit the ascription of that section to "Paul of Merida".[58]

In two surviving MSS of the *VPE* (Evreux 30 and Salamanca BU 2537) several miracle stories from the *VF* are found to be inscribed in the place that in other MSS is normally occupied by the story of the greedy monk of Cauliana.[59] (The same peculiarity was noted also in a manuscript of the work found by Ambrose de Morales in Sigüenza but now lost.) In the Salamanca and Evreux MSS the *VPE*

---

[55] Most emphatically by R. Godding, *AB* 106 (1988), p. 215.
[56] *Ibid.*
[57] *Op. cit.*, p. 35.
[58] *Op. cit.*, p. 215.
[59] For fuller discussion of the complex questions concerning the MSS referred to here, cf. *PsGD*, pp. 140–1.

is included, as was usual, in the standardized group of texts inaccurately called the *Compilación Valeriana*. Studying the Evreux MS, which was formerly in the abbey of Lyre and dates from the eleventh century, I observed some interesting variants. The last part of the text is lost, but the full content of the original is set out in a table of contents at the beginning of the MS.[60] Whereas in the Sigüenza MS the *VF* material replaced the story of the monk of Cauliana, in the Evreux MS the Cauliana tale is not missing, but the Fructuosus material is inserted after it. There are other interesting features of the Evreux MS, in which the scribe inserted some further observations of his own. After retailing miraculous events concerning Fructuosus, he added a reference to a miracle recounted by Pope Gregory in the *Dialogues*: "... *ut egregius vir romanae urbis Gregorius in libris dialogorum testatur*".

The Salamanca MS of the *VPE* also has insertions of *VF* material. The witness of the Evreux and Salamanca MSS (which are among the oldest), coupled with that of the lost Sigüenza MS, may reflect an experimental stage in the redaction of the additional prefix of the *VPE*, which is relevant to the theme of this book because of its references to Gregory and the *Dialogues*. It would appear that at the time those MSS were inscribed the contents of the prefix had not yet been finally settled. The transit from the original short form of the *VPE*, comprising only the *Lives of the Five Bishops*, to the long form attested in those three early mediaeval MSS might not yet have been finalized, so that scribes felt at liberty to rearrange and augment the texts available to them. In this tangled skein of the evolution of the *VPE* the question of the origins of the VF is also entangled.

Lastly, I draw attention to a fact that has a significant bearing on the question of the date of origin of the *Vita Fructuosi*, and in itself provides a cogent argument to show that it was not known in the seventh century, nor for a very long time afterwards. It is the very long delayed appearance of any cult of St Fructuosus himself, or of other saints lauded in the *VF*. Just as the long-delayed appearance of any cult of St Masona tells strongly against the theory that the *VPE* were known in the seventh century and in the two following

---

[60] It can be consulted in *Catalogue générale des manuscrits des bibliothèques publiques de France*: vol. II (Rouen region), Paris 1888, p. 417.

centuries so (and *a fortiori*) does the lack of cult of St Fructuosus tell against the theory that the *VF* was known in the same period. The first tentative signs of such cult date from the later ninth century. An *inventio* of the body of St Fructuosus is reported from the year 878. The Mozarabic calendars of saints had made no mention of him previously to that date, and no Spanish calendar did so until nearly three centuries after it. Diaz y Diaz himself remarks that the neglect of his cult is "curious". He ponders on the problem: "Can we be sure that Fructuosus was an object of cult? It seems proved that this did not commence to any widespread extent until about the twelfth century".[61]

A grant by King Ordono II in 899 to the monastery of San Pedro de Montes in the territory of Bierzo refers to the blessed Fructuosus as first founder of that monastery, which had just been rebuilt. The earliest surviving MS of the *VF* (now in the Biblioteca Nacional in Madrid)[62] was inscribed by a monk named Armentarius in the region of León in the year 902. The earliest mention of a church dedicated to St Fructuosus dates from the year 921. I would suggest that it was the interest in the saint aroused by the *inventio* of his relics in 878 that may have provided the stimulus and setting for the composition of the *VF*, which in turn stimulated the wider flowering of devotion to the saint. By the beginning of the twelfth century devotion to St Fructuosus had evidently developed more widely, since a "pious theft" of his supposed relics was carried out in the year 1102. They were then surreptitiously removed from their humbler burial place and installed in a shrine at Compostela, where they could attract the devotion of the multitudes of pilgrims to the shrine of Santiago. In the course of the following century the abbey of San Millán de la Cogolla, which figures so significantly in the history of the *VPE*, acquired a relic of St Fructuosus to add to its relics of the Fathers of Merida.

Similar to that long and strangely delayed appearance of cult of St Fructuosus himself is the centuries-long neglect of another of the saints lauded in the *VF*. Chapter 15 of that work is devoted to relating the wondrous life and deeds of a saintly abbess, Benedicta. If

---

[61] *Passionnaires*, pp. 54–5; similarly Nock, *op. cit.*, p. 67.
[62] The former *Toletanus* 10.25 (= T); it is now MBN 10007. Another MS from Arlanza, now lost, was dated by Sandoval to 912. Cf. Nock, *op. cit.*, pp. 3–5 & 85; Diaz y Diaz, *Vida*, pp. 32–4.

such a remarkable saint existed in Visigothic history, one would surely expect to find some record of her too in the Mozarabic calendars, or at least some reference to her elsewhere in documents from those centuries. But, as Nock observes, "There appears to be no authentic identification of this Benedicta". Such lack of cult and total silence about so illustrious a saint is readily understandable on the supposition that the only existence she had was in the pages of a fictitious hagiography that was composed some three centuries later than her alleged lifetime, and which even then was available only in a few MSS appearing in a restricted locality in Castile.

That pattern of developments, and other indications, suggest as a likely time for the composition of the legendary life of St Fructuosus the second half of the ninth century. It would fit in well with such a date to suppose that the author of the main section of the *VF* and of the *VPE* was a Mozarabic cleric who was familiar with Merida and with the cult of St Eulalia, and who was one of the many Christians who had passed over to join their coreligionists in the northern regions of Spain during the second half of the ninth century. There his hagiographical talent could have served to meet the eager desire of the faithful for edifying narratives about the Spanish saints in the imagined golden age of the Visigothic monarchy, now recalled with patriotic nostalgia. Something of a Visigothic myth seems to persist even in the study of early Spanish texts. I am well aware that the questions raised here challenge generally received scholarly orthodoxy in this field, but I nevertheless continue to raise them. At all events, whatever may be deduced from the study of those problematic texts, nothing that has been brought to light from study of them provides reliable evidence of knowledge of the Gregorian *Dialogues* before the last decades of the seventh century.

In conclusion I mention a couple of other texts of obscure origin to which A. de Vogüé makes tentative appeal as "points of contact with the *Dialogues*": namely, the *Vita prima Samsonis*[63] and the *Life of John the Almoner* by Leontius of Neapolis.[64] I have shown in *PsGD*[65] that resemblance of themes found both in the *Dialogues* and those texts certainly does not demonstrate dependence of one on another—

---

[63] Cf. *RHE* 83 (1988), pp. 298–9.
[64] Cf. *SC* 251, p. 121 & note 35.
[65] Pp. 106–8; 109–10.

they could have common dependence on traditional motifs. However, it is quite possible that the Dialogist knew and echoed Leontius. It is more questionable whether he could have known the *Life* of St Samson of Dol; although some scholars think it originated in the sixth century, many others agree with R. Fawtier, who in his critical edition of the work assigns its date of origin to the period between 772 and 850.

PART IV

THE DIALOGIST AND HIS LEGACY:
RETROSPECT AND FUTURE PROSPECT

CHAPTER TWENTY THREE

PROFILE OF THE DIALOGIST IN HIS
HISTORICAL SETTING

a

The mass of internal and external evidences surveyed in the second and third parts of this book converge to support the conclusion that the *Dialogues* were not written by Pope St Gregory the Great. It remains to turn attention more closely to the real author, and to bring together the scattered clues that we possess concerning his character, life-setting and activity. What can we know, or infer with probability, about the elusive Dialogist himself? From what milieu did he come, what was his social and cultural background, what were his special interests and past experience? When and where did he write his world-famous book? What can we deduce about his sources, aims and methods of composition, and about his standing in his own day? In what setting did he compose the work, and how does it relate to other contemporary writings?

We have seen that there is a long and significant silence about the existence of the book from the lifetime of St Gregory until the closing decades of the seventh century. Its first appearance into the light at that time provides a pointer to the date of its composition not long before. Such an indication does not by itself exclude the possibility that the author wrote the book earlier in the seventh century but did not make it public, and that the manuscript was copied and circulated several years later. However, not only the circumstances of the book's emergence but other weighty reasons tell against such a supposition. There are good grounds for concluding that it was not only first published in the last part of the seventh century but was also composed not long before that date. As was shown in Chapter 12, sources in Gregory's lifetime and in the following age that would surely be expected to reveal knowledge of the book if it had then existed fail to do so. In Chapters 21 and 22 specific claims that it was known earlier in the seventh century have been examined, and shown to be unfounded.

The first recorded references to the *Dialogues* surface with relative suddenness during the last two decades of the seventh century, found in works written in England, Scotland, Spain, Burgundy and Aquitaine. If the first codices of the work, doubtless originating from Rome, reached those regions in or around the 'eighties of that century, one must date the composition of that work some time earlier, to allow time for its diffusion. It is in any case a carefully contrived book, unrivalled by any of the other *Gesta* collections in talent and ingenuity, the preparation and composition of which would have taken a considerable time. The author's very real talent and inventiveness, rare indeed in his age, was recognized in a perceptive comment of A. de Vogüé which is relevant here:

> A study of Book II [of the *Dialogues*] which we made some years ago revealed to us the consummate artistry with which that *Life* of St Benedict was constructed. The successive stages in the composition are articulated with distinctive virtuosity. Similar observations could be made about the other three books and about the overall structure of the work.[1]

Although Vogüé supposed that it was the real Gregory who displayed such elaborate literary planning and striving for effect, the pontiff would surely not (as I pointed out above in Chapter 11.b) have had time, opportunity or inclination to concern himself with such contrivance in the fraught months of 593 when he was supposedly writing the *Dialogues*—or indeed at any time during his pontificate.

The first divulgation of that carefully crafted book from its point of origin may reasonably be placed within a period from about 670 to 680. Given the frequent traffic to and from Rome of English scholars and pilgrims in particular, it is unlikely that so fascinating a book, authored by the great pope whom the English honoured as their own patron, should have remained unknown in England for a long time after it had appeared in Rome. There are several other historical pointers which serve to indicate the period in which the Dialogist was active. We have seen evidence that he knew and used anecdotes told in seventh-century writings. Not only does his work reflect knowledge of the stories told in the *Pratum Spirituale* of John Moschus and the *Vita Burgundofarae* of Jonas of Bobbio, but (as shown

---

[1] *RHE* 83 (1988), p. 345.

above, in Chapter 9.d) he incautiously used, as sources and models for some of his tales, several *Gesta* narratives of later seventh-century date. A significant example is his evident indebtedness to the ramified *Gesta* of *Abundius and the Twelve Syrians*, a legendary saga that can be dated after the middle of that century and which, on internal evidence, is attributed by Dufourcq to a writer in the pontifical secretariate. In Chapter 8.c I observed that the *Dialogues* reflect a social, cultural and political situation in Italy that accords with the middle or later years of the seventh century rather than earlier. Although in his writing the author was astute in covering his traces, and took pains to maintain the consistency of his artifice that situated his recital in St Gregory's pontificate, some vital clues yet escape from his pages.

From his text we can infer much about the Dialogist's life-setting, cultural background, experience and personal characteristics. In Chapters 6 and 7 I pointed out several distinctive features in his writing and thinking, showing attitudes and aptitudes clearly different from those of the real Gregory. Among them I recall particularly, as well as his wide familiarity with the plentiful *Gesta*-fables of his age, the following distinctive traits: his stilted and clerkish style of writing; his "socio-religious snobbery" and his unctuously reverential manner of referring to clerical personages; his "cultural class-distinction" and interest in "ecclesiastical power-broking"; his demotic Latinity, with its crudities in style and vocabulary; his literary clumsiness, limping logic and inconsequential arguments; his name-dropping and name-borrowing; his lack of pastoral concern in his writing and his concentration instead on the sensational and the prodigious; his familiarity with the officially proscribed *Gesta*-literature from which he borrowed and adapted many of his themes; and withal his real talent as a story-teller and his remarkable astuteness in sustaining the plausibility of his counterfeit work.

Most significant are the many indications discernible throughout the *Dialogues* text which point to the conclusion that the author was a functionary in the *Scrinium* of the Roman church. That central aspect of his life and work is discussed separately in the following chapter. In this chapter, I first indicate clues to his life-setting and experience that are implicit in incidental references in his text to Italian regional history and topography. I group them here under three heads. First, there are clues discernible in the topographical references in his text. Secondly, it will be instructive to examine his attitude to the Lombards in the light of what we know about the fluctuations in Lombard rule in the peninsula during the seventh century. Thirdly, there is in the Dialogist's text the distinctive feature that I call his "Italian hagiographical chauvinism", implying reaction against the prevalent influence of Greek-speaking Christian culture in Italy during the seventh century. His enterprise can be better understood in the light of what we know about the hellenization of church life in Rome, and of Byzantine relations with Italy, in that period.

The Dialogist shows knowledge of the hills and valleys around Subiaco in which he situated the earlier monastic experiences of St Benedict. In *Dial.* II.7 he mentions a lake over the waters of which Maurus ran at Benedict's bidding to rescue Placidus. (There truly was a lake above Subiaco at that time—as the place-name attests—but it has long since disappeared in the course of the centuries.) Likewise he knows the topography and ruins of the district where Latium Adiectum joined Campania, which in his book is the setting of Benedict's main foundation and later life at Montecassino. Much has been written about the problem of exactly dating the first destruction of Cassino by the Lombards. Paul Warnefrid, the eighth-century historian of the Lombards, put it in the early years of the seventh century. His dating it not a casual remark, but fits into the wider chronological framework of the events he relates, which is not without extrinsic confirmation.[2] It is usual to dismiss his statement as a blunder, since the destruction is mentioned in the Gregorian *Dialogues* supposedly written in 593–4. But it may well be that in this instance Paul was correct in that dating. It is noteworthy that the author of the *Dialogues* has no wonder-stories located in Sicily to match those that he tells of miraculous happenings in the Italian peninsula. This contrasts with Pope Gregory's own personal concern for that island and its people. No other region claimed a greater share of his pastoral care. As well as the important Sicilian patrimony of the Roman Church, he himself had family estates in the island and founded monasteries on them. Had he written the *Dialogues*, we should surely expect some reflection of that concern. The Dialogist's own neglect of Sicily may well reflect the changed political situation of that island in the second half of the seventh century. From the

---

[2] *Historia Langobardorum* VI.40.

time that the emperor Constans landed in Italy in AD 664 Sicily became a main Byzantine base. The papal patrimony there suffered from the harsh imperial presence. Those circumstances may serve to explain the Dialogist's neglect of that island in his narrative— despite his claim that Bishop Maximian of Syracuse, Gregory's vicar in Sicily, was a principal informant for that narrative.

The Fathers of Italy whose wondrous deeds are related in his book, are found to be almost all rural saints and thaumaturges dwelling in *loci minores* in central Italy. The Dialogist's narrative does eventually include events in Rome, but in the main his miracle-working Fathers do not dwell there. Roman episodes are introduced as Book III progresses, and in Book IV the phenomena are mainly related from a vantage point in Rome. St Peter's basilica then has a special place in his story. He says he could relate many more marvellous events which occurred in that church, but since to do so would prevent him from relating anything else, he must return to narrate the miraculous lives of modern Italian Fathers beyond Rome "in the provinces of Italy"—which, he implies, is his main intent.[3] Thus, while his narrative is primarily concerned with saints and wonders outside Rome, it also reflects his own experience of ecclesiastical life in the city itself and his own familiarity with the pontifical Curia.

b. *Clues from the topography of the* Dialogues

"One can say that, essentially, it is the legend of the regional hinterland of Rome that the *Dialogues* narrate". A. Dufourcq's percipient comment[4] points to a distinctive feature of the book which accords ill with the supposition that its author was Gregory the Great. From many indications it appears that the author had first-hand knowledge of the rural localities in which so many of his stories are set. One may infer that he had a particular connection with the hill country of Tuscia, Valeria (Umbria), Sabina and Samnium.[5] (Indeed

---

[3] "*Sed si cuncta, quae in eius ecclesia gesta cognovimus, evolvere conamur, ab omnium iam procul dubio narratione conticescimus. Unde necesse est, ut ad modernos patres, quorum vita per Italiae provincias claruit, narratione se nostra retorqueat*" (*Dial.* III.25.3).

[4] *Op. cit.*, III, p. 288.

[5] Useful maps are appended to F. Lanzoni's *Le Origine delle Diocesi antiche d'Italia*, Rome 1923; cf. also J. Petersen's first map, *op. cit.*, p. XXII, and A. de Vogüé's in *SC* 251.

he explicitly claims close acquaintance with the inhabitants of Samnium in *Dial.* III.26, when relating the miracles and sanctity of the Samnite hermit Menas: "I have almost as many witnesses to attest his way of life as there are people familiar with the province of Samnium".) Those regions are the setting of much of his narrative in the first three books of the *Dialogues*. It is possible that he himself was a native of one of those provinces to the north of Rome. As I argue in the following chapter, there are many indications that he was a clerk writing in the Roman secretariate in the second half of the seventh century. (Did he join the papal service in the middle years of that century, when Martin I, who was a native of Todi in Umbria, was pope?) In any case he could have gained fuller local knowledge of those provinces, and also his knowledge of the upper valley of the Aniene and of Campania, shown in his third book, through experience as a curial official employed on administrative journeys to the papal patrimonies or to the rural domains possessed by individual Roman churches.

Even after a century of Lombard occupation of large tracts of Italy, considerable sectors of the once vast patrimonies of the Roman Church still survived in central Italy and in the region south-east of Rome. They were, most relevantly, the *patrimonium Tusciae* (which underwent "a curious expansion in the course of the seventh century", as Dufourcq remarks),[6] the *patrimonium Sabinum et Carseolanum* and the *patrimonium Appiae*, as well as some remaining parts of the *patrimonium Campaniae*, which had been much reduced by encroachments of the Lombard duchy of Benevento.[7] Through the vigilance and energy of the exarch Isaac of Ravenna in the third and fourth decades of the seventh century, the corridor of imperial territory running diagonally across Italy from Ravenna to Rome and Campania remained a fairly cohesive political unity, although flanked and eroded by the Lombard duchies.[8] The setting of some of the Dialogist's stories in that corridor fits well with what we know of the untidy territorial and political situation, in which, as will be recalled more fully in the fourth section of this chapter, Lombard aggression was still a constant reality, but in which church life continued in the decayed

---

[6] *Op. cit.*, III, p. 314.
[7] Cf. O. Bertolini, *Roma di fronte a Bisancio e ai Longobardi*, Rome 1941, p. 264.
[8] *Ibid.*, pp. 295–6.

towns and their surrounding countryside. With that unsettled and remote society we sense that the Dialogist had familiarity and affinity. Although his concern in writing was not to record secular history but to entertain his readers with his fabulous *Gesta*-tales, his pages give us vivid glimpses of the Italian countryside in his age—of that rough-and-ready world of peasants, travellers, servants, soldiers, robbers and others, seen from the viewpoint of clerics and monks.

One fascinating chapter of the *Dialogues* (I.4) can be seen to reflect the distaste of the provincial countryman for the bureaucracy of the city. S. Boesch Gajano observes that the author there presents Rome as not only the seat of pontifical authority "but also as that of an adulatory and malign clergy, who throw doubt on a [provincial] saint and induce the pontiff to an unjust action".[9] She also observes, that while the *Dialogues* and the almost contemporary legends of the Roman *Gesta Martyrum* share certain basic characteristics, there is a significant difference in the location of the two similar hagiographical collections. In the *Gesta* the setting of the stories is urban; in the *Dialogues* it is not. Even the episodes there narrated which take place in towns, she comments, are not presented "*urbanicamente*"—that is, in the setting of urban society.

c. Italian "hagiographical chauvinism" in the Dialogues

The emphatic claim that Italy was a land of spiritual heroes, made by the *soi-disant* Gregory of the *Dialogues* both in the title and explicitly in the prologue, is another distinctive feature of the book. The author would provide a golden legend of Italian saintly wonder-workers to rival the fables about such worthies that abounded in the Greek-speaking world. He would further assert his Italian religious patriotism by presenting narratives of miracle-working saints to outstrip those related about the saintly heroes of Gaul by Gregory of Tours in the previous century. He tells the surprised Peter that he has a superabundant store of information about the wonder-working saints of their native land, and throughout his book his hagiographical perspective remains almost exclusively Italian. When he does introduce a solitary thaumaturge of non-Italian origin, the holy stranger

---

[9] *Op. cit.*, ("*La proposta agiografica . . .*"), p. 635.

Isaac who came to Spoleto from Syria, he feels the need to excuse his rehearsal of the prowess of a foreign saint: "Now this venerable Isaac was not born in Italy, but I will narrate the miracles he performed while living in Italy". (*Dial.* III.14.1.)

We have seen that the Dialogist was well acquainted with the legends of other lands, particularly those in the mainstream of hagiographical piety that had originated in the eastern Church. While imperial administrative control from the exarchate of Ravenna waned, the religious and cultural influences from the Byzantine world increased during the seventh century. It is well documented, and has become clearer through recent research. J.M. Wallace-Hadrill comments: "It is not too much to say that Rome was hellenized afresh between 600 and 750".[10] During that period no less than thirteen of the popes were Greek-speaking. Several factors accounted for this hellenizing wave which flooded into Rome and Italy anew during the century following the pontificate of Gregory I. It was a time of accelerating decline in Roman and Italian culture, under the pressure of Lombard barbarism and the continuing break-up of the old order. The beacon of Christian civilization and learning was Constantinople, the heartland of the Empire in the East. Seventy-five years after the death of Gregory the Great a Roman pontiff, Agatho, sent to the imperial capital a sad acknowledgement of the level of theological and cultural inferiority to which his church had by then descended.[11]

From the middle of the seventh century onwards a new factor further stimulated the influx of clerics and monks from the East into Rome and southern Italy: namely, the meteoric rise of Islam and the conquest by the Arab armies of the ancient Christian provinces of the Levant and North Africa. At the same time there was sporadic Byzantine intervention in the affairs of Italy, culminating in the dramatic arrest, deposition and harsh treatment of Pope St Martin I by the imperial authorities in 653. The exarchate of Ravenna, though in decline, was for a while made an instrument of this hellenization of Italy. In 664 the emperor Constans II himself arrived in Italy with an army of 20,000 men and paid a state visit to old Rome. Although Byzantine influence in Italy thereafter decreased in

---

[10] *The Barbarian West, 400–1000*, London 1952, p. 64. The Greek monastic influence is examined in detail by J.M. Santerre, in *Les Moines grecs et orientaux à Rome aux époques byzantine et Carololingienne* (*milieu du VIe siècle au IXe siècle*), 2 vols. Brussels 1983.

[11] Text in P. Jaffe, *Regesta Pontificum Romanorum*, n. 2109.

the political and administrative sphere, it continued to increase in the cultural sphere. As Latin monasticism declined in the Italian peninsula, Greek-speaking monastic foundations arose and flourished, especially in Rome, southern Italy and Sicily. Greek art and the cult of eastern saints began to dominate the devotional life of Rome, as still-surviving church decoration shows. The importation of eastern art-forms and techniques was further promoted by refugees from the Arab invasions.[12]

The prevalence of Byzantine iconography in seventh-century Rome reflected the popularity of literary hagiography from the East, which the Greek-speaking monks and clerics popularized in Italy, and which can be seen to have powerfully influenced the authors of the contemporary legendary *Gesta* of the duchy of Rome. This was the background against which the Dialogist wrote his own hagiographical composition, in a spirit of sturdy Italian reaction against that tide of foreign pietism. In this respect he stands out in contrast from the other *Gesta*-spinners of that age. In writing their tales they accepted the current presupposition of superior eastern sanctity, but he would not. He would show the proud ecclesiastical immigrants and his diffident fellow-countrymen that Italy could also boast a multitude of saintly thaumaturges. To rival and even to excel St Anthony of Egypt (and likewise St Martin of Gaul) he would promote for Italy the figure of the great wonder-working abbot St Benedict, and of many other previously unknown Italian saints such as Libertinus, Equitius, Nonnosus, Anastasius, Bonifatius, Fortunatus, Sabinus, Cerbonius, Euthicius, Florentius and Sanctulus. This purpose of the author of the *Dialogues* in writing his narrative is observantly described by M. Van Uytfanghe as follows:

> Fundamentally he intends *to prove a thesis*: that is, that in the sphere of thaumaturgy the West in no way yields to the East . . . It seems indeed that his thesis is not self-evident, but it is *necessary* for him to prove it by giving circumstantial reports.[13]

Nevertheless the Dialogist's own enterprise was strongly influenced by the thought-forms of the eastern hagiographers. In order to exalt the spiritual renown of his own land and Church he borrowed models

---

[12] P. Llewellyn, *op. cit.*, (1971), pp. 197–8.
[13] From Van Uytfanghe's contribution to the *Acts* of the 1982 Chantilly colloquy, *Grégoire le Grand*, Paris 1986, p. 318.

from the rich tradition of *Lives* of the Fathers of the East. J. Petersen observes: "The picture of Italian monasticism which emerges from the *Dialogues* strongly suggests that Gregory had in mind a corpus of material emanating in Eastern Christendom".[14] The author's narrative reflects the eastern mystique of "the holy man". Peter Brown has pointed out the special position, prestige and social function of the living spiritual hero in the Greek-speaking world of late antiquity. He also shows that this charismatic phenomenon was distinctive of the eastern Church, and he remarks that (in the special sense in which he is using the term), "No holy man was active in Dark Age Rome".[15]

Indeed in Gregory's age Roman piety had still looked rather to the sanctity of the relics of the Apostles and other martyrs and saints as a source of present spiritual power. It had not yet followed eastern Christendom in legendary exaltation of living or recent charismatic personalities. For the real Gregory (and still for some of the Dialogist's contemporaries, whom he pillories in his story of the detractors of Equitius in *Dial.* I.4.11–12), the faithful were not to look for religious leadership from such extra-canonical holy men, but from the ecclesiastical rulers vested with apostolic authority who exercised the *culmen regiminis*. The Dialogist, on the other hand, depicts as idealized spiritual leaders his rootless and charismatic Fathers of Italy, who have sacredness and effectiveness strangely independent of canonical commission. They are presented as wielders of prodigious power in their contemporary world, who emerge victorious over all adversity and provide a dramatic spectacle for the admiration of the ordinary faithful. In the Italian countryside setting that he evokes they have the same aura and supernatural immediacy as the holy men whose legendary lives awed and fascinated the communities of eastern Christendom. A main merit of J. Petersen's study is in bringing out the affinity of the *Dialogues* to that contemporary climate of eastern hagiographical tradition.[16] She stresses, for instance, the striking parallels between stories in the *Dialogues* and in the *Religious History* of Theodoret. The real Gregory could not have read Theodoret's work; nor, as we have seen, does he evince interest in such fanciful

---

[14] *Op. cit.*, p. 154.
[15] "The rise and function of the holy man in late antiquity", in *The Journal of Roman Studies*, 61 (1971), pp. 80–101.
[16] Cf. especially her sixth chapter and pp. 116–7.

tales. The Dialogist, however, writing in the re-hellenized Rome of the later seventh century, would have picked up those, and other stories of eastern provenance, from contact with the monks and clerics of Greek origin who were then numerous in the city. From such sources, I infer, he would have known of the narrative themes from the *Spiritual Meadow* of John Moschus that are reflected in the pages of his work, though probably not yet available in Latin translation in his day. His religious thought-world reflects that of the hellenizers of the seventh century, even when he reacts against it.

It was not only in the ecclesiastical and devotional sphere that native-born Romans and other Italians were reacting against Byzantine influence and interference in that period. The development of Italian political resentment, leading at times to military resistance, can be traced from the third decade of the seventh century onwards. It was inflamed by the Emperor's persecution of Pope Martin I, when for the first time, as Bertolini observes, "Rome was prepared for even a political breach with Byzantium and its sovereign".[17] It was heightened later in the century, and led to the first serious insurrection of Italy against Byzantium in 692.[18] Into this context of nascent regional patriotism in the social and political spheres the Dialogist's enterprise of hagiographical chauvinism fits appositely. He does tell a tale of a miracle worked long ago by Pope John when making a ceremonial entry into Constantinople (*Dial.* III.2.3), but in his book there is virtually complete silence about imperial authority and institutions, which loom so large in the *Registrum* of letters of Pope Gregory the Great.

Assertion of a specifically Italian or Western religious loyalty is not something that is found in the writings of Gregory the Great, and would have been be alien to his spiritual and cultural outlook. "God's Consul", as his epitaph described him, embraced the whole Christian world in his pastoral concern. His distaste for fictitious *Gesta* tales, in continuation of the sternly critical attitude of the *Gelasianum*, has been discussed in Chapter 9.c. Very revealing is a remark that he made in a personal letter to the Greek count Narses concerning the differing attitudes of authorities in East and West to

---

[17] *"Riflessi politici delle controversie con Bisancio nelle vicende del secolo VII in Italia"*, in the symposium, *Caratteri del secolo VII in Occidente*, Spoleto 1958, p. 744.

[18] Diehl, *op. cit.*, pp. 360 & 401–11.

such frauds: "Our Roman codices are more accurate than Greek
ones: we have neither your talents nor your counterfeits".[19] That
trenchant remark shows, first, Gregory's acknowledgement of the
superior brilliance of Greek culture (no Italian cultural chauvinism
there), and secondly, his contemptuous rejection of spurious religious
texts. And yet those who assert his authorship of the *Dialogues* ascribe
to him the very counterfeiting that he himself condemned.

d. *Clues from Lombard history*

Lombard history also affords clues to the period of the Dialogist's
activity. The Lombards are indeed the villains of the *Dialogues*. The
author writes with consistent abhorrence of them and of their blood-
thirsty wickedness—"*sicut sunt nimiae crudelitatis*" (III.37.13). Although,
as S. Boesch Gajano points out,[20] he relates stories of the perfidy
and cruelty of both the Goths and the Lombards, there is a significant
difference in his attitude to those two tribes of Germanic invaders
of Italy. She observes that his stories about the Goths have as a
sequel a kind of acceptance of their entrance into the religious world
that he describes: "In the end they are inserted and involved in that
very religious reality that they seek to destroy or ridicule, often coming even to see the error of their ways". For the Lombards, on the
contrary, she shows that there is no such mitigation in the judgement of the author of the *Dialogues*: "They are completely extrinsic
to the world he describes". The miracles of his saintly heroes ter-
rify the Lombards, thwart them, put them to flight, but (with a single exception in *Dial.* III.37.17) have no salutary effect on them.
Those supernatural signs do not incline the cruel barbarians to moderation, repentance or conversion. "Spiritually insensitive to sanctity", Boesch Gajano comments, "they only experience its punitive
power". The reason for this difference in the author's attitude to the
two tribes of barbarian invaders, she justly observes, is that the Goths
were more remote in history, defeated and departed, with their resid-
ual elements assimilated into the Italian population. The Lombards,

---

[19] Epist. VI.14. P. Meyvaert cites that sentence, but despite Gregory's acknowledgement in it of superior Greek wits, takes it as a proof of his "Italian chauvinism" (*JEH* 39, 1988, p. 371).
[20] *Op. cit.*, ("*Dislivelli*"), pp. 400–1.

by contrast, were still present, a hostile occupying power still in the Dialogist's lifetime oppressing the native people and institutions of northern and central Italy.

A horror-story such as that told in *Dial.* III.28, of the slaughter by the Lombards of 440 Italian rustics who had refused to participate in their demonic rites, does not belong to the realm of history. It does reflect a loathing for those barbarian invaders and their very real savagery. The author was evidently writing at a time when bitter memories and fears of them were still alive in Italian minds and hearts. The Lombards first descended on northern Italy in AD 568. They established their strongholds in the centre and south of the peninsula about twenty years before the ostensible date, 593–4, at which the *Dialogues* are supposed to have been written by Gregory. Those who assume his authorship of the book naturally assume also that the accounts of the Lombards' cruelty must reflect the first period of their conquest, namely the last quarter of the sixth century. That assumption is too facile. From study of the subsequent phase in the Lombards' rule in Italy it can be seen that the Dialogist's attitude to them concords aptly with the situation in the middle years of the seventh century and even later.[21] Before outlining that situation, I observe that, on the hypothesis that Gregory was writing the *Dialogues* in 593–4, it is odd that when denouncing the Lombards and their misdeeds the author should make no reference to their siege of Rome at that very time, or to the atrocities that the real Gregory saw with his own eyes and described in graphic and harrowing detail in his *Homilies on Ezekiel* as the siege progressed. He eventually had to bring his sermons to an abrupt end because of those dreadful events.

After the siege had been lifted and the threatened sack of the city averted, Gregory achieved during the last years of his pontificate an uneasy peace with the Lombard kingdom, which continued after his death. The first quarter of the seventh century was, relatively speaking, a period of unwonted social and religious peace for the inhabitants of the regions of the main Lombard kingdom to the north, thanks to the pro-Catholic policy of Queen Theodelinda and later of King Adaloald. However, the tolerance of the court of Pavia had

---

[21] In what follows I draw on the massive researches of G. Bognetti, *L'Età Longobarda*, 4 vols. Milan 1966–68.

only indirect and limited effect in mitigating the harshness of Lombard overlordship in the separate feudal duchies of Spoleto and Benevento, where the rulers were Arian (or in some cases pagan). In the first phase of the Lombards' conquest, the seat of their power in central Italy, Spoleto, had been held by the fierce duke Faraold. Although in that duchy too there was a temporary *modus vivendi* for the Catholics after the uneasy truce of 598, the regime remained repressive in the following age. There was reaffirmation of Arianism and severe oppression of the native populace throughout the Lombard domains during the reigns of the kings Arioald (625–636) and Rothari (636–652). In those years, writes G. Bognetti, "it was worse for Tuscia, Spoleto and Benevento, which were obliged, as our sources show, to endure a period of the most radical 'Germanization' of the population, unalleviated by the slightest possibility of action on behalf of the Catholics".[22] That period, I conclude, was in all probability that of the Dialogist's youth. There are indications from his narrative of familiarity with the regions included in the Lombard domains of Tuscia, Spoleto and Benevento. He may well have had personal recollections of those turbulent times, when the fierce soldiery of the Lombard duchies were still laying an iron heel on the necks of the people of those regions. He made his anti-Lombard diatribes apply to the early Lombard invaders of Italy in Gregory's lifetime, but they reflect the antipathy of his own generation to the long-bearded oppressors still in their midst.

During Rothari's reign the Lombards re-emphasized their sense of a national identity throughout the peninsula and their domination over the native inhabitants. For the first time a Lombard king exercised effective power over all the territories occupied by them between the Alps and the gulf of Taranto. Arianism was strongly reasserted against the native Catholicism of the Italian population, and Arian bishoprics were everywhere established. For all his Arian resolution, however, Rothari sought order and stability in his realm. He allowed restoration of the Catholic bishoprics which had been suppressed in many regions during the course of the Lombard conquests. Paul Warnefrid later recorded that during Rothari's reign there were two bishops, one Arian and one Catholic, in almost all

---

[22] *Ibid.*, I, p. 162; III, p. 326.

the towns of the Lombard territories.[23] This period of vigorous but mitigated resurgence of Arianism, during which the region around Spoleto was thoroughly Lombardized, was very probably the background for the story told in *Dialogues* III.29.1–4, referred to above in Chapter 8.d. It tells how an aggressive Arian bishop, at the head of a band of followers, attempted to seize by force one of the Catholic churches in Spoleto, but was foiled by a miracle. In the *Dialogues* the episode is inappositely placed in the period of the first Lombard conquests. It is anachronistic to imagine such ecclesiastical rivalries at that time, when the Lombards were not concerned with church rivalries but with slaughter and conquest. The Dialogist's inclusion of that episode in his narrative provides one more item of evidence showing that he was writing at a time long after the pontificate of Pope Gregory.

After Rothari's systematic restoration of Arianism as the dominant religion of this realm, and the brief reign of his successor Rodoald, there came a swing of the pendulum with the accession to the Lombard throne in 653 of the Catholic king Aripert I. During his reign of nearly ten years he disestablished Arianism and favoured Catholicism. Then, most relevantly for the purposes of our present investigation, the pendulum swung back again and there followed the last and major period of oppression under the tyrannical and Arianizing king Grimoald (662–671), who drove Aripert from the throne. He was a barbarian chief as ruthless as any of his predecessors in the first period of the Lombard invasion of Italy.[24] Before seizing the throne of Pavia with the help of the Lombard viceroys of Spoleto and Tuscia, he had been (since 657) duke of Benevento, and had brought renewed strife and tribulation to the southern part of the peninsula. It is related that in his ducal palace he, and his son Romoald, "adored the pagan viper".[25] As king, Romoald again united all the Lombard dominions under a strongly centralized rule. His campaign against the Byzantine emperor and his exarch in Ravenna, and against the Franks, brought widespread havoc and pillage. His rule was a reign of terror for the subject Catholic population. We know details of one of his atrocities, a massacre in the

---

[23] *Historia Langobardorum* IV.42; *MGH* ed. p. 134.
[24] Bognetti, *op. cit.*, III, p. 490.
[25] *Ibid.*, I, p. 166.

baptistery in Forimpopoli, carried out in revenge for opposition from
that town during one of his military expeditions in the south. Surprising
the Catholic deacons as they stood baptising during the paschal cer-
emonies, he slew all present without mercy.[26]

The recrudescence of Lombard barbarity under Grimoald between
the years 662 and 671 may well have provided the immediately
proximate background to the composition of the *Dialogues*. The author
would have vividly in his mind the recent events of Grimoald's ruthless regime and a deep-seated Italian resentment to give force to his
horrendous tales of Lombard savagery in a previous age. What
Bognetti describes as "the barbarian restoration" under Grimoald
was finally brought to an end when, in 671, the pro-Catholic king
Perctarit ascended the Lombard throne.[27] This time the reversal of
the political and religious situation was to have permanent effect.
The definitive conversion of the Lombard chiefs and people to
Catholicism was not achieved suddenly, but was still to be a gradual and irregular process. Native Italian hatred of the alien con-
querors was slow to die away. Even though Perctarit's reign (671–688)
ushered in a new age, the old animosities, especially in the Lombard
duchies of Spoleto and Benevento, still fed on the grim memories
of the past. The *Dialogues*, composed probably before his mitigating
measures began to have effect, would reflect those animosities, still
very vivid.

---

[26] *Ibid.*, II, p. 343.
[27] *Ibid.*, I, pp. 100 ff.; II, pp. 345–6.

CHAPTER TWENTY FOUR

THE DIALOGIST AS *SCRINIARIUS, GESTA-SPINNER* AND *"TAM PERITUS FALLENDI ARTIFEX"*

a

I focus now on evidence that is central in the quest for the profile and life-setting of the author of the *Dialogues*: namely, that which indicates that he was a clerical functionary in the secretariate of the Roman Curia. Many times in the preceding pages reference has been made to that evidence. In this chapter I recall the main indications that have already been mentioned, and cite further corroborating evidence to the same effect. From internal references in the text of the *Dialogues* and from external indications, there are substantial reasons for locating the Dialogist in the *Scrinium* of the Roman see, among the clerks who worked in it. Since that institution can be seen to be of central relevance in this investigation, I begin by summarizing what is known about it and its personnel in late antiquity, and especially in the seventh century.

In classical Latin the term *scrinium* referred originally to a chest or press in which documents and books were kept. In later Latin it had a wider connotation, being used to refer to the office or secretariate in which scribes and librarians worked. The papal *scrinium*, as it originated in the earlier centuries, was an ecclesiastical parallel of the civil *scrinium memoriae*, or archival office, in which were kept the official codices of the Roman imperial court. There is record that as early as AD 338 Pope Julius I gave organized status to the *"sanctum scrinium"* of the Roman Church. St Jerome referred to that office as the *chartarium ecclesiae romanae*. From at least the fifth century not only the pope's letters, sent and received, but also other official papers—legal, fiscal, administrative as well as literary and theological—were kept in what was now ordinarily called the *scrinium* (or *scrinia*) *sedis apostolicae*. In the preface to his Gospel *Homilies* Gregory uses the phrase *"in scrinio ecclesiae nostrae"*. In his letters he also refers to the *scrinia* of other local churches, and to the *regalia scrinia* of the Frankish kingdom.[1]

---

[1] Cf. *Registrum*, EH I.229; II.373.

The salient facts about the Roman *Scrinium* can be gleaned from a valuable (but little known) nineteenth-century monograph by J.B. De Rossi, entitled "On the Origin and History of the *Scrinium* and Library of the Apostolic see".[2] It was at the same time the secretariate of the reigning pontiff, the archives in which past and present records were housed, the papal library, and a workshop for the transcription of texts. Writing his *Vita Gregorii* in the ninth century, John the Deacon recorded that at that time archives going back to Gregory's time could still be consulted "in this most sacred *Scrinium* of the Lateran palace", and that it was there that he studied the fourteen books of the great pope's letters.[3] Also in the *Scrinium* multiple copies of codices were produced. (Others were of course transcribed in monasteries.) Gregory himself had copies of his own works made there, for sending as gifts to fellow bishops and friends. The scribes also replicated copies of the scriptures, of conciliar acts, of patristic writings and of ecclesiastical records. When Gregory sent a *magna copia voluminum sacrorum* to Augustine in Canterbury he must have had recourse to a stock of codices already transcribed and available for such a purpose, as B. Bischoff observes.[4]

The officials of the *Scrinium* were the *notarii*. According to an early redaction of the *Liber Pontificalis* there were in the administration of the Roman Church, as well as seven deacons and seven subdeacons, the "Guild of the Seven Notaries". The chief of the latter was called the *primicerius notariorum*, followed by the *secundicerius*. Although a *notarius* named Aemilianus was one of those who took down in writing Gregory's *Homilies on the Gospels*, the seven officials entitled *notarii* were no mere pen-pushers, but were often sent on responsible missions by the pontiffs. In more general usage, the term *notarius* was not restricted to the seven officials who constituted the *schola notariorum* but could also be applied more loosely to other clerks in the papal administration. There were several lower grades within the *Scrinium*, again paralleling those in the imperial civil administration. For the humbler tasks of taking down dictated discourses and official pro-

---

[2] Prefaced to his monumental work, *Codices palatini latini bibliothecae Vaticanae*, Rome 1886. I follow De Rossi for many of the details recalled here. Cf. also R.L. Poole, *Lectures on the History of the Papal Chancery down to the time of Innocent III*, Cambridge 1915, pp. 13–25.

[3] "... *in hoc sacratissimo Lateranensis palatii scrinio*"; *Vita*, II.30; *PL* 75.98.

[4] *Mittelalterliche Studien*, Stuttgart 1966–7, II, p. 319.

ceedings there were the *exceptores*, stenographers trained for their task from their youth. Other grades were those of *scriba, regendarius, scriniarius and chartularius*. *Scriniarius* seems to have been used also as a generic name for clerks in the secretariate.

It is among those *scriniarii* that I locate the Dialogist. Whether he was a minor cleric of Roman origin who in the course of administrative journeys gained contact with the legends of the regions lying to the north and south-east of the city, or whether (which seems more probable) he hailed from the rural hinterland of Rome and brought knowledge of regional traditions with him when he entered the curial service in the papal city, he can be recognized as one of the school of clerical scribes who busily plied their pens in the papal court in the later seventh century. He may have had the duty of accompanying the senior *notarii* on official business in the papal patrimonies and other regions, especially in the provinces of central Italy in which so many of his stories are placed.

During the seventh century and later the organization and functions of the Roman *Scrinium* were still basically as they had been in the age of Gregory I, but with further developments.[5] "In the seventh century", wrote De Rossi, "the *Scrinium* and the library of the Apostolic see, over which the *primicerius notariorum* presided, was certainly in the patriarchal palace of the Lateran. In the formulae that were used in that century and are recorded in the *Liber Diurnus*, the 'Archivum of the Roman Church' and the 'sacred Lateran *Scrinium*' were one and the same".[6] An impressive illustration of the complexity and efficiency of the organization of that office comes from the Acts of the Council of Rome held under Pope Martin I in 649. The *primicerius* Theophylactus was called upon to provide for the use of the assembled Fathers a large number of documents, including acts of councils, patristic and heretical writings, charters and other records. That he was able to do so, promptly and repeatedly, testifies both to the literary resources of the *Scrinium* and to the competence of its staff.[7]

The *Scrinium* was also, so to speak, a "publishing house" with a wider scope. It was, as De Rossi observed, "an abundant source

---

[5] De Rossi devotes a chapter of his monograph to this period, entitled, "*De scrinio et bibliotheca sedis apostolicae saeculo septimo*". Cf. also O. Bertolini, *op. cit.*, pp. 372–3.

[6] *Op. cit.*, p. LXVI.

[7] De Rossi, *op. cit.*, pp. LXVI–LXX.

from which codices could be copied for those who requested them.
Thus at the same time the library of the Apostolic see was a centre from which sacred books were disseminated throughout Europe,
especially northern Europe".[8] The importance of the Roman *Scrinium*
as such a centre increased during the seventh century with the ever-
growing demand for books from the bishops, clergy and monks of
the new regions of Christendom—resulting especially from the Merovingian renaissance and new monastic movement in Francia, and
from the conversion of the Anglo-Saxon kingdoms farther north. At
times the demand outstripped the supply. When a northern bishop
wrote to Pope Martin I asking for a copy of a codex, the pope had
to reply regretfully that the stock of that particular book was exhausted,
and that there would be some delay before more transcriptions were
available.[9] The enterprise of producing books and supplying them
to the clergy and monasteries in the new provinces of Christendom
must have brought considerable economic benefit to the Roman
Curia and its employees. In the sixth century the main source of
revenue for the church and city of Rome had been provided by the
estates of the papal patrimonies. Those revenues, however, had been
much reduced by Lombard depredations, imperial confiscations and
the general disorder of the age. With the rise of the new Christian
nations to the north new sources of revenue opened.

Study of the central role of the Roman *Scrinium* as supplier of
books to buyers from all over Europe throws light on the situation
and background of the author of the *Dialogues*, whose work reflects
that ambience. With the surging wave of legendary *Gesta* and *Passiones
martyrum* in the seventh century, it is not surprising to find evidence
that the *scriniarii* were involved not only in transcribing such literature but also in composing it, in order to meet the eager demand.
Here again the value of the researches of A. Dufourcq, once derided,
is now more justly recognized. I recall here what was said in Chapter
9 about his findings in this field, and about those of U. Moricca,
which are very pertinent to our search for the Dialogist's sphere of
activity. S. Boesch Gajano points in particular to the importance of
the link, established by Dufourcq, between the Roman *Scrinium* and

---

[8] *Ibid.*, p. LXXIII. There were, of course, copyists in the monasteries everywhere;
it appears that there was also a bureau for book production attached to St Peter's
basilica.
[9] De Rossi, *op. cit.*, p. LXXIII.

the production of such texts.[10] One of Dufourcq's conclusions was that "the middle ranking Roman clergy" were involved in the literary compositions issuing from what he miscalled "the Gregorian legendary movement". He also observed that there was a close connection between the martyrological legends relating to the city of Rome and the wider hagiographical literature that developed in the seventh century relating to the "duchy" of Rome, the rural hinterland in central Italy. In a passage which has clear relevance to our quest for the elusive Dialogist, he recognized the influence that the earlier productions of legends concerning the city of Rome had on the development in the seventh century of legends relating to the rural districts further afield:

> There is nothing surprising in that, given that it was Roman clerics who composed some of our texts. The Roman churches possessed domains in diverse regions of Italy. The clerics who were responsible for their administration came to learn the legends that were related there; they edited them on the model of the Roman legends. Rome was the religious metropolis and military capital. Its influence could not fail to be felt. We can discern its traces.[11]

In the *Gesta* produced by that later legendary movement, Dufourcq observes, there was "a tendency to separate the themes of martyr and saint". He cites notable instances of venerated saints who were no longer represented as martyrs, such as John Penariensis and Laurence of Spoleto. The *Dialogues* can be seen to be the fullest development of that trend. Dufourcq also notes the indirect influence on this new Italian hagiography resulting from the religious compromise of the Lombard king Rothari in the mid-seventh century, which allowed the restoration of the Catholic bishoprics in the previously unsettled regions.[12] Other scholars now agree with Dufourcq's discernment of that school of *Gesta*-writers. H. Delehaye writes: "What is incontestable is that the authors of those Roman legends belong to one and the same school; that in psychology, motivation and culture they are at the same level; and that they even have in common a characteristic phraseology".[13] G. Lucchesi likewise judges that

---

[10] Cf. her article, "*La proposta agiographa . . .*", p. 657, note 173.
[11] *Op. cit.*, III, p. 283.
[12] *Ibid.*, pp. 283–5.
[13] *Op. cit.*, (*Le Legendier . . .*), p. 12; cf. also his *Les Passions des martyrs*, pp. 236–64.

the fictional accounts of Umbria, Tuscan and Roman saints were the work of writers of one recognizable school.[14]

There must undoubtedly have been an eager demand for this type of literature, which the legend-writers did their best to satisfy. While Dufourcq was mistaken in attributing to Gregory the Great the composition of such counterfeit hagiography, he rightly placed the author of the *Dialogues* in the company of those *Gesta*-spinners. I recall here his scathing judgement, already cited in Chapter 9 above, which does indeed aptly apply to that author: "The writer who takes pleasure in writing so many trivial or futile stories, who records them without making any comment—but rather, who presents them as worthy of faith and praise—that man is on the same level as the compilers of the Roman *Gesta*. What wonder that he underwent their influence?" The authors of those other legendary *Gesta*, like the Dialogist, constantly insisted on the veracity of their fictions and piled up spurious testimonies to authenticate them. Some, like him, ascribed their counterfeits to illustrious authors: for instance at least five fantastic *passiones* were put out under the name of St Ambrose.[15] The Dialogist not only excelled them in the scale and design of his hagiographical project, but his achievement was unique inasmuch as he had lasting success in passing off his literary creation as the work of the great pope Gregory.

b. *The Dialogist's sources and experience: the* scriniarius

There are many indications pointing to the conclusion that the author of the *Dialogues* had personal experience of the work of the Lateran *Scrinium*. There is in the first place, the tell-tale "*style de notaire*" or officialese phraseology pervading his text, so acutely described by A. de Vogüé, which I discussed in Chapter 5.b. Furthermore, there are frequent mentions in his text of ecclesiastical officialdom, including specific mention of scribes. I mentioned in Chapter 7.h the passage in *Dial.* I.8.1 in which he introduces "a notary of the holy Roman Church" named Anastasius, who, wishing to dedicate himself wholly to God, "deserted the *Scrinium* and entered a monastery".[16]

---

[14] *BS* IV, col. 778.
[15] Cf. Lanzoni, *op. cit.*, p. 36.
[16] "... *sanctae romanae ecclesiae notarius fuit. Qui soli vacare desiderans, scrinium deseruit [atque] monasterium elegit*" (*Dial.* I.81).

There are several references (some of them critical) to senior Church officials. In *Dial.* IV.55 a discreditable story is told about an ecclesiastical *defensor* of Milan, who was "an extremely licentious man, given over to every kind of worldliness", and whose body, when buried in a church, was dragged out of it at midnight by demons. In the story of the officials sent by a pope to summon the holy Valerian abbot Equitius to Rome for disciplinary correction (*Dial.* 1.4.13), there is an incidental reference which reflects the Dialogist's interest in scribes and copyists (who were doubtless among his potential readers). When the curial *defensor* and his overbearing assistant arrive at the monastery they do not find Equitius there, and have to seek him elsewhere. Though it has nothing to do with the story he is telling, the author adds the titbit that they did find there "*antiquarios scribentes*"—that is, monks engaged in transcribing documents from past times.

Although the Dialogist writes favourably of monks and extols the virtues of the monastic saints in his narrative,[17] it does not appear that he himself was a monk. Undoubtedly he had cloistered readers in view, but he also envisaged readers of other conditions and classes, especially from among the clerics and officials of the ecclesiastical establishment. I noted in Chapter 5.e that the question of the readership for whom the *Dialogues* were intended has been put on a new footing in recent years. The older assumption that the author, supposedly St Gregory, wrote at a popular level with the main pedagogical intent of bringing a pastoral message to the multitude of the simple and unlettered faithful, is now discredited. I cited in that earlier chapter the well-founded conclusion of A. de Vogüé that his literary ambitions, interests and prejudices were not populist but élitist. He despised the rustics and had scant interest in the common herd of townsfolk. It was especially for an ecclesiastical caste that he was writing. The hypothesis that he was himself a functionary in the Roman *Scrinium* fits very well with the character of his book. He stresses the "venerability" of the higher and middle ranks of the clerical order, and also the dignity of secular nobles, with an obsequiousness that Vogüé finds heavy and monotonous. For all that, the *Dialogist* can be critical of the arrogance of those of superior

---

[17] Indeed A.J. Kinnerey commented: "The *Dialogues* may be said to reflect a monastic *Sondersprache*" (*op. cit.*, p. 124).

rank, commenting that "in some persons nobility of birth is wont to
bring forth baseness of mind".

He reveals by a number of incidental remarks that he is an author
sensitive to critical scrutiny of his writing. He explains in his prologue that in narrating the wondrous experiences of provincial "Fathers
of Italy", he will when necessary paraphrase the homespun phrases
of his informants, since to repeat such crude parlance "would ill
become the style of a writer"—"*haec rusticano usu prolata stilus scribentis non apte susciperet*". (Do the defenders of the authenticity of the
Dialogues really suppose that St Gregory himself would have voiced
such a concern?) In a number of places in his text the Dialogist
takes care to acknowledge that expressions he is using are demotic,
and he explains the meaning of some of them.[18] While many of his
heroes wielding spiritual power are abbots, bishops and dignatories,
his pages also contain much that would appeal to other ranks in the
Church's service who could find their counterparts in his pages: to
priests, deacons, subdeacons and clerics of all degrees, to *scriniarii*
and officials of different ranks, and even to those humbler functionaries, the *mansionarii* and *custodes* who were responsible for the
material care of the churches and other ecclesiastical buildings, whom
he also includes among his characters. Three sacristans are among
his thaumaturges. There is an imaginative touch, found in two of
the stories about the latter, in which the sacristans are depicted as
standing on wooden step-ladders ("*in ligneis gradibus*") and tending
their lamps when a prodigious event occurs.[19]

Further light on the personality and career of the Dialogist can
be gained by studying his text for traces of the sources that he used,
and especially for indications of his own sphere of activity and experience. We have seen that, as well as borrowing some of his themes
for miracle-stories from Scripture, he was steeped in the genre of
fictitious hagiography and that it was his preferred field of interest.
In this his mentality differed most decisively from that of St Gregory
the Great, whose life gave witness to the principle that he stated in
his *Moralia* (12.37), cited earlier: "God has no use for a lie; for Truth
does not seek the aid of falsehood". It is often assumed that the

---

[18] Among these expressions, some of which have been cited in earlier pages are
the following: "*verbo rustico*" (*Dial.* I.12); "*psyatio quod vulgo matta vocatur*" (II.11); "*vas-
cula quae vulgo flascones vocantur*" (II.17); "*quae usitato nos nomine vangae vocamus*" (III.12).
[19] *Dial.* I.5.4 & III.24.1. Cf. Chapter 8.e above.

Dialogues were based on oral folk-traditions going back to the age of the Ostrogoths. The author may have made some use of such traditions, heard during his travels in the provinces of central Italy, but this factor should not be exaggerated. Such unwritten "sources" would be a minor part in the composition of a work spun largely from the author's fertile imagination, in which he adapted the themes of his tales from the earlier and contemporary literary models referred to above, especially the legendary *Gesta*. As well as on those fanciful hagiographies he also drew on genuine Gregorian texts, including the *reportata* and *inedita* in the Lateran library from which he took his IGPs, and most obviously from the *Homilies on the Gospels*, from which he copied verbatim his seven narrative IGPs (while omitting the moral with which Gregory had concluded each passage in the original context). He also knew and borrowed names and references from the archive files in which Gregory's letters were preserved. His access to and knowledge of those otherwise inaccessible records is another significant pointer to his situation within the Lateran *Scrinium*. In previous pages I have noted several instances of his knowledge and reuse of items from that source. One especially notable instance (mentioned above in Chapter 8.e) is the formal phrase applied in two of Gregory's administrative letters from the year 599 to an abbot named Theodosius: "*abbas monasterii quod a Liberio quondam patricio in Campaniae partibus ... constructum*".[20] The identical phrase, with only the name changed, is gratuitously brought into an anecdote in *Dial.* II.35.1, where the Dialogist makes it refer not to that real abbot Theodosius but to a character of his own creation, whom he names as an abbot Servandus. A further instance of inept reuse of details from the file of Gregory's official papers is found in *Dial.* I.8.1. Then, while telling the tale of supernatural portents preceding the death of the former notary Anastasius, he makes Pope Gregory bring into it a solemn reminder of his own sacred dignity as Roman pontiff presiding by divine authority over the Roman Church, in the court of which Anastasius had been a functionary: "*... sanctae Romanae Ecclesiae, cui Deo auctore deservio, notarius fuit*". The first seven words of that phrase were a standard formula of the papal secretariate before and after the age of Gregory the Great. E. Dobschütz notes that it is found in that stylized form in the oldest part of the *Liber Diurnus*

---

[20] *Epist.* XI, 162 & 164; EH II.162–3.

and also long afterwards—as late as the time of Gregory II and III. The Dialogist's misappropriation of it closely parallels its use in an administrative letter sent by Gregory in a letter dated July 591.[21]

The Dialogist would have at hand the biographical notices of the sixth-century popes in the *Liber Pontificalis*. It was probably from that source that he took his references to the journeys of Popes John and Agapitus to Constantinople, in *Dial.* III.2.1 and 3.1. By attending to the dates of the Indiction years given in the archive of Gregory's letters he was able, for the most part, to observe chronological consistency in relating his narrative to the events of Gregory's lifetime. Why, it may be asked, would a falsifier of that age bother to do so? A critical researcher of today would discern inconsistency, but eager and uncritical readers in the seventh century would have no opportunity or thought of verifying such details. A likely answer to this objection is that the Dialogist had in mind possible doubts from critical superiors and peers in the *Scrinium*, who had the same access to the archives that he had, and who could be reassured about the provenance of a hitherto unknown Gregorian work by being referred to the Gregorian letters preserved there in which supporting reference could be found.

There is also the question of the Dialogist's knowledge of the *Regula Benedicti*, demonstrated in *Dial.* II.36. Although he there refers, with the highest praise, to a rule for monks admirably written by a holy abbot Benedict, whose life he recounts in that book, he does not mention its observance anywhere at the time of writing. We have seen that the *RB*, hitherto unknown, had been introduced into the monastery of Altaripa by a magnate named Venerandus in southwest France around AD 625–630, and that in later decades it was in partial use in several Merovingian monasteries in conjunction with the rule of St Columban. There is no trace of its observance in Italy during the whole of the seventh century. How then was the Dialogist familiar with it? A reasonable answer is that as clerks in the Lateran *Scrinium* he and his colleagues would have heard of it from book-seeking visitors and pilgrims from Francia. He may even have had knowledge of a codex of the monastic rule bearing the name of St Benedict preserved in the Lateran library. Such a codex of the *RB* was stated by Paul Warnefrid in the later eighth century to have

---

[21] *Epist.* I.63; EH I.85, line 1.

been donated by Pope Zachary (741–752) to the newly founded abbey and shrine of St Benedict at Montecassino; he boldly asserted that "the blessed father Benedict wrote it with his own holy hands". Whatever its true origin, that codex in the archive may even have been the archetype from which earlier in the seventh century Venerandus had obtained "from the parts of Rome" his copy of "the rule of holy Benedict, a Roman abbot". Since in the middle and second half of the seventh century the *RB* was esteemed and increasingly used in Francia, it is quite likely that the Roman *librarii* who supplied the needs of the book-questors from north of the Alps found that monastic rule to be one of the texts for which there was a growing market. Thus the text of the *RB* in the *Scrinium* would have been quite well known to the personnel of that office. (That the Dialogist had seen the actual text of the *RB* is suggested by a possible echo of its phrasing in *Dial.* IV.57.11.)[22] One may further surmise that it was this quickening of interest in that monastic rule, leading to requests for information about its saintly but otherwise unknown author, that prompted the inventive Dialogist to supply a biography of that saint in his book narrating the miracles of the Fathers of Italy.

c. *The Roman* Scrinium *in four pontificates*

Here I offer reflections relating to four relevant pontificates, the first two antedating the indicated date of origin of the *Dialogues* and the other two postdating it. The Dialogist may well have been reaching maturity in his service in the Lateran *Scrinium* during the twenty years spanned by the pontificates of Vitalian (who was pope from AD 657 to 672) and Adeodatus II (672–676). Indeed it was probably in the latter part of that period that he embarked on his imaginative and ambitious literary project. Vitalian was a friend and promoter of monks, and Adeodatus was himself a monk—the first monastic pope of the seventh century. Vitalian, "one of the greatest of the popes" in Bognetti's judgement,[23] was a native of Campania, and a friend and admirer of the learned abbot Hadrian who, (as

---

[22] "*Nullus ex fratribus se ad eum . . . iungat, nec sermonem . . .*". This may be compared with *RB* 25.2: "*Nullus ei fratrum . . . iungatur . . . nec in colloquio . . .*".

[23] *Op. cit.*, IV, p. 283.

recalled above in Chapters 16.c and 18.c) helped to reinvigorate the Anglo-Saxon church—and who, though coming from the same region, had no knowledge of a great Campanian saint and abbot called Benedict. The phrase in the *Liber Pontificalis* describing Pope Adeodatus II says much: "*natione Romanus, ex monachis*". It is not difficult to visualise the Dialogist, with his monastic sympathies and his familiarity with the rural hinterland of Rome, as finding a congenial place in the Roman Curia during that period.

During the pontificate of Pope Sergius I (AD 687–701) the Roman *Scrinium* was divided into two departments, as we know from the *Liber Pontificalis*.[24] It seems probable that it was the great expansion of the work of book transcription, resulting from the ever increasing demand for codices from the new monasteries and centres of culture in Francia, England and Germany, that led to the eventual distinction of the library and book-production department of the Roman *Scrinium* from the notarial department which performed the administrative work of the papal secretariate. Surviving records,[25] which indicate precisely when and how the two departments were separated, serve to throw light on the circle and circumstances in which the Dialogist would have worked—and also on the ambience in which the *Dialogues* first began their rise to fame.

Pope Sergius committed the care of the library and book-production section to a rising official, the future pope Gregory II, who had been one of the seven subdeacons and *sacellarius*, or treasurer, of the Roman Church. He was to have a major place in the history of the *Dialogues* and the spread of Benedictine monasticism. Of patrician family, he was trained from an early age in the papal palace. His appointment to the new post of curator of the *Scrinium/* library suggests that he was already familiar with the work of that department. He was an able theologian, described as "*divinae scripturae eruditus*", whose learning impressed the Emperor Justinian II and his advisers when, now a deacon, he accompanied Pope Constantine to Constantinople in 710, and who later was esteemed for his defence of orthodoxy in the Iconoclastic controversy.[26] In the year 715, on the death of Pope Constantine I, he was elected pope—the first Roman to be bishop of Rome after a succession of seven popes of

---

[24] Duchesne's edition, I, Paris reprint 1955, p. 396.
[25] Cf. De Rossi, *op. cit.*, pp. LXXIX–LXXX.
[26] Cf. H.K. Mann, Lives of the Popes in the Early Middle Ages, I/2, pp. 141–4.

Greek origin. Gregory II was devoted to the memory and example of his great predecessor whose name he took, Pope St Gregory I. He also became the principal patron of the new devotion to the major saint of the supposedly Gregorian *Dialogues*, St Benedict of Montecassino, which he kindled as soon as he became pope. He then set about the building the new abbey of Montecassino, indicated in the *Dialogues* as the place of Benedict's tomb. It was during his pontificate that the saint's biography in that book began to exercise the great influence that would eventually lead to the exaltation of the *Regula Benedicti* as the pre-eminent rule for western monks. Evidently it is very relevant to discuss his part in the unfolding history of the *Dialogues*.

d. *Placing of the "supporting forgery" in the Roman* Scrinium

Since the *Dialogues* were already known in England, Spain and Francia about ten years before Gregory the former *sacellarius* became a chief curator of the Lateran *Scrinium*, one may naturally infer that the book had been known in Rome some considerable time before the date of his appointment. However, there may have been some reservations about it there. The Romans, the literate curial officials in particular, would have been more critically aware of the novelty of that ostensibly Gregorian work than were the eager book-seekers who came to the city from north of the Alps. They knew well the currency of fictitious and pseudonymous *Gesta*, some of them composed in the *Scrinium* itself. The Church of Rome had not yet abandoned its official attitude of reserve to the wave of legendary hagiography and spurious *Gesta* that had flooded in during the two previous centuries. Some officials in the Curia may well have looked askance at the hitherto unknown hagiographical collection bearing Gregory's name. Because of such suspicions the newly emerged book *De miraculis patrum italicorum* would have been slow to gain acceptance in Rome itself, and some time would have to elapse before it gained wider credence there. It seems probable that it was precisely to counter such reservations and suspicions that the Dialogist took great pains to give his fictitious composition impressive verisimilitude; and that it was for the same reason that he concocted and placed in the scrinial register of papal letters the pseudo-Gregorian *Letter to Maximian* as a supporting forgery to accredit the authenticity of the *Dialogues*.

In his critique of *PsGD* P. Meyvaert, while admitting that "the production of one forgery to support another was a procedure well known to mediaeval forgers that has resulted in some splendid compilations", nevertheless ridiculed my conclusion in the case of the *Letter to Maximian*, objecting: "I know of no other mediaeval forger who would have proceeded in so incoherent a fashion, almost making sure that his forgery would never see the light of day".[27] I answer that far from being incoherent, it appears very likely that it was an astute and carefully planned stratagem on the part of the Dialogist to place the forged letter of authentication in the file of Gregory's letters in the *Scrinium* in order to be able to refer doubting colleagues and superiors to that document for reassurance. They would be well acquainted with hagiographical fictions, some of which were invented in the *Scrinium* itself, and they might naturally suspect that the *Dialogues* were a daring addition to the abundant *Gesta* fictions. Some of them, familiar with and even involved in such counterfeits, would doubtless not have been perturbed; it was the others, especially the Dialogist's superiors, whom he would have had chiefly in mind when crafting his supporting forgery. Their doubts would be allayed when it was pointed out to them that one of Gregory's letters in the scrinial archive explicitly proved his authorship of the work, and moreover that several passages written in Gregory's distinctive rhythm were contained in the text of the *Dialogues* itself. More alert than Meyvaert to the parameters of the question was A. de Vogüé, who pertinently objected to my case: "Strangest of all is that the clergy of the Roman Church, and in particular the personnel of the *Scrinium*, should have conceived no suspicion or raised any objection."[28] I reply that it was precisely to disarm such suspicion and objection that the Dialogist would have crafted the *Letter to Maximian* for placement in the curial file of Gregory's letters. Far from it being the case, as Meyvaert objects, that in the circumstances envisaged the author's supporting forgery would be pointless and necessarily unknown, one may reply that it was most astutely and accurately directed, and in the event proved to be the most permanently effective and influential of all such artifices. Truly was that author described, in the seventeenth-century controversy, as "*tam peritus fallendi artifex*".[29]

---

[27] *RHE* 39 (1988), p. 348.
[28] *RHE* 83 (1988), p. 346.
[29] Cf. Chapter 8.a above.

While we are indeed in the field of speculation here, it is by no means uninformed speculation. We have considerable knowledge of the structure and functioning of the *Scrinium* in the Lateran palace in the seventh century. We know too that it was accessible to visiting scholars, like Tajo of Saragossa, and that that they were able to read and transcribe there the *schedae* of the works of Pope Gregory, both published and *inedita*, and likewise the register of his letters. Many cues point to that curial office as the place where the *Dialogues* originated in the later seventh century. It was Pope Gregory II who gave the impulse in the second decade of the eighth century which both launched the *Dialogues* on their trail of fame and at the same time initiated the cult of St Benedict, thereby spurring the breakthrough of his monastic rule from semi-obscurity to widespread observance and eventual pre-eminence. Speculation naturally focuses on that pope, who was the prime agent in those eighth-century developments and who was also the most eminent *scriniarius* of all. What, we may wonder, were the relations between the patrician cleric and former director of the *Scrinium* who eventually became Pope Gregory II, and the *scriniarius* who composed the *Dialogues* bearing the illustrious name of Pope Gregory I? When and how did the future pope become acquainted with that book? When would he first have come across its text, and how could he have come to accept it as authentic? What relevant inferences can be drawn from his later initiative at Montecassino and his vigorous patronage of newly resurgent Benedictine monasticism?

It would seem that there was an age gap between the *Dialogist* and the scrinial dignatory who became supreme pontiff. Gregory II, elected pope in 715, died in 731. Even if he were aged about 60 when elected and lived to 80 years (unusual in that age) it would follow that he was not born until the middle of the seventh century or later. It is reasonable to estimate, from the evidence of the dates at which the *Dialogues* became known in England, Francia and Spain, that their author had composed them around the period of the pontificate of Adeodatus II (AD 672–676), which would indicate his probable date of birth as well before the middle of that century. Those reckonings point to the probability that the Dialogist was considerably older than his superior in the *Scrinium*, the future Gregory II. The latter was a patrician who, like the first Pope Gregory in the sixth century, established a community of monks in his family home in Rome. It is less probable that he would have been on

familiar terms with the Dialogist. At some point the future pope
became acquainted with the text of the recently discovered *Dialogues*,
and came to accept it as a genuine work of St Gregory the Great.
It is quite possible that by the time he became a principal official
of the *Scrinium* that ascription had become widely accepted, even in
Rome. That he himself accepted it as genuine seems evident from
his enthusiastic devotion to St Benedict, whose life was known solely
from that book. It is surely unthinkable that he would have sponsored the building of a great shrine and pilgrimage centre at Montecassino in honour of St Benedict if he suspected that the basis for
such devotion was a fabulous history recently written and falsely
attributed to St Gregory the Great. We may suppose that by the
time he assumed the direction of the new department of the *Scrinium*
in the last decade of the seventh century the Dialogist's "supporting
forgery" was already having its desired effect in reassuring doubters
in that office. We may even speculate (and it is a real possibility)
that it was above all with that eminent curial official and chief *scriniarius* principally in mind that the Dialogist inserted the supposititious
Letter to Maximian into the archive of Gregory's letters; and that it
was his success in assuring the future Pope Gregory II that the
Dialogues were genuinely the work of his great predecessor that eventually established the permanent fame of that book and led to the
spectacular rise of the new Benedictine movement.

CHAPTER TWENTY FIVE

THE PAST AND FUTURE OF A COUNTERFEIT SAGA ETCHED INTO THE HISTORY OF CHRISTENDOM

a

In the course of this study I have repeatedly emphasized that the case presented in these pages rests on the combination of a very large number of arguments, which both singly and collectively serve to demonstrate that Pope St Gregory the Great did not write the *Dialogues* that have been traditionally ascribed to him. Many of those arguments are solidly probative even taken singly. Some indicate probabilities rather than certainties. It is, I submit, the coherence and convergence of all of them together that gives to the total case its massive unity and force, and which thus establishes the conclusion beyond any reasonable doubt. It may even seem to some readers, coming to the question with no *parti pris*, that I have needlessly multiplied my evidences and have presented a superfluity of proofs when even a few of those given here would have sufficed. Nevertheless, because of the age-old tradition and present-day common assumption of Gregory's authorship of the *Dialogues* I have felt it necessary to marshal a very large number of those mutually corroborating arguments to show the conclusive force of the total case.

My internal critique of the text shows decisively that it bears the stamp of an author other than Pope Gregory the Great; while my study of the external historical data shows that the book was unknown in the age of Gregory himself and for a considerable time afterwards, and that it first emerged into the light nearly a century after his lifetime. That is the kernel of the case. Even if it could be shown, from some genuine documentary record, that the book was in existence earlier in the seventh century, the essential substance of the case would not be weakened. In fact, my historical argument is not merely a negative argument from silence. There is positive evidence showing that seventh-century sources which list Gregory's writings and which would surely be expected to mention the Gregorian *Dialogues* if the work existed, do not do so; and that the significant

absence of mention of it in those sources was later remedied by
interpolations in the manuscript tradition. Moreover there is the positive and very significant evidence that, despite the *Life* of St Benedict
in the *Dialogues* allegedly written by St Gregory in 593, cult and liturgical honour of that great saint and monastic founder was unknown
for a century after that date, and began only in the early eighth
century, following the belated emergence of the book into the light
of day.

The humanist and Protestant scholars who challenged the authenticity of the *Dialogues* in the sixteenth and seventeenth centuries were
right in their basic judgement, which was founded on recognition of
the radically non-Gregorian character of the book's language, style
and reasoning, as well as of its religious perspectives. They did not
win the debate at that time because, lacking the fuller historical and
literary resources now available, they could not pursue their demonstration in sufficient depth. In particular, they could not at that time
adequately refute the counter-arguments of the defenders of the book's
authenticity who appealed to the evidence of many documents that
have since been shown to be spurious or misdated. In any case, the
eventual withering away of that earlier controversy was not simply
the consequence of scholarly argumentation but was due to other
and less academic factors.

G. le Bras has pertinently observed: "No century appears more
obscure in the history of Christianity than that which extends from
the death of Gregory the Great to the time of Gregory II".[1] It is in
the latter part of that dark post-Gregorian age that I situate the origin and emergence of the *Dialogues*. My hope is that my work will
provide stepping stones for other researchers to explore further. I
have found in my own long investigation of this question that the
more I have probed, compared and challenged the sources the more
discoveries I have made of the discrepancies between the data of
the *Dialogues* and the actual historical and literary facts. Undoubtedly
there are further discoveries still to be made concerning the Dialogist's
counterfeits, other pieces still to be fitted into this fascinating mosaic.

While not a few eminent scholars and other interested readers
have studied the arguments of *PsGD* and found them conclusive,
other eminent scholars and interested readers continue to assume

---

[1] *"L'Église romaine et les grandes églises occidentales après la mort de Grégoire le Grand"*,
in *Caratteri del secolo VII in Occidente*, Spoleto 1948, p. 184.

that those arguments cannot be valid. Two major obstacles stand in the way of acceptance of the conclusions of that book. The first is the weight of "received scholarly orthodoxy"; the other is the rampart of the age-old loyalties of Benedictine monasticism. I offer reflections on each in turn.

b. *A crumbling rock and a turning tide*

It has been calculated that, since printing began, some 2,800 books about St Gregory have been published, and of those 61% are specifically concerned with the *Dialogues*. In that vast and ever-increasing literature all aspects of that fascinating and problematic book have been minutely investigated, almost always with the common and unquestioned premise that Gregory was its author. In the past, historians and patristic scholars, despite recognizing the strange disparity in language and content between the *Dialogues* and all Gregory's other works, have assumed the certainty of that premise because they supposed that a solid chain of testimonies ascribing the work to him could be traced back to his own age. To show that such a supposition is mistaken is to remove the traditional and uncritical presumption in favour of the book's Gregorian origin and to expose its contents to unclouded and truly critical scrutiny. Then the deep and ever-recurring unease felt by so many readers in the past (and still today) when confronted with that problematic work, which contrasts so incongruously with both the spirit and the letter of Gregory's genuine writings, need no longer be stifled by conformism to received scholarly orthodoxy.

Scholars who have searchingly analysed and criticized the contents of the *Dialogues*, while accepting unquestioningly the traditional ascription of the book to Gregory, have been constrained, almost inevitably, to accept an estimate of his mentality and character that does him serious injustice. They have had to come to terms with the disconcerting nature of the narrative while still seeking to attribute religious value to it. They have had to admit naïve credulity, or—worse—deviousness and deceit, on the part of its illustrious author, while still wishing to praise his greatness of soul and depth of insight. They have thus been led on to attribute to him a religious psychology that is alien not only to the spiritual insight of other contemplative saints and masters of prayer, but to that of St Gregory himself in his pastoral and theological writings. There is no longer need for those uneasy apologias. Once the traditional assumption of the Gregorian authorship of the *Dialogues* has been exposed as mistaken, the real Gregory can be seen as he truly is: not as a spiritual and cultural schizophrenic, not as a strange mixture of greatness and puerility of soul, but as a saintly teacher of transparent integrity, of extraordinary mental acuity and as a master of faith and religious experience, whom all Christians can honour, without the serious reservations and pejorative admissions that so many authors have felt obliged to make.

From the discrediting of the traditional ascription of the *Dialogues* to Gregory many other consequences will be seen to follow. Much fictitious religious history that has been based on that book, concerning saints and holy sites of sixth-century Italy, and the state of the Church and its institutions before and during the pontificate of Gregory I, will have to be discarded. The calendars of saints to which many miracle-working and legendary heroes of the *Dialogues* were admitted in later ages, especially during the sixteenth century, should be critically revised. In the theological sphere, too, there will be needful reassessments. Some developments of the doctrine of purgatory, and their practical implications, will come under renewed criticism—as is already happening.[2] The grossly realistic anecdotes in the *Dialogues* about souls found imprisoned in torrid places of torment, and especially the story of the sinful monk freed from penal fire by a trental of Masses, were supposed to be vouched for by the authority of the great pope and doctor of the Church. Accordingly they had a considerable influence on the manner in which the doctrine of purgatory, and the practice of Mass-suffrages for the souls detained there, were developed in the mediaeval Church. Those developments will require critical reappraisal: for instance, belief in the special efficacy of a numerical series of Masses offered for deceased souls, which was supposed to be vouched for by the authority of St Gregory in the *Dialogues* narrative. Although the Catholic doctrine of purgatory itself does not depend on the *Dialogues*, the way in which it was interpreted in popular piety owed not a little to the circum-

---

[2] Cf. the article of P. McEniery cited in Chapter 7.c above, "Pseudo-Gregory and the doctrine of purgatory", in which he points out the necessary consequences of the conclusions established in *PsGD*.

stantial accounts supposedly related by Gregory in the fourth part of that work.

So too popular notions about demonology which were widespread in later Christendom, not only in the Middle Ages but also after the Reformation, were much influenced by the tales in the *Dialogues* about the devils' malevolent activity even in the small vicissitudes of life. Responsibility for encouraging those and other bizarre notions can no longer be laid at the door of Gregory the Great. His own sober and sombre exposition of scriptural teaching about the powers of evil can no longer be associated with such alien accretions. When tracing the onward march and fascination of the *Dialogues* through the centuries, G. Dufner remarked on the need for a detailed study to bring out more fully the influence exercised by that book on the socio-religious concepts of the mediaeval world. The need is still there, since that influence was undoubtedly great, but it must now be recognized that it was not a Gregorian influence.

A new critique must be made of the pejorative judgement of Adolf Harnack and the other Protestant historians who, assuming his authorship as certain, denounced Pope Gregory the Great as *pater superstitionis* and as "a very little great man", and who saw in that book the chief source of *Vulgärkatholizismus* and of the debasement of mediaeval religious sensibility. The sub-Christian character of much of the *Dialogues* narrative (like that of the other contemporary *Gesta*-literature) should indeed be frankly admitted, as also the widespread influence of that book in later centuries. Those Liberal Protestant critics were right in their assessment of the religious character of the book, but wrong in accepting its attribution to one of the greatest popes and doctors of the Roman Church. Their negative judgement on popular Catholicism as a whole was exaggerated; nevertheless it must be admitted that in so far as the *Dialogues* exercised a baneful influence on Christian piety and sensibility in later centuries, it was largely due to the universal assumption that the book bore the authority of St Gregory the Great. For the author of the *Dialogues*, as Harnack rightly objected, "miracle was the distinguishing mark of religious reality". From the colourful fantasies in that book mediaeval Christians would too often draw a delight in legendary religion and a thirst for tales of strange preternatural phenomena. By the Dialogist's successful pseudepigraphy, the stamp of official approval was thus illegitimately conferred on a semi-superstitious mentality that placed stress on the marvellous and the sensational in religion rather than on the everyday call of the Gospel message to lead the life of Christian virtue in response to God's grace—a message which was indeed the constant theme of Gregory's own teaching.

c. *Changing monastic perspectives*

Also formidable and still widely influential is the second of the two chief obstacles mentioned above as standing in the way of acceptance of the cogent case for the spuriousness of the *Dialogues*: namely the age-old loyalties of Benedictine monasticism. In Chapter 2 I discussed the continuing force of that factor in the centuries-old debate. The second book of the *Dialogues* is the sole documentary source for knowledge about the life, deeds and person of St Benedict, the author of the monastic code that has shaped western Christendom, who is honoured as patron of Europe. Through the centuries, generations of monks have dwelt with filial piety on the details in the life of their great founder related so graphically in that narrative and vouched for by the authority of St Gregory the Great. Countless references to it are to be found in books of monastic devotion and history. To affirm that the venerable *Life* of the founder was a legendary composition of an unknown pseudepigrapher in a later age seems to many whose own lives and vocations are informed by the spiritual wisdom and genius of the Benedictine tradition to be an affront to that hallowed tradition. It is understandable if many of them assume that such a case must be false, and not worth studying attentively. When first presenting that case, in *PsGD*, I remarked that I must expect something of the obloquy that Abbot Benedict Haeften heaped upon the heads of those scholars who challenged the authenticity of the *Dialogues* in the sixteenth and seventeenth centuries, and I foresaw that present-day monastic critics might feel provoked to apply to me what he said of Huldreich Coccius who first presented that challenge: "*Affectata enim, ne dicam maligna, est haec dubitatio*".[3] That expectation has been verified in some quarters.

However, such negative reactions are by no means general among present-day monastic scholars. In Chapter 2 I cited the judgement of several of them who have either been fully convinced by the argu-

---

[3] *S. Benedictus illustratus*, Antwerp 1644, p. 7.

ments of *PsGD* or at least regard its conclusions as probable and worthy of serious attention. Typical of that scholarly objectivity are the comments of Dom Claude Peifer cited there, who serenely applies to this controversy his principle: "It is always a gain for us to discover the truth." Not a few of them have expressed their agreement with the comment on *PsGD* of Henry Wansbrough, Master of St Benet's Hall, Oxford, cited earlier: "For this Benedictine at any rate, its conclusions are liberating". Since 1997 there has been a notable swing in monastic opinion towards open-minded acceptance of the conclusions of that book, especially following the disconcerting retraction by its two chief critics, A. de Vogüé and P. Meyvaert, of their previous emphatic assertion that Gregory was the composer of the commentary *In 1 Regum*, which they had presented as a main buttress of their case for the authenticity of the *Dialogues*. Vogüé's documentary discovery which made that retraction necessary served to confirm that I had been right in ascribing the composition of that text to a mediaeval Benedictine abbot, and served also to confute those who had argued that Gregory knew of St Benedict and his rule because of his supposed authorship of that commentary on *Kings*. His retraction has led some scholars to greet with a sceptical smile the eminent critic's subsequent pronouncement: "Now as previously, there is not the slightest doubt that the *Dialogues* are entirely the work of the holy pope." They recall his very similarly worded affirmation, also pronounced with magisterial assurance: "One may affirm the entire Gregorian authenticity of the commentary *In 1 Regum*".[4]

A sign of the times was the even-handed and warm welcome given by the editors of the *Revue Bénédictine* to an article by myself pointing out the significant relevance of those developments to the controversy over the authenticity of the *Dialogues*. With similar openness the editors of the *American Benedictine Review* welcomed an article from me commenting directly on the widening debate as it related to

---

[4] In the introduction to vol. I of his *Commentaire des Rois*, *SC* 351, p. 48. I must confess here that the scholar whom I would most dearly wish to come to recognize the truth of the case argued in *PsGD* and in this book is Dom Adalbert de Vogüé. Courteously expressing "*une véritable admiration*" for my argumentation, he even avowed: "*Celui-ci est si brillant et si vigoureux qu'on a peine à lui résister*" (*RHE* 83, 1988, p. 346.) He has unflinchingly retracted his previous emphatic certainty about the Gregorian authorship of *In 1 Regum*; I do not despair of his eventual retraction of his equally emphatic certainty about the Gregorian authorship of the *Dialogues*.

monastic piety and tradition, entitled "Saint Benedict's biography and the turning tide of controversy".[5] These and other similar developments can be seen as indications of the changing climate of debate in the circles of monastic scholarship. It is now generally recognized that Christian devotion to St Benedict, and the honour paid to him by the Church, is not dependent either on the veracity or on the authorship of the picturesque biography that has been handed down by tradition. Nor do the monks of the West, whose way of life has been shaped through the centuries by the *Regula Benedicti*, look to the *Dialogues* for spiritual light or guidance. I recall the comment of J.B. More, cited above in Chapter 2, that Benedictine monks of today consider the biography of St Benedict in the *Dialogues* to have "little relevance and no normative value in connection with their calling". Indeed, as Dom C. Peifer pointed out in a passage also cited in that chapter, monastic scholars have been in the forefront of the critical revision of early monastic history that has taken place in recent years.

d. *The future of a gilded legend*

In these pages I have used not a few pejorative terms when referring to the person and work of the fabricator of the *Dialogues*. I have called him pseudepigrapher, dissembler and forger. I have referred to his cunning and deceit, and spoken of his writing as spurious and counterfeit. These terms are objectively applicable, but they do not imply indignant censure of that far-off and anonymous author. After 50 years of familiar acquaintance with his work and wiles, I seem to know him and his foibles very well. Whatever I have to say about his literary forgeries, I do not see him as a sinister impostor. I appreciate the painstaking application with which he conned and culled the writings of St Gregory, for whom he seems to have the admiration that was common in his age. He was, as we have seen, one of the fairly numerous tribe of spinners of legendary *Gesta*; indeed, he may be said to be the most talented and astute of them all. The pseude-

---

[5] *Rev. Bén* 108 (1998) and *ABR* 53.3 (2002). Another sign of the times was an invitation to me from the Monastic Institute of Sant' Anselmo in Rome to give an address on the subject at an international conference on "Classical Texts in the Monastic Tradition" held there in 2002.

pigrapher who placed his own writings under the assumed mantle of a great name, in order to ennoble them and to commend them to posterity, is a well known figure in the literary history of the ancient and early mediaeval world. The Dialogist, Pseudo-Gregory, is in the company of the unknown authors who wrote the earlier Jewish and Christian apocrypha, and of later Christian pseudepigraphers such as Pseudo-Athanasius, Pseudo-Macarius, Pseudo-Ambrose, Pseudo-Jerome, Pseudo-Isidore and Pseudo-Dionysius the Areopagite. His pseudepigraphy, surviving to the present day, has been more successful than theirs. Moreover, he had the considerable advantage of having access to a store of genuine literary remains of the author whose persona he adopted, and was able to weave them into the fabric of his own composition in order to give it exceptional verisimilitude.

In the balance sheet of Christian history we cannot, indeed, fail to take account of the debasement of religious sensibility to which the Dialogist made a major contribution. His success in fathering his book of bizarre miracle-stories on Pope St Gregory did have the undesirable effect of legitimizing the genre of sensationalist legend in mediaeval piety. One may also reflect, more indulgently, that his inventive talent and piquant tales brought entertainment to countless readers and hearers, lettered as well as unlettered. His literary counterfeit had at least two beneficial effects, the second of which has been of major importance for the Church. First, it preserved for posterity not a few gems of genuine Gregorian wisdom then still stored in the Lateran *Scrinium* (the "IGPs") which otherwise would not have survived. The second unintentional but truly great benefit that has come to the Church from the success of his artifice can be stated as follows: in the providential unfolding of Christian history, the emergence of his *Dialogues* in the late seventh century served as the catalyst for the development of the new cult of St Benedict at Montecassino under Pope Gregory II, followed by the meteoric rise of the Benedictine observance in Francia and its eventual hegemony in western monasticism, thus permanently enriching the life and mission of the Church.

I observed in my conclusion to *PsGD* that in a work of such complexity, ranging over a vast field of religious and cultural history in late antiquity and the early Middle Ages, there would inevitably be some errors and omissions which would call for correction. A number of such flaws have been pointed out by critics, none of them substantially affecting my main conclusions. With due appreciation, I have taken account of those criticisms when writing this volume, and have made amendments accordingly. While welcoming any further corrections and clarifications to the present volume that may prove necessary, I urge that they be seen in due proportion. To point out flaws and misapprehensions in points of detail and in particular lines of reasoning will not avail to overthrow the essential conclusions of this book, founded as they are on a multitude of cogent and convergent arguments mutually corroborating one another. I hope that a continuing dust storm of cavils about minor details will not be allowed to obscure the massive solidity and overwhelming force of that case.

Although an increasing number of scholars are satisfied that the evidence I have presented conclusively exposes the *Dialogues* as counterfeit, I fully realize how great is the weight of the traditional assumptions that stand in the way of general acceptance of my findings. I am under no illusions about the wide extent and indignant zeal of those convictions, nor do I foresee their speedy abandonment. I quite expect that what Dom Claude Peifer memorably called "the heavy artillery", which bombarded *The Pseudo-Gregorian Dialogues* when that book first appeared, will again open fire on this present volume. That formidable first salvo, which seemed to many at the time to be decisive, has signally failed to obliterate its target; the zealous artillerymen can hardly hope that a second salvo against a reinforced stronghold will be any more effective in the long run. To change the metaphor, I turn to Galileo, with whom in my own little corner I have some fellow-feeling. A *ben trovato* anecdote relates how, when required by his inquisitorial critics to abandon his Copernican opinion that the earth was a spinning planet orbiting the sun, and to affirm as established certainty that it was the stationary centre of a universe revolving around it, Galileo murmured as he left the tribunal, ". . . *eppur' si muove*"—". . . but all the same, it does move". As I prepare to leave the arena of this long dispute about the origin and nature of the *Dialogues*, I likewise murmur, with all due deference to the reputed authorities who indignantly arraign me and continue to pronounce as certain St Gregory the Great's authorship of the work, my own parting demurral: ". . . *eppur' non è di Gregorio*"—". . . but all the same, he didn't write it".

"*Habent sua fata libelli*". The fortunes of the famous book entitled *The Dialogues of Pope Gregory concerning the Miracles of the Fathers of Italy*, which first emerged from obscure beginnings some thirteen hundred years ago, have through the intervening centuries become interwoven with the history, literature and religious culture of Christendom. What is its further destiny? I look forward to calmer and surer judgement in the future. As a number of scholars have recalled, it took some 40 years of controversy and the publication of many hundred scholarly studies to bring about the final and general acceptance of another seemingly iconoclastic thesis: namely the disconcerting discovery that the *Regula Benedicti* was posterior to and even dependent on the *Regula Magistri*. I would hope that it will not take so long before the falsity of the age-old ascription of the *Dialogues* to St Gregory the Great is generally accepted. I do not expect to live to see that final turn in the *fata* of the famous *libellus*, but I am confident that it will eventually come about.

TABLE OF SIGNIFICANT DATES RELATING TO THE ORIGINS OF THE *DIALOGUES* AND OF BENEDICTINE MONASTICISM

AD

590   Gregory elected pope.

590–604   During his 14-year pontificate Gregory writes more than 200 letters relating to the regulation of monastic observance, but nowhere in them does he make mention of the Benedictine rule, so highly praised in the *Dialogues*; rather he enjoins provisions which are at variance with that rule.

593   <u>Early months</u>: completion of Gregory's Gospel *Homilies*.
<u>July</u>: dating of the suspect *Letter to Maximian*, allegedly indicating the composition of the *Dialogues* in that year.
<u>Autumn</u>: Gregory preaches his *Homilies on Ezekiel*, ended by the Lombard invasion and siege of Rome.

604   Death of Gregory.

      During the following 70 years and more no authentic reference to the existence of the *Dialogues* can be found in any document, nor any reference to the life of St Benedict, nor any cult or pilgrimage to his tomb.

610   (*circa*) The *Liber Pontificalis* lists Gregory's writings but omits mention of the *Dialogues*. (The title is later interpolated in the MSS.)

616–618   In his *De viris illustribus* Isidore lauds Gregory's works but is silent about the *Dialogues*. (The title is later interpolated in the MSS.)

620–630   First (disputed) historical record of the existence and observance of the *Regula Benedicti*, at Albi in SW Gaul.

640–650   (*circa*) Tajo of Saragossa visits Rome to obtain transcripts of Gregory's writings.

650–665   (*circa*) Braulio studies Tajo's findings, and updates Isidore's *De viris illustribus*—but still omits the *Dialogues* from the list of Gregory's writings. (The title is later interpolated in the MSS.)

655–660   (*circa*) Earliest sure evidence of the use of the text of the *RB*, as one element in the tripartite *Regula Donati*. Thereafter increasing use of the *RB* in Francia as a component of monastic rules.

657–667   Ildefonsus of Toledo, in his *De virorum illustrium scriptis*, lists and lauds Gregory's writings but does not include the *Dialogues* among them. (The title is later interpolated in the MSS.)

670   Abbot Hadrian arrives in England from Rome, and there introduces the Neapolitan sanctoral calendar, including saints venerated in Campania—but does not include St Benedict among them.

670–680   (*circa*) Period indicated with probability as that in which the *Dialogues* were composed by a Roman *scriniarius*.

680–695   (*circa*) Period during which the six earliest recorded testimonies to the existence of the *Dialogues* appeared—in England, Spain and Francia. Thereafter references to the work multiply.

695   (*circa*) The future pope Gregory II appointed curator of the Lateran *Scrinium*/library.

700   ("around the turn of the century") Dating of the four earliest surviving MS fragments of the *Dialogues*.

715   Gregory II elected pope, and soon afterwards sends Petronax to restore the abbey of Montecassino and to inaugurate a shrine for St Benedict's body in the place indicated in the newly famous *Dialogues*.

720   (*circa*) First mention of St Benedict's name in a calendar of saints—in an interpolated addition to the Echternach codex. Thenceforward rapid development of veneration of the saint and pilgrimage to his tomb.

720   onwards: Spreading fame of the *Dialogues* and of the new Benedictine movement, inspired by the new "mystique of Montecassino".

730–740   (*circa*) First mention of an "*adventus*" of St Benedict's relics to Fleury.

731–741   Pontificate of Gregory II: completion of the first phase of the establishment of Montecassino.

740   Willibald joins Boniface in Germany, and together they promote Benedictine monasticism in that mission field.

741–752   Pontificate of St Zachary: his translation of the *Dialogues* into Greek; completion of the second phase of the establishment of Montecassino.

743   The "German Council" prescribes the sole observance of the *RB* in the eastern Frankish realm.

745–775   The favour of the rulers leads to the predominance of the Benedictine observance throughout the Frankish realms and beyond, and eventually to its established hegemony in the ninth century.

APPENDIX: ANNOTATED LIST OF THE INSERTED GREGORIAN PASSAGES ("IGPS") WITHIN THE NARRATIVE TEXT OF THE *DIALOGUES*

In Chapter 3 the presence of numerous genuinely Gregorian passages, inserted by the pseudonymous author within the non-Gregorian narrative text of his *Dialogues*, was established, and questions relating to their origin and recognition were discussed. Constituting approximately 24% of the total wordage of the *Dialogues*, those inserted Gregorian passages", or "IGPs", are about 80 in number. Detailed discussion of each of them may be found in Chapters 14–17 of *The Pseudo-Gregorian Dialogues*. In this Appendix they are listed in numbered sequence, with brief annotations on their usage by the Dialogist. This summary is provided for readers who wish to make a deeper study of the composite structure of the book. (For those wishing to consider a few preliminary examples of the intrusive passages, I suggest half a dozen representative instances: e.g. the discussion of IGPs 1, 21, 26, 64, 69 and 71.)

In the list that follows the opening and closing words of each of the fourscore IGPs are cited in each case, with references given to their place in the *Sources Chrétiennes* edition of the *Dialogues*, citing the numbers of the book, chapter and lines of the text as printed there.[1] Where the imported passage is divided into separated sections by the Dialogist, I mark the division by distinguishing letters (e.g. IGP 9a, 9b etc.) Usually the opening words of an IGP are preceded in the same sentence by introductory words of the Dialogist's own composition, which I omit from the quotation of the opening sentence. (I likewise identify words and phrases within the IGPs that are evidently intrusive.) After each locating reference I add a summary description of the subject matter of the IGP in question, and give references to the pages in *PsGD* where it is discussed more fully. Then short comments are made on points of particular note arising

---

[1] I refer to the qualifications made above in Chaper 3.c, concerning (a) the exact demarcation of the beginning and end of some IGPs; and (b) the presence within the narrative text of many discrete phrases of evidently Gregorian provenance in addition to the 80 (81) self-contained pericopes.

from scrutiny of the IGP in its context. Two features can be recognized in the *Dialogues* text which serve to mark the introduction
of an IGP. First, the insertion of the Gregorian passage is prefaced
by a cue question or comment by Peter the Deacon, often lamely
contrived, to make it seem relevant to the context. The Dialogist
often makes *soi-disant* Gregory address an IGP to his interlocutor
personally by inserting the vocative "*Petre*", or by connecting phrases
in the second person singular. Secondly, the conclusion of the IGP
is often signalled by a comment of smug self-congratulation supposedly written by Gregory and put into the mouth of Peter. Those
two features are recurring "markers" to the beginning and end of
the IGPs and thus serve as confirmation of their extraneous character, which is internally evidenced by their unmistakably Gregorian
phrasing and style.

The IGPs in Book I

IGP 1: Book I, Prologue, paragraphs 3–6; from line 14, ". . . *moerorem
[Petre] quem cotidie patior . . .*" to line 53, ". . . *laboribus noluit occupari*".
Gregory laments his lost contemplative peace. For fuller commen-
tary, cf. *PsGD* pp. 441–3. Points of note are the following:—

- Here at the beginning of the *Dialogues* is the first use of the intrusive and tell-tale vocative "*Petre*" to introduce a genuine Gregorian
  pericope.
- In Peter's introductory query, asking whether something new has
  happened to make Gregory sadder than usual and using the words
  "*novi aliquid*" and "*moeror*", is a clumsy cue to link with the Gregorian
  lament that follows, which includes the words "*moerorem*" and "*novus*"
  in the first sentence.
- There are several parallels to IGP 1 in Gregory's genuine writings: some of the phrases used are verbatim echoes of the wording of three letters written by him in October 590, just after his
  reluctant acceptance of the burden of the papacy. The borrowed
  pericope may well have been originally in such a letter.
- The abrupt change from the elevated spiritual reflections cited in
  IGP 1 to the immediately following editorial rubric (in lines 44–6),
  giving the Dialogist's plan for writing his dialogue, marks the resumption of his narrative.

IGP 2: Book I, Prologue, para. 9. From line 70, *"in expositione quippe..."* to line 79, *"... cognoverit, humiliatur"*. The word *"signorum"* in line 79 is an evident substitution for *"exemplorum"* (cf. Chapter 7.d above, note 27). On the "examples of the Fathers" and their spiritual value, see the fuller commentary in *PsGD*, pp. 443–7. Points to note in IGP 2 are:—

• It is a rare instance of a substantial paragraph of Gregorian prose put into the mouth not of Gregory himself but into that of Peter the Deacon.
• The Dialogist's introductory cue in lines 67–70, and his use and understanding of the expression *"exempla patrum"*, contradict the teaching of the real Gregory. (See Chapter 7.d above.)

IGP 3: Book I, Chap. 1, para. 6–7. From line 43, *"... lege non stringitur..."* to line 65 *"... veneranda sunt, non imitanda."* On the Holy Spirit as inward master. Cf. *PsGD*, pp. 447–8. Main points:—

• Awkwardness of Peter's introductory cue: after relating the sensational deeds of the miracle-working Honoratus, the interlocutor asks abruptly whether the holy man previously had a master. This is used as a peg on which to hang the insertion of the Gregorian reflections in IGP 3 about the inward master, the Holy Spirit. (The cue word in Peter's question is *magister*, referring proleptically to its repeated use in the coming IGP.)
• There is close parallelism between IGP 3 and another Gregorian passage in *In 1 Regum* IV.183. The two texts may be alternative forms of *reportata* of the same discourse.
• Note self-congratulatory concluding comment by *soi-disant* Gregory in line 66.

IGP 4: I.2.7. From line 76, *"Heliseus [quoque] magistri pallium..."* to line 85, *"... et ipse fecit"*. On the humility of Elisha, which rendered him worthy to wield power like that of this master Elijah. Cf. *PsGD*, pp. 449–50. *Notanda*:—

• There is crass incongruity in the Dialogist's use of Gregory's exposition of *2 Kings* 2.13–14 to illustrate his own account of the miracle worked by Libertinus, who restored to life a dead boy by placing on his breast the shoe of his master Honoratus.
• Likewise incongruous is the author's adducing of a supposedly Gregorian comment on the miracle of Elisha as if relevant to his

own assertion that when Libertinus placed his master's shoe on the boy's corpse "he counted on the soul of Honoratus to obtain what he prayed for".

- Key cue words pointing forward to their usage in the IGP are "*de magistri . . . virtute*". Note intrusive "*Petre*" in line 81 and self-congratulatory concluding comment by *soi-disant* Gregory in line 86.

IGP 5: I.4.9. From line 103, "*Opus [Petre] ex dono est . . .*" to line 106, "*. . . dona succrescunt*". On grace prevenient to works. Cf. *PsGD*, pp. 450–1.

- The Pauline/Augustinian axiom enunciated by Gregory in the sentence cited is here brought in ineptly.
- Cue words "*opus*" and "*dona*" are inconsequentially introduced in lines 101–2 to link with their coming use (each thrice) in the Gregorian statement of the axiom.

IGP 6: I.4.18. From line 210, "*. . . in quanta Dei . . .*" to line 218, "*. . . est ante Deum*". On the contrast between the heavenly honour of the humble and the outward vainglory of the proud. Cf. *PsGD*, pp. 451–2.

- This IGP is a doublet of a passage in Gregory's *Homilies on the Gospels*, 28.2–4, and may have been taken from a variant *scheda* in the scrinial file.
- At first sight the Gregorian pericope seems to be an apt comment on the preceding tale of the humiliation of Equitius, but placed as a comment on the *denouement* of that tale it is inept.

IGP 7: 1.4.19. From line 221, "*Quid miraris . . .*" to line 233, "*. . . in multis occupatur*". On the proneness of the human mind to be deceived, and how a busy prelate may easily be imposed upon. Comment in *PsGD*, pp. 452–3.

- Peter's introductory cue "*subripi*" in line 219 foreshadows Gregory's theological reflection (inconsequential here) on our proneness to "subreption" in the turmoil of our daily duties.
- Very similar to IGP 7 in content and expression is the discrete passage of evidently Gregorian reflection inserted earlier in the chapter (I.4.19, lines 134–6): "*. . . moris est . . . citius repulsa*". That snippet probably came from the same original source as IGP 7.
- Gregory draws the same moral that is drawn here from *2 Samuel* 16.1–4, with verbatim parallels, in *In 1 Regum* 4.3.

- "*Petre*" in line 221 is intrusive; "*miraris*" in the same line is a substitute for "*mirum*", used to personalize the citation.
- Note the instance of the constantly recurring self-congratulatory comments by *soi-disant* Gregory's at the conclusion of the IGP, in line 234.

IGP 8: I.5.6. From line 56, "*Qualis enim quisque . . .*" to line 62, ". . . *semetipsos habuerunt*". The truly humble rejoice at being despised. Cf. *PsGD*, p. 453.

- In this instance, there is no introductory cue from Peter; the words "*humilitatis*" and "*despicientem*" in lines 55–6 provide pointers to the short excerpt to follow, linking with "*humiles*" and "*despectione*" in lines 58–9. Peter adds his connecting comment after the IGP, in lines 63–4.
- Similarity of subject matter suggests that, in the store of Gregorian *schedae* in the Lateran *Scrinium*, IGP 8 belonged to the same original context as IGP 6.

IGP 9: I.8.5–6. IGP 9a is from line 39, ". . . *ea quae sancti viri . . .*" to line 45, ". . . *disposuit donare*"; IGP 9b is from line 49, "*Certe etenim [nosti] quia ad Abraham . . .*" to line 63, ". . . *filius habere potuisset*". On the place of men's prayers in God's predestinatory decrees, illustrated from the history of Isaac and Rebecca. Cf. *PsGD*, pp. 450–1.

- IGP 9 is one of the most revealing in the whole series of borrowed Gregorian pericopes in the *Dialogues*. It is a profound yet limpid theological explanation of the place of human prayers in the working out of God's predestinatory plan. Gregory explains that divine predestination does not mean that human prayers are otiose; but that the prayers of the just have a true efficacy because they are the foreordained means by which God's immutable decrees of predestination are fulfilled. (St Augustine had given a similar explanation in *De Civitate Dei* 5.10.) Gregory's measured cadences, his theological insight and his scriptural illustration of the doctrine by reference to the *Genesis* history of Isaac and Rebecca, present a striking contrast between this pericope and the Dialogist's surrounding text, which reflects his homelier style and his lower level of theological perception. The application that the Dialogist makes of the Gregorian passage, in the context of his tale about the supernumerary monk added to the list of the elect by a heavenly voice calling from a crag, is naïve and theologically unsound. (Cf. comments above in Chapter 7.h.)

- In this instance the Dialogist provides two prefatory cues to introduce the two sections of the divided pericope. The first (in lines 37–8) he puts into Peter's mouth, and the second (in lines 48–9) into Gregory's.

- IGP 9 is found in the Gregorian anthologies of both Paterius and Tajo. (References in *PsGD*, p. 454). Both those compilers begin the pericope with the words "*Ea quae sancti viri orando efficiunt . . .*". The Dialogist, on the other hand, who doubtless took it from the same *schedae* in the Lateran archives that they used, prefixed to it some additional words to link with the leading cue that he put into Peter's mouth.

- When reproducing the original text neither Paterius nor Tajo separates IGP 9a from IGP 9b, as the Dialogist does with his second intrusive cue by Peter in lines 48–9. Moreover both of them cite the first three words of IGP 9b as "*Certe etenim novimus . . .*"; but he changes "*novimus*" to "*nosti*" to conform to his dialogistic adaptation of the passage. This is one of the many recurring indications that his work postdated theirs.

- When Peter asks, at the beginning of IGP 9b, "I should like to know whether predestination can be helped by prayers", the Gregory of the *Dialogues* answers at once with un-Gregorian self-assertion: "What I have set forth can be quickly proved". IGP 9b then follows. After it the author, allegedly Gregory, smugly makes Peter exclaim: "Since your reasoning has laid bare the hidden truth, no trace of doubt remains in my mind" (lines 64–5).

- In Chapter 21.b I pointed out that IGP 9, as cited in the anthology of Paterius, immediately follows another expository passage on the same theme from the same scriptural context. This is another confirmation that the Dialogist's presentation of the argument, interrupted in *Dial.* I.8.5–6, is of later date.

IGP 10: I.9.6–7. From line 59, ". . . *redemptor noster*" to line 79, ". . . *exemplum dedit*". Lines 55–7 also seem to be authentic. Resolution of a theological query arising from *Matthew* 9.27–31. Cf. *PsGD*, pp. 456–7.

- IGP 10 is a notable example of a Gregorian doublet: a closely parallel passage is in *Moralia* 19.36.

- It is unusual in that the first five lines of the IGP are put into the mouth not of Gregory but of Peter, following straight on from his introductory question: "Because an apt occasion presents itself, I ask what it means to say..." The Dialogist had evidently put in lines 50–4 to provide such an opportunity, but did not find a way to insert his Gregorian gem more appositely.

- Note the customary expression of appreciation for the IGP put into Peter's mouth in line 80.

IGP 11: I.9.9. From line 106, "...*pensandum est*" to line 112, "...*invalidus non est*". To provoke the wrath of one in whom God dwells is to provoke the wrath of God. Cf. *PsGD*, p. 458.

- In its original context IGP 11 was evidently a comment on one of the scriptural texts concerning the righteous anger of the prophets as reflection of the wrath of God. Just such a text is *I Samuel* 11.6: "And the spirit of the Lord came upon Saul...and his anger was exceedingly kindled". In his commentary on that text in *In 1 Regum* 5.13 (*CCL* 144, p. 424), Gregory teaches the same lesson as in IGP 11 in very similar terms. It may well be that it was his possession of this short Gregorian excerpt that prompted the Dialogist to compose the dramatic though disagreeable tale that precedes it in his text, about the strolling minstrel who unwittingly offended the venerable Bishop Boniface of Ferentis and was punished by death from a fall of masonry.
- As so often, there is the tell-tale "*Petre*" immediately before the beginning of the IGP. I do not point them all out in the remaining 78 IGPs.

IGP 12: I.9.19. Lines 215–7, "*Hoc [Petre] ex magna...maiora debeamus.*" An axiom concerning the divine pedagogy. Cf. *PsGD*, pp. 458–9.

- Brief though it is, IGP repays attentive study. The same pedagogy of the divine *dispensatio*, which leads on from smaller graces to greater, is explained more fully by Gregory in his Gospel *Homilies*, 32.4. He explains that Christ first promised to his novice disciples that they would see God's visible kingdom on earth as an earnest of eventually seeing his invisible kingdom in heaven. The Dialogist's perspectives are on a different plane. He goes straight on to make the Gregorian axiom apply to the hopes of a "holy and simple boy" who lamented to the Lord that a fox had just snatched one of his mother's hens that he was hoping to eat, whereupon the fox at once returned to restore its prey, and then dropped dead.

IGP 13: I.10.7. IGP 13a is from line 75, "*Multa [Petre] videntur...*"
to line 80, "*...rectum esse videatur*"; IGP 13b is from line 84 "*Sunt
namque nonnulli...*" to line 87 "*...qua ceteros premunt.*" On perverse
intention which vitiates actions even if they appear to be good. Cf.
PsGD, pp. 459–60.

- In its original setting IGP 13 was evidently one continuous paragraph, phrased in Gregory's usual objective style, stating general
  moral principles. The gloss that the Dialogist has interposed (in
  lines 80–4 between the two separated parts of the pericope) is
  clearly different from the Gregorian pericope in language, style
  and level of thought, as also is the comment that he adds at the
  end of the excerpt.
- The passage is a typical statement of Gregory's teaching on the
  decisive influence of antecedent intention on the moral quality of
  an act. There are at least three other passages in Gregory's authentic works which give similar teaching, with similar phraseology.
- The Dialogist bizarrely distorts Gregory's spiritual message by making it a comment on his tale about a disguised demon who threw
  to his death in a fire the infant son of a householder, who had
  made an apparently charitable act with a faulty intention, and was
  thus justly punished by that dreadful event.

IGP 14: I.10.19. From line 222, "*post mortem melius...*" to line 228,
"*...ossa sua perseverat*". On miracles at a saint's tomb, testifying to
his better life in union with God.

- Cf. *PsGD*, pp. 461–3, where I give reasons for concluding that,
  despite appearances to the contrary, these lines were borrowed by
  the Dialogist from a genuinely Gregorian source. Discounting the
  preceding clauses, IGP 14 has a fairly close resemblance to similar eulogies pronounced by Pope Gregory at the tombs of Roman
  martyrs and included in his Gospel *Homilies*. Its use here is incongruous.

IGP 15: I.12.4–5. IGP 15a is from line 46, "*Vitae namque...*" to
line 49, "*...dispares non sunt*"; IGP 13b is from line 53, "*Paulus apos-
tolus...*" to line 63, "*...non est in coelo*". (Intrusive are the interjec-
tions "*nescis quoniam*", "*Scio plane*" and "*Quod ipse bene reminisceris*" in
lines 53, 56 & 58.) Performance of miraculous signs is not the cri-
terion of virtue and heavenly merit. (Cf. *PsGD*, pp. 463–5.)

- The Dialogist has found and reproduced in IGP 15 a pericope which is similar in phrasing and teaching to several other passages in Gregory's genuine works, yet which contradicts the basic suppositions of his own enterprise of legendary invention. His futile attempt to deny the contradiction is discussed above in Chapter 7.d.

The IGPs in Book II

IGP 16: II.2.3–4. IGP 16a from line 27, "*Unde et per Moysen . . .*" to line 30 ". . . *custodes vasorum fiant*"; IGP 16b is from line 34 "*Liquet [Petre] quod in iuuentute . . .*" to line 41, ". . . *doctores animarum fiunt*".[2] Exposition of *Numbers* 8.24–6, concerning quinquagenarian Levites. Cf. *PsGD*, pp. 666–9.

- Both IGP 16 and the related extract in the collection of Paterius (on *Numbers* 8.24–6.) can be seen to be closely related to the received text of *Moralia* 23.12. The intricate question of the dependence both of Paterius and *Dialogues* on a fuller text of the *Moralia* is discussed in *PsGD*, pp. 466–8. It appears that they both used a somewhat longer text of the *Moralia* surviving in the archives of the *Scrinium*, and that the Dialogist's shorter text betrays its later origin.
- The Dialogist's use of the passage of Gregorian exposition of the *Numbers* text is in any case inapposite here. He applies the typology of that text to St Benedict, whom he likens to the quinquagenarian Levites who had passed beyond the temptations of the flesh. But since Benedict's victory over carnal temptation was at an earlier age, near the beginning of his monastic life, the typology is incongruous.
- Peter is made to interject after IGP 16a a request for fuller explanation. This duly follows in IGP 17b and is significantly marked with an intrusive "*Petre*" to personalize the quotation.

IGP 17: II.3.5–9. IGP 16a is from line 48, "*Nam quotiens . . .*" to line 59, ". . . *ad se rediit?*"; IGP 17b is from line 64, ". . . *de Petro apostolo . . .*"

---

[2] I now recognize that IGP 16b begins 3 lines earlier than marked in *PsGD*.

to line 78, "... *prius fuit*". Explanation, with scriptural illustrations, of what was meant by the saying that Benedict "lived to himself" ("*habitavit secum*"). Cf. fuller discussion in *PsGD*, pp. 670–4.

• The incongruity of IGP 17 in the Dialogist's context is discussed at length in *PsGD* (pp. 47–4). The whole sequence that follows Peter the Deacon's initial request for elucidation of the meaning of "*habitavit secum*" has a puzzling quality. The Dialogist attempts by glosses to make Gregory's reflections on Luke 15.17 and Acts 12.11 seem relevant to Peter's initial request in lines 40–1 of *Dial.* II.3, but without success.

IGP 18: II.3.10–11. IGP 18a is from line 85, "... *ibi adunati* ..." to line 90, "... *ferre meliorem*"; after the intrusive sentence in lines 90–92, IGP 18b is from line 93, "*Et saepe agitur* ..." to line 107, "... *campum quaesivit*". How the apostolic labourer, finding that he is labouring fruitlessly, may move to another field of greater spiritual fruit. Cf. *PsGD*, pp. 474–5.

• The magisterial self-assertiveness of the phrase which introduces IGP 18, taking up the cue given to Peter the Deacon in lines 83–4, is typical of the Gregory of the *Dialogues* but not of the real Gregory: "*Ut ego, Petre, existimo* ..."
• A passage which IGP 18 closely resembles with (some verbatim agreement) is in *Moralia* 31.58–9. In that longer passage Gregory adds warnings about the danger of grave fault if we desert our field of apostolic labour for another when the balance of spiritual advantage does not warrant it. It may well be that in his careful revision of the *Moralia* text Gregory replaced IGP 18 with a fuller exposition because, lacking the additional pastoral warnings contained in the latter passage, it could have been taken amiss by some prelates. His letters show his constant concern about churchmen tempted to abandon vexatious responsibilities.

IGP 19: II.8.9. IGP 19a is from line 75, "... *unius spiritum [habuit] qui* ..." to line 79, "... *omnes accepimus*"; IGP 19b is from line 79, "... *sancti Dei homines* ..."[3] to line 87, "... *gloriam potestatis*". There are two themes: the first, the one spirit of Christ in the hearts of the elect; the second, the difference between the signs shown by

---

[3] I now place the beginning of IGP 19b 2 lines earlier than in *PsGD*.

Christ to his proud enemies and to his humble followers. Cf. *PsGD*, pp. 475–7.

- It appears that the Dialogist has conflated IGP 19 out of two unrelated Gregorian fragments. IGP 19b, though following directly on from IGP 19a, is from a different context. The introductory cue given to Peter the Deacon in lines 68–73 has verbal links with IGP 19a only. (When he remarks of Benedict, "*spiritu iustorum omnium plenus fuit*", the word *spiritu* links with *spiritum* in line 77 of IGP 18a, *iustorum omnium* links with *electorum omnium* in line 76, and *plenus* links with both *implevit* in line 76 and *plenitudine* in line 78.) IGP 19a may have been taken from an expository comment by Gregory on the expression "*unus spiritus*" which occurs in several Pauline texts (e.g. *I Corinthians* 6.17, 13.9 & 13.13; *Ephesians* 2.18, 4.4; *Philippians* 1.27; cf. comment on IGP 21 below). In IGP 19b the real Gregory is not speaking of indwelling Spirit in the just but of Christ's witness of his mission, which was diversely received by the humble and by the proud. The Dialogist has managed to make IGP 19a seem relevant to Peter's cue, but not 19b, which is inconsequentially appended.

IGP 20: II.15.3. From line 25, "*Cuius prophetiae mysteria . . .*" to line 29, "*. . . prosternantur videmus*". How in the decay of the city of Rome a scriptural prophecy is mystically fulfilled. Cf. *PsGD*, pp. 477–9. Cf. *PsGD*, pp. 477–9.

- In Chapter 7.h above, I pointed to the original source of both IGPs 20 and 22, namely Gregory's expository interpretation in his *Homiliae in Ezechielem* (II.6.22–3) of two biblical prophecies as mystically portending the ruin of the city of Rome. One of those biblical prophecies related to the coming destruction of Nineveh, foretold in *Nahum* 2.11; the other related to the coming destruction of Jerusalem,[4] foretold in *Ezekiel* 1–14. I also pointed out in that earlier chapter that the phrase "*prophetiae spiritus*" is used by the Dialogist when presenting both those IGPs, in both of which "the spirit of prophecy" is attributed to St Benedict; but it is never applied by the real Gregory to any but scriptural prophets.
- The aptness of IGP 20 to the use the Dialogist makes of it strongly suggests that he composed his story of the colloquy between Benedict

---

[4] The text of the *Homilies* has "Samaria".

and Sabinus of Canosa, in which Benedict corrects the mistaken prediction of Sabinus and utters his own spirit-inspired prophecy of the eventual decay and ruin of Rome, precisely in order to find a niche for the genuine fragment of Gregorian exegesis that lay ready to his hand in the Lateran *Scrinium*.

IGP 21: II.16.3–4. From line 27, "*Quid adhaeret Domino . . .*" to line 79, "*. . . occultata non possunt*" ("*tibi*" in line 56 is intrusive.) To what extent do the Apostles and saints know the mind of God? Cf. *PsGD*, pp. 479–81.

- One of the longest IGPs in the first three books of the *Dialogues* (52 lines), this passage has the unmistakable pattern of Gregory's heuristic exegesis, whereby he considers apparent contradictions arising from contrasted texts of Scripture, in order to resolve them in a doctrinal synthesis. He meditates on the Pauline question (in *Romans* 11.34): "Who has known the mind of the Lord and who has been his counsellor?"
- There is only a tenuous connection between IGP 21 and the preceding narrative to which it is appended as a supposedly relevant sequel. The Dialogist has just told the tale of a cleric possessed by a demon, who had sought in vain for deliverance at numerous shrines of martyrs before he was exorcized at last by St Benedict. The saint warned him never to receive sacred orders, under pain of being repossessed by the evil spirit. When, years later, he disregarded Benedict's warning and obtained ordination, he was straightway seized by the devil and shaken to death. Thereupon Peter the Deacon provides the strained cue for the introduction of IGP 21 by remarking that to be able to predict that eventuality Benedict must have "penetrated even the secrets of the Deity". The Gregory of the *Dialogues* replies, "Why would he not know the secrets of the Deity, since he observed the commandments of the Deity?"; the genuine Gregorian passage, expounding scriptural texts concerning union with God and knowledge of his mind, is placed immediately after that remark.
- Thus IGP 21, which was evidently composed for a very different context, is here a long digression merely juxtaposed to the Dialogist's narrative.
- He divides into sections this long Gregorian pericope by putting ten lines of it into the mouth of Peter the Deacon. However, the searching reflections made in those ten lines are quite out of character for the obtuse Peter of the *Dialogues*.

IGP 22: From line 21, "*Prophetiae spiritus . . .*" to line 37, ". . . *sint de semetipsis*". ("*Petre*" in line 21 is intrusive.) God sometimes withdraws his spirit of prophecy from the minds of the prophets. Cf. *PsGD*, pp. 481–2.

- This pericope is a doublet of what Gregory says elsewhere: indeed it is a "triplet", since the same theme and the same explanation is found in *Moralia* 2.89 and in *Homilies on Ezekiel* I.1.15–6. The two biblical illustrations used in IGP 22 (namely, the nescience of the prophets Nathan and Elisha) are both included in the fuller series of example given in those other two texts.
- The similarity of subject matter of IGP 22 with that of IGP 21 suggests that their original provenance was from the same source.
- Despite his earlier affirmation that "It was patently clear to everyone that nothing could remain hidden from the venerable Benedict", the Dialogist now makes Peter the Deacon introduce IGP 22 by asking whether Benedict possessed the prophetic spirit at all times or only intermittently. His reason for contriving this question is that the IGP about to be cited is about the intermittent ignorance of the prophets. Since Gregory gives in it only a general conclusion on the divine reasons for withdrawal of prophetic powers from the scriptural prophets, Peter's question about Benedict receives no answer.
- As so often, the Dialogist picks out a phrase from the borrowed pericope to use as a preliminary cue question to be spoken by the interlocutor. He chooses the opening two words of IGP 22, "*Prophetiae spiritus [Petre] . . .*", and makes Peter echo them it twice in his leading question (in lines 18–20). As when commenting on IGP 20, I recall again that the real Gregory never applies the title of "*propheta*" to a post-biblical saint. His illustrations of prophecy are always drawn from the pages of holy writ; even "false prophets" are only mentioned in contrast to the true prophets of God whose words and deeds are recorded in that sacred history.

Supernumerary IGP (= "IGP 22 *bis*"): In addition to the 80 IGPs listed in *PsGD*, I now add a further passage which also has the hallmark of Gregorian authenticity.[5] It is in II.22.4, line 38, "*Liquet*

---

[5] R. Godding drew my attention to it, in *AB* 106 (1988), p. 222, note 44. I pass over his surmise that I purposely omitted discussion of it! His percipient discernment of it is an implicit recognition of the *sui generis* character of the IGPs, despite the protests to the contrary made by him and his fellow-critics.

profecto . . ." to lines 42–3, "*. . . iterum invenit*". This biblical example, used to illustrate the independence of spirit from material confinement, is typically Gregorian. As in so many other cases, the pericope has the usual "markers": namely, an introductory cue by Peter the Deacon and a concluding exclamation of his admiration for his master's wisdom. The preceding story of Benedict's levitational visits to the abbot and prior of Terracina seems to have been contrived by the Dialogist to provide an opening for this Gregorian excerpt.

IGP 23: II.23.6. From line 52, "*Numquidquam . . .*" to line 61, "*. . . est firmitas Dei*". ("*Petre*" in line 52 is intrusive.) On the awesome authority that is given to men on earth to pass judgements valid even in heaven. Cf. *PsGD*, pp. 482–5.

- The Dialogist crassly misapplies this jewel of Gregorian theology concerning the sublime power given to Peter and the Apostles, and to their successors, to share in Christ's power to pass judgement valid both on earth and in heaven. He makes it apply to his tale of the two bad-tempered nuns whom Benedict threatened to excommunicate if they did not curb their mordant tongues but who died without doing so. When during Mass non-communicants were dismissed, their spectres were seen to rise from their tombs and depart. Hearing of this, Benedict relented and lifted their excommunication; the spectres were thereafter at peace and "received communion from the Lord". As I observed when discussing the story in Chapter 7.c, Pope Gregory would certainly not have given any credit to such a bizarre and theologically aberrant yarn.
- By implication, *soi-disant* Gregory accords to the unordained abbot Benedict a share in the apostolic power of "governing the Church in matters of faith and morals" (lines 56–7). The real Gregory declared that "In the Church the place of the Apostles is now held by the bishops. In it the power of binding and loosing is acquired by those who possess that ruling power" (*Homilies on the Gospels* 26.5).

IGP 24: II.30.2–3. From line 18, "*Qui devota mente . . .*" to line 32, "*. . . illi reddidit orando*". On two modes of miracle working: one by prayer, the other by direct power. Cf. *PsGD*, pp. 485–6.

- The distinction that Gregory makes in this pericope between the two modes of miracles, one "*ex potestate*", the other "*ex prece*" (cf. lines 20–1 & 30–1), provides the Dialogist with the motif for three successive tales of miracles procured by Benedict. The first, telling of a miracle "*ex potestate*", precedes IGP 24 and serves as occasion for inserting it; the other two are narrated in the immediately following chapter (II.31). One of them is also "*ex potestate*" (worked by a glance, which instantly untied a captive's bonds), the other "*ex oratione*" (when by a prayer Benedict instantly raised a dead boy to life). The Dialogist repeatedly alludes here to this distinction and to its application in his tales.

- The leading question of Peter the Deacon which is the cue for introducing IGP 24 is ineptly placed. He has just heard his master recount a miraculous exorcism of an old monk solely by an act of Benedict's own will ("*solummodo*", in II.20, line 12—which links proleptically with the real Gregory's "*solummodo*" in IGP 24, line 29). Nevertheless Peter goes straight on to ask whether Benedict "always impetrated such great miracles by the power of his prayer, or did he sometimes produce them by the sole act of his will"— regardless of the fact that he has just heard his master relate such a miracle.

IGP 25: II.3.31. From line 1, "*Quisnam erit . . .*" to line 3, "*. . . non valuit?*" Even St Paul did not obtain all that he asked of God in prayer. Cf. *PsGD*, pp. 486–9.

- IGP 25 parallels two passages in Gregory's published works concerning St Paul's unanswered prayer: *Moralia* 19.11–2 and *Homiliae in Evangelia* 27.6.
- The cue preceding IGP 25 is Peter's question in the preceding sentence, asking whether holy men are able to obtain by prayer all that they wish. The single Gregorian sentence which follows as response to that naïve question has been excerpted by the Dialogist to use it as a prelude to one of the most substantial and pleasing stories in his book, which follows immediately—namely, the story of how Scholastica succeeded by her prayers in constraining her brother Benedict to remain in her abode against his will to spend a night in spiritual colloquy. In narrating that episode he expressly refers back (in II.33, lines 5–6) to the wording of IGP 25. In *PsGD*, pp. 488–9, I point out incongruities in his use of the Gregorian pericope in that narration.

IGP 26: II.35.6. From line 51, "*. . . animae videnti creatorum . . .*" to line 59, "*. . . humiliata non poterat*". (There are also clear echoes of Gregorian phrases in para. 2 lines 19 to 27 and para. 3, lines 24–7.)

On the mystical vision of divine light, in which the soul is taken up into the greatness of God and realizes the littleness of all else. Cf. *PsGD*, pp. 489–92.

- IGP 26, rightly famous as a gem of Gregory's mystical theology, has been inserted by the Dialogist into his celebrated account of the "cosmic vision of St Benedict". There are several tell-tale features that mark it out as extraneous to the narrative, which I discuss at considerable length in *PsGD*, pp. 490–4. There I also discuss some other phrases and allusions in *Dial.* II.35 that closely resemble passages in Gregory's genuine writings, especially in *Homiliae in Evangelia* 34.18.
- The insertion of IGP 26 is prepared for by phrases in II.35.2 & 3, and by an explicit cue from Peter in lines 45–9. After its citation, there follow two paragraphs serving to make it appear relevant to the preceding story of Benedict's vision of the soul of Bishop Germanus of Capua being carried up to heaven in a ball of fire while a dazzling light lit up the whole world.
- The Dialogist's account of the sensational events following Benedict's ecstatic experience, describing how the saint shouted loudly and repeatedly for Servandus to come and see the miraculous spectacle, is in a fantasy world very different from the vision of the real Gregory, as evidenced by his reflections on the state of the contemplative soul returning to itself after mystical rapture.[6]
- As so often after an IGP, Peter the Deacon comments admiringly on its distinctiveness and on his master's sagacity: "I see that it was beneficial that I did not understand what you were saying, seeing that from my incomprehension followed so excellent an explanation. But now that you have so clearly poured these truths into my mind, please return to the order of the narrative" (lines 74–5).

IGP 27: II.38.4. From line 29, "*Unde ipsa quoque...*" to line 39, "*...discitis spiritualiter amare*". Solution of an apparent theological difficulty concerning the eternal procession of the Holy Spirit. Cf. *PsGD*, pp. 494–5.

---

[6] On the desolation of the *anima reverberata* returning from mystical contemplation, according to the authentic teaching of St Gregory, cf. R. Gillet, *SC* 32b, pp. 50–4.

This passage has been discussed in full detail in Chapter 3.d above, as a prime and representative example of all the IGPs in the *Dialogues*. I refer to that discussion for demonstration of its manifest incongruity in this context.

The IGPs in Book III

There are only two short IGPs in the first 13 chapters of Book III, after which several long Gregorian passages are introduced into the Dialogist's narrative.

IGP 28: III.7.1. From line 5, "...*qui corpus suum*..." to line 8, "...*formae famulatur*". A disciplinary warning to those committed to celibacy. Cf. *PsGD*, p. 496.

- This fragment has the authentic stamp of a disciplinary admonition delivered by Gregory to enforce clerical chastity. In his letters of pastoral instruction there are several parallels (e.g. Epist. IX.110; EH II, pp. 115–6.) It may have been excised from a filed draft of such a letter.
- IGP 28 is inserted as a preface to the tale of the risky slap given by Bishop Andrew of Fondi to a consecrated handmaid, and his subsequent correction by a Jew who had overheard a report of the bishop's fault related in a demonic conclave. Although *soi-disant* Gregory claims to have heard the story from countless witnesses from Fondi itself, it is manifestly modelled on earlier forms of the same racy story in Cassian and the *Vitae Patrum*.[7]
- The admonitory tone of IGP 28 makes it somewhat difficult to introduce into the Dialogist's text. He solves this difficulty by disregarding in this instance his chosen literary convention by which Gregory's remarks are addressed to Peter the Deacon in a dialogue, and addressing them to his "readers"—whom he envisages as dedicated to celibate continence. (This is a revealing indication of his "target audience".)

IGP 29: III.7.10. From line 88, "...*oportet et de Dei*..." to line 92, "...*stabilitate fiducia*". Diffidence in our weakness and trust in God's mercy must go together. Cf. *PsGD*, pp. 496–7.

---

[7] Cf. Vogüé, *SC* 251, pp. 129–30, 132–4 & *SC* 260, pp. 283–5.

- As IGP 28 provided a hortatory exordium for the chapter on Bishop Andrew's temptation, so IGP 29, unmistakably Gregorian in its style, provides a suitable hortatory conclusion to it. Peter's introductory cue (in lines 86–7), reflecting also on the previous tale, links with the "fear and hope" that are enjoined in the coming IGP.
- The allusion to "the cedar of paradise, shaken but not overthrown", seems to be a Gregorian comment based on the Latin text of *Ezekiel* 31. 8–9.

IGP 30: III.14.12–14. From line 125, "*Magna est [Petre]* . . ." to line 158, ". . . *damno servetur*". Those to whom God gives great gifts he leaves with certain imperfections, in order that they should always have incentive to do better. Cf. *PsGD*, pp. 497–9.

- The elevated doctrine and stately Latinity of this long IGP is made relevant to the preceding narrative (which so markedly contrasts with it) by paragraph 10, "*Hic igitur . . . nullo modo crederetur*", which is interposed to provide a peg on which to hang this choice passage of Gregorian spirituality.
- Since in IGP 30 the real Gregory refers to minor faults which remain in the just (using *Judges* 3.1–4 as an apt scriptural reference), the Dialogist makes his Gregory remark beforehand that in the midst of all his virtues the holy abbot Isaac had one fault— occasionally immoderate gaiety. Then he introduces IGP 30 by making Peter ask (in lines 121–4) whether Isaac gave himself to such gaiety willingly or was swept into it involuntarily. Although IGP 30 follows as the response to that leading question, it does not in fact answer it, since it is an impersonal statement of general principle.
- IGP 30 is one of the Gregorian passages found both in the *Dialogues* and in the *Libri Sententiarum* of Tajo. (Cf. Chapter 21.c above.) The passage has verbal differences in the two works.

IGP 31: III.15.9–10. IGP 31a is from line 125, ". . . *cum Paulus dicat* . . ." to line 77, ". . . *a regno vitae*"; IGP 31b is from line 81, "*Si apud districtum iudicem [Petre] otiosus* . . ." to line 84, ". . . *utilitatis vacat*". On the grave malice of uttering a curse. Cf. *PsGD*, pp. 499–500.

- In the original source IGP 31b evidently led straight on from IGP 31a, without the question interposed by Peter—which mars the sense by introducing a query not answered in the Gregorian original. In IGP 31b Gregory does not envisage any such distinction between malicious cursing and non-malicious but careless cursing.

• There are at least four parallels to IGP 31 in Gregory's genuine works. His teaching there shows its true import, which is obscured by the Dialogist's use of it.

• The Gregory of the *Dialogues* gives a very strange reason why God ordained the death of the four envious monks who had slain the pet bear of the holy hermit Florentius, a horrible death in the sight of all which followed as the consequence of his lethal curse, and which led to his lifelong remorse. The reason given is: "We believe that God did this in order that the simple man should never again, however much he might be moved by sorrow, presume to hurl the weapon of a curse" (lines 69–71). Here we are very far from the spiritual vision and lucid reasoning of St Gregory the Great.

IGP 32: III.15.13–17. From line 107, "*Apud omnipotentis . . .*" to line 143, "*. . . nullo modo audimus.*" (Intrusive "*Petre*" in line 108.) From purity of heart and simplicity comes the prayer that is acceptable to God. Cf. *PsGD*, pp. 501–2.

• This lengthy and profound passage of Gregorian teaching is here in an alien setting. It is presented as a comment on the prayer of Florentius which leads to the miraculous extermination of the multitude of snakes which infested his cell and to the disposal of their remains. Peter asks what must be the virtue and merit of a man whose prayers were thus heard by God. IGP 32 is presented as the answer, but the Dialogist's explanation of it becomes entangled.

• Towards the end of the IGP Gregory draws a moral from *Proverbs* 28.9. The Dialogist immediately adds a further moral of his own to make the text also apply to his tale about Florentius.

• There are several parallels to IGP 32 in Gregory's writings. Vogüé percipiently remarks of it "*Le présent commentaire est inédit*"; and indeed it seems probable that it came from the *schedae* of unedited Gregorian drafts in the *Scrinium*.

• It is also probable that IGP 32 had a common source with IGP 31: in both we find mention of "*otiosa*" and "*noxia verba*". A similarity can also be observed between IGP 32 and IGP 1, as Vogüé also observes.

IGP 33: III.17.7–13. From line 59, "*maius est miraculum . . .*" to line 91, "*. . . interius vivificetur.*" It is a greater miracle to convert a sinner than to raise the dead. Cf. *PsGD*, p. 502.

- Peter's cue question in lines 53–6 picks out words from the coming Gregorian pericope, which is presented as the corrective to his rash assertion there.

IGP 34: III.18.3. From line 22, "*tres pueri...*" to line 29, "*...ad tormentum*". How the element of fire can, by divine dispensation, produce contrary effects. Cf. *PsGD*, pp. 502–4.

- It appears that IGP 34 presents a more abbreviated form of a passage in *Moralia* 9.102, which it closely resembles in language and argument. The fragment is not relevant to the tale it is supposed to illuminate.

IGP 35: III.19.5 & 20.3. IGP 35a is from III.19 line 38, "*Sine labore certaminis...*" to line 43, "*...accusator existat*"; IGP 35b is from III.20 line 20, "*contra inimici...*" to line 28, "*...virtute terreatur*". On the spiritual combat we always have to wage against the ancient enemy. Cf. *PsGD*, pp. 504–6.

- The two sections of the IGP, each introduced by a cue from Peter, doubtless belonged to an originally continuous passage, which the Dialogist has divided by interposing his quaint tale of the invisible devil who unlaced a priest's boots.
- The first cue is laboured. In order to bring in the Gregorian pericope on resistance to the "*antiquus hostis*" (III.20, line 25) Peter asks earlier, apropos of nothing in particular, "Since I am hearing about so many men in Italy of admirable virtue, I should like to know this: did they have to suffer no cunning assaults from the ancient enemy, and if so did they turn such assault to good account?" (III.19, lines 34–7). The cue words are repeated (in II.20, line 16) after the tale of the bootlaces has been told, in order to introduce IGP 35b.
- That tale is interposed in the middle of the Gregorian passage because it would be inconsequential after IGP 35b.

IGP 36: III.21.4. From line 31, "*Propositae regulae...*" to line 42, "*...per humilitatem*". All things are subject to God; the malign spirit has no power except by his permission. Cf. *PsGD*, pp. 506–7.[8]

- It may well be that both IGPs 35 and 36 came from the same source. The foregoing tale, quaintly imitating the Gospel episode

---

[8] I now do not press the argument proposed in the second paragraph on p. 507.

of the Gadarene swine, has evidently been composed to provide an opening for use of IGP 36.

- The noble and typically Gregorian lesson in the concluding sentence of IGP 36 is irrelevantly placed as an answer to Peter's cue question relating to the devil cast into a pig by a holy nun.

IGP 37: III.24.3. From line 21, "*cum Daniel propheta . . .*" to line 28, ". . . *non valet, infirmetur.*" The flesh cannot perceive what pertains to the spirit. Cf. *PsGD.* pp. 507–9.

- This short commentary on the text of *Daniel* 8.27 has parallels in *Moralia* 4.67 and *Homiliae in Ezechielem* I.8.19. In it the real Gregory speaks of a mystical experience of the Spirit which leaves the human vessel conscious of its infirmity. The Dialogist crassly applies it to his concocted tale of an apparition of the Apostle Peter which so frightened an early-rising sacristan that he had to keep to his bed for many days.

IGP 38: III.26.7–9 & 28.2–4. IGP 38a is from III.26 line 52, "*Duo sunt [Petre] martyrii . . .*" to line 68, ". . . *mortuus non est*"; IGP 38b is an incomplete fragment, from line 70, "*si persecutionis . . .*" to line 75, ". . . *martyres fuerunt*"; IGP 38c is from III.38 line 14, "*Quid est mirum . . .*" to line 30, ". . . *virtute persisterunt*". On two kinds of martyrdom. Cf. *PsGD,* pp. 509–12.

- I have remarked on IGP 38 above in Chapter 3.c, pointing to Peter's preliminary cue in lines 50–1, introducing the coming *excursus* of Gregorian wisdom concerning spiritual martyrdom, as a ploy that is abrupt and inept. A. de Vogüé finds it "*un peu inattendue*" (cf. Chapter 3.c above).
- In three of Gregory's Gospel *Homilies* (3.4, 11.3. 35,7) we find reflections on spiritual martyrdom very similar to those developed in IGP 38.[9] The last passage is a very close parallel to it, both in wording and in reasoning. It may well be that IGP 38 was originally in one of the sermons preached by the pontiff at the tombs of martyrs.
- The interrupted sentence into which IGP 38b is inserted is in uncouth Latin contrasting with the enclosed Gregorian fragment.

---

[9] Cf. also other references in A.C. Rush, "Spiritual martyrdom in St Gregory the Great", in *Theological Studies* 23 (1962), pp. 569–89.

It serves to introduce the fictitious tale of the 440 Italian peasants martyred by the Lombards. The insertion of IGP 38c after that tale is incongruous.

IGP 39: III.34.1–5. From line 1, "*In multis speciebus . . .*" to line 48, ". . . *commemorari debuisset*". On two kinds of compunction. Cf. *PsGD*, pp. 512–7.

- IGP 39 is introduced so artificially that the seams of the Dialogist's cobbling are more than usually visible. The cue given to Peter the Deacon to lead into it is abruptly and clumsily contrived: as Vogüé again comments caustically, "*la demande de Pierre est bien gauche*" (*SC* 260, p. 400.)
- I have noted above, in Chapter 21.b, that the same expository text is cited by both Paterius and Tajo (though with some differences in wording and grammatical usage); and also, in a quite different order, in the letter of Gregory in 593 to Theoctista. There was, it seems, more than one file copy of it in the *Scrinium*. Parallel passages are found in Gregory's *Moralia* and *Homilies*.[10] As placed in the *Dialogues* this elevated passage of Gregorian exposition is indeed an *excursus*, quite extraneous to the context. The Dialogist has used it just because it was there.

IGP 40: III.37.18–20. From line 166, "*quis ille spiritus . . .*" to line 188, ". . . *odorari nesciebat*". (The words "*isdem venerabilis vir Sanctulus*" in line 173 can be seen to be a substitution by the Dialogist.) On the heroic virtue of an unlettered saint who laid down his life for another. Cf. *PsGD*, pp. 417–9.

- For the preliminary cue to the introduction of IGP 40 we have to go back 80 lines—to II.37.9, lines 79–81.
- At first sight the passage seems to be an integral part of the Dialogist's hagiographical narrative, since it is about a named individual brought to martyrdom and seems to fit aptly after the preceding tale about Sanctulus. The language of the relevant section is, however, not the Dialogist's but the real Gregory's (with the exception of the intrusive mention of Sanctulus in line 173). In *PsGD* I show reasons for concluding that in its original setting IGP 40 was part of another of the homilies delivered by Gregory at the shrines of early Roman martyrs on their feast-days.

---

[10] Cf. Vogüé, *SC* 260, pp. 401–3.

- In this case the martyr honoured was evidently one who was simple and unlettered. There are two principal indications of this: (i) in lines 178–82 Gregory cites *I John* 3.16, "...so we too ought to lay down our lives for our brethren...", and says that the unlettered martyr whom he is honouring knew the meaning of that precept not by intelligence but by experience—"*tam sublime apostolicum praeceptum faciendo magis quam sciendo noverat*". (This does not fit the Dialogist's tale, for Sanctulus did not undergo martyrdom in fact); (ii) as was pointed out above, in Chapter 7.h, the real Gregory would never have set up for admiration a priest (as Sanctulus is in the story) who was illiterate and did not even know the Bible. Vogüé also points out an inconsistency in Peter's assertion there, contradicting what the interlocutor had asserted in the prologue to the *Dialogues*.

IGP 41: III.37.21–22. From line 193, "*Malitia remanentium...*" to line 208, "*...mentem traherent*". Why good men are taken out of this world. Cf. *PsGD*, pp. 519–20.

- IGP 41 follows immediately on the heels of IGP 40, but not with any relevance to the context; as Vogüé observantly remarks, Peter's cue query is "*sans lien apparent avec ce qui précède*" (*SC* 260, p. 426).

IGP 42: III.38.3–4. From line 23, "*Mox enim illa...*" to line 43, "*...ne diligatur clamat?*" The signs of the times point to the approaching dissolution of the world. Cf. *PsGD*, pp. 520–24.

- The apocalyptic events which are the subject of this powerful Gregorian passage are presented by the Dialogist as a sequel to an event related in his tale of a spectral apparition of the martyr Iuticus to Bishop Redemptus, announcing thrice "*Finis venit universae carni*". The real setting and expository teaching of IGP 42 is made very clear by examination of the many other passages in Gregory's genuine works which express the same expository teaching about the signs of the Last Days, often using identical words and phrases.
- In *PsGD* (p. 521) I list no less than ten such parallel passages and make detailed comparison of them with IGP 42. There is a particularly close correspondence between IGP 42 with a longer and more developed treatment of that theme found in a passage in the *Homiliae in Evangelia*, I.1, in which Gregory expounds Luke's account of Christ's eschatological discourse. In both those texts there is the

same linking of the Gospel signs of the approaching end of the world with current history. It is reasonable to conclude that IGP 42 was taken from a codex containing an unpublished draft of a discourse similar to the one given in that homily.

The IGPs in Book IV

In the fourth book of the *Dialogues* the inserted Gregorian excerpts constitute a far larger proportion of the text than in any of the other three—approximately 48%. They are there more "free-standing" than in the first three books; many of them are not appended to an antecedent miracle-tale, as was the rule in those other books. In Chapter 7 I discussed the special character of Book IV, the theme and scope of which does not correspond to the overall intention of the author as announced in his prologue to the *Dialogues*. Several of the longer IGPs in this book are verbatim reproductions of *exempla* related by the real Gregory in his Gospel homilies—but in every case shorn of the pastoral moral that was Gregory's purpose when relating them there. There are also two other verbatim citations from his genuine writings.

The programme and contents of the fourth book are clearly stated in the introductory cue put into the mouth of Peter the Deacon at the end of the third. Remarking that "many within the bosom of the Church have doubt concerning the life of the soul after the death of the body", he asks: "I beg that you should, for the edification of many, explain this truth, both from rational proofs and using any illustrative accounts of [disembodied] souls that may come to your mind, so that those who doubt may learn that the soul does not die with the body." That general introductory rubric enables the Dialogist to deploy many of his borrowed IGPs in Book IV without the elaborately contrived cues used in the first three books.

IGP 43: IV.1.1–5. From line 1, "*Postquam de paradiso . . .*" to line 45, ". . . *carceris agnovit*". Fallen mankind suffers blindness concerning the invisible realities, which is healed by the Holy Spirit. Cf. *PsGD*, pp. 528–30.

- This lengthy Gregorian extract, which serves as a splendid exordium for the last and longest part of the *Dialogues*, has no introductory cue as had all the previous IGPs. Nevertheless, it has a different perspective from that implied by Peter's request at the end of Book III. The real Gregory does not assume the premise posited there—namely that doubters need to be taught the truth of the soul's survival after death by rational proofs or by the evidence of ghost-stories. Rather, he teaches in IGP 43 that the reality of the *invisibilia* is now made manifest to our fallen and redeemed race only through the Incarnation of the Son of God, who has sent his Holy Spirit into our minds and hearts "so that we may believe what we can no longer know experientially".

• There are fairly close parallels to IGP 43, frequently verbatim, in at least seven texts in Gregory's known writings. His consistent teaching is that it is only through the Redeemer's grace and by faith that the darkened human mind can transcend its bodily imaginings and gain some inkling of the *bona invisibilia*. The Gregory of the *Dialogues*, however, finds a principal assurance of the existence of the world beyond the grave in his colourful ghost-stories and reports of *revenants* from the other world.

IGP 44: IV.2.1–3. IGP 44a is from line 1, "*Audenter dico . . .*" to line 8, ". . . *absque dubitatione testatur*"; IGP 44b is from line 11, "*Habent etiam . . .*" to line 16, ". . . *videri non possunt.*" Not even the unbeliever lives without a kind of faith. Cf. *PsGD*, pp. 531–2.

• IGP 44 echoes an argument of St Augustine. The cues by which the two separated parts of the passage are brought in by Peter are again clumsy. Like IGP 43, it is at a tangent from the declared theme of Book IV, which was to demonstrate the survival of the soul. The subsequent cue in I.2, lines 17–18, prepares for the resumption of that theme in the following chapters.

IGP 45: IV.3.1–3 & 4.1–8. IGP 45a is from IV.3 line 1, "*Tres quippe vitales . . .*" to lines 19–20, ". . . *sine fine moriantur*"; IGP 45b is from IV.3 line 23, ". . . *quid est quod Salomon . . .*" to IV.4 line 81, ". . . *veritate definivit*". On the three orders of spirits: with an answer to an objection from *Ecclesiastes*. Cf. *PsGD*, p. 532.

• Running to 111 lines, this is the longest of all the IGPs. Matched by clear parallels in the *Moralia*,[11] it is typical Gregorian exposition

---

[11] Cf. Vogüé, *SC* 265, pp. 23–5, 28–9. In particular, IGP 45b (*Dial.* IV.3–6) closely parallels *Moralia* 4, preface, 1.

of holy writ. The obscurities of the *Ecclesiastes* text are reverently discussed, leading by stages to a harmonious resolution of exegetical difficulties. Such passages, bearing Gregory's true stylistic signature, implicitly discredit the pseudepigrapher who tries to fit them into his own very different composition.

- By inserting this long passage of scriptural exegesis the Dialogist digresses widely from his stated intention, which was to prove the immortality of the soul from rational proof and "stories of souls".

IGP 46: IV.4.10. From line 88, "*Cur condescendentem . . .*" to line 93, ". . . *praedicatoris imitaris*". On "condescension" for the sake of one's weaker neighbours. Cf. *PsGD*, pp. 532–3.

- In *PsGD* I give reasons for supposing that IGP 46 was originally a snippet from a letter of Gregory to a prelate whom he addresses with courteous respect and praises for his "*condescensio*"—a virtue that in the *Moralia* he shows to be proper to a superior or preacher who out of charity adapts himself to the lower level of others. In the *Dialogues*, IGP 46 is incongruously addressed to Peter the Deacon. This usage contrasts strangely with the very different attitude habitually shown there by the *soi-disant* Gregory to his obtuse and fawning interlocutor.

IGP 47: IV.5.4. From line 22, ". . . *vis divina implet . . .*" to line 31–2, ". . . *spiritus iustorum*". Invisible ministering spirits pay court to the invisible Creator. (NB intrusive words: "*Ut tamen . . . ad te*" in line 43, and "*tui*" in line 45) Cf. *PsGD*, pp. 533–5.

- This passage is clearly Gregorian. There are verbal parallels in *Homiliae in Ezechielem* and in *Moralia* (cf. Vogüé, *SC* 265, p. 35.) But it is manifestly out of place here as an answer to Peter's cue question in IV.5.3, which it does not address.
- The original context of IGP 47 can be seen to be the same as that from which IGPs 43 and 44 were taken—namely, a Gregorian discourse on the invisible heavenly world, knowledge of which is known to redeemed humankind through Spirit-bestowed faith. That is not the same theme as the one proposed by the Dialogist in Book IV. He himself shows awareness of the inconsequence of his argument, for he introduces IGP 47 with an excuse for its inappositeness: "*Non quidem similiter, sed dissimiliter dico . . .*" (lines 20–1).

IGP 48: IV.5–8. IGP 48a is from line 43, "*Cum Paulus . . .*" to line 42, ". . . *quod videri possit*"; IGP 48b is from line 43, ". . . *nulla visi-*

bilia . . ." to line 66, "*. . . corpora quae videntur*". (Probably intrusive are "*tui*" in line 45 and "*te*" in line 55.) Invisible spirit is the moving principle of visible bodies. Cf. *PsGD*, pp. 535–6.

- Although probably taken from the same original source, IGPa is a separate snippet which does not logically connect with IGPb (as the Dialogist realized, it seems—to judge from the interpolated words in line 43). IGP 48a is about faith in the theological sense, as in the passage from *Hebrews* 11.1 alluded to there. IGP 48b is not about faith but about invisible spirit's priority to and control over visible matter; as placed here, it is inconsequential and digressive. A. de Vogüé duly observes the logical standstill—indeed retrogression—of the argument in IV.5. (*SC* 265, p. 37.)
- There is a parallel passage in *Moralia* 15.52 which throws light on the meaning of IGP 48. There, as in IGP 48b, Gregory's concern is not with the survival of the soul in the future life but with the present certainty of the invisible reality of which God is the summit.

IGP 49: IV.6.1–2. From line 2, "*Numquidnam sancti . . .*" to line 15–6, "*. . . in tot miraculis vivunt*". (Interpolated is the sentence "*Tu ipse inquies . . . corporis agnoscis*".) The posthumous miracles of the saints testify to the reality and quality of their heavenly life. Cf. *PsGD*, pp. 537–9.

- IGP 49, which has the distinctive traits of Gregory's pulpit oratory, is adventitiously introduced into the Dialogist's context. The key to understanding its original bearing is to be found in a closely parallel passage in the *Homiliae in Evangelia*, 32.6. There, in his sermon to the people of Rome gathered at a martyr's shrine, Gregory presents the very same argument drawn from the death and miracles of martyrs. In both passages he is not concerned to establish the philosophical truth of the permanence of human souls after death, but to proclaim the blessed life of the saints in the heavenly realm and to raise the minds of his hearers to aspire to sharing that life.
- IGP 49 terminates the section of Book IV that supposedly presents "rational proof" of the soul's immortality. The Gregory of the *Dialogues* goes on thereafter to a long series of the *animarum exempla* which he promised in III.38.5.

IGP 50: IV.11.1–2. IGP 50a is from line 3, "*Hunc omnipotens . . .*" to lines 9–10, "*. . . sanando monstravit*"; IGP 50b is from line 13, "*Sed* *quia nemo . . .*" to line 21, "*. . . iuste misereri*". Of God's loving care for his chosen children, even while he chastises them. Cf. *PsGD*, pp. 539–41.

- IGP 50b stands out as another treasure of Gregorian spiritual wisdom and eloquence set in the dross of the Dialogist's folklore.
- But what about IGP 50a? Unlike IGP 50b, it does not enunciate universal spiritual truths applicable to all humankind, but refers expressly to one individual, to whom God has shown the extremes both of severity and grace. Is not the application of it in the *Dialogues* to the abbot Spes, who was afflicted with blindness for 40 years and then miraculously cured, evidence that this Gregorian passage originated as an integral part of the legendary narrative? No, the description of the grievous sufferings and chastisements divinely sanctioned for the individual referred to in IGP 50a is ineptly applied to the blindness of Abbot Spes; but it does apply most aptly to the heroic figure of Job, about whose great afflictions under God's merciful *flagella* Gregory repeatedly makes similar reflections in his great *Commentary on Job* (e.g. *Moralia* 3.3–16, 35.22.) IGP 50a may well have been drawn from a filed *scheda* of a Gregorian draft originally intended for that work.

IGP 51: IV.12.5. From line 40, "*. . . plerumque contingit . . .*" to lines 44–5, "*. . . fatigatione salvantur*". On visions of saints seen by the dying. Cf. *PsGD*, p. 541.

- The expression and thought of this fragment are again clearly Gregorian. It is akin to a similar passage in *Moralia* 24.34.

IGP 52: IV.15.2–5. From line 6, "*. . . in ea portico . . .*" to lines 42–3, "*. . . fragrantia non recessit.*" (Intrusive is "*cuius te quoque non ambigo meminisse*" in line 8.) On the heroic and edifying death of the poor paralytic Servulus. Cf. *PsGD*, pp. 541–2.

- By his introductory remarks to IGP 52, in lines 1–6, the Dialogist devises an opening for the first of his series of seven verbatim transcripts of edifying *exempla* taken from Gregory's *Homiliae in Evangelia*, which *soi-disant* Gregory says he "remembers narrating" there. It is taken from Homily 15.5 (cf. Chapter 3.e above.) In line 4 the reference to Peter the Deacon's personal reminiscence of Servulus is of course obtrusive.
- In the original homily Gregory did not narrate Servulus's edifying and consoling death in order to teach the truth of the soul's

immortality, but the Dialogist, omitting the moral that was the purpose of the pontiff's narration, fixes solely on the supernatural manifestations that attended Servulus's passing.

IGP 53: IV.16.1–4. From line 3, "*Eo namque tempore . . .*" to line 75, "*. . . elongata finiretur*". On the hidden virtue and wondrous death of the holy woman Romula. Cf. *PsGD*, pp. 542–3.

• IGP 53 is another word-for-word copy from the text of Gregory's Gospel *Homilies* (40.11). Here we find it inserted with a different intention. From the example of Romula's pious and wondrous death Gregory drew the lesson for his hearers to love and honour the poor and to share their riches with them. The Dialogist's purpose in retelling the story, bereft of its original moral, is to add to his promised dossier of phenomenal proofs for the immortality of the soul.

IGP 54: IV.17.1–3. From line 4, "*Quae inter . . .*" to line 27, "*. . . mortua testabatur.*" On the heavenly visitors who summoned the soul of Pope Gregory's aunt Tarsilla. Cf. *PsGD*, pp. 542–3.

• The third of the "narrative IGPs" copied from Gregory's Gospel *Homilies* (38.5) follows immediately on the first two, but differs from them in that the Dialogist edits and truncates the pious narrative because its main bearing does not suit his purpose. In the full original form Gregory related it to illustrate the Gospel text "many are called but few are chosen" by comparing the holy life and death of his aunt Tarsilla with the contrary course of her unworthy sister Gordiana. Omitting all mention of the latter, the Dialogist copies only the section which tells of Tarsilla's vision of Christ coming to welcome her.

IGP 55: IV.20.1–4. From line 3, "*Fuit enim vir . . .*" to line 36, "*. . . territi fugerunt*". (The Dialogist has added "*isdem Probus et . . . alii*" in line 4.) On the humble virtue, edifying death and heavenly reward of the holy abbot Stephen of Rieti. Cf. *PsGD*, pp. 554–5.

• After two intervening stories (one of which told of a five-year-old boy whose soul departed not to heaven but to hell) the Dialogist presents in IGP 55 the fourth of his series of edifying stories borrowed from Gregory's *Homiliae in Evangelia* (35.8). Only one section corresponds verbatim with the received text of the *Homilies*. Maybe the Dialogist made his transcript from a variant codex.

- As usual, he fastens on the preternatural phenomena reported to have attended a holy death, and omits the lesson of heroic patience and faithfulness, exemplified by Stephen, which Gregory drew from the narrative.

IGP 56: IV.24.2–3 & IV.25.1. IGP 56a is from IV.24 line 11, "*Cum scriptum sit . . .*" to lines 19–20, ". . . *crudelitatis acceperunt . . .*"; IGP 56b is from IV.25 line 1, "*Nam vir Dei . . .*" to line 12, ". . . *cadaver iusti*". How dying can purify the elect, how vengeance awaits their persecutors, and a reflection on *1 Kings* 13. Cf. *PsGD*, pp. 545–7.

- Both IGPs 56a and 56b may well have been taken from the same Gregorian original, since both include reference to death's purifying power for the elect. However, they could not have been consecutive there, since the transit from the first to the second is inconsequential.
- There is a parallel passage to 56a in *Moralia* 16.69. The Dialogist makes Gregory's reference to the divine sanction awaiting reprobate persecutors apply to the case of the Lombard who slew a saintly deacon. To support this application he invokes the testimony of Scripture in *1 Kings* 13, as expounded in IGP 56b, which is a commentary on the purgation by death of an erring prophet. In *PsGD* p. 547 I surmise that this pericope may have been set aside by Gregory because he had a scruple about its theological speculations.

IGP 57: IV.26.1–4. IGP 57a is from line 1, "*Hoc neque de omnibus . . .*" to line 19, ". . . *aeternam in caelis*"; IGP 57b is from line 23, "*Hoc eis nimirum . . .*" to line 36, ". . . *gloria laetabuntur*". The souls of the just enter heaven immediately after death, with the exception of some who are temporarily delayed. Cf. *PsGD*, pp. 547–8.

- In order to deploy this theological passage the Dialogist makes Peter request it with a cue which abruptly digresses from the stated theme of Book IV. In his *SC* commentary A. de Vogüé duly observes: "*Cette nouvelle question de Pierre déborde sa demande initiale*" (i.e. in III.38.5).
- IGP 57 may well reflect Gregory's pruning of drafts of the *Moralia*. There are two passages closely resembling it in that work (Preface, 20 & 35.25), where the same scriptural texts and the same arguments are adduced in very similar language. Peter's second cue question marks a move to a later paragraph in the original text.

IGP 58: IV.27.14. From line 118, "*Quis occulta . . .*" to line 120, ". . . *discutere debemus*". A short reflection on the mystery of God's judgements. Cf. *PsGD*, p. 548.

• The introduction of this fragment about God's "*occulta iudicia*", which has the ring of a genuine Gregorian aphorism, is prepared for by the phrase "*occulto iudicio*" in line 110.

IGP 59: IV.28.1–4. From line 5, "*Fuit namque . . .*" to lines 30–1, ". . . *aromata ferbuissent*". On the death of the pious count Theophanius. Cf. *PsGD*, pp. 548–9.

• Resuming his series of transcripts from Gregory's *Homiliae in Evangelia*, the Dialogist repeats a pastoral *exemplum* given there in II.26.13, about the edifying death of an official. Whereas in the original sermon Gregory took the exemplary life of the man as occasion to reflect on St Paul's teaching about the married in *I Corinthians* 7, the Dialogist omits the moral and adds a further confirmatory story of his own to attest the worthy official's preternatural prescience. Vogüé again notes the divergence from the tenor of the story in the *Homilies*: "The conclusion in the homily is that is possible to live in the world without having its spirit. The perspective in the *Dialogues* is different . . ." (*SC* 265, pp. 98–9).

IGP 60: IV.29.1 and 30.2–3 & 5. IGP 60a is from IV.29 lines 3–4, ". . . *ex retributione aeterna . . .*" to line 7, ". . . *reprobos exurat*"; IGP 60b is from IV.30 line 6, "*Si incorporeus spiritus . . .*" to line 24, ". . . *ignibis neget?*"; IGP 60c is from IV.30 line 38, "*Certe reprobis . . .*" to line 43, ". . . *sentire tormenta*" ("*Petre*" is intrusive in line 6.) The souls of the wicked are punished in hell before Judgement Day. Cf. *PsGD*, pp. 550–1.

• Probably IGP 60 belonged to the same original source as IGP 57, a source in which Gregory discussed *novissima hominis*. It has notable parallels in *Moralia* 9.95–104 & 15.35–6. In those cases, however, he did not discuss the question of how the separated soul can be said to be punished by fire, whereas in IGP 60 he explicitly addresses it. This IGP may be one of those passages, referred to by R. Étaix, which Gregory decided not to publish because of his sensitive theological caution.
• The see-saw of dialogue in IV.30.4 is the Dialogist's own composition. 60b seems out of its original order as placed here.

IGP 61: IV.34.1–5. From line 3, "... *cum dictum esset* ..." to line 51, "... *scientem omnia sciunt?*" (Intrusive is the Dialogist's aside "*quod nequaquam ipse requisisti*" in lines 32–3.) In the next world both the good and the wicked have knowledge of others. Cf. *PsGD*, pp. 551–2.

- IGP 61 is introduced after three tales describing how wicked men were justly consigned to penal flames immediately after their death. It is a doctrinal *excursus*—beyond the Dialogist's stated theme—on the knowledge possessed by souls, both good and wicked, in the after-life. It seems to belong to the same original source concerning the Last Things from which came a number of the other IGPs in Book IV.
- The Dialogist is aware that he is here straying from his stated theme, and once more puts in a excusatory aside by which his Gregory says to Peter "... you did not ask me this" (lines 32–3).
- IGP 61 ends with a pithy rhetorical question in the real Gregory's familiar rhythm, expressing a reflection which is found in many variant forms elsewhere in his writings: "*Quid est quod ibi nesciant ubi scientem omnia sciunt?*" The Dialogist's immediately following "*Nam* ..." makes this saying applicable to the story in his next paragraph of a dying saint's vision of three prophets.

IGP 62: IV.36.12. From line 73, "... *prae ceteris locis* ..." to line 82, "... *credere recusant*". Increasing volcanic activity is a sign of approaching doom. Cf. *PsGD*, pp. 552–3.

- The approaching end of the world is a theme Gregory sombrely expounds in several places in his *Moralia* and *Homilies*. In its original meaning IGP 62, like those other passages, does not naïvely assert that the volcanic craters of Sicily and its neighbouring islands are literally the gates of hell—as the Dialogist supposes, here and in *Dial.* IV.31.2–4. Gregory presents those widening volcanoes as symbols to the living ("*ad correctionem viventium*") of the eternal torments prepared for sinners as Judgement Day draws near. The same analogical sense of the fire of hell is conveyed in IGP 60b—"*ex igne visibili ardor ac dolor invisibilis trahitur*" (IV.30, lines 12–3).

IGP 63: IV.36.13–14. From line 86, "*Ipsa quippe propter* ..." to lines 106–7, "... *ad conburendum ligant*". The blessed in heaven all enjoy the same beatitude, but with difference of quality; likewise the punishments of the damned are distinguished according to the gravity of their sins. Cf. *PsGD*, pp. 553–4.

- To understand the original bearing of IGP 63 it must be compared with a parallel but longer passage in the *Moralia*, 9.98, where Gregory also comments on *Matthew* 13.30. One sentence there sums up the lesson also given in IGP 63: "As there are many mansions in the Father's house according to diversity of virtue, so disparity in evildoing subjects the damned to diversity of torment by the fires of hell."
- The Dialogist has concocted his two preceding tales to cap them with IGP 63. In the first tale it is made clear by a deathbed prodigy that two holy monks who died at the same moment "because they were equal in merit, just as they died together, would also live together in one dwelling in heaven". In the second tale two evidently wicked associates also die at the same moment and are invisibly ferried to Sicily, there to enter the gates of hell together.
- In IGP 63 Gregory's original concern was not to stress separation of places but the qualitative differences—"*dispar retributionis qualitas*"—that exist within the unitary recompense or retribution which souls receive in the next world.

IGP 64: IV.38.4–5 & 39. IGP 64a is from IV.38 line 28, "... *eamdem delectationem . . .*" to line 36, "... *superna patiatur*". [The phrase "*constat . . . eorum habitacula*" in lines 31–2 is intrusive.] IGP 64b is from IV.39 line 1, "... *libro Geneseos*" to line 7, "... *delectationem tradisset*". Metaphor of the stinking vapour of carnal sin. Cf. *PsGD*, pp. 554–7.

- The graphic narrative that intervenes between IGPs 63 and 64 has been designed to prepare for the introduction of the latter. The original bearing of IGP 64 (which is significantly changed in the Dialogist's use of it) is clear from comparison with parallel and often verbatim parallels to it found in *Moralia*, 14.23 & 16.83. In the latter text Gregory cites the same words from *Job* 24.20, "*Dulcedo illius vermis*", that are cited in IGP 64, line 30. Likewise he expounds the word "*foetor*" as used there in the same sense as in *Job* 8.15, referring to brimstone sprinkled on the tents of the wicked. He takes brimstone, emitting a foul stench and serving to kindle fire, as a symbol of the foulness of carnal sinfulness, which "while it diffuses in the wicked mind the vapour of its stench" ("*foetoris sui nebulam*") brings fuel, as it were, to the flames to come" (*CCL* 43a, p. 711). He gives similarly symbolic exegesis of the term "*foetor sulphuris*" in his commentary on the punishment of the Sodomites related in *Genesis* 19.24, which is also referred to in IGP 64b. Both the expressions "*foetoris nebula*" and "*foetor sulphuris*" are found verbatim in IGP 64.

- However (as I have pointed out in Chapter 7.b above) a very different and bizarre application of that distinctive Gregorian phrase "*foetoris nebula*" is made by the Dialogist in his tale that immediately precedes IGP 64. In that tale the "*foetoris nebula*" is the stinking vapour that arises from the infernal river separating the saved from the damned. Some who, while still sullied by the delight they took in impure thoughts while still on earth, have managed to escape damnation and to cross the fateful bridge over the Stygian boundary to arrive on the heavenward side, but are still subject to the lesser penalty of being afflicted with that "*foetoris nebula*".
- The phrase "*foetoris nebula*" is also expressly cited by Peter the Deacon as the cue for introducing IGP 64. This grotesque alteration of the meaning of that phrase taken from Gregorian exegesis is surely clear enough indication that the author of the *Dialogues* narrative was not the original author of the inserted exegetical passage that he appends to his tale. (He vainly tries to make it seem relevant by inserting into it the inapposite mention of "*habitacula*" in line 32.)

IGP 65: IV.40.2–5. From line 8, "*. . . in meum monasterium . . .*" to line 46, "*. . . carne soluta* est". The deathbed deliverance of a dissolute young monk. Cf. *PsGD*, pp. 57–8.

- IGP 65 is the sixth in the series of seven *exempla* from Gregory's *Homilies on the Gospels* inserted in the fourth book of the *Dialogues*. The source here is Homily 38.16; there is an interesting parallel in Homily 19.7, where Gregory tells the same story but in different words. There is also a somewhat similar story in the letter sent by him to a pious benefactress of St Andrew's monastery in 601 (Epist. XI.26). Once more the Gregory of the *Dialogues* begins by remarking that he "remembers" having told the story in his sermons to the people, and then proceeds to reproduce it verbatim from Homily 38.
- The Dialogist's interest in repeating the story is not for its original moral (which he omits) but because it tells of a departing soul who saw "something penal in the realm of spirits".

IGP 66: IV.40.6–9. From line 49, "*. . . vir in hoc mundo . . .*" to line 79, "*. . . petiit non accepit?*" The desperate end of Chrysaurius. Cf. *PsGD*, p. 558.

- The story that follows at once after IGP 65 is similar to it but with a different conclusion. It is the seventh of the "narrative IGPs" or genuine Gregorian *exempla* taken verbatim from the Gospel *Homilies* (12.7).
- In the story in the *Homilies* Gregory simply says that he learned the facts from "a religious man". The Dialogist gives his authority for the story as Probus, doubtless intending to refer to a monk of that name whom he has mentioned in *Dial.* IV.13.1, a nephew of Bishop Probus of Rieti. He adds that Probus the informant was related to Chrysaurius; in Chapter VI.13.1 he also says that the father of Probus the bishop was named Maximus. The latter name was the same that, as Gregory himself mentioned in his homily, was borne by the son of a real Chrysaurius. (Cf. Vogüé, *SC* 265, pp. 53, 71, 143). Here we see the Dialogist's liking for circumstantial details and for the reuse of names taken from genuine sources.

IGP 67: IV.41.1–6. From line 1, "*In evangelio . . .*" to line 46–7, "*. . . obtineat promereatur.*" (Instead of "*purgatorius ignis credendus*" in line 14, an original reading such as "*purgatio credenda*" is probable.) Even after death there can be purgation from light faults. Cf. *PsGD*, pp. 558–61.

- Here the Dialogist suddenly changes the subject and puts in a cue question from Peter to enable him to reproduce a long passage of Gregorian exegesis. A. de Vogüé again remarks on the abruptness and inconsequence with which the question is interjected (*SC* 251, p. 73).
- The penultimate paragraph of IGP 67 (IV.41.5) is one of the otherwise unknown Gregorian passages that are not only found in the *Dialogues* but were copied by Tajo of Saragossa when scanning Gregorian literary remains in the Roman archives in the mid-seventh century, and reproduced in his *Libri Sententiarum* (V.21). Tajo records a short but significant phrase that is not in the *Dialogues*. From its omission by the Dialogist I argue in *PsGD* (p. 560) that Tajo's fuller text reflects an original that was probably a discarded draft of the text of *Moralia* 16.39.

- This discussion of a purgatorial fire after death has no close parallel in Gregory's other works. If the passage was an earlier draft from the *Moralia* which was later excised, the reason may have been that Gregory had some misgivings that his exegesis of *I Corinthians* 3.13–15 was somewhat novel. We know from his letter to Secundinus of 593 how scrupulously he retracted and corrected his exegesis of a Gospel text which he felt he had earlier explained "*sub quadam ambiguitate*" (Epist. IV.17a).

IGP 68: IV.43.2. From line 6, "*. . . quantum praesens*" to lines 21–2, "*. . . ante solem videmus*". Gleams of spiritual realities before the dawn of the world to come. Cf. *PsGD*, pp. 561–2.

- The Dialogist seeks to make Gregory's references to the portents of the present world's approaching end apply to his own collection of reports of spectral apparitions of the after-life, such as the extraordinary tale he has just told of the ghost of the deacon Paschasius being released from his steamy purgatory in the baths. In the IGP the real Gregory is not speaking of such reports but of the manifest signs of the coming "end times" to which he refers in IGP 42 and *passim* in his expository writings.

IGP 69: IV.44.1–3. From line 1, "*Hac de re . . .*" to line 26, "*. . . infernus credatur*". On the location of hell. Cf. *PsGD*, p. 563.

- Peter's introductory question for IGP 69 expressly harks back to the phrase "*de locis poenalibus*" in IGP 63. IGP 69 belongs to a series of pericopes of Gregorian exposition referring to hell which began in IGP 60 and is now resumed after an intermission of several chapters devoted mainly to tales of preternatural clairvoyance by dying persons. Vogüé remarks on this puzzling interruption of the discussion of "the question of hell" (*SC* 251, p. 70). He also remarks that just as the chapters on purgatory were introduced abruptly by Peter without apparent connection with what had preceded, so "in a manner just as abrupt he passes from purgatory to the questions concerning hell" (*SC* 251, p. 73).
- The explanation of the puzzle lies in awareness of the Dialogist's "scissors and paste" method of bringing in nuggets from the treasure trove of Gregorian passages that he has ready for insertion into his narrative. Now, resuming his deployment of extracts from a Gregorian discussion of aspects of hell, he inserts in succession IGP 69 on the location of hell, IGP 70 on the diverse manners

of penal torments in hell, IGP 71 on the perpetuity of hell, and
IGP 72 on how the damned soul, though immortal, can be said
to suffer perpetual death.

- IGP 69 is another of the Gregorian passages that are common to
the *Dialogues* and to the *Libri Sententiarum* of Tajo (V.20). As I show
in *PsGD*, p. 563, Tajo's text gives some words lacking in the
Dialogues and has a better word order—another probative indication of the fallacy of supposing that he copied from the *Dialogues*.

IGP 70: IV.45.2. From line 5, "*Unus quidem . . .*" to line 14, ". . . *dissimiliter exurat*". The same hell-fire afflicts the damned in different
manners. Cf. *PsGD*, p. 563.

- Peter's woodenly catechetical cue question, picking out the phrase
"*unus gehennae ignis*" from line 3 of the IGP, is again inconsequential.
- IGP 70 is closely paralleled in *Moralia* 9.98; it also has echoes of
IGP 63, which links with that text.

IGP 71: IV.46.1–9. From line 4, ". . . *sicut finis . . .*" to line 72–3,
". . . *subtilitate discordat*". [The words "*Scire velim . . .*", put into Peter's
mouth in IV.46 line 18, are intrusive.] On the eternity of punishment in hell. Cf. *PsGD*, pp. 563–5.

- Peter's next catechetical question introduces one of the most intriguing and significant of all the IGPs. It takes us into the Dialogist's
workshop, so to speak. What makes it of unique interest in our
investigation is the fact that this long dialogistic exchange, in which
Gregory shows awareness of Augustine's previous treatment of the
same question, faithfully reproduces a dialogue placed by Gregory
himself in *Moralia* 34.35–8, where he answers objections put by
"Origenists" against the doctrine of the eternity of hell. In IGP
72 the very same dialogic exchanges are reproduced that are set
out in that *Moralia* text, with the same arguments, in the same
order and often in exactly the same words. What is different is
that the Dialogist has inserted the name of Peter the Deacon wherever in the *Moralia* text Gregory introduces the objections of the
Origenists with the phrase, "*At inquiunt . . .*"—"But they say . . .".
The Gregory of the *Dialogues* gives no hint that the IGP has already
appeared in the *Moralia* under different guise. Understandably commentators (e.g. Vogüé, *SC* 265, p. 161) are taken aback by this
covert duplication.
- In *PsGD* (pp. 564–5) I argue from some textual differences that,

rather than culling his extract directly from the published text of the *Moralia*, the Dialogist used a variant draft of this sequence of dialogue, which he may have found apart in the *Scrinium* files.

IGP 72: IV.47.1–2. From line 3, "... *quoddammodo anima immortalis* ..." to line 17, "... *finis infinitus*". How the damned soul, though immortal, suffers perpetual death. Cf. *PsGD*, p. 565.

• The last of the group of Gregorian pericopes on theological questions concerning hell, IGP 72 is introduced by Peter with an abruptness that contrasts with the smooth flow of genuinely Gregorian dialogistic exchanges in the preceding IGP. There are again resemblances here with statements about the unending death of the damned soul in *Moralia* 4.5 & 15.21.

IGP 73: IV.48 & 49.1. IGP 73a is from IV.48 lines 1–2, "... *plerumque de culpis* ..." to line 3, "... *iustorum purgat* ..."; IGP 72b is from IV.39 line 1 "*Nonnunquam vero* ..." to line 3, "... *minime pertimescant*". On the fear of death in the just. Cf. *PsGD*, pp. 565–6.

• IGPs 73a and 73b were probably one undivided fragment, matching a similarly balanced sentence in *Moralia* 24.34. There is recognizable Gregorian phraseology also in IV.49, lines 5–6 and 9–11. It may be that the whole of IV.49.1–3 is Gregorian in origin. The *exemplum* concerning Antonius is sober and unsensational; it resembles the story told by Gregory in his Gospel *Homilies*, 34.18, and may be taken from the draft of one of his unpublished sermons.

IGP 74: IV.50.2–6. From line 3, "*Sciendum [Petre] est* ..." to line 45, "... *falsitate laqueare*". On the discernment of dreams. Cf. *PsGD*, pp. 566–72.

• Comparison of IGP 74 with closely connected passages in the *Moralia*, as copied by Tajo and also by the Dialogist, is very revealing. (The relevant passages in the earlier texts are: *Moralia* 8.42–3; Tajo, *Libri Sententiarum* IV.7.) In *PsGD* I devote seven and a half closely reasoned pages (pp. 566–72) to that comparison. I invite researchers to examine that intricate pattern of evidence, which clearly shows that the Dialogist's use of IGP 74 is derivative from the earlier sources. There is a long paragraph (Section Y in my presentation of the three texts) which is clearly integral to the sense of the whole argument, yet which is found only in *Moralia* and

Tajo, not in *Dialogues*. This is another proof that the *Dialogues* text is posterior to Tajo's mid-seventh century compilation.

• The way IGP 74 is introduced by a cue question from Peter is again awkward. In the three preceding stories about apparitions the Dialogist has repeatedly used the phrase "*nocturna visio*" (IV.49, lines 12, 24, 33–4, 38–9) in order to link proleptically with Peter's cue question for IGP 74, in which he asks whether "*nocturnae visiones*" should be taken seriously. In the context it is a strange question, in view of the fact that his master has just related three episodes in which he related nocturnal visions which, he declared, brought true revelations from heavenly sources.

IGP 75: IV.52 & 55.5. IGP 75a is from IV.52 line 5, "*Quos gravia . . .*" to lines 11–2, "*. . . in ecclesiis ponuntur*"; IGP 75b is from IV.55 line 23, "*. . . si in sacro . . .*" to lines 25–6, "*. . . temeritatis accuset*". On burial in church. Cf. *PsGD*, p. 572.

• IGP 75b, eloquently reinforcing the last sentence in 75a, clearly belongs to it as a single lesson, in which Gregory (following Augustine) seeks to counter superstitious belief about the eternal value of being buried in a church. The Dialogist has widely separated the two parts of the passage by interposing three cautionary tales of dreadful sanctions which followed the burial of wicked people in church.

• From Chapter 57 onwards the concluding part of Book IV is concerned with the offering of Mass and its salutary effects for the dead. It is presented as an extended response to the question put by Peter in IV.57.1, "What can there be that may avail to benefit the souls of the dead?". A number of supernatural occurrences are related to illustrate the efficacy of requiem Masses. The first two stories are the Dialogist's own, telling of liberation from otherworldly (and even earthly!) prisons by eucharistic oblation made for them. Then follow IGPs 76 and 77, which retell in abbreviated form two edifying *exempla* taken from Gregory's Gospel *Homilies*.

IGP 76: IV.58.1–2. From line 3, "*Cassius, Narniensis . . .*" to line 12, "*. . . e corpore exivit*". A bishop's eucharistic devotion. Cf. *PsGD*, p. 573.

• IGP 76, an edited "narrative IGP", is a condensed and impoverished version of the story of Bishop Cassius of Narni related by Gregory in the *Homilies* (37.9), with some phrases reproduced

verbatim. Its insertion does not fit well into the Dialogist's con-
·text. He is adducing examples to show how the Mass-oblation
benefits the souls of the dead, but in the case of Cassius (as Gregory
explains at length in the fuller text of the homily) it was the bishop's
piety *before* his death, shown not only in his devout offering of
Mass but also in his good deeds and compunction, that merited
for him a blessed future in eternal life.

IGP 77: IV.59.1. From line 1, "*. . . audivimus quemdam . . .*" to line 7,
"*. . . sacrificium recognovit*". Temporary relief for a chained captive
through the Mass-oblation. Cf. *PsGD*, pp. 573–4.

• This short passage, the last of the borrowed "narrative IGPs" in
the *Dialogues*, may be called a Gregorian passage only in a looser
sense, since it is a very abbreviated paraphrase of an *exemplum* in
Gregory's Gospel *Homilies*, 37.8. There he relates a story for which
he gives no more precise authority than "*fertur*—"it is said". It is
about a captive in a foreign land whose wife procured the offering
of Mass for him on certain days. On those very days his chains
were loosened. In the original sermon Gregory referred to that
commonly told story to argue *a fortiori*: if the sacred oblation could
thus temporarily loosen those material chains, how much more
must it avail to loosen in us the shackles of the heart.
• Although, like IGP 76, the story in IGP 77 is not relevant to his
stated theme of the lot of souls after death, the Dialogist reuses it
because it tells of a prodigy connected with the offering of Mass;
he omits the spiritual moral that Gregory drew from it for the
hearers of his sermon.

> After telling one more story of rescue granted to the living, the Dialogist
> devotes the rest of his book to citing a number of genuine Gregorian
> passages of theological reflection on the efficacy of the Mass-offering
> for the succour of departed souls. The remaining text consists wholly
> of IGPs. IGPs 78, 79 and 80 are all evidently related to one another,
> forming parts of an original Gregorian discourse, the order of which
> has been rearranged. The tone of homiletic earnestness and pastoral
> exhortation in these concluding passages of Book IV suggest that their
> original source was a sermon to the people akin to the 37th of Gregory's
> Gospel *Homilies*.

IGP 78: IV.59.6, 60.1–3 & 61.1. IGP 78a is from IV.59 line 55,
"*. . . si insolubiles culpae . . .*" to IV.60 line 8, "*. . . hostias immolare*"; IGP
78b is from IV.60, line 9, "*Haec namque . . .*" to IV.61 line 5, "*. . . hos-*

tiam fecerit". On the efficacy of the mystical sacrifice of Christ. Cf. *PsGD*, pp. 574–7.

- The logic of the sentence with which the Dialogist introduces IGP 78 (lines 53–5) is odd. *Soi-disant* Gregory argues that the purpose of the prodigies he has just related was "to show to those living persons who were involved in them while unaware of what was being done" (e.g. the chained captive and the sailor Varaca) that the eucharistic oblation was beneficial even to the dead.
- IGP 78b is very similar—evenwith identical phrasing—to a section of the 37th of Gregory's Gospel *Homilies*. It may well have been part of the unpublished *reportata* of another homily on the same theme. In *Homily* 37 he links the same theological lesson to the *exemplum* relating to the eucharistic piety of Bishop Cassius (which the Dialogist has detached and placed earlier, in IGP 76). Both the passage in that homily and the doublet in *Dial.* IV.59 became classical *loci* for the development of the Catholic theology of the Mass.[12]

IGP 79: IV.61.2. From line 6, "*Sed studendum . . .*" to line 15, ". . . *quod poposcit*". On keeping the mind vigilant after times of prayer. Cf. *PsGD*, pp. 577–8.

- Although IGP 79 is presented as a rider to IGP 78, it seems to have been taken from another context, not directly referring to the eucharistic sacrifice. It is paralleled by two other Gregorian texts, *Moralia* 33.43 and *Homilies on Ezekiel* I.11.27. In both of the latter passages there is similar mention of compunction and tears, and in both Gregory uses the same scriptural example of Hannah's seriousness, as given in the Vulgate version of *1 Samuel* 1.18. In neither of those two passages does the warning for the need for vigilance after prayer refer to liturgical prayer during the eucharistic rite. In *Moralia* 33.43 the phrase "*post orationis tempora*", which reoccurs verbatim in IGP 79, clearly refers to private petitionary prayer.

IGP 80: IV.62.1–3. From line 1, "*Sed inter haec . . .*" to line 30, ". . . *hostia ipsi fuerimus*". The path to peace before the coming of the divine judge. Cf. *PsGD*, pp. 578–9.

---

[12] Cf. *Eucharistic Sacrifice and the Reformation* by Francis Clark, pp. 405, 520, *et alibi*.

- IGP 80, referring to the evangelical prerequisites *before* making offering before the altar, should logically precede IGP 79, which relates to due mindfulness *after* offering prayer.
- There are indications, from verbatim correspondence in lines 10–15 and 25–30 of IGP 80, that it was drawn (like IGP 78) from an unpublished discourse of Gregory's closely akin to the 37th of his Gospel *Homilies*. (They are spelt out in *PsGD*, p. 578.) That homily clarifies the sequence of thought in IGP 80. The argument drawn from *Matthew* 5.23–4 is also used by Gregory in three of his known works: *Regula Pastoralis* 3.23, *Homiliae in Ezechielem* I.8.9 & Epist. VII.5.
- With its urgent Gregorian exhortation and stately cadences, IGP 80 provides an impressive climax to the fourth book of the *Dialogues*, a final jewel of Gregorian spiritual wisdom set in the Dialogist's legendary paste.

BIBLIOGRAPHY

Primary Sources

Aldhelm of Malmesbury: *Opera*, ed. R. Ewald. *MGH* Berlin 1919.
Bede: *Historia Ecclesiastica, Historia Abbatum*, etc., ed. C. Plummer, 2 vols. Oxford 1896, reprinted 1946.
Codices latini antiquiores: ed. E. Lowe, 7 vols. & *Supplement*, Oxford 1934–71.
Diplomata, chartae et instrumenta aetatis Merovingicae: ed. J. Pardessus, 2 vols. Paris 1843–9.
Gesta martyrum romanorum: ed. A. Dufourcq; see below, in secondary bibliography.
Gregory of Tours: *Opera*, ed. W. Arndt & B. Krusch, *MGH* Hannover 1884; *PL* 71.
Gregory the Great: *Dialogues*: edited, with commentary, by A. de Vogüé; Latin text and French trans. by P. Antin: *Sources Chrétiennes*, vols. 251, 260, 265, Paris 1978–80. Also ed. of U. Moricca, Rome 1924.
—— *Moralia in Job*: ed. M. Adriaen, *CCL* 143, 143A, 143B, Turnhout 1979–85; *PL* 75–6.
—— *Homiliae in Hiezechielem*: ed. M. Ariaen, *CCL* 142 (1971).
—— *Homiliae in Evangelia*: ed. H. Hurter, *Sanctorum patrum opera selecta*, Innsbruck 1892 (= *PL* 76, cols. 1075–1312).
—— *Regula Pastoralis*: ed. N. Turchi, *Bibliotheca sanctorum patrum* VII, Rome 1908 (= *PL* 77, cols. 13–128).
—— *In Cantica Canticorum* & *In librum primum Regum*: ed. P. Verbraken, *CCL* 144, Turnhout 1963.
—— *Registrum epistularum*: ed. P. Ewald & L. Hartmann, *MGH, Epistulae*, I–II, Berlin 1891–99; ed. D. Norberg, *CCL* 140 & 140A, Turnhout 1982.
Ildefonsus of Toledo: *El 'De viris illustribus' de Ildefonso de Toledo, estudio y edición crítica*, ed. C. Codoñer Merino, Salamanca 1972.
Isidore of Seville: *Opera omnia*, ed. F. Arevalo, 7 vols. Rome 1797–1803; also *PL* 81–84.
—— *De viris illustribus*, ed. C. Codoñer Merino, Salamanca 1964.
—— *Etymologiae*, ed. W. Lindsay, 2 vols. Oxford 1911.
John the Deacon: *Vita Gregorii, PL* 75.
Jonas of Bobbio: *Vita Columbani, etc.*, ed. B. Krusch, Hannover and Leipzig, 1905; also *PL* 87.
Liber Pontificalis: ed. L. Duchesne (1886); 2nd ed. with revisions by C. Vogel in supplementary volume, Paris 1955–7; also ed. T. Mommsen, *Gesta pontificum romanorum* I/1, *MGH* Berlin 1898.
Martyrologium Hieronymianum ad fidem codicum: ed. J. De Rossi & L. Duchesne, in *AA.SS*, November II/I, Brussels 1894.
Moschus, John: *Pratum spirituale*, ed. P. Pattenden, *CCG* 1989; French ed. M.J. Rouet de Journel, *SC* 12 (1946).
Paterius: *Liber testimonorum*, ed. P. Vander Plaetse, *CCL* 145A.
Paul Warnefrid: *Historia Langobardorum*, ed. G. Waitz, *MGH* Hanover 1898; *PL* 95.
Regesta Pontificum Romanorum, ed. P. Jaffe, Graz 1956.
Sanctuarium (legendary *passiones martyrum*) ed. B. Mombritius, Paris 1919.
Sulpicius Severus: *Vita Martini*, ed. J. Fontaine, *SC* 133–5, Paris 1967–9.
—— *Dialogi*: ed. C. Halm, *CSEL* 1, 1866.

Vita Fructosi: ed. F. Nock, *The Vita sancti Fructuosi*, Washington 1946; ed. M. Diaz, *La Vida de san Frutuoso de Braga*, Braga 1974.
Vita sancti Bonifati: ed. W. Levison, Hanover 1905.
Vitae Patrum: PL 73.
Vitas patrum Emeretensium: ed. C. De Smedt in *AA.SS* 63, November 1, Paris 1887; ed. J. Garvin, Washington 1946; *PL* 80.

Secondary Sources

Aherne, C. *Valerius of Bierzo*, Washington 1949.
Auerbach, E. *Literatursprache und Publicum in der lateinischen Spätantike und im Mittelalter*, Bern 1958.
Batiffol, P. *St Gregory the Great* (trans.), London 1929.
Boesch Gajano, S. *"Dislivelli culturali e mediazione ecclesiastiche nei Dialoghi di Gregorio Magno"*, in *Quaderni Storici* 41 (1979), pp. 398–415.
——. *"La proposta agiografica dei Dialoghi di Gregorio Magno"*, in *Studi Medioevale* 21 (1980).
Bognetti, G. *L'Età Longobarda*, 4 vols. Milan 1966–8.
Borchardt, C. "The ongoing debate on the Gregorian *Dialogues*", in *Studia Historiae Ecclesiasticae* 18 (1992), pp. 96–107.
Bruys, F. *Histoire des Papes*, La Haye 1732.
Bruzzone, A. *Sulla lingua dei Dialoghi di Gregorio Magno* in *Studi Latini e Italiani* (1992), pp. 181–283.
Cave, W. *Scriptorum ecclesiasticorum historia literaria*, London 1688.
Chapman, J. *St Benedict and the Sixth Century*, London 1929.
Clark, F. *Eucharistic Sacrifice and the Reformation*, London 1960 (3rd ed. 1981).
——. "The authenticity of the Gregorian *Dialogues*: a reopening of the question?", in *Acts* of the 1982 Chantilly conference on St Gregory, *Grégoire le Grand*, Paris 1986, pp. 429–44.
——. "The authorship of the Gregorian *Dialogues*: a challenge to the traditional view": paper at the Oxford Patristic Conference of 1983, published in *Studia Patristica* 18 (1990), pp. 120–32.
——. *The Pseudo-Gregorian Dialogues*, 2 vols. Leiden 1987.
——. "The authorship of the Gregorian *Dialogues*: an old controversy renewed", in *The Heythrop Journal* 30 (1989), pp. 257–72.
——. "St Gregory and the enigma of the *Dialogues*: a response to Paul Meyvaert", in *JEH* 40 (1989), pp. 323–43.
——. "The renewed debate on the authenticity of the Gregorian *Dialogues*", in *Augustinianum* 30 (1990), pp. 75–105.
——. "The renewed controversy about the authorship of the *Dialogues*", in *Gregorio Magno e il suo Tempo*, Rome 1991, vol. II, pp. 5–25.
——. "The authorship of the Gregorian *Dialogues*: the state of the question", in *Studia Patristica* 33 (1997), pp. 407–17.
——. "Authorship of the *Commentary In 1 Regum*: implications of A. de Vogüé's discovery", in *Rev. Bén* 108 (1998), pp. 61–79.
——. "R.A. Markus, Gregory the Great and *In 1 Regum*", in *The Heythrop Journal*, 40 (1999), pp. 207–9.
——. *Godfaring: on Reason, Faith and Sacred Being*, Washington and London 2000.
——. "The unmasking of the pseudo-Gregorian *Commentary on Kings* and its relevance to the study of Benedictine origins", in *Studia Patristica* 36 (2001), pp. 3–8.
——. "Saint Benedict's biography and the turning tide of controversy", in *ABR* 53.3 (2002).

Clarke, H. & Brennan, M. *Columbanus and Merovingian Monasticism*, Oxford 1981.

Cooke, R. *Censura quorundam scriptorum*, London 1614.

Cracco, G. "*Francis Clark e la Storiographia sui Dialogi di Gregorio Magno*", in *Rivista di Storia e Letteratura Religiosa* 27 (1991), pp. 115–24.

Cremascoli, G. *Novissima hominis nei Dialoghi di Gregorio Magno*, Bologna 1979.

——. "*Se i Dialogi siano opera de Gregorio Magno: due volumi per una vexata quaestio*", in *Benedictina* 36 (1989), pp. 179–92.

Dagens, C. *Saint Grégoire le Grand: culture et expérience chrétiennes*, Paris 1977.

Delehaye, H. *Sanctus: essai sur le culte des saints dans l'antiquité*, Brussels 1927.

——. *Les Légendes hagiographiques*, Brussels 1905.

——. *Étude sur le légendier romain*, Brussels 1936.

Deshusses, J. & Hourlier, J. *Saint Benoît dans les livres liturgiques*, *SM* 21 (1979), pp. 143–204.

Díaz y Díaz, M. *De Isidor al Siglo XI*, Barcelona 1956.

——. *Index scriptorum latinorum medii aevi Hispanorum*, 2nd ed. Madrid 1959.

——. "*La Compilación hagiografica de Valerio de Bierzo*", in *Hispania Sacra* 4 (1931), pp. 3–25.

Diehl, C. *Études sur l'administration byzantine dans l'Exarchat de Ravenne (568–751)*, Paris 1888.

Dobschütz, E. *Das Decretum Gelasianum*, Leipzig 1912.

Dudden, F. Holmes. *Gregory the Great: his Place in History and Thought*, 2 vols. London 1905.

Dufner, G. *Die Dialoge Gregors der Grossen im Wandel der Zeiten und Sprachen*, Padua 1968.

Dufourcq, A. *Étude sur les Gesta Martyrum romains*, Paris, vol. I 1900; vols. II–III 1907; vol. IV 1910.

Dunn, Marilyn. *The Emergence of Monasticism: from the Desert Fathers to the Early Middle Ages*, Oxford & Malden 2000.

Dunn, M.B. *The Style of the Letters of St Gregory the Great*, Washington 1930.

Dzialowski, G. von: *Isidor und Ildefons als Literaturhistoriker*, Münster 1898.

Ebert, A. *Geschichte der christliche-lateinischen Literatur*, vol. I Leipzig 1894.

Étaix, R. "*Le Liber Testimoniorum de Paterius*" in *RSR* 32 (1958), pp. 66–78.

Ferrari, *Early Roman Monasteries . . . from the V through the X Century*", Rome 1957.

Fontaine, J., Gillet, R. & Pellistrandi, S. (editors), *Grégoire le Grand*, Paris 1986.

Funk, J. (ed. & trans.) *Gregor der Grosse vier Bücher Dialoge*, Munich 1933.

Geary, P. *Sacra Furta. Theft of Relics in the central Middle Ages*, Princeton 1978.

Gillet, R. "*Spiritualité et place du moine dans l'Eglise selon saint Grégoire le Grand*", in *Theologie de la vie monastique*, Paris 1961, pp. 323–52.

——. "*Grégoire le Grand*" in *DS* VI (1967), cols. 872–910.

——. Introduction to *Moralia* of St Gregory in *SC* 32, pp. 81–109.

——. "*Grégoire le Grand*" in *DHGE* vol. 21, cols. 1387–1420.

——. "*Les Dialogues sont-ils de Grégoire?*", *Revue des Études Augustiniennes* 36 (1990), pp. 309–14.

Godding, R. "*Les Dialogues de Grégoire le Grand: à propos d'un livre récent*", *AB* 106 (1988), pp. 201–29.

——. *Bibliographia di Gregorio Magno (1890–1989)*, Rome 1990.

Goffart, W. *The Le Mans Forgeries*, Cambridge Mass. 1966.

Gregorovius, F. *A History of the City of Rome in the Middle Ages* (trans.), vol. II, London 1894.

Guevin, B. "A new Gregorian controversy: the authorship of the *Commentary on First Kings* in doubt", *ABR* 50 (1999), pp. 437–43.

Hallinger, K. "*Papst Gregor der Grosse und der heilige Benedikt*", in *SA* 42, 1957, pp. 231–319.

——. "*Römische Voraussetzungen der bonifatianischen Wirksamkeit im Frankenreich*", in the symposium *Bonifatius: Gedenkgabe zumzwölfhundertsen Todestag*, Fulda 1954.

——. "*Benedikt von Monte Cassino. Sein Aufstieg zu Kult und Verehrung*", in *RBS* 10/11 (1984), pp. 77–89.

Kessler, S. "*Das Rätsel der Dialoge Gregors des Grossen*", in *Theologie und Philosophie* 65 (1990), pp. 566–78.

Kinnerey, A. *The Late Latin Vocabulary of the Dialogues of St. Gregory the Great*, Washington 1935.

Leclercq, J. *Cultura monastica e desiderio di Dio. Studio sulla letteratura monastica del Medio Evo*, Florence 1983.

Le Goff, J. *La Naissance du Purgatoire*, Paris 1981.

Llewellyn, P. *Rome in the Dark Ages*, London 1970.

——. "The Roman Church in the 7th century: the legacy of Gregory I", in *JEH* 25, 1974.

Mabillon, J. *Annales ordinis S. Benedicti*, vol. I, Paris 1723.

Mahler, M. "*Evocations bibliques et hagiographiques dans la Vie de saint Benoît par saint Grégoire*", *Rev. Bén.* 83 (1973), pp. 398–429.

Malnory, A. *Quid Luxovienses monachi discipuli Sancti Columbani ad regulam monasteriorum atque ad communem ecclesiae profectum contulerint*, Paris 1894.

Manitius, M. *Geschichte des lateinischen Literatur des Mittelalters*, Munich 1911.

——. *Zu Aldhelm und Baeda*, Vienna 1886.

Markus, R. *Gregory the Great and his World*, Cambridge 1997.

Masdeu, J. de. *Historia Critica de España y la Cultura Española*, Madrid 1794.

Mayr-Harting, N. *The Coming of Christianity to Anglo-Saxon England*, London 1977.

McCready, W. *Signs of Sanctity: Miracles in the Thought of Gregory the Great*, Toronto 1989.

Mélanges Colombaniens, Actes du congrès international de Luxeuil 1950, Paris 1950.

Meyvaert, P. "The Enigma of Gregory the Great's *Dialogues*: a response to Francis Clark", in *JEH* 39 (1988), pp. 335–81.

Murray, P. "The miracles of St Benedict: may we doubt them?", in *Hallel* 11 (1983), pp. 64–8.

Norberg, D. *In Registrum Gregorii Magni studia critica*, Uppsala 1937.

——. "*Qui a composé les lettres de saint Grégoire?*", in *Studi Medioevali*, Series 3, 21 (1980), pp. 1–18.

O'Carroll, J. "Monastic Rules in Merovingian Gaul", in *Studies* (Dublin) 42 (1953), pp. 407–19.

Peifer, C. "The origins of Benedictine monasticism: state of the question", in *ABR* 51 (2000), pp. 293–315.

Penco. G. "*La prima diffusione della Regula di San Benedetto*", in *SA* 42, 1957, pp. 321–45.

——. *Storia del Monachesimo in Italia*, Rome 1960.

Petersen, J. *The Dialogues of Gregory the Great in their late antique cultural Background*, Toronto 1984.

Pfeilschifter, G. *Die authentische Ausgabe des 40 Evangelien-homilien Gregors der Grosse*, Munich 1900 (reprinted 1970).

Pin, Ellies du. *Nouvelle bibliothêque des auteurs ecclésiastiques*, vol. V, Paris 1691.

Prinz, F. *Kirchengeschichte Deutschlands*, 8th ed, Leipzig-Berlin 1954.

——. *Frühes Mönchtum in Frankenreich*, Munich-Vienna 1965.

Quentin, H. *Les Martyrologes historiques du moyen âge*, Paris 1908.

Reuter, T. (ed.) *The Greatest Englishman. Essays on St Boniface*, Exeter 1980.

Richards, J. *Consul of God*, London 1980.

Rivetus, A. *Critici sacri specimen*, Leipzig (?) 1612; augmented ed. Geneva 1642.

Rossi, J. De. "*De scrinio et bibliotheca apostolicae saeculo septimo*"; prefixed to *Codices palatini bibliothecae Vaticanae*, Rome 1886.

Salvarorelli, L. *San Benedetto e l'Italia del suo tempo*, Bari 1929.

Schmitz, H. *Histoire de l'ordre de saint Benoît*, Maredsous 1948.

Schrörs, H. "*Das Charakterbild des heiligen Benedikt von Nursia und seine Quellen*", in *ZKT* 42 (1921), pp. 169–207.

Sepulcri, A. *Le alterazione fonetiche e morfologiche nel latino di Gregorio Magno e del suo tempo*, in *Studi Medioevali* (Turin), I (1904), pp. 171–235.

Talbot, C. The *Anglo-Saxon Missionaries in Germany*, London 1954.

Tateo, F. "*La Struttura dei Dialoghi di Gregorio Magno*", in *Vetera Christiana* 2 (1965), pp. 101–27.

Tausch, H. *Benediktinisches Mönchtum in Österreich*, Vienna 1949.

Traube, L. *Textgeschichte der Regula S. Benedicti*, Munich 1898; in *Abhandlungen der königliche Bayerischen Akademie der Wissenschaften*, XXXV, no. 2, Munich 1911.

Vitale Brovarone, A. "*La forma narrativa dei Dialoghi di Gregorio Magno: problemi storico-letterari*", in *Atti della Academia delle Scienze di Torino*, 108 (1973–4), pp. 95–173.

Vogüé, A. de. *Vie de saint Benoît*, Bégrolles-en-Mauges 1982.

——. "*Grégoire le Grand et ses 'Dialogues' d'après deux ouvrages récents*", in *RHE* 83 (1988), pp. 281–348.

——. "*Les Dialogues, oeuvre authentique et publiées par Grégoire lui-même*", in the symposium, *Gregorio Magno e il suo tempo*, Rome 1991, vol. II, pp. 27–40.

——. "*L'Auteur du Commentaire de Rois attribué à S. Grégoire: un moine de Cava?*", *Rev. Bén.* 106 (1996), pp. 319–31.

——. "*Du nouveau sur les Dialogues de saint Grégoire?*", in *CC* 62 (2000), pp. 193–8.

Wallace-Hadrill, J. *Early Mediaeval History*, Oxford 1975.

——. *The Frankish Church*, Oxford 1983.

Wansbrough, H. Review of *PsGD* in *The Heythrop Journal* 30 (1989).

Wasselynck, R. "*Les Compilations des 'Moralia in Job' du VIIe au XIIe siècle*", in *Recherches de théologie ancienne et médiévale* 30 (1982).

Wilmart, A. "*Le Recueil Grégorien de Paterius*", in *Rev. Bén.* 39, (1927), pp. 81–104.

Zelzer, M. "*Die Regula Donati, der alteste Textzeuge der Regula Benedicti*", in *RBS* 16 (1989), pp. 23–26.

Zibermayr, I. *Noricum, Bayern und Österreich*, Munich-Berlin 1944.

Zimmermann, A. *Kalendarium Benediktinum*, vol. I, Mettern 1933.

INDEX NOMINUM

Studies in the History
of Christian Thought

EDITED BY HEIKO A. OBERMAN

46. GARSTEIN, O. *Rome and the Counter-Reformation in Scandinavia*. 1553-1622. 1992
47. GARSTEIN, O. *Rome and the Counter-Reformation in Scandinavia*. 1622-1656. 1992
48. PERRONE COMPAGNI, V. (ed.). *Cornelius Agrippa, De occulta philosophia Libri tres*. 1992
49. MARTIN, D. D. *Fifteenth-Century Carthusian Reform*. The World of Nicholas Kempf. 1992
50. HOENEN, M. J. F. M. *Marsilius of Inghen*. Divine Knowledge in Late Medieval Thought. 1993
51. O'MALLEY, J. W., IZBICKI, T. M. and CHRISTIANSON, G. (eds.). *Humanity and Divinity in Renaissance and Reformation*. Essays in Honor of Charles Trinkaus. 1993
52. REEVE, A. (ed.) and SCREECH, M. A. (introd.). *Erasmus' Annotations on the New Testament*. Galatians to the Apocalypse. 1993
53. STUMP, Ph. H. *The Reforms of the Council of Constance (1414-1418)*. 1994
54. GIAKALIS, A. *Images of the Divine*. The Theology of Icons at the Seventh Ecumenical Council. With a Foreword by Henry Chadwick. 1994
55. NELLEN, H. J. M. and RABBIE, E. (eds.). *Hugo Grotius – Theologian*. Essays in Honour of G. H. M. Posthumus Meyjes. 1994
56. TRIGG, J. D. *Baptism in the Theology of Martin Luther*. 1994
57. JANSE, W. *Albert Hardenberg als Theologe*. Profil eines Bucer-Schülers. 1994
59. SCHOOR, R.J.M. van de. *The Irenical Theology of Théophile Brachet de La Milletière (1588-1665)*. 1995
60. STREHLE, S. *The Catholic Roots of the Protestant Gospel*. Encounter between the Middle Ages and the Reformation. 1995
61. BROWN, M.L. *Donne and the Politics of Conscience in Early Modern England*. 1995
62. SCREECH, M.A. (ed.). *Richard Mocket, Warden of All Souls College, Oxford, Doctrina et Politia Ecclesiae Anglicanae*. An Anglican Summa. Facsimile with Variants of the Text of 1617. Edited with an Introduction. 1995
63. SNOEK, G.J.C. *Medieval Piety from Relics to the Eucharist*. A Process of Mutual Interaction. 1995
64. PIXTON, P.B. *The German Episcopacy and the Implementation of the Decrees of the Fourth Lateran Council, 1216-1245*. Watchmen on the Tower. 1995
65. DOLNIKOWSKI, E.W. *Thomas Bradwardine: A View of Time and a Vision of Eternity in Fourteenth-Century Thought*. 1995
66. RABBIE, E. (ed.). *Hugo Grotius, Ordinum Hollandiae ac Westfrisiae Pietas (1613)*. Critical Edition with Translation and Commentary. 1995
67. HIRSH, J.C. *The Boundaries of Faith*. The Development and Transmission of Medieval Spirituality. 1996
68. BURNETT, S.G. *From Christian Hebraism to Jewish Studies*. Johannes Buxtorf (1564-1629) and Hebrew Learning in the Seventeenth Century. 1996
69. BOLAND O.P., V. *Ideas in God according to Saint Thomas Aquinas*. Sources and Synthesis. 1996
70. LANGE, M.E. *Telling Tears in the English Renaissance*. 1996
71. CHRISTIANSON, G. and T.M. IZBICKI (eds.). *Nicholas of Cusa on Christ and the Church*. Essays in Memory of Chandler McCuskey Brooks for the American Cusanus Society. 1996
72. MALI, A. *Mystic in the New World*. Marie de l'Incarnation (1599-1672). 1996
73. VISSER, D. *Apocalypse as Utopian Expectation (800-1500)*. The Apocalypse Commentary of Berengaudus of Ferrières and the Relationship between Exegesis, Liturgy and Iconography. 1996
74. O'ROURKE BOYLE, M. *Divine Domesticity*. Augustine of Thagaste to Teresa of Avila. 1997
75. PFIZENMAIER, T.C. *The Trinitarian Theology of Dr. Samuel Clarke (1675-1729)*. Context, Sources, and Controversy. 1997
76. BERKVENS-STEVELINCK, C., J. ISRAEL and G.H.M. POSTHUMUS MEYJES (eds.). *The Emergence of Tolerance in the Dutch Republic*. 1997
77. HAYKIN, M.A.G. (ed.). *The Life and Thought of John Gill (1697-1771)*. A Tercentennial Appreciation. 1997
78. KAISER, C.B. *Creational Theology and the History of Physical Science*. The Creationist Tradition from Basil to Bohr. 1997
79. LEES, J.T. *Anselm of Havelberg*. Deeds into Words in the Twelfth Century. 1997
80. WINTER, J.M. van. *Sources Concerning the Hospitallers of St John in the Netherlands, 14th-18th Centuries*. 1998

81. TIERNEY, B. *Foundations of the Conciliar Theory*. The Contribution of the Medieval Canonists from Gratian to the Great Schism. Enlarged New Edition. 1998
82. MIERNOWSKI, J. *Le Dieu Néant*. Théologies négatives à l'aube des temps modernes. 1998
83. HALVERSON, J.L. *Peter Aureol on Predestination.* A Challenge to Late Medieval Thought. 1998.
84. HOULISTON, V. (ed.). *Robert Persons, S.J.: The Christian Directory (1582)*. The First Booke of the Christian Exercise, appertayning to Resolution. 1998
85. GRELL, O.P. (ed.). *Paracelsus*. The Man and His Reputation, His Ideas and Their Transformation. 1998
86. MAZZOLA, E. *The Pathology of the English Renaissance.* Sacred Remains and Holy Ghosts. 1998.
87. 88. MARSILIUS VON INGHEN. *Quaestiones super quattuor libros sententiarum*. Super Primum. Bearbeitet von M. Santos Noya. 2 Bände. I. Quaestiones 1-7. II. Quaestiones 8-21. 2000
89. FAUPEL-DREVS, K. *Vom rechten Gebrauch der Bilder im liturgischen Raum*. Mittelalterliche Funktionsbestimmungen bildender Kunst im *Rationale divinorum officiorum* des Durandus von Mende (1230/1-1296). 1999
90. KREY, P.D.W. and SMITH, L. (eds.). *Nicholas of Lyra*. the Senses of Scripture. 2000
92. OAKLEY, F. *Politics and Eternity*. Studies in the History of Medieval and Early-Modern Political Thought. 1999
93. PRYDS, D. *The Politics of Preaching*. Robert of Naples (1309-1343) and his Sermons. 2000
94. POSTHUMUS MEYJES, G.H.M. *Jean Gerson – Apostle of Unity*. His Church Politics and Ecclesiology. Translated by J.C. Grayson. 1999
95. BERG, J. VAN DEN. *Religious Currents and Cross-Currents*. Essays on Early Modern Protestantism and the Protestant Enlightenment. Edited by J. de Bruijn, P. Holtrop, and E. van der Wall. 1999
96. IZBICKI, T.M. and BELLITTO, C.M. (eds.). *Reform and Renewal in the Middle Ages and the Renaissance*. Studies in Honor of Louis Pascoe, S. J. 2000
97. KELLY, D. *The Conspiracy of Allusion*. Description, Rewriting, and Authorship from Macrobius to Medieval Romance. 1999
98. MARRONE, S.P. *The Light of Thy Countenance*. Science and Knowledge of God in the Thirteenth Century. 2 volumes. 1. A Doctrine of Divine Illumination. 2. God at the Core of Cognition. 2001
99. HOWSON, B.H. *Erroneous and Schismatical Opinions*. The Question of Orthodoxy regarding the Theology of Hanserd Knollys (c. 1599-169)). 2001
100. ASSELT, W.J. VAN. *The Federal Theology of Johannes Cocceius (1603-1669)*. 2001
101. CELENZA, C.S. *Piety and Pythagoras in Renaissance Florence the* Symbolum Nesianum. 2001
102. DAM, H.-J. VAN (ed.), *Hugo Grotius, De imperio summarum potestatum circa sacra*. Critical Edition with Introduction, English translation and Commentary. 2 volumes. 2001
103. BAGGE, S. *Kings, Politics, and the Right Order of the World in German Historiography c. 950-1150*. 2002
104. STEIGER, J.A. *Fünf Zentralthemen der Theologie Luthers und seiner Erben*. Communicatio – Imago – Figura – Maria – Exempla. Mit Edition zweier christologischer Frühschriften Johann Gerhards. 2002
105. IZBICKI T.M. and BELLITTO C.M. (eds.). *Nicholas of Cusa and his Age: Intellect and Spirituality*. Essays Dedicated to the Memory of F. Edward Cranz, Thomas P. McTighe and Charles Trinkaus. 2002
106. HASCHER-BURGER, U. *Gesungene Innigkeit*. Studien zu einer Musikhandschrift der Devotio moderna (Utrecht, Universiteitsbibliotheek, MS 16 H 94, olim B 113). Mit einer Edition der Gesänge. 2002
107. BOLLIGER, D. *Infiniti Contemplatio*. Grundzüge der scotus- und scotismusrezeption im werk huldrych zwinglis. 2002
108. CLARK, F. *The 'Gregorian' Dialogues and the Origins of Benedictine Monasticism*. 2002

Prospectus available on request

BRILL — P.O.B. 9000 — 2300 PA LEIDEN — THE NETHERLANDS